READINGS IN ART EDUCATION

READINGS IN

GINN–BLAISDELL A XEROX COMPANY

Waltham, Massachusetts / *Toronto* / *London*

Elliot W. Eisner, STANFORD UNIVERSITY

David W. Ecker, THE OHIO STATE UNIVERSITY

ART EDUCATION

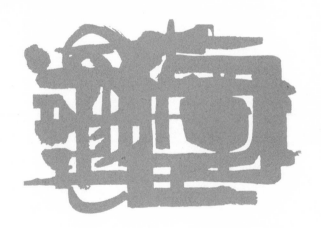

for Ellie and Gloria

Consulting Editor

JOHN I. GOODLAD

Foreword

A GOOD BOOK OF READINGS in any field is a product of wise choices. These choices, in turn, depend upon and are guided by the rationale of those persons who make them. The reputations of authors and the recency of selections are insufficient criteria in seeking to create a definitive anthology. Clearly, Professors Eisner and Ecker knew what they were after when they turned to the literature and then applied rigorous criteria in choosing among alternatives.

Their stated purpose is to involve the reader in an inquiry into some of the major issues in art education. Doing the job economically — that is, with a minimum number of selections — requires keen sensitivity both to the issues and to the subtleties of each author's point of view. After all, it is the rare protagonist who announces that he is about to discuss such-and-such an issue, is going to take this side rather than that, and then proceeds to describe the tenets of his position. Few significant issues lend themselves to such bold treatment. No, the writer reveals himself through values implicitly applied to commonplaces which, more often than not, do not protrude readily through the discourse: commonplaces such as the nature of knowledge, knowing man, and the good life. Professors Eisner and Ecker — largely because of their unique combination of backgrounds and abilities in art, art education, curriculum, and philosophy — have brought together a collection of readings which is both elegant and spare: elegant in that each selection serves a specific purpose, spare in that no two selections serve precisely the same purpose.

The two editors have done much more, however, than invite participation in the issues. They have suggested the fields that appear to have something to say about the issues. And they have taken a significant step toward defining the range of art education itself. In the process, they reveal vital gaps in both inquiry and practice. For example, the field of evaluation in art education is virtually a desert.

The Eisner-Ecker manuscript reveals almost dramatically that art education is so very much more than the study and teaching of drawing and painting for children and youth. It opens up new vistas for the education of teachers and of teachers of teachers, giving to both of these rather practical activities a substantive base which is but dimly perceived in schools and colleges across the land.

For me, the insightful editorial comments written by Professors Eisner and Ecker to precede each section of the book are alone worth "the price of admission." They weave the various points of view — at times, even the language — of the collected authors into a cohesive narrative, whetting the appetite but leaving authors to speak for themselves and reader to think for himself. One could profitably read either the editorial introductions or the selected readings, but to read both is to appreciate the creative synthesis that has been effected.

Institute for Development of Educational Activities at Los Angeles   JOHN I. GOODLAD

Preface

IN PREPARING THIS VOLUME we have attempted to identify some of the major issues in the field of art education and to select resource materials that speak to these issues from diverse points of view. The problems associated with helping human beings grow in their ability to experience and produce art are to be resolved, in part, by methods and knowledge derived from fields outside of art education. The problem of clarifying or developing an adequate conception of art, for example, is a problem that must be treated with the methods of philosophy in general and aesthetics in particular. Identifying effective teaching strategies in the art classroom or studio may be facilitated by knowledge from the field of psychology. Determining the nature of creativity and the conditions that foster it is, in part, both a psychological and a sociological problem. The problem of identifying and applying criteria for the evaluation of art products is a curricular as well as an aesthetic problem, and the relationship between art and society is an educational problem in the broadest sense of the term. Thus, the problems encountered in art education rely for their resolution upon the skills and products of workers outside of art education as well as upon those within art education.

By no means have we intended to select resources that present a unified position vis-à-vis these problems. In fact, we have found no single theoretical orientation, discipline, or practice wholly adequate for their resolution. We have, instead, attempted to select materials that approach these problems from different vantage points, hoping that the volume would have a dialectical character which would challenge the reader to examine critically the alternative positions that are offered. These selections are therefore meant to be "invitations to inquiry" rather than a "rhetoric of conclusions" taken as certain and final answers to perplexing problems.

The selections have been arranged in most cases to contrast with one another. Thus, in Part IV, How CAN ART BE TAUGHT?, Walter Smith's highly programed approach to art instruction is contrasted to the "natural" approach of Kimon Nicolaides. By examining and comparing the diverse views contained in each part of the anthology, the reader may be better able to develop his own approach to the problems of art education. Although such new approaches might be eclectic in character, they might also be more than this. The intent of the authors is not to suggest that a "via media" is desirable or that eclecticism is necessary, but rather to provide positions that will stimulate critical thought in the hope that from such thought new and useful ideas may be generated. The field of art education like most other fields needs fresh and useful formulations from which to view and resolve its problems.

The material selected for this volume has come from a variety of sources. Although some material previously published in book form has been included, many of the books from which this material has been drawn are now out of print and very difficult to obtain. Most of the selections in this volume have appeared earlier as articles in professional and academic journals in the fields of art education, education, psychology, sociology, philosophy, and aesthetics. Such journals are frequently inaccessible and, for this reason among others, they have not been widely used by students of art education. One piece, Weitz's "The Nature of Art," originally presented as an address, appears here in print for the first time.

Some of the material has been selected partly for its historical value as an indication of some of the changes that have taken place in the field. We felt that the perspective afforded by the classical statements included here would be of use to those working in the field today, especially in appreciating the progress that has been made and in sensing the direction in which the field is moving. Thus, selections by Walter Smith and Florence Goodenough exemplify in their separate ways what was frontier thinking prior to and after the turn of the century. Norman Meier's work at the University of Iowa in the third decade of this century exemplifies a significant effort to understand art aptitude and represents perhaps the most extensive and intensive research effort carried out on artistic aptitude.

The use of concepts, methods, and theories from the fields of psychology, sociology, anthropology, and aesthetics has not been common within the field of art education. There are many reasons for this. Art education as a field has been atheoretical in the main. Theory and scientific methodology have not been a part of the art teacher's stock in trade. Art educators, like those working in other disciplines, have had a tendency to dichotomize the cognitive and the affective, the thought from the emotion, and to look upon science with skepticism, especially as it might be applied to artistic experience. In addition, language used in scientific journals has been unfamiliar to many art educators, and statistical methods have appeared an anathema. Art, they have claimed, cannot be boiled down to science, much less to numbers. Claims such as this reveal a fundamental misconception regarding the goals and functions of the behavioral scientist concerned with the artistic activity of man. Nevertheless, such claims have tended to create barriers to an understanding and appreciation of highly relevant work in fields outside of art education. It has been our hope that these barriers might be lowered by bringing findings relevant to art education to the attention of those working within the field.

This volume is intended, therefore, for undergraduate and graduate students in art education as well as for others concerned with the artistic development of man. We believe that undergraduates especially would benefit by examining the diversity of viewpoints concerning problems in the field, for if students were to believe that an adequate and widely accepted answer now exists for each of the problems here identified, they would be courting future disappointment as art teachers in the public schools. The problems in art education are far from resolved and the sooner the student realizes this and recognizes the need to engage in his own inquiry into these problems, the better. That there is a need for critical inquiry by graduate students in art education goes without saying.

The articles have been arranged in a manner that seemed most appropriate to us. But deviation from this order is readily accomplished since most of the articles are complete units in themselves. The present arrangement is by no means meant to be prescriptive for the instructor.

PREFACE

We are especially grateful to Manuel Barkan and Jerome Hausman for their encouragement in preparing this book of readings. Ivan Johnson, June McFee, Lambert Brittain, Howard Conant, Vincent Lanier, Ronald Silverman, and Robert Saunders, from the field of art education, were quite helpful in their thoughtful criticism of the initial selections we assembled. In subsequent revisions, Eugene Kaelin, Francis Villemain, and Nathaniel Champlin offered useful suggestions from the vantage point of their own disciplines of aesthetics and philosophy of education.

And, of course, we are deeply indebted to the authors and publishers who gave their kind permission to use the material that we have ultimately selected for this volume.

E. W. E.

D. W. E.

Contents

PART I

WHAT IS ART EDUCATION?

Some Historical Developments in Art Education

In order to understand what art education is today, it would be useful to examine some of the developments which have occurred in its history. By becoming familiar with the major developments of art in American public education, the character of present-day theories and practices can be seen more clearly because a basis for comparison will have been established. With a clearer view of the present, those responsible for art education programs will be better prepared to make intelligent decisions regarding its future.

Art education, like all other subject areas in the curriculum, functions in at least two contexts. One of these contexts is that of the school and the other the society within which the school functions. Although what happens in the school has some influence upon society, the rapid and dramatic changes in American society have greatly influenced the school. These changes have incurred new and evolving expectations of the school and of the various subject areas that constitute its curriculum. We shall see as the chapter proceeds that the teaching of art has been affected by these changing expectations and that the goals which art educators have tried to attain have been shaped, in large measure, by developments — political, social, economic, and intellectual — in society. Indeed, the very facts that one seeks and the moral ends one hopes to attain through education cannot be understood or realized apart from the milieu in which one lives.

The Introduction of Art in the Schools

Although instruction in art was advocated as early as 1770 by Benjamin Franklin (1), the formal introduction of art in the public schools of America begins with the nineteenth century. During the first half of the nineteenth century art was taught in public and private schools when individual teachers elected to do so. During this period no national organizations of art teachers existed, no state laws requiring the teaching of art were in force, and the type of art instruction that did occur was based upon the personal views and aspirations of individual teachers (2).

Those teachers who taught art in their classes, such as William Minifie (3) of Philadelphia and William Bently Fowle (4) of Boston, conceived of art as drawing: to engage in the teaching of art was to engage in the teaching of drawing. This conception of drawing as art and art as drawing continued well into the twentieth century in many of the nation's schools. For Minifie, art was valuable because it was an aid to industry, and in the Baltimore Boys High School in which he taught in 1848–49, he based his teaching of drawing on geometric principles. As the students developed skill in geometric or mechanical drawing Minifie thought that they would be better able to meet the industrial demands of an increasingly industrial society. And Fowle, in addition to using geometric drawing as a basis for his teaching, also used monitorial techniques, a method whereby groups of students seated around large tables could be taught by a student monitor who in turn was instructed by the headmaster (5). Thus, one headmaster might instruct twenty monitors who in turn would instruct ten students each, an arrangement which when first initiated promised to be highly effective as well as economical.

In addition to the teaching of art through monitorial methods and through the practice of having students copy geometric designs, drawing was also taught because some teachers thought that it contributed to better writing habits. After all, in order to draw well one needed to control the pencil, to develop skill of hand and eye; weren't the same skills necessary for writing legibly, and couldn't, therefore, drawing be used as an aid in developing a graceful and legible penmanship?

These were not the only functions art performed in the schools during the first half of the nineteenth century; art was also taught in some schools as a mark of refinement, as a social nicety (6). In private schools, especially for upper class young ladies, art was seen as a cultural accomplishment, something to symbolize the finer things of life, and in such schools art included more than drawing. Art also included fancy stitching and painting on velvet and on glass. As these young, future debutantes were to learn the social graces, the proper way to dance, to sit and to eat, so were they to learn to create pretty things, to engage in the cultivated arts of painting and sketching.

With the growing industrialization of America in the 1850's and the 1860's the vocational value of drawing instruction was emphasized even further. Although the methods of instruction remained much the same as when Minifie taught it as geometric drawing in Baltimore in the 1840's, the justification for art as a subject to be taught in the school — especially in the industrial states in New England — was that it was necessary for the development and prosperity of American industry. Minifie himself pointed out that in 1852 Americans had imported $36,000,000 worth of textiles from Great Britain alone and $11,000,000 worth from France (7). If America as an industrial nation was to compete with the nations of Europe she needed craftsmen and designers who could produce products that were attractive to people abroad as well as to those in this country. And in 1864 drawing became a required subject in the Boston Public Schools: slates and tablets for drawing were provided at the primary grades, drawing books at the grammar grades, and special teachers of art at the high school level. By 1874 a U. S. Bureau of Education Bulletin (8) stated:

In addition to the increased competition arising from steam-carriage, new and cheaper methods of manufacture, and increased productiveness, another element of value has rapidly pervaded all manufacturers, an element in which the United States has been and is woefully deficient — the art element. The element of beauty is found to have pecuniary as well as aesthetic value. The training of the hand and of the eye which is given by drawing is found to be of the greatest advantage to the worker in many occupations and is rapidly becoming indispensable. This training is of value to all the children and offers to girls as well as boys opportunity for useful and remunerative occupations, for drawing in the public schools is not to be taught as a mere "accomplishment." The end sought is not to enable the scholar to draw a pretty picture, but to so train the hand and eye that he may be better fitted to become a bread-winner.

Owing to the economic changes of the nation, art took on an unprecedented significance. ·Art was placed in the service of industry, and competence in drawing was seen as an important vocational skill. Thus, one of the most significant episodes in the historical development of art education in this country occurred when the State of Massachusetts, under pressure from the leading industrialists of the state, passed a state law requiring that art be taught to boys over 15 years of age living in cities over 10,000.

To find leadership for the newly founded state program, the legislature sent to England in 1871 to invite Walter Smith — a teacher of Industrial Drawing and Crafts at the time at the South Kensington School — to come to America to direct the program. After a short visit, Smith accepted the post — an unenviable one which entailed being not only Director of Art for the State of Massachusetts but also Supervisor of Art for the City of Boston and principal of the Art Normal School, a school designed to prepare teachers of art. In his contractual arrangements Smith was to devote three-fifths of his time to the city of Boston and two-fifths of his time to the state. Like most academic part-time jobs, his probably turned out to be three full-time jobs. But Smith was an energetic and imaginative man who not only managed to oversee the teaching of art in the state and to establish new curricula for the training of art teachers; he also managed to write several books on the teaching of art which had an influence well beyond the borders of Massachusetts (9).

To Smith drawing and writing had certain parallels. As writing has its alphabet and its grammar, so too does drawing have its alphabet — the straight and the curved line — and its form. To teach the student to write, he believed, one should progress from the simple to the complex so that the student would gradually be able to arrange the individual units together to create a sentence; so too in the teaching of art must one move from the simple to the complex, making sure that the student first masters the single straight and curved lines and then their combinations until

he is able to construct a well-proportioned design. For Smith the objective of
drawing was practical: the acquisition of a useful vocational skill; and the methods
were clear-cut: a highly systematic and prescribed curriculum which teachers were
to follow scrupulously. The creation of art was not essentially a matter of talent but
of training, and if effective training methods could be developed (which Smith
didn't question for a moment), students could be trained to produce art.

Needless to say, Walter Smith, an Englishman with definite and clear-cut ideas
about art education in an America not yet one hundred years old, made an impact.
The Art Normal School, of which he was the head, opened in 1873 and by the time
of the Philadelphia Centennial Exposition of 1876, at which his course of studies
was displayed, his reputation was well established. But his relationship to the State
legislature did not remain satisfactory and, for reasons that are not altogether clear,
he was relieved in 1885 of the three posts he had worked so hard to develop and returned to his native land to take up the role of headmaster in a large English art
school.

The direction and emphasis that Walter Smith provided in art education lasted a
great many years. Indeed, even today in some schools in both rural and urban
areas art is taught in a copybook manner similar to Smith's, and drawing is the sole
or dominant mode of activity used for instruction. But America in the eighties and
nineties was changing rapidly. New ideas were crossing the seas from Europe, im-
migration increased, and industrialization continued at an even faster pace.

The Growth of Professional Education Movements

There developed, therefore, in the 1880's forces both social and intellectual which
began to change the general character of art education in the United States. It was
during the 1880's that the Child Study Movement got underway under the leadership of the eminent American psychologist G. Stanley Hall (10). As a movement
within psychology and education its main concerns were with the child and his
development both mental and physical. Its work, building upon the ideas of
Pestalozzi, Herbart, and Froebel, developed a new conception of the child. It was
a conception which saw the child as being an individual who had particular and
even unique needs and whose mind differed qualitatively from that of an adult. To
many in education the child was still viewed as a miniature adult and hence expectations were set for children that they could not possibly attain. Indeed, Walter
Smith described his own daughter's performance in drawing this way (11):

... a young lady of the mature age of three ... [with] the advantage of being quite unprejudiced in the matter of style of execution and perfectly fearless in the expression of what
she believes to be the truth, whilst the firmness of her natural touch is something tremendous. ... Her mental disadvantages arise from an altogether too exalted opinion of her
own works causing a self-satisfaction which hinders her progress and blinds her to defects
in style, and her imperfect execution; and she is wildly indignant with me at any faults I
point out, and simply turns round and thrashes me if I point out a faulty line.

Unless references to a "mature young lady of three," "her mental disadvantages," "too exalted opinion" and "defects in style" be an attempt at gentle irony, by current standards Mr. Smith had quite inappropriate expectations for his young daughter! Yet with the Child Study Movement and with what was to develop in the field of education through the work of John Dewey, a newer and quite different view of the child emerged. It was a view which began to take an interest in not only what could be *im*pressed upon the child through instructional methods, but also what the child had to *ex*press. The Child Study Movement and the developments which were to follow liberalized the art curriculum, initiated an interest in the role of imagination, and paid greater attention to the stages through which children normally develop in their visual expression. These concerns, buttressed by the availability of inexpensive crayons and water colors, dramatically changed the general character of art education, all within a twenty-year period. By the turn of the century *The Applied Arts Book*, *The Voice of the Applied Arts Guild of Worcester, Massachusetts* (which was later to become *School Arts* magazine) could state as its doctrine that it advocated "taste in all matters relating to Applied Arts. It stands for beauty in American life." But more, it also urged teachers to have students draw from *nature*, to draw objects in their environment, to study color, and to learn the principles of art, e.g., "harmony — Nature's use of straight lines for strength and curved lines for beauty" (12). Although such exhortations seem quaint by today's standards they were a far cry from the geometrically inspired directions prescribed by Smith.

In addition to the Child Study Movement and the availability of new art media in America, education itself was expanding. And with this expansion came the growth of educational organizations, education journals, and art magazines. The National Education Association formed an art department with Langdon S. Thompson as its first president; the manual training movement gained even greater impetus and later developed as an independent organization; and these, together with the Columbia Exposition of 1893, boosted interest in the art of the child by displaying hundreds of portfolios of art work produced by American schoolchildren.

Thus, by the turn of the century art education had developed another type of concern. As it once was concerned solely with enabling students to develop manual skills useful in industrial vocations, art education now became concerned about helping children "appreciate beauty." Where is beauty found? These men and women had the answer — in nature and in art. Thus began that aspect of art education known as *picture study*.

Art Education for Art Appreciation

In picture study the students were shown "masterpieces" painted by the world's "greatest" artists and were encouraged to familiarize themselves with the lives of these artists and with the story depicted in each painting. It should be noted that the paintings that the students studied, even as late as 1927, were not those of the Impressionists, the Cubists, or those of the then contemporary American artists.

They were, more often than not, the works of the Renaissance artists, those of the genre school of painters in France and those Victorians who told interesting tales in their paintings. "*Picture Study in the Grades,*" wrote its author Oscar Neale in 1927, "aims primarily to develop in the children of our schools an appreciation of the great masterpieces of art so that they may know the joy that comes from such an appreciation and so that their ideals may be influenced by the patriotism, the sympathy, the courage, the piety, and the beauty which the great artists of different ages have given to the world" (13). Thus, not only were the significant modern artists of the age — who by 1927 had already established themselves — absent from picture study, but the study itself was directed to issues that present-day art educators would be inclined to call extraneous to the concerns of art. If picture study was designed to teach something about art history, it was mostly used to inculcate certain ethical values the paintings were believed to reflect.

It is important to mention here that until very recently art education as a field has been quite unresponsive to contemporary developments in the world of art. Even as late as the 1940's the styles of art work held in high esteem in art education were the genre paintings of Millet and Dupre and the works of the Florentine and Venetian masters, especially those which had some sort of visual narrative. That art educators were receptive to such work rather than to the contemporary art of their time is evidenced not only in the paintings selected for picture study but also in the type of art work displayed in the schools and the type of art work published in school art journals. Art education until as late as the middle of the twentieth century was more a reflection of lay artistic tastes than it was a leader in shaping those tastes and in enabling students to experience the work on the artistic frontiers of their day.

Art Education for Art Production

The turn of the century not only brought picture study but also brought a number of men to the fore who had a profound effect on art education. Arthur Wesley Dow, Professor of Fine Arts at Columbia University, was such a man. Dow was concerned with trying to understand the principles which were incorporated in successful works of art. What were their ingredients? What needed to be considered in constructing an art product that displayed harmony and beauty? Dow found an answer and it was *composition* (14). To construct a composition that was successful — and to be successful the composition was to display harmony — three elements must be considered: (1) Line, (2) Value, and (3) Color. Line referred to the contour of drawn objects, value to lights and darks, and color to the hues incorporated in the picture. To obtain harmony in composition five principles were to be employed: (1) Opposition, (2) Transition, (3) Subordination, (4) Repetition, and (5) Symmetry. By identifying the elements that constituted successful works of art Dow believed he was in a position to teach such principles systematically, thus enabling students to produce harmonious compositions.

Dow was not alone in his efforts to understand the nature of art and to formulate a systematic way in which it could be taught. But as Dow focused on the finished work of art in order to identify the order it seemed to possess, Walter Sargent, Professor of Aesthetic and Industrial Education at the University of Chicago, focused upon the process through which children learned to draw. Sargent was interested in the psychology of children's art and in the methods that would help them produce art. To Sargent, "Drawing is a language, a mode of reproducing ideas, and as such is a means of forming and developing these ideas. . . . Drawing thus becomes a tool with which to think." And again, "Drawing an object means translating one's perceptions into terms which have been evolved by the race, and which demand careful selection. It means organizing one's sensations so as to determine what produces the impression and the modes in which that impression can be interpreted. To draw an object requires a mental activity comparable to that which occurs when a thought is translated from one language into another" (15).

The tenor of Sargent's discourse about art and the process through which art is created places him very close to the field of psychology. His conception of drawing as a language and as a *tool with which to think* is a remarkable conception considering the historical context in which it was made. And it should be recognized that even today the idea that art is a cognitive activity is not widely recognized or well understood. Walter Sargent, through his work in *Fine and Industrial Arts in Elementary Schools* (16) and in *How Children Learn To Draw* (17) developed a level of sophistication about art that has since then been matched too rarely. According to his theory, three factors influence children in their ability to learn to draw. First, the child must want to say something, he must have some idea or image he wants to express through drawing. Second, the child needs to use devices such as three-dimensional models or pictures to work from in making his drawings. And finally, he claimed that children often learn to draw one thing well but not others, so that skill in drawing is specific; a person could be good at drawing houses or boats and and not good at drawing other things.

Walter Sargent's inquiry grew out of an interesting intertwining of two important but distinct branches of American psychological thought (18). One branch in psychology stems from the work done by German psychologists and scientists such as Gustav Fechner, Hermann Von Helmholtz, and Wilhelm Wundt, an orientation which emphasized laboratory methods, the significance of the mental event and the mind. The other branch stems from the English, from the work of John Locke, Charles Darwin, Francis Galton, and Herbert Spencer, and emphasizes the importance of natural observation and of the environment in shaping human behavior. The German experimental orientation with its concern for the mind and introspection is perhaps best exemplified by the work of G. Stanley Hall, who studied with Helmholtz, Fechner, and Wundt. The English tradition is reflected in greater degree in the work of such psychologists as Edward Lee Thorndike and John Watson, the latter interested in purging psychology from the German interest in introspection and in replacing it with objective methods for the study of human behavior. These traditions were in the air, in modified American form, when Sargent was writing, and his concern with both the mind and its product, thought, and with the use of objective methods for teaching art suggest the influence of these two historical traditions.

Art Education for Creative Development and Mental Health

The work in psychology by Hall and by the Child Study Movement, with its interest in children's development and the factors that affect it, found support from two major forces, each of which influenced art education in the first half of the twentieth century. One of these influences emanated from the writings of John Dewey and the other from the writings of Sigmund Freud.

Dewey, influenced by the work of Charles Darwin and William James, saw man's nature as being biological (19). For Dewey man was an organism that not only lived *in* but *through* an environment. And since that environment was not always friendly, since it did not automatically meet the organism's needs, the organism needed to control the environment or to adjust to it. Man's basic need, for Dewey, was to come to terms with his environment, to attain equilibrium, and to grow. In order to grow and to cope with the problematic situations that arose during one's life, the organism needed to behave intelligently. And since human intelligence was based, in large measure, upon the experience and past resolutions to problems the individual had achieved, the role of experience in education became a crucial issue for Dewey.

What Dewey saw when he viewed the schools in the 1880's and 1890's was institutions that made little provision for the individual experiences of the child. He saw institutions that did not provide for the child's needs nor for the child's unique view of the world. Schools, Dewey thought, were pervaded by a formalism that was inappropriate for meaningful learning. In these schools children were considered miniature adults who were to pay attention and be still. They were arranged in rows, seated in immovable desks, and restrained from both the psychological and physical freedom that they needed in order to develop into intelligent human beings. Schools were bookish, teachers dogmatic and pedantic, and instruction was crammed with inert ideas unconnected with the lives of the children.

In developing his conception of man's nature, the nature of knowledge and how it was achieved, Dewey concerned himself with education and conceived of education as a process of expanding human intelligence, thereby increasing its capacity to experience. For him schools needed to provide physical, emotional, and intellectual freedom for the pupil, freedom that could be attained only if the student had the opportunity to exercise his intelligence on problems that were meaningful to him. Not only this, but the child could not be thought of as part mind and part body; the child is whole, a thinking and feeling organism that could not be artificially carved into neat categories.

Dewey's thinking represents one of the major influences on art education in the twentieth century because it provided the ideological leadership for the Progressive

Education Association. Dewey's ideas, although carried at times to extremes he never intended, encouraged educators to reconsider the means and ends of education. Dewey's interest in helping educators provide for the uniqueness of the child and the significance of experience in his life grew into a movement which eventually considered self-expression and noninterference by the teacher an important tenet of its program. Indeed, many of the practices advocated in the journals of the Progressive Education Association and in other progressive publications were exaggerated to such a degree that Dewey felt compelled, in 1938, to write a book, *Experience and Education* (20), which was intended to clarify his views regarding the nature of education. Art education shifted from a concern with correct drawing, picture study, and hand-eye coordination to an emphasis upon unlocking the *creative* capacities of children. Creativity, a concept seldom found in the literature prior to the twenties, now became one of art education's major organizing ideas. If a child, by nature, had the capacity for creative intelligent action, perhaps art education could be instrumental in helping the child realize his latent creativity.

A number of progressives writing on art education articulated the role of creativity in art and education. Margaret Mathias (21), Bell Boas (22), Florence Cane (23), and, later, Victor D'Amico (24) pointed to the creative abilities of the child and to the unique cognitive world which he possessed. Art, they claimed, could unlock these latent creative capacities and what is more, once developed, these abilities could be applied to areas other than the arts. Thus, art education was important not only because it developed creativity in art but also because it developed creativity in general. That was a most significant shift. With this subtle but crucial shift the teaching of art became an instrumentality for creative development in all walks of life; it was to be a process-oriented activity which was to have as one of its major goals the development of children's creative thinking. "Creative self-expression" was soon to become the watchword of the new art education that emerged during this period.

With the concern for the creative development of the child there developed an interest in the relationship of art to the other subject areas of the curriculum. The progressives, concerned as they were with meaningful learning and with eliminating the artificial dichotomies of the traditional curriculum, tried to build their program around problems or projects. The project method developed by William Heard Kilpatrick (25), a disciple of Dewey and a Professor of Education at Columbia, was a means whereby students would investigate a problem area by bringing to bear upon it the tools and methods of a host of disciplines. If students studied the Middle Ages, they were encouraged not only to understand the social arrangements between the master and his serfs but were encouraged also to build a castle or to construct figures of knights and their armor. Here, art had an important function to perform. Through art the students could learn more clearly about the practices and ideas that animated the medieval period. Art was to be a correlated activity and not "cubby-holed" as an independent subject area unrelated to the projects in which children engaged. With this conception of the role and function of art, art was again used as an instrumentality, but this time not so much a means for developing the general creative abilities of the child as a means of teaching important ideas. With this view of educational method, art was in the service of concept formation.

There was still another type of emphasis that characterized art education during the twenties and thirties; this was an emphasis on the therapeutic aspects of work in art. Freud, whose *On the Interpretations of Dreams* was published in 1900, had a slow but growing influence on American intellectuals concerned with education (26). This influence grew steadily from the turn of the century on and was given an important thrust forward when Hall, as President of Clark University in 1909, invited Freud to come to America to lecture on his work. By a decade or so later the intellectuals in the East were quite familiar with his concepts of ego, id, and superego. In art education people such as Margaret Naumberg (27) saw the relationship between the art of the child and the unconscious needs and desires that underlie his behavior. To the child experiencing stress under the rigors of growing up and in the confines of the school, the visual arts could serve as a form of release. Art could, if used intelligently, contribute to the mental health of the child by giving him an opportunity to alleviate those tensions and communicate those meanings that he could not articulate in discursive language. Art in the schools could be a type of therapy, a preventive medicine that contributes to the psychological comfort of the child. On this view, art was in the service of mental health.

The Recognition of Modern Art, Technology, and Scientific Inquiry

Developments in art education since the thirties have been various. The trends initiated in the twenties and early thirties continued as did some of the practices that were begun before the turn of the century. But two developments stand out as being especially important. One of these was the slow but growing recognition of those artists who worked in the modern idiom and the second was the writing and stature of Viktor Lowenfeld.

The date of the birth of the modern movement in art is a disputed issue. Whether it started with Delacroix and the practice of going directly to nature for one's subject matter or with the Impressionists and their concern with light, with Cézanne and his emphasis on form, or with Kandinsky and the abstract movement has not been settled. This dispute need not concern us here. If it is recognized that artists working in Europe in the 1880's and 1890's developed a style and approach to visual art that differed radically from the realism of the middle of the nineteenth century, this will be sufficient. The work of the Post-Impressionists, the Fauves, the Cubists, and the Expressionists was not new by the thirties. Indeed, in 1913 the famous Armory Show, held in New York, Chicago, and Boston, displayed paintings by the foremost moderns. Yet art education in both its aesthetic tastes and its practices seems to have been well insulated from the then current (and not so current) artistic movements. If one is to judge the type of aesthetic values held in

art education by the kinds of projects advocated and the type of work displayed in
art education journals, art education's insulation from the mainstream of modern
art did not change from its neo-Victorian character until the late forties. Puppetry,
egg coloring, leather tooling, and stencil designs were characteristically advocated
and displayed on the pages of the most widely circulated art education journals.
But the influence of the modern artist could not be held back. By the early fifties
art educators began to recognize the "new," sixty-year-old aesthetic, and the influence of Cubism, Surrealism, and Expressionism began to affect the type of instruction taking place in the schools and the type of work which the students were
producing.

The use of varied materials in the classroom, well beyond standard art media,
was now being advocated. The materials approach to art was seen as a device for
furthering the creative capacities of students and developing their sensitivity to
texture, form, and design. The ideas generated in the Bauhaus (28), a school of
design in Germany which attempted to prepare designers to meet the needs of a
technological society, began by the fifties to affect some art education programs in
the schools of the United States. Explorations to determine the constructive possibilities of new, "non-art" materials were advocated, the construction of purely
formal or abstract three-dimensional sculpture was introduced, and the experimental treatment of visual qualities in two-dimensional media was pursued.
Modern art began its slow but steady advance into the art curriculum, and the
present-day character of art instruction in the public schools of America had found
its beginning. Art education not only attempted to develop the creative capacities
of students through the use of novel visual problems, but it could also sensitize them
to a host of media previously considered outside the scope of the field of art.

The work of Viktor Lowenfeld in American art education is significant for
several reasons: first, because through the three of his four books that were printed
in English he, more than any other, laid a psychological foundation for the way in
which children develop in and through art; second, because he crystallized much of
the teaching about art education that had developed through the progressive era;
and third, because his system became one of the major psychological systems in
which teachers of art were trained during the late forties and fifties in the United
States and Europe. *The Nature of Creative Activity* (29) and *Creative and Mental
Growth* (30) are hallmarks in the literature of art education, the latter having been
translated into several languages and having undergone three revisions by the time
of Lowenfeld's death in 1960. It is difficult to summarize the work of a man in a few
sentences, yet the major thesis of Lowenfeld's work is clear-cut. He was interested
in the creative and mental growth of the child and saw art as a vehicle for facilitat-
ing this growth. Although art was important to him in his own life, and although he
valued it for students, his primary concern was in the growth of the child as a seeing,
thinking, and feeling human being — concerns that were not alien to those who
were brought up on the educational philosophies of Dewey and Kilpatrick. Art
education, as Lowenfeld saw it and as he encouraged teachers to view it, should

not lose sight of the child and what was happening to him in the *process* of working with art media. The child was paramount, the art instrumental. Copying and using coloring books were forbidden, and art contests for children were deemed inappropriate if not downright harmful.

Lowenfeld's ideas, contained in his widely read books, articles and speeches, set the stage for current practices and assumptions among art educators in the fifties. Creative activity and self-expression in art gained a new stature through his publications, and the significance of the child was again re-emphasized in the programs that prepared teachers of art.

Lowenfeld influenced art education not only through his writing but also because he provided a model for careful, scholarly inquiry in art education. Much of Lowenfeld's work as an art educator was scientific, and he was one of the few who published in psychological journals. Furthermore, in his position as chairman of one of the largest graduate programs in art education, he was in a position to influence future art educators who themselves would be responsible for the education of teachers of art. In short, Lowenfeld not only wrote two of the most significant books in the field of art education and provided a model for scholarly inquiry into the field, but also worked directly with those who were later to become professors of art education in the colleges and universities in the United States and in Europe.

What we have seen in this overview of some of the significant developments in the history of art education is a past characterized by a variety of practices, theories, and objectives. As American society has changed, new responsibilities have been placed upon the school. Art education as one of the instrumentalities within the school has, as a consequence, changed with the institutions. If society saw education as a means of creating an individual of culture, art was seen as a tool for developing cultured tastes and cultural accomplishments. If schools were to prepare citizens to contribute to the economic welfare of the nation, art was to be taught as an important vocational skill. If the schools' major task was to develop man's creative intelligence, art became a means for unlocking the child's potential creativity. Art education, inescapably, operates within the context of the school and within the context of the society. We can expect that as American society changes in the future, new and different objectives and practices for art education will be advocated.

One of the crucial tasks for art educators is not one of finding ways to resist change but, rather, to employ critical procedures by which wise choices may be made among competing proposals for change. In matters of fact the body of conclusions provided by research in the behavioral sciences may be the most appropriate resource to consult. But where critical answers to factual problems relevant to art education are not available, art educators must themselves engage in scientific research. Likewise, in matters of value, art educators must pursue philosophic research. Art education, especially since the early fifties, has considered a part of its task the provision of relevant data through empirical research. But to determine with any clarity the ends worth pursuing is not a problem to be solved by the massing of scientific data. However important such data may be, the problem of what ends are worth pursuing is reasonably managed by philosophic inquiry. Indeed, the extent to which *this* inquiry should or should not, can or cannot, employ various scientific procedures is itself a philosophic problem. So we can see that neither scientific nor philosophic inquiry should be considered alien to the field of art education. When art educators engage in research into both factual and value problems, they more firmly establish — and even enlarge — the traditional domain of art education. The second and third sections of this chapter deal, respectively, with the need for and the limits of scientific research and with the need for and character of philosophic research in art education.

Research in Art Education

The Need for Research

We have seen, in the preceding section, how the field of art education has grown toward intellectual maturity, how it has become sophisticated to the point of recognizing that there is no single authoritative source of information on educational theory and practice. It has become clear that there are many sources of viable ideas in a multi-valued society. Some of these sources are highly visible to teachers — the curriculum guide, the art education textbook, the directives of the principal and board of education; other sources are almost indistinguishable from the social and political fabric of American life; still others lie buried in the literature of psychology, sociology, philosophy, and education. The sophistication results when school people find that simple "black and white" answers will no longer do. The increasingly complex operation of the schools forces them to look beyond the prevailing ideas, opinions, and beliefs about education in their immediate environments to ideas having more power — ideas supported by evidence, ideas justified by reason, ideas that lead to resolutions of the most basic questions one can ask about art education.

But intellectual sophistication is not merely the recognition of the need for critically worked-out answers to our problems. It is also a characteristic of that mode of thought able to tolerate, work with, and choose among competing ideas — ideas that represent divergent or even contradictory answers. In this regard, there is no room for complacency, for an awareness of conflicts in educational thought, while a necessary condition for their resolution, is not sufficient for it. Not only must art educators be able to identify and test the major available ideas bearing upon the problems in their field, but, as some of these ideas are found to be inadequate, art educators must be able to generate and test new ones. Thus, the need for continuing research becomes increasingly apparent.

Attitudes Toward Research

In art education attitudes toward scientific research cluster around two poles. One group tends to view research with fear, the other with confidence; one with apprehension and skepticism, the other with assurance and faith. Some claim scientific research can only stifle creativity; others see it as the saving grace for a field too deeply steeped in romanticism. But amidst the discussions, researchers in art education go about their work studying the problems in art education, and since the 1950's an impressive body of scientific literature has been produced (31). Schools that once had little or nothing to do with research are beginning to prepare future teachers of art who are not only competent in art but who are also literate in science. Those who embrace scientific research look upon knowledge as the cornerstone of correct action. Since knowledge is desired, it is only reasonable that the method of science should be used as the primary tool in knowledge-making. Indeed, according to some philosophers of science, it is the only way in which knowledge can be produced, for it is the only way in which warrant can be obtained for belief. All knowledge claims that are untestable are thereby unwarranted, and hence inadmissible as knowledge. Furthermore, since scientific knowledge is theoretical, that is, propositional and predictive, it is not difficult to understand why such knowledge should be considered useful in the education of the teacher of art. Propositions are communicable, and when predictive, powerful. Thus, it is held as a truism that the most useful tool for good teaching is good theory. To the extent to which it contributes to the modification and expansion of theory, research is held to contribute to good teaching. Teachers who understand such theory are thought to be better able to make more accurate predictions, obtain better control, and therefore are able to get on more efficiently with the educational task.

It seems clear that scientific research in art education will continue to grow. But with this growth there are certain potential pitfalls, among which is the possibility that we may expect too much from research or that we may expect too little. The first attitude breeds disappointment; the second, neglect or rejection. In our efforts to improve art education through the improvement of the art teacher's education, we need to maintain a realistic stance regarding the limitations as well as the potential usefulness of scientific research. It would therefore be important to identify some of these limitations and then to indicate what kinds of research might contribute to the education of future (and present) teachers of art.

Limitations of Present Research

The situation with which a teacher is concerned in the classroom has some similarity to the experimental situations in research since both function as change agents. If, through *experimental* research, it were possible to identify the necessary and sufficient conditions for achieving desired ends, teaching would be much easier. The teacher would decide what he wanted to achieve, read the literature to determine what conditions would bring it about, and employ those conditions to attain his desired ends. Armed with such knowledge teachers could enter the classroom assured of success. But as yet such knowledge does not exist. It does not take long to find that significant experimental studies in education are exceedingly rare.

They are rare partly because human populations are difficult to obtain for experimental purposes and partly because of the difficulty of meeting the criteria necessary for experimentation in the human behavioral sciences. It is an extremely difficult task to obtain both internal and external validity under truly controlled conditions with equivalent samples. Experimental research in teacher education which would be *directly* useful would not only identify the kinds of teacher-controlled conditions which effect lasting change on the part of pupils; it would also identify the conditions employed in the teacher education program that caused the changes in the teacher which subsequently caused desired changes in pupil behavior. Thus, such research would identify *two* types of experimental conditions, one treating the teacher-in-training and the other treating the student directly. An examination of research yearbooks in art education, past issues of *Studies in Art Education*, and issues of *Psychological Abstracts* and *Child Development* reveals that such research simply is not available.

The second type of research, namely, *descriptive* research, is much more plentiful in both art education and general education but is far less directly useful. Descriptive research reports conditions and relationships *as they are* and has no direct implications for identifying the kinds of conditions that will change the very conditions described. Yet the task of the teacher is not essentially to be able to describe behavior or even to understand it, but to change it. The move from comprehension of descriptive findings to experimental action in particular situations relies upon a careful and artful interpretation and transformation of descriptive data by the teacher.

The making of such transformations is no easy task, for as Getzels and Jackson (32), Oliver and Shaver (33), and Tyler (34) have pointed out, many of the descriptive studies end up with findings that are conceptually barren. For example, discovering that the well-liked teacher is energetic, friendly, courteous, kind, and good-humored tells us really very little because such findings are frequently unrelated to a larger theoretical model that would be useful for understanding their meanings. When research findings do not contribute to the verification, modification, or refutation of a theoretical model, their utility is severely curtailed. In short, the findings of experimental research which would be the most useful are the least available, while the findings of descriptive research which are the most available are the least useful.

Even when significant descriptive and experimental research findings are available, however, two major problems remain. The first is a problem of methodology; the second, a problem of values. Let us examine these problems in that order.

Most research carried out in the behavioral sciences uses statistical methodologies. These methodologies generate findings that are directly relevant to populations or samples rather than to individuals. Yet the teacher is concerned not only with groups (and in the teaching of art he is perhaps even less concerned than in some of the academic areas) but with the concrete reality of a particular student in a particular classroom. Findings from statistical research must be treated with the utmost care in making teaching decisions designed to affect particular cases. The usefulness of such findings is realized only if artfully transformed. This kind of transformation is difficult because some of the actions the teacher employs in the teaching act may be only tenuously influenced by the findings he may want to use in the classroom. That is, his own behavior as a teacher may not be controlled, in the main, by a rational consciousness logically guiding his day-to-day, personal interactions with students. While the conscious use of self may be a worthy goal to strive for in the classroom, there may be limits as to how conscious one can be about the self-in-action. And it may not be too far-fetched to entertain the thought that some of the preconscious aspects of teacher behavior may be among the most artful and beneficial of the teaching act.

That teaching behavior does not improve directly with increased comprehension of research findings may be observed by checking the teaching behavior of the "haves" and "have-nots" of research, by observing the teaching behavior of those most and those least sophisticated in research in the behavioral sciences. It has been our impression that no important differences in teaching behavior exist for *groups* of individuals teaching in college departments of English, Art, and Music as compared to those in departments of Psychology, Education, and Sociology. Knowledge of research is clearly not a sufficient condition for teaching competence, and the extent to which it is a necessary condition still needs to be determined.

A second limitation of scientific research concerns the value problem. We cannot look to scientific research to determine what we *ought* to do because science cannot presently tell us what kind of an education children ought to have. More generally, science cannot presently deal with normative problems. Knowing what is or what can be does not tell us what ought to be. *Science can help us attain the desired but cannot help us determine the desirable.* But even if this were not a problem, we would still find little widespread agreement on what we mean by the good or effective teacher of art. For example, do we mean by the good teacher of art one who nurtures artistic creativity or one who nurtures creativity in other areas? It may not be possible to do both simultaneously. Do we mean by the good teacher one who encourages a liking for art or one who helps the student learn to discriminate among works of art? The two may not be related. Do we mean by the good teacher of art one who enables children to turn out high quality art work or one who leads the child to a healthy psychological adjustment? One end might be achieved at the cost of the other. And if it were possible to achieve all ends without excluding any, we would still have to decide which ought to have priority. In short, the very concept of who and what a good teacher of art is — the very concept which is needed for directing the use of research findings and theory — is itself an issue of contention.

Does this mean that empirical research is of no use in the education of the teacher of art? We think not. Present research does not have much to say *for* the education of the teacher of art, but it has a great deal to say *to* the art educator and to those who educate him.

The theoretical models and empirical findings emerging from the work of the behavioral scientist are important and useful for the same reasons that any of the good scientific theories are important and useful. Such theories *may* provide the teacher with new frames of reference for viewing human behavior. New theories *may* open up new ways of viewing the world. The power of such views is clearly evident in the dramatic contributions of a Freud or a Dewey, but it is also evident in the more subtle and perhaps not as dramatic contributions of a Schachtel or a Kubie (35). Indeed, new theoretical cosmologies or world outlooks and the findings that they generate can open up new behavioral vistas to the teacher of art. This is not to imply that with new vistas the teacher's problems become simpler. To the contrary, precisely because of the new vistas, new problems arise. Teachers who once believed simply that the artistically diffident child was untalented has a much simpler answer than teachers have who are aware of the multitude of factors affecting the human condition. It is paradoxical that a science committed to the creation of laws of high generality and simplicity should effectuate complexity. It is in this sense that the products of scientific research do not simplify the teacher's task; they make it more complex, and in the *short run*, more difficult.

But such contributions from research can, *in the long run*, improve things; they can militate against the superstitions that otherwise may be difficult to resist. For example, knowing that the relationship between creativity and IQ is only moderate (36) can weaken the myth that only the intellectually gifted student, as measured by IQ, can be creative. Findings such as these have no direct application in the classroom. Such findings, by themselves, suggest nothing for teaching action. These kinds of findings — and these are of the general type produced by research — need to be artfully translated by a sensitive and artistic teacher of art. While the problem of making such translations is difficult, it is not impossible, and given the present state of theory and method in the behavioral sciences we can do little more. Scientific research is useful in teaching *not* because it can provide directives, but because it can provide perspectives: it can provide new ways to look at old problems and can help us identify some new ones at the same time. What the teacher does after he sees these worlds through the windows of research is dependent upon his own artfulness as a teacher and perhaps on his own motives for teaching.

We believe art education, as a profession, has two kinds of responsibilities regarding research and the education of the teacher. The first is to prepare students in a manner that will help them become literate in research. Students of art education need to be able to understand the language of research if they are to be effective in utilizing the conclusions of research. Second, we in the field cannot afford the luxury of having others do our work. People in psychology, general education, and sociology don't have our problems as their central concern. Moreover, they are not generally aware of our problems. We will have to continue to learn how to deal with our own problems. Thus, we will have to prepare teachers of art who are not only able to read research but who also have the research skills to be able to deal with their theoretical problems directly. In our enthusiasm for science it would be ironic if we forgot that in the final analysis it takes an artful teacher of art to extract, judiciously and with wisdom, the implications research has for improving the education of children in and through art.

Methods of Research Appropriate for Art Education

To the extent we can assume that people do research because they seek to answer questions, the method of research one uses depends upon the kind of question one asks. For example, to answer the question: "How many jars of each color of paint do I have in the storeroom?" requires only a simple inventory — you just count what's there. The question, "How much paint will the students in my school district probably use next year?" requires a prediction based on past performance. Record-keeping of the number of students and amount of paint used over several years and simple arithmetic will do. ("They use as much paint as you let 'em," is an interesting but probably unsatisfactory answer.) Selections in Parts II–VII of this anthology provide answers to more basic questions. "What factors influence human development in art?" the central question of Part III, is basic in the sense that answers entail claims having far greater ranges of generality and, hence, wider applicability than answers to those questions above. The answers apply not merely to this or that situation but to all possible situations involving the same conditions. If the question concerns description, explanation, or prediction with respect to attributes, objects, or events, it may require scientific inquiry. The scientific methods exhibited in the selections in Part III are characteristic of behavioral research in general (37).

But, to expand upon the value problem identified earlier, there are *other* kinds of basic questions art educators can ask that are not answered by scientific inquiry. To illustrate one kind of question, which is in an important sense "nonfactual," we may note, first, that scientific researchers in art education *operationally define* their key terms; that is, the entire meaning of their central conceptions is stipulated as (1) certain measurable elements (variables) to be found in school situations and (2) the procedure by which these elements will be measured. For example, *art* may be defined as "all paintings and drawings produced by 100 students during 20 weeks of instruction," *art learning* as "the increase in scores, as measured on a scale, for degrees of expressiveness between first and last art products as judged by experts," *teaching* as "specified behavior the art teacher displays to students." Without operational definitions such as these the phenomena to be investigated cannot be measured and empirical research cannot proceed. However, before — or even after — all the "facts" are in, one may legitimately ask: How is one to *justify* labeling as "art" the paintings and drawings of these students, operational definitions notwithstanding? Or, more generally, one may ask: What is art, or more exactly, what is worthy of being judged art? This is a central question of Part II. One answer, Croce's, is that art is a nonphysical intuition which cannot be scientifically measured.

Implicit value assumptions in empirical research may be revealed by such philosophic questions, and if pursued with rigor, they call for philosophical inquiry. Their resolution depends upon logical analysis and criticism of alternative concepts of art, learning, curriculum, and the like, and possibly they might require the proposal of new objectives of human endeavor. Philosophic questions about art education, as with other areas of human experience, characteristically center on *value* problems. Art experience, perhaps more than other kinds of experience, is an affair to be intrinsically valued. Thus, questions about the nature of what it is that is to be valued for its own sake and problems arising when views concerning this nature conflict with one another require much more carefully wrought answers than our common sense can provide.

But there are many other value questions of interest to art teachers besides the question of what is of intrinsic worth. How should artistic performances be evaluated? What ought to be the role of art education in the curriculum, in the community, in society? These questions typically do not arise as a result of an examination of the value assumptions and factual conclusions of research in the behavioral sciences. They arise when the art teacher, curriculum specialist, or school administrator is confronted with the task of identifying, justifying, defending, proposing, or rejecting goals for art education in relation to other educational goals or values. Yet it would seem that scientific facts about learning and the learner and about the school and society are highly relevant to the achievement of adequate value judgments in art education. It remains to suggest how they may be relevant.

The Problem of the Relationship Between Fact and Value

Art teachers make value judgments every day of their professional lives. Some of these judgments concern such relatively simple matters as the choice of art materials and tools to have available for the children's use; other judgments are much more complex, such as the planning of the sequence of art lessons, the evaluation of progress made, and decisions as to how to handle individual differences among students. The alert art teacher will want to take advantage of the known facts about child growth and development in art, about learning, creativity, and so on, in order to be more effective in his work. In his eagerness to incorporate what established facts there are into his day-to-day teaching he may overgeneralize these facts, as we have already mentioned. But a potentially more serious error that characterizes much of our thinking in art education is the logical error of attempting to derive value judgments solely from factual claims. It is potentially serious because even if our beliefs about the facts are true, some of our chief arguments for the value of art and art education can be discredited because they are logically unsound, i.e., our conclusions do not validly follow from our premises.

To illustrate with a typical argument one might well expect to hear from an art teacher informed in the area of creativity:

Research has shown that creative behavior is promoted by establishing X, Y, and Z conditions in the classroom.

Therefore, the principal ought to allow me the freedom to establish these conditions in my art classroom.

This argument, as it stands, is invalid; nothing about what anyone *ought* or *ought not* to do logically follows from what *is* the case. It is an invalid argument even if, in the above case, empirical research conclusively establishes that X, Y, and Z conditions promote creativity. The general logical rule is that nothing can appear in the conclusion of a valid argument which does not appear in its premises. Applying this rule to the above argument we may note that, while an "ought" appears in the conclusion, no "oughts" or other value words appear in the premise. Viewed as a categorical syllogism the argument is missing its major value premise. Art teachers, of course, would have no trouble in supplying one. Thus, a complete and now valid argument might look like this:

Art teachers ought to establish whatever conditions promote creative behavior. Conditions which promote creative behavior are X, Y, and Z.
Therefore, art teachers ought to establish X, Y, and Z.

But in the process of making explicit one's value premise in order to establish a valid argument, the argument becomes vulnerable to another kind of attack. Now that the value premise is visible, the principal, other teachers, students, and parents may view it with something less than enthusiasm and conceivably might argue for one which would require conditions that could suppress creativity. As a matter of fact, some research indicates that teachers, students, and parents tend to place a low value on creative behavior and may even oppose those conditions that promote it (38). They believe that conformity — not creativity — makes for social acceptance and success in adult life. And the conditions which promote conformity in thought and action may well be antithetical to creativity. Thus, advocates of conformity could argue just as well against the art teachers' conclusion by starting with *their* premises.

Now what? If correct reasoning is to be identified with valid syllogistic argument, then evidently one is free to prove that he ought to act in a certain way merely by choosing the appropriate premises. It would seem, then, that the choice among moral premises is arbitrary, at least with regard to reason. At this point in our analysis of the relation between fact and value the reader will no doubt be mumbling something to the effect that reason has no business in matters of ultimate value anyway. It so happens that he could marshal much philosophic support for this view, from positions as diverse in other respects as ethical hedonism and existentialism. For example, David Hume, the eighteenth-century empiricistic philosopher (who was the first modern philosopher to call attention to the logical mistake of deriving the "ought" from the "is"), went so far as to say that "Morals excite passions, and produce or prevent actions. Reason of itself is utterly impotent in this particular. The rules of morality, therefore, are not the conclusions of our reason" (39). His ethical theory was based on the idea that human actions were decided by what proved to be agreeable or disagreeable.

On the other hand, Aristotle argued that man's "intuitive reason" grasped first principles, while man's "philosophical wisdom" was capable of combining intuitive reason and logical demonstration to discover the nature of the good. Other ethical theories depend upon such notions as an innate moral sense or conscience, an absolute moral law, subjective psychological sensations, and the like. While there is no general consensus among philosophers as to the nature and justification of values such as there is among physicists about the nature of the atom, they do tend to agree that questions of value *cannot be reduced without remainder* to the kinds of questions that the behavioral sciences seek to answer (40). While an understanding of precisely how various philosophic positions differ and how they agree on matters of value would be an invaluable aid for critical inquiry into value problems in art education, this is not the place for more than the brief analysis of the relationship of fact and value presented here. Nevertheless, we hope it persuades the reader that if one intends to pursue value questions in art education in a critical manner, he will inevitably be engaged in philosophic inquiry into philosophic issues.

Research and the Future of Art in the Public Schools

Determinism and Its Possible Effects on Research

The efficacy of science is certainly a central belief of modern man. Perhaps it is the one belief that distinguishes him as modern. For of all the diverse beliefs entertained in human history concerning man's power to control his worldly fortunes, it is this belief that appears to be a candidate for universality. Even now there is widespread agreement among the educated peoples of the world — whether Western, Asiatic, Middle-Eastern, or African — that scientific knowledge, even the apparently "impractical" sort, does give man the power to change much of his environment. Now there can be little doubt that, through inquiry into fossils, the nucleus of the atom, or the future course of a hurricane, man derives his most reliable knowledge about *what was, what is,* and *what is possible.* But does he also discover *what will be?* Can he, for instance, discover his fate?

The answers to be found are ambiguous to say the least: in some contexts modern man does seem to believe that science can reveal a predetermined future; in other contexts, however, he believes implicitly in his ability to change or modify the future. Of course, art teachers are as concerned as anyone else with "the future." And some of them, graduate students and others, do research with an eye to the future of art in the public schools. Because their beliefs and attitudes — including their answer to the "cosmic" question above — provide the motivation for much of their research and even affect the kind of research problems they attack, we would like, in this section, to raise a few caution flags about the attitudes that may develop as we ponder our future as art teachers and researchers. Then we will conclude with some problems for research which we believe are relevant to the future of the field.

Perhaps that about which we are concerned may best be illustrated by a story of free enterprise. It seems that there was a man who came to this country many years ago as an immigrant. He decided to start a hot dog stand. Money was scarcer then than now, for this was during the depression. But by dint of imagination and trial and error — but mostly by hard work — he managed to build up his stand. First, he added items to the menu; then he hired waitresses; then he built additions on to his original stand. While all of his decisions were not immediately successful — the time he raised the price of a hamburger from fifteen to twenty-five cents, business really slumped — he did manage to establish a thriving "drive-in" business. He also raised a family. Now this fellow remembered how hard it was to succeed without an education, and vowed that he would send his boy to college. And he did! A B.A., M.A., and Ph.D. in business economics were successfully won at a famous university. The father, impressed with his son's learning, decided to ask for *scientific advice* on how to run his drive-in restaurant. The boy, having knowledge of a predicted slump in the national economy, advised his father to economize by firing the waitresses. This was done. And, sure enough, business at the drive-in fell off sharply. The father was grateful for his son's wisdom. Shortly thereafter the son again offered some expert advice: "Dad, you had better cut down on the menu; another slump is coming." The old man did, and — sure enough — business got terrible! After a few more "scientific predictions" the old man went bankrupt. But his losses were only slight; think what they might have been! He remained eternally grateful for the business forecasts of his son.

How many educators, in their amazement over recent scientific achievements — which, in a sense, are the result of true predictions — are not prone to act either like the father or the son in the story? Now, it *is* statistically probable that the school population will double in the near future. It is also probably true that there will be an increasing emphasis on the so-called "hard" subjects — the "three R's," languages, and the sciences. And teaching machines, TV classrooms, and other devices will no doubt facilitate this shift. Certainly art teachers will be hard-pressed to maintain their business of teaching art to the youth of our country. But, even if we are all aware of these impending events in the public schools, meaningful questions are still before us: What course should *we* follow? What ought *we* to do?

There is, of course, a philosophic argument underlying this central problem which is at least as old as early Greek thought. It is the argument between those who believe in free will and those who believe in determinism, and it is very much alive today (41). Translating the situation in art education in these terms, we might on the one hand believe that the future of art in the public schools is decided by the immutable course of history. Thus, this argument runs, certainly no one art teacher alone in a public school could possibly alter the fact that science is becoming more and more important in the curriculum. So we might as well resign ourselves to coming events. "Anyway," the art teacher might say, "I've got a certificate to teach social studies!" On the other side of the argument, art teachers may believe that *everything they do professionally* — the special art exhibition they put up in the community, the talk they give to the P.T.A., that extra effort in the classroom, the research problems they undertake — has some effect on the future of their students, on the school, and even on the community.

Without dragging out the technical arguments for and against determinism, we think it fair to say that science does not stand or fall on whether events are conceived as determined or not. As a matter of fact, scientists themselves take different sides on this philosophic problem and still manage to work in science. Our own position is that man is free to choose much of his future. For example, the art teacher may choose to set up that special exhibit; he can choose to try to interest children in an art career, and so on. Our point here is that the future of art in the public schools will be decided not by cosmic forces at work in the universe, but rather by people struggling to secure their futures against the contingencies of the cold war, a rising population, automation, or whatever. A major problem is that we tend to take the attitude that the *value* of art in the schools is self-evident; so the researchers among us are after the *facts* of art education. But others among these people are members of school boards and citizens committees, submarine builders, administrators, and taxpayers, who may agree with our facts, but who may not share our attitudes and beliefs about the value of art in the school. Here we should be careful: we are not necessarily the "good guys." We have already seen, in the preceding section, how valid conclusions may be drawn from premises we may not want to accept. And the "goodness" or "badness" of our attitudes and actions is someone's judgment based on certain criteria. Thus, to raise the problem of how, or in what ways, we should act suggests a prior question: *On what criteria should we act?*

Before we propose some such criteria, it would be wise to state explicitly what perhaps was only implicit in the foregoing discussion. We believe it is characteristic of human experience that ultimately all decisions concerning alternative ethical values are our *own*. That is, we personally adopt them. Others may decide, for example, that everyone *ought* to believe in communism, democracy, or pacifism. But only we as individuals finally decide. (Existentialists have made much philosophical hay over this simple fact of life.) And our crucial educational problems are much like other ethical problems in that they arise whenever there are conflicts among alternative sets of values. Thus, the art teacher in his own classroom inescapably makes ethical choices: he will teach in a certain manner according to the criteria or standards he chooses. The choice may be to acquiesce to the choices of others or to propose new alternatives. The consequences may range from a raise and tenure to a dismissal from his position. Yet he is free to choose to let even this come about.

Minimal Criteria for Critical Thinking in Art Education

If people in the field of art education want to claim that they have more than a conventional understanding of art and art education — if they aim at better than the layman's conception of their subject matter, then they are obliged to measure their theorizing, or anyone's professional writing or talk, against those minimal criteria for theoretical adequacy that are implicitly agreed upon by those researchers and scholars who work with scientific or philosophic theory. Our aim here is to help in the evaluation and possible reconstruction of contemporary art education theories (42).

First, professional theorizing should proceed in light of the major alternative theories of art and art education, and offer a basis for choice among these alternatives (e.g., reasons should be given for holding that art is intuitive knowledge, or that art cannot be learned). This basis itself must be subject to criticism, or fallible.

Second, professional theorizing should be offered and evaluated in view of the full range of practices of art education. Talk is irresponsible and incompetent when it presents ideas without accounting for these ideas in relation to the broad educational context.

Third, professional theorizing about art education should reflect a significant understanding of the history of art, the practices of artists, and the conditions under which they have worked.

Fourth, professional theorizing should meet the conditions of scientific inquiry where that inquiry is applicable. No theory or criticism of theory or practice should ignore or contradict established scientific facts where these facts are relevant to the theory or criticism.

Fifth, professional theorizing should meet the minimal conditions of logic (e.g., the principles of coherence and consistency).

Sixth, professional theorizing need be only as precise as present or anticipated problems or situations demand.

Seventh, professional theorizing should be concerned to establish or propose specific means, ends, and methods in art education; i.e., goals should be stated so as to suggest the means or teaching procedures by which these goals are to be achieved.

The eighth criterion is that all criteria for evaluating critical thinking, whether that thinking is about student performance, curriculum proposals, learning goals, or other aspects of the art program in the schools, should in principle be publicly available to students, parents, teachers, and administrators alike. This does not imply, of course, that everyone is qualified to establish adequate standards of scientific, philosophical, artistic, or teaching performance.

By way of contrast and further clarification, it would be profitable to identify briefly what we consider to be typical *unsound* criteria that guide too much of our professional thinking. Some of these false standards are operating when: (1) we accept or reject an idea about art because of its source (e.g., when a famous artist pleads: "Art will save mankind," or when Harry Truman comments on modern art: ". . . merely the vaporings of half-baked, lazy people . . . the ability to make things appear as they are is the first requisite of an artist," the person is judged rather than the evidence offered in support of his statement); (2) we confuse the soundness of ideas with demonstrated depth of conviction, or the literary or aesthetic merit of their author (e.g., the style of Plato or Santayana); (3) we disparage reasonable talk about art while presenting our own reasons for doing so (e.g., the reasoned skepticism of some contemporary artists over the role of reason in art talk).

At this point it may be asked: Granting these criteria, how does one go about establishing his goals, means, and methods? Given the above standards, the answer is that the art teacher must initiate his own inquiry. This brings us to our underlying proposal concerning the *kind* of research needed here.

Now we think the field *ought* to have more scientifically established facts available than we now have on matters relevant to art education — facts about creativity, artistic learning, and social forces affecting art. But this statement itself is a value judgment that cannot logically be derived solely from the descriptive findings of the social sciences, as we have seen earlier; likewise neither can other judgments as to what matters — facts, criteria, problems — are relevant to art education be so derived. *Philosophical inquiry*, on the other hand, is chiefly concerned with the significance of knowledge for the value problems of men, evaluation of the adequacy of value judgments, and the generation of proposals for what *ought to be*. Thus, its methods are analytical, critical, and speculative. So our proposal is just this: The art educator as researcher must inquire into those ethical problems resulting from the competing value orientations abroad in his school and society. His inquiry must result in a conception of an art program meeting at least the above-named minimal criteria. Philosophic inquiry, we are arguing, provides a rational basis for securing the future of art in the public schools.

REFERENCES

1. See *Writings of Franklin*, A. H. Smyth, ed. New York: The Macmillan Co., 1905.

2. For a competent treatment of the history of art education see Frances Bland Belshe's unpublished dissertation, "A History of Art Education in the Public Schools of the United States," Yale University, 1946.

3. William Minifie. *A Text Book of Geometrical Drawing*. Boston: Hilliard, Gray, Little, and Williams, 1830.

4. William Bently Fowle. *The Eye and the Hand; Being a Series of Practical Lessons in Drawing, for the Training of These Important Organs, Adapted to the Use of Common Schools*. Boston: W. B. Fowle, 1847, 94 pp.

5. For a discussion of Fowle's work on monotorial schools see, *Manual of Mutual Instruction: Consisting of Mr. Fowle's Directions* by William Russell. Boston: Wait, Greene, and Co., 1826.

6. For a history of the arts in American life see Holger Cahill, editor. *American Folk Art*. New York: Museum of Modern Art, 1932.

7. Belshe, *op cit.*

8. "The Relation of Art to Education," *Circulars of Information of Bureau of Education*, No. 2. Washington: Government Printing Office, 1874, pp. 86, 88.

9. Perhaps the most influential was Walter Smith. *Teachers Manual of Free Hand Drawing and Designing*. Boston: Charles Osgood and Co., 1873.

10. For an excellent treatment of Hall's work as it related to the child study movement see Lawrence Cremin's, *The Transformation of the School*. New York: Alfred A. Knopf, 1961, as well as Hall's own writings which include *Educational Problems*. New York and London: D. Appleton and Co., 1911.

11. Quoted from Frederick M. Logan's *The Growth of Art in American Schools*. New York: Harper and Bros., 1955, p. 70.

12. *The Applied Arts Book, The Voice of the Applied Arts Guild of Worcester, Massachusetts,* Vol. 1, No. 1 (September 1901), p. 4.

13. Oscar Neale. *Picture Study in the Grades.* Milwaukee: O. W. Neale Publishing Co., 1927. From the Preface.

14. Arthur W. Dow. *The Theory and Practice of Teaching Art.* New York: Teachers College, Columbia University, 1908.

15. Walter Sargent. *Fine and Industrial Arts in Elementary Schools.* Boston: Ginn and Co., 1912, pp. 5–7.

16. *Ibid.*

17. Walter Sargent and Elizabeth Miller. *How Children Learn To Draw.* Boston: Ginn and Co., 1916.

18. For a history of European and American psychology see Gardner Murphy. *An Historical Introduction to Modern Psychology.* New York: Harcourt, Brace and Co., 1932.

19. The books and articles written by John Dewey are too numerous to list. *The School and Society, Democracy and Education, Logic: The Theory of Enquiry,* and *Art as Experience* are a few of his more important works.

20. John Dewey. *Experience and Education.* New York: The Macmillan Co., 1938.

21. Margaret Mathias. *The Teaching of Art.* New York: Scribner, 1932.

22. Bell Boas. *Art in the School.* New York: Doubleday, 1924.

23. Florence Cane, "Art — The Child's Birthright," *Childhood Education,* 7 (May 1931) pp. 482–485.

24. Victor D'Amico. *Creative Teaching in Art.* Scranton, Pennsylvania: International Textbook Co., 1942.

25. William Heard Kilpatrick. *The Project Method: The Use of the Purposeful Act in the Educative Process.* New York: Teachers College, Columbia University, 1919.

26. Sigmund Freud. *The Interpretation of Dreams.* New York: The Macmillan Co., 1933.

27. Margaret Naumberg. *The Child and the World.* New York: Harcourt, Brace and Co., 1928.

28. For a history of the Bauhaus see Herbert Bayer, and Walter and Ise Gropius. *Bauhaus 1919–33.* New York: Museum of Modern Art, 1938.

29. Viktor Lowenfeld. *The Nature of Creative Activity,* First Edition. London: Routledge and Kegan Paul Ltd.

30. Viktor Lowenfeld. *Creative and Mental Growth,* First Edition. New York: The Macmillan Co.

31. Perhaps the best examples of such research are to be found in *Studies in Art Education,* published by the National Art Education Association.

32. J. W. Getzels and P. W. Jackson, "Research on the Variable Teacher, Some Comments," *The School Review,* 68 (Winter 1960), pp. 450–462.

33. D. W. Oliver and J. P. Shaver, "A Critique of Practice in Teaching," *Harvard Educational Review,* 31 (Fall 1961), pp. 437–448.

34. Fred T. Tyler, "Teacher Personalities and Teaching Competencies," *The School Review,* 68 (Winter 1960), pp. 429–449.

35. For significant statements regarding the nature of creativity see Ernest G. Schachtel. *Metamorphosis.* New York: Basic Books, Inc., 1959; also Lawrence S. Kubie. *Neurotic Distortion of the Creative Process.* Lawrence, Kansas: The University of Kansas Press, 1958.

36. Jacob Getzels and Philip Jackson. *Creativity and Intelligence: Explorations with Gifted Students.* London and New York: John Wiley and Sons, Inc., 1962.

37. For a valuable source of information and guidance on problems of scientific inquiry in education see N. L. Gage, ed. *Handbook of Research on Teaching.* Chicago: Rand, McNally and Co., 1963; for a systematic and critical essay on the nature of scientific inquiry see Ernest Nagel. *The Structure of Science: Problems in Logic of Scientific Explanation.* New York and Burlingame: Harcourt, Brace and World, Inc., 1961.

38. Jacob Getzels and Philip Jackson, *op. cit.*

39. David Hume. *A Treatise of Human Nature,* Book III, Part I, Section 1.

40. For a good survey of leading philosophical orientations in twentieth century ethics, see Wilfrid Sellars and John Hospers, eds. *Readings in Ethical Theory*. New York: Appleton-Century-Crofts, Inc., 1952.

41. For examples of the major contemporary arguments for and against determinism by leading philosophers, scientists, and scholars see Sidney Hook, ed. *Determinism and Freedom in the Age of Modern Science*. New York: New York University Press, 1958.

42. A similar purpose motivated the drafting of "The Distinctive Nature of the Discipline of the Philosophy of Education," a statement by a committee of the Philosophy of Education Society which appeared in *Educational Theory*, Vol. IV, No. 1 (January 1954), pp. 1–3. Our list of criteria for critical thinking in art education is modeled in some respects on this statement.

PART II

DO ART TEACHERS NEED
A THEORY OF ART?

Perhaps the safest general observation one could make about art teachers and their characteristic beliefs is that, for all the diversity of ideas they entertain about how children develop in art, how art can be taught, how art should be evaluated, and how education in art relates to society, they share one belief in common: art is expression and what is expressed is one's feelings or emotions. This belief now dominates our field to such a degree that the question "Do art teachers need a theory of art?" will probably strike most of us as something less than a burning issue in art education, if not a wholly trivial one. Indeed, one may anticipate the impatient reply of some: "Of course, we need a theory. Art teachers must know what art is; otherwise how could we teach what we don't know? You ask: What's our theory? Call it expressionism."

Overlooking for the moment what may be a case of question-begging (each of the writers in Part II will provide or suggest different interpretations to this question and answer), we may note immediately that some of the arguments supporting the current belief in expressionism are persuasive enough. Much of modern art does appear to consist of individual or personal expressions if nothing else; children do seem to be expressing themselves through their artwork — even children unexposed to adult art, modern or otherwise; and one may cite statements of contemporary artists and critics to the effect that what is wanted is not a theory about artistic expressions but a genuine emotional response to them. All parties involved tend to disparage purely intellectual efforts to arrive at conceptual truths concerning the nature of art.

But it is one thing to persuade oneself and others that art is expression and quite another thing to justify this view, especially when one is confronted by persons who argue just as persuasively (if one would only listen) for alternative views, for example, that "art should look like something." This sort of confrontation does not pose a crisis for the professional artist; in fact it may provide a psychological stimulus for his contrary artistic efforts. The art teacher, however, does find it disconcerting when parents vent dissatisfaction with the art their children produce under his guidance. Young children themselves often ask how they can learn to draw realistically or, later, demand to know what utility art has, how much money they can make as artists, and the like. Even more unnerving to the enthusiast for art expression in the classroom are the typical responses of his school associates: since they are typically provided little or no theoretical justification for his teaching goals, they can find little of educational value in the achievement of these goals. Anti-intellectualism anywhere in the operation of the school has become untenable, and the art teacher finds that his belief about art and its value is not the same as having a viable theory of art, which stands up under criticism and vindicates the expense, space, and time consumed in the business of having children draw, paint, and sculpt in the school.

In sum, it has become a pressing need for present and future art teachers to develop more than common-sensical or merely personal conceptions of art and art education. And it would seem logical that we begin this enterprise first by defining the nature of art, then by moving on to develop a conception of art learning and appropriate methods of instruction, and finally by posing a conception of the role of art education in society.

An early lesson the art student or teacher learns in attempting to move beyond his own deeply felt experiences with art or teaching is that some opponents of artistic expression are not just insensitive Philistines or uneducated laymen. He discovers a host of art theories held by philosophers, historians, and aestheticians that are unsympathetic or that flatly contradict his notion of art and the way he has been teaching it. For instance, he finds that the "layman's belief" that art should look like something, or that art should serve as a means to social ends, is given convincing support in Plato's conception of art as imitation of reality. He soon may become intrigued with the subtleties he finds in the various historical theories of art.

The study of aesthetics is of course interesting in itself, and several adequate anthologies are available to provide the reader with a general survey of the problems of aesthetics. The more specialized need here, however, is to identify major contemporary alternative answers or analyses regarding a question professional art educators can no longer avoid: Do art teachers need a theory of art? The following five papers are presented as alternative answers.

Several assumptions underlie the way Part II (and subsequent sections) has been organized. First, the editors are assuming that there *are* alternative answers to the questions making up the titles of each part of the anthology, and that it is urgent for art students and teachers to consider them in a critical light. If critical thinking begins in the awareness of a problem, a contradiction of facts or values, an anomaly of some kind which disrupts the normal course of events, then the editors are also assuming that art education has now reached the stage where its problems require theoretical solutions. It follows from these two assumptions, for example, not that we necessarily believe art is expression, but rather that Benedetto Croce has the clearest and most powerful conception of art as expression and, further, that R. G. Collingwood has been successful in working out the implications of this concept in terms of artistic activity.

After studying these first two selections the student of art education may well ask: "Where is the problem? I agree with the theory of art as expression; it supports what I've believed all along!" A series of theoretical problems is raised only when Morris Weitz denies that there can be any theory of art, arguing that a true theory of the nature of art is more than just difficult, i.e., requiring only greater diligence and attention to art works, but that it is *logically impossible* to name the "necessary and sufficient properties" that will truly define art. He does, however, point out the uses art teachers can make of the various aesthetic theories and suggests how they might teach art — not by appealing to a "true" theory of art, but by appealing to "paradigm cases" or art masterpieces which exhibit the characteristic features of different art styles. Croce, it turns out, is not so much wrong as wrong-headed; his theory is not false, it is not a theory.

David W. Ecker takes the tack that generalizations about art may serve many purposes, but that one purpose especially relevant to art educators is methodological; for "if it is possible to describe the artistic process as a series of problems and their controlled resolution" then the result may have practical bearings for teachers of art. Thus he shifts the reader's attention from the preoccupation of Croce and Weitz with true definitions of the art objects — the one offering one and the other denying the possibility of even doing so — to the empirical evidence leading to his characterization of the artistic method as contrasted to the scientific method.

Eugene F. Kaelin follows with a critique of the preceding articles as examples of "some of the current philosophical theories concerning the nature of art which continue to militate against a consistent theoretical approach to art education." He takes them in the order in which they are presented, calling them the idealistic, the linguistic or analytic, and the "neo-pragmatic" positions. He goes on to demonstrate how the latter position "needs further amplification in an existential, phenomenological concept of an aesthetic object for a complete, workable theory of education in art."

Further readings are listed at the end of Part II with the hope that once the reader accepts the challenge to think critically about the question, Do art teachers need a theory of art? he will not be satisfied with the answers given here but will continue to seek out, reflect upon, and develop a more adequate understanding of the problem of art theory and its relation to art teaching.

1. Art as Expression

Intuition and Expression

Knowledge has two forms: it is either
intuitive knowledge or *logical* knowledge;
knowledge obtained through the *imagination*
or knowledge obtained through the *intellect;*
knowledge of the *individual* or knowledge of
the *universal:* of *individual things* or of the
relations between them: it is, in fact,
productive either of *images* or of *concepts.*

In ordinary life, constant appeal is made
to intuitive knowledge. It is said that we
cannot give definitions of certain truths;
that they are not demonstrable by syl-
logisms; that they must be learnt intuitively. The politician finds fault with
the abstract reasoner, who possesses no
lively intuition of actual conditions; the
educational theorist insists upon the necessity of developing the intuitive faculty in
the pupil before everything else; the critic
in judging a work of art makes it a point
of honor to set aside theory and abstractions, and to judge it by direct intuition; the practical man professes to live
rather by intuition than by reason.

But this ample acknowledgment, granted
to intuitive knowledge in ordinary life,
does not correspond to an equal and
adequate acknowledgment in the field of
theory and of philosophy. There exists a
very ancient science of intellectual knowledge, admitted by all without discussion,
namely, Logic; but a science of intuitive
knowledge is timidly and with difficulty
asserted by but a few. Logical knowledge
has appropriated the lion's share; and if
she does not slay and devour her companion
outright, yet yields to her but grudgingly
the humble place of maid-servant or
doorkeeper. — What can intuitive knowledge be without the light of intellectual
knowledge? It is a servant without a
master; and though a master find a servant
useful, the master is a necessity to the
servant, since he enables him to gain his
livelihood. Intuition is blind; intellect
lends her eyes.

Now, the first point to be firmly fixed in
the mind is that intuitive knowledge has no
need of a master, nor to lean upon any one;
she does not need to borrow the eyes of

✻SOURCE: Reprinted from *Aesthetic*, translated by Douglas Ainslie. Copyright, 1909 by The Macmillan
Company, Ltd., London. "Intuition and Expression" (Ch. 1) and "Intuition and Art" (Ch. 2).
The title of this Reading was devised by the editors as an overall title for the material used here.

others, for she has excellent eyes of her own. Doubtless it is possible to find concepts mingled with intuitions. But in many other intuitions there is no trace of such a mixture, which proves that it is not necessary. The impression of a moonlight scene by a painter; the outline of a country drawn by a cartographer; a musical motive, tender or energetic; the words of a sighing lyric, or those with which we ask, command and lament in ordinary life, may well all be intuitive facts without a shadow of intellectual relation. But, think what one may of these instances, and admitting further the contention that the greater part of the intuitions of civilized man are impregnated with concepts, there yet remains to be observed something more important and more conclusive. Those concepts which are found mingled and fused with the intuitions are no longer concepts, in so far as they are really mingled and fused, for they have lost all independence and autonomy. They have been concepts, but have now become simple elements of intuition. The philosophical maxims placed in the mouth of a personage of tragedy or of comedy perform there the function, not of concepts, but of characteristics of such personage; in the same way as the red in a painted face does not there represent the red color of the physicists, but is a characteristic element of the portrait. The whole is that which determines the quality of the parts. A work of art may be full of philosophical concepts; it may contain them in greater abundance and they may there be even more profound than in a philosophical dissertation, which in its turn may be rich to overflowing with descriptions and intuitions. But notwithstanding all these concepts the total effect of the work of art is an intuition; and notwithstanding all those intuitions, the total effect of the philosophical dissertation is a concept. The *Promessi Sposi* contains copious ethical observations and distinc-

tions, but does not for that reason lose as a whole its character of simple story or intuition. In like manner the anecdotes and satirical effusions to be found in the works of a philosopher like Schopenhauer do not deprive those works of their character of intellectual treatises. The difference between a scientific work and a work of art, that is, between an intellectual fact and an intuitive fact, lies in the difference of the total effect aimed at by their respective authors. This it is that determines and rules over the several parts of each, not these parts separated and considered abstractly in themselves.

But to admit the independence of intuition as regards concept does not suffice to give a true and precise idea of intuition. Another error arises among those who recognize this, or who at any rate do not explicitly make intuition dependent upon the intellect, to obscure and confuse the real nature of intuition. By intuition is frequently understood *perception*, or the knowledge of actual reality, the apprehension of something as *real*.

Certainly perception is intuition: the perceptions of the room in which I am writing, of the ink-bottle and paper that are before me, of the pen I am using, of the objects that I touch and make use of as instruments of my person, which, if it writes, therefore exists — these are all intuitions. But the image that is now passing through my brain of a me writing in another room, in another town, with different paper, pen and ink, is also an intuition. This means that the distinction between reality and nonreality is extraneous, secondary, to the true nature of intuition. If we imagine a human mind having intuitions for the first time, it would seem that it could have intuitions of actual reality only, that is to say, that it could have perceptions of nothing but the real. But since knowledge of reality is based upon the distinction between real images and unreal images, and since this distinction does not at the first moment exist, these intuitions would in truth not be intuitions either of the real or of the unreal, not perceptions, but pure intuitions. Where all is real, nothing is real. The child, with its difficulty of distinguishing true from false, history from fable, which are all one to childhood, can furnish us with a sort of very vague and only remotely approximate idea of this ingenuous state. Intuition is the undifferentiated unity of the perception of the real and of the simple image of the possible. In our intuitions we do not oppose ourselves as empirical beings to external reality, but we simply objectify our impressions, whatever they be.

Those, therefore, who look upon intuition as sensation formed and arranged simply according to the categories of space and time would seem to approximate more nearly to the truth. Space and time (they say) are the forms of intuition; to have an intuition is to place it in space and in temporal sequence. Intuitive activity would then consist in this double and concurrent function of spatiality and temporality. But for these two categories must be repeated what was said of intellectual distinctions, when found mingled with intuitions. We have intuitions without space and without time: the color of a sky, the color of a feeling, a cry of pain and an effort of will, objectified in consciousness: these are intuitions which we possess, and with their making space and time have nothing to do. In some intuitions, spatiality may be found without temporality, in others, *vice versa;* and even where both are found, they are perceived by later reflection: they can be fused with the intuition in like manner with all its other elements: that is, they are in it *materialiter* and not *formaliter*, as ingredients and not as arrangement. Who, without an act of reflection which for a moment breaks in upon his contemplation, can think of

space while looking at a drawing or a view? Who is conscious of temporal sequence while listening to a story or a piece of music without breaking into it with a similar act of reflection? What intuition reveals in a work of art is not space and time, but *character, individual physiognomy*. The view here maintained is confirmed in several quarters of modern philosophy. Space and time, far from being simple and primitive functions, are nowadays conceived as intellectual constructions of great complexity. And further, even in some of those who do not altogether deny to space and time the quality of formative principles, categories and functions, one observes an effort to unite them and to regard them in a different manner from that in which these categories are generally conceived. Some limit intuition to the sole category of spatiality, maintaining that even time can only be intuited in terms of space. Others abandon the three dimensions of space as not philosophically necessary, and conceive the function of spatiality as void of all particular spatial determination. But what could such a spatial function be, a simple arrangement that should arrange even time? It represents, surely, all that criticism and refutation have left standing — the bare demand for the affirmation of some intuitive activity in general. And is not this activity truly determined, when one single function is attributed to it, not spatializing nor temporalizing, but characterizing? Or rather, when it is conceived as itself a category or function which gives us knowledge of things in their concreteness and individuality?

Having thus freed intuitive knowledge from any suggestion of intellectualism and from every later and external addition, we must now explain it and determine its limits from another side and defend it from a different kind of invasion and confusion. On the hither side of the lower limit is sensation, formless matter, which the spirit can never apprehend in itself as simple matter. This it can only possess with form and in form, but postulates the notion of it as a mere limit. Matter, in its abstraction, is mechanism, passivity; it is what the spirit of man suffers, but does not produce. Without it no human knowledge or activity is possible; but mere matter produces animality, whatever is brutal and impulsive in man, not the spiritual dominion, which is humanity. How often we strive to understand clearly what is passing within us! We do catch a glimpse of something, but this does not appear to the mind as objectified and formed. It is in such moments as these that we best perceive the profound difference between matter and form. These are not two acts of ours, opposed to one another; but the one is outside us and assaults and sweeps us off our feet, while the other inside us tends to absorb and identify itself with that which is outside. Matter, clothed and conquered by form, produces concrete form. It is the matter, the content, which differentiates one of our intuitions from another: the form is constant: it is spiritual activity, while matter is changeable. Without matter spiritual activity would not forsake its abstractness to become concrete and real activity, this or that spiritual content, this or that definite intuition.

It is a curious fact, characteristic of our times, that this very form, this very activity of the spirit, which is essentially ourselves, is so often ignored or denied. Some confound the spiritual activity of man with the metaphorical and mythological activity of what is called nature, which is mechanism and has no resemblance to human activity, save when we imagine, with Aesop, that "*arbores loquuntur non tantum ferae.*" Some affirm that they have never observed in themselves this "miraculous" activity, as

though there were no difference, or only one of quantity, between sweating and thinking, feeling cold and the energy of the will. Others, certainly with greater reason, would unify activity and mechanism in a more general concept, though they are specifically distinct. Let us, however, refrain for the moment from examining if such a final unification be possible, and in what sense, but admitting that the attempt may be made, it is clear that to unify two concepts in a third implies to begin with the admission of a difference between the two first. Here it is this difference that concerns us and we set it in relief.

Intuition has sometimes been confused with simple sensation. But since this confusion ends by being offensive to common sense, it has more frequently been attenuated or concealed with a phraseology apparently designed at once to confuse and to distinguish them. Thus, it has been asserted that intuition is sensation, but not so much simple sensation as *association* of sensations. Here a double meaning is concealed in the word "association." Either association is understood as memory, mnemonic association, conscious recollection, and in that case the claim to unite in memory elements which are not intuited, distinguished, possessed in some way by the spirit and produced by consciousness, seems inconceivable: or it is understood as association of unconscious elements, in which case we remain in the world of sensation and of nature. But if with certain associationists we speak of an association which is neither memory nor flux of sensations, but a *productive* association (formative, constructive, distinguishing), then our contention is admitted and only its name is denied to it. For productive association is no longer association in the sense of the sensationalists, but *synthesis*, that is to say, spiritual activity. Synthesis may be called association; but with the concept of productivity is already posited the distinction between passivity and activity, between sensation and intuition.

Other psychologists are disposed to distinguish from sensation something which is sensation no longer, but is not yet intellectual concept: the *representation* or *image*. What is the difference between their representation or image and our intuitive knowledge? Everything and nothing: for "representation" is a very equivocal word. If by representation be understood something cut off and standing out from the psychic basis of the sensations, then representation is intuition. If, on the other hand, it be conceived as complex sensation we are back once more in crude sensation, which does not vary in quality according to its richness or poverty, or according to whether the organism in which it appears is rudimentary or highly developed and full of traces of past sensations. Nor is the ambiguity remedied by defining representation as a psychic product of secondary degree in relation to sensation, defined as occupying the first place. What does secondary degree mean here? Does it mean a qualitative, formal difference? If so, representation is an elaboration of sensation and therefore intuition. Or does it mean greater complexity and complication, a quantitative, material difference? In that case intuition is once more confused with simple sensation.

And yet there is a sure method of distinguishing true intuition, true representation, from that which is inferior to it: the spiritual fact from the mechanical, passive, natural fact. Every true intuition or representation is also *expression*. That which does not objectify itself in expression is not intuition or representation, but sensation and mere natural fact. The spirit only intuits in making, forming, expressing. He who separates intuition from expression never succeeds in reuniting them.

Intuitive activity *possesses intuitions to the extent that it expresses them*. Should this proposition sound paradoxical, that is partly because, as a general rule, a too restricted meaning is given to the word "expression." It is generally restricted to what are called verbal expressions alone. But there exist also nonverbal expressions, such as those of line, color and sound, and to all of these must be extended our affirmation, which embraces therefore every sort of manifestation of the man, as orator, musician, painter, or anything else. But be it pictorial, or verbal, or musical, or in whatever other form it appear, to no intuition can expression in one of its forms be wanting; it is, in fact, an inseparable part of intuition. How can we really possess an intuition of a geometrical figure, unless we possess so accurate an image of it as to be able to trace it immediately upon paper or on the blackboard? How can we really have an intuition of the contour of a region, for example of the island of Sicily, if we are not able to draw it as it is in all its meanderings? Everyone can experience the internal illumination which follows upon his success in formulating to himself his impressions and feelings, but only so far as he is able to formulate them. Feelings or impressions, then, pass by means of words from the obscure region of the soul into the clarity of the contemplative spirit. It is impossible to distinguish intuition from expression in this cognitive process. The one appears with the other at the same instant, because they are not two, but one.

The principal reason which makes our view appear paradoxical as we maintain it, is the illusion or prejudice that we possess a more complete intuition of reality than we really do. One often hears people say that they have many great thoughts in their minds, but that they are not able to express them. But if they really had them, they would have coined them into just so many beautiful-sounding words, and thus have expressed them. If these thoughts seem to vanish or to become few and meager in the act of expressing them, the reason is that they did not exist or really were few and meager. People think that all of us ordinary men imagine and intuit countries, figures and scenes like painters, and bodies like sculptors; save that painters and sculptors know how to paint and carve such images, while we bear them unexpressed in our souls. They believe that anyone could have imagined a Madonna of Raphael; but that Raphael was Raphael owing to his technical ability in putting the Madonna upon canvas. Nothing can be more false than this view. The world which as a rule we intuit is a small thing. It consists of little expressions, which gradually become greater and wider with the increasing spiritual concentration of certain moments. They are the words we say to ourselves, our silent judgments: "Here is a man, here is a horse, this is heavy, this is sharp, this pleases me," etc. It is a medley of light and color, with no greater pictorial value than would be expressed by a haphazard splash of colors, from among which one could barely make out a few special, distinctive traits. This and nothing else is what we possess in our ordinary life; this is the basis of our ordinary action. It is the index of a book. The labels tied to things (it has been said) take the place of the things themselves. This index and these labels (themselves expressions) suffice for small needs and small actions. From time to time we pass from the index to the book, from the label to the thing, or from the slight to the greater intuitions, and from these to the greatest and most lofty. This passage is sometimes far from easy. It has been observed by those who have best studied the psychology of artists that when, after having given a rapid glance at anyone, they attempt to obtain a real intuition of him, in order, for example, to paint his portrait, then this ordinary vision, that seemed so precise, so lively, reveals itself as little better than nothing. What remains is found to be at the most some superficial trait, which would not even suffice for a caricature. The person to be painted stands before the artist like a world to discover. Michelangelo said, "One paints, not with the hands, but with the brain." Leonardo shocked the prior of the Convent of the Graces by standing for days together gazing at the "Last Supper," without touching it with the brush. He remarked of this attitude: "The minds of men of lofty genius are most active in invention when they are doing the least external work." The painter is a painter, because he sees what others only feel or catch a glimpse of, but do not see. We think we see a smile, but in reality we have only a vague impression of it, we do not perceive all the characteristic traits of which it is the sum, as the painter discovers them after he has worked upon them and is thus able to fix them on the canvas. We do not intuitively possess more even of our intimate friend, who is with us every day and at all hours, than at most certain traits of physiognomy which enable us to distinguish him from others. The illusion is less easy as regards musical expression; because it would seem strange to everyone to say that the composer had added or attached notes to a motive which was already in the mind of him who is not the composer; as if Beethoven's Ninth Symphony were not his own intuition and his intuition the Ninth Symphony. Now, just as one who is deluded as to the amount of his material wealth is confuted by arithmetic, which states its exact amount, so he who nourishes delusions as to the wealth of his own thoughts and images is brought back to reality, when he is obliged to cross the *Pons Asinorum* of expression. Let us say to the former, count; to the latter, speak; or, here is a pencil, draw, express yourself.

Each of us, as a matter of fact, has in him a little of the poet, of the sculptor, of the musician, of the painter, of the prose writer: but how little, as compared with those who bear those names, just because they possess the most universal dispositions and energies of human nature in so lofty a degree! How little too does a painter possess the intuitions of a poet! And how little does one painter possess those of another painter! Nevertheless, that little is all our actual patrimony of intuitions or representations. Beyond these are only impressions, sensations, feelings, impulses, emotions, or whatever else one may term what still falls short of the spirit and is not assimilated by man; something postulated for the convenience of exposition, while actually nonexistent, since to exist also is a fact of the spirit.

We may thus add this to the various verbal descriptions of intuition, noted at the beginning: intuitive knowledge is expressive knowledge. Independent and autonomous in respect to intellectual function; indifferent to later empirical discriminations, to reality and to unreality, to formations and apperceptions of space and time, which are also later: intuition or representation is distinguished as *form* from what is felt and suffered, from the flux or wave of sensation, or from psychic matter; and this form, this taking possession, is expression. To intuit is to express; and nothing else (nothing more, but nothing less) than *to express*.

Intuition and Art

Before proceeding further, it may be well to draw certain consequences from what has been established and to add some explanations.

We have frankly identified intuitive or expressive knowledge with the aesthetic or artistic fact, taking works of art as examples of intuitive knowledge and attributing to them the characteristics of intuition, and *vice versa*. But our identification is combated by a view held even by many philosophers, who consider art to be an intuition of an altogether special sort. "Let us admit" (they say) "that art is intuition; but intuition is not always art: artistic intuition is a distinct species differing from intuition in general by something *more*."

But no one has ever been able to indicate of what this something more consists. It has sometimes been thought that art is not a simple intuition, but an intuition of an intuition, in the same way as the concept of science has been defined, not as the ordinary concept, but as the concept of a concept. Thus man would attain to art by objectifying, not his sensations, as happens with ordinary intuition, but intuition itself. But this process of raising to a second power does not exist; and the comparison of it with the ordinary and scientific concept does not prove what is intended, for the good reason that it is not true that the scientific concept is the concept of a concept. If this comparison proves anything, it proves just the opposite. The ordinary concept, if it be really a concept and not a simple representation, is a perfect concept, however poor and limited. Science substitutes concepts for representations; for those concepts that are poor and limited it substitutes others, larger and more comprehensive; it is ever discovering new relations. But its method does not differ from that by which is formed the smallest universal in the brain of the humblest of men. What is generally called *par excellence* art collects intuitions that are wider and more complex than those which we generally experience, but these intuitions are always of sensations and impressions.

Art is expression of impressions, not expression of expression.

For the same reason, it cannot be asserted that the intuition, which is generally called artistic, differs from ordinary intuition as intensive intuition. This would be the case if it were to operate differently on the same matter. But since the artistic function is extended to wider fields, yet does not differ in method from ordinary intuition, the difference between them is not intensive but extensive. The intuition of the simplest popular love-song, which says the same thing, or very nearly, as any declaration of love that issues at every moment from the lips of thousands of ordinary men, may be intensively perfect in its poor simplicity, although it be extensively so much more limited than the complex intuition of a love-song by Leopardi.

The whole difference, then, is quantitative, and as such is indifferent to philosophy, *scientia qualitatum.* Certain men have a greater aptitude, a more frequent inclination fully to express certain complex states of the soul. These men are known in ordinary language as artists. Some very complicated and difficult expressions are not often achieved, and these are called works of art. The limits of the expression-intuitions that are called art, as opposed to those that are vulgarly called non-art, are empirical and impossible to define. If an epigram be art, why not a simple word? If a story, why not the news-jottings of the journalist? If a landscape, why not a topographical sketch? The teacher of philosophy in Molière's comedy was right: "whenever we speak, we create prose." But there will always be scholars like Monsieur Jourdain, astonished at having spoken prose for forty years without knowing it, who will have difficulty in persuading themselves that when they call their servant John to bring their slippers, they have spoken nothing less than — prose.

We must hold firmly to our identification, because among the principal reasons which have prevented Aesthetic, the science of art, from revealing the true nature of art, its real roots in human nature, has been its separation from the general spiritual life, the having made of it a sort of special function or aristocratic club. No one is astonished when he learns from physiology that every cell is an organism and every organism a cell or synthesis of cells. No one is astonished at finding in a lofty mountain the same chemical elements that compose a small stone fragment. There is not one physiology of small animals and one of large animals; nor is there a special chemical theory of stones as distinct from mountains. In the same way, there is not a science of lesser intuition as distinct from a science of greater intuition, nor one of ordinary intuition as distinct from artistic intuition. There is but one Aesthetic, the science of intuitive or expressive knowledge, which is the aesthetic or artistic fact. And this Aesthetic is the true analogue of Logic, which includes, as facts of the same nature, the formation of the smallest and most ordinary concept and the most complicated scientific and philosophical system.

Nor can we admit that the word *genius* or artistic genius, as distinct from the non-genius of the ordinary man, possesses more than a quantitative signification. Great artists are said to reveal us to ourselves. But how could this be possible, unless there were identity of nature between their imagination and ours, and unless the difference were only one of quantity? It were better to change *poeta nascitur* into *homo nascitur poeta:* some men are born great poets, some small. The cult of the genius with all its attendant superstitions has arisen from this quantitative difference having been taken as a difference of quality. It has been forgotten that genius is not something that has fallen from heaven, but humanity itself. The man of genius who poses or is represented as remote from humanity finds his punishment in becoming or appearing somewhat ridiculous. Examples of this are the *genius* of the romantic period and the *superman* of our time.

But it is well to note here, that those who claim unconsciousness as the chief quality of an artistic genius, hurl him from an eminence far above humanity to a position far below it. Intuitive or artistic genius, like every form of human activity, is always conscious; otherwise it would be blind mechanism. The only thing that can be wanting to artistic genius is the *reflective* consciousness, the superadded consciousness of the historian or critic, which is not essential to it.

The relation between matter and form, or between *content* and *form*, as is generally said, is one of the most disputed questions in Aesthetic. Does the aesthetic fact consist of content alone, or of form alone, or of both together? This question has taken on various meanings, which we shall mention, each in its place. But when these words are taken as signifying what we have above defined, and matter is understood as emotionality, not aesthetically elaborated, or impressions, and form as intellectual activity and expression, then our view cannot be in doubt. We must, that is to say, reject both the thesis that makes the aesthetic fact to consist of the content alone (that is, the simple impressions), and the thesis which makes it to consist of a junction between form and content, that is, of impressions plus expressions. In the aesthetic fact, expressive activity is not added to the fact of the impressions, but these latter are formed and elaborated by it. The impressions reappear as it were in expression, like water put into a filter, which reappears the same and yet different on the other side. The aesthetic fact, therefore, is form, and nothing but form.

From this was inferred not that the content is something superfluous (it is, on the contrary, the necessary point of de-

parture for the expressive fact); but that *there is no passage* from the qualities of the content to those of the form. It has sometimes been thought that the content, in order to be aesthetic, that is to say, transformable into form, should possess some determined or determinable qualities. But were that so, then form and content, expression and impression, would be the same thing. It is true that the content is that which is convertible into form, but it has no determinable qualities until this transformation takes place. We know nothing about it. It does not become aesthetic content before, but only after it has been actually transformed. The aesthetic content has also been defined as the *interesting*. That is not an untrue statement; it is merely void of meaning. Interesting to what? To the expressive activity? Certainly the expressive activity would not have raised the content to the dignity of form, had it not been interested in it. Being interested is precisely the raising of the content to the dignity of form. But the word "interesting" has also been employed in another and an illegitimate sense, which we shall explain further on.

The proposition that art is *imitation of nature* has also several meanings. Sometimes truths have been expressed or at least shadowed forth in these words, sometimes errors have been promulgated. More frequently, no definite thought has been expressed at all. One of the scientifically legitimate meanings occurs when "imitation" is understood as representation or intuition of nature, a form of knowledge. And when the phrase is used with this intention, and in order to emphasize the spiritual character of the process, another proposition becomes legitimate also: namely, that art is the *idealization* or *idealizing* imitation of nature. But if by imitation of nature be understood that art gives mechanical reproductions, more or less perfect duplicates of natural objects, in the presence of which is renewed the same tumult of impressions as that caused by natural objects, then the proposition is evidently false. The colored waxen effigies that imitate the life, before which we stand astonished in the museums where such things are shown, do not give aesthetic intuitions. Illusion and hallucination have nothing to do with the calm domain of artistic intuition. But on the other hand, if an artist paints the interior of a wax-work museum, or if an actor gives a burlesque portrait of a man-statue on the stage, we have work of the spirit and artistic intuition. Finally, if photography have in it anything artistic, it will be to the extent that it transmits the intuition of the photographer, his point of view, the pose and grouping which he has striven to attain. And if photography be not quite an art, that is precisely because the element of nature in it remains more or less unconquered and ineradicable. Do we ever, indeed, feel complete satisfaction before even the best of photographs? Would not an artist vary and touch up much or little, remove or add something to all of them?

The statements repeated so often, that art is not knowledge, that it does not tell the truth, that it does not belong to the world of theory, but to the world of feeling, and so forth, arise from the failure to realize exactly the theoretic character of simple intuition. This simple intuition is quite distinct from intellectual knowledge, as it is distinct from perception of the real; and the statements quoted above arise from the belief that only intellectual cognition is knowledge. We have seen that intuition is knowledge, free from concepts and more simple than the so-called perception of the real. Therefore art is knowledge, form; it does not belong to the world of feeling or to psychic matter. The reason why so many aestheticians have so often insisted that art is *appearance* (*Schein*) is precisely that they have felt the necessity of distinguishing it from the more

complex fact of perception, by maintaining its pure intuitiveness. And if for the same reason it has been claimed that art is *feeling*, the reason is the same. For if the concept as content of art, and historical reality as such, be excluded from the sphere of art, there remains no other content than reality apprehended in all its ingenuousness and immediacy in the vital impulse, in its *feeling*, that is to say again, pure intuition.

The theory of the *aesthetic senses* has also arisen from the failure to establish, or from having lost to view, the character of expression as distinct from impression, of form as distinct from matter.

This theory can be reduced to the error just indicated of wishing to find a passage from the qualities of the content to those of the form. To ask, in fact, what the aesthetic senses are implies asking what sensible impressions are able to enter into aesthetic expressions, and which must of necessity do so. To this we must at once reply, that all impressions can enter into aesthetic expressions or formations, but that none are bound to do so of necessity. Dante raised to the dignity of form not only the "sweet color of the oriental sapphire" (visual impressions), but also tactual or thermic impressions, such as the "dense air" and the "fresh rivulets" which "parch the more" the throat of the thirsty. The belief that a picture yields only visual impressions is a curious illusion. The bloom on a cheek, the warmth of a youthful body, the sweetness and freshness of a fruit, the edge of a sharp knife, are not these, too, impressions obtainable from a picture? Are they visual? What would a picture mean to an imaginary man, lacking all or many of his senses, who should in an instant acquire the organ of sight alone? The picture we are looking at and believe we see only with our eyes would seem to his eyes to be little more than an artist's paint-smeared palette.

Some who hold firmly to the aesthetic character of certain groups of impressions (for example, the visual and auditive), and exclude others, are nevertheless ready to admit that if visual and auditive impressions enter *directly* into the aesthetic fact, those of the other senses also enter into it, but only as *associated*. But this distinction is altogether arbitrary. Aesthetic expression is synthesis, in which it is impossible to distinguish direct and indirect. All impressions are placed by it on a level, in so far as they are aestheticized. A man who absorbs the subject of a picture or poem does not have it before him as a series of impressions, some of which have prerogatives and precedence over the others. He knows nothing as to what has happened prior to having absorbed it, just as, on the other hand, distinctions made after reflection have nothing whatever to do with art as such.

The theory of the aesthetic senses has also been presented in another way; as an attempt to establish what physiological organs are necessary for the aesthetic fact. The physiological organ or apparatus is nothing but a group of cells, constituted and disposed in a particular manner; that is to say, it is a merely physical and natural fact or concept. But expression does not know physiological facts. Expression has its point of departure in the impressions, and the physiological path by which these have found their way to the mind is to it altogether indifferent. One way or another it comes to the same thing: it suffices that they should be impressions.

It is true that the want of given organs, that is, of certain groups of cells, prevents the formation of certain impressions (when these are not otherwise obtained through a kind of organic compensation). The man born blind cannot intuit and express light. But the impressions are not conditioned solely by the organ, but also by the stimuli which operate upon the organ.

One who has never had the impression of the sea will never be able to express it in the same way as one who has never had the impression of the life of high society or of the political arena will never express either. This, however, does not prove the dependence of the expressive function on the stimulus or on the organ. It merely repeats what we know already: expression presupposes impression, and particular expressions, particular impressions. For the rest, every impression excludes other impressions during the moment in which it dominates; and so does every expression.

Another corollary of the conception of expression as activity is the *indivisibility* of the work of art. Every expression is a single expression. Activity is a fusion of the impressions in an organic whole. A desire to express this has always prompted the affirmation that the work of art should have *unity*, or what amounts to the same thing, *unity in variety*. Expression is a synthesis of the various, or multiple, in the one.

The fact that we divide a work of art into parts, a poem into scenes, episodes, similes, sentences, or a picture into single figures and objects, background, foreground, etc., may seem opposed to this affirmation. But such division annihilates the work, as dividing the organism into heart, brain, nerves, muscles and so on, turns the living being into a corpse. It is true that there exist organisms in which division gives rise to other living beings, but in such a case we must conclude, maintaining the analogy between the organism and the work of art, that in the latter case too there are numerous germs of life each ready to grow, in a moment, into a single complete expression.

It may be said that expression sometimes arises from other expressions. There are simple and there are *compound* expressions. One must surely admit some difference between the *eureka*, with which Archimedes expressed all his joy at his discovery, and the expressive act (indeed all the five acts) of a regular tragedy. Not in the least: expression always arises directly from impressions. He who conceives a tragedy puts into a crucible a great quantity, so to say, of impressions: expressions themselves, conceived on other occasions, are fused together with the new in a single mass, in the same way as we can cast into a melting furnace formless pieces of bronze and choicest statuettes. Those choicest statuettes must be melted just like the pieces of bronze, before there can be a new statue. The old expressions must descend again to the level of impressions, in order to be synthesized in a new single expression.

By elaborating his impressions, man *frees* himself from them. By objectifying them, he removes them from him and makes himself their superior. The liberating and purifying function of art is another aspect and another formula of its character as activity. Activity is the deliverer, just because it drives away passivity.

This also explains why it is usual to attribute to artists both the maximum of sensibility or *passion*, and the maximum of insensibility or Olympian *serenity*. The two characters are compatible, for they do not refer to the same object. The sensibility or passion relates to the rich material which the artist absorbs into his psychic organism; the insensibility or serenity to the form with which he subdues and dominates the tumult of the sensations and passions.

2. Expressing One's Emotions

R. G. COLLINGWOOD

Expressing Emotion and Arousing Emotion

Our first question is this. Since the artist proper has something to do with emotion, and what he does with it is not to arouse it, what is it that he does? It will be remembered that the kind of answer we expect to this question is an answer derived from what we all know and all habitually say; nothing original or recondite, but something entirely commonplace.

Nothing could be more entirely commonplace than to say he expresses them. The idea is familiar to every artist, and to everyone else who has any acquaintance with the arts. To state it is not to state a philosophical theory or definition of art; it is to state a fact or supposed fact about which, when we have sufficiently identified it, we shall have later to theorize philosophically. For the present it does not matter whether the fact that is alleged, when it is said that the artist expresses emotion, is really a fact or only supposed to be one. Whichever it is, we have to identify it, that is, to decide what it is that people are saying when they use the phrase. Later on, we shall have to see whether it will fit into a coherent theory.

They are referring to a situation, real or supposed, of a definite kind. When a man is said to express emotion, what is being said about him comes to this. At first, he is conscious of having an emotion, but not conscious of what this emotion is. All he is conscious of is a perturbation or excitement, which he feels going on within him, but of whose nature he is ignorant. While in this state, all he can say about his emotion is: "I feel ... I don't know what I feel." From this helpless and oppressed condition he extricates himself by doing something which we call expressing himself. This is an activity which has something to do with the thing we call language: he expresses himself by speaking. It has also something to do with consciousness: the emotion expressed is an emotion of whose nature the person who feels it is

＊SOURCE: Reprinted from R. G. Collingwood, *The Principles of Art*, Copyright 1938 by The Clarendon Press, Oxford, pp. 109–115 and 121–124.

The title of this Reading was not taken from the original work but was devised by the authors of this reader as a title for the material used here.

no longer unconscious. It has also something to do with the way in which he feels the emotion. As unexpressed, he feels it in what we have called a helpless and oppressed way; as expressed, he feels it in a way from which this sense of oppression has vanished. His mind is somehow lightened and eased.

This lightening of emotions which is somehow connected with the expression of them has a certain resemblance to the "catharsis" by which emotions are earthed through being discharged into a make-believe situation; but the two things are not the same. Suppose the emotion is one of anger. If it is effectively earthed, for example by fancying oneself kicking someone down stairs, it is thereafter no longer present in the mind as anger at all: we have worked it off and are rid of it. If it is expressed, for example by putting it into hot and bitter words, it does not disappear from the mind; we remain angry; but instead of the sense of oppression which accompanies an emotion of anger not yet recognized as such, we have that sense of alleviation which comes when we are conscious of our own emotion as anger, instead of being conscious of it only as an unidentified perturbation. This is what we refer to when we say that it "does us good" to express our emotions.

The expression of an emotion by speech may be addressed to someone; but if so it is not done with the intention of arousing a like emotion in him. If there is any effect which we wish to produce in the hearer, it is only the effect which we call making him understand how we feel. But, as we have already seen, this is just the effect which expressing our emotions has on ourselves. It makes us, as well as the people to whom we talk, understand how we feel. A person arousing emotion sets out to affect his audience in a way in which he himself is not necessarily affected. He and his audience stand in quite different relations to the act, very much as physician and patient stand in quite different relations towards a drug administered by the one and taken by the other. A person expressing emotion, on the contrary, is treating himself and his audience in the same kind of way; he is making his emotions clear to his audience, and that is what he is doing to himself.

It follows from this that the expression of emotion, simply as expression, is not addressed to any particular audience. It is addressed primarily to the speaker himself, and secondarily to anyone who can understand. Here again, the speaker's attitude toward his audience is quite unlike that of a person desiring to arouse in his audience a certain emotion. If that is what he wishes to do, he must know the audience he is addressing. He must know what type of stimulus will produce the desired kind of reaction in people of that particular sort; and he must adapt his language to his audience in the sense of making sure that it contains stimuli appropriate to their peculiarities. If what he wishes to do is to express his emotions intelligibly, he has to express them in such a way as to be intelligible to himself; his audience is then in the position of persons who overhear him doing this. Thus the stimulus-and-reaction terminology has no applicability to the situation.

The means-and-end, or technique, terminology too is inapplicable. Until a man has expressed his emotion, he does not yet know what emotion it is. The act of expressing it is therefore an exploration of his own emotions. He is trying to find out what these emotions are. There is certainly here a directed process: an effort, that is, directed upon a certain end; but the end is not something foreseen and preconceived, to which appropriate means can be thought out in the light of our knowledge of its special character. Expression is an activity of which there can be no technique.

Expression and Individualization

Expressing an emotion is not the same thing as describing it. To say "I am angry" is to describe one's emotion, not to express it. The words in which it is expressed need not contain any reference to anger as such at all. Indeed, so far as they simply and solely express it, they cannot contain any such reference. The curse of Ernulphus, as invoked by Dr. Slop on the unknown person who tied certain knots, is a classical and supreme expression of anger; but it does not contain a single word descriptive of the emotion it expresses.

This is why, as literary critics well know, the use of epithets in poetry, or even in prose where expressiveness is aimed at, is a danger. If you want to express the terror which something causes, you must not give it an epithet like "dreadful." For that describes the emotion instead of expressing it, and your language becomes frigid, that is inexpressive, at once. A genuine poet, in his moments of genuine poetry, never mentions by name the emotions he is expressing.

Some people have thought that a poet who wishes to express a great variety of subtly differentiated emotions might be hampered by the lack of a vocabulary rich in words referring to the distinctions between them; and that psychology, by working out such a vocabulary, might render a valuable service to poetry. This is the opposite of the truth. The poet needs no such words at all; the existence or non-existence of a scientific terminology describing the emotions he wishes to express is to him a matter of perfect indifference. If such a terminology, where it exists, is allowed to affect his own use of language, it affects it for the worse.

The reason why description, so far from helping expression, actually damages it, is that description generalizes. To describe a thing is to call it a thing of such and such a kind: to bring it under a conception, to classify it. Expression, on the contrary, individualizes. The anger which I feel here and now, with a certain person, for a certain cause, is no doubt an instance of anger, and in describing it as anger one is telling truth about it; but it is much more than mere anger: it is a peculiar anger, not quite like any anger that I ever felt before, and probably not quite like any anger I shall ever feel again. To become fully conscious of it means becoming conscious of it not merely as an instance of anger, but as this quite peculiar anger. Expressing it, we saw, has something to do with becoming conscious of it; therefore, if being fully conscious of it means being conscious of all its peculiarities, fully expressing it means expressing all its peculiarities. The poet, therefore, in proportion as he understands his business, gets as far away as possible from merely labeling his emotions as instances of this or that general kind, and takes enormous pains to individualize them by expressing them in terms which reveal their difference from any other emotion of the same sort.

This is a point in which art proper, as the expression of emotion, differs sharply and obviously from any craft whose aim it is to arouse emotion. The end which a craft sets out to realize is always conceived in general terms, never individualized. However accurately defined it may be, it is always defined as the production of a thing having characteristics that could be shared by other things. A joiner, making a table out of these pieces of wood and no others, makes it to measurements and specifications which, even if actually shared by no other table, might in principle be shared by other tables. A physician treating a patient for a certain complaint is trying to produce in him a condition which might be, and probably has been, often produced in others, namely, the condition of recovering from that complaint. So an "artist" setting out to produce a certain emotion in his audience is setting out to produce not an individual emotion, but an emotion of a certain kind. It follows that the means appropriate to its production will be not individual means but means of a certain kind: that is to say, means which are always in principle replaceable by other similar means. As every good craftsman insists, there is always a "right way" of performing any operation. A "way" of acting is a general pattern to which various individual actions may conform. In order that the "work of art" should produce its intended psychological effect, therefore, whether this effect be magical or merely amusing, what is necessary is that it should satisfy certain conditions, possess certain characteristics: in other words be not this work and no other, but a work of this kind and of no other.

This explains the meaning of the generalization which Aristotle and others have ascribed to art. We have already seen that Aristotle's *Poetics* is concerned not with art proper but with representative art, and representative art of one definite kind. He is not analyzing the religious drama of a hundred years before, he is analyzing the amusement literature of the fourth century, and giving rules for its composition. The end being not individual but general (the production of an emotion of a certain kind), the means too are general (the portrayal, not of this individual act, but of an act of this sort; not, as he himself puts it, what Alcibiades did, but what anybody of a certain kind would do). Sir Joshua Reynolds's idea of generalization is in principle the same; he expounds it in connection with what he calls "the grand style," which means a style intended to

produce emotions of a certain type. He is quite right; if you want to produce a typical case of a certain emotion, the way to do it is to put before your audience a representation of the typical features belonging to the kind of thing that produces it: make your kings very royal, your soldiers very soldierly, your women very feminine, your cottages very cottagesque, your oak trees very oakish, and so on.

Art proper, as expression of emotion, has nothing to do with all this. The artist proper is a person who, grappling with the problem of expressing a certain emotion, says, "I want to get this clear." It is no use to him to get something else clear, however like it this other thing may be. Nothing will serve as a substitute. He does not want a thing of a certain kind, he wants a certain thing. This is why the kind of person who takes his literature as psychology, saying "How admirably this writer depicts the feelings of women, or busdrivers, or homosexuals...," necessarily misunderstands every real work of art with which he comes in contact, and takes for good art, with infallible precision, what is not art at all.

Expressing Emotion and Betraying Emotion

Finally, the expressing of emotion must not be confused with what may be called the betraying of it, that is, exhibiting symptoms of it. When it is said that the artist in the proper sense of that word is a person who expresses his emotions, this does not mean that if he is afraid he turns pale and stammers; if he is angry turns red and bellows; and so forth. These things are no doubt called expressions; but just as we distinguish proper and improper senses of the word "art," so we must distinguish proper and improper senses of the word "expression," and in the context of a discussion about art this sense of expression is an improper sense. The characteristic mark of expression proper is lucidity or intelligibility; a person who expresses something thereby becomes conscious of what it is that he is expressing, and enables others to become conscious of it in himself and in them. Turning pale and stammering is a natural accompaniment of fear, but a person who in addition to being afraid also turns pale and stammers does not thereby become conscious of the precise quality of his emotion. About that he is as much in the dark as he would be if (were that possible) he could feel fear without also exhibiting these symptoms of it.

Confusion between these two senses of the word "expression" may easily lead to false critical estimates, and so to false aesthetic theory. It is sometimes thought a merit in an actress that when she is acting a pathetic scene she can work herself up to such an extent as to weep real tears. There may be some ground for that opinion if acting is not an art but a craft, and if the actress's object in that scene is to produce grief in her audience; and even then the conclusion would follow only if it were true that grief cannot be produced in the audience unless symptoms of grief are exhibited by the performer. And no doubt this is how most people think of the actor's work. But if his business is not amusement but art, the object at which he is aiming is not to produce a preconceived emotional effect on his audience but, by means of a system of expressions, or language, composed partly of speech and partly of gesture, to explore his own emotions: to discover emotions in himself of which he was unaware, and, by permitting the audience to witness the discovery, enable them to make a similar discovery about themselves. In that case it is not her ability to weep real tears that would mark out a good actress; it is her ability to make it clear to herself and her audience what the tears are about.

This applies to every kind of art. The artist never rants. A person who writes or paints or the like in order to blow off steam, using the traditional materials of art as means for exhibiting the symptoms of emotion, may deserve praise as an exhibitionist, but loses for the moment all claim to the title of artist. Exhibitionists have their uses; they may serve as an amusement, or they may be doing magic. The second category will contain, for example, those young men who, learning in the torment of their own bodies and minds what war is like, have stammered their indignation in verses, and published them in the hope of infecting others and causing them to abolish it. But these verses have nothing to do with poetry.

Thomas Hardy, at the end of a fine and tragic novel in which he has magnificently expressed his sorrow and indignation for the suffering inflicted by callous sentimentalism on trusting innocence, spoils everything by a last paragraph fastening his accusation upon "the president of the immortals." The note rings false, not because it is blasphemous (it offends no piety worthy of the name), but because it is rant. The case against God, so far as it exists, is complete already. The concluding paragraph adds nothing to it. All it does is to spoil the effect of the indictment by betraying a symptom of the emotion which the whole book has already expressed; as if a prosecuting counsel, at the end of his speech, spat in the prisoner's face.

The same fault is especially common in Beethoven. He was confirmed in it, no doubt, by his deafness; but the cause of it was not his deafness but a temperamental inclination to rant. It shows itself in the way his music screams and mutters instead of speaking, as in the soprano part of the Mass in D, or the layout of the opening page in the *Hammerklavier* Sonata. He must have known his failing and tried to overcome it, or he would never have spent so many of his ripest years among string quartets, where screaming and muttering are almost, one might say, physically impossible. Yet even there, the old Adam struts out in certain passages of the *Grosse Fuge*.

It does not, of course, follow that a dramatic writer may not rant in character. The tremendous rant at the end of *The Ascent of F6*, like the Shakespearian[1] ranting on which it is modeled, is done with tongue in cheek. It is not the author who is ranting, but the unbalanced character he depicts; the emotion the author is expressing is the emotion with which he contemplates that character; or rather, the emotion he has toward that secret and disowned part of himself for which the character stands.

[1]Shakespeare's characters rant (1) when they are characters in which he takes no interest at all, but which he uses simply as pegs on which to hang what the public wants, like Henry V; (2) when they are meant to be despicable, like Pistol; or (3) when they have lost their heads, like Hamlet in the graveyard.

3. *The Nature of Art*

MORRIS WEITZ

It is easier to teach art than to talk about its nature. Even so, teachers of art agree that it cannot be taught, or at least effectively taught, unless they can state truly its nature.

Critics, artists, philosophers, and interested amateurs concur with these teachers that no one can talk meaningfully or intelligibly about art without knowing what art is — what defines its real nature. Clive Bell, a distinguished critic of painting, epitomizes the general attitude toward this dependence of discourse about art upon a theory of it:

For either all works of visual art have some common quality, or when we speak of "works of art" we gibber. Everyone speaks of "art," making a mental classification by which he distinguishes the class "works of art" from all other classes. What is the justification of this classification? What is the quality common and peculiar to all members of this class?

Is Bell right? Do we talk nonsense when we teach or criticize art without knowing its nature or at least without assuming that it has a nature?

Bell's question certainly suggests a flattering invitation to the philosopher, since the whole point of it is to request of the philosopher a true definition of art that will guarantee our meaningful discussions and arguments about it. Probably one reason you have so kindly asked me to address you today is that you would like from me — as a philosopher — some sort of true, up-to-date definition of the nature of art so that your assumption, that intelligent teaching of art is rooted in a true theory of art, might be defended and justified.

Now, philosophers are notoriously prone to this sort of flattery that solicits from them wise, definitive solutions of problems. They are only too anxious to please, as even the history of aesthetics from Plato on shows, so many answers has it put forth.

David Hume, a great sceptic, enjoined philosophers long ago that they must resist, to the very core of their intellectual integrity, this sort of compliment because, unless they do, they simply return flattery for flattery; a pleasing reply to a pleasing request. Such intellectual goings-on, while comforting, to be sure, are on the far side of truth. The philosopher's first task, perhaps his primary intellectual obligation,

∗SOURCE: Address given to the National Committee on Art Education Conference at Columbus, Ohio, on March 24, 1961.

49

is not to provide desiderated solutions to difficult problems, but to clarify, ruthlessly if need be, the problem posed. The solution, if forthcoming, will take care of itself.

With Hume as my model, I want to examine the pervasive assumption that talk about art is gibberish without a statement or supposition of its nature.

Let us begin with the concept of the nature of art. Notice, first, how ambiguous the key terms are. "Art," as is well known, stands for a number of different things, among them, the creation of art, the work of art, the visual arts, or great art. "Nature," too, refers to different things: the essence of a thing, the shared, common qualities of the members of a class, and the origin, function, and value of a thing.

Why are these ambiguities important? Because until they are resolved, no precise sense can be given to the question, Can we teach or talk about art without knowing or being able to state its nature? Are we asking, for example, Can we teach painting or music without knowing or being able to state the essence of these arts?; Can we talk about the origin or value of art without knowing what all works of art have in common?; Can we say of something that it is art, and not, say, merely some paint on a canvas, without knowing what great art is?; and so on? I think that those artists, critics, philosophers, and teachers of art who believe that we cannot teach or talk about art without knowing its nature or at least assuming it has one, also sub-scribe to the view that we cannot discuss intelligently the creation of art, the work of art — whether a poem, a painting, or a statue, etc. — or great art, without knowing what all works of art share, their origin, value, and function.

I have no intention here of dealing with all these questions as they arise in any adequate unraveling of the ambiguities of our seemingly simple question about the nature of art. Instead I shall choose one

strand of the ambiguity and ask, Do we need a true theory of the essence of works of art to be able to render intelligible our talk about them as teachers, critics, artists, or philosophers? Must we know what makes a work a work of art, or assume there must be something that makes every work of art art, if we are to discuss it in any way whatever?

I have no doubt that most of you agree with Bell that we do need a theory of works of art in order to talk about them intelli-gently: to teach them, to interpret them, and to evaluate them.

What does this conviction come to? It comes to this, I think: First, that there is a class of objects in the world which has, as subclasses, painting, poetry, music, architecture, sculpture, the dance, and so on; and whose subclasses have, as members, particular poems, paintings, statues, com-positions, and so on. This whole class is the class of art works in the world. Second-ly, that this class is distinguishable from everything else — God, man, trees, viruses, and so on and so forth — which class is the class of nonart works in the world. Thirdly, that each of the members of the subclass or the class has a certain property or properties that are shared by all the members. These properties — what Bell refers to as qualities common and peculiar to all members of the class of works of art — are conceived of as the essential or defining ones of works of art.

It is this third doctrine that is crucial in the whole problem of the nature of art. Indeed, aesthetic theory, whether pur-sued by artists, critics, or philosophers, considers it basic, as its persistent attempt to define art reveals.

I began by asking whether we need to know the nature of art or even to assume it has a nature in order to guarantee the intel-ligibility of our diverse discourse about art. Because of the multiple range of ambiguity involved in "nature" and "art," I pinned down the question to this: Do we need to know or to assume that there is a theory in the sense of a true definition or statement of the essential properties of all works of art — i.e., the necessary and sufficient properties with which there are works of art and without which there are not works of art — in order to be able to teach or talk effectively and intelligibly about works of art?

I believe it is the case that almost all teachers, artists, critics, and philosophers concur that we do need such a theory; otherwise, as Bell said, we gibber. I want now to try to convince you that this assumption is false: that we do not need a theory in order to say all that needs to be said about works of art. Indeed, I wish to go further and try to convince you that such a theory is impossible — that there not only is not but cannot be a true statement of the necessary and sufficient properties of all works of art.

First, let us ask whether there is such a theory, i.e., such a true definition of the nature or essence of works of art?

Our best lead here is the great theories of the philosophers of art. The history of aesthetics contains many such theories. The most important and influential ones are: Imitationalism, Expressionism, Emotionalism, Formalism, and Organicism. I think it is a correct generalization to say that every theory of the nature of art, from Plato on, as well as every theory of the nature of any of the subclasses of art, for example, painting, music, sculpture, is a variant of one or other of these above theories.

Imitationalism is the doctrine that the defining properties of works of art are certain features that imitate the world outside of art. For Plato, the founder of the doctrine, these features comprise images of appearances of the ideal forms, hence, are far removed from the truly real. For Aristotle, the imitative features that define works of art are their organic structures; i.e., works of art resemble actual objects in that they,

too, have a beginning, middle, and end; form and matter, and the four causes — the material, efficient, formal, and final; works of art also imitate reality in that they embody certain universals. For Plotinus, imitations are manifestations of the oneness of things. For Reynolds and Dr. Johnson, works of art are also essentially imitations, but only of the ideals suggested by and abstracted from the actual world.

Expressionism is a repudiation of Imitationalism. Art, it maintains, is an imitation of nothing — at least in its essence. It is primarily imaginative, the product of the creative imagination. Croce, one of the great exponents of Expressionism, argues that works of art are actually identical with the process of their creation; as such, they are the expression or clarification of the sensations and images of the creative artists.

Emotionalism — probably the most popular of contemporary theories — defines a work of art as the embodiment in a public, sensuous medium, like canvas, stone, words, tones, of an emotion or a collection of them. Indeed, some Emotionalists define the whole of the aesthetic experience, from artistic creation, through the art object, to the spectator, reader, or listener, as emotional. Tolstoy is the best representative of this view.

Formalism is the doctrine that works of art are essentially certain organizations of elements that produce a certain effect. There are many varieties of Formalism in aesthetics as there are of Imitationalism. One version stresses the relations of a work; another, the purity of the medium; a third, harmonic relations; and what Bell calls "significant form," i.e., the right combinations of lines and colors in painting or of tones in music. Bell's view, superbly developed by Roger Fry, has achieved the status of a dogma at the present time among certain practitioners and theorists of abstract art.

Organicism, also an ancient theory, is the doctrine that works of art are essentially unities. Their defining property is their integration of all the elements of a single work of art, and not any one element or any abstracted collection of elements.

Most of you are especially interested in painting. It may be helpful, therefore, to apply some of these general theories of all works of art to the sub-class of paintings. Here, too, one finds the same overall theories, the same purportedly true statements of the exhaustive sets of necessary and sufficient properties of all paintings, the same essentialist definitions.

Bell and Fry, we have already noted, define painting — state what all paintings have in common and what distinguishes them from everything else — as those combinations of lines, colors, masses, space, volume, and light that produce the aesthetic emotion in the beholders of these combinations. At one stage of his career, Fry went so far as to reduce the defining essence of all painting to compositional structure.

According to another theory of painting, that of A. C. Barnes, painting is essentially color; everything else is a modification of it: line, drawing, composition, movement, volume, design — these are essentially aspects of coloration in painting.

To both Barnes and Fry, Berenson, certainly a powerful theorist of the art of painting, says that painting is essentially decoration, by which he means the embodiment on a surface of certain pictorial elements that invite the spectator to project his tactile imagination into them. For him, volume, because it suggests the solidity of things, is all-important; color is unessential.

Clearly, the theories of Bell, Fry, Barnes, and Berenson, and there are plenty more, are not idle, for they have their effects on criticism as well as on creation of paintings. If Barnes' view can lead to a negative assessment, for example, of Botticelli's achievement, on the ground that Bot-

ticelli had no grasp of the centrality of color in painting; if Berenson's theory yields a denigration of medieval and modern abstract painting as well as a good deal of non-Florentine Renaissance painting; and if Bell's and Fry's definition requires the repudiation of all representational elements in painting because they constitute a violation of it; we cannot but conclude that theories are powerful instruments in our discourse about art.

So much for our Cook's tour through the realm of theory about works of art. Do any of these theories strike us as imposing monuments of truth? How can we tell? What are the criteria of adequacy of a true theory or definition of the essence of works of art? Here are at least the minimal criteria: the theory or definition must contain clear, precise, empirical, and testable terms; the definition must not be circular; it must cover all cases and all properties of works of art; and it must not include clear cases of things that are not art.

Now, it seems to me, as I'm sure it does to many of you, that none of these theories satisfies all these minimal criteria. Some involve unclear, unempirical, untestable terms. Some, e.g., the Bell-Fry one, are circular. Some are overly inclusive in that they allow almost anything to be a work of art. All are restrictive, leaving out something that many think is essential to works of art.

I submit to you that none of the theories does the job it was supposed to do: to state the defining properties of all works of art. Further, that no meticulous, detailed exposition of any of these theories or any eclectic combination of their best ingredients does the job either. Indeed, I do not know of one theory in the whole history of aesthetics that states truly the necessary and sufficient properties of the class of art works or of any of its sub-classes: no one has yet defined truly all the arts or any of the separate ones of painting, music, poetry, the dance, the motion picture, sculpture, or architecture. Nor, I believe, has anyone ever proposed a theory which is a true definition of any of the other strands twisted into the nature of art; i.e., there is no true statement of the exhaustive, essential, defining properties of art creation or of the function, significance, or value of art.

If we require a true theory of works of art, creation of art, and the function and value of them, in order to justify our teaching and talking about them, we must admit, then, that we are sunk, for there simply is no such theory.

Are we sunk? Do we really require a theory of the essence of works of art in order to justify our teaching and other serious talk about them?

It seems to me that we do not: we can say what needs to be said about works of art without knowing the necessary and sufficient, the defining, properties of them, or without assuming that there is such a set of exhaustive, definitive properties. We can explain our discourse about works of art; we can render it intelligible by simply examining how we do talk about them. How do we actually talk about them? Not, I suggest, as Bell and others claim, by picking out a class of objects and probing their essence, but by pointing out established, recognized examples, about which there can be no question of their being works of art for the all-important reason that they are intrinsically connected with the home base of the concept, "work of art," itself. In the sense in which we can correctly ask whether, say, *Death of a Salesman* is a tragedy but not whether, say, *Oedipus Rex* is a tragedy, because the very concept of tragedy was invented or, to be more accurate, adapted to cover this paradigm case; we can ask whether, say, Duchamps' urinal, placed in exhibition, is a work of art, rather than a misplaced convenience, but not whether Michelangelo's

Last Judgment is a work of art. The concept, "work of art," functions in our discourse about art on the assumption, absolutely warranted, that there are established paradigm cases of works of art, not on the assumption, absolutely unwarranted, that there are established necessary and sufficient properties of works of art.

Our responsible teaching and talk about the classes and subclasses of works of art rest primarily upon established, paradigm cases. What is a work of art? or What is a painting? can be best understood as questions by comparing them to What is a collage? or What is a mobile? No one even dreams of answering these latter questions with a definitive statement of their essential properties, but simply by directing attention to the examples that gave birth to the concepts themselves.

Our teaching and talk about works of art are buttressed also by examples other than the paradigms. These examples have properties that are similar to those of the paradigms. But they may also have properties that differ from those of the paradigm cases. The first collage, with all its many properties, was nevertheless similar enough to paintings so that, in spite of its differences from all previous paintings, it was designated as a new member of the class of paintings. The first mobile, on the other hand, departed radically from one of the properties of sculpture, namely, aesthetic immobility, hence, was given a new name to distinguish it from traditional sculpture. It was called a mobile, however, not because it did not satisfy the necessary and sufficient properties of sculpture, but because, in spite of great similarities to previous sculptures, it substituted the one property of being subject to motion for the property of immobility.

Consider a more traditional example. Someone asks, What is a painting? The answer, I have suggested, is not some purportedly true statement of what all paintings have in common as their essential properties. The correct answer is: Michelangelo's *Last Judgment* and things like it. The *Last Judgment* — let us call this "*A*" — has certain properties: it is made by a man; it involves skill or craft and imagination; it is paint on a publicly observable surface; it has lines, color, drawing, composition, volumes, space, light, movement, and representation; it embodies a particular conception of a central theme of the Christian epic; and so on. Let us call these and its other discernible properties "1, 2, 3, 4, 5, etc." Now, "things like the *Last Judgment*" refers to objects *B–N* that contain properties 1–5; or properties 1–3, but not 4 and 5; or properties 1–5, plus new properties 6–8, say. Thus, objects *B–N* — roughly much of the history of painting — are paintings because they have properties 1–5; or 1–3; or 1–3, plus 6 and 7; and so on. But they are not paintings because they have properties 1–5, which are necessary and sufficient ones of all paintings. Object *N* + 1 (e.g., an abstraction by Mondrian or Kandinsky) is a painting, then, not because it contains any set of essential properties of painting but because it is like recognized paintings *A–N* in some respects, although it differs from them in others. Knowing what painting is, consequently, is not knowing a true theory of painting but knowing indisputable examples and how to decide on the basis of similarities what else is to count as a painting. And teaching or talking about paintings is also independent of a theory of painting (i.e., a true statement of its essential properties); it depends only on established examples and their strands of similarities of properties.

We can now generalize: What is a work of art? can also be answered by examples and statements of sets of properties. It need not be answered by some purportedly true statement of what all works share as their essential properties. What is a work of art? is best answered by: The *Last Judgment*, the *Parthenon*, *Don Giovanni*,

Anna Karenina, *Hamlet*, Martha Graham's *Letter to the World*, Chaplin's *Modern Times*, etc. These are indisputable examples. They have many individual properties. Some of these properties are present in all the examples; some are present only in a few. None adds up to necessary and sufficient properties. What ties them together are certain strands of similarities. It is these strands that we refer to when we include new examples under the class of works of art. Thus, every question of the form, Is *N* + 1 a work of art? is answered by an appeal to previous, established examples, with their collections of properties, where none of the properties constitutes the essence of art.

There is no true theory of works of art. There need be no such theory to guarantee our teaching and talk about works of art. I want now to persuade you that there can be no theory of art, i. e., no true statement of the necessary and sufficient properties of all works of art.

If we turn, as we must, to the concept "work of art," and inquire into its functions in our teaching and talk about art, we shall see that "work of art" is employed by us to describe or to evaluate certain objects under certain conditions. One of these conditions is that there exist paradigm cases. Another is that there exist certain strands of similarities among properties. Still another condition is that new examples of works of art with their new properties are allowed for. The concept, "work of art," operates on the condition that it can be used to describe or evaluate works that will be made tomorrow where these works bring into being absolutely new properties. It is this condition that precludes the very possibility of a definition in the sense of a true statement of the necessary and sufficient properties of works of art, for any such statement forecloses on the very functioning or use of the concept itself, namely, to cover new examples with their new properties. We cannot state the essential criteria of that concept whose very employment demands that there shall be no exhaustive set of essential criteria. Every real, purportedly true definition or theory of works of art represents an attempt to state the necessary and sufficient criteria of the concept of works of art, which concept, as its actual functioning reveals, demands that it shall have no such criteria. Thus, every theory of works of art violates the logic of the concept it sets out to elucidate, by trying to define that which cannot be defined. "Work of art" and "art" itself are open concepts, i.e., concepts whose very use depends on their not having a closed set of essential criteria in order for them to do the jobs we have assigned to them.

The relevance of my remarks on the indefinability of works of art to artistic creation or creativity — a problem that many of you take very seriously — should be obvious: there is no theory, no true statement, about the essence of creativity. How could there be? Such a statement would contradict the very point of the concept itself, that it be applicable to all sorts of new, unforeseen conditions, conditions which are neither necessary nor sufficient ones for the correct understanding of the concept. To state truly the essence of creativity is logically impossible, for this would be tantamount to denying that there is such a thing as creativity altogether. We cannot state all the properties of that whose primary property is novelty itself.

If there are no satisfactory theories of works of art, if there need be no such theories in order to teach and criticize works of art, and if there can be no such theories, what, then, is the point of these theories? Are they all total failures?

In spite of the fact that all of them fail to accomplish what they set out to do — to give a true definition of works of art — these definitions are nevertheless helpful and well worth intensive study. For behind every one is a redefinition of "work of art"; i.e., an attempt to get us to concentrate on certain criteria or properties of works of art as against others. If we attend to these criteria or properties and forget the unsuccessful attempts at true, essentialist definitions, we can learn a great deal from the theories, especially as to what we should look for in works of art and how we should look at them. Indeed, the great contribution of theories of works of art is precisely in their teachings, not in their definitions, of art: each of the theories represents a set of explorable criteria which serve to remind us of what we may have neglected or to make us see what we may not have seen. To do this, I should think, is the primary job of teaching. Here, then, is the relation between teaching and the nature of art or, to use the title of your conference, the nature of art and its implications for teaching: that the great theorists of the nature of art have served as the great teachers as well, in telling us, through their definitions of art, what we are to learn from them about the arts. Their emphases on the properties of imitation, emotion, form, organic unity, skill, intelligence, imagination — if we do not identify these with essential properties of art — can function as perennial pointers in the teaching of art. As general as these emphases are, they can still help us to pinpoint specific features of works of art, e.g., the expressive or emotional dimension of them or their organic relations. I can think of nothing more important in the teaching of art, for example, than to remind students as well as myself that in art everything counts, everything plays a role in relation to everything else in any single work of art; consequently, that isolation or abstraction as a method of teaching or criticism violates one of the features of a work of art.

The theorists of painting also serve primarily as teachers. For hidden in their purportedly true definitions of painting are also recommended criteria or suggested properties that we should attend to if we are to get the most from painting. When Bell and Fry tell us that painting is essentially significant form, we need not construe their definition as a true statement about all paintings, but, more importantly, as a primer for our visual training: Their definition teaches us how to seek out all the relationships of line and color, along with the other purely pictorial elements before we start reducing the picture to predominantly representational elements. From their teaching we learn what joy awaits us once we experience the purely formal values of painting and, through these, the purely formal values of all the arts. We can learn from Barnes and Berenson, too. Barnes' definition is a persistent reminder not to neglect the dynamic, building power of color in painting, to refuse to see color as mere ornament; and Berenson's is a similar invitation, this time to project our tactile sensations into the visual, pictorial elements of painting, an invitation which, once acted upon, may very well inspire the life-enhancing experience he promises us if we follow his teachings in painting.

Our circle is drawn and I can stop. I began by asking whether the teaching of art rests on a true theory of it. I then tried to show that the teaching of art does not, cannot, and need not, rest on such a theory. Rather, that the theories of art comprise different sets of directions—indeed, the best there are — for the richest possible participation in the arts. If my argument is correct, teachers of art should go to the theories of art not for nonexistent true definitions but for all their fertile suggestions about the very teaching of art, since the theorists themselves have been the best instructors.

4. *The Artistic Process as Qualitative Problem Solving*

DAVID W. ECKER

The statements of artists on art have served many purposes. Promotion and protest, instruction, criticism and reflection, even calls for aesthetic revolution, have issued forth on those occasions when artists have been moved to express themselves in words. The diversity of purposes or intentions of the artist-as-writer persuades the critical reader that different kinds of criteria are appropriate for the evaluation of such a wide variety of discourse.

When judged by literary criteria the literary efforts of artists are found to range from the grotesque to the polished and, at times, the elegant. For examples of this stylistic range one need only compare the Dada manifestoes with Delacroix's *Journal*.

When judged by philosophical criteria the generalizations of artists rank from the superficial, and occasionally the incoherent, to the profound. This intellectual gamut is readily noted by comparing a random sample of the flood of statements by contemporary artists

published in catalogues and magazines with Leonardo's *Notebooks*.

When judged by educational criteria treatises on art run from the highly specific to the broadly theoretical. One thinks of Cennini's *Book of the Art*, the original "how-to-do-it" manual for painters, on the one hand and on the other Paul Klee's almost spiritual *Pedagogical Sketchbook*, whose sub-title is "Initial plan for a section of the theoretical instruction at the German Bauhaus."

It is apparent, however, that statements of artists on art and art itself may serve functions other than those sought by the artists. For instance, the purpose of the researcher into art may well involve criteria for assessing the writings or works of art that are not relevant to the artist's purposes. The artist may be concerned with the qualities of his personal experience or he may be preoccupied with the unique character of his artistic production. The art critic could well be chiefly interested in the completed work

＊SOURCE: The following pages are a revised version of a paper read at the annual meeting of the American Society for Aesthetics, held at Wayne State University on October 28, 1961.
Reprinted from *The Journal of Aesthetics and Art Criticism*, XXI/3, Spring 1963.

as an example of a stylistic movement, as a type of art activity that lends a common character to the work of many artists. Given this interest criteria come into play that have more inclusive applicability than those confined to a few cases. The philosopher is concerned with the status of a work of art as part of the furniture of the world and, more recently, with the status of *talk* about art. The sociologist, historian and psychologist of art will work with quite different hypotheses and, consequently, look for and find evidence of very different sorts in the same material.

The general impression one gets from a survey of writings of artists and nonartists alike is that the closer the writer has stood to the work of the studio, the more the techniques and means of production are appreciated. Conversely, it seems that the farther he moves back to view the role of art in education, society, or civilization, the more the writer becomes concerned with the ends of art, its ultimate value to mankind.[1]

My interest in artists' discourse is methodological. By this I mean to indicate that my problem is one of formulating warranted generalizations about the controlled process of artistic production. These perspectives may be usefully merged. A close examination of the shop talk and the work of the studio will provide certain data about the process of constructing an art object. These generalizations will be expanded to a level of abstraction inclusive of the immediacies of any given artistic production. I will call the latter qualitative problem solving. It is my contention that careful study of what painters *do* when ordering their artistic means and ends, as well as of

what they *say* they are doing, will provide the bases for significantly improving our generalizations about the plastic arts and our conceptions about education in the arts. If it *is* possible to describe the artistic process as a series of problems and their controlled resolution, the ensuing generalizations may be of no small consequence to the teaching of art. Thus, my interest in and criteria for the evaluating of the verbal and qualitative materials of the artist will be methodological: my interest will be in artistic means and ends and my criteria that which will evaluate discourse in terms of its ability to explain and describe deliberately conducted procedures involved in artistic production.

I

Henry Moore, writing on "the problems that have concerned me from time to time," claims that the sculptor "must strive continually to think of and use form in its full spatial completeness. . . .he knows while he looks at one side what the other side is like; he identifies himself with its centre of gravity, its mass, its weight; he realizes its volume, as the space that displaces air."[2] Moore speaks of the sources of his "sculptural problems" as follows:

. . . I sometimes begin a drawing with no preconceived problem to solve, with only the desire to use pencil on paper, and make lines, tones and shapes with no conscious aim; but as my mind takes in what is so produced a point arrives where some idea becomes conscious and crystallizes, and then a control and ordering begins to take place.

Or sometimes I start with a set subject; or to solve, in a block of stone of known dimensions, a sculptural problem I've given myself, and then consciously attempt to build an ordered relationship of forms. . . .[3]

Thus Moore refers to what Dewey would call qualitative thought — thinking *in* the particular qualities of the artist's medium

[1]This generalization is not entirely true, however, since from the nineteenth century on artists in their writings reveal an increasing concern with the ends served by art, often expressing quite diverse opinions. See *Artists on Art From the XIV to the XX Century*, ed. Robert Goldwater and Marco Treves (New York, 1947), and *The Creative Process*, ed. Brewster Ghiselin (New York, 1955).

[2]*The Creative Process*, p. 74.
[3]*Ibid.*, p. 77.

FIGURE 4.1 Henry Moore, "Reclining Figure" (Elmwood, 1935). Room of Contemporary Art Collection, Albright-Knox Art Gallery, Buffalo, New York.

FIGURE 4.2 Henry Moore, "Recumbent Figure" (Hornton stone, 1939). Courtesy of the Trustees of the Tate Gallery, London.

FIGURE 4.3 Henry Moore, "Reclining Figure" (Bronze, 1957). Working Model for Sculpture for UNESCO Building in Paris.

(in this case, stone). Moore's sculptural ideas are not necessarily "preconceived," but nevertheless at some point in the proceedings an "idea becomes conscious and crystallizes" and "ordering begins." Here, one thinks of Moore's various wood, bronze, and stone solutions to his long-time problem with the theme of the human torso — his "reclining figure" series.

Turning to a painter, the following is a recorded conversation with Picasso.

It would be very interesting to record photographically, not the stages of a painting, but its metamorphoses. One would see perhaps by what course a mind finds its way towards the crystallization of its dream. . . .

The picture is not thought out and determined beforehand, rather while it is being made it follows the mobility of thought. . . .

When one begins a picture one often discovers fine things. One ought to beware of these, destroy one's picture, recreate it many times. On each destruction of a beautiful find, the artist does not suppress it, to tell the truth; rather he transforms it, condenses it, makes it more substantial. . . .[4]

Here Picasso gives an illuminating account, part shop talk and part speculative, of his painting procedures. Yet what is perhaps even more significant from a methodological point of view is a comparison of his paintings of the 1910's with those of Braque and Juan Gris. For it seems justified to claim that, at this period in the history of modern art, these three painters shared cubistic problems — shared them even to the point of making it difficult for the viewer to distinguish the work of one painter from another save through signature.

Another painter, Yasuo Kuniyoshi, states:

There are numerous problems that beset the artist in his work. Consciously or unconsciously each artist tries to solve them. Lately I have come to the stage where I actually take a problem and try to solve it. For instance I was interested in painting a dark object within the dark. In order to carry this out successfully it may take me

several years. Once accomplished to my satisfaction, however, it becomes an integral part of me, enabling me to go on to another problem.[5]

This last statement about going on to another problem suggests the notion of a development — or learning sequence — whereby the artist increases his control, over a period of time, by solving problems which are qualitatively related to one another in technique, style, or theme. It also suggests a conception of art history as a series of problems and solutions; those solutions which provoke the most artists in succeeding generations to work at related problems are named "masterpieces." Successive problems with perspective, modeling, proportions, color, composition, expression, and so on, are literally a part of art history.

Is this not the case in the series of paintings shown here? Cézanne's *Village of Gardanne*, painted in 1885–1886, with its flattened perspective and color — the same green is used in the distant hill as in the trees in the foreground — is clearly a precursor of Picasso's cubistic *The Reservoir*, painted in 1909. In turn, Cubism, as a pervasive quality of the work of Picasso, Braque, and Gris, prompted Mondrian to move toward "pure" painting in *Eucalyptus Tree in Grey + Tan* (1912), and in his *Oval Composition* done in 1914. Even in this sequence of only four paintings one can see why Cézanne is called the father of modern painting. His work, as summed up in his dictum: "Nature must be treated through the cylinder, the sphere, the cone," has led many painters ultimately to reject nature as subject matter altogether. Yet with respect to "volume" the new qualitative alternatives gained by Cézanne — the qualities of flatness and "local" color without light or shadow — have influenced quite diverse schools of painting. These "surface" or component qualities have, together with the pervasive "expressive" qualities of Van

[4]*Ibid.*, pp. 56–57.

[5]*Ibid.*, p. 62.

FIGURE 4.4 Paul Cézanne, "Village of Gardanne" (1885–1886). Courtesy of the Brooklyn Museum.

FIGURE 4.5 Pablo Picasso, "The Reservoir. Horta de Ebro" (1909). Courtesy Fernand Hazan, Paris.

FIGURE 4.6 Piet Mondrian, "Eucalyptus Tree in Grey + Tan" (1912). Courtesy of Sidney Janis Gallery, New York.

FIGURE 4.7 Piet Mondrian, "Oval Composition" (Picture 111, 1914). Courtesy of Fernand Hazan, Paris.

Gogh and the "decorative" qualities of Gauguin, directly influenced the *Fauve* movement of 1905–1907 (Matisse, Derain, Vlaminck, Dufy, Marquet, Rouault, Braque, Friesz, van Dongen) and, by way of Cubism, have also influenced the geometric, nonobjective *De Stijl* movement (Mondrian, van Doesburg, Vantongerloo, the architect, Oud, and the *Bauhaus*). One is impressed by the *continuity* of artistic thought, as these new pervasive qualities are seen to emerge from older qualities — sometimes dramatically, sometimes almost imperceptibly. By extending this analysis of qualitative relationships it is conceivable that the history of art could be viewed as a record of the highest achievements of man's qualitative problem-solving behavior.

If this conception of the art process as a problem-solution-problem continuum is warranted by the qualitative evidence of art history, much of the shop talk between artists is verbal evidence. For shop talk is largely a by-product of their mutual problems of painting or sculpting. The words incorporated into this shop talk have common sense meanings, or, rather, sense common to fellow artists. That is, the words refer to the shared qualities of their work. Consider the empirical character of the following examples of shop talk: "If you use a cool green here you can get this plane to recede." "My painting is beginning to get a cubist quality." "This jagged shape contrasts sharply with those open volumes." The things dealt with by such language are what I choose to call the means and ends of artistic production, the *qualities* artists manipulate, orchestrate, modify, and create in solving their problems. Even the limited sample of artists' statements reviewed thus far suggests the broad features of the artistic thinking that is involved in the production of plastic art.

Given these initial data it seems plausible to suggest that: (1) Artists at their work think in terms of relations of qualities, *think*

with qualities; their thought, in a word, is qualitative. (2) This thought is exercised on behalf of the construction of further qualities — the qualitative problem. (3) Qualitative problems are not so much "in the mind" as they are "mindings." Artistic problem solving takes place in the artist's medium — line, plane, color, texture, form are the qualities distinctive to or possible for such materials as stone, wood, paint, or fabric. (4) Qualitative problems are not "inner conflicts" or "states of confusion" but awareness of elements or prospects within a range of qualities with regard to some intended order, end-in-view, or pervasive quality. Thus qualitative problems, like theoretical problems, are publicly available to student and instructor alike for shared criticism and work. (5) The means for the resolution of a qualitative problem are component qualities. Words as qualities may, of course, enter into the art, say, of collage, or the poster. (6) While language may be of help in the definition of the qualitative problem, that is, in its location or delimitation, the ability to describe verbally a qualitative problem is not a necessary condition for having one. (A painting may be labeled after its completion.) (7) Critical judgment is not necessarily antecedent, nor totally subsequent, to a creative act, but often occurs during the act. Judgment, or judging, is choosing among alternative actions and qualities, choosing among alternative qualitative means-ends and methods. Cubism as a style has acted to determine what elements, planes, structures may be organized. As such the style regulates or controls the production of a given canvas. Because of this control one would identify the canvas as cubistic. The painter may, at any time, choose to destroy his canvas, that is, embrace *another* control. Or he may indicate verbally his satisfaction with its development or otherwise *affirm* his control. (8) None of the laws of formal logic as such seems to be directly applicable to the qualitative thought of the artist. While logic can order the theoretical symbols used in scientific inquiry and control statements and assertions, whether about art objects or other subject matters, it is not applicable to the qualitative ordering that yields a piece of sculpture. (9) One may locate within the history of art the history of art criticism; the historical series of qualitative solutions to artists' problems sets the qualitative standards for evaluation of art.

II

John Dewey is one of the few modern philosophers who have offered us some methodological analyses of controlled production both in the arts as well as in scientific inquiry. These analyses are exceedingly pertinent to the theme of this paper. Dewey held that all thinking depends upon the awareness of qualities. He claimed it is the unique quality that pervades a situation that acts as a control over all means to ends-in-view ordering. But in his most systematic effort to explain thought processes Dewey is essentially occupied with the nature of the "pattern of inquiry," or *scientific* problem solving. Dewey's analysis of the steps of inquiry are well known: "(i) a felt difficulty; (ii) its location and definition; (iii) suggestion of possible solution; (iv) development by reasoning of the bearings of the suggestion; (v) further observation and experimentation leading to its acceptance or rejection; that is the conclusion of belief or disbelief."[6] As to his conception of artistic thinking he leaves only a series of rather unsystematic, albeit seminal, ideas, which suggests the possibility of extending the conception of "problem" to include both scientific and artistic aspects of human intelligence. For example one reads:

The artist has his problems and thinks as he works. But his thought is more immediately em-

bodied in the object. Because of the comparative remoteness of his end, the scientific worker operates with symbols, words and mathematical signs. The artist does his thinking in the very qualitative media he works in, and the terms lie so close to the object that he is producing that they merge directly into it.[7]

Dewey finds many similarities between art and science and he often identifies the two. He insists that

. . . science is an art, that art is practice, and that the only distinction worth drawing is not between practice and theory, but between those modes of practice that are not intelligent, not inherently and immediately enjoyable, and those which are full of enjoyed meanings. . . .[8]

According to Dewey the method of inquiry is the method of art: "Scientific method or the art of constructing true perceptions is ascertained in the course of experience to occupy a privileged position in undertaking other arts. . . ."[9] Furthermore, he claims that artists and scientists have much in common:

There is . . . a tendency among lay critics to confine experimentation to scientists in the laboratory. Yet one of the essential traits of the artist is that he is born an experimenter. Without this trait he becomes a poor or a good academician. The artist is compelled to be an experimenter because he has to express an intensely individualized experience through means and materials that belong to the common and public world. This problem cannot be solved once for all. It is met in every new work undertaken. Otherwise an artist repeats himself and becomes esthetically dead. Only because the artist operates experimentally does he open new fields of experience and disclose new aspects and qualities in familiar scenes and objects.[10]

Having stated the basic similarities between artistic and scientific activities, Dewey does not ignore their differences, although perhaps he fails to draw the line to the de-

[6]*How We Think* (Boston, New York, Chicago, 1910), p. 72.

[7]*Art As Experience* (New York, 1934), p. 16.
[8]*Experience and Nature* (Chicago, London, 1926), p. 358.
[9]*Ibid.*, p. 379.
[10]*Art As Experience*, p. 144.

gree of sharpness his critics might desire. Between the two,

> ... the only significant distinction concerns the kind of material to which emotionalized imagination adheres. Those who are called artists have for their subject-matter the qualities of things of direct experience; "intellectual" inquirers deal with these qualities at one remove, through the medium of symbols that stand for qualities but are not significant in their immediate presence.[11]

Inasmuch as the theme of intelligence as the one valid instrument to control and enrich human experience is central to all Dewey's writings, it is quite understandable that we find him insisting throughout these passages on the indispensable part thought plays in the production of art. He insists that "the odd notion that an artist does not think and a scientific inquirer does nothing else is the result of converting a difference of tempo and emphasis into a difference in kind."[12] Or again, when he writes, "any idea that ignores the necessary role of intelligence in production of works of art is based upon identification of thinking with use of one special kind of material, verbal signs and words."[13] Citations such as these could be continued, but nowhere does one find a systematic analysis of the method of "artistic" thinking.

III

Two students of Dewey's thought, N. L. Champlin and F. T. Villemain, of Wayne and Toledo Universities respectively, have exploited these suggestions by extending methodological analysis to include the controls in "qualitative thought" and the formal character of qualitative ordering. Following Peirce and Dewey, they define intelligence as a human process or activity rather than as some kind of entity within humans. But intelligence is not limited to

arranging theoretical symbols — that with which scientists think primarily.

The artist, too, exhibits deliberate control over his materials: he arranges qualitative *means* such as lines, colors, planes, and textures, to achieve his qualitative *end*, which we might name "cubist," "impressionist," or "expressionist." In his selecting, rejecting, and relating of qualitative means, he is guided by a quality which is common to his previous work or to a particular style, such as Cubism. Thus, a certain kind of general or "pervasive" quality acts as his *method*. Just as the laws of logic are the controls by which theoretical symbols are arranged in scientific inquiry, so these pervasive qualities act as *controls* — directive criteria — by which component qualities are arranged in the artistic process. The artist utilizes qualitative methods to arrange the qualitative means toward qualitative ends. Art, therefore, is an affair of intelligence — it is intelligence in qualitative ordering.

The arts can now be seen as *specialized* products of qualitative intelligence. Dewey's idea that the pervasive quality of experience is the "regulative principle of all thinking," and that this quality provides the necessary conditions for scientific knowing as well as qualitative operations, forms the basis for Villemain's and Champlin's theory of education. The traditional distinction between scientific and artistic activities — that science has to do with "reason" and "intelligence," while art traffics with "feelings" and "emotions" — is rejected as inherently untestable. (The latter terms do not have publicly shareable referents.) In its place, their theory establishes qualitative (aesthetic) and theoretical (scientific) intelligence as operating in *all* areas of human experience.[14]

[11]*Ibid.*, p. 73.
[12]*Ibid.*, p. 15.
[13]*Ibid.*, p. 46.

[14]This section is, of course, a highly schematic presentation of some features of their theory. For a more comprehensive view, see F. T. Villemain, "The Qualitative Character of Intelligence," and and N. L. Champlin, "Controls in Qualitative Thought," both unpubl. diss. (Columbia, 1952). Also see their article, "Frontiers for an Experi-

IV

With the broad features of the artistic process staked out and with a conception of art as qualitative means-ends relating as our theoretical base, we may now undertake to generalize the statements of artists into a statement of qualitative problem solving in methodological terms. It may be noted that, historically, much attention has been given to the description of the parts of word or number ordering. For example, there are the labels *verb, noun, adjective; hypothesis, assertion, deduction; division, multiplication, addition; assumption, verification, proof.* Many writers have wanted to use these or similar terms to describe artistic ordering. And although it is true that much talk about the arts incorporates the terminology of theoretical ordering — such terms as "artistic truth," "visual statement," "aesthetic validity," "perceptual knowledge" are terms which come to mind — this is no doubt due to the vague morphological resemblance noted between artistic and scientific procedures. The reflections of artists and scientists alike point up striking similarities in all original thinking. But the use of these quasi-scientific terms to refer to qualities of art is, I think, grossly misleading.

The initial stages of art may appear to be random, uncontrolled behavior; but the appearance of an object is not a stage of artistic problem solving any more than the indeterminate situation was, strictly, a stage of inquiry for Dewey. A problem has to be taken in thought as either (1) *an object* such as a painting, costume, or table setting, or (2) *a situation* in which the relations of component elements seem present not in virtue of an ordering. In painting, for instance, if the work is to proceed, choices must be

made; the alternatives are many and varied before the initial brush stroke (and the artist often may be in a hurry to make even "aimless" marks on the paper or canvas to gain a basis for future choice). But after these first elements — whether a bit of color, a line of a poem, or a bar of music — the alternatives diminish in number.

Here is a sequence of photographs of a painting by Saul Horowitz. Not all of the stages of the painting are shown. However, the qualities of the final painting *are* present in the beginning sketch. Other qualities have been modified considerably, or in some places completely painted over. Yet the total quality of each state is related to the extent that, were they mixed up with photos of other paintings, they could be reordered into the original sequence by inspection and comparison. It seems entirely plausible, therefore, to hold with Dewey that "The doing or making is artistic when the perceived result is of such a nature that *its* qualities *as perceived* have controlled the question of production."[15] Also plausible is Champlin's notion that the final painting, even if hazily "conceived" or *there* at the time of the initial sketch, could, nevertheless, act in some kind of controlling capacity — as a criterion — for the selection and rejection of qualitative elements (line, color, distribution of shapes and textures).

Artistic thinking, then, occurs when present and possible qualities are taken as means, or ways of proceeding, toward a qualitative end-in-view, a total quality. The pervasive quality directs artistic behavior from stage to stage until a coherent whole is realized. This purposive activity may be conducted entirely in qualities — component, pervasive, and total. However, there *may* be ordering of theoretical symbols which may not be found as elements of the art work itself, but which are, nevertheless, helpful and in some cases demanded for the

mentalist Philosophy of Education," *The Antioch Review*, XIX (1959), pp. 345–359. Of further interest is "John Dewey Centennial: A Special Section," co-ed. Villemain and Champlin, *Saturday Review*, November 21, 1959, pp. 16–26.

[15]*Art As Experience*, p. 48.

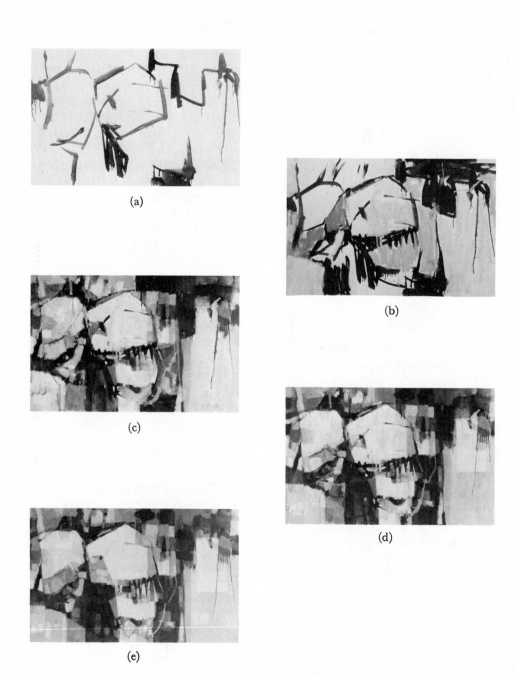

(a)

(b)

(c)

(d)

(e)

FIGURE 4.8 Sequence of photographs of five stages
of a painting by Saul Horowitz.

66

solution of a qualitative problem. It may be necessary, for example, for a painter to test a certain new formula for a particular gesso ground so as to achieve a highly *mat* finish when colors are applied over the canvas.

Qualitative problem solving is, as Dewey insisted of scientific inquiry, not a neat progression of steps but a single, continuous means-ends progression, sometimes hesitating, halting, groping; it may be rethought, move forward again, start over, in short, it is *experimental* behavior. And all that one can attempt is a logical analysis of distinguishable phases of the artistic process, as Dewey did in his description of scientific processes of thought. Rules, or recipes, as such, for producing good art (or science, for that matter) have never been established, and are perhaps anathema to the genuinely creative art of each age.

To reinterpret Dewey's definition of "inquiry": The artistic process is qualitative problem solving; it is the controlled procedure of instituting qualitative relationships as means to the achievement of a qualitative end or total. Not all of the following steps or stages are to be taken as necessarily proceeding in the order of presentation; but they are herein held to correspond with what Dewey has called "the stages of a complete act of reflective thinking":

1. *A presented relationship.* The initial and perhaps rambling phase is the instituting, taking, selecting, the discrimination of component or total qualitative relationships — the confrontation of that quality or those qualities which achieve candidacy for alteration, reconstruction, or change. These qualities (including those sometimes designated by the term "materials") vary, of course, from medium to medium, from substantive context to substantive context, and are components to be developed.

2. *Substantive mediation.* There follows, sometimes quickly or sometimes over a prolonged period, the instituting of new qualitative relationships. In some instances these

relationships become, however hazily, candidates for means, whose status as means is dependent upon having an end-in-view. The choice for *these* relationships rather than some other possible relationships conditions succeeding choices among qualities. A future choice, however, may involve the "destruction" of a previous choice in the sense that another quality appears to compete with the initiating quality.

3. *Determination of pervasive control.* The controlling pervasive quality may emerge more clearly *as a pervasive* — as a control — at any time of the process' development; it results from the qualitative components being introduced, manipulated, and related to *other* components and the qualities emerging from *these* respective relations. "Components" of a unique end-in-view gain identity as such by virtue of the envisioned total quality now emerging. The *pervasive* quality may, however, be that of some "traditional" or already available art form or style. Nevertheless the total sought may maintain its uniqueness as a total quality. (The achieved total may appear as unique in the sense of being a distinctive forming according to a pervasive quality already available historically, *e.g.*, impressionism, and thereby contribute to that pervasive control, or it may be unique as a total which itself becomes a pervasive or control quality for future orderings, *i.e.*, the appearance of a new style.)

4. *Qualitative prescription.* Given a pervasive quality, whether arriving early or late in the art production, future mediations follow according to patterns of qualitative relatedness. The artist "infers" quality from quality in the sense that future "qualitative steps" are anticipated or intended by virtue of presently instituted qualities.

5. *Experimental exploration.* With each brush stroke, push of the thumb, touch of the key, tap of the mallet, gouge of the burin, voice inflection, gesture, a "testing" operation is being performed. Such testing takes place as component qualities (now here or

yesterday there) are thought in relation to total and/or pervasive quality also empirically there.

6. *Conclusion: the total quality.* The work is judged complete — the total achieved — the pervasive has adequately been the control. It is a tentative affair because future evaluations may yield a conclusion for future modifications. (Indeed, some artists have maintained that they have never really "finished" a canvas.)

In this attempt to establish methodological generalizations about artistic processes, I have argued for a discrimination between two kinds of problem solving — the scientific and the qualitative, each with its distinctive controls. These distinctions together with the analysis of qualitative procedures extend Dewey's conception of method and flow from the general theory of intelligence being explored by Villemain and Champlin.

To summarize the methodological conception of the artistic process advanced here, it may be said that qualitative problem solving is a mediation in which qualitative relations as means are ordered to desired qualitative ends. Thus to choose qualitative ends is to achieve an artistic problem. Whenever qualitative problems are sought, pointed out to others, or solved, therein do we have artistic endeavor — art and art education.

5. *Aesthetics and the Teaching of Art*

E. F. KAELIN

The precarious position of the creative arts in the educational curriculum is a well-attested fact. Government, foundation, and university support is slow to come; and when it does, the persons who are most likely to benefit from such institutional largesse are the already established artists, who more and more are playing the role of artist-teacher. The assumption seems to be that only the person who has proved himself as an artist is capable of teaching other artists. And the facts of history give good reasons for making the assumption: the greatest teachers of art have been those masters whose pedagogical interest was dictated by the necessity for the cheap labor apprentices have always afforded. Since the subject of the commissioned works was usually ordered by the patron or purchaser, the master could lay out the composition of the piece and turn over the tedious task of filling in the detail to the eager student who had already mastered the techniques of his enterprising teacher. What was taught under these circumstances was a technique, and what was learned was formulable in a series of rules for the craft. That this noble tradition of craftsmanlike preparation has been discredited in theory — although a quick walk through any gallery displaying a student art show is sufficient to show that it has not been discredited in fact — indicates that history has witnessed a changing conception of the role of the creative artist. Nor is this change in conception a recent phenomenon: like French politics, the more the situation changes, the more it remains the same.

The English language is full of aphorisms which indicate the intellectual bases for the changing conception. All the while enrollments in our art schools are on the increase, there is heard the reverberating echo of the anonymous cliché: artists are born, and not made. And if the wisdom of the ages does not suffice to indicate the art educator's difficulty, the wit of G. B. Shaw is more mordant still: his "Those who can, do, and those who can't, teach," may be read as adding nothing more to the foregoing commonplace than his evaluation of those teachers who had never heard of it, and who, as teachers of art, must be caught in a doubly compromising pose if the old adage is correct. Within the realm of philosophy itself the

⁕SOURCE: Reprinted from *Studies in Art Education*, V (Spring 1964), p. 2.

same belief has had widespread acceptance. To mention only two philosophers, Plato and Kant.

It will be remembered how Plato has Socrates con the young Ion into accepting the fact that he (Ion) interprets Homer so successfully only because he has been inspired, as the poet himself has been inspired by the muse. Ion's original claim, that he interprets the poet by rule and knowledge, is reduced to absurdity. And Kant's famous dictum, couched in his definition of genius as " . . . the talent (or natural gift) which gives the rule to art,"[1] leaves very little room for educability of the aesthetic sensibility: "Since talent, as the innate productive faculty of the artist, belongs itself to nature, we may express the matter thus: Genius is the innate mental disposition (*ingenium*) through which nature gives the rule to art."[2] Kant's predecessor, Baumgarten, suggested to would-be artists looking for inspiration to ride on horseback, to drink wine in moderation, or, providing they remain chaste, to contemplate beautiful women.[3]

Multiplication of such examples would not be difficult. There seems to be a deeply felt conviction that art is a discipline which cannot be taught, while on the other hand the conviction is belied by many examples of successful artists who have learned at least the rudiments of their craft from some kind of teacher. Thus there results a problem, defined by the inconsistency between belief and action, which it is the province of philosophical analysis to clarify and of educational institutions to solve.

I shall attempt the clarification of the issues involved by examining some of the current philosophical theories concerning the nature of art which continue to militate against a consistent theoretical approach to art education — the idealistic and the linguistic, or analytic; then, after having shown the shortcomings of these views, I shall consider the claims of neo-pragmatism for having solved the noted deficiencies. My own claim is that the thesis of "qualitative problem solving" deriving from the aesthetic theory of John Dewey needs further amplification in an existential, phenomenological concept of an aesthetic object for a complete, workable theory of education in art. The remainder of this essay, then, will be devoted to these three tasks.

* * *

Idealism in aesthetics has as its distinctive mark a separation of the artifact — a physical thing — from "the work of art," or original idea of the artist, which is communicated to some audience via the artifact. As likely as not, an idealistic aesthetics will find the value of works of art to be expression or embodiment of feelings in a sensuous construct. The Croce-Collingwood theory of expression is perhaps the most influential of its kind.

For Croce, an artist expresses feeling in the form of intuitions by giving form to the multitudes of impressions playing upon his psychic processes; until formed, however, the impressions remain unknown matter, a limiting concept postulated to fulfill the theoretical requirements of Croce's general philosophy of spirit. The essence of the human spirit is its activity: theoretical, in forming intuitions or concepts; and practical, in achieving ends of a particular sort (the realization of an end following its conception by a single individual) or of the general good (the working out of a moral life by the general community). The four divisions of the philosophy of the spirit are in consequence dedicated to aesthetics, logic, "economics," and morality. Any consideration of Croce's aesthetics which ignores the relatedness of the spheres of human activity is likely to miss the necessary con-

[1]*The Critique of Judgment*, translated by J. H. Bernard, New York, Hafner Classics, 1951), p. 150.
[2]*Ibid.*
[3]Cited by Croce, *Aesthetic*, translated by Douglas Ainslie (London: The Macmillan Company, Ltd., 1953), p. 103.

nection between art and economics, between the intuitions of an artist and his "externalization" of them, that has been the bane of professional art educators. Finally, the relation between aesthetics and logic is not without some import for the conception of education in art.

If an artist is passive before the impressions which play upon him, his mind is active in giving form to them. The feelings of the impressions undergone are transmuted into feelings expressed in the intuition of individual forms. As individual, these intuited forms are not previsible, nor are they translatable into other terms; the artist, in this scheme, creates, finding "himself big with his theme, he knows not how; he feels the moment of birth drawing near, but he cannot will it or not will it."[4] And not only can he not will his creation, whatever he does to incorporate his idea into a physical means is no longer art:

The aesthetic fact is altogether completed in the expressive elaboration of impressions. When we have achieved the word within us, conceived definitely and vividly a figure or a statue, or found a musical motive, expression is born and is complete; there is no need for anything else. . . . It is usual to distinguish the internal from the external work of art: the terminology seems to us infelicitous, for the work of art (the aesthetic work of art) is always *internal;* and what is called *external* is no longer a work of art.[5]

Technique considered as a means for achieving in external form the content of an internal artistic intuition represents the incursion of "economic" activity in the realm of the aesthetic. In Croce's technical terms, technique is "knowledge at the service of the practical activity directed to producing stimuli to aesthetic reproduction."[6]

The complete artistic process, then, may be divided in Crocean terms into the following steps: (a) impressions, (b) expression (the spiritual aesthetic synthesis), (c) hedonistic accompaniment (pleasure of the beautiful), (d) translation of the aesthetic fact into physical phenomena, such as sounds, tones, movements, combinations of lines and colors, etc.[7] The resultant physical object then becomes a stimulus to the reproduction of the original expression, and may be designated as (e). At this point, a viewer may reverse the process by perceiving the physical phenomena, which are "together the aesthetic synthesis already produced," the resynthesis of which will reproduce the original hedonistic accompaniment.[8]

A moment's reflection on Croce's system will show both its appealing and its nonappealing features. As theoretical activity, aesthetic intuitions are considered a kind of knowledge, the basis for all further knowledge given in conceptual awareness; as objects of logic, furthermore, concepts are nothing more than relations between intuitions. Moreover, aesthetics is the beginning of language (the formulation and communication of an intellectual content), and as such the basis for a general science of linguistics. If all of these claims are true, art is at least *worthy of* being taught. The difficulty of Croce's point of view is that his conceptual analysis of the artistic process makes it *impossible* to teach: his account leaves the relation between the internal synthesis of impressions and the construction of the physical artifact in midair. The least we should be led to suppose is that some relationship obtains: presumably the artifact may be read as a sign or symbol of the internal spiritual act. Unfortunately, however, since the internal fact remains internal, there is really no ground for understanding the relationship between the vision of the artist and what he constructs as a translation of it.

[4]*Ibid,* p. 51.
[5]*Ibid.,* pp. 50–51.
[6]*Ibid.,* p. 111.

[7]*Ibid.,* p. 96.
[8]*Ibid.,* p. 97.

Collingwood takes up the theory at this point. Although admitting that art is a language having no technique, he doubts in fact that Croce's description of technique in the process of painting is adequate to the facts of the matter. First, Croce's stand:

It might be objected to the explanation of the physically beautiful as a simple aid to the reproduction of the internally beautiful, or expressions, that the artist creates his expressions by painting or by sculpturing, by writing or by composing, and that therefore the physically beautiful, instead of following, sometimes precedes the aesthetically beautiful. This would be a somewhat superficial mode of understanding the procedure of the artist, who never in reality makes a stroke with his brush without having previously seen it with his imagination. . . .[9]

Collingwood's transformation of this thesis may be made clear in a series of steps. First of all, the artist expresses emotion which he has experienced without knowing what it is; in expressing the emotion, he "gets it clear." "A person expressing emotion . . . is treating himself and his audience in the same kind of way; he is making his emotions clear to his audience, and that is what he is doing to himself."[10] But this process is not guided by a technical analysis of the problem:

The means-and-end, or technique, terminology . . . is inapplicable. Until a man has expressed his emotion, he does not yet know what emotion it is. The act of expressing it is therefore an exploration of his own emotions. He is trying to find out what these emotions are. There is certainly here a directed process: an effort, that is, directed upon a certain end; but the end is not something foreseen and pre-conceived, to which appropriate means can be thought out in the light of our knowledge of its special character. Expression is an activity of which there can be no technique.[11]

So far, so much agreement with Croce. The second step, where their differences begin

to emerge, is Collingwood's attempt to show that in drawing a line, juxtaposing colors, etc., the painter is in fact making his emotion clear; his work will succeed (and thus be good) if his emotion becomes clear, and will not if it does not. A test for aesthetic goodness, then, is possible:

Any theory of art should be required to show, if it wishes to be taken seriously, how an artist, in pursuing his artistic labor, is able to tell whether he is pursuing it successfully or unsuccessfully: how, for example, it is possible for him to say, "I am not satisfied with that line, let us try it this way. . . ." A theory which pushes the artistic experience too far down the scale, to a point below the region where experience has the character of knowledge, is unable to meet this demand.[12]

Croce, it may be assumed, came too close to the line, having failed to observe that, for a painter,

The watching of his own work with a vigilant and discriminating eye, which decides at every moment of the process whether it is being successful or not, is not a critical activity subsequent to, and reflective upon, the artistic work; it is an integral part of the work itself. A person who can doubt this, if he has any grounds at all for his doubt, is presumably confusing the way an artist works with the way an incompetent student in an art-school works. . . .[13]

In short, following the suggestion of one of the interpreters of the Croce–Collingwood theory, an artist thinks with some consequence as an artist when he thinks in terms of the symbols of his medium,[14] and he knows that he has succeeded in his expression when his "statement" is clear.

Surely, no other test is made for the teaching of the simple skills of verbal expression at whatever level of rhetorical instruction. The only difference would seem to be that, using language almost since birth, we are all

[9]*Ibid.*, p. 103.
[10]Collingwood, *The Principles of Art* (New York: Galaxy Books, 1958), pp. 110–11.
[11]*Ibid.*, p. 111.

[12]*Ibid.*, p. 281.
[13]*Ibid.*
[14]Hospers, John, "The Croce-Collingwood Theory of Art," *Philosophy*, XXXI (October 1956), pp. 10–11.

most apt to perceive clarity in the use of linguistic symbols, whereas recognition of artistic clarity is learned late, if at all. What is needed, then, for an adequate curriculum in the education of art, is a well-founded theory of aesthetic judgment which would enable both teacher and student to perceive the clarity of a successful aesthetic expression.

The artist's work ends when he judges that his work is good, and there is no reason to assume that the viewer judges in any way different from his: the guarantee that this judgment is the same would be the fact that both artist and viewer consider the artistic object in terms of the symbols of the medium used to make the expression, and the clarity of the statement made. What a philosopher of art has to contribute to the curriculum of art students is a way of justifying the validity of artistic expressions. Whether or not technique can be learned, and whether or not technique is relevant to the activity of the artist in forming his intuitions, only that part of an artist's technique which has produced the object of judgment will have an effect upon the judgment of the object.

In sum, idealist aesthetics has failed art educators in that it has situated the work of art in an artist's head, where it can never be judged; has declared irrelevant any artistic techniques for the construction of physical analogues to the work of art, which might be judged; and has, even in Collingwood, produced no clear-cut statement of the manner in which the artist and his audience do in fact judge the success or unsuccess of aesthetic expressions. A corrective to the idealist separation of artifact and work of art would be possible if it could be shown that technique is not irrelevant to art, but necessary, and so closely correlated with the forming activity of the artist that no distinction may be drawn between technique and form. This is the position maintained in the experimentalist aesthetics of John Dewey; but before considering the manner in which Dewey's theory is being treated by contemporary art educators, it behooves us to examine the case of the linguistic philosophers against the educability of art.

Morris Weitz is one of the philosophers in our own time who tried to establish the conditions necessary for judging the success of artistic expressions. His early answer to the problem was couched in terms of "organicism," a theory judging the excellence of expression in terms of the maximal relatedness of the elements funding into an integral experience.[15] Following a study of the logic of discourse about art, however, he disavowed his prior work, along with all other traditional attempts at aesthetic theory. His second point of view was most forcefully presented in his Matchette prize essay, "The Role of Theory in Aesthetics."[16] There he claims that all theory about art, whether it be his own or that of others — "Formalism, Voluntarism, Emotionalism, Intellectualism, Intuitionism, Organicism" — is based upon a mistake, upon the attempt to list a set of conditions both necessary and sufficient for defining the concept "art." His own denial is as strongly put as one dare:

Aesthetic theory — all of it — is wrong in principle in thinking that a correct theory is possible because it radically misconstrues the logic of the concept of art. Its main contention is that "art" is amenable to real or any kind of true definition is false. Its attempt to discover the necessary and sufficient properties of art is logically misbegotten for the very simple reason that such a set and, consequently, such a formula about it, is never forthcoming. Art, as the logic of the concept shows, has no set of necessary and sufficient properties, hence a theory of it is logically impossible and not merely factually difficult. Aesthetic theory tries to define what cannot be defined in its requisite sense.[17]

Hence, instead of a fixed, "closed" concept capable of precise application to all works

[15]Weitz, Morris, *Philosophy of the Arts* (Cambridge, 1950).
[16]First printed in the *Journal of Aesthetics and Art Criticism*, XV (September 1956), pp. 27–35.
[17]*Ibid.*, pp. 27–28.

of art, empirical observation of the matter suggests an open concept applicable to many different sorts of objects which may resemble each other in some ways and yet contain significantly different aspects one from the other and each from the class. There is no essence, or nature, of art, but only a "family resemblance" of many things alike enough to be compared and different enough to be seriously contrasted. In conclusion, "To understand the role of aesthetic theory is not to conceive it as definition, logically doomed to failure, but to read it as summaries of seriously made recommendations to attend in certain ways to certain features of art."[18] Thus, if a certain concept cannot be precisely defined, if its nature cannot be stipulated, then it cannot be taught in the most strict interpretation of conveying knowledge concerning the objects of our inquiry; all one need do is point to outstanding cases in which the term is used properly — either descriptively or normatively — to cover "paradigm" cases in order to discover what is meant when we use the term.

So far, so good; but the student would feel extremely ill at ease, if not flattered beyond all bounds, if his instructor were to point to one of his works as a paradigm case for the application of the word "art" in its normative sense. The logic of the concept "paradigm" precludes this possibility — unless the instructor were capable of justifying his evaluation in terms of an experience of the work's excellence; and note, please, that the instructor is likewise precluded from comparing the student's work with some other paradigm case, for in such an instance two difficulties arise: if the student's work is comparable to the paradigm case, then the student's work is derivative; and unless the instructor is capable of establishing the validity of his paradigm case, nothing is learned from the comparison. I conclude

that Weitz' prize-winning essay is a mistake; and its basic error is the assumption that we can learn anything about the concept of art merely by inquiring into the manner in which people actually use the term. Discourse about discourse is futile unless there is good ground for assuming that we are capable of recognizing when discourse is being used properly in the first instance; and the only way to judge whether a term is being used correctly is to examine the nature of the experience the term is intended to designate. Instead, therefore, of replacing aesthetics of the traditional kind, Weitz' second thoughts on the matter merely serve to point out the importance of finding an adequate aesthetic terminology applicable in the first instance. How ironical to discover what Immanuel Kant had already written in 1790: that aesthetic judgment is reflective, not determinant! In contemplating a work of art we are presented with an object for which no concept is adequate.[19]

Still, analytic philosophers are fond of pointing out the fact that real or true definitions are impossible to find. According to their preferred manner of proceeding, only family resemblances can be found, not essences of things capable of definition according to the strict logical requirements set down in a list of necessary and sufficient conditions. It is perhaps appropriate to point out that Croce, idealist and definer that he was, was convinced of the same fact:

Resemblances exist, and by means of them, works of art can be arranged in this or that group. But they are likenesses such as are observed among individuals, and can never be rendered with abstract determinations. That is to say, it would be incorrect to apply identification, subordination, coordination and the other relations of concepts to these resemblances, which consist wholly of what is called a *family likeness*, derived from the historical conditions in which the various works have appeared and from relationship of soul among artists.[20]

18*Ibid.*, p. 35.

19Kant, *op. cit.*, pp. 15, 184 ff.
20Croce, *op. cit.*, p. 73.

The same kind of family resemblances, it might be noted, are to be found among the sciences. That is, the logic of the concept of science admits of no more certainty in individual applications of the term than does that of art; and no one has yet presented himself as a defender of the proposition that, for this reason, the philosophy of science rests on a mistake. Yet the philosophy of science and the philosophy of art are strictly analogous as intellectual disciplines. If one is impossible, then so is the other. I conclude that "philosophical analysis" has yet to refute the claims of Croce's aesthetics or those of his logic. The point is simply that there is much work to be done on the concept "work of art," and, if one may dare say so, equally as much to be done on the concept "object of science." The fiction that the way people use the term, or learn how to use the term, is a solution of the problems involved is a bald deception.

Consider the case of scientific objects. The concepts we use to designate them are no less open textured than is the concept of "art" even in the evaluative sense of the two terms involved. It is apparent that, descriptively, astronomy is a science, and so is physics. But not all critics are agreed on the propriety of the concept for covering the case of sociology, anthropology, and economics. There is a family resemblance, true; but no essence anyone would call "science" unequivocally. What corresponds to the normative terms of aesthetics within the discipline of scientific behavior, on the other hand, is the notion of truth, or perhaps verified law. Both "truth" and "law" are equally open-textured concepts, no less than "beauty" and "successful expression." The nature of truth varies with the frame of discursive reference — in Humean terms, with whether statements relate our ideas or record our observations of matters of fact; and even within the area of matters of fact alone, some hypotheses are considered "laws" if they summarize different areas

of observation and predict wider ranges of future observations. One can only infer that if the scientific discipline is thought any more teachable than the artistic, one is misusing a term; if not "artistic," then "scientific."

The discovered laws of traditional science are, of course, teachable; and they can be used to make utilitarian objects, as the law for the conversion of matter into energy could and was used in the construction of the Bomb. But this kind of scientific teaching reads the word "scientific" to mean *technology*. If my analogy is correct, some artistic styles can be taught in the same manner; but if they are, this kind of artistic teaching reads the word "artistic" to mean *industry*, as Kant so correctly put the matter so long ago.[21]

The result of this analogous reasoning, of course, is not to indicate that Weitz is wrong in his central contention: "art" is an open-textured term. His ultimate mistake is based upon the faulty conclusions he draws from this banal fact. The first was to demand a logical rigor — the stipulation of the necessary and sufficient conditions for the definition of an entity, which is possible perhaps only in the formal disciplines of mathematics and logic, where the notion of a "real" or "true" definition may be interpreted as making some sense; and the second was in supposing that if such definition is impossible, the instruction of art (or science) is therefore impossible.

When a concept is open textured, the only conclusion to be drawn is that each individual case must be considered in terms of the experience it affords, and how the human subject behaves in controlling the experience. It is true, for example, that theoretical controls are relatively more fixed in scientific behavior than in artistic; but no one yet has given a *logical* explanation of the formation of workable hypotheses. At rock bottom they may be nothing more than

[21]*Op. cit.*, p. 153.

hunches or lucky guesses, not to say complete accidents. An idealist like Croce
would take this to be an indication of the
fact that the imagination must function even
in the controlled experiments of basic scientists. The only difference from the behavior of the "lucky" artist (or pregnant one,
as one prefers) is that the model which comes
to form in the scientist's mind is capable, if
successful, of being applied to many repeat-
able instances, whereas the intuition of an
artist is of a unique, unrepeatable object
which lesser critics may then take as a "paradigm case," or touchstone.

The only recent American thinker to give
a great deal of thought to both the scientific and the artistic process of human creativity is John Dewey. His five-step process of
human behavior in problem solving indicates that a man observes a situation; discovers and refines a problem; considers and
compares alternative, hypothetical solutions; and tests them in thought and in action.[22] "Inquiry," which is Dewey's name for
the process of problem solving, is obviously
an open concept; the situation determines
what the inquirer is to observe, and what he
must do if his hypotheses are to be verified.
But in each case, it is the experience of the
problem, and of the observed predictions,
made on the basis of a hypothesis, which
determines the particular character of the
solution: its workability or nonworkability,
hence its "truth" or "falsity."

At this point it may be of some import to
indicate the obvious comparisons with the
preceding approaches to aesthetics. If the
analogy between "science" and "art" is
maintained, as Dewey insists that it must be,[23]
there is no longer any basis for the distinction
between "theory" and "practice" as Croce
draws it. The scientist must do something

to his situation in order to gain his knowledge. Any solution to a problem that is
merely prevised is only tentative; it must
work out in experience in order to be accepted. As Collingwood put it, the artist, in
order to get his emotions straight, must
think with the counters of his medium by
manipulating them.

The most explicit statement of the analogy
I have been suggesting between the work of
the scientist and that of the artist has already
been elaborated to some extent by Francis
Villemain, Nathaniel Champlin and David
Ecker. The latter's essay, "The Artistic Process as Qualitative Problem Solving,"[24] puts
in succinct compass the theoretical problem
of conceiving the manner in which an artist
solves his qualitative problems. In short,
it contains a philosophical presentation of
the *process* of art. Now since talk about the
artistic process is truly a theoretical affair, if
the talk is an accurate description of what
happens in general when an artist works,
the case will have been made for the possibility of education in art. The only question remaining, then, is whether Ecker's
talk appropriately covers the situation involved.

The crux of Ecker's problem was to find
an analogue within "the artistic process as
qualitative problem solving" for the role
played in theoretical problem solving of the
basic scientist by the successful hypothesis:
a workable means of summarizing and predicting observed or observable data. Dewey
had already indicated in the essay referred
to above that a "pervasive quality" per-
meates every situation recognizable as such;
just as the laws of logic by which inferences
are drawn from the supposed truth of a hypothesis may be said to "control" our theoretical analysis of scientific problem solving,
so, says Ecker, the controls of qualitative
problem solving derive from the relatedness

[22]Dewey, John, *How We Think* (Boston, New York,
Chicago: D. C. Heath and Company, 1910), pp.
72 ff.
[23]In "Qualitative Thought," *Philosophy and Civilization* (New York and London, 1931), pp. 96 ff.

[24]In *Journal of Aesthetics and Art Criticism*, XXI
(Spring 1963), pp. 283–290.

between component qualities and the pervasive quality defining the artistic situation.[25]

In the completed analogy, Ecker finds six
steps are needed to capture the essence of
Dewey's five-step process of reflective
thought:[26] an artist is said to begin with a
presented relationship between the counters of
the medium being worked with (line to line,
line to color, color to line, color to color,
etc.). In this phase, thinking with his materials, the artist is "playing around with"
the symbols of his craft. Next is *substantive
mediation,* in which certain emerging relations tend to dominate; certain choices are
destroyed, others opened up. In the *determination of pervasive control,* a single dominant
qualitative relationship emerges: "'Components of a unique end-in-view gain identity as such by virtue of the envisioned total
quality now emerging.'"[27] And this quality
may be either a traditionally definable style,
or "it may be unique as a total which itself
becomes a pervasive or control quality for
future orderings, i.e., the appearance of a
new style...."[28] The hypothesis (of the
analogy) is now present. There follow the
steps of *qualitative prescription:* from here on
only those components consistent with the
pervasive quality are acceptable choices;
through *experimental exploration,* while one
continues to work the medium in explora-
ation of the possibilities of the pervasive
quality; to the *conclusion: the total quality,* or
finished work of art.

Professor Ecker's lucubrations on the process of artistic thought constitute a clear-cut
gain over the two theoretical approaches
evaluated above. In showing how what the
artist does is necessary to what an artist
thinks in making a work of art, he obviates
some (but not all) of the difficulties attending the distinction between technique
and inspiration which vitiates the idealist's

aesthetic as a tool for educational theory.
Likewise, since he is not afraid to make some
general prescriptions for the achievement of
controls in artistic thought, he has more to
offer art educators than an idea of "what to
look for" as indicated by the more traditional aesthetic theories of representation
(imitation), form, emotion, and the like.
Any further evaluation of his description of
artistic problem solving must come from an
inquiry into the adequacy of his six-step process to cover our notions of what an expressive or successful artistic object is and does:
we must bring further light on the function
of the object itself in controlling our vision.
It will come as no surprise, then, that the
nub of the new problem is to weigh the relative importance of steps (3) "determination
of pervasive control," and (6) "the total
quality."

Ecker's statement that pervasive control
is formally determined, and recognizable
as a "style" — either of the tradition or of a
new mannerism which may be further elaborated into a tradition of its own — is the first
questionable point. He illustrates his thesis
with examples of work by Henry Moore,
Pablo Picasso, Paul Cézanne, Piet Mondrian
and Saul Horowitz. In the work of the first
four named artists we are presented with the
total quality (photographically abstracted
into value discriminations only), while that
of the latter is presented so as to make the
pervasive quality visible in various stages of
the work's completion.

Why is the pervasive style, or quality,
that is already established easier to achieve
than the invention of a new; and why are
there good and bad paintings achieved in the
various styles, whether old or new? The
grounds for the second of these questions
seem fairly well attested in the history of art;
for the first, in the paucity of artists who
might truly be said to have initiated new and
significant developments in the arts. *Prima
facie,* then, the questions appear meaningful
for our inquiry.

25 *Ibid.,* p. 289.
26 *Ibid.,* pp. 288–289.
27 *Ibid.,* p. 289.
28 *Ibid.*

In giving an answer to them, as consistent as possible with Ecker's scheme, one could say that the pervasive quality, although effective as a means of ordering relations of (component) qualities toward an end-in-view, has failed in the case of unsuccessful paintings to yield an end-in-view (the total quality) worth the ordering. Thus, it is the total quality of the piece which guides or controls when the artist is to stop his "experimental exploration" and not the pervasive quality which, from the point of view of the total expressive object, is only another of the components, and, moreover, constantly changes throughout the stage of experimental exploration. This is the case I shall try to make in interpreting the series of stages in the development of Horowitz' painting. As a parenthesis, it may now be stated that Ecker has not so much solved the problem of the idealists as indicated where in the process of painting it really occurs; for in distinguishing technique from inspiration the idealists were only making the point that before a work is achieved (in the mind, for Croce; on canvas, for Collingwood) there is no way of ordering physical means for the attainment of an end, even if we call the end an "end-in-view." This process of envisaging, imagining, or perceiving an end remains as mysterious in the neo-pragmatic scheme as it appeared in the idealistic one examined above. And, surely, it is for this reason that an existing style is easier to recognize and to judge (the token with respect to the type) than to explain the expressiveness of an entirely new and different work of art.

For the clue to our interpretation let us start with the analogy being pursued. In Dewey's scheme, thinking arises in an unsettled and ends in a settled situation. To be accurate in our rendering of his thought within an artistic frame of reference, the perception of the finished status of the art object must correspond to the settledness of the problematic situation; the final per-

ception must in some sense satisfy the inquirer that his problem is solved. Thus, the workability of the hypothesis and the success of the expression are the correlates standing in analogous relation. Since the success of the scientific hypothesis is to be judged in action, there is no reason to suppose that the success of the total expressiveness of the art work is to be judged in any other way. In other words, both kinds of situations must be lived, or experienced, if the problem is to be felt in the first place, and if the hypothesis or pervasive quality of both kinds of situations are to succeed in settling the respective kinds of problem in the second. Judgment, then, must begin with the experience of the finished quality of every problematic situation; and to be able to judge we can do no better than follow the phenomenologist's prescription to go back to the things themselves as they appear to our vision.

Accordingly, let us look at the series of steps in the development of Saul Horowitz' painting. Ecker is firm in his statement:

> Here is a sequence of photographs of a painting by Saul Horowitz (see page 66). All of the stages of the painting are not shown. However, the qualities of the final painting *are* present in the beginning sketch. (Italics his.)[29]

But, what appears to our vision; what is the case? Are all the qualities of the final painting present in the beginning sketch? Not to my vision; nor, I would wager, to the vision of the artist at this stage of the painting's development. The final painting, of course, contains the "total quality," but at what stage is the pervasive quality first apparent? One might be forgiven for assuming that the pervasive quality is present in the first exposure since the qualities of the last are supposed to be in the first. But that too would be an error of visual judgment. The first stage is at most an experience of three planes: the grayish background, the blackish lines and forms appearing on the ground,

[29] *Ibid.*, p. 288.

and the space tensional plane between. Although in the last stage the first two of these planes are still *generally visible*, a great deal has been done to them as well as to the interstitial space tensional plane. In the final stage, the initial background no longer serves as ground; it is no longer a single plane. It has been modified by the addition of other forms on the various receding planes (the variety of the planes being determined by the relative value discriminations in the variety of forms placed between the initial fore- and backgrounds), so that it appears as if it were a light perceived from behind the picture plane. What one perceives of it is now controlled by the action of the interposed solid black or deeper gray forms. The point is that the ground now functions in a way different from the way it did in the first exposure; there it appeared as a deep space against which the action of the lines is set. And, to bring this analysis to a sharp halt, these original lines have been lost, as lines acting against the inert gray of the original ground, and even for the most part as interacting with each other as tensional forces on the same plane, since they now serve to create space as outlines of solid forms, where they are visible at all.

My suspicion is that Ecker has judged the painting as a "flat" design rather than for what it is and does to our attentive vision. And if this is true, it would be more proper to say that some of the linear action taking place on the first plane as it is constituted in the first stage of the painting has been retained in the last, but what has been lost is more significant for the total quality of the work than what has been retained. Since the work is nonobjective, no "depth" or representational elements appear. The sensuous surface of the painting has, however, undergone a complete transformation from the beginning to the last stage.

The pervasive quality and the total quality of the *painting* (in its finished state) are the same; and neither is apparent until the work has been achieved. Dewey, it will be recalled, maintained that *every* situation is known by virtue of its pervasive quality — the moodal sense of wholeness within which we are capable of making distinctions and marking associations. Only when the painting has been achieved could it be imitated or copied in many variations, and thus become a "pervasive or control quality for future orderings."[30] But then, future orderings will produce other pervasive (or final) qualities. An idealist, in reading these scribblings, would be tempted to say that the pervasive (total) quality of the painting is *implicit* in the first stage and *explicit* only in the last. Furthermore, we judge that a quality is implicit in a situation only by grasping an *imaginary* modification of the given situation; and all explicit qualities are immediately visible to our *perceptive* faculties. The trick, of course, is to be able to grasp imaginatively those modifications of a given situation which will enable a painter to perceive ultimately that a total satisfying situation has been achieved. What takes place between the first strokes on a virgin canvas and the final perception is precisely the essence of painting. Many mistakes will be made, and some of them will be erased; but which strokes are mistakes and how they are to be erased is still a matter of aesthetic judgment. If, therefore, the aesthetician has anything to offer an art educator it will be a procedure for judging an object of art — no matter at which stage of development that object happens to be. The only requirement for being able to judge a visual object is that it be visible. And it is for this reason that a painter must know what constitutes the visibility of the seen.[31]

[30]*Ibid.*, p. 289.
[31]A phenomenological analysis of the structures of a visual field as exemplified in paintings of a representational, nonobjective, and "abstract" character may be found in E. F. Kaelin's essay, "The Visibility of the Seen," in *An Invitation to Phenomenology*, edited by James M. Edie (Chicago: Quadrangle Books), 1965.

In sum, the neo-pragmatic description of the *artistic process* demands completion by a phenomenological account of visibility. It is by virtue of the appearance of structures within a visual field — the description of which is missing in Ecker's account — that the *product* of art is to be judged: if not by the painter, then by his critics, who may not be so kind.

SUGGESTED READINGS FOR PART II

ALDRICH, VIRGIL C. *Philosophy of Art.* Englewood Cliffs: Prentice-Hall, 1963.

CROCE, BENEDETTO. *Aesthetic,* trans., Douglas Ainslie. London: Macmillan, Ltd., 1909.

DEWEY, JOHN. *Art As Experience.* New York: Minton, Balch, 1934.

KAELIN, EUGENE F. *An Existentialist Aesthetic: The Theories of Sartre and Merleau-Ponty.* Madison: The University of Wisconsin Press, 1962.

LANGER, SUSANNE K. *Feeling and Form: A Theory of Art.* New York: Charles Scribner's Sons, 1953.

MARGOLIS, JOSEPH. *Philosophy Looks at the Arts: Contemporary Readings in Aesthetics.* New York: Charles Scribner's Sons, 1962.

MUNRO, THOMAS. *Toward Science in Aesthetics: Selected Essays.* New York: The Liberal Arts Press, 1956.

WEITZ, MORRIS. *Problems in Aesthetics: An Introductory Book of Readings.* New York: Macmillan, 1959.

PART III

WHAT FACTORS INFLUENCE HUMAN DEVELOPMENT IN ART?

Does the human being develop essentially from the outside in or from the inside out? Is the process of maturation essentially one of unfolding capacities latent within the individual, or is it one which is shaped predominantly by forces outside of the individual? These questions have puzzled teachers, psychologists and philosophers ever since Plato advanced his theory of education as a theory of recollection. And in modern times these notions are reflected in the nature-versus-nurture controversy. This controversy has centered upon the problem of determining the relative importance of the individual's nature as compared to the importance of environmental influence in shaping his abilities and in determining his levels of performance.

For art educators as for all others concerned with the education of man, this is a question of the utmost importance, for the way in which it is answered will have a great effect in determining who shall be educated, where, in what manner, and for how long. If the ability to create or to experience art is a gift of the limited few, one could argue that art instruction should be reserved for those possessing such a gift. If, however, art ability is primarily a function of the kinds of experiences one has had in life, then one could arrive at a very different conclusion.

The problem of identifying the factors that influence human development in art not only is important for determining who shall be educated in art, but is also important for determining how instruction in art should proceed. If one conceives of the child as an organism that goes through predictable stages of perceptual maturation and that each state is characterized by particular perceptual abilities, instruction in art will be likely to be adapted to the particular level at which the student is and will avoid providing tasks for students which demand more than their perceptual level of maturation will permit. Furthermore, if the visual art that is produced by the child is affected by his personality dispositions, and if these dispositions are not easily changed, then one might expect a fairly consistent type of artistic output from a given child over a period of several years.

If, on the contrary, visual perception is primarily a function of the types of tasks children have had an opportunity to engage in, if their art work is reflective of their immediate state of mind, of the immediate condition of the organism, and if such conditions are primarily a function of the particular situation in which they live, then by changing that situation one might expect important changes both in the perceptual skills the child is able to employ and in the qualitative characteristics of his art work.

The quickest and most ready answer to the problems posed above is that it is not *either* the environment *or* the organism's nature that is important in determining artistic behavior but both. While this is undoubtedly true, it is of little help in resolving the problems of teaching in art. The teacher needs to be in a position to make reasonably adequate predictions concerning what can be changed in the child's art learning and what is unlikely to be changed — no matter what is done in the classroom. The easy answer that both the child and the environment are important in learning provides little guidance to the teacher and is of little consolation.

The philosophic underpinnings of American thought tend to accept the environment as being the most important influence in an individual's life. Reacting against some of the European beliefs in *inborn* class distinctions and in the merits of a highly stratified and relatively immobile social class, the founders of this nation tended to lay greater stress on the importance of opportunity for man and founded this nation upon some of the philosophic principles laid down by John Locke. This philosophy, in part, saw man as a product of his environment; man, in a sense, was what he experienced. A society, they felt, built upon the ideal of opportunity would be one where no man would be condemned to a menial position in life merely because of his station at birth. If experience is the important shaper of a human's ability, then each man, as it were, could start life on more or less equal terms.

The general philosophic view laid down by Locke and built into the Declaration of Independence has found much support from those working in the field of sociology. Sociologists are among the first to point out the ways in which the environment affects attitudes, values, and behavior in general. They point out that what people see is, in part, a function of what they value. They have described how certain ethnic groups and social classes reward and punish particular forms of behavior and that when what is rewarded outside of the school is inconsistent with what is rewarded inside the school, the child faces problems that may be especially difficult to overcome. Sometimes these problems are resolved by revolting against one of the two parties contending for the child's allegiance.

Linguists, too, have emphasized the importance of experience in shaping human behavior. Their concern with determining the role of language in experience has culminated in data indicating that the language models from which one learns greatly affect the kind of abstractions one is able to make. Still others have argued that the child's environment, especially during his preschool years, is so important that it determines the type of academic future the child will have in school. In short, those who have been most concerned with environment — anthropologists, psychologists, sociologists, and more recently linguists — have tended to emphasize the role of culture and society in shaping the behavioral patterns of human beings.

Others, however, such as geneticists, physiologists, and some psychologists have emphasized hereditary factors as the primary determinant of human behavior. They have pointed out that the ability to deal with abstraction and the incidence of artistic ability is not randomly distributed. Parents who have high-level cognitive abilities have a significantly higher proportion of children with high-level cognitive abilities than those parents who are not so gifted. Parents who have artistic ability and whose ancestors were so gifted also tend to have children with artistic talent. Herman J. Muller, the world famous geneticist, has suggested that since the environment does not perform the natural selective role it used to perform, modern man would do well to establish formal methods to control the procreation of social deviates which could enable intelligent parents to plan the type of offspring they would like to have. The establishment of sperm banks is one such suggestion.

It would seem, then, that one's personal theory and his vocational choice greatly affect his answer to the question: What factors influence human development in art? The readings in Part III were selected to acquaint the reader with a variety of views, and should, at the very least, serve to bring his own theory into sharper focus.

6. Growth

RUDOLF ARNHEIM

Recent progress in the field of the psychology of perception makes it possible to describe the artistic process more adequately. In the past an oversimplified concept of this process was based on a double application of what is known in philosophy as "naïve realism." According to this view, there is no difference between the physical object and its image perceived by the mind. The mind sees the object itself. Similarly, the work of the painter or the sculptor is considered simply a replica of the percept. Just as the table seen by the eye is supposed to be identical with the table as a physical object, so the picture of the table on the canvas is simply a repetition of the table the artist saw. At best the artist is able to "improve" reality or to enrich it with creatures of fantasy by leaving out or adding details, selecting suitable examples, rearranging the given order of things. As an example, Pliny's famous anecdote, so widely quoted in Renaissance treatises, may be cited. The Greek painter Zeuxis, unable to find any one woman beautiful enough to serve as a model for his painting of Helen of Troy, "inspected the maidens of the city naked and chose out five, whose peculiar beauties he proposed to reproduce in his picture."

The manipulations ascribed to the artist by this theory may be called "cosmetic," because in principle they could be performed just as well on the object itself. There is no notion of any basic difference between the world of reality and its image in paint or marble.

The approach was not basically changed by what optics and physiology contributed to a better understanding of the process of vision. It became clear that the physical object could no longer be identified with the image received by the eye; but the role of the physical object was taken over by its equally physical projection, and the conviction prevailed that a visual experience was identical in all its properties with the picture projected upon the retinae. Just as the retinal image of the table was complete in all its detail and distorted in size and shape by perspective, so the subjective per-

*SOURCE: Reprinted from *Art and Visual Perception*, pp. 126–35, 165–68. Copyright 1954 by University of California Press, Berkeley.

cept of the table was assumed to be mechanically complete and perspectively deformed.

This theory encountered puzzling contradictions in the field of the arts. If spontaneous perception corresponded to the projective image, it was reasonable to expect that naive pictorial representation at early stages of development would tend toward completeness and perspective distortion. Modifications of the elementary experience would not be expected to occur until later when the maturer mind became free to elaborate the perceptual raw data. The opposite, however, was found to be true. Representation started genetically with highly simplified geometric patterns, and realism was the late and laboriously accomplished product of such sophisticated cultures as Hellenism and the Renaissance.

Why Do Children Draw That Way?

The early drawings of children show neither the detail nor the perspective deformations to be expected. What is the explanation? Since it was taken for granted that the drawings do not correspond to what the children actually see, a reason for the deviation had to be found. For example, it was suggested that children are technically unable to reproduce what they perceive — just as they cannot hit the bull's-eye with a gun because they lack the concentrated glance and the steady hand of an adult marksman, so their eyes and hands do not have the skill to hit the right lines with a pencil or brush. Now it is quite true that the drawings of young children show incomplete motor control. Their lines sometimes steer an erratic zigzag course and do not meet exactly where they should. Much of the time, however, the lines are accurate enough to indicate what the drawing is supposed to be like, particularly if many drawings of the same kind are compared. Moreover, at an early age the former imprecision of the stroke gives way to an

exactness that is more than sufficient to show what the child is trying to do. There can be no doubt that none of these drawings is an unskillful attempt at projective realism. They all clearly try to do something else. The reader is invited to put a pencil in his mouth or between the toes of one of his feet and copy a realistic picture of a human ear. The lines may turn out to be so crooked as to be totally unrecognizable; but if the drawing is at all successful, it will still be basically different from the usual way in which the child draws an ear as two concentric circles. Thus lack of motor skill cannot explain the phenomenon.

Others have maintained that children make straight lines, circles, and ovals because these simple shapes are easier to draw. This is perfectly true, but does not indicate what mental process induces the children to identify the complex objects of reality with the very different geometric patterns.

Neither can lack of interest or careless observation be cited. I have referred earlier to the sharpness of children's observation. Whoever has seen the expression of breathless fascination in their eyes or the concentration they devote to their art work will agree that the explanation is unsatisfactory. It is true up to a certain age that if the child is asked to draw a man he will pay little attention to the particular man put in front of him as a model. This behavior, however, does not prove the child's incapacity or unwillingness to observe his environment; instead, it is due simply to the fact that fresh information is neither needed nor usable for what, in the opinion of the child, the drawing of a man is supposed to contain.

Then there are explanations that sound convincing but are really little more than a play with words, such as the assertion that children's pictures look the way they do because they are not copies but "symbols" of real things. The term "symbol" is used nowadays so generously that it can serve indiscriminately whenever one thing stands for another. For this reason it has no explanatory value. There is no way of telling whether the theory is right, wrong, or no theory at all.

The Intellectualistic Theory

The oldest — and even now most widespread — explanation of children's drawings is that since children are not drawing what they are assumed to see, some mental activity other than perception is responsible for the modification. It is evident that children limit themselves to representing the overall qualities of objects, such as the straightness of legs, the roundness of a head, the symmetry of the human body. These are facts of generalized knowledge; hence the famous theory according to which "the child draws what he knows rather than what he sees." In substituting intellectual knowledge for sensory perception, the theory follows the kind of thinking that Helmholtz popularized in the 1860's. Helmholtz explained the "constancy" phenomena in perception — that is, the fact that we see objects according to their objective size, shape, color — as the effect of unconscious acts of judgment. According to him, persons obtain a "correct idea" of an object's actual properties through frequent experience; since the actual properties are what interests them for practical purposes, they come to overlook their own visual sensations and to replace them unconsciously by what they know to be true. In a similar intellectualistic vein children's drawings have been described by hundreds of investigators as representations of abstract concepts.

It is a strange theory indeed; for it is well known that a main characteristic of the mind at early stages of its development is its thorough dependence upon sensory experiences. To the young mind, things are what they look like, sound like, move like, or smell like. Of course, children also think and solve problems. They also generalize

because their biological interest, like that of all creatures, is in the typical rather than in the unique; but this thinking, problem solving, and generalizing go on largely within the perceptual sphere itself rather than at the level of intellectual abstractions. For example, the child learns how to keep his upright body in balance without formulating any abstract rules on the subject. He learns to distinguish men from women without isolating their distinctive traits by induction. Abstract intellectual concepts referring to concrete facts are likely to be very few in children, considering how rare they are in adults of our Western culture. An example of such a concept might be the fiveness in the statement "a hand has five fingers." The visual concept of a hand usually contains the radial spreading out of fingers without specification of their number, and in a picture of the hand the correctness of the number is usually ascertained by counting. Here, then, a visual fact is known mainly or exclusively by means of the intellect, which is called upon for the purpose of correct picturing. Another example: my memory image of my Uncle John may not contain the information on what side he parts his hair; but I may remember from a conversation the words "Uncle John parts his hair on the right side," and in drawing a portrait of him from memory I shall supply by conceptual knowledge what my visual knowledge fails to offer.

We need only mention such examples to realize how untypical they are. It is also significant that they refer to facts that are visually undistinguished, such as numbers above three or four or the difference between right and left. Most of the time man, child, and animal rely on visual knowledge. Parents are taller than children, men wear pants, a face has two eyes above the mouth, the human body looks symmetrical from the front — all these facts are known visually, even though words also may be available to express them. There is certainly no evidence that young children possess the rather advanced intellectual concepts necessary to think abstractly of symmetry, proportion, or rectangularity. According to the intellectualistic theory, the child, in drawing the picture of a human head, relies on his knowledge of the words "a head is round" and draws the roundness rather than a head. But even if the child possessed the intellectual concept of roundness, the theory would fail to answer the question "Where did he derive the circular shape by which roundness can be adequately represented?"

The theory has been applied not only to children's drawings but to any kind of highly formalized, "geometric" art, particularly that of primitive peoples. And since it could not be very well asserted that all art was derived from nonvisual concepts, the theory led to the contention that there existed two artistic procedures that were different from each other in principle. Children, Neolithic painters, American Indians, and African tribesmen worked from intellectual abstractions; whereas Paleolithic cave dwellers, Pompeian muralists, and Europeans during and after the Renaissance represented what they saw with their eyes. This absurd dichotomy was one of the main drawbacks of the theory, for it obscured the essential fact that well-defined form, which is so prominent in the work of many primitives, is indispensable and exactly of the same kind in any "realistic" representation that deserves the name of art. A child's figure is no more a "schema" than one by Rubens — it is only less differentiated.

On the other hand, the theory neglects the fact that perceptual observation contributes to even highly stylized work. When a South Sea Islander paints the sea moved by the wind as a rectangle striped with oblique parallel lines, essentials of the model's visual structure are rendered in a simplified but entirely un-"symbolic" manner. And Albrecht Dürer's highly naturalistic studies of hands, faces, and birds' wings are works of art only because the innumerable strokes and shapes form well-organized, even though complex, patterns that interpret the subject.

It will be apparent now that the formula "The child draws what he knows rather than what he sees" would be invalid even if the word "knowledge" had a connotation different from what the promoters of the theory meant and mean by it — if it referred to visual rather than to intellectual knowledge. Even then the theory would be misleading, because it would still assume between perceiving and knowing a dichotomy that is alien to the perceptual and the artistic processes. It is in the very nature of these processes that every particular act of seeing involves the grasping of overall features — that is, of generalities. Conversely, all visual knowledge, as remote as it may be from any individual percept, requires the concrete realization of certain structural features. The indivisible unity of visual perceiving and visual knowledge is basic for the processes I am discussing. Therefore any theory that attempts to account for the "geometric" styles of representation by asserting that they spring from a procedure different in principle from that of so-called realistic art is a misinterpretation.

They Draw What They See

The intellectualistic theory would hardly have monopolized the writings on the subject for such a long time if another theory had been available as an alternative. To work out a better explanation it was necessary: first, to revise the conventional psychology of perception; second, to become aware of the conditions imposed on artistic representation by the particular medium in which it occurs.

The first point requires only recapitulation of what I have said before. Vision as experience differs in two important ways from "photographic" projection. It does not register the complete set of individual detail contained in the retinal image. Evidence has been given to show that perception does not start from particulars, which are secondarily processed into abstractions by the intellect, but from generalities. "Triangularity" is a primary percept, not a secondary concept. The distinction between individual triangles comes later, not earlier. Doggishness is perceived earlier than the particular character of any one dog. If this is true we can expect early artistic representations, based on naïve observation, to be concerned with generalities — that is, with simple, overall structural features. Which is exactly what happens.

Another distinction between retinal image and visual experience concerns perspective. The image created by the lenses of the eyes shows the projective distortions of a photograph, whereas in vision not much influence of distance on size and shape is observed. Most objects are seen approximately in their objective shape and size: a rectangular suitcase looks rectangular, and distant persons in a room look no smaller than those close to the observer. It is quite difficult for many persons to visualize the working of perspective, even when it is demonstrated to them with a yardstick. Recently an intelligent and sensitive young college student, to whom I tried to show the oblique shape of a box on the table, finally hid her face in sudden terror and exclaimed: "It is true — how horrible!" If perspective plays so small a part in vision, the same can be expected to happen in early stages of art, which is exactly what we find.

Children and primitives draw generalities and undistorted shape precisely because they draw what they see. But this is not the whole answer. Unquestionably children see more than they draw. At an age at which they easily tell one person from another and notice the smallest change in a familiar object, their pictures are still quite

undifferentiated. The reasons must be sought in the process of representation.

In fact, as soon as we apply our revised notion of visual perception, a peculiar difficulty arises. I said that perception consists in the formation of perceptual concepts, in the grasping of integral features of structure. Thus, seeing the shape of a human head means seeing its roundness. Obviously roundness is not a tangible perceptual thing. It is not materialized in any one head or in any number of heads. There are shapes that represent roundness to perfection, such as circles or spheres. Even these shapes stand for roundness rather than being it, and a head is neither a circle nor a sphere. In other words, if I want to represent the roundness of an object such as the head, I cannot use the shapes actually given in it but must find or invent a shape that will satisfactorily embody the visual generality "roundness" in the world of tangible things. If the child makes a circle stand for a head, that circle is not given to him in the object. It is a genuine invention, an impressive achievement, at which the child arrives only after laborious experimentation.

Something similar is true for color. The color of most objects is anything but uniform in space or time; nor is it identical in different specimens of the same group of things. The color the child gives to the trees in his pictures is hardly a specific shade of green selected from the hundreds of hues to be found in trees. It is a color that matches the overall impression given by trees. Again we are not dealing with an imitation but an invention.

The Medium

The circle and the sphere represent the structural features of roundness most purely by their curved boundaries and centric symmetry. The same task can be accomplished, more or less perfectly, by various patterns. The one chosen will depend upon the medium. For example, a pencil creates objects by circumscribing their shape with a line. A brush, which creates broader spots, may suggest a disk-shaped patch of color. In the medium of clay or stone the best equivalent of roundness is a sphere. A dancer will create it by running a circular path, spinning around his own axis, or by arranging a group of dancers in a circle. In a medium that does not yield curved shape, roundness may be expressed by straightness. Figure 6.1 shows a snake pursuing a frog as represented in a basketry pattern by the Indians of British Guiana.

FIGURE 6.1

A shape that expresses roundness best in one medium may not do so in another. A circle or disk may be the perfect solution in the flat picture plane. In three-dimensional sculpture, however, circle and disk are combinations of roundness and flatness and thus imperfect representations of roundness. A black-and-white apple becomes "colorless" when transferred from a monochromatic lithograph to an oil painting. In a painting by Degas a motionless dancer is a suitable representation of a moving dancer, but in a film or on the stage a motionless dancer would not be in movement but paralyzed.

Furthermore, the term "medium" refers not only to the physical properties of the material but to the style of representation used by a specific culture or individual artist. A flat-looking patch of color may be a human head in the essentially two-dimensional world of Matisse; but the same patch would look flat instead of round in one of Caravaggio's strongly three-dimensional paintings. In a cubist statue by Lipchitz a cube may be a head, but the same cube would be a block of inorganic matter in a work of Rodin. Figure 6.2 shows Picasso's drawing *The End*

FIGURE 6.2

of a Monster. The way in which the head of the monster is drawn serves in other works by the same artist to represent undistorted, nonmonstrous shape (compare the bull of Figure 6.3). There is no contradiction in this fact. A pattern that produces a monster in a relatively realistic picture may stand for "straight" anatomy in a work that applies the same manner of distortion to everything.

FIGURE 6.3

Representation never produces a replica of the object but its structural equivalent in a given medium. Apart from other reasons, this is true because replication is possible only if the object is duplicated in its own medium. Anywhere else there are considerable differences between model and image. Some of these are so common that we are hardly aware of them. We do not notice, let alone resent, the fact that most images are smaller or larger than the things they stand for. We accept without questioning a flat picture for a round body or a bunch of lines for a solid object. This is not an esoteric convention thought up by artists but common usage everywhere in life. Scale models, line drawings on blackboards, or road maps deviate most strongly from the objects they depict. The young child spontaneously discovers and accepts the fact that a visual object on paper can stand for an enormously different one in nature, provided it is its

structural equivalent in the given medium. I shall presently demonstrate the unerring logic and consistency of the child in this matter.

The psychological reason for this striking phenomenon would seem to be, in the first place, that in human perceiving and thinking similarity is not based on piecemeal identity but on the correspondence of essential structural features; secondly, that an unspoiled mind spontaneously understands any given object according to the laws of its context.

It takes a great deal of "spoiling" before we come to think that representation is not only an imitation of the object but also of its medium, so that we expect a painting not to look like a painting but like physical space, and a statue not like a piece of stone but like a living body of flesh and blood. This unquestionably less intelligent concept of representation, far from being natural to man, is a late product of the particular civilization in which we happen to have lived for a while.

Representational Concepts

Earlier I spoke of "perceptual concepts," by which I meant the overall structural properties that are grasped in vision. Now I must consider also "representational concepts" — that is, the conception of the form by which the perceived structure of the object can be represented with the properties of a given medium. Representational concepts find their external manifestation in the work of the pencil, the brush, the chisel.

The formation of representational concepts, more than anything else, distinguishes the artist from the nonartist. Does the artist experience world and life differently from the ordinary man? There is no good reason to think so. He must be deeply concerned with — and impressed by — these experiences. He also must have the wisdom of finding significance in individual occurrences by understanding them as symbols of universal truth. These qualities are indispensable, but they are not limited to artists. The artist's privilege is the capacity to apprehend the nature and meaning of an experience in terms of a given medium and thus make it tangible. The nonartist is left "speechless" by the fruits of his sensitive wisdom. He cannot congeal them in adequate form. He can express *himself*, more or less articulately, but not his experience. In the moments in which a human being is an artist, he finds shape for the bodiless structure of what he has felt. "For rhyme can beat a measure out of trouble."

Why do some landscapes, anecdotes, or gestures "ring the bell"? Because they suggest, in some particular medium, significant form for a relevant truth. In search of such telling experiences, the artist will look around with the eyes of the painter, the sculptor, the dancer, or the poet, responding to what fits his form. On a walk through the fields a photographer may look at the world with camera eyes and react only to what will "come" photographically. The artist is not always an artist. Matisse was once asked whether a tomato looked to him when he ate it as it did when he painted it. "No," he replied, "when I eat it I see it like everybody else." The ability to capture the "sense" of the tomato in pictorial form distinguishes the response of the painter from the frustrating, shapeless gasping with which the nonartist reacts to what may be a very similar experience.

The formation of adequate representational concepts makes the artist. In this sense I would answer in the affirmative the old question whether Raphael would have been an artist if he had been born without hands. It cannot be maintained, however, that the representational concept always precedes the actual realization of the work. The medium itself is a powerful source of inspiration. It often supplies form elements that turn out to be usable for the expression of experience. There is nothing illegitimate about a rhyme suggesting a content, and there are great artists — for example, Paul Klee — of whom it is tempting to say that their ideas sprang primarily from the medium. But what counts is not the chronology of steps in the process of creation. If in the final product a valid content has found adequate form, the goal has been attained.

Perhaps it is necessary to point out again that by using the term "concept" I am not subscribing to the intellectualistic theory of the artistic process. Neither perception nor representation in a given medium is based on intellectual abstraction. Nothing but our particular one-sided tradition suggests that concepts are formed only by the intellect. All the cognitive instruments of the mind operate by grasping overall features of a phenomenon or a group of phenomena through form patterns of a medium. The medium may consist of the stock of "perceptual categories" or the shape patterns of a means of representation or the abstractions of the intellect. The word "concept" refers to an operation performed by all kinds of cognition rather than serving to reduce them all to intellectual processes.

The nature of representation is illustrated most simply and clearly in the drawings of young children. For this reason, this chapter will deal in detail with the development of their work. Throughout the analysis, however, the true subject will be the growth of artistic form in general, even though it will not be possible here explicitly to refer to the larger subject. In particular, striking similarities between the art work of children and of peoples at early stages of artistic development ("primitive art") have been demonstrated. This kind of comparison is not popular today because of a fashion of thought according to which it is more scientific to talk about differences than about similarities. Undoubtedly there are considerable differences of various kinds between the art work of the child and the adult; but it would seem that there is no way of under-standing differences anywhere as long as the common ground has not been determined. In fact, I can think of no essential factor in art or artistic creation of which the seed is not recognizable in the work of children. The following investigation deals with some of these factors.

The example of children's drawings makes it particularly evident that pictorial repre-sentations cannot be described and under-stood simply by their distance from the ob-ject they purport to portray. Rather must they be related, on the one hand, to the ex-perience they reflect and, on the other, to the medium in which they are done. The representation offers a structural equivalent of the experience that gave rise to it, but the particular concrete form in which that equivalent appears cannot be derived only from the object. It is also determined by the medium.

Credit is due Gustaf Britsch for having been the first to demonstrate systematically that pictorial form grows organically ac-cording to definite rules of its own, from the simplest to more and more complex patterns, in a process of gradual differentiation. Britsch showed the inadequacy of the realis-tic approach, which found in children's drawings nothing but charming imperfec-tion and which could deal with the phases of their development only in terms of in-creasing "correctness." Being an art educa-tor, Britsch did not avail himself of the psychology of perception, but his findings support and are supported by the newer trends in that field. Like many pioneers, Britsch seems to have carried his revolution-ary ideas to the opposite extreme. As far as can be determined from the writings that have been published under his name, there is little room in his analysis for the influence of the perceived object upon pictorial form. To him the development of form was a self-contained mental process of unfolding, similar to the growth of a plant. This very

one-sidedness makes his presentation all the more impressive; and as I try to describe some phases of formal development as an interplay of perceptual and representational concepts, I acknowledge that I am pro-ceeding from the base laid by Britsch.

Educational Consequences

The preceding detailed analysis of the growth of form in the drawings of children fulfills its purpose only if its wider implica-tions are evident. It has been undertaken mainly for two reasons. In the first place, there seems to be no more striking demon-stration of the fact that pictorial representa-tion cannot be understood merely in relation to the realistically conceived model object. I have tried to show how form develops with-in its medium and according to the condi-tions of the medium. Misinterpretations are inevitable if the picture is considered a more or less correct replica or derivative rather than a structural equivalent of the object in terms of the medium. This holds true not only for the work of children, but for all art including the realistic.

In the second place, it seemed useful to describe how pictorial form develops or-ganically from the simplest to increasingly complex patterns. Thus the process of growth gives further evidence of the ten-dency to simplicity, which was demonstrat-ed earlier in visual organization. Step by step, the maturing mind requires greater complexity, but the higher stage can be reached only by way of the lower ones. The mastering of a given stage creates need and readiness for the next. The mind proceeds at the rate at which it can comprehend, and at any point of the rising path it is handling a medium that seems fitting and natural. Willful interference with this pro-cess creates disturbance. The old-fashioned teacher who imposes on his student ad-vanced tricks of the trade is just as guilty as the new-styled primitivist who admonishes the child: "This is a nice picture, but we do not make noses in second grade!" The art student who copies the manner of an admired teacher will be in danger of losing his intuitive sense of right and wrong by wrestling with a form of representation that he can imitate but not master. His work, instead of being convincing and congenial, is puzzling to him. He has lost the honesty of the child, which every successful artist preserves and which gives the simplest possible shape to any statement, complicated as the result may be objectively. Arnold Schönberg, the composer of some of the most intricate music ever written, told his students that their pieces should be as natural to them as their hands and feet. The simpler they seemed to them, the better they would be. "If something you have written looks very complicated to you, you do well to doubt its genuineness right away!"

The formal features already discussed are derived from the cognitive functions of the mind: the sensory perception of the outer world, the elaboration of experience in visual and intellectual thinking, and the conservation of experience and thought in memory. Considered from this angle, pictorial work is a tool for the task of identifying, understanding, and defining things, investigating relationships, and creating order of increasing complexity. More commonly psychologists have been using art work for a different purpose. They have studied it — particularly in mentally disturbed or diseased individuals — as a manifestation of a person's social attitude, his mood and temperament, the equilibrium or disequilibrium of motivational forces, his fears and desires. These studies have opened a promising field of research, likely to be of great value for the understanding of both art and the human personality.

Until now there has been little coordination between the two approaches. Some investigators have examined pictorial form as though it was detached from the vital aims of living, whereas others have treated art as a diagnostic tool without giving attention to the perceptual and representational factors. Because of the youth of the enterprise, such one-sidedness may be necessary and useful, except for the misinterpretations resulting from it. It is true that a complex whole cannot be understood without an analysis of the factors that are integrated in it. Understanding will not get beyond a first stage, however, unless a more comprehensive view is taken. General psychology has paved the way. It is well known by now that such cognitive functions as intelligence, learning, or memory cannot be dealt with apart from the total structure of wishes, needs, attitudes. "Personality" has been shown to manifest itself in the individual's way of perceiving the world. On the other hand, the range of a person's outer experiences and the level of intelligence are considered in their effect upon his or her overall attitude.

The need for such integration may be illustrated by an example, chosen at random, among many to be found in the literature on the subject. In a book on art education Herbert Read comments on a drawing of a girl who is a little less than five years old. A tiger is represented very simply by a horizontal stroke for the body and two verticals for the legs. The lines are crossed' with short stripes, meant to depict the tiger's skin. Read speaks of the "wholly introvert, inorganic" basis of the picture. The child, he says, has given no regard to whatever image of a tiger she may have had; she has created "an expressive symbol which corresponds not to her perceptual awareness or conceptual knowledge of the tiger. . . ." The picture is a typical example of the horizontal-vertical stage, at which the average child will represent an animal in just this way. Very often no differentiation between organic and inorganic shape is possible at this level; straight lines stand for both. Pictures of this kind are meager in content, not because the child is unable or unwilling to observe and to use his observations, but because the elementary stage of representation does not permit him to use much of what he has seen. Whether or not this particular child is a withdrawn introvert cannot be determined on the basis of his drawing and his age alone. Introversion may retard differentiation of form, but undifferentiated form in itself does not suggest introversion. The same drawing could come from a noisy extrovert, passionately interested in the way animals look and behave.

The perceptual and representational characteristics already discussed are more universal — because they are more elementary — than most pictorial effects of "personality." The development of pictorial form relies on basic properties of the nervous system, whose functioning is not greatly modified by cultural and individual differences. It is for this reason that the drawings of children look essentially alike throughout the world, and that there are such striking similarities among the early art products of different civilizations. A good example is the universal occurrence of circular, concentrically arranged figures, to which Jung has applied the Sanskrit word "mandala." It is found in Eastern and Western art, in Egypt as well as in the drawings of children or American Indians. Jung refers to this pattern as one of the archetypes or collective images that appear everywhere, because the collective unconscious, of which they are a part, "is simply the psychic expression of identity of brain structure irrespective of all racial differences." The reader will recognize the mandala as a form of the sunburst pattern, which was found to be characteristic for an early stage of differentiation. The universal occurrence of the pattern in children's drawings would seem to be sufficiently explained by the need

of the young mind for visual order at a low level of complexity. At the same time such patterns are able to symbolize deepest insights into the nature of the cosmos as they are intuited and shaped by the unconscious and the conscious mind. This demonstrates the unity of the mind, which needs and creates the same forms in the outermost layers of sensory perception and in the hidden core, from which dreams and visions originate.

Visual symbols cannot be studied adequately without consideration of perceptual and representational factors. The psychoanalyst who assumes that the child starts his art work with circles in remembrance of his mother's breasts, which were the first important objects of his experience, neglects the elementary visual and motor conditions that favor the circle. Early symbols, like the sun wheel or the cross, reflect basic human experiences by means of equally basic pictorial form. There is no point to engaging in a priority struggle as to what came first, the content or the form.

Modern art education is profiting from the methods and findings of psychology, but to now there has been one-sided emphasis on art as an expression of emotions, conflicts, needs, and so on. For this reason something like a monopoly has developed for technical tools that foster the spontaneous stroke, the impulsive flash, the raw effect of amorphous color, and interfere with the precision of visually controlled form. Broad brushes and dripping easel paints compel the child to create a one-sided picture of his state of mind, and the possibility cannot be excluded that the kind of picture he is permitted to make may, in turn, influence the state of mind he is in. Unquestionably the modern methods have given an outlet to aspects of the child's mind that were crippled by the traditional procedure of copying models with a sharpened pencil. But there is equal danger in preventing the child from using pictorial work for clarifying his observation of reality and for learning to concentrate and to create order. Shapeless emotion is not the desirable end product of education, and therefore cannot be used as its mean either. The equipment of the art room and the mind of the art teacher should be comprehensive and variable enough to let each child act as a whole person at any time.

7. Tests for Visual and Haptical Aptitudes

VIKTOR LOWENFELD

The following presentation deals with a series of aptitude tests, growing out of more extensive investigations reported elsewhere.[1] There I have demonstrated the existence of two distinct creative types, based upon two unlike reactions toward the world of experience. In the course of this study it was found that imaginative activity, including the ability to give objective reference to creations of the imagination, by no means depends upon the capacity for perceptive observation. Furthermore, it was shown that the inability inspectively to notice "visual" objects is not always inhibitory of creative activities. On the contrary, the very fact of not paying attention to visual impressions may become the basis of a specific creativeness of the haptic or haptical type.

It is obvious that it would disturb and greatly inhibit a visually minded person to be stimulated only by means of haptic impressions, or to be asked not to use sight and to orientate himself only by means of touch, bodily feelings, muscular sensations and kinesthetic fusions. It is, however, not so clear that "seeing" may also become an inhibitory factor when forced upon an individual who does not use his visual experiences for creative work. Both facts are established by experiments in the work already cited.

Further studies have shown that the distinction which is true for creative types can also be made among individuals. In the following tests an attempt has been made to discriminate between persons whose tendency is to use their eyes as the main intermediaries for their sense impressions and those who, though with normal sight, do not use their eyes but are more concerned with those perceptions that derive from haptical experiences.

An extreme haptical type of individual — by no means rare — is a normal-sighted person who uses his eyes only when he is compelled to do so; otherwise he reacts as would a blind person who is entirely dependent upon touch and kinesthesis. An extreme visually minded person, on the other hand, is one who is entirely lost in the dark, one who depends completely on his visual experiences of the outside world.

[1] V. Lowenfeld, *The Nature of Creative Activity: Experimental and Comparative Studies of Visual and Non-Visual Sources*, 1939, 1–272.

*SOURCE: Reprinted from *American Journal of Psychology*, **58** (1945), pp. 100–111.

It is evident that most persons fall between these two extreme types. Investigations have proved, however, that there are few individuals who have equal amounts of visual and haptic predisposition. In about 75 percent of the Ss tested, there is an appreciable tendency toward the one or the other. (See Tables I, II and III.) Since the tendency toward these two antipodes of experience plays a vital part in life, especially in the proper choice of occupations, it seemed desirable to design tests to determine the degree and amount of preference for the one or the other type of perceptual and imaginal experiences.

There are occupations in which visual control not only is impossible but would interfere with the efficiency of the worker; mechanical jobs which are done inside a case with the hands as the only control, work in the darkness, work on switchboards. It is also clear that there are occupations which place the main emphasis on the use of the eyes. They deal with ocular observation, estimation of distance, orientation, surveying. Certainly a great number of occupations require both abilities; yet it is often possible to determine which of these aptitudes is dominant and of greater importance.

If a special ability stands out as necessary for the proper execution of a certain job, and if this ability is tested by a single one of our tests, then this test can be given separately from the whole series. For instance, if a mechanical job, done inside a case or in darkness where visual control is impossible, requires merely the ability to recognize different forms by means of tactile experience, then the Tactile Impressions Test (Test V and Figure 7.7) would be suitable.

If the preference of the individual for visual or haptic experience is doubtful, then the S should. undertake the whole series of tests.

One factor in visual observation is the ability to see first the whole without the awareness of details, then to analyze it into detailed or partial impressions and to build these parts up again into a new synthesis of the whole. You see first the general shape of a tree, then the single leaves, the twigs, the branches, the trunk, and finally everything incorporated in the synthesis of the whole tree. Partial impressions thus are integrated into a simultaneous image.

The first of this series of tests deals with this ability. It is a test which proves whether or not a person can integrate partial impressions, which are perceived successively, into a whole.

I. Test of Integration of Successive Impressions[2]

Behind a narrow slot (see Figure 7.1) a series of symbols is moving. The items increase in complexity as the test proceeds. Each symbol is shown separately. Through a narrow slot only a small section of each moving symbol is visible. After the whole symbol has passed behind the slot, S is instructed to recognize the correct symbol out of several similar figures. Figures 7.2 and 7.3 are samples out of ten such sets. The score is so determined that more complex symbols have an adequate higher score than simpler ones. The final score shows to what amount and degree S is able to integrate the partial impressions into a whole image.

II. Test of Subjective Impressions

An experience which is perceivable to the same degree haptically or visually will be apprehended in one way or the other, depending on the aptitude of the individual, provided always that no other associations interfere with the process. For instance, in

[2]This test has been adapted by the author for pilot training and has been put into motion-picture form by the U. S. Air Force, where it is being used on aviation cadets.

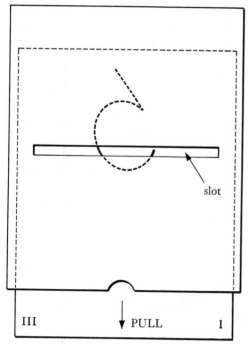

III ↓ PULL 1

FIGURE 7.1 Exposure apparatus for successive impressions. The folder has a slot behind which the symbol is seen moving. The cards with sets of symbols are interchangeable. There are ten sets of symbols altogether.

thinking of a mountain I can think of the mountain as I have *seen* it, or I can think of myself *climbing* the mountain. In drawing, this aptitude can clearly be seen by the kind

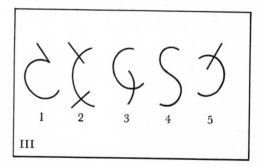

FIGURE 7.2 Symbol Set No. III.

of drawings made by *S*. In haptic representations, *S* draws the object in its proportions and view (plan, elevation or sideview) in accordance with his tactile impression, whereas in visually perceived pictures he

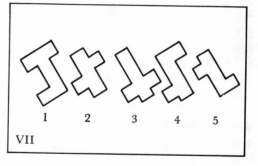

FIGURE 7.3 Symbol Set No. VII.

TABLE I

Reactions of 224 Individuals to Visual-Haptic Tests

Group Tests

Kind of Test	Visual	Percentages of the various reactions Haptic	Indefinite	Discarded	Total
Table Test	50.00	32.04	16.52*	1.44	100
Think-of-a-Building Test	52.67	30.36	14.73†	2.24	100
Word-Association Test	48.21	30.80	18.79‡	2.20	100
Total of reactions	50.30	31.10	16.52	2.08	100

*Most *Ss* drew only the objects, neglecting the table entirely.
†Merely counted the floors.
‡These reactions show no clear tendency to either experience.

draws an objective view which does not change according to its meaning. Thus he will always draw a table with a top and legs if he is visually minded, whether his emphasis is on the top or on the legs. He will draw it in the same way whether there is a glass of water on it or a chessboard, the one sketch calling for a side view, the other without doubt better perceivable from above.

A group of 224 adults was given the following test (Table I).

"When you are supposed to draw something, remember that this is a psychological test and that it does not depend on your drawing ability. The most primitive drawing will give the same insight as the most perfect. Just draw it as you would do it if nobody asked you to.
Draw: A table with a glass on top.
Draw: A table with a chessboard on top.

Approximately a third of the group, 72 Ss, drew only the top of the table and did not draw table-legs at all when they were asked to draw a table with the chessboard. When they were asked to draw the table with the glass on it, however, they drew a table in side-view, a mere line representing the top of the table. On the other hand, in 112 drawings the representation of the table changed neither with the glass nor with the chessboard. See Figure 7.4. *In the first group of drawings the representation of the table changed according to the meaning the thing had for the Ss.* Since the most distinct and clear representation of a chessboard is the top view, the table is represented in plan. On the other hand, since the most distinct way of drawing a glass is in sideview, the table with the glass is drawn in elevation. In the second group, no such change occurred. They drew an objective view of the table. The visually minded person does not change his impression of the table according to the thing which is on it (Figure 7.5). The num-

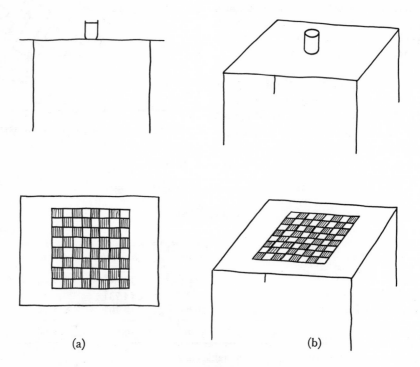

(a)   (b)

FIGURE 7.4   (a) Representations by haptically minded person.   (b) Representations by visually minded person.

TABLE II

Individual Reactions to Visual-Haptic Test

Kind of Test	Number of Ss	Percentage of score below 12 (indefinite)	Percentage of score 12–18	Percentage of score 18–20
Integration-of-Successive-Impressions Test	176	35.22	52.26	12.52
Test for Visualization of Kinesthetic Experiences	142	38.02	58.45	3.53
Tactile-Impressions Test	138	60.87	33.34	5.79

ber of different reactions almost completely coincided in another test of the same category, however, with no drawings involved.

The Ss were given the following pencil-and-paper test.

Think of a very familiar building (house of your friend, court house, town hall, dormitory), a building which you know from outside and inside, which is neither your home nor your school nor office building.

   1. How many floors has the building?

   2. Were you (a) sure; (b) not quite sure; (c) unsure of the given number?

   3. When you thought of the number of floors, did you think of

      (a) how many floors you have to climb?

      (b) did you count the floors singly?

      (c) did you think of the whole building as it appears from the outside?

Almost the same number, 118 Ss, and also the identical Ss who drew the objective view of the table, considered the building as it appears from without. The 68 who checked (a), the "climbers," however, were those who omitted the table legs and made the "subjective" representation of the table top.

Highly interesting was the fact that of the 36 Ss who did not draw the table at all but drew only the glass and chessboard, 24 checked (b) in Question 3 (counting the floors). This result indicates that these Ss were more the abstract type, whose sensory experience is of a subordinate nature. Counting the floors singly relates neither to visual nor to haptic experience in the same way

that the representation of the glass and chessboard without the table indicates the act of naming.

More experiments of this type with similar outcome have been reported elsewhere.[3]

TABLE III

Numbers and Percentages of Reactors to All Tests

Kind of reaction	Number	Per cent
Visual	530	47.0
Haptic	263	23.3
Indefinite	321	28.5
Discarded	14	1.2
Total	1,128	100

As an outcome of these experiments a more suitable paper-and-pencil test was designed in the form of verbal associations. Since this test is closely correlative with the former, it can be accepted as a means of partial determination of visual or haptic aptitude.

III. Test of Visual vs. Haptical Word Association

The problem here was to find words which incite associates equally from haptic and visual experience. Haptic experience usually refers to the bodily self; visual experience to things outside which are perceivable by ocular means. For example, you can "walk

[3]Lowenfeld, op. cit.

fast" but also "walk on the floor"; you can "climb a mountain" but also "climb hard."

The instruction ran:

Write down your immediate reaction after reading each single word; if nothing comes to mind, leave the space blank.

greeting...................	pulling...................
walking...................	swimming.................
looking...................	riding...................
climbing...................	running...................
talking...................	jumping...................
lifting...................	listening.................
thinking...................	reaching.................
drawing...................	touching.................
catching...................	stretching................
hearing...................	breathing................

The score is determined by adding up first the visual responses (reactions to environment, e.g. climbing — mountain) and secondly the haptic (reactions to the bodily self as indicated in actions, e.g. climbing — hard). If S gave at least 12 answers in one direction (visual or haptic), he was considered to show visual or haptic aptitude. Each additional reaction counted as one point: if he gave less than 12 answers in one direction, then he was considered as "indefinite."

From the 224 Ss, 108 reacted visually, 69 haptically and 42 were indefinite. Five had to be discarded because of reactions which could not be classified (cf. Table I).

IV. Visualization of Kinesthetic Experience

Visually minded persons have a tendency to transform kinesthetic and tactile into visual experiences. Haptically minded individuals are, however, completely content with the tactile or kinesthetic modality itself, as experiment has shown.

If, for instance, a visual person acquaints himself with an object in complete darkness, he tries to visualize all tactual or kinesthetic experiences. "How it looks" is the first reaction to any object met in darkness. In other words, he tries to imagine in visual terms what he has perceived through other senses. A haptically minded person, on the other hand, might use this kind of imagery only when forced to report in visual terms. Normally he remains satisfied with his haptic experience. A visually minded person who encounters an object in darkness tries immediately to visualize the object which he has met; a haptically minded person merely withdraws, perhaps, with some feelings of the surface structure of the obstacle or with partial impressions of the object which he has touched. A pilot who is visually minded is likely to visualize his kinesthetic experience while going through a flight curve, while a haptically minded pilot may have the body-feel of going through the curve without translating it into visual terms.

FIGURE 7.5   Test for visualization of kinesthetic experiences.

TABLE IV

Tests of Visual vs. Haptic Aptitude

Kind of Test	Ss showing haptic aptitude	Ss showing visual aptitude	Indefinite aptitude
I. Integration-of-Successive-Impressions Test			
10 figures, each counts 2			
(a) positive reactions		12–20	below 12
(b) negative reactions	12–20		below 12
II. Subjective-Impressions Test			
1. Table Test			
(a) change of table representation:* top and side view	10		
(b) objective view without change		10	
(c) no table drawn, objects only			indefinite
2. Think-of-a-Building Test			
(a) outside view		10	
(b) thinking of climbing	10		
(c) counting the floors singly			indefinite
III. Word-Association Test			
(a) actions	12–20		
(b) environment		12–20	
(c) neither action nor environment			indefinite
IV. Visualization-of-Kinesthetic-Experiences Test		12–20	below 12
V. Tactile-Impressions Test	12–20		below 12
Total	80*	80*	

*Highest score possible.

The following test is designed to prove the extent to which a person can visualize kinesthetic experience.

Different stencils of geometric figures of increasing complexity are cut into a thick cardboard or plywood. On a tablet the same geometric figures are drawn in scale. When blindfolded, S follows with one finger the line along the cut stencil while a finger of his other hand remains at the starting point as a guide. After returning his moving finger to the starting point, he must be able to recognize visually the figure which he has perceived kinesthetically. No longer blindfolded, a tablet with 5 different figures then is shown to him. Out of them he has to recognize the object previously explored.

Simple symmetrical figures have lower scores than irregular ones. If from 20 scores at least 12 are positive, we may regard S as possessing visual aptitude. Below 12 points he is considered to be "indefinite."

V. Test of Tactile Impressions

This test determines whether or not a person can recognize figures which were perceived through tactile experience. The cutout figures of Test IV are used. Single figures as large as the palm of a hand (narrow touch space) are singly put into a bag. S has before him the same tablet used in the next preceding test. He puts his hand into the bag, and by holding, touching, and moving the figure in his hand, he is required to recognize the correct figure on the tablet which is before him. (See Figure 7.7.)

The score is determined as in Test IV, with the exception that *S* gets haptic scores.

These tests can be applied singly or as a series. When they are given singly, they are designed to measure aptitude toward a particular perceptual experience, as indicated by the description of each test. When they are given as a series, however, a total score may be determined by adding up the visual or haptic scores. The total score will then show whether or not there is a predominance of the one or the other aptitude.

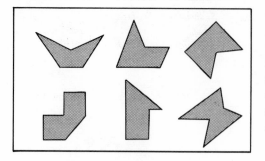

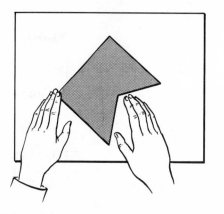

FIGURE 7.6   Test for tactile objectification.

Summary

From 1128 reactions, 47 per cent of the *S*s were clearly visual, 23 per cent were haptic, and 30 per cent either received a score which was below the line where a clear identification was possible or was otherwise not identifiable. In other words, approximately half of the individuals tested reacted visually, whereas not quite a fourth reacted haptically. Thus it would appear that — so far as our evidence goes and under our conditions — one among four individuals depends upon touch and kinesthesis rather than upon vision.

8. Factors in Artistic Aptitude: Final Summary of a Ten-Year Study of a Special Ability[1]

NORMAN C. MEIER

Introduction

With passage of time permitting a decade of observation on the same subjects and a wide variety of approaches to test other hypotheses on considerable groups it is now possible to lay down certain observations on the nature of artistic aptitude, which, in the sense that anything in science may be "final," epitomize the complete findings. The principal conclusions rest mainly on the experimental work of research assistants, the case-study records of six talented and six nontalented children, and the life histories of forty-one American artists, although

much more data enter into specific phases of the findings.

The finding of greatest interest is a new theory of talent which, for the first time, clearly indicates the specific interaction of the inherited aspects of talent with the learned phases. There can be no adequate understanding of artistic aptitude *without both being taken into account.* The view presented herein places the greater emphasis upon heredity, but extreme care must be taken by the reader to note the particular aspect of heredity involved — *constitutional stock* inheritance — not direct inheritance, in the commonly assumed sense, from parents. Only one of the six factors is strongly referable to inheritance — manual skill — yet it is to be noted further that three of the other factors are to some degree *conditioned* by heredity: that is to say, their development is at least partially influenced by the peculiar nature of the inherited traits. There is hence presented for the first time a theory (for which there is con-

[1]The research program, "Genetic Studies in Artistic Capacity," at the University of Iowa, under the author's direction. The various activities referred to include cooperative relations with the public schools of Des Moines, St. Louis, Milwaukee, Nashville, Chicago, and other places. Most of the case studies were made in Iowa City and Des Moines. The program was sponsored by the Spellman Foundation and the Carnegie Foundation for the Advancement of Teaching with funds of the former and of the Carnegie Corporation.

✳SOURCE: Reprinted from *Psychological Monographs*, LI (1939), pp. 140–58.

siderable substantiation) which suggests a unique and peculiar *interlinkage* of factors that exhibit both inherited and acquired characters.

Artistic aptitude is viewed as resting upon the possession of six factors: manual skill or craftsman ability, energy output and perseverance in its discharge, general and aesthetic intelligence, perceptual facility, creative imagination, and aesthetic judgment. It is readily recognized that these are not mutually exclusive categories but are general terms descriptive of a number of recognizable functions which overlap considerably and are not strictly independent variables. In future analyses of mental functions there will no doubt be breakdowns, of some of these at least, into more specific and simple functions.[2] Of the six general factors the first three (manual skill, energy-perseveration, and intelligence) refer *primarily* to heredity. The latter three (perceptual facility, creative imagination, and aesthetic judgment) refer principally to acquired nature, but as it will be developed later, are conditioned in their specific development by factors having a definite reference to heredity. This is particularly applicable to perceptual facility and aesthetic judgment, less to creative imagination.

The Factors in Aptitude

I. Manual Skill

Obviously no work of art is possible without some manual skill. This ability is regarded as primarily inherited, *but not inherited as a skill* directly from parents. It comes as a phase of general constitutional stock inheritance from a *line* of ancestry which in the individual members may not neces-

sarily include artists but *does include a comparatively* large or above average number of individuals having *craftsman ability*. The line, traced back through a half-dozen or more generations, may have included such occupational interests as toy-making; wood-carving and cabinetmaking; watch and instrument making; diamond-cutting; textile design and manipulation; jewelry making, repairing or adjusting; or any of the arts; lithography, engraving, drafting and related activities. The essential fact is the craftsman nature of the work, whether it touches upon any of the recognized "arts" or daily occupations such as carpentry or rug-weaving.[3] The following of these occupations successfully by members of a line is *prima facie* evidence that these were individuals *to whom such skill came easily* in their youth. It also denotes that in such regions of the world (*e.g.*, Central Europe, Japan) where craftsman activities have long been prominent there was a social selective factor operating in matings that would tend to concentrate and perpetuate the better and (economically) more successful "strains"; the youth who quickly attained economic competence by virtue of his ready acquisition of the needed skill would marry into a family likewise (economically) established.[4]

The heredity involved is simply that of social selection in a consistent direction. Morphological characters alone are involved: the individuals come from stock that is well adapted for work requiring fine eye-hand coordinations; they transmit the same

[2]Suggested by the progress made by Thurstone at the University of Chicago and others. Thurstone, *The Vectors of Mind* (1935) and *The Primary Mental Abilities* (1938). (Chicago: University of Chicago Press.)

[3]It is to be noted that the distinction between "fine" and "applied" art is of comparatively recent origin; in fact the word "art" carried the connotation of anything well done (shaped, engraved, sculptured, designed) as recently as 1880. Dictionaries prior to that time did not force a distinction between "artist" and "artisan."

[4]This sociological phenomenon has been discussed by Giddings who refers to such concentrations of like-mindedness (more properly here: like-skilled) as "familial aggregations." (The medieval household industry and later communal industries of the upper Danubian and Rhineland regions constitute excellent examples.)

characteristics, in some instances reinforced. Each new individual does not come into life with preformed skills; he merely inherits the kind of neurophysical constitution that is *readily adaptable* to the *acquisition* of such skills.[5] In actual instances today it is not expected that clear cases of perfect craftsman ancestry will appear in great numbers, but evidence is consistent in the prevalence of considerable craftsman activities in the ancestry of both artists and the talented children studied.

Perfect craftsman ancestry need not be expected, nor should one look only to gainful employment as evidence of craftsman nature. Since the Industrial Revolution with its de-emphasis upon handwork and its dissipation of pride in workmanship, many a potential craftsman interest has been stifled — in some instances to emerge as an avocational interest.[6] Hobbies are frequently eloquent in indicating deep-seated interests, which for one reason or another cannot become the bread and butter vocation.

Specific evidence of the relation of craftsman ancestry to manual skill is of four types: early appearance in talented children, early appearance in adult established artists, relatively more craftsman activities in ancestry, and the case study of Loran Lockhart.

A small group of children early identified (at ages 4 and 5 years) as exhibiting an interest in drawing, modeling or arranging[7] have now been followed for a period of ten years; likewise a group approximately equal in chronological and mental age who

had not at the same initial period shown any interest. Individual cases have been under intermittent observation in Des Moines for about seven years. The Iowa City groups have been reduced slightly by removal from the city, but of those still available for record the original classifications have been borne out practically without change.[8] It is of utmost significance that these children now still exhibit the same high degree of unstimulated interest and high proficiency in production as at any time throughout the period. In the case of the nontalented the interest is still nominal or lacking and the performance average or less.

Among established adult artists only a few failed to recall early artistic endeavors; others were able to lay out for the author's inspection water colors and paintings made during the age of five to eight years. To others less specific in their memory, the expression "as far back as I can remember" was frequently asserted. Only in one instance[9] was the earliest remembered artistic production given as late as sixteen. The other striking fact is that in no instance were the individual's interest and activity urged upon him by an adult.

Information blanks filled out by 283 art students, chiefly in the high schools of St. Louis, disclosed more craftsman activities in recent ancestry (seldom going beyond three generations) than in a group taken at random from classes in commercial subjects and mathematics in the same high schools. Among the art students a total of 358 blood relatives listed such occupations as against

[5]From the viewpoint of genetics this is in harmony with the principle of orthogenesis or directional evolution, about which there is no serious question as to principle but only differences of opinion regarding specific manner of functioning (Haldane, to writer).
[6]Witness the surprising interest in home power tools and machines, which permit professional people and businessmen to indulge their propensity outside of workday hours, and the well attended businessmen's evening art classes in the larger cities.
[7]See *Psychol. Monogr.*, **45**, No. 200, 1933, studies by Grippen, Rodgers and Tiebout. (Studies in the Psychology of Art, Vol. I.)

[8]Some of the Z-children (nontalented) subjects in the Saunders experiment were given intensive training over a two-year period. Although that experience resulted in some of the subjects attaining a measure of proficiency, the significant fact is that four years *after* the termination of the experiment and the withdrawal of stimulation those children have not carried on the activity nor demonstrated any continuance of particular interest in art production. (See *Psychol. Monogr.*, **48**, No. 213, 1936. Article by Saunders.)
[9]The late Irving Couse of Taos, New Mexico.

TABLE I

Craftsman Ancestry of Artists, Art Students and the General Population

	N	N (zero)	Ave. N Cr.
General population			
Unselected college students	153	36%	2.05
Unselected high school students	23	35%	1.61
Totals	176	35.8%	2.00
Art population			
Artists (limited sample)	58	15%	3.59
Art students — art schools	282	9%	4.74
Art students — colleges	230	13%	3.98
Art students — h.s. and n.s.	43	13%	4.07
Art staff — engraving firm	31	6%	5.64
Totals	644	11.02%	4.37

N = number of subjects.
(zero) = number having no known craftsmen in ancestry.
Ave. N. Cr. = average number of known craftsmen in ancestry.

120 for the nonart group; taking the occupations most closely related to art (*e.g.*, engraver, lithographer, etc.) the numbers are respectively 152 as against 37.[10]

In order to test the hypothesis further, a personal data blank was prepared with space provided for checking off the number of craftsmen in the ancestry, listing the following activities — cabinetmaker, carpenter, engraver, weaver, architect, jeweler, lithographer, potter, draftsman, watch repairman, artist, technician — with additional space for any occupation of a craftsman nature not listed, and with provision for hobbies of both the parents and the person addressed, as well as further data on training and future occupational interests, and

[10]It should be pointed out that these results are on "art students," that is, high school students taking art courses. The assumption does not follow that they are necessarily *talented* in art. In view of this circumstance it is reasonable to assume that if only the definitely talented were singled out the results would probably be more striking. It is entirely possible also that there are some cases of potential talent among the nonart students.

information to be supplied by teachers on the subject's ranking in creative ability and in technical ability.

This blank was sent to a number of artists, to art students in both private and college art schools, to a limited number in high schools and normal schools and also to a sampling of the general population taken from the high school and college ranks of individuals who have not had any training and have little or no interest in art. A further group of 31 constituting the art staff of a large engraving house was also secured.

It is believed that the great prevalence of craftsmen ancestry among art people would be indicated in at least two ways — first by the proportion of subjects having no craftsmen ancestors whatever and by the average number of craftsmen for the individuals in each group. The results of this survey are given in Table I.

It should be understood that the expectation in these returns would be short of true conditions because of the following conditioning circumstances:

A. Lack of extensive records. Most persons know little of their ancestors beyond three generations.

B. Failure to include true inheritance through female line because activities that are significant in this connection are usually occupationally nonclassifiable. For instance, fine embroidery work may require the same skill as engraving but would not be classifiable and recorded in this study except in a few instances where the alertness of the subject caused it to be included among hobbies of mother. Hobbies, however, were not tabulated in the totals, and in many instances they have decided significance. It is very probable that hobbies of ancestors, other than father and mother, would be known in very few instances.

C. Individuals may put varying interpretations upon some occupations, as for instance carpenter, jeweler or technician — undoubtedly some were included when they should not have been while others were excluded when they

should have been included. The list of craftsman occupations furthermore was not exhaustive.

D. Obstruction of the true occupational interest of the ancestor through necessity to work at more available or in more remunerative activities. A sustaining occupation is enjoyed by relatively few artists. The real interest would show up in hobbies, had that end been explored further and recorded in the data.

In making comparisons between the art groups and general population, however, errors which may creep into the data because of the conditions enumerated will probably cancel since there is no reason to assume that they would not be approximately as prevalent on one side as the other.

The records of several hundred students whose teachers supplied ratings on the basis of standing in the upper tenth, upper third, or average of the class were examined in order to see if a greater number of ancestors accompanied the higher standings. In other words, would persons with ten craftsmen in the ancestry rank more consistently in the upper tenth of their classes than would students with no craftsmen ancestors? This was done by assigning twenty points for standing in upper tenth in both creative ability and technical ability and values ranging down to ten of the various combinations (10-10, 10-7, 7-7, 7-5,5-5). The number of students so studied was too limited, however, to draw conclusions from the findings. The averages of the standings of the art students from both the private art school and the college student groups classified on the basis of number of ancestors are shown in Table II.

Apparently, at least from the data at hand, it is not possible to generalize on the number of craftsmen in a quantitative way. In the limited high school sampling there is evidence of a slightly higher average number of craftsmen in the superior group as compared to the average (3.73 as against 3.32).

The returns from the nationally known artists were somewhat disappointing because of faulty addresses, a large number of

TABLE II

Number of Craftsmen in Ancestry and Average Rank in Class*

	Groups			
	Students — P†		Students — C‡	
N. Cr.	N	Ave. Rank	N	Ave. Rank
0	21	16.1	29	14.9
1	21	14.3	30	15.2
2	29	16.0	26	14.4
3	25	15.2	23	16.0
4	21	15.7	25	15.3
5	25	16.5	24	14.8
6	16	15.0	15	16.7
7	7	12.0	5	13.4
8	8	16.0	6	15.0
9	8	16.7	6	13.1
10	8	16.1	3	16.3
11-31	15	13.5	12	14.2

*Rank in both creative and technical ability.

†Private art schools.

‡College art schools.

the requests being returned undelivered.[11] The returns, while including a number of the country's great artists, were lacking in other famous ones. It will be noticed that nine out of the fifty-eight artists reported no craftsmen. An inspection, however, of their record sheets shows that in seven out of these nine the hobbies of parents are distinctly of a craftsman nature, the following being cited as examples: painting (m), weaving (m), photographer (f — artist himself is a portrait painter), gardens (m), mounting of rare birds (f), and wood carving (f), (m, mother; f, father). Subsidiary data on the blanks yields other interesting and significant facts that tend to explain some of the instances which statistically do not show craftsmen ancestry.

The case of Loran Lockhart[12] can be explained in no other way than by the acceptance of the theory now presented. This boy, blind up to his seventh year, was enabled to have imperfect vision by a series of operations for double complete cataract. He then began drawing and painting at a level equal to or above normal children of his age. This ability has continued. A thorough investigation failed to reveal any possibility of environmental help or stimulus. Presence in the ancestry of craftsman ability and other aspects of his general constitutional inheritance provides the only means of accounting for the facts of the case.[13]

II. Energy Output and Perseveration

One of the striking characteristics of the work habits and energy outflow of the talented child and adult is the concentration upon the task at hand for indefinite periods. The usual time for staying with any activity on the part of preschool children is brief. A few marks on the paper with crayon or a brush satisfies many children; some do not bother to spend any time at the easel.[14] The artistically talented children referred to above were first identified by their frequent use of the easel and the length of time working at it. The predisposition to occupy oneself at such activity is so pronounced that in a number of cases the child on reaching third grade was denied the usual art period for a time because he was neglecting other activities. In summary it may be said that the artistically competent child discloses early in life a proclivity to spend concentrated effort frequently in work on art activities and does so in preference to almost any rival interest. At the early teen age the activity may temporarily follow interests other than drawing or painting, such as model building or specimen collecting and mounting. But even these are closely related to the craftsman pattern of activity and serve to enhance the possibilities for development of creative imagination in later endeavors. The same tendency toward deep concentration and care for detail is strikingly in evidence.

In the adult artist the same characteristics prevail. From the extensive notes and observations gained by personal contacts with forty-one established artists[15] the same ability to focalize great energy upon a

[11]The address list was taken from the American Art Annual for 1936, and apparently artists are prone like any other group to move frequently and fail to leave forwarding addresses.

[12]Presented in *Psychol. Monogr.* **48**, No. 213 (1936). See Meier, "Art Ability without Instruction or Environmental Background"; Case Study of Loran Lockhart, 155-163.

[13]Loran attended the Missouri School for the Blind, at St. Louis, learned Braille, and was visited by the author in April, 1937, three years after the first contact. His vision, as stated by the superintendent, is about 70% normal, but he will have to depend upon Braille for his major reading activities. Now eleven, he is a very popular student and regrets that the requirement of Braille learning prevents his giving time to his drawing and painting which are, however, indulged in during summer months.

[14]Based upon observations at the University of Iowa Preschool laboratories and supplemented with observations of others at other places, and upon individual children. The "situation" assumes an easel usually available, and nearly always available if the child desires it.

[15]Chiefly at Taos, Santa Fe, Laguna Beach, and Carmel-Monterey; but also in New York City, Toronto, Chicago, St. Louis, Denver, San Francisco region, Minneapolis, and other places. Seven of them represent European birth and training.

theme until it is brought to completion is evident. One typical example is presented. Thomas Benton received the commission for the Indiana murals for the state exhibit at the Century of Progress exhibition six months before the date of the fair's opening. He spent three months in research (visiting scenes, and people; uncovering historical events in libraries for planning the theme; drawing sketches of the panels). He then spent less than three months in the actual painting (egg-tempera) of the 240 lineal feet of eight-foot murals, requiring an uninterrupted energy-outflow of astonishing magnitude. Other instances might be supplied of concentration and persistence that would serve to refute the popular stereotype of the artist as a temperamental, emotionally unstable, long-haired dreamer.

III. Aesthetic Intelligence

The Tiebout-Meier study of the relation of general intelligence to artistic ability disclosed a definite tie-up between the two.[16] The relation was in evidence in the high school field but was prominently in evidence in the ascertained scores of fifty-one nationally known artists, representative of various types and all of definitely high standing. Although in the test instrument used[17] it was not found by a breakdown of the test elements into categories that the artists as a group were particularly strong or weak in any one category. It is possible that the more detailed analyses of mental functions now being studied may show the artist type of mental habits probably stronger in *visualizing, speed in perceiving*, and possibly several more, than in others like *facility with numbers* or *verbal fluency*.

The studies of the talented children in the Iowa City group disclosed one subject who tested variously[18] as having an IQ of 154,

136, 140, 155, 166, 141, 140, 130 when tested at different times, which averages 145 or near genius intelligence. Another tested at different times disclosed IQs of 133, 132, 135, 149, 116 or an average of 131 which is in the very superior category. Others disclosed average IQs of 134, 133 and 124. These are children who have been followed for a period of over ten years. These were paired with children in the same environment and with comparable IQs (as 112 and 111; 124, 124; etc.) who have not exhibited artistic preference to any considerable degree even when stimulated, indicating that intelligence alone does not account for superior artistic talent.

Both in the case of the talented child and the adult artist superior intelligence conditions the rate of development and the functioning of other factors.[19] It ordinarily determines the artist's competency in handling a given theme and the adequacy of his treatment. Other things being equal it may mark the general effectiveness of the work on the whole.[20] It may partially mark the degree of originality (entering into creative imagination) and the range of possible ways of treating a given subject.

IV. Perceptual Facility

By this factor is meant the relative ease and effectiveness with which the individual responds to and assimilates experience which has potential significance for present or future development in a work of art. The Tiebout investigation disclosed that one of the significant differences between the talented and the nontalented was the relative effectiveness in response to the visually experienced subject matter coming before the subject.[21] The talented children not only "carried away" more of identical objective material visually experienced but also

---

[16]*Psychol. Monogr.*, 1936, **48**, No. 213.
[17]Otis Self-Administering.
[18]Administered by Iowa Child Welfare Research Station.

[19]Aesthetic judgment and creative imagination.
[20]A conclusion arrived at by Manual. See Manual, H. T., *A Study of Talent in Drawing.* (Bloomington, Ill., 1919.)
[21]*Psychol. Monogr.*, 1933, **45**, No. 200, pp. 108–133.

retained it in approximately the same ratio. The Grippen study supplied additional supporting evidence.[22] The artistically superior child is thus one who "drinks in" more of a vacation trip, movie, or graphically presented story and retains the impression better than does the "average" child. His perceptions of this type are therefore more adequate, and his memory for visual experience more lasting and to a greater extent available for recall.

With the adult artist this facility takes the form of more realistic and adequate "note taking" when in the presence of a scene, interesting "character" or imagined or reconstructed historical episode. On meeting a person for the first time, and in the event that the person met constitutes a possible subject for a later painting, the impression may be one, compared to that ordinarily experienced, of considerable clarity, in which most of the distinctive features and details are well noted.[23] In the case of the landscape painter the possibilities of a given landscape as a subject for a painting would be quickly reviewed, and the trial-and-error procedure in actual sketching considerably reduced.

An example may clarify the trait. Again Thomas Benton: many of the themes of his paintings have been gleaned from his many leisurely automobile sketching trips in the Appalachians, the southern States and in the southwest. Whenever he chanced upon a scene, a bit of local color, a "character" or a meeting place of a religious sect the sketch would be made, to be added to the rich collections obtained in his various trips. Back in his studio he organizes this material into compositions, models them in clay, makes a color sketch and paints the picture. Probably but little of the original experience is lost. The ability to work in this fashion pre-supposes a facility for keen observation, for entering into the personality he is studying (empathy), and for making many subtle observations without appearing to do so.

The factor of *perceptual facility* is well illustrated in the description by Benton of his impression of a New Mexico sunrise which is quoted in part below.[24] The contrast with the perceptually deficient individual is noteworthy.

The next morning I woke up before dawn. Against the whitish sky to the east a chain of black mountains rose. As the sky turned pink the mountains became blue. There was a bright star hanging in the sky above them. This dawn on the desert was the most beautiful thing I have ever seen. It was moving. It was like the music of some old chant of the early Church, delicate, exquisite, and sad. I walked away from the car. I cherished the sense of great peaceful loneliness the scene gave. I felt like wandering off into the blue, violet, and orange-pink planes that hung in transparent sheets from the top of the sky to within a few yards of my feet. The earth and the sky were as one. There was no distinction between what was solid and what was not. The universe stood revealed to sense as a great harmonious unity, as one thing. . . .

When the sun came over the mountains to the east, the world became what it is. In the place of the one thing there were many things big and little. There were ants at my feet, there were yucca plants and clumps of sparse grass. Way over on the side of a hill, little round bumps of pinon pine squatted in black irregular rows. Beneath another hill about a half mile ahead was a ranch house with a windmill. A scrubby cottonwood tree grew by the windmill. We felt as if we were utterly removed from the possibility of further contact with civilization. Yet the highway from Albuquerque to Gallup was just the other side of the hill below which the ranch house lay. We found it in fifteen or twenty minutes after we started. Where our trail joined it there was a store and a gas station. The boy in charge there was from Newark, New Jersey. He hated the country.

'This place is too lonely for me,' he said. 'There ain't a damn thing to see.' I judged he had not been up in the dawn of that morning.

---

[22]*Ibid.*, pp. 63–81.

[23]It is recognized that much of this is learned; probably the functioning of a set of observational habits would be difficult for the person not so natively equipped to foster—perhaps next to impossible in some.

[24]By permission of the author. From T. H. Benton. *An Artist in America* (New York: McBride, 1937), pp. 236 ff.

V. Creative Imagination

Inasmuch as this term is in wide use and is perhaps little understood by its users, it is proposed that the simple designation be given as the ability to utilize vivid sense impressions effectively in the creation (organization) of a work having some degree of aesthetic character. There is no need for mystification, nor assumption of creation "out of one's mind" — which does not make any particular sense. One does not construct "out of" unless some basis for such construction is there. And that can come only from one's experience, or as is usually the case from composites of experience.

Because the experience of children is usually simple, uncluttered and vivid many of their constructions have a naïvete and charm to adults which the work of older children and other adults does not have. Similarly the emotionally charged but simply experienced observation of a charging or grazing animal afforded primitive man the material for an expressive picture which excites admiration in modern people. The Grippen study[25] presents the various ways in which creative imagination functions in children's art experiences. It is evident in the child's sphere as well as in the adult's that the adequacy of perceptions is a fundamental precondition for effective creative imagination, but it should be noted that the manner of retention of experience does not necessarily lead to an effective organization of this material. In the case of the small child, organizations recognizable as effective are probably accidental in many instances, although the ability to manipulate sense-data and bring in new material may come into the work of an artistically superior child at almost any period.

The dependence of creative imagination upon elements entering into the past experience of the individual is well illustrated in the methods of Hovsep Pushman who is

[25]*Op. cit.*, pp. 69 ff.

regarded as one of the great still-life painters of all time. Mr. Pushman has traveled widely and has accumulated an extensive collection of objects of art from various parts of the world but particularly from China, India and the Near East. This collection in his New York studio constitutes a veritable private museum and includes several hundred frames which are of such variety and character as to make it possible when his painting is completed to select one that is extremely well-fitted to the tonal and textural character of the painting. The still-life is thus a product of his unerring selection of objects from his museum, his unfailing aesthetic judgment in arranging these objects to form not only a marvelously beautiful composition but also to provide the material basis for a flawlessly painted composition. In the process perceptual facility, creative imagination, and aesthetic judgment function as a unit guided by a superior aesthetic intelligence. There is also present in the situation a constantly high outflow of energy which utilizes superior manual skill.

An example of creative imagination motivated by an emotional initiation of the theme itself characterizes the production of Grant Wood's *Daughters of Revolution*. Irked by public criticism of persons regarded by Wood as good Americans, Mr. Wood proposed in his own mind to construct a satire which would have the broad significance of depicting the contrast between comfortably housed, elderly ladies who discuss people and issues at teas, with the actual hardship experienced by ancestors five or six generations removed. Hence the employment of contrast of color and the inclusion of Leutze's *Washington Crossing the Delaware*. It is to be noted that the incentive for this picture was a succession of news items; the creative part wherein imagination functions is in the manner in which Mr. Wood sought out and utilized photographs which would serve as a vehicle for the satire. The three faces in the picture are constructs though based upon a study of many photographs, the actual identity of the persons being unknown.

VI. Aesthetic Judgment

As a factor in artistic competence, aesthetic judgment is probably the most important. The two best established tests for artistic ability have singled out this quality for almost exclusive treatment.[26] Simply defined, aesthetic judgment is the ability to recognize aesthetic quality residing in any relationship of elements within an organization. It is vital to the artist in that good aesthetic judgment permits him to know when his composition is good or unsatisfactory and what might be done to improve it. It is also the basis for art criticism and underlies the appreciative aspect of the aesthetic response. Studies[27] show that it is present in children to some degree but it undoubtedly is subject to considerable development through learning and experience. It is probably never completely mastered by anyone.

In the interests of clarification it should be understood that aesthetic judgment is not the application of a series of rules but is something which the individual acquires on the basis possibly of some innate neurophysical constitution. His own individual manner of attaining aesthetic quality is always his own in the sense that a quality such as balance even with the same materials may not be attained in exactly the same way even by repetitions of the same organization. It is likewise true that the general goal of all aesthetic organization — namely unity — is seldom arrived at by preconceived design but simply emerges on the completion of a composition. Unity is probably never perfect but is attained in varying degrees of success.

[26]Meier-Seashore and the McAdory.
[27]*Psychol. Monogr.* 45 (1933). Studies by Daniels, Jasper, Whorley, and Walton.

From repeated observations on artists in their manner of work, their personal habits, tastes, and manner of arriving at their aesthetic judgments, the author proposes that there is a probably hitherto unsuspected relationship between craftsman heredity and the higher degrees of aesthetic judgment constantly in evidence on the part of many artists. Viewed in this sense aesthetic judgment is fundamentally referable to pride in orderly arrangement. Craftsman skill being a care for nicely proportioned relationships, good all-over design, and infinite and persistent effort in the attainment of good finish, it appears reasonable to assume that the same personal concern for orderly arrangement in a painting or a simplified and unified design characterizes the artist. If this is true then the six factors all become more or less related.

It is not to be assumed that artistic aptitude consists in high degrees in all six factors, but it is necessary to assume that at least some of them must be present in any kind of individual who will make any kind of headway in the field. We may expect that the ultimate progress of the individual is somewhat related to and conditioned by the degree to which he possesses most if not all of the six factors.

Undoubtedly there may be instances of conspicuous success in art which will not be explained on the basis of the factors as set forth. In such cases these factors may be operating, but in a manner not readily discoverable. It may be, moreover, that a strong drive, motivated either by intense ambition or by social pressure, may have urged the person on to extraordinary effort to achieve in the art field. Possibly also he may have been motivated by unusually stimulating and expert training. The writer believes, however, that in all such cases some of these factors would be found present if the manner of work of the individual were studied closely and if all of the facts of his life and ancestry were known.

General Implications of
the Interlinkage Theory

Inasmuch as the theory set forth touches upon the nature–nurture controversy, it is desirable that certain aspects be clearly understood. The writer has long shared the conviction of careful students of this problem that the explanation of psychological phenomena is not to be found in an all-or-none explanation. It is as wrong to assume that artists are "born" as it is that artists are "made." A public which insists upon extreme simplification has seemingly demanded an answer in one direction or another. Neither long study of hereditary charts nor the supposedly rigid control of environmental influences has offered convincing evidence in either case. Nor does it seem profitable to attempt to find which is the more influential of the two.

In the case of artistic capacity as investigated over a fifteen-year period, such evidence as presented and checked against the known viewpoints of present-day biology seems to suggest that some aspects of the capacity are largely attributable to the factor of *stock inheritance* and others are more attributable to learning, but the writer wishes to point out that the hereditary factor referred to is not heredity in the sense of direct inheritance; furthermore, that the environmental aspect is not environmental influence in the usual sense, but a relationship between the individual and his aesthetically significant environment wherein the individual himself takes the initiative. Nature and nurture are here not separate elements since neither acts directly, but rather interact in a dynamic, total situation. The six factors outlined above are therefore more a *series of conditions which*, when present, *interact with the energies of the individual to develop* his artistic competence. The individual therefore, not the inheritance nor the environment, is the final determiner in the situation. The person may have the consti-

tutional stock in the same manner possessed by a long line of craftsmen ancestors, but he may not wish to develop the potential skill present; he may prefer to sell bonds or engage in law practice. He may have the temperamental trait of perseveration with inexhaustible energy reserves; but he may wish to apply it to scientific research. He may have the general intelligence demanded of the higher grades of artistic activity, but he may wish to use it in teaching or business. He may have the peculiar perceptual facility which goes with the artist-personality; but he may wish to use it for nature study or biological research. The special ability known as artistic capacity refers therefore to developmental potentialities which when used through the volition of the individual lead to extraordinary accomplishment in the area. It is up to the individual and to no one else to bring this about.

It is the thesis of the writer that the person with the six factors *can* bring this end about and that the person without these factors *cannot* bring this about to any great degree The position is, therefore, a deterministic point of view — deterministic in the sense that certain neurophysical and developmental factors seem to be normally a *precondition* for the rest of the total development and that these predisposing conditions are not present equally in all persons nor if absent can they be established. The nature-nurture aspect is hence anything but a simple matter. Not only are the factors interlinked in the gross aspects, but they are interlinked and condition one with the other in a dynamic sense — *i.e.*, the interrelationships may change with time and may exist in varying potencies with different individuals. There are probably no two individuals who present identical composites of factors to begin with, and these composites are probably different at each stage of development. It is firmly believed nonetheless that in all cases the *general pattern* is that described above, involving the factors of motor skills, the volitional-temperamental traits of energy output and perseveration, intelligence, habits of perceiving, special utilization of imagination and a special disciplining of judgment and critical processes. Paradoxical as it may seem, it is yet noteworthy that while the basic fact remains that artistic capacity rests upon a general stock inheritance, even the *acquired phases* relating to perception, imagination and judgment are themselves *conditioned by this inheritance*. The unique contribution which these ten years of investigation have made is the knowledge that all these factors are in a peculiar and unique manner *interlinked* and the entire dynamic process is a closely knit, interdependent and evolving development.

9. Easel Painting As an Index of Personality in Preschool Children

ROSE H. ALSCHULER *and* LA BERTA A. HATTWICK

Orientation

Those who work with children's paintings are well aware of the fact that young children do not paint to express ideas, but rather to express *what* they feel and *how* they feel. This fact is particularly apparent in children's earliest representations. Children *first tend to represent themselves.* They exaggerate, usually by size or number, those parts of the representation — eyes, mouth, thumb, hat, etc. — which from their own experience have become particularly important to them. They omit parts which have not played a felt role in their personal experiences.

As children move on from the age of earliest representation toward adolescence, they become increasingly aware of the world as it is, they become concerned with reproducing what they objectively see rather than what they feel, and the self-expressive qualities of painting decrease. Lowenfeld's studies[1] suggest that the peak in this transition occurs by the age of nine. At that time, children tend to be so conscious of the external world and so bent upon exact reproduction of that world that they become blocked in attempts at self-expression. Art teachers support this finding in their observations that age nine is a particularly difficult year in which to obtain self-expressive, really creative products.

Acceptance of the above trends is fast becoming established. But what of painting *before* the age when recognizable representation begins? What of painting during the preschool years? From the developmental standpoint, we would expect painting during the preschool years to be more revelatory than painting at any other time. For

[1]See particularly Lowenfeld, Viktor. *The Nature of Creative Activity.* (New York: Harcourt, Brace and Co.), 1939.

*SOURCE: Reprinted from the *American Journal of Orthopsychiatry*, XIII (1943), pp. 616–25.

This is a descriptive report of a study in final stages of completion. It was possible only through the cooperation and efforts of the Winnetka Public School Nursery Staff, the supervisory and teaching staffs of the WPA Nursery Schools of Chicago, sponsored by the Chicago Board of Education, the research personnel of the WPA Nursery School Project, and several skilled volunteers.

children are functioning more naturally at an impulsive, self-expressive level during the preschool years — particularly between the ages of two and four — than at any other stage of their development. We would expect their creative activities to reflect the impulsive, self-expressive patterns which are evidenced in everything they do.

As we look into the paintings of preschool children, we discover that each child has his own individual pattern. These patterns differ from one another not on the basis of what is represented, but rather on the basis of the children's feelings, which are individually expressed in their abstract use of color, space, line, and form.

The fact that during the preschool years children work largely in abstract patterns rather than through recognizable representations tends to heighten one's recognition of the self-expressive quality and the subjective interpretive value of painting during the preschool years. After all, the very process of representation involves an awareness of outside stimuli. Even though the child who makes a representative painting expresses how he feels about the object represented, the act of representing nonetheless involves ideas or conscious intent, in other words, awareness of the outer world. It is only as the child uses creative media without intending to represent that he is likely to express pure feelings unmodified by conscious content.

Rorschach and others, particularly Harms, have clearly demonstrated that abstract expression brings us closer to an emotional or feeling level than does representative work. It is the abstract qualities of the Rorschach ink-blots which bring forth deep-felt emotional reactions on the part of the subjects. Harms,[2] for diagnostic purposes, has trained juvenile patients to break away from representative work and to use paints or

crayons freely in an abstract way. He has been able to gain insights from the abstract products of these patients that were not apparent in their more realistic forms of expression.

In the case of the Rorschach material and of the Harms experiments, it was necessary to *set the stage* with test materials in order to secure material which would reveal unalloyed feelings. But in the case of children between the ages of two and four the stage is naturally set. No breakdown of established habits is necessary. Expression in abstract rather than representative terms and expression of unalloyed feelings both tend to be typical of children who are in the impulsive, self-expressive stage of development.

With the above facts in mind, the authors have undertaken an extensive study for the purpose of determining (1) if and in what ways the free activities of two, three and four year old children with certain creative media — easel paint, crayons, clay, blocks, and dramatic play[3] — may be related to and give insights into individual personalities; (2) what generalized tendencies, if any, may be found between activities with these creative media and personality.

The study was carried on with 150 preschool children in eight different nursery groups. Records were secured for each child daily over a period of one school year. Twenty children were studied daily over a period of two school years. Follow-up material is still being obtained for these children.

Records include actual preservation of painting and crayon products, sketches of block work, photographs of painting, crayon, clay, block, and dramatic play activities, detailed records of children's behavior while using the indicated media, records of their

[3]Finger painting was not frequent in these nursery school groups, but has also been studied to the extent made possible by existent circumstances. Other creative interests—language, music, and play—were also included to the extent that they predominated in given children's activities.

[2]Harms, Ernst. "Child art as aid in the diagnosis of juvenile neuroses." *AM. J. Orthopsychiatry*, II, 2, 1941, pp. 191–209.

choice or preference for given media, records of overt behavior in the school situation and at home, and social and developmental history data. Both case analyses and quantitative group comparisons have been made from these data.

The study has indicated that helpful clues to personality and to personal problems may be obtained from individual children's (1) *choice* of creative media, (2) *behavior* while using creative media, and (3) *characteristic products or patterns with given media*.

The present report touches upon only one finding in regard to choice — the difference between crayons and easel paints at the preschool level — and upon products in only one area — easel painting.

Significance in Use of Crayons and Easel Paints at Preschool Level

Our data, both qualitative and quantitative, indicate that very young children choose and use crayons to express quite different needs, moods, and meanings from those expressed when they work with easel paints. Crayons tend to be associated with awareness of outside standards and with the desire to communicate with others. In contrast to when they paint, when children crayon they more often tend to name their work and show it to adults, are concerned about the finished product, and are perhaps critical of it themselves. Relatively soon they turn to representation with crayons. Even before they can make representative forms they will tease out their wavy scribbling and call it writing. They are seemingly conscious of crayons as a medium for communication, for expressing ideas.

With painting, on the other hand, children tend to express how they feel, regardless of what others think. The child who sits at the crayon table and makes a recognizable, detailed human being may on the same day go to the easel and produce only a colored mass. Our data reveal crayons as a medium for expressing ideas, whereas easel painting is more often a medium for expressing feelings.

We have noted that most of the nursery school children who show a predominant interest in crayons tend to be relatively new to the group. They usually come from homes with standards overly high for children. Those predominantly interested in crayons are usually tense in the group. They seem most at home with crayons, perhaps because this is a hard, tense medium, as they themselves are tense and somewhat hardened by tensions. Pressure or tension is required to use crayons as compared to paints. As children become freer in the group they invariably lose their major interest in crayons and develop an interest in more fluid materials. A change in major emphasis from crayons to easel painting almost always parallels more freedom and better adjustment within the nursery school group.

Many factors might contribute to the above distinctions, one being that children often use crayons before they come to school, usually through suggestions from parents or siblings. Paints, on the other hand, are more often experienced for the first time after a child enters school. They are not associated as yet with outside or adult standards and expectancies.

The two media, paints and crayons, are also available under different conditions in the nursery school group. Crayons are usually provided at a table where other children may be crayoning and where social stimuli are likely to be present, whereas easel painting tends to be one of the more solitary activities in the nursery school. In the present investigation, nursery groups were limited in general to two easels apiece. These were primarily back to back easels, and there was little interaction between the two children painting at any given time. The easel was usually off to a side of the room, away from more active kinds of play.

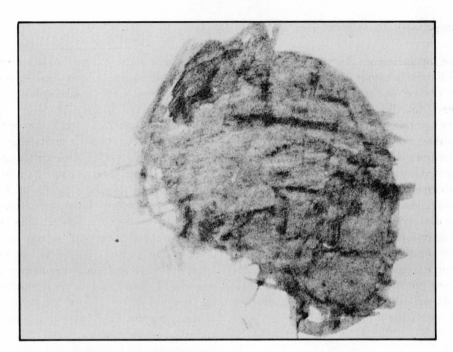

FIGURE 9.1 *10-11-37*. Aileen: 3 years, 6 months. This ovular red mass pattern characterized 133 of the 187 paintings Aileen made during the first year of observation. Through repeated verbalizations and other data we learned that this form meant *home* to Aileen.

FIGURE 9.2 *4-2-40*. Aileen. This left-right pattern with red oval on left and blue form on right suggests that Aileen was trying to push her emotional problems away from awareness and was trying to accept educational standards.

Still other factors which might account for the above distinctions are differences in the nature of the materials themselves. Crayons more easily lend themselves to line and form. Easel paints, with their fluid quality, more readily lend themselves to colored-mass techniques.

While children usually tend to show the above distinctions in the use of paints and crayons, there is a notable exception warranting examination. When children are so emotionally disturbed that everything they do is distorted by the emotional factor, crayon and painting products are likely to show similarities. In such cases the crayon products parallel and take on the colored-mass techniques of the easel paintings.

The above discussion shows the need for separate consideration of crayon and painting products at the nursery level. In fact, it is often the comparison of differences or similarities in expression between these two media which gives the most important clues to the child's personality, particularly as to how well, if at all, his inner feelings are integrated with his overt behavior.

To simplify the present report, the findings on products presented below are limited, unless otherwise specified, to easel paintings.

Illustrative Case Data

Many leads for quantitative comparisons in the present study, and all qualifications which we have found necessary in interpreting the quantitative findings, have come from individual case analyses. Two illustrative cases are given.

Aileen, a three year old girl, showed a major interest in easel paints. Her characteristic painting pattern was a crude circular or oval form outlined in red and then filled in with red (Figure 9.1). She made 187 paintings during the first year of observation, two to three times as many as any other child in her group. In 133 the above described form appeared. She most often called this product "House."

During the second year of study, Aileen produced more varied and more realistic representa-

tions. There were days, however, when she dropped back to the ovular mass. Even in follow-up studies two years later, she was observed to incorporate her ovular red mass in her painting theme (Figure 9.2). It was noted that she usually returned to this form during upset, depressed periods. One day she went from the easel to blocks and built a structure of which she said, "This is a house for my people. Nobody else can come in here. This is a house for my people who haven't any other place to stay."

The significance of the painting theme and naming of it became obvious when seen against her own background. She came from a broken home; both parents remarried; she spent weekdays with one parent, weekends with another. Frequently she lived in a third home, with grandparents. In none of these homes was Aileen the center of attention. Her own father soon had a child by his second wife; her own mother was more absorbed in professional interests than in her child. The grandfather died during the course of the study and the grandmother, suffering from cancer and depression, made two attempts on her own life. Both mother and grandmother came to the teachers perplexed as to what to do about Aileen's apparent confusion regarding home. They said she would remark, "I don't want to go home," when she was home. Occasionally she would ask if they were going home when they were actually there.

Aileen's paintings seem an obvious expression of her basic need: her craving for a stable home, with adequate affection and love.

Several questions for quantitative study are raised by the analysis of Aileen's paintings. Her work was limited to a restricted mass. In the group her typical behavior was to withdraw. Is work in a restricted space typical of children who tend in other activities to withdraw and to function in a relatively restricted area?

She emphasized red and was focused on an emotional problem: a craving for affection and for love. Does red tend to be emphasized by children who are emotionally involved or driven? Can emphasis on red usually or frequently be related to a specific emotion, such as observed in this case? She persisted in fanciful rather than realistic representation (a) beyond the age when realis-

FIGURE 9.3 *Spring, 1940.* Aileen. On noting that Esther was building a hen coop, Aileen announced that she, too, would build one. Hers became the fanciful, pedestaled structure at left, with chickens perched on top. In blocks, clay, paint, and dramatic play, Aileen's pedestal-like projections expressed her self-centered feeling of being apart and aloof from life around her.

FIGURE 9.4 Aileen: 4 years, 9 months. Like the early representations of many other children, this was a self-portrait. Both the crying eyes and open mouth were true to life. Children tend in the early years to paint themselves as they feel from within.

tic patterns became usual, and (b) in block work and other media in addition to easel painting (Figure 9.3). Is such an emphasis a clue to strong emotional drive and to emotional difficulties (Figure 9.4)?

Ann was another child with a particularly interesting and persistent pattern. She characteristically painted a restricted mass in yellow and then overlaid her yellow mass with blue and green (Figure 9.5). In crayoning, likewise, the overlay of yellow with blue and with green prevailed. In block building, which she seldom did at school, Ann would also attempt to hide her work (Figure 9.6).

She was one of the most repressed children in the study. At the time she began to paint she had been in school a year and a half and was still not talking in the group. Her mother reported she talked freely at home when only the family was present.

Ann spent her time standing inactive and apart. Her first participation in school activities came through teacher stimulus. For several days she had been eyeing the crayon table, but seemed unable to bring herself to take an active part. Finally the teacher, sensing the conflicting urge to remain apart and to participate, sat her down forcibly in a chair at the crayon table. From then on Ann felt free to use the crayons. Introduction to other activities, including paints, came about in somewhat the same fashion.

Toward spring she brought for a visit the kitty she loved very much, with which she felt relaxed and secure. This apparently was one of the final things needed to help her open up in the group, for that day she began to talk at school. For the remainder of the school year she showed outgoing behavior of a teasing, aggressive sort. She threw children's hats outside the fence, followed and kicked at adults. Her last easel painting product that year came just when she was beginning to talk and assert her feelings. She then did the first *monochrome* nonoverlaid painting. It was a single mass of brilliant yellow, larger than the usual masses, but clear and not overlaid by any other color.

From analysis of Ann's paintings, and those of other children who consistently overlaid one color with another, one wonders whether such overlay may usually reflect the personality of children who cover over their own basic feelings, i.e., repressed chil-

dren. Would the underlying color and the color used to overlay give any specific clue as to the nature of the repression, the nature of the overt behavior pattern, and their relationship to one another?

Ann was a child with apparently outgoing, happy potentialities, judged by the mother's description of her in the home, yet she was cold and unresponsive in school. She covered the warm color, yellow, with the colder colors blue and green. In two other children in this series there were home records of anxieties, often expressed in night terrors, whereas in the group the children were quite gay and clownish. Each of these children tended to splash over underlying cold and somber colors with dashes of yellow. An attempt to study specific color placement in overlay as a guide to the overt and repressed behavior tendencies in a given child seems justified by these cases.

The above types of constellation are perhaps not new to the psychoanalyst or the psychiatric worker. But such relationships have not been extensively explored in preschool children, nor have they before, to the authors' knowledge, been studied in a quantitative manner. The description which follows summarizes trends which have for the most part been suggested by our individual case studies and substantiated by statistical group analyses.

Generalized Tendencies

Both the statistical analyses and the case studies indicate that children's use of color, line, and form and space can give distinctive insights into personality. Color has been found to give the clearest insights into the child's emotional life. Our case and quantitative data show that children who emphasize color tend to have a strong emotional orientation. Specific color preferences and specific patterns of color placement give clues to the emotional makeup of the child. Our data support the view that red is the most emotionally toned of all the colors. From a developmental standpoint, red is a preferred color during the early preschool years, when children are naturally functioning on an impulsive level. Interest in red decreases and interest in the cooler colors increases as children outgrow the impulsive stage and grow into the stage of reasoning and of greater emotional control.

One child in this study who went through cycles of being emotionally disturbed because of specific situations within her family, and then of being very happily adjusted and self-controlled when the disturbing situations had cleared, showed alternation between red-yellow-orange masses and blue or otherwise cooler colored forms and representations. The warm masses paralleled emotionally disturbed periods. The forms and lines in cooler colors paralleled periods of happy adjustment and of constructive relationships.

Emphasis on red has been found to be associated with either of two extremes: (a) feelings of affection and love; (b) feelings of aggression and hate.

Aileen's emphasis on red seemed related to a craving for affection and love. Other examples of the relation of red to love and affection or to aggression and hate appear when we single out the one or two red paintings in a series otherwise characterized by cold colors, and when we note what happened to the children on those particular days to make them turn to red. In one series we find that the only red painting was done by a rejected, neglected child who usually painted in somber colors in keeping with her predominantly dejected feelings. The one red painting occurred on a day when this child was receiving an undue amount of affection and attention. In the case of another unloved child, the only emphasis on red paralleled a birthday. In another case it occurred after a morning spent in the doll corner, in which the child was the baby, and everyone cuddled and made a fuss over her.

One case was that of an unusually small child who in his drive to be a big man was hiding all emotions under a cold, dominating exterior. His paintings were usually in bold but dirty colors. One morning he had started to paint in a nondescript, grayish black. As he was about to leave the easel, he did something which brought a gentle reprimand from the adult standing near. Angrily he turned back to the easel and smeared his painting with heavy red. He appropriately called his painting "Fire-works"!

While emphasis on red seems related to strong emotional drives, emphasis on blue seems more often associated with drives toward control. Children frequently select blue as they turn away from mass and begin to work with more effort toward control in line and form. Another interesting observation is that many children who come from particularly high-standard homes, i.e., homes geared to adults rather than children, will turn to blue after an absence from school when they have been home, and gradually work away from blue as they again adjust to school and begin to function more freely and at the more impulsive level natural for children of their age.

One of the greatest adjustments children must make during preschool years is that between their own impulsive desires on the one hand and educational pressure toward control on the other. Many times this conflict is reflected in children's contrasting use of blue with a warmer or dirtier color in easel paintings.

Rita's conflict between impulses and educational demands was reflected in easel paintings. She lived completely in her mother's shadow. Except for school hours, she was with her mother every minute of the waking day. Her play activities were planned and directed by the mother, herself particularly interested in drawing. When giving the social history, the mother asked for a pencil and paper so she might impress the interviewer with how quickly she could draw Betty Boop.

In school Rita was completely lost and extremely unhappy during free play. She functioned easily in adult-directed groups. Her earliest painting work showed the human representations and attempts to write which had been stimulated by her mother. As she became freer in painting, a struggle between these trends in representation and her own impulsive drives became apparent. She painted controlled forms, with emphasis on blues and greens, on the left of her paper, and smeared with dirty orange and brown on the right half. She made controlled forms in blue, then smeared them with orange or brown. Once she spent a great amount of time on a painting, practicing alphabet letters. Next she made a precise rectangle filled with blue, and then — apparently in reaction — covered the entire form with heavy red. One time the mother led her to the easel and encouraged her to paint. Rita outlined a house all in black. Her very next painting — the last obtained in the study — began with the placement of precise blue dots all over the painting page. Then she took the orange paint and splashed each dot with orange.

The drive toward control involves emphasis on cleanliness and is therefore opposed to children's natural tendency to smear and play in dirt. Often, at the preschool level, the drive toward control is also opposed to children's feelings in the matter of bowel control. Blue and brown seem to be outstanding choices of children who are working out this conflict. A number of children in the the present investigation evidenced this trend.

The drive toward control also comes in conflict with desires to remain infantile and dependent. We have observed many painting patterns in which yellow and blue were used together — particularly yellow overlaid with blue — to parallel and apparently express this conflict.

Generalized trends have also been suggested by the children's use of other colors. Green, like blue, tends to be used by children who are functioning on a relatively controlled level and show few unusually strong emotional reactions. However, children who emphasize blue may give evidence of very strong underlying emotions which they have redirected, i.e., sublimated, whereas those who emphasize green often lack all

evidences of a strong underlying emotional core. It appears that green (seemingly the least emotionally expressive color) and red (the most emotionally toned color) are used to express polar qualities in a personality sense as they express polarity in the color scale. Green further tends, it appears from case analyses, sometimes to be associated with elimination or with eating difficulties in preschool children.

Orange tends to be used by children who show tempered emotions such as sympathy and friendliness, rather than intense or extreme emotional reactions, and is usually used by children who turn more to fantasy and imaginative pursuits than to more direct overt reactions. Black has been found to be a favorite color with which to overlay, and it has been most persistently sought and used by children with intense anxieties or fears.

Color placement, as well as color choice, gives clues to personality. Consistent overlay usually reflects repression. Separate placement suggests outgoing but highly controlled or directed emotions. Intermingling suggests an outgoing, less controlled emotional flow.

While color seems to give keenest insights into emotions, children's *use of line and form is particularly helpful in giving clues as to the nature of the child's control.* Most of us recognize increased use of line or form as an indication of greater physical or motor or muscular control, but we fail to realize that emphasis on form is also a reflection of increased emotional control, i.e., *self-control.* Our quantitative data indicate that children who emphasize form are turning away from impulsive reactions and are functioning on a more logical, rational basis. We find that children emphasizing form in easel painting tend to be interested in discovering relationships in the outside world and of conforming to the outside world. Usually these are children who are also showing a constructive interest in the use of blocks. The direc-

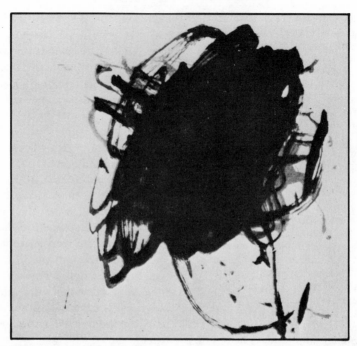

FIGURE 9.5   *5-12-38*. Ann. Greater isolation, as well as more aggression, is reflected in this more heavily painted and more restricted form. At this time Ann was beginning to be aggressive in attacking others, destroying their structures, etc.

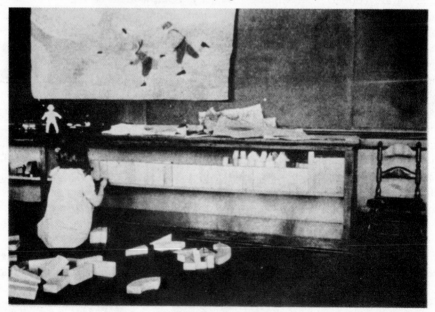

FIGURE 9.6   Ann. Just as Ann had concealed her thoughts by not speaking and had covered over her natural basic color, yellow, so she often covered her block structures with her skirts while theoretically busy putting the blocks away. Note how Ann built and concealed a structure back of the other blocks in the right-hand corner of the upper shelf.

FIGURE 9.7 *1-27-39*. Ann. A sister was born on 1-17. Note yellow verticals smeared on right. On the second painting of the same date, yellow verticals on left were crossed out. Clear, unsmeared red circles on right remained.

tions which children emphasize, the forms which predominate, also give clues to the nature of their drives and personalities. Emphasis on circles tends to be associated with the more submissive, more effeminate types of behavior. Emphasis on verticals reflects the more assertive, more masculine type of personality.

Next in obviousness to the struggle between impulse-action and control among preschool children is seemingly the submissive-assertive struggle, often crystallized as a conflict in the drives to be a girl or a boy. This conflict shows up particularly when there are sibling rivalries, e.g., when the preschool child has a sibling, notably one of the opposite sex. Sometimes it seems stirred by the arrival of a baby, regardless of sex. In the cases of boy-girl conflict circles and verticals tend to be used by the same child in alternating or conflicting ways; e.g., circles on one side of the page, and verticals on the other.

Or one may be overemphasized to the exclusion of the other. Circles and verticals both may be used, the circles being smeared and the verticals left untouched. Circles may be overlaid with verticals, or used to smear out verticals.

Howard illustrates the boy-girl conflict, paralleled by the contrasting use of circles and verticals in easel painting. He was a jovial, outgoing boy, who usually sought the locomotor toys or the blocks, having no apparent interest in easel paints. This remained true until January 4, when he sought the easel and for many days afterward showed a persistent drive to paint. A recurrent pattern of smeared verticals and of unsmeared circles appeared (Figure 9.7). During this time his sociable, outgoing behavior gave way to solitary play. His locomotor interests were abandoned for tea parties and play with doll and buggy. On January 17 a baby sister was born. The painting pattern of smeared verticals and of unsmeared circles continued, and now the boy began to verbalize his feelings. On February 1, while working with clay, he

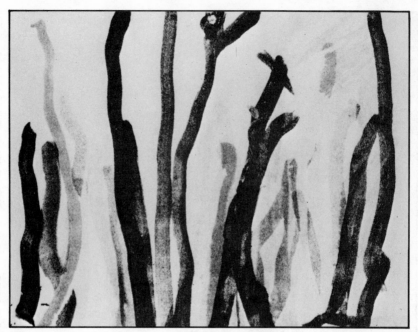

FIGURE 9.8a *10-28-38.* Jessica. A characteristic painting of this period, when entire focus was on verticals. Jessica, an assertive girl who obviously desired to be a boy, wore boy's clothes, and stood to urinate.

FIGURE 9.8b *3-13-39.* Jessica. As she began to desire social acceptance and to meet adult expectancies, she began to smear her verticals. Verticals then became fewer, shorter, and less firmly painted. Like various other children who showed alternation between vertical and circular patterns, she tended to show corresponding alternation between assertive and submissive behavior.

remarked to a cousin, "If you didn't have a ribbon and those yellow curls, you'd be a boy." On February 6, at morning inspection, he told the teacher, "My mother is going to buy me a dress and I'm going to get yellow curls and then I'll be a girl too." The last painting with circular-vertical theme appeared on this date. Following this his interest in painting disappeared and he gradually returned to his former interests. It was as though his problem had been brought to a verbal, conscious level through the painting experience, and that once at this level, it had begun to be resolved in more direct ways than through easel painting.

Jessica is illustrative of several girls observed with strong masculine interests and assertive drives who tended in easel painting to emphasize verticals during their most assertive periods, and to smear verticals or turn toward circular work during their rare submissive periods (Figure 9.8 a and b).

Space usage also gives us distinctive insights into children's personalities and helps give a picture of individual children's reactions to their environment. It seems valid to think of the painting page as a *sample of the child's usage of his environment. How he reacts to this part of his environment is likely to indicate his reaction to the larger environment.*

The child who can not function freely in his whole environment, who finds it necessary to cut out for himself a narrower environment, who perhaps limits himself to a single adult, to another child, or to a few selected bits of equipment such as the doll buggy and the swing, is the child who is likely to outline a narrow area of the painting page and work within that area.

The child who functions most freely and effectively in his general environment is likely to be one who makes the freest use of the painting page. Such a child does not cut off an area in which to work, nor does he seem bound, consciously, by the limits of the painting page. He seems to make an unconscious adjustment to the limits of the painting paper, leaving perhaps an unpainted border around the edge, yet not seeming cramped in the execution of his work by so doing.

We have had several children whose paintings were a wild scramble of lines which ran in every direction, off as well as on the page. These paintings were also characterized by work in every color; they used a little of every color, not much of any particular one. The effect was much the same as one might get by tangling various colored threads in a sewing basket.

These paintings were made by children who were highly distractible, who flitted from one activity to another, tried a little of everything, and concentrated on nothing. Were we to chart the footpaths of one of these children on the playground in a given morning and use a different color each time the child left one activity and began another, the effect would probably be much the same as the easel paintings show.

Integration of Quantitative and Case Study Trends

This report began with the statement that children paint what they feel. In our quantitative study, we have related children's painting characteristics not to feelings alone but to overt behavior patterns, on the assumption that during the self-expressive phase of development children primarily behave as they feel. The fairly consistent trends which appear in our quantitative study justify the belief that this is true.

Our case studies, however, keep us continuously aware of the fact that even during the preschool years there are many exceptions to the above tendency. Even preschool children sometimes have feelings which may be expressed in easel painting but which may not be receiving an "out" in more overt behavior. An example in point was an exceedingly submissive, infantile four year old boy whose paintings with their heavy full-page strokings in red reflected the assertive, aggressive feelings which he was not free to show in more direct reactions.

These various findings suggest that easel painting products by themselves may not safely be used to predict behavior. They suggest, however, that if we regard painting products as a possible clue to understanding the child's personality and his emotional flow, and integrate the painting facts with all other available information about the child, these painting products may supply some of the missing clues needed to build a workable understanding of the child.

The above findings, we believe, also have important implications for all adults who tend to impose patterns of work on children rather than encourage them to express themselves freely in creative media.

10. Reactions of Middle and Lower Class Children to Finger Paints As a Function of Class Differences in Child-Training Practices

THELMA G. ALPER, HOWARD T. BLANE, AND BARBARA K. ABRAMS

During the past decade a new philosophy of child training has come into prominence. Variously termed "developmental," "permissive," "self-demand" or "child-centered," its two major tenets are: (a) habit training should be started when the child is physiologically ready to comply, not before; and (b) the emotional climate in which the training takes place should be one of unconditional acceptance of the child, of tolerance for failure, not coercive adherence to rigid schedules. The first is consistent with the findings of a number of co-twin control experiments (see, e.g., 10 and 17). For the second there is some support from clinical studies (e.g., 12, 19, 24) but the experimental evidence is still equivocal.[1] The psychological advantages and disadvantages of per-missive as compared with rigid child-training practices cannot yet, therefore, be clearly evaluated.

During this same period sociologists have been reporting striking social class differences in child-training practices (3, 5). Middle class parents, they find, are coercive, lower class, permissive. Middle class parents begin habit training earlier, set higher standards for achievement, and are less tolerant of failure. These studies, based only on what mothers say their practices are, include no data on how the children react to the parental demands. That class differences in training might result in class differences in personality development, however, is suggested by the sociologists. Davis and Havighurst generalize from their data, as follows: "We would say that middle class children are subjected earlier and more consistently to the influences which

[1]See Orlansky's (20) cogent criticisms of the experimental literature; also, Harris (11, pp. 12–19) and Koch (14, pp. 6–11).

*SOURCE: Reprinted from *Journal of Abnormal and Social Psychology*, LI (1955), pp. 439–48.

make a child an orderly, conscientious, responsible and tame person. In the course of this training, middle class children *probably* suffer more frustration of their impulses" (3, p. 707). Ericson's conclusions, based on the same population samples, are similar: "Middle class children are *probably* subjected to more frustrations in the process of achieving these learnings and are probably more anxious as a result of these pressures than are lower class children" (5, p. 501).[2]

To test the validity of these generalizations, the reputed class differences in a specific area of habit training, namely bowel training, were selected as the focus of the present study. The rationale of the study was as follows: if the cleanliness standards of middle class parents are more rigid from infancy on, and if these standards are "frustrating," then an experimental task which requires the child to get dirty should elicit measurably different behaviors in middle and lower class children.

Three major differences in behavior were predicted:

1. Middle class children would more often try to avoid the task (refuse to enter into it, or be slower to accept it);

2. Middle class children would show more concern about getting dirty once in the task (maintain minimal contact with the materials);

3. Middle class children would show more concern about getting themselves cleaned up afterwards (go to the bathroom oftener).

Two experiments were designed to test these predictions. In the first, Experiment I, the child was required to use finger paints; in the second, Experiment II, a control experiment, crayons. It was predicted that the behavior of middle and lower class children would differ significantly in Experiment I, not in Experiment II.

[2]The editors have added the italics to this and to the preceding quotation.

TABLE I

Median Age in Months for Beginning and Completing Bowel Training in Lower- and Middle-Class White Children*

	Present Sample		Davis and Havighurst Data	
	Middle Class	Lower Class	Middle Class	Lower Class
Bowel Training Begun	9	11.2	7.5	10.2
Bowel Training Completed	27	18.0	18.4	18.8

*Present data compared with data from Davis and Havighust (3).

EXPERIMENT I: THE FINGER-PAINTING STUDY METHOD

Subjects: Thirty-six four-year-old white nursery school children served as Ss.[3] Eighteen were attending a university-sponsored nursery school in Cambridge, Massachusetts; the other 18 attended social-agency-supported day nursery schools situated in lower class residential areas in Boston, Massachusetts.

Occupational, educational, residential, and other pertinent socioeconomic data, as outlined by Warner *et al.* (30), obtained through parent interviews, teacher interviews, and school records, support the designation of the first group as middle class, the second as lower class.[4] Both boys and girls were included, but not in equal numbers. All were within, or above, the normal IQ range.

As evidence of class differences in toilet training, parental time schedules, reported in median age in months for beginning and completing

[3]The sample was restricted to white children since the data for Negro parents are not as consistent. Duvall (4) reports that Negro mothers at all class levels are less permissive than white mothers, whereas Ericson (5) finds that lower class Negro mothers are coercive in toilet training, though permissive in other areas.
[4]The middle class sample was primarily upper-middle; the lower class, primarily middle-lower.

bowel training,[5] are presented in Table I, along with the corresponding data from Davis and Havighurst (3, p. 701). In both samples, middle class parents start training significantly earlier than do lower class parents. In the present sample, the middle class child achieves control significantly *later;* in the Davis and Havighurst sample, the two groups achieve control at about the same time. The first tenet of the new philosophy of permissiveness in child training, then, is seemingly more frequently violated by middle than by lower class parents in our sample, since it is the former who start the training too early; *cf.* Spock (26), and Gesell and Ilg (9). The fact that middle class *S*s achieve voluntary control later than do lower class *S*s may be indirect evidence that the second tenet, a permissive emotional climate, is also being violated by our middle class parents.[6]

Materials: The Shaw (25) finger paints, red, orange, yellow, green, blue, purple, brown, and black, were used. The paper was the usual 22- by 16-inch glazed paper recommended by Napoli (18) for finger painting.

Procedure: Each *S* was tested individually in a small examining room where *E* had put out the materials in advance. These consisted of a sheet of dampened paper on the work table, the paints, in eight small jars, arranged in random order on a stand beside the table, and a smock, the latter being customary in these schools during painting sessions.

The *E* began the session by engaging *S* in conversation about finger paints: did he know what finger paints were, how to use them, etc. Regardless of *S*'s answers, *E* illustrated how both hands, both arms, and even the elbows could be used in this kind of painting.

To maximize contact with the paints, *S* was required to use his fingers for scooping the paints out of the jars.

The experimental task consisted of two finger paintings. For the first, the "free painting," the

instructions were: "Paint anything you want to paint." For the second, the "family painting," the instructions were: "Paint a picture of your family — your brothers and sisters, mother and daddy."[7] If *S* seemed uncertain of what was required of him, *E* asked: "Who are the people who live in your house?" *S* was then encouraged to enumerate these people and to draw them.

The *E* attempted to maintain an informal and permissive atmosphere during the experimental session.

Variables Measured: Sixteen formal variables were included for measurement. The list, including operational definitions, is given below.

1. Time to begin painting: measured from the moment *E* completes the instructions to the time *S* begins actually to apply paint to paper; 10 sec. or less scored as "immediate," over 10 sec. as "delayed"; measured only for the "free painting."

2. Acceptance of task: scored as accepted if *S* does finger-paint; if *S* refuses to paint, or if in the second painting the content is something other than "a family," performance scored as "task not accepted."

3. Requests help: *S* asks *E* for help at some stage in the drawing.

4. Use of whole hand vs. finger-tip approach: *S* uses fingers and palm for smearing vs. only finger tips.

5. Use of both hands: *S* uses both hands in whole or part, simultaneously or successively.

6. Use of whole sheet vs. partial use of sheet: finished product covers whole sheet of paper vs. only a restricted portion.

7. Use of warm vs. cold colors: *S* makes more frequent use of red, orange, and yellow than of green, blue, and purple, as measured by a frequency count.

8. Use of monotones: *S* uses only one color.

9. Use of brown and/or black: *S* uses brown, black, or both.

10. Separate placement of colors: *S* applies paint in daubs, streaks, or patches, keeping each color separate against the white background of the paper.

---

[5]Ericson's (5, p. 499) definition for "training completed" was followed: the child can inhibit defecation voluntarily and can indicate to the mother the need to defecate.

[6]Direct measures of the emotional climate, unfortunately, were not included in the study.

[7]Having ascertained the family constellation in advance, *E* altered these instructions to fit the individual *S*.

11. Intermingling of colors: the colors border on each other, but each is retained in the finished product; overlapping of edges is included, "overlay," is not. (See 1, p. 47.)

12. Indiscriminate mixing of colors: the identity of the separate colors is lost; the finished product characteristically looks "muddy." (See 1, p. 47.)

13. Names "free drawing"; S spontaneously announces what the drawing represents; scored only in the first painting.

14. Mutilation: S defaces finished product by smearing or overlay of fresh paint; original content unrecognizable in whole, or in part, by E; scored only in the second painting.

15. Asks to take paintings home: S asks permission to take his paintings home.

16. Washing-up behavior: S leaves task, goes to the bathroom, washes hands, face, etc., during or after task is completed. For purposes of analysis and interpretation, the variables were grouped as follows: a. Measures of S's willingness to undertake the task: variables 1 and 2; b. Measures of S's willingness to remain in the situation: variables 3, 4, 5, and 6 in the free painting and 3, 4, and 5 in the family painting; c. Measures of color usage and color placement: variables 7, 8, 9, 10, 11, and 12; d. Measure of S's tolerance for an unstructured situation: variable 13;[8] e. Measures of S's tolerance for the finished product: variables 14 and 15; f. Measure of S's tolerance for "the state of being dirty": variable 16.

Results

The S was scored in terms of presence or absense of each variable. The scores are presented in Table II along with the probability values for significance of the differences between the two groups of Ss, computed by Fischer's (7) exact test.

Free Painting Task

a. Willingness to undertake the task (variables 1 and 2). The behavior of the two groups differs significantly on one of these

[8]Since E imposes structure in the second task, this measure applies only to the first painting.

variables. Both groups comply with the instruction to paint a picture (variable 2), but more lower class Ss accept the task immediately (variable 1, $p = .001$).

b. Willingness to remain in the situation (variables 3, 4, 5, and 6). Three of the differences are significant in the expected direction. More lower class Ss use the whole hand for smearing (variable 4, $p = .02$) and, indeed, smear with both hands (variable 5, $p = .001$). More lower class Ss smear the paint over the entire surface of the paper (variable 6, $p = .001$). Neither group requests help with the free painting (variable 3).

The use of the finger tip, not the whole hand (variable 4), and of a different finger tip for each separate color, is a middle, not a lower class behavior. Lower class Ss more often use a whole arm, "into-the-paints-to-the-elbow" technique. They apply the paints in wide swirling motions, using both hands, palms down, fingers spread, as contrasted with the constricted, small movements of middle class Ss (variable 6).

c. Color usage (variables 7, 8, and 9) and color placement (variables 10, 11, and 12).

Only one color usage variable yields a significant difference: lower class Ss more often use warm colors, red, orange, yellow; middle class Ss cold colors, green, blue, purple (variable 7, $p = .001$). The use of monotones (variable 8) is rare in both groups. Both groups use browns and blacks (variable 9).

All of the color placement variables yield statistically significant differences. When clear separation of the colors occurs (variable 10, $p = .05$), it does so only among middle class Ss. When the middle class S permits colors to come into contact he intermixes them in such manner that the colors lose their separate identity in the finished product (variable 12, $p = .02$). The lower class S more often intermingles the colors (variable 11, $p = .02$). As a consequence, the total effect of the two sets of

TABLE II

Comparison of Middle and Lower Class Four-Year-Old Children
on Two Finger-Painting Tasks

Variable	Free Painting Task			Family Painting Task		
	Middle Class Ss (N = 18)	Lower Class Ss (N = 18)	p*	Middle Class Ss (N = 18)	Lower Class Ss (N = 18)	p*
1. Begins to paint immediately	5	17	.001	—	—	—
2. Accepts task	18	18	1.000	4	12	.010
3. Requests help	0	0	1.000	8	3	.030
4. Use of whole hand	11	17	.020	12	17	.040
5. Use of both hands	8	17	.001	13	17	.090
6. Use of whole sheet	9	18	.001	—	—	—
7. Use of warm colors	1	10	.001	2	7	.060
8. Use of monotones	2	2	1.000	3	2	>.200
9. Use of brown and/or black	11	11	1.000	12	12	1.000
10. Separate placement of colors	4	0	.05	3	0	.110
11. Intermingles colors	2	13	.001	3	10	.020
12. Mixes colors indiscriminately	10	3	.02	8	5	>.200
13. Names free painting	14	7	.02	—	—	—
14. Mutilates painting	—	—	—	10	4	.040
15. Asks to take drawing home	—	—	—	18	1	<.001
16. Washing-up behavior	5	0	.02	18	18	1.000

*Computed by means of Fischer's (7) exact test.

paintings is strikingly different. The paintings of middle class Ss typically consist of daubs, streaks, or somewhat constricted wavy lines of paint widely separated from each other, or of dark, muddy-looking, formless masses with much overlay of one color on another, the original colors no longer being recognizable in the final product. The paintings of the lower class Ss, on the other hand, are more often warm and bright in color tone, and the original colors are recognizable in the finished product.

d. The S's tolerance for an unstructured situation (variable 13).

Giving a name to the painting (variable 13), is used as a measure of S's intolerance for the unstructured situation. The difference between the two groups is statistically significant: more middle class Ss name the free painting (p = .02).

Sometimes the naming occurs right away, S announcing what he will paint. Sometimes it occurs only after the product is finished, when E routinely asked if the picture had a name.

e. The S's tolerance for the finished product (variables 14 and 15).[9]

f. The S's tolerance for the state of being dirty (variable 16).

A frequency count of the number of Ss who left the task to go to the bathroom (variable 16) revealed a class difference. No lower class Ss went to the bathroom during, or at the end of the free painting task. Nor did they talk about wanting to go. This be-

[9]Not measured for the first painting.

havior occurs only among middle class Ss ($p = .02$).[10]

Family Painting Task

a. Willingness to undertake the task (variables 1 and 2). As noted earlier, variable 1 was not measured here. Variable 2 did yield a significant difference in the expected direction: more lower class Ss comply with E's instruction to paint a picture of the family ($p = .01$).[11]

b. Willingness to remain in the situation (variables 3, 4, and 5). Two of these variables yield significant differences in the expected direction. As in the free painting, more lower class Ss use the whole hand for smearing (variable 4, $p = .04$). Use of both hands for applying the paints, however, now only shows a tendency in favor of lower class Ss (variable 5, $p = .09$).

c. Color usage and color placement (variables 7, 8, 9, 10, 11, and 12).

None of the color usage variables yields a significant difference. One approaches significance: more lower class Ss tend to use warm colors (variable 7, $p = .06$).

The direction of the differences for color placement variables (variables 10, 11, and 12) remains the same in both paintings. But only intermingling (variable 11, $p = .02$) reveals a significant between-class difference in the second painting.

d. The S's tolerance for the finished product (variables 14 and 15).

More middle class Ss mutilate the family painting (variable 14, $p = .04$).[12]

All middle class Ss asked for permission to take their paintings home (variable 15). Only one lower class S made this request. The p here is beyond the .001 level of confidence.

e. The S's tolerance for the state of being dirty (variable 16).

After completing the second task, all Ss voluntarily entered the bathroom and washed up before returning to the classroom.

The results of Experiment I indicate, then, that the behavior of middle and lower class Ss does differ in the predicted ways: middle class Ss more often tried to avoid the finger-painting task and more often tried to avoid getting dirty while they were painting. They were apparently also more concerned than lower class Ss to get clean afterwards.

EXPERIMENT II: THE CRAYON
STUDY METHOD

Subjects: Forty white four-year-old nursery school children served as Ss. Twenty were enrolled in private schools in Worcester, Massachusetts, the other twenty in the social-agency-sponsored schools used in Experiment I. The sociological criteria for selecting the two groups, the one middle class, the other lower, were the same as in Experiment I.[13]

---

[10]While the record of S's questions and remarks during the painting process is not complete enough for statistical analysis, it may be noted in passing that middle, not lower class S's carry on a running commentary, replete with self-references, while painting. Typical remarks are the following: "Look at me, I'm all dirty"..."My hands are green"..."I'm all muddy"..."Will the paint come off?"

The vocalizations of lower class S's were more often squeals, grunts, or laughs. When they talked it was usually to ask why E was there or when E would come again, rather than to direct attention to themselves.

[11]In no case do we find a family, or reasonable facsimile thereof, in the final products of middle class Ss. The four who did accept the task mutilated the drawing at the end of the session.

[12]The content data support the view that S's mutilation is intentional. Like many middle class Ss, middle class Ann, for example, paints a house, not her family. Her house has four windows. She identifies each as she paints: "This is my mommy's, this is my daddy's, this is brother's and this is mine." Next she smears black paint across three windows, leaving undefaced only the window of her own room.

Lower class Suky draws her mother, starting with the feet. She then says, "She is too big." Where the body should be Suky smears with a kind of scribbling motion. Suky's mother, the teacher has told us, is pregnant.

[13]As in Experiment I, the middle class group was primarily upper-middle; the lower class, primarily middle-lower.

TABLE III

Mean Age in Months at Which Bowel
Training Was Begun and Completed

	Middle Class		Lower Class			
	N	Ss	N	Ss	t	p
Bowel Training Begun	18	10	17	9	1.04	.30
Bowel Training Completed	18	25.9	16	17.4	4.49	<.01

The toilet-training time schedules are presented in Table III.[14]

Comparison of Tables I and III reveals some schedule differences. Experiment I was completed in 1948, Experiment II in 1951. In the 1948 sample (Table I), the middle class parent began the training earlier and completed it later than did the lower class parent. Both differences were significant. In 1951 (Table III), the middle class parent started and completed training later.[15] But now only the completion data differ significantly for the two social classes. The reversal in starting-time, while not statistically significant, however, may have some importance.

In 1951, some middle class mothers volunteered during the interview that they had read "The Books" and that they were "following" them. By "The Books" they meant Gesell and Ilg (9) and/or Spock (26, 27). In 1948, these books were not mentioned. Nor did lower class mothers mention them in 1951. Yet, if the attitudes of our 1951 middle class mothers were as consistently permissive as self-demand theory requires, and if the lower class mothers were continuing to be permissive, then logically, training should be completed approximately at the same time in the two social classes. But, as Table III shows, this is not the case. As in 1948, middle class Ss still achieve control significantly *later* ($p = .01$). What seems likely, therefore, is that the middle class delay in starting training may stand alone in "taking over" the new philosophy of child care. The attitudes and emotional cli-

[14]It was not possible to complete these data for all Ss. The teachers were of the opinion, however, that the incomplete cases were not atypical.

[15]The Maccoby et al. (16) social class training data gathered in the same year are also in this direction.

TABLE IV

Comparison of Middle and Lower Class Four-Year-Old Children
on Two Crayon Drawing Tasks

Variable	Free Drawing			Family Drawing		
	Middle Class Ss (N = 20)	Lower Class Ss (N = 20)	p*	Middle Class Ss (N = 20)	Lower Class Ss (N = 20)	p*
1. Begins to draw immediately	18	19	>.20	17	13	.14
2. Accepts task	20	20	1.000	16	12	.15
3. Use of whole sheet	15	14	>.20	13	9	.15
4. Use of warm colors	4	3	>.20	6	2	.12
5. Use of monotones	2	6	.12	6	11	.10
6. Use of brown and/or black	15	13	>.20	14	9	.10
7. Separate placement of colors	3	2	>.20	2	1	>.20
8. Intermingling of colors	11	6	.10	11	5	.05
9. Indiscriminate mixing of colors	4	6	>.20	2	0	>.20
10. Names free drawing	14	15	>.20	—	—	—
11. Mutilates drawing	5	4	>.20	2	0	>.20

*Computed by means of Fischer's (7) exact test.

mate may still be coercive.[16] This will be considered again in a later section.

Materials: Milton-Bradley Trutone Crayons were used. The colors were the same as in Experiment I. The drawing paper was of the newsprint variety. The size of the paper corresponded to that customarily used in the given nursery school.

Procedure: The procedure was the same as in Experiment I, adjustments being made only for the difference in medium. For example, no demonstration of crayoning was given.

Variables Measured[17]

1. Time to begin crayoning.
2. Acceptance of task.
3. Use of whole sheet vs. partial use of sheet.[18]
4. Use of warm vs. cold colors.
5. Use of monotones.
6. Use of brown and/or black crayons.
7. Separate placement of colors.
8. Intermingling of colors.
9. Indiscriminate mixing of colors.
10. Names "free drawing."
11. Mutilation.
12. Takes initiative in cleaning-up: at end of session *S* spontaneously offers to put away crayons and/or to clean the table.
13. Asks to take drawings home.
14. Asks to do an extra drawing: at end of session, *S* asks if he may make one more picture.

As in Experiment I, *S* was scored in terms of presence or absence of each variable.

These scores constitute the data for analysis.

Results

The data for variables 1–11, analyzed by means of Fischer's (7) exact test, are summarized in Table IV. Postsession behavior,

---

[16]Klatskin's (13) data support this possibility. The values and attitudes of middle class mothers who participated in the rooming-in plan seemed to remain "middle class" (coercive, nonpermissive) even though their practices followed the precepts of self-demand scheduling.
[17]Only variables new to Experiment II will be defined.
[18]Because the crayon drawings typically had content, the entire sheet was rarely covered. If a drawing occupied at least two thirds of the paper, it was scored as using the whole sheet.

variables 12–14, is presented in Table V. As these tables show, of the 24 differences analyzed, only two were statistically significant. Since this could occur by chance alone, no further discussion of these data will be presented.

TABLE V

Comparison of Postsession Behavior of Middle and Lower Class Nursery School Children Following Crayon-Drawing Tasks

Variable	Middle Class Ss (N = 20)	Lower Class Ss (N = 20)	p
12. Takes initiative in cleaning-up process	5	11	.05
13. Asks permission to take drawings home	3	7	.14
14. Asks to do an extra drawing	5	8	>.20

Computed by means of Fischer's(7) exact test.

The hypothesis Experiment II was designed to test, therefore, is supported: middle and lower class *S*s behave in the same way when the drawing medium does not necessitate getting dirty.

Discussion

As predicted, finger paints, not crayons, yielded statistically significant differences in the behavior of middle and lower class nursery school children. Middle class *S*s do appear to be made anxious by the smearing requirement: they have a lower tolerance for getting dirty, for staying dirty, and for the products they produce while dirty. Among the more obvious variables to reveal these differences are the slower acceptance by middle class *S*s of the finger-painting task, the maintenance of only minimal contact with the paints (e.g., a single finger tip, not a whole-hand approach), the substitution of a different content for the "family" painting and /or final mutilation of it. Differences yielded by other variables also support the thesis of tolerance differences, as can be seen by relating these variables to the empirical findings of other studies, as discussed below.

While investigators are not in complete accord about the psychological significance of color usage (23), many make a distinction between warm and cold colors. Cold colors in children's drawings have been associated with depression (21), delinquency (22), poor adjustment (29), and controlled reactions as opposed to free emotional expression (1); warm colors, with cheerfulness and good adjustment (1, 2, 22, 28, 29, 31). The parsimonious application of these findings to our results is that middle class Ss by using more cold colors in Experiment I are attempting to control their feelings.[19] The greater use of warm colors by lower class Ss is consistent with absence of situational anxiety.

Our color placement data fall into the three patterns previously noted by Alschuler and Hattwick (1). One pattern, separate placement, they suggest, is the response of the emotionally more mature child who has an "extreme sense of order and cleanliness" and "repressed desires to smear and to soil" (1, p. 82). A second pattern, indiscriminate mixing, is the response of the emotionally immature child who is still functioning "on a manipulative, smearing level" (1, p. 47). Both the more controlled separate placement and the uncontrolled indiscriminate mixing occurred in middle, not lower class Ss in the present study. Lower class Ss more often resorted to a third pattern, the intermingling of colors. According to Alschuler and Hattwick (1, p. 47), intermingling is not associated with "strain or emotional tension."

Constricted use of the drawing paper has been found to characterize the behavior of the timid child (15), the rejected and deprived child (2), the withdrawing, emotionally dependent child (1); use of the whole sheet, the "uninhibited" child (31), the "relatively outgoing, assertive, self-reliant personality" (1). In our results, middle class Ss resort to the constricted pattern, lower class to the unconstricted.

The assigning of a name to the "free" painting, a variable which characterized middle class Ss, is reminiscent of Frenkel-Brunswik's (8) concept of intolerance for ambiguity. The structuring of an unstructured situation by giving it a name may help S control or contain the anxieties aroused by smearing. By naming, S may be saying: "I have drawn *something;* I have not just been smearing."

The more frequent request of middle class Ss for help with the family painting suggests another mechanism of defense: only if the adult gets dirty, too, is it all right for middle class S to get dirty!

The middle class S's lack of spontaneity about cleaning up the examining room would seem to be consistent with the rest of his behavior. It may mean that he wants to get away quickly from the scene of his smearing misdoings. Or, like the middle class child in the Fisher *et al.* (6) balloon film, he departs without helping, knowing that "somebody else will clean up." Characteristically, for the middle class child, someone else does. Teachers in the lower class schools tell us that these children are taught to clean up after themselves. They appear here to do so willingly.

Two different explanations occur to us with respect to the middle class S's more frequent request to take his drawings home: (a) he may want to use his products as a gift to appease the parent who disapproves of his getting dirty; or (b) he may wish to destroy the evidence himself. To choose between these alternatives, we would have to know

[19]The studies cited above have limited value for comparative purposes. In some, abnormal populations only were sampled. Some use watercolors, some crayons, others a combination of media. Social class factors also were not controlled.

the "take-home policies" of these schools, as well as what, in fact, S would do with his products were he allowed to retain them.

Consistently, then, the finger-painting data support the thesis of social-class tolerance differences for getting and staying dirty. Middle class Ss are seemingly made more anxious by the smearing task. As predicted, however, behavioral differences break down when crayons are used as the drawing medium. Yet since some middle class mothers in the crayon study tell us that they are following "The Books," the argument could be made that the crayon study does not serve as an adequate control, that we are no longer dealing with coercively vs. permissively reared children. Indeed, there are no differences now in the parental time schedules for starting toilet training. Differences in time for completing training, however, persist. This latter fact, we feel, supports the argument that the emotional climate in which the training is taking place is different in the two social classes.

Middle class mothers, influenced by modern parent-oriented literature, may be *trying* to be more permissive. Yet if their attitudes toward dirt and messiness are still traditionally middle class—and Klatskin's (13) study done during the same time interval suggests that they are—the likelihood is that these parents would resort either to inconsistent permissiveness or to a laissez-faire policy. In either case, we would expect control to be delayed, since "the rules" for winning parental approval would not be clear to the child. Class differences in the atmosphere in which the training is taking place would still pertain. Exposure to a new philosophy of training, as Klatskin (13) notes, does not insure the proper attitudes for applying it.

A study by Maccoby *et al.* (16), however, raises some important questions. It overlaps in time, and to some extent in geographical sampling, our crayon experiment. On the basis of interviews with middle and lower class mothers, they report a shift "toward greater warmth and permissiveness, and less severity in socialization among upper-middle families with the more severe training occurring among the lower group" (16, p. 392). As in our crayon study, bowel training is started a little later by middle class mothers, but not significantly so. Unlike our study, training is completed by middle and lower class children at about the same time. This latter difference is an important one. Yet we cannot fully account for it.

In comparing their data with those of Davis and Havighurst (3), Maccoby *et al.* (16, p. 394) raise the question of sampling differences. Davis and Havighurst, they suggest, may have been dealing with a "lower-" lower class sample. But Ericson (5, p. 496) used the Davis and Havighurst sample and describes it as "for the most part, upper-lower class." Our lower class sample was primarily middle-lower. The linear relationship between severity of training and class membership, from lower-lower as to upper-middle, as reported by Maccoby *et al.*, moreover, would fit neither the Davis and Havighurst data, nor ours. Sampling differences, therefore, would seem not to be the crucial factor.

A more promising lead is suggested by the Maccoby *et al.* question as to whether "upper-middle mothers were telling the interviewers not what they actually do but what they believe would be the right thing to say to the interviewer" (16, p. 392). In telling us that they are following "The Books," our middle class mothers may also have been telling us "the right thing." Yet, since they report an even later age for completing bowel training, may this not mean that their standards for cleanliness are very high indeed?

We raise a final and perhaps the most basic question for future research. Judging from recent informal discussions with parents at PTA meetings, for example, middle class parents *are* reading "The Books." But they seem to be equating permissiveness and laissez faire. They mistake the "let the child do anything he wants to do, lest we frustrate him by imposing rules" for permissiveness. The consequences of permissiveness and laissez faire for personality development, however, theoretically should be quite different. Laissez faire, with its absence of rules, absense of any sort of guidance, should make for insecurity, indecisiveness, and feelings that the parents are not interested enough to help.[20] Yet from the parents' point of view the training procedures might seem permissive because they are "lenient." Consistent with this possibility are the Maccoby *et al.* findings of statistically significant class differences in techniques of discipline. Upper-lower mothers more often use what Maccoby *et al.* describe as "negative techniques" (16, p. 387): physical punishment, ridicule and deprivation of privileges; upper-middle mothers more often use scolding statements involving withdrawal of love (16, Table 6, p. 388). That the latter can make children very anxious indeed is clinically now well recognized.

To gain further insight into the problems raised by this discussion necessitates additional research. Among the studies which might profitably be undertaken are (*a*) a repetition of the original finger-painting study in which the consequences of different parental attitudes as well as of different training procedures are investigated; (*b*) a study of the behavioral consequences of social class differences in habit training areas other than toilet training; and (*c*), a systematic study of the extent to which present-day parents are confusing permissiveness with laissez faire.

Summary

Starting with the findings by sociologists that child-training practices differ markedly in middle and lower class families, two related experiments were designed to measure behavioral consequences of the reputedly coercive, rigid middle class procedures as contrasted with the more permissive lower class procedures. The conjectures of Davis and Havighurst (3, p. 707) that middle class children "probably suffer more frustration of their impulses," and of Ericson (5, p. 501) that middle class children "are probably more anxious as a result of these pressures," were tested, using class differences in toilet-training procedures as the basis for the experimental design.

In the first experiment, eighteen middle and eighteen lower class white nursery school children used finger paints for painting two pictures. The *S* chose his own content for the first picture. For the second, he was asked to paint a picture of his family. Quantitative analysis of the formal aspects of the painting reveals statistically significant differences in the performance of the two groups of *S*s. The middle class *S*s show a lower tolerance for getting dirty, for staying dirty, and for the products they produce while dirty, as measured by such variables as time to begin painting, color usage, mutilation of the family painting, bathroom behavior, etc.

In the second experiment, crayons were used as the drawing medium. As predicted, the class differences obtained in the first experiment do not persist in the second experiment. The class differences in Experiment I, therefore, reflect differences in reactions "to getting dirty," not differences in drawing, as such.

The results are interpreted to mean that soiling and smearing behavior does arouse more anxiety in middle than in lower class children. The mechanisms used by the middle class child to handle this anxiety are discussed.

[20] A quotation from the senior author's unpublished counseling records of a young college student epitomizes the feelings of rejection laissez faire can entail: "My parents do not restrict me at all. They never ask me where I'm going, with whom I'm going or where I've been. I guess they don't love me enough to care."

REFERENCES

1. ALSCHULER, ROSE H., & LA BERTA B. W. HATTWICK. *Painting and Personality.* Vol. I, II. Chicago: University of Chicago Press, 1947.

2. BRICK, N. The mental hygiene value of children's art work. *Amer. J. Orthopsychiat.*, 1944, **14**, 136–146.

3. DAVIS, W. A., & R. J. HAVIGHURST. Social class and color differences in child-rearing. *Amer. Sociol. Rev.*, 1946, **11**, 698–710.

4. DUVALL, EVELYN M. Conceptions of parenthood. *Amer. J. Sociol.*, 1946, **52**, 193–203.

5. ERICSON, MARTHA. Child-rearing and social status. In T. M. NEWCOMB, E. L. HARTLEY & others (Eds.). *Readings in Social Psychology.* New York: Holt, 1947.

6. FISHER, M. S., L. J. STONE, & J. BACKER. Balloons: demonstration of a projective technique for the study of aggression and destruction in young children. New York: New York Film Library, 1941 (Film).

7. FISCHER, R. A. *Statistical Methods for Research Workers* (6th ed.). Edinburgh: Oliver and Boyd, 1936. Also in A. C. EDWARDS. *Experimental Design in Psychological Research.* New York: Rinehart, 1950. pp. 84–85.

8. FRENKEL-BRUNSWIK, ELSE. Intolerance of ambiguity as an emotional and personality variable. *J. Pers.*, 1949, **18**, 108–143.

9. GESELL, A., & FRANCES ILG. *Infant and Child in the Culture of Today.* New York: Harper, 1943.

10. GESELL, A., & HELEN THOMPSON. Learning and growth in identical infant twins. *Genet. Psychol. Monogr.*, 1929, **6**, 1–124.

11. HARRIS, D. B. Child psychology. *Ann. Rev. Psychol.*, 1953, **4**, 1–30.

12. HUSCHKA, MABEL. The child's response to coercive bowel training. In S. S. TOMKINS (Ed.). *Contemporary Psychopathology.* Cambridge: Harvard Univer. Press, 1947.

13. KLATSKIN, ETHELYN H. Shifts in child care practices in three social classes under an infant care program of flexible methodology. *Amer. J. Orthopsychiat.*, 1952, **22**, 52–61.

14. KOCH, HELEN L. Child psychology. *Ann. Rev. Psychol.*, 1954, **5**, 1–26.

15. LEMBKE, W. Über zeichnungen von "frechen" und "schuchteren" kindern. *Zscht. f. pod. Psychol.*, 1930, **31**, 459–462.

16. MACCOBY, ELEANOR E., PATRICIA K. GIBBS & others. Methods of child-rearing in two social classes. In W. E. Martin & Celia B. Stendler (Eds.). *Readings in Child Development.* New York: Harcourt Brace, 1954.

17. McGRAW, MYRTLE B. Neutral maturation as exemplified in achievement of bladder control. *J. Pediat.*, 1940, **16**, 580–590.

18. NAPOLI, P. J. Finger-painting and personality diagnosis. *Genet. Psychol. Monogr.*, 1946, **34** 129–230.

19. NAUMBERG, MARGARET. Studies of the free art expression of behavior problem children and adolescents as a means of diagnosis and therapy. *Nerv. Ment. Dis. Monogr.*, 1947, **71**, 1–225.

20. ORLANSKY, H. Infant care and personality. *Psychol. Bull.*, 1949, **46**, 1–48.

21. PFISTER, O. Farbe und Bewegung in der Zeichnung Geisteskranker. *Schweiz. Arch. Neurol. Psychiat.*, 1934, **34**, 325–365.

22. PHILIPS, E., & E. STROMBERG. A comparative study of finger-painting performance in detention home and high school pupils. *J. Psychol.*, 1948, **26**, 507–515.

23. PRECKER, J. A. Painting and drawing in personality assessment. *J. Proj. Tech.*, 1950, **14**, 262–286.

24. RIBBLE, MARGARET A. *The Rights of Infants.* New York: Columbia Univer. Press, 1943.

25. SHAW, RUTH F. *Finger-Painting.* Boston: Little, Brown, 1934.

26. SPOCK, B. *Pocket Book of Baby and Child Care.* New York: Pocket Books, 1948.

27. SPOCK, B. *The Common Sense Book of Baby and Child Care.* New York: Duell, Sloan and Pearce, 1946.

28. TRAUBE, T. La valeur diagnostique des dessins des enfants difficiles. *Arch. Psychol.*, 1937, **26**, 285–309.

29. WAEHNER, TRUDE S. Interpretations of spontaneous drawings and paintings. *Genet. Psychol. Monogr.*, 1946, **33**, 1–70.

30. WARNER, W. L., K. MEEKER, and K. EELLS, *Social Class in America.* Chicago: Science Research Associates, 1949.

31. WOLFF, W. *Personality of the Preschool Child.* New York: Grune and Stratton, 1946.

11. The Psychological Interpretation of Children's Drawings

FLORENCE L. GOODENOUGH

An attempt to trace the development of the mental processes which govern the child's first attempts at representative drawing leads us back to the period of very early infancy. The mental life of the new-born child can be little more than an unorganized series of sensations which force themselves upon the developing consciousness with greater or less insistence, according to the intensity of the physical stimulus and the immediate condition of the receiving organism. Little by little, however, certain groups of sensations begin to single themselves out from the others. Vaguely but surely the child begins to differentiate between his mother and other persons with whom he is brought into contact, between familiar and strange surroundings, etc. These first associations and recognitions are perhaps more nearly related to the conditioned reflex than to the conscious reasoning of later life; yet in them we can trace the beginnings of analysis, of differentiation and comparison, which, as will

be shown, are among the basic processes in the type of activity with which we are concerned.

From the recognition of individual objects the child progresses by imperceptible stages to the recognition of classes of objects, and, later on, to the recognition of pictorial representations of objects. Perez[1] and Darwin[2] considered that the time when objects seen in a mirror are clearly recognized as images, and not as the objects themselves (as is shown by the child's turning away from the mirror to look for the source of the reflection), marks one of the earliest stages in the development of the ability to recognize objects in pictures. This development is characterized by an increasing ability to analyze, to abstract certain elements from the total impression made by an object, and

[1]Perez, M. B. L'Art et la Poesie chez l'Enfant. (Paris, 1888).
[2]Darwin, Charles. "A Biographical Sketch of an Infant." *Mind*, Vol. 2 (1901), p. 828–832.

*SOURCE: Reprinted from Florence Goodenough, *Measurement of Intelligence by Drawing*, pp. 67–80. Copyright 1954 by Harcourt Brace and World, Inc., New York.

to reconstruct the whole in terms of those parts which experience has shown to be essential to it. The infant of a few weeks can recognize his mother only through the combined action of a large number of sensory impressions — visual, tactual, auditory, and, it may be, olfactory as well. Little by little he becomes able to substitute a single group of sensations for the total, so that the sight of his mother or the sound of her voice is alone sufficient to awaken the response which was formerly elicited only by actual contact. By a like process of abstraction and substitution, not the less important because it is for the most part unconscious, the child becomes able to dispense with more and more of the usual concomitants of the sensory impression and to replace them by centrally initiated equivalents, so that eventually a small photograph of his mother is sufficient to arouse recognition, in spite of the difference in size, the absence of color, and the changes in ocular accommodation incident to the elimination of the third dimension.

We are accustomed to speak of this type of recognition as "association by similarity." More precisely defined, it is association by the similarity of certain parts of elements, in spite of the dissimilarity of other parts. Many writers on primitive art have called attention to the importance of this factor in the development of representative drawing. A number of instances are extant, especially among the prehistoric rock drawings which have been found in the caves of Southern France, in which advantage has been taken of some natural fissure of discoloration in the rock itself to lessen the labor of drawing or carving — the fissure serving as a partial outline, and the remainder of the drawing being added by the artist. Koch-Grünberg[3] has shown that in certain South American petroglyphs the grooves which have been worn in the rocks by fishing

lines have been used in this way. Similar instances have been found in primitive sculpture, especially in wood carving, where a peculiarly shaped knot or twisted branch frequently appears to have served as the original suggestion for the work.

In the early drawings of very young children a circumstance somewhat analogous to the foregoing has frequently been reported. The child whose work has previously consisted only of random scribbling suddenly sees a resemblance between the incoherent lines obtained by chance and some known object. He tries to complete or to perfect the resemblance, and in this way the first real attempts at graphic expression come into being. It is not necessary to suppose that these associations are entirely spontaneous in all instances. It is probable that in many cases they are directly aroused by the questions or comments of older persons, and it can hardly be doubted that the child's previous acquaintance with pictures is a factor of much importance. It must be remembered, however, that these external circumstances can be effective only in case the mind has developed to a stage at which it can profit by them; otherwise they are comparable to the many "inadequate stimuli" of the physical world, whereof the inadequacy consists, not in the stimuli themselves, but in the nonadaptation of the organism to their reception. While variations in external conditions may retard or accelerate the development of graphic expression to some degree, especially in the first stages, the conditions of modern life are such that few children fail to grasp the idea of pictorial representation because of its unfamiliarity.

An experiment which appears to indicate that "association by similarity" plays an important part even in decorative art is reported by Paulsson.[4] Paulsson is of the

[3]Koch-Grünberg, Theodor. Anfangen der Kunst im Urwald (Berlin, 1905).

[4]Paulsson, Gregor. "The Creative Element in Art." Scandinavian Scientific Review, Vol. 2 (1923), pages 11–173.

opinion that the first impulse toward graphic expression has its origin in the desire for emotional outlet, the pleasure derived from the objectification of emotion. In order to determine the nature of the specific stimulus which serves to direct this impulse toward a particular type of performance two experiments were carried out by Paulsson under carefully controlled conditions. Adult subjects were used in both instances, most of whom were accustomed to psychological experimentation. Several artists were included. In the first experiment, in which nine subjects took part, a series of ten ink blots were exposed, one at a time, for a brief interval. After each exposure the subjects were told to draw from memory what they had seen, and to "make their drawing beautiful." It was found that each interpreted the blots according to his individual interests. A doctor drew one of them as a section of the spinal cord; an art theorist made them into an example of his art theory; etc. But little similarity could be observed between the drawings of the same blot as made by different subjects. In the second experiment, in which fourteen subjects took part, a tachistoscope was used and two hundred ink blots were shown, but the subjects were told that they need draw only as many of them as they liked. Again the instructions were to "make them beautiful." Introspective results showed that in this experiment only those blots were drawn which suggested a meaning of some sort to the observer. In the actual drawing everything was subordinated to this meaning — unrelated elements being minimized or omitted, while other parts, which furnished, as it were, the cue to the idea, were emphasized. From these data Paulsson concludes that it is the meaning which furnishes the aim. "It is the meaning, therefore, that guides the graphic 'structures' in their development from the primitive schematic stages to the highest manifestations of the artistic mind."

Albien,[5] in a somewhat similar experiment in which unfamiliar geometrical figures were used as the stimuli and the subjects were children of from nine to eighteen years of age, obtained much the same results. He decided that directed observation and analysis, followed by apperception and assimilation of many partial elements into a unified whole, are the primary factors in the ability to reproduce the figure. Observation itself is less important than the relationships observed. It would seem that "relationship," as he uses the term, is somewhat analogous to "meaning" as used by Paulsson.

Meumann[6] has given us a very useful summary of the factors which tend to produce inability or defective ability in drawing. He classifies these factors as follows:

1. Analytic observation is lacking, because of either inability to analyze or unwillingness to observe.
2. Visual imagery is defective or transitory.
3. Eye-hand coordination is defective.
4. The imperfection of the actual work interferes with the memory image as the drawing progresses.
5. Related drawing schemes are lacking.
6. There is inability to understand and portray three-dimensional space; inability to escape from the childish idea that all that exists must be shown.
7. Manual skill is defective.

A later study by Meumann[7] analyzes the drawing act from the positive standpoint. He concludes that it is dependent upon three groups of factors, as follows:

[5]Albien, Gustav. "Der Anteil der nachkonstruierenden Tatigkeit des Auges und der Apperception an dem Behalten und der Wiedergabe einfacher Formen." *Zeitschrift für experimentelle Padagogik*, Vol. 5 (1907), pages 133–156, and Vol. 6 (1908), pages 1–48.
[6]Meumann, Ernst. Vorlesungen zur Einfuhrung in die experimentelle Padagogok, Vol. 2 (Leipzig, 1907). (See pages 360–397.)
[7] Meumann, Ernst. "Ein Programm zur psychologische Untersuchung des Zeichnens." *Zeitschrift für padagogeische Psychologie*, Vol. 13 (1912), pages 353–380.

1. Visual activity, as eye movements which underlie appreciation of distance, direction, etc.

2. Activity of eye and hand; accuracy of motor coordination.

3. Apperceptive ideas, involving a strong intellectual element.

Hence, he adds, there must be:

1. Association of eye and hand movements.

2. Association of visual memory and hand movements.

3. Association of these elements and apperceptive factors.

It should be noted that Meumann's experiments were carried on with children of grammar school age and had to do only with drawing from copy or directly from the object itself, followed by work in immediate recall. His analysis, therefore, has only partial application to the present experiment, that of drawing a man without model or copy and with no suggestions apart from those arising spontaneously in the child's mind from the concept which has previously been formed. Under these circumstances the performance is seen to be only indirectly dependent upon visual activity (assuming, of course, reasonable normal visual acuity), the importance of eye-hand coordination is greatly lessened, and the intellectual element becomes the predominating factor in determining the result. As has been said before, drawing of this sort is for little children a language, a form of expression. Art it may be called, but its purpose is not primarily aesthetic; nor is it, in the beginning, a simple matter of the reproduction of a visual image. Repeated experiments have demonstrated the truth of the saying that "the child draws what he knows, not what he sees."

One of the simplest, as well as the most convincing, of these experiments is that carried out by Professor A. B. Clark of Stanford University.[8] Clark had several hundred children draw an apple with a hatpin run

[8]Clark, A. B. "The Child's Attitude toward Perspective Problems," in *Studies in Education* by Barnes, Vol. 1 (1902), pages 283–294.

through it. The hatpin entered the apple on the side turned toward the children, and emerged on the side turned away from them. To none of the children could it be seen as entering or leaving exactly at the edge. When the drawings were examined, however, it was found that the younger children had, in almost all instances, drawn the hatpin extending straight through the apple from side to side and visible throughout its length. Those slightly older had realized that the portion of the hatpin which was within the apple could not be visible, but had paid no attention to its apparent point of entrance. In drawings of this type the pin stopped at the outline of the apple on one side, and began again at a roughly corresponding point on the opposite side. Only in the upper grades was it found that the visual image of the object actually before the children had served any other purpose than that of giving the cue for the idea; given the idea, the nature of the drawing was no longer dependent upon the image immediately present.

Kerschensteiner found no perceptible difference between the memory or, to speak more precisely, the "concept" drawings of little children and those made when a model was placed before them. Children who were accustomed to draw the human figure in full face continued to do so even when the model was placed in the profile position.

It seems evident, then, that an explanation of the psychological functions which underlie the spontaneous drawing of little children must go beyond the fields of simple visual imagery and eye-hand coordination and take account of the higher thought processes. It has been said that the ability to recognize objects in pictures, an ability which must obviously precede any real attempt to represent objects by means of pictures, is dependent upon the ability to form associations by the similarity of certain elements which are common both to the picture and to the object, in spite of the dissimilarity of other elements. Analysis and abstraction are clearly involved, but only the final result is present in consciousness. The three-year-old child who recognizes the photograph of his mother cannot tell you by what means he is able to do so, and even the adult finds such a task difficult. In order to represent objects by means of pictures there must be, however, a conscious analysis of the process, of the intermediate steps by means of which the desired result is to be obtained. It is necessary to select from out of the total impression those elements or features which appear to be characteristic or essential. This analysis must be followed or accompanied by observation of relationships. The relationships to be observed are of two kinds, quantitative and spatial. The former determine the proportion, the latter the position, of the various parts of the drawing with reference to each other. Very great individual differences are found among children with respect to the extent to which these functions keep pace with each other. In general it may be said that the brighter the child, the more closely is his analysis of a figure followed by an appreciation of the relationships prevailing between the elements which are brought out by his analysis. Backward children, on the other hand, are likely to be particularly slow in grasping abstract ideas of this or any other kind. They analyze a figure to some extent, and by this means are able to set down some of its elements in a graphic fashion, but the ability to combine these elements into an organized whole is likely to be defective and in some instances seems to be almost entirely lacking. It is this inability to analyze, to form abstract ideas, to relate facts, that is largely responsible for the bizarre effects so frequently found among the drawings of backward children — the "*Zusammenhangenlosigkeit*" to which Kerschensteiner has called attention.

If we accept the theory that a child's drawing of an object during this early, or, as it has been called, "pre-artistic," period is dependent primarily upon his concept of that object rather than upon immediate visual imagery or artistic appreciation, it becomes possible to explain the fact that the developmental changes which take place in children's drawings do not remain fixed from the time of their first appearance. Instead, any new characteristic usually goes through a longer or shorter period of fluctuation, during which time it is sometimes shown, sometimes not. Only gradually does it become a consistent feature of all the drawings which the child makes. This fluctuation is, however, a necessary accompaniment of any intellectual manifestation which is in reality continuous, but which is measured only in discrete steps. Memory for digits is an example. There is no sudden leap from the stage in which only five digits can be remembered to that in which it is always possible to remember six. On the contrary, it will be found that the person who can always, or practically always, remember five digits after a single reading will occasionally be able to remember six, or, more rarely, even as many as seven. The same principle holds good in children's drawings. The progress from the simple concepts which govern the crude productions of the four-year-old, to the comparatively complex and highly developed ideas of the ten-year-old, is indicated in the drawings by a series of rather marked changes. At first these changes appear only sporadically; later on they tend to become fixed. When a child, whose drawing of the human figure has consisted only of head, legs, and trunk, first begins to add the arms, he does not do so invariably. As his concept develops, however, the arms tend more and more to become an essential part of it, with the consequence that they are shown more and more frequently until a period is reached when the child no longer regards his drawing as complete without them. It may thus be said that at any given time a child's drawing will consist of two parts — the first part embracing those characteristics which have already become an integral part of his concept of the object drawn, and consequently appear invariably; the second part including the elements which are in process of becoming integrated and are therefore shown with more or less irregularity. The frequency with which any given characteristic tends to appear is a function of the extent to which it has become integrated into the developing concept, and a measure of the weight which should be given to it as an index of concept development.

The "frequent retrogressions to an inferior stage" which Rouma finds characteristic of the drawings of backward children are easily explained if we assume that the integration of the various elements into the total concept takes place at a less rapid rate with backward than with normal children. A similar explanation would account for the qualitative differences found in drawings made by children in special classes for defectives, which Burt[9] has described in the following paragraph:

Compared with drawings from ordinary schools, those obtained in the special schools resemble the work of children from two to three years younger. . . . There are, however, in the drawings of defectives special differences in kind and character, as well as a general deficiency in degree, so that it is usually possible to distinguish the drawing of an older defective from that of a younger normal child. These differences well deserve study. They may, perhaps, be most briefly epitomized by saying that the drawings of the defective are apt to include inconsistent features, characterizing stages of development which among normals are distinct and even remote.

It is evident that the child does not show in his drawing all the facts which he knows about the object, but only those which to him are so essential or characteristic that they occur to him spontaneously without suggestion from outside sources. A three-year-old child will point to his hair when asked to

do so, but 50 per cent of nine-year-old children are entirely content to draw the human figure without a vestige of hair, although these same children include in their drawings such nonessential features as flashing scarfpins, elaborate hat bands, pipes, canes, etc. The problem which the child has to meet is primarily one of selection, of determining which ones of a vast number of items really furnish the key to the situation. Knowledge of a fact does not in itself guarantee that this fact shall be shown in a drawing; its importance must also have been evaluated. Terman[10] has shown that the majority of seven-year-old children *know* the number of their fingers when the question is put to them; yet only 31 per cent of unselected seven-year-olds show the correct number in their drawings when no suggestion is made. The difference can hardly be due to technical difficulty; at least it is hard to see why it should be any more difficult to draw five fingers than to draw four or six, or, as occurred in the case of one kindergarten child, twenty-nine on one hand and thirty-six on the other! Carelessness, in the sense of lack of appreciation of the importance of details, is undoubtedly one of the factors involved; yet when one notices the care with which some of these drawings have been finished, and the effort which has apparently been expended upon them, it appears evident that carelessness, in the ordinary sense of the term, is not an adequate explanation for the discrepancy in the findings by the two methods. The determining factor appears to be the presence or absence of the definite stimulus, "How many?" In the one instance, that which is measured is the memory of a particular percept; in the other, the integration of that percept into the concept of which it is a part. By referring to Table I (point 10 *b*), it will be seen that as large a proportion of accelerated six-year-olds as of retarded ten-year-olds have been

[9]Burt, Cyril. "Mental and Scholastic Tests." Report of the London County Council, 1921.

[10]Terman, L. M. *The Measurement of Intelligence* (Boston: Houghton Mifflin Company, 1916).

TABLE I

Per Cent Succeeding with Each of the Separate Points in the Scale by Age and School Progress. Original Group.

Age	4		5		6		7		8			9			10	
Key No.	N	A	N	A	N	A	N	R	A	N	R	A	N	R	N	R
1	94	100	99	100	100	100	100	98	100	100	100	100	100	100	100	100
2	85	100	96	100	99	100	100	96	100	100	100	100	100	100	100	100
3	55	80	64	87	83	96	88	80	92	91	81	100	92	91	98	90
4 a	59	100	74	100	87	100	99	92	100	99	98	100	100	98	100	100
4 b	10	20	22	49	33	55	48	42	65	49	51	88	62	57	75	53
4 c	0	0	1	6	2	13	7	2	29	12	7	52	25	10	46	19
5 a	21	70	44	82	66	93	85	73	93	87	79	100	92	89	97	89
5 b	2	30	9	17	12	33	24	14	54	33	23	72	47	28	59	38
6 a	5	40	14	32	26	61	44	26	80	66	39	88	74	57	83	59
6 b	0	0	1	16	6	17	16	7	49	32	17	72	45	24	65	36
7 a	81	100	93	100	98	100	98	96	100	98	98	100	99	98	100	99
7 b	54	100	78	93	90	100	95	93	100	97	96	100	100	97	100	98
7 c	58	90	80	96	90	96	91	91	97	92	90	100	94	91	96	90
7 d	0	0	0	9	2	18	18	0	43	24	7	55	35	30	73	44
7 e	2	0	4	15	3	19	8	5	22	13	3	56	22	10	27	15
8 a	16	0	13	22	16	46	22	21	46	45	25	64	45	35	58	41
8 b	0	0	0	1	0	5	5	0	17	10	5	52	17	5	35	13
9 a	27	90	35	91	75	99	94	78	99	98	92	100	98	98	100	90
9 b	0	20	0	2	2	17	8	2	38	19	9	64	42	19	58	26
9 c	0	0	0	0	0	1	1	0	6	3	0	36	7	0	24	3
9 d	0	0	0	2	0	5	3	0	31	11	6	68	26	10	49	18
9 e	0	0	0	0	0	0	0	0	2	0	0	20	5	0	15	3
10 a	32	60	49	83	69	90	77	72	90	78	75	95	86	79	93	78
10 b	4	10	10	37	19	47	35	16	49	41	29	50	45	36	57	37
10 c	0	0	3	17	7	19	14	6	22	19	13	44	26	16	41	25
10 d	0	0	0	1	1	3	1	0	6	3	0	12	5	2	13	3
10 e	6	20	5	14	12	26	14	6	40	29	12	60	36	22	48	28
11 a	1	10	2	6	5	30	18	5	48	26	14	68	48	26	64	30
11 b	1	20	3	13	8	22	13	7	45	31	17	64	40	26	53	32
12 a	20	40	33	49	38	66	53	37	70	69	49	80	72	63	76	58
12 b	1	20	8	16	13	42	23	14	35	30	22	45	44	29	47	34
12 c	8	50	29	52	39	57	50	38	68	62	49	67	62	52	64	53
12 d	12	70	27	42	42	59	60	49	74	64	55	80	67	65	76	74
12 e	9	60	27	66	50	87	66	51	95	86	68	100	92	84	98	80
13	1	20	4	10	10	36	18	10	45	37	19	64	52	37	66	38
14 a	2	40	18	50	35	70	54	47	91	77	61	100	88	74	93	76
14 b	0	0	0	0	0	0	0	0	3	0	0	8	2	0	9	1
14 c	0	0	0	2	1	9	5	3	25	17	6	56	33	12	44	27
14 d	0	0	0	9	2	16	8	3	46	17	7	48	35	14	48	28
14 e	0	0	1	1	1	1	2	1	17	3	2	20	14	5	23	16
14 f	0	0	0	0	0	0	0	0	2	2	1	56	4	1	23	5
15 a	14	10	10	22	24	39	27	24	40	32	28	40	35	29	36	32
15 b	1	0	1	4	2	13	9	4	31	14	7	36	14	12	28	15
16 a	2	20	9	43	26	57	42	26	63	55	37	72	58	52	68	56
16 b	3	10	7	15	9	24	15	6	40	21	12	80	35	20	37	27
16 c	0	0	1	6	4	8	9	4	25	16	6	60	26	10	33	18
16 d	0	0	0	2	0	2	1	0	3	1	0	12	4	0	7	2
17 a	7	20	18	43	39	54	56	41	74	66	57	90	84	66	90	78
17 b	0	0	0	2	0	7	5	1	18	15	10	30	24	12	31	19
18 a	0	0	0	0	1	12	2	1	14	7	4	28	20	4	28	11
18 b	0	0	0	0	0	1	0	0	1	1	0	12	3	0	10	3

A = Children accelerated in school.   N = Children who have made normal school progress.
R = Children retarded in school.

found to show the correct number of fingers in their drawings of the human figure. This indicates that the ability to evaluate the importance of facts such as the foregoing is one of the elements in determining school success.

It is interesting to compare the above facts with certain unpublished vocabulary data collected by Mr. L. G. Schussman of Stanford University. Mr. Schussman had about one hundred children of the eighth and ninth grades write definitions of a number of words, choosing for this purpose words in such common use as to make it highly unlikely that any of the children would ever have had occasion to look them up in a dictionary. The failure to give proper evaluation to facts which were almost certainly well known was very evident in the nature of the responses received. The word *mother*, for example, was variously defined as "a female," "a parent," "a woman who takes care of her children," etc. It may almost be taken for granted that eighth and ninth grade children know, and if specifically questioned could state, that a mother is not simply a female or a parent, but a female parent. They know that a father is also a parent, and in ordinary conversation they never confuse the two. Nevertheless, they are entirely satisfied with a definition which includes only one, or perhaps neither, of the two essential characteristics of an adequate "mother" concept — parenthood and femaleness. There is a distinct difference between knowledge of facts and appreciation of their relative significance.

Turning again to the specific problem under consideration — that of the child who is given the task of drawing a picture of a man without aid or suggestion — we see that the psychological processes involved may be classified as follows:

1. *Association by similarity.* The child sees a resemblance between a series of lines on paper and the concrete object which is represented by them. This is the preliminary stage, which must precede any active attempt at representation on the part of the child himself.

2. *Analysis into its component parts* of the object to be drawn.

3. *Evaluation of these parts* and selection of those which appear to be essential or characteristic. This process is largely an unconscious one as far as the child is concerned, but it is significant, since it is determined by the nature of his interests and by his fundamental habits of thought.

4. *Analysis of spatial relationships; of relative position.*

5. *Judgments of quantitative relationships; of relative proportion.*

6. Through *further process of abstraction,* reduction and simplification of the several parts into graphic outlines.

7. *Coordination of eye and hand movements* in the drawing act.

8. *Adaptability,* the capacity to adjust the drawing scheme to the new features which are added from time to time as the concept develops.

Considered as a whole, the process is quite analogous to that described by William James in his classic distinction between "reasoning" and "common associative thinking." Of the former he says:

It contains analysis and abstraction. Whereas the merely empirical thinker stares at a fact in its entirety, . . . the reasoner breaks it up and notices one of its separate attributes. This attribute he takes to be the essential part of the whole fact before him. . . . Reasoning may then be very well defined as the substitution of parts and their implications or consequences for wholes. And the art of the reasoner will consist of two stages:

First, *sagacity,* or the ability to discover what part, M, lies embedded in the whole which is before him.

Second, *learning,* or the ability to recall promptly M's consequences, concomitants, or implications.

In a footnote James adds the following:

To be sagacious is to be a good observer. J. S. Mill has a passage which is so much in the spirit of the text that I cannot forbear to quote it.

"The observer is not he who merely sees the thing which is before his eyes, but he who sees what parts that thing is composed of. . . . One person, from inattention or from attending only in the wrong place, overlooks half of what he sees; another sets down much more than he sees, confounding it with what he imagines or with what he infers; another takes notes of the *kind* of all the circumstances, but being inexpert in estimating their degree leaves the *quantity* of each vague and uncertain; another sees, indeed, the whole, but makes such an awkward division of it into parts, throwing things into one mass which require to be separated, and separating things which might more conveniently have been considered as one, that the result is much the same, sometimes even worse, than as if no analysis had been attempted at all."

In the foregoing pages an attempt has been made to point out some of the psychological factors involved in the spontaneous drawing of young children, and to show their relationship to general intellectual development. It is believed that these drawings afford a means for the study of mental growth which is of value both to the practical educator and to the psychologist. The former will find that they throw additional light on the factors which govern school success and failure; the latter will find them useful in the analysis of specific mental functions and in the study of the development of conceptual thinking during early childhood. It is felt that the present experiment, which has dealt chiefly with the intellectual side, has by no means exhausted the possibilities which these drawings possess for the study of child development. On the contrary, it is the writer's opinion that, if properly understood, they would contribute much to our knowledge of child interests and personality traits. It is hoped that the experiment which has been described will point the way to further research into this very fundamental type of childish expression.

12. The Relation of Intelligence to Art Ability

ROBERT C. BURKHART

Introduction

The history of research investigation concerned with intelligence and art ability raises some important questions concerning the present concept of intelligence, as it is represented by the common tests now in use in the grade schools, high schools, and colleges of our nation. These studies have a bearing, because of the research done in the field of art education, on the extent to which tests of intelligence are measuring creativeness.

Early Studies

Practically all the early studies were limited in their measures of intelligence to teachers' estimates of general ability or standing in high school subjects, since intelligence tests had not yet been developed. Those of Kerschensteiner done in 1905 and Kir done in 1909 were of this kind.

Not many years afterwards, several studies appeared which included measures of intelligence by standardized tests. However, these studies did not use any objective method for determining the kind and quality of art ability which existed within the group studied. For instance, both Terman (26) and Manuel (20) used selected groups for their studies which were formed solely upon the basis of recommendations of the students' art teachers. Terman employed 15 pupils with "special ability" and Manuel 19 "talented subjects" in their respective researches. It would seem that they employed too small a sample also to support any strong generalizations on this topic.

Objectivity of Measures in Studies after 1925

After the year 1925, a number of important researches were done with larger popu-

*SOURCE: Reprinted from *The Journal of Aesthetics and Art Criticism*, XVII, 2 (December 1958), pp. 230–41. This article is derived in part from an unpublished doctoral dissertation done by Burkhart at Penn State University entitled "An Analysis of Individuality of Art Expression at the Senior High School Level."

lations, and the measures of intelligence and art ability employed appear to be, in so far as it is possible, of an objective nature. The intelligence tests used were established and standardized measures, and the criteria employed in determing art ability were, for the most part, reasonably objective in character. Methods such as counting the number of items which appear in a drawing were often employed, or in the case of aesthetic criteria, a number of qualified judges were used. The extent to which they agreed, regarding the works judged, helped establish the reliability of the evaluations made. In these researches, criteria were employed as well as trained judges. Carefully prepared visual scales were also employed in some of these studies. For the most part, these studies confined themselves to the elementary grades where the evaluation of the art works could be based upon existing knowledge of the developmental chacteristics of child art.

Studies at the Elememtary Level Using Objective Measures

The researches done at the elementary level have been included here because they have a close relationship to the few studies that have been done at the senior high school level and beyond. These studies are also important because they tend to show the differences in the various factors of creativity which predominate in childhood as contrasted with those which are dominant during and after adolescence.

Probably the best known study done with children's drawings is that of Florence Goodenough(9). Her "Draw a Man" test is still being used. She found close relationship between the conceptual development shown in children's drawings and their general intelligence up to about the age of ten. After this age, there is a sharp decrease in this relationship. She felt the drawings appeared to take on characteristics of special ability in adolescence in which aesthetic considerations

might be thought of as becoming increasingly of more importance (9, pp. 33–34). Her analysis of the characteristics or factors which lead to a high score on her test is of particular interest as it reveals that her test is probably mainly a measure of the child's powers of observation and memory for detail. She states (9, p. 53):

Examination of drawings which make unusually high scores on the test leads to the opinion that keener powers of analytic observation, coupled with a good memory for details, are the more potent factors in producing high scores than is artistic ability in the ordinary sense of the term.

It has not been sufficiently emphasized that one of Goodenough's important findings in support of the reliability and validity of her intelligence test is that this test is not a measure of art ability. This is stated with some clarity in her conclusion. She states in this connection that (9, p. 82):

The correlation with teachers' judgements of art ability was found to be .444 within the first three grades, but in grades above the third, the correlations with teachers' judgements was too low to be significant.

This is very significant in that later findings tended to show very low correlations of intelligence with art ability after the third grade level. In order to emphasize this point for all ages, Goodenough (9, p. 82) also states in her conclusions that, "Art ability is a negligible factor at these ages as far as influencing the score is concerned."

An important study which followed that of Goodenough was done by Tiebout and Meier in 1936. They used a sample of a hundred children in each grade from the first through the seventh in their research. Each subject made three paintings to be judged on the basis of aesthetic quality achieved. The judgments were made upon the carefully prepared visual scale development by Tiebout. They found zero correlations between art ability and intelligence after the third grade. Tiebout and Meier (28, p. 108) conclude:

Thus while a close relationship does not exist between ability to achieve aesthetic quality in compositions and general intelligence, as is the case with drawings used as a general means of expression at the younger ages, there is a tendency toward some relationship in the lower grades in contrast to the upper where the correlations are approximately zero.

Bird's (3) study done about the same time tends to confirm these findings as he finds a drop from .510 to .140 in the correlations with intelligence made on the Dearborn group test after the third grade. His drawings were judged on a more representational basis than Tiebout and Meier's, and this may account for a slightly higher correlation which he finds after the third grade. He used three drawings: the first from memory of a cat running after a ball, the second from a model, and the third from memory after the model had been used. These drawings were scored for accuracy of representation and portrayal of action. He states in reference to the findings he made in the early grades that those on the Dearborn test were about half those made with the Goodenough in every case (3.81). Apparently no greater relationship to general intelligence exists for ability in representational drawings as analyzed by Bird than exists for achievement in aesthetic quality as it is determined by Tiebout and Meier.

Some clarity is given to these findings by the studies of Hurlock and Thomson(13) done about the same time. Their research is of particular importance in that they analyzed the drawings in regard to specific kinds of characteristics and ran correlations between each of these characteristics. They studied 2,292 drawings produced by children from four schools. Their drawings were obtained from the kindergartens, the first and second grades. These are the grades in which the very high correlations are found by Goodenough and in which lower, but

significant, correlations were found by Tiebout, Meier, and Bird. The specific value of their findings is that they tend to clarify what specific factors are contributing, and are not contributing, to the significant correlations made in these studies. The first group of their conclusions to be discussed is closely related to the findings of Goodenough and tends to explain their significance as she does in terms of accuracy of observation and memory for detail. Hurlock and Thomson conclude (13):

The tendency to perceive the specific rather than the general increased with age.
The tendency to perceive details increases with age and to a lesser degree with intelligence.
The accuracy of perception increases with age and to a lesser degree with intelligence.
Between the ages of four and a half and eight and a half years inclusive, the ability for accurate and detailed perceptions shows a more constant relationship to chronological age than to intelligence.

This suggests that what Goodenough has tapped is a mainly developmental factor which is related to the changes which take place in the child's perceptual activities. This would tend to account somewhat for the fact that Goodenough finds that art ability is a "negligible factor" in determining the scores on her tests, for the qualitative differences in children's art abilities cannot be determined by developmental characteristics. For instance, that a base line appears at a certain age for most children is a developmental fact. Certainly, no qualitative distinction in regard to children's art can be made, at an age at which it is normal for a base line to appear, between drawings on the basis that they include the base line. The same distinction holds with regard to the increased accuracy and tendency to perceive the specific rather than the general at these age levels. However, this only becomes apparent when a norm is established for the number of details that appear at a given age level. The fact that fewer or more details appear for a particular child at that age level indicates that that child is either advanced or behind his general age group. Still, developmental characteristics are so closely related to general intelligence at early ages that it is difficult to distinguish between them.

Hurlock and Thomson made other findings which tended to explain the lower correlations which Tiebout, Meier, and Bird made at these ages as compared with Goodenough's, which were almost double those reported by these investigators (9, p. 137). Hurlock and Thomson state, "The tendency to perceive associated objects and design increases with age, but shows little relationship to intelligence." They conclude that in general, "The ability to give artistic expression through drawing shows little relationship to age or intelligence."

In this respect, they confirm Goodenough's belief that at these levels, art ability is a "negligible factor" in determining the relationship between intelligence and the "Draw a Man" test. This suggests that developmental changes account for the relationship of the "Draw a Man" test to intelligence tests.

This tends to explain the reason why low positive correlations are sometimes found as high as the fifth grade and occasionally beyond in studies such as McVitty's. McVitty found a correlation of .396 (22, p. 72). McVitty employed both developmental and aesthetic criteria in the judgment of art works, and his correlation may be accounted for on the basis of developmental differences alone as Goodenough gets a correlation with her criteria at this level of .728 (9, p. 20) and at age ten of .849. It would be well if in the future developmental criteria were kept separate from aesthetic criteria so that the relationship of intelligence to each of these factors could be determined with greater accuracy.

The studies at this level are summed up well by Lewerenz (19) who conducted a very comprehensive study concerning the relation of measures of art ability and intelligence. The research extends from the third grade through the twelfth using criteria for judgment which were largely aesthetic. He employed 939 pupils in this research as a means of evaluating his *Tests in the Fundamental Abilities in Visual Arts*. He found a correlation of .155, which is clearly not significant, between art ability and general intelligence on these measures. His conclusion is very interesting in that it is a good summation of the findings made beyond the third grade level from 1928, which was the year in which he completed his study, to the present day. He states (19, p. 490).

It is probably true that anyone who succeeds exceptionally well in art will also rank rather high on an intelligence test. However, a high intelligence score does not bring necessarily a corresponding ability in art. The fact is that there are a great number of people whose intelligence quotients range from 85 on up who have equal chances for achieving moderate success in art work. It may be said, therefore, that predicting the success of students in an art class on the basis of intelligence quotients alone probably would yield results little better than a random guess.

Studies at the Senior High School Level

Perhaps the most extensive study done at the senior high school level in the 1930's was by Tiebout and Meier (28). In conjunction with their study at the elementary level, for which Tiebout was mainly responsible, Meier conducted the first careful study at the senior high school level. The subjects were derived from a list made up by the art supervisors and art teachers in the high schools in Milwaukee, Wisconsin (28, p. 95). They were divided into two groups, those designated as outstanding or unusual and those regarded as less outstanding but superior. The intelligence test results gave an average IQ on the Kuhlman-Anderson Series of 109.35 in the case of the twenty-four starred or unusual subjects, and of 107.3 for the remaining subjects. These data show that the artistiçally superior tend to be somewhat superior in intelligence. Meier states that the group average falls at the upper limit of average IQ according to the classifications given by Terman. Yet he concluded (28, p. 111):

Rank and intelligence apparently give little indication of the degree of artistic superiority since the starred subjects have only a slightly higher average IQ than the remainder of the group. Within this group of starred subjects, also, the subject indicated as most outstanding had an IQ of 101 on the Kuhlman-Anderson and of 105 on the Stanford series. On the basis of their IQ's one of the group of twenty-four outstanding students would be included in Terman's classification of dull; ten, average; eight, superior; and five, very superior. While there is a slight preponderance of these subjects in the superior and very superior groups, it is obvious that an average IQ does not preclude the possibility of successful artistic performance at the high school level.

The major shortcoming of Meier's study is, of course, that he used a group which was determined on the basis of teacher recommendations, rather than on the basis of criteria judgments.

Winslow (33) to some extent in his study avoids this problem by using a revised version of the Kline-Carey scale and a special method for evaluating the drawings of ninth graders by compositional arrangement. In studying the relationship of the twenty ranked highest according to their drawings, as compared with the other students included in this study, he concludes (33, p. 306):

When all the drawings had been rated and the scores tabulated, the marked superiority of the artistically superior group over the group of pupils of equal intelligence was at once apparent. It was surprising, however, to see how closely the scores of the later group compared with those of pupils who made the poorest drawings. This would seem to indicate that individuals of approximately the same general intelligence are capable of making drawings of varying degrees of artistic excellence, the superior group in art being superior because of certain factors peculiar to art ability.

His superior group had an IQ of 105.5 and the twenty lowest students in drawing ability had an IQ of 103.5. However, Winslow did not correlate the IQ and drawing scores in his study.

If Meier's and Winslow's study and the other studies done in the upper grades were to have a predictive value, we might expect to find that the outstanding students in art ability found in other researches would have an average IQ of between 105.5 and 109. We would expect that there would be a low correlation found between intelligence and art ability. We might predict that the correlation found would be close to zero, according to their conclusions and those made by other investigators in the upper grades such as Bird, Tiebout, and Lewerenz.

One hundred and nineteen students were employed in a recent study by Brittain (4). This includes those used in the cross-validation. This is a somewhat larger sample than those employed by Meier or Winslow.

TABLE I

Correlation with IQ .064 or No Correlation with Criterion Judgment

N	Group	Means for IQ	Standard Deviation for IQ
17	Outs.	107.41	11.05
42	Aver.	105.28	11.90
21	Low	106.29	11.06
21	Low	106.29	11.06
80	Total	106.00	11.64

The measure for individuality of art expression at the senior high school level that was developed consisted of ten verbal criteria; these criteria carefully evolved during four revisions and trial runs. Using these criteria, five expert judges scored the works of 80 high school students from grades 9 through 12 over a 27-week period. Eighteen sample pictures were then selected by score according to standings from the total range of scores. These were then ranked by 29 art educators on a preference basis. The art educator's preference ranking of the works correlated .89 (significant at the .01 level) with the judgment of the works by the verbal criteria. This acted to establish the lower bound for reliability of this judgment which can be no less than its correlation with another independent measure.

When the IQ scores were correlated with those for the criterion judgment, the result was a .064 correlation which is interpreted as showing no correlation. This means that IQ as measured by Otis tests had no relationship to achievement in art as judged in this study, and the examination of the mean scores on the IQ tests for the three groups shows them to be only one point apart (note Table I). The mean for the total group is 106 and the greatest difference from this score is represented by the mean IQ of the outstanding group which is 107.4. The standard deviation for these scores for the total group is 11.64. All the groups have a standard deviation of around 11.0 points which means that 68 per cent of the IQ scores in these groups varied from the mean as much as 11 points, this indicating that there was some real range within the IQ scores of the members of each of these groups.

Since a correlation is usually found between academic average and intelligence at the high school level, such a correlation was run between these two measures for the students in this group to determine if they were in any way an atypical high school population in regard to their academic achievements in general. This correlation was .530 which is significant at the .01 level and, therefore, this group should be considered quite usual in regard to the relation of their academic work to their intelligence quotients.

In order to check further the findings made in this study regarding the relationship of IQ and art achievement, a cross-validation was made using the scores from another research in this same area. Willard,

a graduate student, had recently completed a study at Penn State in which he used the works of 37 students. He had them judged as they were judged for this study; and fortunately, he also had their IQ's measured with the Otis test. The mean score of the group was 100.2 and the standard deviation 10.7. Since both measuring devices were exactly the same as those in the present study, a correlation was made and found to be .067 which is almost exactly the figure reported in this study. The importance of this finding is that it rules IQ out as being a factor in determining individuality of art expression for the students used in these researches. Achievement in art is evidently then the result of intelligence factors other than those measured by standardized tests. It may be that some kind of intelligence not measured by the usual group IQ test is involved in creative performance.

Studies beyond the High School Level with Findings of Special Value for Further Investigations

Introduction

Two studies have been done in which special attention has been paid to aspects of this subject not treated extensively in the studies which have been discussed. The findings made are suggestive ones which have important implications and which appear to justify further investigation.

Woods: The Role of Language Handicap in the Development of Artistic Interest

Woods (35) had several concepts of importance which he investigated by studying with some care a hundred young male veterans for whom he was a special counselor. He believed that "art is a space-relations language" and wanted to determine if "artistic interest is often developed as a result of deficiency in the use of other symbols" (35,

p. 240). The results would give the impression that artistic interest is marked by a low academic intelligence (35, p. 242). To arrive at this conclusion he used the art interest test from the Kuder Battery and the Army Alpha test of intelligence.

Evidence presented in this study indicates that a negative correlation exists between artistic interest and academic accomplishments measured in terms of school grade completed and ability in the Army Alpha test. The data also tends to indicate that a negative correlation exists between artistic interest and verbal and computational interests, due to an initial handicap in the use of English.

Of course, he is measuring art interest and not art ability and it may be argued that he deals with a special population. However, Meier and Tiebout found indications of the same thing at both the elementary and high school levels. They conclude, "In the light of the oft-expressed opinion that the artist is

FIGURE 12.1

The Relation of Factors in Creativity to Those Found in the Block Design Test

Guilford	*Brittain*	*Kohs* *Factor Analysis of Kohs Block Design* *Test*
1. Fluency Rapid production of word meeting specific requirements	Fluency	Mental Productiveness "Fluency of expression and speed of operation" on "speed and number of ideas which come to mind that pertain to the problem" (found by Corter)
2. Flexibility "In easily changed set"	Flexibility Definition the same as Guilford	Flexibility "The ability to change set" (found by Corter)
3. Analysis "Redefinition of organized works"	Ability to Abstract	Analytic Function (Found by Kohs and Armitage)
4. Synthesis Ability (Organizing ideas into large more inclusive patterns)	Closure	Synthetic Functions (Found by Kohs and Armitage)
5. Sensitivity to Problems	(Same as Guilford)	Conceptual Ability "The ability to grasp the essential similarity between variables, to abstract them and to generalize them" (found by Corter)
6. Redefinition	Ability to Rearrange	Changing Gestalts "The manipulation of two configurations simultaneously or in succession" (found by Thurstone)
7. Originality	Originality	(Not found as a factor)
8. Penetration	(Not found as a factor)	(Not found as a factor)
9. (Not found as a factor)	Intuition	(Not found as a factor)
10. (Not found as a factor)	(Not found as a factor)	Spatial Factor Very high — maybe related to art ability (found by Thurstone, Armitage and Corter)

visually rather than verbally minded, it is interesting to note that the vocabulary test was more often failed at both levels than any other test" (28, p. 119). This may be one possible explanation of the way art ability does not apparently correlate with general intelligence.

deWit: The Block Design Test and Art Ability

In his study deWit (7) used the Kohs Block Design to predict the art ability of 63 education students at the college level in introductory courses in art education. This is of particular interest as the Block Design Test has been found to have a strong "space factor" in factor analyses run independently by Kohs (16), Armitage (2), Thurstone (30), and Corter (6). The study is of additional interest because its findings vary somewhat from those made in previous studies. The difference, however, is mainly that deWit found what appears to be a somewhat reliable measure of art ability. His findings are very close to all previous findings in regard to the relationship of art ability to intelligence as he reports a correlation coefficient of .097 (7, p. 23) which is clearly not significant. However, he found a correlation coefficient of .606 between the Block Design Test and drawing ability (7, p. 23).

The Kohs (16) Block Design Test has a number of factors other than the spatial one which have been analyzed by means of factor analysis. Kohs himself found two fundamental factors, a synthetic factor and an analytic factor.

Armitage (2) also found synthetic and analytical factors on the Block Test. Thurstone (30) found a CG factor which he calls "Changing Gestalts." He defined this factor as the "manipulation of two configurations simultaneously or in succession."

Corter (6) found several other factors including those found by other investigators. The first (6, p. 65) and most important, he names "mental productiveness," which he defines as "speed of operation and fluency of

expression," or "speed and number of ideas which come to one's mind that pertain to the problem" (6, p. 65). He also finds a factor which he calls "flexibility" which he defines as "the ability to change one's mental set" (6, p. 57). In addition to this he finds a factor which he names "conceptual ability," "the ability to grasp essential similarity between discrete variables, to abstract them and generalize them."

These factors are of particular interest to those in art education. Guilford's (11) study of creative ability in science and Brittain's (4) art education show the presence of eight factors, some of which appear very similar to some found in Kohs Block Design Test.

The common factors found by Guilford and Brittain which have been demonstrated by factor analysis to be present in the Block Design Test are shown on Table I.

These findings are of further importance because the Kohs Block Design Test has been shown to correlate .714 with the Wechsler-Bellevue (32) test of intelligence. This indicates that the test itself is a good measure of intelligence for a representative population. The factors in it are apparently related to general intelligence. Still, deWit's study shows the Kohs Block Design Test is not a good predictor of the intelligence quotient of people with art ability. The reason is apparently that the people with art ability score much higher on this test than the other students with equivalent intelligence. It is just this that suggests that the Kohs Block Design Test is a good predictor of art ability. However, it is just this that evidently makes it a poor predictor of intelligence for those with art ability. They evidently did not score as high on the other tests included in the total pattern used to measure their intelligence. If they had, the correlations found between intelligence and art ability would have been high and positive rather than near zero.

This suggests that people with art ability have a higher than average level of intelligence in a particular area where the spatial factor is high. This is indicated by the analysis of the Block Design Test. Moreover, on this test a number of other factors have been found that have been demonstrated to be characteristic of creative ability. These implications suggest the need for further extensive researches at all levels using the Kohs Block Design Test so that deWit's findings can be rejected or supported, confirmed, and extended. Further studies should employ some measures of verbal ability also, so as to determine if verbal deficiencies relate to art achievement.

Summary and Interpretation of Findings

In summary, intelligence tests are not good predictors of art ability beyond the third grade level. The correlations found beyond the third grade level were not significant. Groups of students with high art ability usually have a mean IQ which is slightly above average. Highly significant correlations were usually found from kindergarten through the third grade in most investigations. In early investigations, an important factor which did correlate significantly with intelligence but not art ability was found by Goodenough. High scores on her tests showed good memory for detail and observational accuracy. Hurlock and Thomson found that an increase in awareness of detail and accuracy of perception took place between the ages of four and a half to eight and a half. Their study showed that this increase correlated more highly with chronological age than intelligence. This suggests that the increases in accuracy of perception and awareness of details of these ages is a developmental tendency which reaches its maximum, and then levels off about the age of ten. The presence of aesthetic factors in paintings and drawings shows an increase with age but shows little relationship to intelligence even at the first and second grade levels, accord-

ing to Hurlock and Thomson. In general, aesthetic factors are not related to intelligence beyond the third grade level.

Two relatively distinct factors have then been found to be functioning with different strengths during childhood and adolescence. The first seems to be a developmental one which involves accuracy of perception and memory for detail, and has no apparent relationship to art ability after the third grade level. The second is a factor which involves aesthetic elements, such as composition and design, manner of handling, originality of ideas, and personal involvement.

An explanation of why significant correlations are found up to the third grade level and not beyond may be supplied by Jones's (14) and Thurstone's factor analysis of intelligence tests. Their studies have established the hypothesis that intelligence becomes more differentiated as age increases. Jones (14) did a factor analysis of the 1937 Stanford-Binet at ages 7, 9, 11, and 13. He concluded that his group factors become more clearly defined and distinct, one from the other, at higher age levels. Thurstone, using 1,154 eighth grade children and a battery of 60 tests, isolated six factors which he considered primary. These factors appeared to function independently, and he describes them as being number, word fluency, verbal, memory, induction, and spatial. He, Armitage, and Corter found the "spatial" factor to be very high on the Kohs Block Test, which supports Woods's belief that art is a "space-relations language." Apparently, in the early grades the different factors function together more or less as a total unit. This would account for the correlations found with art ability. This correlation would tend to decrease as these apparently separate factors become more distinct and differentiated from each other according to their functions.

Separating the developmental factors from the aesthetic factors helps provide an explanation of the changes in the art activity which occur between childhood and adolescence. Developmental considerations clearly predominate in the early grades and are essential to any evaluation of the art of the child. In the upper grades aesthetic considerations become increasingly important because developmental tendencies diminish in their importance. However, aesthetic considerations are important at all levels. Apparently the quality of adolescent art is dependent in a large degree upon the student's ability to take into conscious consideration aesthetic concerns while he works. The aesthetic concerns of the child are not conscious; they may need to be for adolescence. The creative task of the adolescent seems then more conscious and less instinctive than that of the child.

These conclusions result in certain questions of importance in this research area. First, are standard measures of adaptability or capacity to succeed in school correlated with the kind of spontaneous flexibility and sensitivity which are intrinsic to art expression? In particular, this research raises doubts about the relatedness of measures such as academic achievement and IQ to measures of creative expression. According to this study these measurings are not measuring creative ability. In this respect it may be that the generalized concept of intelligence and creativity fits children better while a concept involving specific factors and instances of intelligence and creativity is better suited toward the adult level, especially in regard to individuality of art expression in the senior high school. It might also be suggested that intelligence tests, by and large, have not considered factors related to creativity as of any importance to their assessment of intellect.

REFERENCES

1. ALSCHULER, ROSE H., and LA BERTA WEISS HATTWICK, *Painting and Personality.* Vol. I. Chicago: University of Chicago Press, 1947.

2. ARMITAGE, S., "An Analysis of Certain Psychological Tests Used for Evaluation of Brain Injury," *Psychol. Monogr.*, 1946, **60**, No. 1, 30, 1–48.

3. BIRD, MiHon HAWKINS, "A Study in Aesthetics," *Harvard Monogr. in Education*, 1932, 1.00, **11**, 370–426.

4. BRITTAIN, WILLIAM L., *Experiments for a Possible Test to determine Some Aspects of Creativity in the Visual Arts.* Unpublished doctoral dissertation, The Pennsylvania State College, 1952.

5. BROOKS, F. D., "The Relative Accuracy of Ratings Assigned With and Without Use of Drawing Scales," *School and Soc.*, 1928, **27**, 518–520.

6. CORTER, HAROLD M., *A Factor Analysis of Some Individually Administered Reasoning Tests.* Unpublished Ph.D. dissertation, The Pennsylvania State College, 1949.

7. DEWIT, FRED, *The Block Design Test and Drawing Ability.* Unpublished M.A. dissertation, The Pennsylvania State College, 1951.

8. ELKISH, PAULA, "Children's Drawings in a Projective Technique," *Psychol. Monogr.*, 1945, **58**, No. 1, 1–31.

9. GOODENOUGH, FLORENCE L., *Measurement of Intelligence by Drawings.* New York: World Book Co., 1926.

10. GOUGH, HARRISON, "Mentioned in review by W. W. Putney," *Characteristics of Creative Drawings of Stutterers.* Unpublished Ph.D. dissertation, 1955, 51–80.

11. GUILFORD, J. P., *A Factor Analytic Study of Creative Thinking.* California: The University of Southern California Press, July 1952.

12. GUILFORD, JOY PAUL, "The Nature of Creativity," *Research Bulletin Eastern Arts Association*, 1954.

13. HURLOCK, ELIZABETH BERGNER, and J. L. THOMSON, "Children's Drawings: An Experimental Study of Perception," *Child Development*, 1934, **5**, No. 2, 127–138.

14. JONES, LYLE V., "A Factor Analysis of the Stanford-Binet at Four Age Levels," *Psychometrika*, 1949, **14**, No. 4.

15. KLINE, L. W., and C. L. CAREY, *A Measuring Scale for Free Hand Drawings.* Baltimore: The Johns Hopkins Press, 1922.

16. KOHS, SAMUEL CALMIN, *Intelligence Measurement.* New York: The Macmillan Co., 1923.

17. LANSING, K. M., *The Effect of Class Size and*

Room Size Upon the Creative Drawings of Fifth Grade Children. Unpublished doctoral dissertation, The Pennsylvania State University, 1956.

18. LOWENFELD, VIKTOR, *Creative and Mental Growth.* New York: The Macmillan Co., 1952.

19. LEWERENZ, ALFRED S., "IQ and Ability in Art," *School and Society,* 1928, **27,** 489–90.

20. MANUEL, HERSHEL THURMAN, *Talent in Drawing.* Bloomington, Illinois: Pub. Sch. Pub. Co., 1919.

21. MATTIL, EDWARD L., *A Study to Determine the Relationship Between the Creative Products of Children, Age 11 to 14, and their Adjustment.* Unpublished doctoral dissertation, The Pennsylvania State University, 1953.

22. McVITTY, LAWRENCE, *An Experimental Study on Various Methods in Art Motivation at the Fifth Grade Level.* Unpublished doctoral dissertation, The Pennsylvania State University, 1954.

23. MORGAN, JOHN J., *Child Psychology* (Revised Edition). New York: Farrar and Rinehart, 1937.

24. NAUMBURG, MARGARET, *Studies of the "Free" Art Expression of Behavior Problem Children and Adolescents as a Means of Diagnosis and Therapy.* New York: Coolidge Foundation, Publishers, 1946.

25. ROGERS, MARY JUNE, *An Attempt to Find Drawing Criteria Specific to the Junior High School Level.* Unpublished master's thesis, 1955.

26. TERMAN, LEWIS MADISON, *et al.*, "Genetic Studies of Genius," Vol. I. *Mental and Physical Traits of a Thousand Gifted Children.* Stanford University Press, 1925, P. 37.

27. TIEBOUT, C. E., "The Measurement of Quality in Children's Paintings by the Scale Method," *Psychol. Monogr.,* 1936–37, **48,** pp. 85–94.

28. TIEBOUT, C. E., and MEIER, N. C., "Artistic Ability and General Intelligence," *Psychol. Monogr.,* 1936–37, **48,** pp. 95–125 (review of studies of intelligence before 1925).

29. THORNDIKE, EDWARD L., "The Measurement of Achievement in Drawing," *Teachers College Record,* 1913, **14,** No. 5, 1–38.

30. THURSTONE, LOUIS LEON, *Factorial Study of Perception.* Chicago: The University of Chicago Press, 1944.

31. WACHNER, TRUDE S., "Formal Criteria for the Analysis of Children's Drawings," *American Journal of Orthopsychiatry,* 1942, **12,** No. 1, 95–103.

32. WECHSLER, DAVID, *The Measurement of Adult Intelligence.* Baltimore: The Williams & Wilkins Co., 1944.

33. WINSLOW, LEON LOYAL, *The Integrated School Art Program.* New York and London: McGraw-Hill Book Co., Inc., 1939.

34. WOODRUFF, A. D., *The Psychology of Teaching.* New York: Longman Green and Co., Inc., 1946.

35. WOODS, WALTER A., "The Role of Language Handicap in the Development of Artistic Interest," *Jour. of Consulting Psychol.,* 1948, **12,** 240–245.

13. Children's Art Abilities: Studies at the Cleveland Museum of Art

THOMAS MUNRO

The Aims and Educational Background of the Studies

In a large democracy, it is an urgent problem to select potential leaders in and through the educational process. Mass production, standardization, and leveling constantly threaten to dominate. In art, as in other fields, high grades and promotions, awards and scholarship aids are to be administered. Democracy calls for the giving out of such inducements to the genuinely deserving, the potential leaders, from whatever economic, geographic, or racial group they may come.

But how can we discover the really talented, promising students in art, if possible, at an early age? In most other subjects, ability is more easily recognizable and to some extent measurable, especially when it can be manifested through correct inference or fact-finding, or (as in engineering) by tasks in which the standards of successful performance are clear and accepted. The standards of successful performance and creation in visual art are still obscured by

wide disagreement among artist and critics. The standards of mature artistic value being themselves highly debatable, how can we measure the creative or appreciative performance of children?

Several alleged tests and measures of art ability in production and judgment have been available for several years, but none has been accorded general acceptance by artists or educators. Still the idea remains tempting — of a test or scale on the order of the Binet and later tests of intelligence, aptitude, or probable learning rate, which would deal with ability in the visual arts. Combined with tests of musical and other types of art ability, it might even yield a measure of *aesthetic age*, comparable to "mental age," and a numerical quotient in relation to chronological age.

No such goal was attained by the Cleveland studies, or even sought as a practicable end in view. The resources of the program were far too limited, and the theoretical difficulties too clearly recognized. A few groping steps in that direction were made.

*SOURCE: Reprinted from Thomas Munro, *Art Education: Its Philosophy and Psychology*, pp. 209–36. Copyright 1956, by The Liberal Arts Press, New York.

All the workers were clearly aware of the paramount danger in constructing an art ability test, and studious in trying to avoid it: namely, the danger of assuming in advance that one knows what good art is (or asking a group of supposed experts who claim to know), and then measuring students' ability in terms of approximation to that supposed norm.

Yet, while the difficulties in the way of a standardized test were obvious, another fact was equally so. Art education as an actual process made some sort of evaluation necessary. This had to be done and was being done in thousands of schools, in order that the machinery of promotion and graduation, prize-giving and job-giving might go on. At this end, one might say, "the subjective judgment" of teachers held sway; a process of arbitrary grading with undefined or vaguely defined unsupported standards. At the other end lay the unattainable vision of a purely objective, scientific instrument for exact evaluation of work and measurement of ability. Was not an intermediate, transitional stage possible — some procedure a little more systematic than the ordinary ones, more clearly thought out in its criteria, more informed about the facts of art and of child development, more intelligent in its adaptation to new educational objectives? Would not this be of value to teachers, even though no claims were made to have jumped at one bound to the heights of scientific precision?

A few years ago, it was felt by many educators that the secondary school level had lagged somewhat behind the lower ones in adapting its methods and content to the psychological needs of students. The growing influence on youth of radio, periodicals, screen and stage was being discussed, and that of the art museum as an educational agency. Teachers were asking, for example, how museum visits and loan exhibits could be most profitably fitted into school work in art and other subjects; whether, for example,

the study of old masters in art could be made conducive to original creativeness rather than to imitation. A museum which had some contact with students of secondary age thus seemed to be one promising place to study the evaluation of art ability and performance. The secondary level was to be emphasized, but not exclusively, since it might be illuminated by comparison with the earlier ones. The inquiry was not limited to any single problem, such as testing, but was open to any way of throwing light on children's art and art abilities.

Conditions Under Which the Studies Were Conducted

At no single place, or type of institution, can all aspects of children's art be effectively observed; different ones have peculiar advantages and disadvantages. An art museum has some of each which the ordinary school does not possess. The Cleveland Museum of Art was considered especially favorable as a place for study, because of the unusual extent to which it had emphasized and developed educational work with children. Children unaccompanied by adults had been given free access to all galleries, with permission to draw, and free drawing materials. In well-lighted studios, water color, ink, and modeling clay could be used. Thousands of students, from nursery school through university and art academy, flocked to its classes. School teachers brought their own classes during the week, to derive illustrative material for their work in art, history, and many other subjects. On Saturdays, several hundred children came to draw, paint, model, listen to music and stories, hear illustrated talks, and watch plays, moving pictures, and marionette shows. Some of them attended special classes for children of members; others attended open classes, free to all, and still others attended free classes for those believed to have special talent in art. The racial backgrounds of the children were extremely diverse. For all, cultural development rather than professional training was the principal aim. Classes were graded according to age level, and met on successive Saturdays in various parts of the museum, so as to permit a varied round of activities. In many of them, an attempt was made to interrelate work in visual arts with that in music; and in all, to combine appreciation with creative production. Exact, unimaginative copying from nature or from other works of art was not encouraged, but students could use museum objects as materials and suggestions for adaptive modification. It was not assumed that such an approach to art was necessarily better than completely "free expression," apart from other art; but it was felt that such an approach was the peculiar opportunity of the art museum for experiment, with its wealth of art objects beyond the reach of most schools.

On the other hand, the museum was comparatively limited in its contact with individual students. A child came, perhaps, each Saturday morning for a season of twenty-five weeks. (Some attended a year-round class which met outdoors in summer.) Those who came during the school week, with outside teachers, could receive little individual attention during their short gallery visits. Attendance was voluntary at the Saturday classes, except in so far as parents exerted mild pressure. A considerable number of children came year after year, but others drifted in and out, "shopping around" among the city's varied week-end activities. Thus there was a fairly large annual turnover, and new students were constantly entering the upper age levels without any previous museum instruction. An easy play spirit had to be maintained, for its own sake and to hold attendance; anything like sustained, enforced hard work ran the risk of making students leave entirely. This militated somewhat against the giving of frequent, formal tests. Although the psycho-

logical staff contrived ingeniously to make them short and pleasant, weaving them into the regular art lesson, and although the teachers and students cooperated surprisingly well, nevertheless the fear of imposing too much on the all-too-brief time for regular work restrained the psychologists from pursuing many experiments up to a theoretically adequate stage. Moreover, age-level groups in the Saturday classes were not evenly distributed, or all large enough to provide sufficient data. The peak load was around eleven years old, although classes extended from six to sixteen; older students, especially boys, were much less numerous.

Another advantage of the Cleveland Museum was the fact that examples of children's drawing had been carefully preserved there over a period of twenty years. The development of several individual students was illustrated from childhood to maturity. Some of these, after going through art school, had become successful professional artists, teachers, and writers.

Out of the need to choose students for the "Special" or Advanced Drawing Class for talented children came the recognition of a problem: could this choice be made more scientifically? It had been made rather informally for years, on the basis of interest shown through coming to the museum and drawing, or through recommendations of school teachers. Each fall for years, such recommended children came for an entrance test, which consisted in making several drawings. Museum teachers picked out the drawings and the children they considered most promising, but wished to improve this arbitrary process, if possible. Also, they wished to learn more about children's development in art — its natural course in normal and supernormal cases, and the best ways of enriching it educationally.

The Cleveland Museum of Art was and is not primarily a research institution. It lacked staff and equipment for conducting psychological experiments. Through a foundation grant, these were secured in modest proportions; but it proved surprisingly difficult to secure properly qualified workers, with some training in art as well as in psychology, especially on the short-time tenure necessitated by terms of the grant. Workers came and went, and the work lacked continuity.

Progress of the Studies

Various art tests were given in the first year to hundreds of school children. Supplementary data cards were filled out for as many of these children as possible, with facts as to school IQ and other tests, school record, home environment, etc. All existing devices for testing art ability in production or appreciation were studied and discussed; and several were given museum classes for comparative purposes. The detailed management of the project was given over to Mrs. Betty Lark-Horovitz, who had had experience in both art instruction and psychological research on children's art in the Vienna schools. Dr. Edward N. Barnhart of the University of California came as research associate.

The Seven Drawings Test

This test was an outgrowth of the regular museum entrance test for the advanced drawing classes. It consisted of seven drawings to be made by the child of different subjects, and was designed to bring out different types of drawing ability — for example, to draw from memory, from imagination, from another picture on view, and from a moving, changing object. One was to show some of the child's interest by allowing him freedom to choose a favorite subject. This test was first given by Mrs. Louise M. Dunn and the author in September, 1933. The children were seated in the museum auditorium, with empty seats between them. They were given identical sets of material: a piece of drawing

board, a box of colored pencils, and a pamphlet of blank sheets of drawing paper, each set being serially numbered and each sheet numbered from one to eight. On the back of the last sheet was printed the following questionnaire, to be filled out:

1. Name
2. Address
3. How old are you?......Date of birth (year) .... (month) .... (day)....
4. School ....Grade....
5. Where were you born?
6. Where was your father born?
7. Your father's occupation..............
   When employed......................
8. Where was your mother born?
9. Are you left-handed?
10. Who has encouraged you to draw or study art?

Standardized instructions were read by the examiner, as follows:

Preliminary Instructions; Repeat as Much as Necessary:

1. "Do not mark on these sheets until you are told to do so."
2. "Has everyone a folder of papers, a cardboard, and a box of colored pencils? If not, raise your hand."
3. "Lay your folder on the cardboard so that the blank page with numbers is on top."
4. "Be careful not to look at anyone else's paper."
5. "Don't use any pencils except the ones you were given."

Questions:

1. *Favorite Subject* (time, ten minutes). "Answer the first question on page one. You can use as much of the page as you like. This is the first question. Make a drawing of whatever you like best to draw. It can be a picture of anything at all. Make a picture of whatever you like best to draw. The time allowed is ten minutes. Begin now." ... "You have one more minute to finish this question."
2. *Drawing of a Man* (time, five minutes). "Now turn to page 2. *On this page draw a picture of a man. It does not matter what kind

of man you draw, what he is doing, or how he is dressed." (Repeat from asterisk.) "You will have five minutes. Now begin." ... "You have one more minute to finish this question."

3. *Memory* (time, twenty minutes). "Now turn to page 3. Shut your eyes a minute. Try to remember how your classroom looks at school." (Short pause.) "Now open your eyes. *Make a picture showing just how your classroom looks while the children and the teacher are there." (Repeat from asterisk.) "You have twenty minutes for this question. Now begin." ... "You have one more minute to finish this question."

4. *Imagination* (time, twenty minutes). "Now turn to page 4. On this page make a picture showing what you would like to do next summer. Shut your eyes again for just a minute. Try to imagine something you would very much like to be doing on your next summer vacation. Now open your eyes and draw." ... "You have one more minute to finish this question."

5. *Decorative Design* (time, fifteen minutes). "Now turn to page 5. *On this page draw a design which could be used for a rug. Make a picture of the most beautiful rug you can imagine." (Repeat from asterisk.) "The time allowed is fifteen minutes. Begin now." ... "You have one more minute to finish this question."

6. *Copy of Lantern Slide of a Painting* (time, ten minutes). "Turn to page 6. In just a minute you will see a picture on the screen. (Dim lights and show picture of Chardin *Still Life*.) "Now, while this picture is on the screen, make a copy of it on your paper. Make just as exact a copy as you can. The time allowed is ten minutes. Now begin." ... "One more minute."

7. *Drawing from Moving Picture* (time, ten minutes — while lights are on). "Now turn to page 7. In just a moment you will see a very short moving picture of an animal in motion. This moving picture will be shown several times. While it is being shown, make a drawing of the animal which you see. Make it in any position you like. If you wish to make more than one drawing on this page you may do so. The time allowed is ten minutes. Now begin." ... "One more minute."

This test was given to over thirteen hundred children: in elementary, junior and senior high schools, under conditions closely approximating those in the museum auditorium; to all the museum Saturday morning classes at least once, and to a selected group of the "Specials" or advanced students again after two years. It yielded a vast mass of data in the shape of over nine thousand drawings, plus supplementary information about the young artists. It consumed a considerable share of the staff's time and energy throughout the research, although each new test likewise yielded masses of children's art — easy to get, but hard and slow to interpret.

As a testing device, the Seven Drawings Test (given before the research began) was never regarded as a perfected instrument, worthy of being given out for general use. It immediately disclosed several faults, especially the following: (1) In drawing a man (question 2) children should have been told to draw the whole man; many drew the head only. (2) The moving picture used for drawing 7, of a horse in motion, had been too inferior in quality, too blurred and rapid, for many children to grasp it; yet to change the film would make comparison impossible. (3) The lantern slide of drawing 6 was in black and white, unsuited to the colored pencils and too complex in line and texture for young children to copy. Dimming lights to see the slide made it hard for them to draw. (4) The instructions for drawing 5 were so phrased that some children tried to draw an actual rug in perspective, missing the point of the question, which was to elicit an abstract, decorative design.

Other Experimental Devices

More fundamentally, it was realized that no single test, no set of drawings made on a single occasion, could give more than presumptive evidence of a child's probable success in art. Too many important psychological factors, such as motivation, work habits, and emotional stability, would not appear to any considerable extent in the results. For these, observation over a period of time would still be necessary.

The Seven Drawings Test was obviously faulty, but at least it had brought out a wealth of promising data. The staff questioned whether to lay it aside and work out other tests, in the hope of perfecting some of them, or to neglect the invention of new tests, but study the results of the faulty one as carefully as time allowed. Actually, they took a middle course, trying out several new devices, but not attempting to perfect any one of them. They hoped to build up a series, not of formal tests, but of devices for observing and experimenting on children's production and appreciation of art. These could be partly standardized into definite tasks to be performed at various times, under controlled, uniform conditions. They were aimed at stimulating significant responses from the child, which an intelligent teacher might find enlightening, even though not exactly measurable.

Several such devices were carried to various degrees of completeness, and tried out in museum classes by Mrs. Lark-Horovitz and Dr. Barnhart. The principal ones are as follows:

a. Seven Drawings Test.

b. The *Beautiful Page* experiment: an attempted improvement on question 5 of the Seven Drawings Test, in that it calls for abstract decoration rather than a picture of a textile. The child is simply told to make the sheet of paper as beautiful as possible, and that it need not look like anything else.

c. The *Story Completion* experiment: an attempt to stimulate imagination by telling part of a story, then having the subject complete it (*a*) in pictures; (*b*) in words. (This allows comparison of pictorial with literary ability.) A fairy tale and a fictitious news item, both with vivid imagery, were used.

d. The *Recorder:* a device for preserving a record of consecutive stages in the development of a child's drawing; showing to what extent and how he plans it systematically, rather than adding details at random. The child draws on a sheet of paper, under which are carbon paper and a roll

of white paper which can be shifted at intervals by the examiner.

e. The *Machinery Drawing* experiment: a way of studying children's ability to learn and change their own ways of drawing as a result of observing pictures by others. (This is specially relevant to museum instruction, where children are led to appreciate art of all periods, and then asked to make works of art of their own, which will profit by that appreciation and yet avoid direct copying.) The group is first asked to draw a picture involving machinery of some kind; is then shown museum pictures involving machinery; and is finally (at once or on another day) asked again to draw machinery pictures, without having the museum examples to look at.

f. The *Bear* or *Visual Memory* experiment: a way of studying children's ability to remember and represent an object seen, after various intervals of time. A ceramic figure of a bear is shown from different points of view, then withdrawn. The children are asked to draw it immediately, then after several days, and again after several weeks.

g. The Art Appreciation experiments: In addition to the above ways of studying drawing ability, methods were developed for observing and comparing children's preferences for different types of art. Selected, diversified sets of pictures, textiles, ceramics, and other objects were shown to them with specified comments and questions; their answers were noted down, analyzed, and classified. The aim was not to decide or measure how "correct" their judgments were, but to find out how different types (as to age, sex, etc.) differed in their attitudes toward art.

h. The Project Analysis Record Sheets: for use in school or elsewhere; some for students and some for teachers, as means of systematizing evaluation and records of progress toward chosen objectives. They are, in a broad sense, devices for observation, experiment, and evaluation.

These eight types of instruments (each of them capable of much variation and development) were all aimed at eliciting samples of constructive work or aesthetic response on the part of the student, or at recording and appraising extended programs of work. In addition, the task of interpreting results of the Seven Drawing Test required certain instruments of a different sort.

Evaluation in Practice

Three kinds of problems confronted the staff. One, when the test was first given, was immediately practical. In a few days, before classes started, about fifty students had to be selected for the Museum Special Class of supposedly talented children, eleven through sixteen years of age. The selection was to be made in large part from the drawings of about two hundred children who had applied for admission. There was no time for detailed analysis or theoretical quibbles; decisions had to be quick and arbitrary.

Accordingly, three judges of reputation and experience with children's art were asked to make them. The papers were first divided into piles according to age levels. Beginning with the youngest, paper after paper was inspected by the three judges at once, and assigned by them to an A, B, or C group (good, medium, bad) within the age level. Thus, each age level pile was divided into three. There was usually swift agreement on the verdicts; a few were discussed at some length, or held in suspense until the rest had been judged and the degrees of relative merit seemed clearer. No one simple standard was used; the judges often remarked of a "C" paper that it was "weak," "fumbling," "stereotyped," or "had nothing to say"; of an "A" paper that it had "life," "vitality," "sense of humor," "distinctive point of view," or "decorative quality," "rhythmic lines," or "delicate textures." Fifty best were chosen from all the "A" piles, with approximately equal distribution. As a safeguard, any applicant not chosen for the "Special" class was allowed to enter an "Open" class, with no restrictions. There he was observed for months, and in some cases advanced to the Special class

afterward, while some who had been chosen for the latter proved unworthy in the long run. Such a process of choice could certainly be called arbitrary and subjective, strictly speaking. But at least it involved explicit discussion of standards, a tentative attitude, and systematic comparison of the data.

The Analysis of Children's Drawings; A Manual for Teachers

A second type of problem was to make the Seven Drawings Test, or some altered version of it, into a more workable tool of evaluation for the outside teacher. Ideally, it should be not only capable of yielding exact numerical scores, but also somewhat mechanical and automatic in operation; so that the ordinary teacher, not an art expert, could use it. These results might have been attained through the usual process of "validation" — submitting the papers to many judges, or repeatedly to the same judges, giving the test repeatedly to the same children, and preserving only those features in test and scoring which seemed most "reliable" — that is, which would yield similar results on repeated use. But the staff was convinced that such a test would be specious, merely one more neatly printed device for enforcing established, conservative standards, for glorifying conventional types of "good art," while missing or disparaging the unusual and experimental. At the same time, while avoiding excessive claims to accuracy, the test might perhaps be sharpened up a little for general use.

As a means to that end, the staff worked out a report which was published by the Cleveland Museum of Art under the title *Graphic Work-sample Diagnosis: an Analytic Method of Estimating Children's Drawing Ability*, by B. Lark-Horovitz, E. N. Barnhart, and E. M. Sills. This mimeographed volume of 143 pages, plus appended "check sheets," contains a manual of instructions for teachers to use in checking and diagnosing children's drawings preceded by an introductory explanation of the various types of children's drawing by age levels. It is illustrated with black and colored photographic reproductions and line drawings of various types. It amounts essentially to a scale of graded examples, with verbal comments to point out their distinctive traits, by comparison with which the teacher may grade the work of her own pupils. It was worked out through a study of the Seven Drawings Test papers, with examples taken from them. Hence its proposed age-level norms are applicable, in a strict sense, only to drawings made under the same conditions (as to subject, medium, time allowed, etc.). However, its illustration and definition of types of children's drawing, and of specific traits therein, may be found more widely useful. This book was sent out to a number of teachers, some of whom used the manual and reported to the staff on their results. Certain drawings were sent around to be analyzed and graded by different teachers, with the use of the *Diagnosis*.

Most teachers are not at present sufficiently interested in the careful grading of students' drawings to be willing to take the time necessary for it. To distinguish types of art requires specific training, as it does to distinguish botanical or zoological types. Few classroom teachers and not all art teachers have had it. It cannot be made entirely quick, easy, and automatic without dangerous oversimplification. There are too many kinds of good art, by children as well as by adults; too many important individual differences; too many detailed characteristics worthy of note, for any simple scale of examples to cover them adequately.

The idea of a manual for use in grading pictures runs up against serious difficulties. One is that of nomenclature and definition of terms, in referring to type of art and elements in art. Aesthetic theory is still in a very primitive state on this matter; there is

little or no accepted terminology for the description of adult art, of the masterpieces of art history. There is no recognized technique for analyzing and comparing works of art. If there were, it might be applied with modification to children's art. But whenever we try to analyze a child's drawing in such terms as "design," "realism," "rhythm," "balance," "proportion," etc., we discover radical differences among teachers and critics as to what these terms mean and what aesthetic values are to be attached to them. At least, the staff did try for some clarity and consistency by stating definitions for the principal terms. But outside teachers often could not understand or accept them, and applied the same term to a given example in widely varying ways. It is too much to hope that any single educational device can produce at a single step a generally acceptable technique and terminology for art analysis. That is a long job for aesthetic theory, which must be approached through study of old masters as well as of children's art. A good start was made toward it in Germany and Austria during the twenties; but it has had little effect on American education.

Well aware of this problem, the staff approached the task of analyzing the "Seven Drawings" papers in a careful, indirect way. They had first to work out a definite method of analysis. This was done in the form, first, of a questionnaire or list of charateristics believed to be somehow significant in children's art, for the analyst to notice in the case of each picture.

On the basis of the questionnaire, a number of large blank charts were made: several for each of the first four drawings of the test, as executed by boys, girls, and various age-level groups. Large, representative samplings of the test papers were taken, mostly from the Seven Drawings Test, plus some from the Beautiful Page and other experiments. These were analyzed in minute detail, the results being entered and tabulated on the charts. This was the slow, drudging, time-consuming phase of the process, common to all inductive science.

The questionnaire, the charts, and the tabulation had one primary aim: to show the age level and sex distribution of specific characteristics in children's drawings. By this means, it was hoped, we could begin to generalize in terms of developmental norms. These would doubtless not be capable of exact numerical statement, but would consist of verbal description, illustrated by typical examples, of the kinds of drawing usual on each age level. There would be a range of variation on each level; certain characteristics being nonexistent among younger children, then becoming gradually more prevalent; others perhaps gradually dying out with maturation. With such an account of normal development, the teacher could compare the work of any particular child and find out to what extent it was normal, advanced, or retarded, both on the whole and in specific ways. The *Diagnosis* provides such an account, replete with illustrative detail, and as such provides a suggestive (though not an accurate) instrument for any teacher who wishes to take the trouble to use it. Its indications will be useful in proportion to the care the teacher takes to set up the same conditions as those used in determining the norms.

Developmental Stages in Children's Drawing

Substantial aid was provided for this phase of the work by previous European studies of children's drawing. Psychologists had distinguished roughly between the so-called *schematic* or conceptual and the *true-to-appearance* or visually realistic stages. Historians and anthropologists had gone on to point out resemblances between children's art and primitive art, and some had even suggested that children's artistic development involved a recapitulation of some of the main stages in art history, from crude schematism to the developed realism of the Renaissance, with its three-dimensional modeling and perspective. On the other hand, it had been pointed out that some very primitive art — by the Ice-Age cavemen — was not schematic but realistic in outline. Leaving aside controversial issues in psychology and cultural history, there remained a thoroughly documented, skeleton outline of the normal development of children's drawing ability, which apparently held true of children the world over.

This important conception of artistic development in the individual had never been subjected to verification in America, on a scale comparable to that of the Cleveland studies. It is one accomplishment of these studies to have confirmed, refined, and considerably developed this conception. It can be subdivided into intermediate stages, as follows: (1) the primitive schematic stage; (2) the full or developed schematic stage; (3) the mixed stage (intermediate between schematic and true-to-appearance); (4) the true-to-appearance; (5) the perspective stage.[1]

Not all individuals, even modern adults, pass through all these stages. Many of them remain on a schematic and therefore childlike or primitive stage as regards drawing ability, or regress to one through disuse, although highly educated along other lines, and perhaps capable of appreciating art. But the evidence indicates that no individual can advance to a later stage without going through the earlier ones, in substantially the order named.

Development from stage to stage is apparently not dependent on specific training in art, though probably capable of being affected and somewhat accelerated by it. (Experimental data are lacking on this point.)

[1]These names are capable of further improvement. The fourth is "true-to-appearance" only in a limited sense, especially as to linear outline and modeling and texture. Full visual realism comes only with perspective and deep space representation, if then.

It apparently tends to go on to some extent with little or no art instruction, and whatever teaching methods are used, as a result of general mental and perceptual development, muscular coordination, and observation of popular art. In estimating a child's artistic development, then, we are studying not only his specific achievement or acquired skill in art, but also certain indications of his general mental development.

Maturity, Realism, and Excellence

Can degree of advancement in realism be taken as equivalent to degree of excellence in a picture, and of superior talent in a child? Is a more mature or precocious child or picture necessarily better? These questions recall the old controversies over whether evolution is the same as progress; whether increasing complexity of structure and of civilization are necessarily improvement, or whether (as Rousseau argued) more simple and primitive stages are sometimes better. In many cases no dispute arises: the more mature child and picture seem possessed of all the other possible artistic virtues, and so are unhesitatingly put down as "superior talent." Insofar as this is true, one can use the scale of development as a scale of excellence; that is, as an objective indicator or correlative of excellence, even though the two are not synonymous. But it is not always or necessarily true. A highly realistic work may be found in some ways mediocre; a schematic one may be admired for its decorative or expressive qualities.

In art criticism generally, extreme realism is not considered equivalent to excellence or a necessary sign of greatness. Art history has not stopped short with the realistic modeling and perspective of the Renaissance. It has gone on to modern eclecticism, with its frequent conscious reversion to the decorative distortions and schematism of primitives and children; with deliberate sacrifice of realism to design, expression, and fantasy. Often in the past, sophisticated adult artists have made the same sacrifice, consciously or not — for example, in Byzantine mosaics and Persian miniatures. They have managed to find great scope for development on a level which a scale of stages in realism would describe as relatively childish.

To decide artistic standards and define excellence in general is a problem essentially outside the field of the psychologist, and of all descriptive science. It involves aesthetic and perhaps moral standards, as well as questions of general mental and physical health. But the psychologist can at least analyze its detailed implications. Is degree of maturation regarded as equivalent to excellence in other phases of child development? Certainly we do not always consider precocity a desirable trait in children — for example, in matters of sex. On the other hand, the question does not seem to arise in regard to intelligence tests, where a more mature status is an accepted sign of superiority. Of course, it is open to any school or teacher to adopt as an objective the development of adult ways of drawing. As a matter of fact, this was the main objective in teaching drawing until the time of "free expression" and "progressive methods," with their implication that children's ways of drawing had values of their own and were not merely crude approaches to adult art. The vast majority of people, art teachers included, still think of art value largely in terms of successful realism. If any judge or teacher still wishes to adopt the scale of normal development in drawing as equivalent to a scale of improvement, of increasing ability in general, then the *Diagnosis* will help him evaluate much more precisely and systematically than before.

However, the progressive art teacher, like the "advance guard" artist and critic, will not be satisfied with evaluating children's art entirely on a basis of increasing powers of realistic representation. He will insist, as did the aforementioned judges, who quickly appraised results of the Seven Drawings Test, that one six-year-old drawing can be better than another, even though both are definitely schematic in type and show no signs of advancement to the next stage. Within each developmental type, in other words, there is room for considerable variation in detail, in mode of treatment, which many judges will regard as sufficient to determine a picture's merit. Such characteristics may even outweigh, in the judge's mind, degree of realistic advancement. He may admire a child's drawing as he does an African Negro carving — not with a condescending smile as if to say, "Pretty good for one so young, or for a mere savage"; but on its own merits as superior to the average adult, modern academic piece. Often it is the decorative, design aspect of the childlike or primitive piece which is weak or missing in the academic one. Often (as remarked above) the judges were attracted by an effect of vitality, humor, or a vividly childish way of looking at the world and picking out what seemed important to the childish mind — a net effect of artistry through definite selection, emphasis, and reorganization from direct experience. It seems to manifest itself on any age level beyond early infancy, and not necessarily in proportion to maturity or amount of skill and information. In fact, too often it seems to decline as these increase.

Can these intangible, supposed signs of excellence be described in any objective way? The Cleveland studies have made only a slight beginning, not enough to provide anything like a definite scale or manual. They have called attention to the problem, at least, and have gone a step farther in roughly distinguishing between "developmental," "constant," and "rare" characteristics. In the last two of these categories, perhaps, remain hidden the elusive intangibles which future workers will regard as signs of superior ability regardless of age level. A "developmental" characteristic is one which changes according to age level. A "constant" characteristic appears with considerable frequency in about the same degree in all age levels. A "rare" one appears very seldom on any level. "True-to-appearance" is a developmental characteristic; "smooth areas" is a constant one; and "bold line" is rare. Such classification of specific characteristics was made on the basis of fewer examples than could be wished, especially on the higher age levels, and it is hoped that future study will revise and clarify them considerably. As matters now stand, our understanding of rare and constant characteristics is still vague and fragmentary. It has been hard to describe them without the use of evaluative, subjective terms. Our conception of their importance in relation to giftedness is subject to change in the light of new aesthetic theories.

The term "developmental," as used here, includes characteristics which tend to dwindle and die out with maturation, as well as those which grow. Both, it is felt, are somehow bound up with development in general. One of the most interesting disclosures of the "Seven Drawings" study is the way in which decorative characteristics in general, especially in use of bright colors and rhythmic lines, tend to die out as the child grows older. In the art appreciation study, also, these characteristics gradually lose appeal as reasons for liking a picture. The tendency in both cases is more rapid and pronounced in boys. More and more, with advancing age, the sensuous delight in color, line, and pattern for their own sake is sacrificed to the dominating interest in representing certain types of subject matter, and in doing so with utmost realistic accuracy. The organized grouping of details in a picture also seems to decline in favor of great realism and accuracy in a few details.

Here again, one must notice the apparent recapitulation of certain phases in art history: the decrease of decorative color and line which accompanied the rise of realistic art in the Renaissance. And again one asks, "What next?" If an individual's artistic development goes on, and does not atrophy through disuse in adolescence or before, where will it go after achieving full perspective realism? In the case of modern Post-Impressionists, as we have seen, it can evidently go on to a sort of eclecticism, with possible reversion to certain aspects of the schematic stage, enriched by adult experience and perhaps combined with realistic features. Our studies up through age sixteen throw no light on this problem. But such considerations do deter us from assuming that our present view of normal development tells the whole story.

Moreover, we may ask, suppose our survey had been made in ancient Persia or Byzantium, or even in modern Paris, would the same decline of decorative emphasis have appeared? Is what we have seen due to the local cultural climate, to America's artistic immaturity or Cleveland's, or to faulty art teaching in schools and museums? Is it due to naïve prejudice against decorative art as effeminate? Is it due to some more basic impulse toward realism, bound up perhaps with growing intellectual and scientific powers, which makes decorative beauty seem trivial and distracting? If so, to what extent should the art teacher try to fight against it and preserve a taste for design and decoration in the growing child? How can he present the decorative and formal aspects of art in ways more attractive to older children, especially boys?

At the same time, there is food for thought in an experiment which tended to show that preference or liking is not always favorable to active learning. Pictures which the children at first disliked often changed their attitudes more than ones they liked at first sight. Quick liking is sometimes a sign of familiarity, of having learned how to respond to that sort of thing. Dislike, on the other hand, may be due to unfamiliarity. If the first impulse to brush the thing aside

can be restrained and followed up by careful study, the result may be profoundly unsettling and far reaching educationally. We must not assume that children should be given only types of artistic experience which they accept easily and quickly. How many would go far in mathematics on that basis? We are sometimes justified in persisting for a time against apparent antipathy to a subject on the child's part, if we have good reason to believe he will see its value later. But when possible, it is well to put the dynamic of interest behind his scholastic efforts.

It was evident to the staff that merely grading pictures as more or less advanced or mature in type was not the same as evaluation, and was not a sufficient way of grading from the teacher's standpoint. To bring it nearer to the teacher's needs, the authors of the *Diagnosis* ventured out a little way from the safe shore of objective analysis, and onto the thin ice of evaluative standards. Among the various characteristics they labeled certain ones "desirable" and others as "undesirable." Advanced representational states were declared to be desirable "because there seems to be a strong inclination for children to strive toward a naturalistic representation of objects and figures. The tendency toward expressionism and abstract art, when it occurs at all, seems to grow out of the true-to-appearance drawing." "Outstanding color," "decisiveness and boldness of line and area," "subtlety of line," "clarity of outline," and "highly organized grouping" were declared to be desirable or superior qualities. On the other hand, "hesitating and weak lines," "ragged, smudgy areas," and "inconsistent use of medium" were called undesirable, signs of inferiority. Evaluative significance was thus given to "developmental" as well as to "rare" and "constant" characteristics. By individual diagnosis blanks, the teacher was aided to analyze a given picture, and to appraise it as "superior," "typical," or "inferior."

Probably no one interested in art criticism can read such a list without at once rising to challenge it with exceptions. Is boldness of outline always good? Do not some great artists use ragged, smudgy areas — and so on? Endless debate would certainly be possible on these points, for they merely carry over into children's art perennial issues in the aesthetics of drawing and painting. At the same time, there are other considerations to remember. Granting that a certain characteristic may be good when used in a special context by a sophisticated, adult artist, it does not necessarily follow that the same characteristic is a healthy, promising sign in most children's art. On the whole, and except for occasional atypical cases (which the teacher may evaluate as such), we may be justified by experience in regarding it as a sign of weakness. Occasionally, a great artist may affect a smudgy, fumbling, awkward stroke for a certain purpose, long after he has learned to draw firmly and clearly when he wants to. But if a child draws that way consistently, at an age when most children want to draw clearly and have a hard time doing so, the chances are that he is doing so through inability and not intention. No scale can be relied on completely, and the wise teacher will always supplement its use with a careful eye to the rare, atypical genius.

Moreover, there is no use trying to evaluate and be purely objective at the same time. The two are essentially inconsistent, and if the teacher wants a method of evaluation, he must be prepared to accept some trace of debatable standards in it. The psychologist renders no great service by remaining impeccably objective (if that were possible) and evading all the practical problems of educational grading. The important questions to raise about a proposed method are: "What standards does it imply or assume? Does it state them explicitly as such, conceding their debatable nature, or does it hide them under a mask of pretended scientific objectivity?" If it does state them, we can go on to debate them and decide whether or not to accept them. Evaluation becomes more intelligent, not by trying to avoid debatable standards entirely, but by realizing more clearly what one's standards imply, abstractly and concretely, and what arguments can be advanced for and against them. We are making a step toward objectivity whenever we define our standards in explicit terms, and analyze vague, general ones into specific characteristics. The importance of such analysis is indicated by Mrs. Lark-Horowitz's study of subjective judgments,[2] in which it appeared that judges professing similar abstract standards applied them with very different results.

Gifted and Average Groups Compared

Yet another approach to the problem of evaluation has been made throughout the Cleveland studies. It involves detailed comparison between students in the "Special" classes at the museum, made up of supposedly talented, gifted, superior children from eleven through sixteen, and all others. The others included (a) children in the public schools who had shown no unusual interest in coming to the museum or in taking special art work; (b) students in the museum's Saturday open class for children, free to all and very diversified as to economic, racial, and educational family backgrounds; (c) students in the Saturday classes for children of museum members, coming from high economic and presumably cultural levels in the community. The b and c groups were not wholly unselected in relation to art, since either they or their parents had shown a definite interest in coming, and perhaps in paying to come; but they had not had to show any special art ability. In fact, any child in the open class who had long shown marked ability was likely to have been transferred from there to the

[2] The Journal of Experimental Education, XI. 2 (1942), p. 116.

Special class. Choices for the Special class were made either in this way or, as explained above, through the Seven Drawings Test. In either case, admission to it was based on the arbitrary judgment of museum teachers or judges appointed by them.

What right had we then to assume that the "Special" children were actually more gifted than the "Averages," or that any differences between them were associated with differences in art ability? None, theoretically; and all generalizations were made with this clearly in mind. But it is valid scientific procedure to assume something as a working hypothesis, and see where it leads. Also, lacking evidence to the contrary, it is reasonable to believe that supposed experts have some justification for their views; not to accept their judgment as final, but to examine it carefully as a hypothesis. In the same way, the findings of any art test at all, or any mode of judging talent, may be followed out hypothetically and itself tested by experience. However implausible or unreasonable it sounds, the results may justify it over a long period of time. Such results — for example, a high percentage of successful careers in advanced art study and professional work — are the only real way of confirming the accuracy of any method for evaluating children's art ability. This way itself can never be final, for all judgments of later "success" in art are debatable, even for centuries after the artist is dead. But it is the only one we have. The chief trouble with most of the current art ability tests is that they conceal their assumptions, and the hypothetical nature of their findings, under a cloak of statistical claims to "validity" and "reliability" — terms which are popularly understood, unfortunately, to mean a great deal more than they imply in a strictly technical sense.

The "Specials," then, were a group of children who had been judged (rightly or wrongly) to possess superior talent. We assumed that they at least deserved special study, and set out to discover in what specific, observable ways (if any) they differed from other children in matters concerned with art. The answers would at least show more clearly what kind of children the judges considered gifted. At most, if the judges were right, we might know a few more observable facts about artistically gifted children. These facts might serve in turn as *indicators* of talent — as signs by which other presumably gifted children could be recognized. By a highly diversified set of test or experimental devices — some analyzing work samples, some observing ability to remember visually, to learn a new technique, to defend preferences intelligently, and so on — we might approach the composite of diverse abilities known as "art ability."

Objective differences between the Special and the Average groups were indeed found in a considerable number of experiments. The Specials were on the whole a little, but not much, more intelligent than the Averages; on the other hand, some high IQ groups in the schools did very uneven work in the Seven Drawings Test. The Specials were considerably more advanced in developmental type of drawing than the Averages were. They paid more attention to artistic style, form, mode of treatment than the Averages did, both in their own productions and in judging other works of art, and were correspondingly less concerned with the nature of the subjects represented. They were able to explain and defend their preferences more explicitly, with reference to the artistic qualities of a particular object. They identified themselves less with the subject or scene portrayed, and were more able to take an objective view toward the artist's accomplishments. They observed and learned more quickly, and retained visual memories longer; they were more capable of experimenting with a new medium and adapting their technique to its requirements.

Whether such differences are really typical of artistically gifted children in general is, of course, the crucial question. As mentioned above, that cannot be decided with any assurance unless and until we can compare the later artistic performance of the Specials with that of the Averages. More long-term observation of that sort is to be desired. In the meantime, wherever a group of children is selected as gifted in art, by any test or mode of judgment, it is worthwhile to study them carefully, in order to have the data in hand when their later performance can be appraised.

The Meaning of "Development" in Relation to Art Ability

In a letter to me, Mrs. Lark-Horovitz summarized her impression of the museum "Specials" as follows:

Our findings substantiate the fact that Specials are heightened Averages; that the top-group of Specials represents a still more heightened average (especially as to perception) plus certain intangible qualities — whether inherited or native or acquired — that are, as yet, unexplained. The main difference between the two groups is neither intelligence, nor of a developmental nature. It is the phenomenon that specially gifted children express themselves (and think primarily) in a *visual* medium: that is, they translate all their experience into this mode of expression; while average children lack this ability, even though their experiences are as powerful and their gift of expressing them as strong.[3]

In other words, there appears to be no radical difference in kind between the gifted and the average child in art, but rather a gradual stepping-up of a number of related abilities, plus a strong tendency to experience things visually, and even to try to suggest, represent, and symbolize other types of experience in visual terms. This itself

[3]This refers primarily to children gifted in visual art; those gifted in music would presumably be more inclined to auditory thinking. (T.M.)

might perhaps be called an ability — to interpret the world in visual images — but it also involves a direction of interest and motivation, each no doubt stimulating the other. The importance of interest in the matter has seemed especially important to me in observing children's behavior throughout the tests. I often sensed that many of the high IQ students tested in the schools were simply not interested in the tests or in art at all; that they felt a positive antipathy toward the more decorative, sensuous aspects of art; that this antipathy tended on the whole to increase with age and to be much stronger in boys than in girls. This accords with the obvious fact, so disappointing to art teachers, that large numbers of children who apparently show talent in art at an early age drop it as an activity later on. What may appear in tests and questionnaires as a decline of ability in art may be mainly a decline in willingness to use and exhibit what ability one has. The result, however, is eventually the same, since an ability unused or inhibited tends to atrophy.

Educationally, it seems important to decide, if possible, the question raised above: To what extent are these apparent declines in ability and interest, especially along decorative lines, due to cultural influences? If largely so, then we may hope to counteract them by building up more respect for art, including decorative art, as a respected masculine interest. If the cause goes deeper, the problem is harder. We must decide how much to fight against nature, the nature of adolescent development. Again, we should ask very searchingly whether art is now presented to adolescents, in schools and museums, in a way to attract the changing interests and abilities of that age level. There is no great difficulty in interesting adolescents in sports, moving pictures, clothes, and ballroom dancing, all of which possess features akin to visual arts, including the decorative. What have they which school and institutional types of art lack? Some of the answers are obvious, but what to do about it is not so easy to decide.

In the remark just quoted, Mrs. Lark-Horovitz states that the main difference between the two groups is not "developmental." Although the Specials are a little more advanced on the scale of successive types or stages, this does not seem to be the essential difference. "Developmental" includes diminishing as well as growing abilities, as we have seen, but this again fails to distinguish the two groups. The Specials do not lose their decorative interests faster than the others. Often they seem to hold them longer, especially when explicitly directed to such a task, as in the "Beautiful Page" experiment.

However, the other characteristics which do help to mark them off are also developmental, in another sense. One can say of a certain six-year-old that he has a good all-round development, although he is not at all precocious. He has not developed in any way beyond the typical six-year norm, but differs from certain others of his age in having developed just that far along more different lines at once. Development of the individual, in other words, is potentially a process of growth in many distinct though related functions, bodily structures, and abilities. No one grows equally fast or far in all of them at once. Some go ahead precociously along certain lines, and are arrested, slow, or even regressive along other lines. Now the ability to draw in a visually realistic way, rather than schematically, is apparently an ability which increases rather steadily among all children under present educational conditons. It seems, therefore, to be intimately bound up with the process of maturation, and is therefore called "developmental"; perhaps a better word would be "maturational." The other kinds of characteristics (here called "constant" or "rare") do not seem to vary definitely with age. But, at the same time, they may be more highly developed in one individual than in another. Nearly everyone has a highly developed de-

sire for sweets at an early age, and in some it remains constant all through life. Some have a highly developed musical interest at an early age; no doubt partly due to innately high development of the auditory nerve-systems. In some the high though early development is in visual alertness. Later experience and learning may in a sense develop these early traits by redirecting, complicating, and refining them, while in another sense — that of relative strength or sensitivity — they do not develop, but appear as markedly in childhood as they ever will.

Essentially, then, it is not mere precocity in visual realism that we must look for as a sign of artistic talent (though this may well occur as one indication), but rather such characteristics as perceptual, imaginative, emotional alertness, directed by preference into visual experience and manipulation of visible materials. Such signs will never appear abstractly, in a vacuum, but only in some concrete activity or production. Hence the need for "tests" to call out such behavior. But we must read between the lines of their results, not judging them for obvious signs of maturity, special training, or sophistication. Rather we should look for signs of that vitality, sensitivity, eagerness, inventiveness, and organizing power which distinguish excellence from mediocrity on every age level and at every stage of cultural development.

It is possible that such characteristics, although "constant" or "nondevelopmental" in one sense, can be developed in another sense by proper educational and other influences; that is, stimulated into more active and harmonious exercise. Is not this the essential task of education in art and in other subjects? There would seem to be little value in merely hastening the progress toward visual realism, or other mature ways of drawing, any more than there would be in trying to accelerate physical maturation. It seems a better ideal to help each child achieve maximum fullness of experience, happy and successful living (however these are conceived), on each age level as he comes to it rather than hurrying on to the next. It would seem better to help him draw, think, feel, and play as well as possible in the six-year-old manner while he is a six-year-old. Accordingly, we should not put a premium on mere maturational advancement in drawing or any other ability. We should not, perhaps, even refer to the stages in such advancement as "the development of drawing ability," for that is too broad a term and omits the other phases in drawing ability which we are now considering. On the other hand, any attempt to retard artistic maturation artificially, so as to preserve the decorative charm of schematic art, runs the risk of unexpected repercussions on general mental development.

Much remains to be done in showing the deeper significance of the tendency in children's drawing toward visual realism. Its suggestive analogy to art history through the Renaissance has been mentioned above. More specifically, the schematic stage of early childhood bears certain resemblances to adult drawings of the Neolithic period. Culturally, this was an age of great development in language, including the beginnings of written language. It was an age when humanity was struggling to form its basic set of concepts of the main types of person, animal, plant, inanimate object, action, event, and abstract quality. These emerge later on in Egyptian and Chinese pictographs. Schematic drawings, simplified and apparently crude, were an important means in this process of distinguishing main types and giving them written as well as vocal symbols. Visual realism was not essential at that stage, and would have been an unnecessary encumbrance. In young children, also, the period of schematic drawing is one of recognizing basic types and forming basic concepts. Schematic drawing is concep-

tual drawing, of the way a thing is understood to exist — of what seem to be its most interesting and important features — rather than of how it would look to a disinterested observing eye. Drawing, clay modeling, and other modes of representation play an important part in aiding intellectual and perceptual development as well as manual coordination.

Educational Implications

What, then, should be the role of art education in early childhood? Has it not been an error to urge visually realistic drawing, from a model or otherwise? Would we not be further mistaken to favor such drawing by any scale or test which restricts the idea of "art ability" to realistic drawing ability, or to any other way of conforming to adult standards? The alternative is not to discourage precocity; when it occurs along with signs of health, well and good. But a paramount need may be to utilize schematic drawing itself, while it lasts, as an aid in certain phases of mental development. Indeed, schematic drawing can itself be developed into mature scientific diagramming, mechanical drawing, and other types of expository art involving conceptual realism, without ever yielding place entirely to visual realism.

An associated problem arises in the relation of children's drawing to their ways of appreciating pictures made by others. The present research and supplementary teaching experience indicate that young children do not prefer looking at the kind of pictures they make themselves. While making schematic pictures, they tend to prefer realistic ones. In some ways, they treat adult art as they do the whole outside world of objects: as something to be looked at selectively, in a childlike way, for what interests them. If asked to copy a realistic picture, they will do so with highly abbreviated schematism, and will either not notice or not be bothered by the discrepancy. They can enjoy and appreciate, to a limited extent, much more mature and realistic art than they can produce. Often they tend to look down on primitive art which is nearer their own productive level. They are not much interested in what the adult artist tried to emphasize or how he secured his realistic or decorative effects. They are more interested in the subject represented; they like to project themselves into the scene and perhaps identify themselves with one of the persons. Average older children maintain this type of interest, while Specials tend at an earlier age to adopt the more specialized technical and visual attitude of the adult artist. This of course has been stimulated in the Specials by teaching; but they respond to it more than the Averages do.

Again it would seem wise to consider these psychological hypotheses in working out our teaching methods. To what extent shall we try to influence all children toward liking contemporary nonrealistic art, or toward liking art for its technical and purely visual, formal aspects? Some, with special visual talents and development, may take to such experiences easily and heartily; and if so, well and good. But for the rank and file, and for all in early childhood, there may be psychological values which we do not now understand in using art appreciation as a means to vicarious experience, to enriched

and heightened conscious fantasy — not in isolation, but linked with other studies and practical experiences.

Any light on a student's level of artistic development, and on his peculiar interests and abilities, is of direct value in adapting educational methods and contents to the human factors involved. It brings immediate returns in more successful teaching, whether or not it can be mathematically expressed and verified.

Drawing is not, and perhaps should never be, a required subject for all secondary students. But art appreciation, properly taught, might well be advanced to that status. For young children, drawing, painting, and modeling are already so recognized in a great number of schools. They are not sufficient as media to exercise productive impulses in visual form, and should be supplemented by crafts, dancing, and theater, as well as by music and literature, to give adequate scope to art education in a broad sense. Accordingly, studies like the present one should be supplemented by studies in other arts, to raise there similar questions about normal and accelerated development and other signs of art ability. Children's drawings, however, will remain peculiarly worthy of attention, because of the clear, permanent, easily produced and handled evidence which they present. It is hoped that the present report, inconclusive as it is, will point a few paths for later inquiry.

14. Implications for Change in Art Education

JUNE K. MC FEE

Art educators' increased interest in human behavior in art, as evidenced by the subject matter of this conference, is an encouraging sign of professional growth. It is evidence that we are becoming less afraid of objectivity and can tolerate the idea that our field of *art education* includes both the subjective intuitive expressive aspects of art *and* the analytical study of behavior necessary for education in art.

Edgar Wind, professor of Art History at Oxford[1], in his study of the separation of the intellectual and intuitive in art finds that this dichotomy has been a fairly recent creation starting with the Romantic period. People unaware of this have accepted the separation as a basic fact. He strongly urges that in this age both the *intellectual* and the *intuitive emotional* need to be brought into fuller play. He believes that artists no longer need to fear knowledge, but need to learn to use it without its inhibiting their intuitions.

[1]Edgar Wind, "Art and Anarchy: The Fear of Knowledge," *The Listener* (England) LXIV: 1654, (Dec. 8, 1960), pp. 1039–1041.

Art as Communication

From a behavioral point of view the visual arts are forms of communication. By defintion we may say that art is that form of human behavior by which man purposefully interprets and enhances the quality or essence of his experience through the things he creates. Man's art enhances his experience, and his experience enhances his art. This reciprocal action leads to aesthetic and cultural growth.

The architect deals with a basic aspect of human life — providing shelter. As societies become more complex the style of the shelter becomes symbolic. These symbols identify the kind of activities of those who live or work there, and the kind of behavior that is to be expected. The architect in his special role responds to the needs of his society and his client, and uses his artistry to symbolize the nature and essence of the particular activity for which he designs.

Several types of visual communication take place: (1) everyone who comes in contact with the building receives some informa-

*SOURCE: Reprinted from *Western Arts Bulletin* (September 1962), pp. 16–30.

tion about its function; (2) the people who use it get reinforcement and feedback about their status and role; (3) the building contributes to or detracts from the surroundings through its aesthetic quality.

The painter, depending on his particular school, responds to experience and invents symbols to communicate the way he feels about it. If he is a romantic he takes from experience those things that enhance his viewpoint and communicates them to others and to himself.

The abstract expressionist or action painter whose concern with life is its never-ending interaction — its essence of tactile reaction — *symbolizes* and thus *communicates* his particular interests through his very process of painting. His interests, like the romantic, are the screen through which he sees the world, thus influencing the kind of response he makes.

The craftsman responds to his materials and the function of his product. These are part of life — part of the experiential environment within which he works. His products have meanings which enhance the experience of those who use them.

The recognition of the communicative role of the arts, historically and cross-culturally, has been too long neglected in art education. To make this more starkly apparent let us imagine some situations.

First, contemplate a generation of people, with a large complex society such as ours, in which all art forms were obliterated. It almost is impossible to conceive of such a thing, but let's explore it. They would have no visual record outside of the printed page to help them understand their own attitudes, values, and beliefs which have evolved from the past. To make this more clear, think of what we know of Renaissance man from Renaissance art. Transmission of culture from one generation to the next would be severely limited and human progress drastically impeded, for art is one of the major recording systems through which man de-

lineates his progress and from which he takes off for his next step forward.

Second, such a civilization would have no symbolic communication system for describing status and roles through costume design, architecture, artifacts of jewelry, ceramics, or fabrics. In a complex society this would mean a major breakdown in information about *who* does what. Many of the signs of achievement and reinforcement of self-concepts from the symbols of clothing would be unavailable because the symbolic style of costume design — its art — would be gone. The achievement of adult status through changes of clothing styles, the gaiety of social life, the identification of the law, the judiciary, the military, and even the status of the grey flannel suit would be lost. A value judgment as to whether this is good or bad is not the point here. Our concern is that the art forms do communicate. Perhaps by better understanding this concern we can improve the effects of art on society.

Third, these people would have no art forms to enhance the quality of their *experience*. Through most of history man has embellished his tools for work, his emblems of worship, his ceremonies for important stages of life, and his signs of prestige. Symbols change through time and vary from society to society but symbolic enhancement of experience goes on. The symbols communicate what the essence of experience should be. Without this the nature and cohesiveness of a cultural group would be lost. Thus we see that art is a major communicating force in developing and maintaining society.

Fourth, no sensitive artist would mirror for these people their present culture. No avant garde creators would develop art forms for the future.

Finally in this brief survey of art as communication, we must deal with the growing use of visual art forms in mass media. Within one generation the use of design to influence people's judgment has grown far beyond our ability to respond intelligently. Like subliminal impressions it operates at a pre-cognitive level of awareness. Product, package and industrial design, commercial and interior design, television, magazine advertising, all use form, line, color and texture to subtly influence the individual toward one decision or another.

In no way do I want to deprecate the strides in improved design in industry and advertising. But this language system of design must be understood so people will be able to make intelligent independent choices of products, and be able to reject if necessary the influence being projected to them. These influences of mass media and mass manufacture tend to pull to a national average — a conformity — of values and tastes. In some ways this influence is overshadowing the other forms of visual art.

All of this points to the importance of the language of the visual arts as a major communication system, and one that needs to be part of the education of every individual — beginning early in his experience and continuing in some degree through his education.

A small child, like a great painter, reacts to his experience through his particular readiness to respond. His past experience, culture, personality and development all contribute. His personal art and his response to the art of his society are both dependent on his ability to handle visual information.

As educators we are mainly concerned with the art of children, adolescents and adult students. If we recognize that art is communication, then the behaviors involved in the input and output of information — visual perception and the screen of personality — all become our concern.

Information Handling

A prior speaker has demonstrated to you some of the ways in which man selects from his environment what is important to him, accepting what his system needs and rejecting what it doesn't. He showed the influence of suggestion on what one perceives — and differences between individuals in the acceptance of information. These all point to individual differences that will be found in the classroom. I would like to explore some other areas of perceptual behavior that have particular importance for teaching art.

Perceptual experience is the major well-spring of creative art. The perception of size, shape, texture and color are the means of obtaining basic visual information to be expressed in art, whether its mode be realistic, abstract or expressive.

The physical properties of the human eye are such that the viewer's retinal image of a man standing 20 feet away is *half* the size of the image of the man if he were standing 10 feet away. This is a physical constant for people with normal vision. All of us, as artists, know that things the same actual size appear smaller in visual size as they move farther away from us. If the physical properties of perception were the only factors involved then we could assume that all people would see size differentiation in the same way. Twenty people with normal vision seeing the same object move away from them from the same viewpoint and same surroundings will receive similar physical information, but because other factors intervene we cannot assume they will all handle this information in the same way — so we cannot assume that they are getting the same final cognitive information.

It must be clear that the information reflected on the retina of the eyes is not the totality of visual perception. Through past experience and individual abilities the individual develops a screen through which he views his world. This screen influences what he will look at, and how much he will analyze. After he receives what he has set out to look for he categorizes this information into the concepts he has already developed. Then, if he is an artist, he has to develop or create symbols to express his own percepts. This is what we call perceptual information handling. Personality, training, and culture all influence this process.

Individuals will differ in the degree their training has been more *cognitive* than *visual*, that is, they respond to their visual world more in terms of what they *know* about rather than what they see — and this knowledge actually interferes with the handling of the physical information received.

They differ in the kinds of compromises they make between what they see and what they know. One occasionally finds persons so dependent on what they *know* that they live in flat two-dimensional worlds. Others at the other extreme see perspective as it exists physically. Most people make some kind of a compromise in between. As artists, when we are trying to overcome what we know so we can "see," in physical perception we use a pencil at arm's length to measure the actual size decrease. We are forcing ourselves to block out the effects of our cognitive impressions.

Psychologists call this tendency to compromise between what is known and seen as the perceptual constancies. For example, most of us *know* things are smaller farther away than closer — but we usually do not see them *as* small as they actually *are* in physical perspective. This is the size constancy.

The other constancies, shape, location, and color, are also seen as compromises between what one knows and what one sees. We tend to have constant *concepts* as to what *shapes things are*. We might call these *perceptual stereotypes* — the categories into which we sort our visual information. For example, the stereotyped symbol of an apple is usually a side view — a top view would not give us enough cues to discriminate an apple from other generally round froms. Our stereotypes tend to use those identifying contours

that most clearly separate an object from other similar objects. Because of this stereotyping we utilize only a small part of the available information. We tend to see our stereotypes rather than objects as they exist in light and space. This tendency keeps us from seeing forms change in perspective even though we learn a mechanical system for drawing them.

An elementary teacher once brought me drawings of a second grade class. He was amazed because all the children drew houses in two dimensions with peaked roofs. "Why," he asked, "do they draw them this way when they all live in a housing project of flat roofed houses?" I asked him to look at the nursery school and primary books where children were learning concepts to see what kind of houses were drawn. These were the perceptual stereotypes of *shape* they had learned.

Another form of stereotyping that children learn around age six is to organize things on a line. They are being taught in first grade to put their work symbols on lines and transfer this to their organization of visual symbols, until they learn there are other ways to do it. This is what psychologists call the location constancy. We tend to have stereotyped positions for remembering locations, and so it is not surprising that we tend to draw or paint that way.

The fourth constancy is color perception. We tend to see things in terms of our categories for color. Different societies have different ways of sorting and organizing colors even though physically people may respond to color in similar ways. Thus they will differ widely in the way they will use the color information. Color perception is most relative. We see hue, value and intensity in relation to other hues, values and intensities. Things are only relatively brighter or darker or redder than others depending upon what we are using for a reference.

Again past experience and training will determine how many and what kinds of concepts individuals will have with which to handle visual information of color, of size and shape and location.

All of this leads to a very important point. Visual perception is in large part learned. To learn to see things both cognitively and visually requires training. Unless people use their visual capacities fully they are missing much of the beauty and wonder of nature and art — and can make gross mistakes or remain perceptually illiterate.

I teach representational drawing at my school. It is a general education course taken by students from many of the science fields as well as engineering and architecture. I have experimented by teaching them mainly to *see* — to overcome what they know and really *observe* what actually is there. Most of them are appalled at their visual incompetence. Some, even understanding what is happening psychologically, have to battle their long established habits to see forms change in space, to see size in relation to distance, and the variety and subtle changes in hue, value, and intensity. But, through this process, most everyone does learn to see and draw volumes and spaces with strong three-dimensional structure. In other words, they learn to *see* and *think* and *symbolize* in three-dimensional space.

Cognitive and visual perception need not be in conflict — they complement each other, reinforcing and enriching learning through both channels. The implications of this for us as art educators as I interpret them are as follows:

1. Many people have probably learned they were not artistic because their individual differences in perception were not considered. They were not encouraged to increase their categories for organizing visual information.

2. Students cannot be given drawing assignments and hope to succeed unless

their visual skills are already developed *or* they learn to develop them.

3. Perceptual training probably should begin in the early school years and continue throughout education. Visual communication is no less complex than verbal communication. We find it necessary to continue verbal education throughout the school years — but have ignored the necessity for parallel visual education. As we have seen in the introduction to this paper, *nonverbal communication is increasing in importance,* and we cannot afford to have people literate in one area of communication and illiterate in others, as this avenue could be used to undermine the others.

There are two more areas of visual perception that we should explore before applying this to actual classroom practice. Information theory deals with the uses of bits of cognitive information. Attneave,[2] a psychologist, has done considerable work relating this theory to the use and assimilation of visual bits of information. His main hypotheses are:

1. Visual perception is largely redundant. That is, we get far more information than we actually use. We handle this redundancy at a precognitive level of awareness in three ways:

(a) We group similar things into single units. We tend to focus on likenesses as we attempt to organize the complexity of our visual experience.

(b) We take averages of things that are different. The philosopher Suzanne K. Langer[3] gives an excellent example of this when she describes the averaging

[2]Fred Attneave, "Some Informational Aspects of Visual Perception," *Psychology Review,* 61:3, 1954, pp. 183–193.
"Physical Determinants of the Judged Complexity of Shapes," *Journal of Experimental Psychology,* 53:4, (1957), pp. 221–227.
[3]Susanne K. Langer, *Philosophy in a New Key* (Cambridge: Harvard University Press, 1942).

process we make in driving down a freeway, handling a great complex of visual information and computing averages of other cars' speed and direction, and our special relationships to them.

(c) We make continuations or closures of things we see part of. If we get enough cues from seeing part of a thing we get the cognitive impression of having seen the whole thing. If a cue is very ambiguous we have more freedom to bring our own concepts into play. This is why the Rorschach test gets such varied responses from people. It is random form and each individual makes his own closure from it depending on his past experience. This may be the reason that drawings using small suggestions of form invite the viewer to become more involved in the art because he has to participate by making his own closure. This participation is not necessary in drawings where every detail is handled.

2. Most of the time we sort information into the simplest possible patterns. Most of our visual experience does not allow time for careful analysis. We tend to take just enough information to make a judgment and move on to the next perceptual task.

3. We depend on contour far more than on other cues in identifying objects. We tend to look, according to Attneave, to those points of contour where there is the most identifying information. This is what the cartoonist does when, with a few deft strokes, he captures the essence of the most striking features which identify the individual.

These three sorting processes are closely related to the older Gestalt principles of perceptual organization.[4] I had studied de-

[4]Max Wertheimer and W. D. Ellis, *A Source Book of Gestalt Psychology* (New York: Harcourt Brace, 1938).

sign from an intuitive basis for many years, but it was not until I studied Gestalt psychology that I could analyze intellectually what it was I was doing. At first I studied students' problems and began to realize that their designs became confused when they didn't follow these characteristics of perceptual organization.

The human visual information handling process appears to be the fundamental basis upon which design is built. We cannot assume that all is known about perceptual organization, but we do have some directives. The designer appears to be a mediator between the perceiver and unorganized visual stimuli. He uses design, the grammar of visual communication, to organize his material so that it can direct visual attention, arouse interest and make it more easily assimilated.

Basically the Gestalt categorizing principles are these:

The perceiver tends to see relationships between things that are similar in size, shape, color, texture or pattern. *If these* similar things are close in proximity there is a stronger relationship. For example, if two similar forms are in close proximity the force of the design is stronger than if they are far apart.

The perceiver follows suggestions of continuity or closure, such as when forms are so grouped that they indicate direction or line.

He groups his perceptions into figures from ground, what we artists call foreground and background or the dominant and subdominant.

This grouping activity is necessary to remember images. We know that when people learn things that are structured, they tend to remember them better than when they are given materials that are not organized or structured. We all know how hard it is to read writing that is not organized into sentences and paragraphs. We have the same trouble with disorganized visual information.

The human organism needs some forms of order to be able to respond. His perceptual process itself is an effort to make order out of his visual world. He also needs variety, dominance and subdominance to structure this order. The question then arises — how do these findings help us teach design? Does it help us understand why some people are better designers than others?

We feel that designing is related to the basic perceptual organizing process. Apparently some people use perceptual organizing in their delineation of design. Perhaps what we have called intuitive designing ability is an individual's use of his precognitive perceptual ordering skills in his work. He can recognize when his design is right or wrong but cannot tell you why.

An art education doctoral research in progress at Stanford compared 20 upper division design students in a state college with 20 similar nonart students. These students were all asked to choose between pairs of designs — which ones they liked best and which ones least. The ability to give even a minimal reason for choice appeared to be no more advanced in art students than in nonart students. Most of us would agree, I think, that the design students were good designers and in performance were far ahead of the other group. But apparently their work had mainly been done at the intuitive or precognitive level.

The question remains, should these people be allowed to go on intuitively or should they also be trained to design intellectually as well? This is a matter each teacher will have to decide. Some very highly creative intuitive students should probably be left alone — but if they are going to teach design to others, and be able to teach the nonintuitive students as well as inspire others like themsleves, they need to understand and be able to verbalize about what they do. This cognitive analysis need not take place during the actual creation of design, but it can be on a basis for self-criticism, and this can lead to understanding.

As educators we feel that all students should understand design as every individual uses it daily in his life. How do we teach the students who do not have an intuitive ability?

As part of a study on creativity, we have taught design to academically superior adolescents. In the beginning many of these students were afraid of art. They were not accustomed to using their intuitions. We found that we could get them very involved in designing by explaining the perceptual organizing process. This enabled us to use design as a means for encouraging fluency, flexibility and originality, which we had felt to be major criteria of creativity. Parenthetically you will be interested to know that in a comparison of these students with a matched control group we found that they showed consistently greater shifts toward more creativity than the control group, as measured by creativity tests which allow for divergency.

Though our results were not highly significant on any single test, the fact that we got consistent shifts using a wide range of tests leads us to believe that we may have some support for our hypothesis that a design curriculum which is open-ended and encourages and rewards creativity can increase the creative performance of academically superior adolescents.

This study was done with ninth grade junior high school students. This is the first year that grades count for college entrance. Most of the students are college bound, particularly those in our groups who are in the upper ten per cent on the School and College Ability Tests. The pressure to conform to what the teacher wants in the competition for top grades hardly seems conducive to creativity. To get any consistently greater increase in mean shifts for the experimental group in this kind of a situation is encouraging.

Those who work with smaller children feel that many of them design intuitively, but often appear to lose this sensitivity when they reach the upper elementary grades. We have found that helping children understand what it is they are doing, at a very simple level, helps these 4th, 5th, and 6th grade children continue their interest in design at the same time that their drawings may be becoming more realistic. We need research in this area to see what personality differences are most related to the intuitive vs. the nonintuitive approach.

Again this points out to me that we need to find more effective ways for teaching design and ways to do this at all levels of education.

Every student is expected to learn the English language no matter what his potential. The importance of the visual arts as communication would indicate that most students also should understand this language system. We must devise ways to make design understandable by students with wide differences in ability.

Individual Differences

Individual differences are found in almost every kind of perceptual behavior that is used in art activities. There is considerable evidence that people learn to use different kinds of cues to relate themselves to space. This is a basic mode of orienting themselves to their environment. Some people can use freely their bodily sensory, kinesthetic cues of uprightness and use less information from the visual field. They more easily separate figure from ground.

At the other extreme are people who ignore bodily cues of uprightness and are dependent on the cues in their visual field. Placed in rooms that are tilted they try to adjust themselves to the way the room appears, and have much more difficulty separating figure and ground. A large majority of people make compromises of the information received from visual and bodily cues. But we cannot assume that all these people are getting the same kind of information from their visual field because of the differences in the kinds of cues they are using. It is quite well established that these differences occur as early as eight years. To my knowledge, this has not been tested at an earlier age.

As a group, children are more dependent on the field than adults even though differences occur among them. Witkin[5] and his associates, who are the major researchers in this area, have found that dependency on field clues is found more among boys whose mothers were restrictive and limiting in the amount of freedom given them as children. These boys were much more dependent than those who had more freedom and had learned to separate themselves from their environment.

With the relationship found between dependency and independency, we can have some assurance that by helping a child become more independent we can also help him learn to use both kinds of cues effectively. For an important contribution of this research is that these tendencies are mainly learned. Witkin found that people who are very field dependent can use bodily cues when blindfolded. This further substantiates our point of view that people can be trained. We could not assume, though, that a person who was very field dependent could immediately profit or succeed in a task that required free independent use of kinesthetic cues.

For example, the motivating technique of asking students to imagine the feeling of movement to improve their drawing of action figures might well be frustrating to the

[5]H. A. Witkin, "Perception of the Upright," *Scientific American* (February 1959), pp. 50–56. *Personality Through Perception* (New York: Harper and Brothers, 1954).

student who has not developed the use of such kinesthetic cues.

A second area of individual differences is in the use of intuition or sensory evidence in responding to the environment. A new experimental personality inventory of the Educational Testing Service — the Myers-Briggs Test Inventory — indicates that only about 25% of the population responds intuitively to their environment while the other 75% stop with the sensory evidence insofar as they are able to see it. The intuitive person is more creative, using the cues he gets to see relationships and organizations, while the person dependent on sensory evidence tends to stop with that and not go on. Two people responding to cues in such opposite ways would get the same information. More interesting we probably would find that they would succeed or fail in an art assignment depending on the requirements. The intuitive person may have a very hard time analyzing details, and the person who is satisfied with sensory details may have difficulty in improvising on or abstracting from nature.

The personality factor of rigidity operates in perception. There is a considerable body of evidence that people who are behaving rigidly or anxiously will accept less perspective distortion from what they know about the things they see than people who are not rigid. If he is a rigid individual he will be less open to new information. If he is flexible and visually inquisitive he will look for new information, and if he doesn't have a concept for dealing with it he will create one.

Individual differences in perception also include the relationship between individual IQ and the ability to handle visual complexity. Unfortunately, this area has not had as much research as it should, but we do have some rather broad indications of trends. This requires that we think carefully as we weight different information. There is some evidence that people of higher IQ can handle more complex visual information than

people of lower IQ[6] and that they can assimilate more asymmetrical material. This does not mean that everyone of lower IQ cannot handle complex visual material. It only means that there is some relationship between higher intellectual abilities as measured within the limits of IQ tests and ability to handle visual detail. It could mean that these people have developed more categories for structuring their visual information. On the other hand many of us have seen individuals of very low IQ who can draw realistically in perspective with great skill. This may mean that they are freer from cognitive interference and can observe more directly. What they know doesn't get in the way of what they see. Here again we must watch our generalizations. We certainly cannot assume that everyone who is an excellent draftsman has a low IQ. More appropriately a Leonardo da Vinci, a Raphael or a Paul Klee has very high intellectual capacities, but has also developed the ability to use his perceptual skills to a very high degree.

All of this points to the complexity of human behavior in art and the great need for art educators to understand as much as possible of this behavior in order to create art experiences that will have meaning for all children and adolescents.

It must not be assumed that these are the only areas where research on perceptual information handling can help us. They are the areas, as I have reviewed the literature, that seem helpful to me. Others using the same research will see more and other ideas. New research is constantly being made available.

The next question is what use can we make of these studies in curriculum development and practice? They do suggest new dimensions to our objectives for art in general education — the art education of all American youth.

[6]June K. McFee, *Prepartaion for Art* (Belmont: Wadsworth Publishing Co., 1961).

1. If art is the complex communication system that it appears to be, then one of our objectives should be making students aware of its communicating functions.

   To do this they need to—understand art as a part of society's culture;—understand design as the form or organizing system through which communication takes place; —have the visual skills necessary to respond both to art and to nature.

2. In an age of mass communication and influence, individuality and independence of aesthetic judgment and taste need to be carefully preserved;

   Through understanding design and opportunity to use this understanding creatively, students should have a better potential for resisting the conforming and leveling pressures of mass media.

3. Since we can no longer assume that perception is unlearned, perceptual training through the arts becomes a necessary objective in the education of all children and youth. All students can increase their ability to handle complex detail and the concepts they use in categorizing visual information.

4. Since design is now seen as a basic communication system, all students should have design instruction at both elementary and secondary levels.

5. Since art is so important in our lives, we must discover and encourage the artistically talented who will make the contributions of the future.

These five objectives lead to problems of curriculum development. We need to ask ourselves for each of them:

1. How can we structure an overall curriculum so each objective can be introduced in its simplest forms in the primary grades, and be enriched and added to throughout the elementary and secondary schools?

2. How can we keep the curriculum open-ended so individual and creative teachers can use the material without being hampered?

   Also how can we structure it so that at any given level the material can be introduced to children of diverse abilities?

3. How can we group students or organize curriculum so that these differences can be handled?

This year I have worked with the National Association of Secondary School Principals Curriculum Committee which is trying to devise ways to increase education in the arts in the face of the other pressures on education. They showed growing interest in flexible scheduling as one possible solution.

Briefly, flexible scheduling means adjusting class time and number of session per week to subject matter and student needs. This would allow more time for the arts for all high school students. It would allow for large group motivation and small group application. It would allow for grouping of students as to aptitude for art — giving the more able students more opportunities for small group and individual instruction. It would also give teachers who can stimulate and interest large groups opportunity to do so, while teachers who work best in small groups could work in depth. It would give those art teachers who are particularly skilled in reaching the emotionally disturbed and slow learners a chance to work with these students without the responsibilities of teaching them in regular classes. Flexible scheduling is advantageous for the individual students as well. Students may be shifted to more advanced classes any time their ability warrants it.

With this kind of grouping and scheduling taking away some of the more obvious differences and teaching problems, it would seem easier for us to allow for the subtler differences in perception, in the use of intuition or sensory evidence. It would allow us to structure the curriculum leading to our objectives for the ability levels of our groups.

When we can break away from thinking of course work grouped into one 50-minute period per day per week, many new possibilities become evident. We need to be prepared to answer questions such as this: If every student in a high school should be given 160 hours of art instruction, how can we best use this time? One possibility might be core courses in understanding art to large groups meeting once a week for two or three years — plus small group activity courses depending on ability and interest. Do we know if one year of required work in art at the 7th grade is the best way to teach art in general education?

As new possibilities for class scheduling arise we must be prepared to use them in the most effective ways. I do believe that if we are ready as these changes take place we will be able to increase the amount of art in the high schools.

At the high school level particularly there are two serious problems. One, we have not analyzed adequately our subject areas to be able to develop a structure of sequential basic concepts which will support art learning from the elementary through the secondary school. This to me is our most pressing challenge, as it challenges every field of education. Jerome Bruner's book, *The Process of Education*, has some important ideas in this respect.[7] He feels that each field should look for its underlying structure and devise ways to present it at all educational levels. This will certainly be necessary if we are to move into long term art instruction in the high school.

The second problem is our need to preserve the fanciful, and imaginative, and the intuitive activities as we help students increase their understanding of the arts. As teachers we must cherish the emotional, yet be willing to use our intellect as well, if the arts are to be preserved in education. We cannot defend them from the standpoint of

[7]Jerome Bruner, *The Process of Education* (Cambridge: Harvard University Press, 1960).

personal experience alone, nor can we meet the new curriculum demands solely from a personal philosophy of education.

In the elementary grades, different problems exist, and are more varied depending on state requirements and the use of specialized art teachers. It has been found to be effective to have three kinds of art activities for children:

Art learning experiences in which children's perceptions are stimulated and cultivated — where the interaction of the elements of design are discovered — and new techniques and materials are explored.

Self-directed art in which each child has time for his own inventing and has time to stay with activities until he is ready to go on.

Integrated art activities in which children learn about the role of art in society. For example, as they learn the major roles in society such as the law, and the military, they also need to understand the contributions of the architect, artist, designer and craftsman. They can learn to understand another society through its art and thus gain sensitivity to the function of the arts in their own society.

In all three kinds of art experiences, children are using art as a means of learning as well as expressing. Art is an important avenue for analyzing and discriminating perceptions, for organizing these concepts in their interactions, and then symbolizing them so they can be understood by others. Painting a picture or a mural is as good a summary of learning as a written report. In some ways its richer symbolism may increase retention. Certainly children can organize in drawing more complex ideas than they can in writing.

The elementary teacher who understands children's individual differences in art, understands learning through art, and has had adequate art training herself is probably the best teacher, as she knows her own students best. Unfortunately such teachers are not in the majority, so other solutions must be found, such as the art specialist in the elementary schools, or the combined consultant teacher. Whatever the solution, it does seem important that all those who work with children understand both the content of art and the differences in the children who receive the content.

Whatever the curriculum design and grouping of students, individual differences will exist.

In providing motivation we must allow for these differences.

Cognitive and visual learning need to be encouraged, with special help for students who depend strongly on one or the other.

Motivation in drawing classes should include activities for students who use either bodily or visual cues. After some success has been achieved, they can be encouraged to develop their use of the other cue as well. Dancing, rhythm activities, moving with eyes shut, all encourage the development of kinesthetic bodily cues. All students need to learn to *see* and *think* in three-dimensional space.

Students who are particularly rigid need special help in going beyond the perceptual constancies to see form, color, size and location change in space.

Students of design need avenues for learning it intellectually, intuitively or both, depending on their particular readiness and future goals.

The introduction of new motivating subject matter and experiences needs to be geared to the class's general ability to handle visual detail and the range of individual differences in it. Sudden shifts in kinds of art activity may be difficult for more rigid students so the sequence of activities needs to be carefully watched.

I hope these dimensions of individual differences are not discouraging to you. Actually they make the teaching of art far more exciting as it is possible to reach more students.

All art educators would agree, I'm sure, that our major challenge is to increase the aesthetic sensitivity of American society through education. We are attempting to do this during a period of great unrest and conflict over the role of education. Our strengths lie in the increase of the quality of art in general education. Three directives emerge from the materials discussed in this paper:

1. We need to increase our understanding of the roles and functions of the arts in society so we can teach it more effectively.

2. We must increase our awareness of the behaviors used in responding to and expressing through art so that we may make art have more meaning in the lives of more people.

3. Finally we must develop curricula that will provide for individual differences, meet the new changes in education, and reach our major goals.

SUGGESTED READINGS FOR PART III

ALSCHULER, ROSE H., and LA BERTA W. HATTWICK. *A Study of Painting and Personality of Young Children.* 2 vols. Chicago: The University of Chicago Press, 1947.

ANASTASI, ANN, and JOHN P. FOLEY, JR. "An Analysis of Spontaneous Drawings by Children in Different Cultures," *Journal of Applied Psychology*, XX (1936), 689–726.

BARRON, FRANK. "Some Relationships between Originality and Style of Personality," *American Psychologist*, IX (1954), 326.

LINDSTROM, MIRIAM. *Children's Art.* Berkeley: University of California Press, 1957.

LOWENFELD, VIKTOR, and W. LAMBERT BRITTAIN. *Creative and Mental Growth* (fourth edition). New York: The Macmillan Company; London: Collier-Macmillan Limited, 1964.

McFEE, JUNE. *Preparation for Art*. San Francisco: Wadsworth Publishing Company, Inc., 1961.

MORRIS, DESMOND. *The Biology of Art: a study of the picture making behaviour of the great apes and its relationship to human art*. London: Methuen and Company, Ltd., 1962.

SCHAEFER-SIMMERN, HENRY. *The Unfolding of Artistic Activity*. Berkeley: University of California Press, 1948.

PART IV

HOW CAN ART·
BE TAUGHT?

Art teaching practices today run the gamut from laissez-faire approaches involving little more than provision of time, space and art materials to approaches involving highly organized lessons or units of study, with a number of variants falling between these two extremes. Conceivably, the entire range — from nondirected to directed practices — could be exhibited over a period of time by one and the same teacher, who might insist, quite plausibly, that the method should vary according to the art activity; that (say) fingerpainting and drawing in two-point perspective require quite different latitudes in the freedom allowed the student, with corresponding degrees of specificity in instruction. More commonly, however, art teachers will be found to have more or less consistent personal methods or styles of teaching whatever the activity to be taught, and typically their methods or styles are not dictated by curriculum theory or justified by any conscious appeal to pedagogical principles.

Nevertheless, it can be reasonably argued that the current profusion of teaching methods — and nonmethods — does in part stem from diverse notions, however vague and ill-defined, of what the content of art is and how humans learn or otherwise acquire this content. And clarification among teachers of the alternative concepts and analyses contained in Parts II and III would probably sharpen the differences in their methods. Our claim here is not that there should be widespread acceptance of a single true method of art instruction, but rather that at least a part of the preparation of the art teacher should involve a conscious and deliberate attention to alternative methods.

The point of this claim would hardly have been understood in earlier more stable periods in art history when art schools, guilds, and studios were required to turn out artists who could produce work that met well-established aesthetic standards of church, state and aristocratic patrons. Methods varied in each era, to be sure. But they did not stand in radical opposition to one another as do some current approaches to art instruction. Much of Ancient, Medieval, and Renaissance art was susceptible to codification into principles of appreciation and formulas of production; now any didactic effort in the arts is suspect because all methods seem so transitory. Modern art presents a bewildering array of rapidly changing styles, techniques, subject matters and functions — each with vociferous champions and equally vocal critics. The art teacher who views this kaleidoscopic scene is hard-pressed to decide just what the content of art is, not to mention the problem of how to teach it. Expressionistic and formal painting, Hard Edge, Neo-Dada, Pop and Op Art, the return to the figure and "happenings" — all compete for his attention. His aesthetic preferences are bound to affect his method of art instruction.

The articles in this section were chosen not only because they offer the sharpest contrasts in approach but also because they are worthy of study on their own merits. Yet the difference between the teaching methods Walter Smith and Kimon Nicolaides recommend is striking. We think it important that art teachers be prepared to make intelligent choices among these methods, or, at least, become sophisticated enough to offer a rationale for their own method of instruction in the face of the competing methods available to them. School personnel, parents, and students are entitled to know what justification there is for any pedagogical method employed in the school, from reading instruction to art instruction.

It will become evident to the reader that if one accepts the premises of a Walter Smith, the strict "copybook" drawing exercises follow as a valid conclusion. If, on the other hand, one were to accept Nicolaides' premises, his "natural" method of drawing would follow with equal validity. Both methods are valid because they are implied by the premises — by their respective conceptions of art and art learning. But the reader should also notice that the question, "How can art be taught?" is not merely a matter of logic (the deduction of pedagogical conclusions from conceptual premises) because determining the truth of an answer necessarily involves testing by experience and experiment. Answers range from "Art can be taught this way because in my experience students learned under this method" to the following from Beittel, Mattil, et al.(see page 256).

These experimental findings indicate some of the conditions necessary for progress in art. Where a drive for depth and involvement is made possible through sustained work in a limited area of creativity it is possible to hold and perhaps develop a positive, aesthetic, self-determining orientation. Only over a series of work where progress can be discerned and evaluation can take place is it likely that an entire group of students will grow not only in their creativity in art but perhaps as individuals.

The first answer characterizes the type of statement provided by the artist-teacher. It is convincing when the artist-teacher has, in fact, turned out students who have gone on to make contributions to the art world or who have in some other way benefited by his instruction. The second answer illustrates the cautious, corrigible and generalizable statement of the educational researcher, and can be convincing for the same reason — it has been tested and is testable. The obvious differences of language in the two kinds of statements — the different degrees of rigor and abstractness of terminology — should not be allowed to obscure the reciprocal relationship possible. The informal reflections of the successful artist-teacher can suggest some of the most significant hypotheses for researchers to test under controlled conditions; researchers, in turn, can transmute these reflections-*cum*-hypotheses into explicit formulations having applicability to a large number of teacher-learning situations.

Specific answers to the question of how art can be taught range in applicability from the teaching of drawing to children to teaching drawing in general (presumably to any student), from creative art teaching to the aesthetic method in education, from a comparison of methods of art instruction at the ninth grade level to an analysis of the logic of teaching in the fine arts. All of the articles included in this section are suggestive of approaches to art teaching that could be undertaken in the public schools; some of the articles propose methods of instruction while other articles (i.e., Taylor, Read, Smith) offer a critique of existing methods.

15. Freehand Drawing

WALTER SMITH

Introduction

That it is practicable to teach drawing in the public schools is no longer a matter of doubt; and that the study is one of great industrial and educational value, when properly taught, no person, who has carefully investigated the subject, questions for a moment. The drawing, however, must be wide in its range, rational, and systematic. It must be much more than simple copying: indeed, it must be, in the main, something wholly different from that; and it must be much more than picture-making, — even good original picture-making. Those who think otherwise sadly misapprehend the scope and value of one of the most practical studies.

It will be observed, as characteristic of this course of drawing, in both its primary and advanced grades, that the picture-element, as such, is almost entirely excluded. The author is well aware that, in excluding many pretty things which have usually been considered proper for drawing exercises, he sacrifices something of superficial attrac-

tiveness; but he omits them because the best artistic, practical, or educational results cannot otherwise be produced. He excludes them from even this primary course, because he would here lay a sound basis for more advanced and severer work, when pupils reach the grammar schools. Hence, while the author is aware that pupils are anxious to begin what may be called "pretty work" as early as possible, he wishes teachers clearly to understand that picture-making, so far as the public schools are concerned, should always be regarded as a secondary matter. He also wishes teachers to remember that the correct representation of any object, as really seen, involves principles of perspective, with light and shade, which young pupils cannot understand; which cannot, indeed, be understood by anyone without much hard study. Hence, to set children drawing from copies involving these features is to set them to reproducing, in a merely mechanical way, what they cannot possibly comprehend. Instead of leading learners into such ruts, the author desires, first of all, to make them acquainted with the beauties of pure

*SOURCE: Reprinted from Walter Smith, *Freehand Drawing*. James R. Osgood and Co., Boston (1875), pp. 5–31, 146–149.

form and with the principles of good design. Therefore it is that the exercises in this primary course are principally such as deal with mere outline representation, based on geometrical forms, and illustrating leading principles of practical design. It is only when pupils have well mastered this stage that they are prepared to take up intelligently, and in a thorough manner, perspective, and model and object drawing.

Drawing Should Be Taught by Regular Teachers

Drawing can, and should, be taught by the regular teacher. One who understands the general principles of teaching can teach drawing successfully, without any special artistic gifts. Thousands of persons teach arithmetic successfully who possess no special mathematical gifts; and there is nothing about drawing so difficult to master as some of the features of mathematics. Let it, then, be accepted as true, that there is nothing about drawing to prevent any person of fair capacity becoming proficient enough to teach it intelligently and with success. It is clear, from the present movement in favor of art education, that the teaching of drawing will soon be required in all public schools; and it must, therefore, be taught by the regular teachers. Indeed, it is best, for various reasons, that it should thus be taught.

The Object of This Primary Course

This Manual, with the cards which accompany it, is intended for a course of instruction in slate-drawing in primary schools. The exercises are so simple, and so gradually progressive, that teachers, though they may have had no previous instruction in drawing, can master them, if they choose, without assistance, and intelligently lead any class of young pupils who happen to be under their charge. There is no better way to teach one's self than teaching others. With the cards in

the hands of the pupils, furnishing them good copies, it is not at all essential that teachers should be extraordinarily skillful in drawing on the blackboard. The Manual will acquaint them with all the principles involved: these principles they can explain orally to the pupils. It is the clear setting forth of these principles that constitutes the feature of chief importance in teaching drawing. The pupils, with their card copies before them, aided by the oral explanation, and by such illustrations (even though they be rude) as the teacher may give on the board, will make very satisfactory progress.

It is the leading object of these cards to teach proportion, the simple figures of plane geometry, the principles of practical design, and to familiarize the pupil with beautiful forms. To immediately follow these cards in the upper classes of primary schools, or in intermediate schools, the author has prepared three small books in freehand drawing, to be used by pupils in beginning to draw on paper. The exercises in these books apply the principles of the instruction given in the card-exercises, and teach more fully the drawing in outline of objects with regular features.

Reduction and Enlargement

Teachers should make themselves sufficiently familiar with the exercises, by drawing them, to be able to point out their features readily and clearly. When working on the blackboard, they should proceed slowly, explaining each point as they go along, and requiring the whole class to work together, even though some are obliged to execute their drawings very rudely.

It is intended that the figures given in the first chapter of the Manual shall be drawn on the blackboard by the teacher to a scale of one foot for every half inch of the copy. Then the pupils are to copy them on their slates, making them of a definite size stated by the teacher. The size of the figures will be governed by the size of the pupils' slates. This will teach *reduction*. It is intended that the forms on the cards shall be copied by the pupils from the cards, the teacher indicating the proportions, or scale, which should be much larger than in the copy. This will teach the pupils *enlargement*. The two features of practice, reduction and enlargement from copies, should go together: both are essential to good progress in drawing. If each pupil is supplied with card copies, the labor of the teacher will be greatly abridged; since all can be taught the same thing at the same time, while the advancement of the whole class will be more satisfactory than it can be otherwise. The figures given in the other chapters of the Manual, and not found on the cards, are intended for blackboard copies, to be drawn by the teacher as introductory exercises to the use of the cards, or for dictation exercises to accompany the cards.

Geometrical Definitions

The definitions of plane geometry, illustrations of which are employed as a basis of freehand drawing, should be given to, and repeated by, the youngest pupils. They should be explained, not so much by words, as by freehand illustrations drawn on the blackboard as accurately as possible. Figures of this kind, when seen, children readily understand. The copies in the first chapter may be repeated as often as writing lessons; but, instead of continued repetitions of the same exercise, the whole series in the first chapter should be gone over once, and then be taken again from the first, with a better understanding and increased skill. When teaching children to draw, above all things avoid wearying them by repetition of uninteresting elementary work. They have no appreciation of abstract truths, nor of the words used to express such truths; but they are exceedingly sensitive to visible forms, and

readily acquire a knowledge of them. It is possible to reach their understanding through the sense of sight sooner than by appeals to either of the other senses, or by logical explanations. Geometric accuracy in freehand or model drawing is not to be expected of any one: the standard by which the efforts of little children are judged should, therefore, be a very merciful one.

Power of Observation

Since intelligent drawing is always an expression of knowledge, the power of observation must be cultivated from the outset. Pupils must be trained to discover the features of whatever they are to draw before they begin their work. To take a simple illustration: When the pupils have learned the names of the different straight lines and angles, the square may be given as an exercise. The teacher should draw it on the blackboard, requiring the pupils to name each line drawn, and, when the figure is completed, to give the number and names of the angles it contains. After the diameters and diagonals have been drawn, the pupils should then be required to state the effect of these lines upon the original angles, and to give the number and names of the new angles and triangles. Other exercises may be treated in a similar manner.

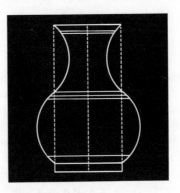

FIGURE 15.1

Class Analysis of Forms

When the cards are used, a class analysis of the figure should frequently precede the drawing; that is, the pupils should be required to describe the general geometrical form of the figure, and the various lines which it contains.   Take figure 15.1 for example: The analysis would show the pupils, before they began to draw, that an oblong would enclose the vase; that the vase is symmetrically arranged on an axis, its two sides being alike; that it is composed of compound curves and horizontal lines; that the top and bottom have the same width; that the widest part is near the bottom; that the narrowest part is the neck near the top; that it has a base; that the compound curves make both the widest and narrowest parts; that they do not reach to the bottom; that there is no ornament on the vase except the horizontal lines. It will be seen at once that this preliminary analysis must develop the observing powers, must firmly fix in the mind the principles of drawing and design, must enable the pupils to do their work intelligently.

First of all, then, the eye is to be educated to distinguish form, and the mind to comprehend principles: the correct manual rendering of the form is a simple matter which will come by practice. In the early lessons, therefore, teachers whould lay more stress upon developing observation and understanding than upon mere dexterity in execution. It is rare, almost accidental, for young pupils to draw clear unbroken lines; while lines varying in thickness must be expected from them for a long time. In criticizing their efforts, form, irrespective of beauty of execution, should be mainly considered at first. When form has been fairly mastered, then teachers may begin to insist upon better lines and more careful workmanship. One thing should thus be taken at a time.

Drawing on the Blackboard

Drawing on the blackboard should be practiced at least once a week by all the pupils; a section working on the board every time a lesson is given, the others working at the same time on their slates. Pupils will be delighted with this, while it will afford them variety of practice, which is important. It will, in particular, allow them to make their drawings on a large scale. This work on the board may be termed the completest exemplification of freehand drawing.

Length of Lessons

Short lessons, often repeated, are better for young pupils than long ones at greater intervals. Four lessons a week, of half an hour each, or six of twenty minutes each, will be a fair amount of time for children under ten years to give to drawing. After that age the lessons may be longer and not so frequent, while new subjects may be taken up. When instruction is given at all in drawing, the lessons should be sufficiently frequent and sufficiently long to keep the pupils alive to their work, and thoroughly interested. Two short lessons a week will not do this. Four lessons will much more than double the results, and six lessons much more than treble them. This is not only true of drawing; but every teacher who has tried the experiment knows that it is also true of arithmetic or geography, for example. In neither of these studies would any one expect to make any satisfactory progress with only two short lessons a week. Indeed, the time would be regarded as, perhaps, worse than wasted, since the little progress actually made would not compensate for the disgust many of the children would acquire for the study thus treated. If then, drawing is to be taught at all, it should be taught in earnest, and not as a merely tolerated study. Even its decided attractiveness will not fully compensate for the lack of earnest work.

Again, if any new study, whatever, is to be put into a school, it should receive for a while, if possible, special attention, in order to emphasize its importance in the minds of the pupils, and to make a strong beginning. To begin well is half the battle. When the new study is thus once firmly established, it may then take its place with the other regular studies. Thus should the schools welcome drawing, which is destined to contribute so much towards the future prosperity and culture of the country.

Dictation Exercises

It is remarkable how few persons can accurately describe the true form, size, proportions, color, and character of any thing which the eye sees. People have general impressions, which, brought to the test of description, are found to be vague and altogether unreliable. Drawing, preceded by criticism and analysis of copies or objects, in which well-chosen terms describe details, cannot fail to educate even the reasoning powers as well as the imitative and artistic. For this purpose, lessons should also be frequently dictated by the teacher, without illustration in books, on cards, or on the blackboard.

For this kind of instruction, artificial objects, having geometric forms, are better suited than natural objects. For example, houses of simple proportions may thus be dictated and drawn. When such a drawing has been executed, it is then advisable to require the pupils capable of doing so to write a minute description of it, giving its form, size, proportions, etc. There could not possibly be a better subject for a composition, when it is desired to teach exactitude in the use of language.

A simple illustration of the dictation exercise is here given. The drawing of the annexed geometrical form may be dictated

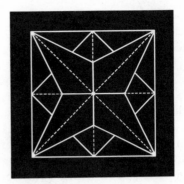

FIGURE 15.2

thus: Draw a square, its diameters and diagonals. Halve the semidiameters. From each corner of the square, draw a straight line to the nearest point of division on each diameter. On the diameters of the first square, as diagonals, draw a second square. Erase the diagonals of the first square, and the outer divisions of its diameters; also those parts of the inner square which go behind the points of the star. If the pupils heed what is dictated, they will produce the required figure; if not, they will draw something else. After the pupils have finished their work, the teacher will draw the figure correctly on the blackboard.

The object, then, of dictation exercises is to show that forms and words are interchangeable, both being mediums for the expression of thought; to teach pupils to use either language with equal facility; to translate and retranslate from one into the other. Such exercises, beginning with simple geometric forms, may be continued, until the most elaborate irregular forms can be drawn from dictation, if the language describing them be accurate and terse. Artisans have constant use for the power which is acquired from dictation exercises.

Memory Exercises

Pupils should be frequently required to produce, from memory, exercises which they have previously drawn. This will show the teacher how much of previous instruction is retained, while it is valuable simply as a means for developing the power of memory. Therefore, as soon as pupils have got a limited knowledge of forms, they should begin to reproduce these forms without seeing the copies and within a specified time. It is also urged that the pupils, leaving their cards at school, be occasionally required to do their drawing exercises at home, from memory, and, putting them into a little book provided for the purpose, bring them to the teacher for inspection.

Ruling and Measuring

With each series of cards there is a five-inch scale, the inches divided into halves, quarters, and sixteenths. This scale should be used only for correcting lines after they have been drawn, and not to help in first drawing the lines. Teachers must see that pupils do not use the scale in the manner prohibited. It is essential that the first lines of any drawing should be approximately correct, otherwise the remaining lines will be wholly out of place. Hence, when the first proportional lines have been drawn as nearly correct as possible by the eye alone, pupils should be permitted to measure them, and to correct them if they need correction. It is to be distinctly understood, however, that the measuring is not to be permitted until the lines have been drawn.

Some teachers say, "Never draw a straight line freehand if you have the means of ruling it;" yet it is better thus to draw straight lines than to rule them, unless it is absolutely essential, for some special reason, that they be mathematically straight, both because it is good practice for the eye and hand, and makes the pupil independent of rulers. The same may be said of drawing circles. Of course, when any thing of importance depends upon a circle being perfectly drawn, it is best to use a pair of compasses; but a circle practically

exact may be drawn freehand with very little experience, and it is educational thus to draw it. In practice, it will be found more difficult to rule either vertical or horizontal straight lines, than to draw them by the aid of the eye alone. A somewhat extended experience in teaching, with continued observation of the work of many pupils, has convinced the author that those who draw vertical and horizontal lines freehand, besides doing their work in less time, generally make their lines more nearly upright and level than those who rule them. Those only draw well who draw intelligently.

Position

When vertical and horizontal lines are drawn, the slate or paper should be kept in one position in front of the pupil, its edge parallel with the edge of the desk. When oblique lines are drawn, the slate or paper may be kept in the same position, while the hand is turned so that the vision may not be obstructed. When curves are drawn, it will be best to allow the slate or paper to be put in any position the pupil may prefer, in order that the hand may form the center of the curve drawn, which can be, in some cases, only when the drawing is turned sidewise or upside down.

Pencils and Models

The slate pencils should be soft, long, well-pointed, and held about an inch and a half from the end, far enough to keep the fingers from obstructing the vision.

For the purpose of illustrating many of the exercises, and accelerating the advance of the pupils, every primary school should have a box of models, which can be procured of the publishers of this book. Such a box would contain a sphere, cube, oblong block, triangular prism, hexagonal prism, cone, cylinder, rectangular pyramid, square frame, cross, and some other pieces.

※　※　※

In conclusion, the author would say that the child who draws from five years of age to fifteen ought to be able to draw any created thing, and will be able to do so when we teach well what every child ought to know. There is no royal road to drawing; and those who profess to offer such a road to us may be suspected of a desire to mislead with a regal name which represents nothing.

Center, Points, and Straight Lines

When young children begin to draw, teach them first the meaning of the word "center." Require them, by way of illustration, to touch the center of their slates with the end of their pencils. This center we will call a point.

A POINT *is simply position or place, without size, and may be indicated in different ways.*

Explain, next, the meaning of the words "right" and "left." Draw a vertical line on the blackboard; to the right of this line draw another, explaining that the last is to the right hand of the first. In the same way illustrate the meaning of the word "left." Next, draw a horizontal line, and in a similar manner explain the meaning of the words "above," "below."

Always make certain, in some way, that children have a clear understanding of whatever is used for the purpose of further extending their knowledge. It is well to take nothing for granted, but to explain the simplest things. When the celebrated Faraday lectured before children at the Royal Institute, London, he was accustomed to illustrate the most common phenomena. He would not take it for granted that the children knew that an apple, when unsupported, will fall to the ground; but he would actually illustrate the fact.

Straight Lines

A VERTICAL LINE *is a straight line which runs up and down, inclining neither to the right nor to the left, neither backwards nor forwards* (a).

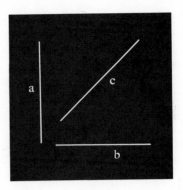

FIGURE 15.3

A HORIZONTAL LINE *is a level straight line, inclining neither up nor down* (b).

AN OBLIQUE LINE *is a straight line, neither vertical nor horizontal, but slanting* (c).

First, draw the three kinds of lines on the board, and give their names. Then require the pupils to draw them on their slates, without turning their slates. Each line should be drawn many times, until the pupils can instantly distinguish between the different lines; until they can instantly name them when drawn by the teacher, or instantly draw them when named by the teacher. A straight stick held in different positions will serve nicely to illustrate the meaning of the words "horizontal," "vertical," "oblique." Request the pupils to name objects in these different positions.

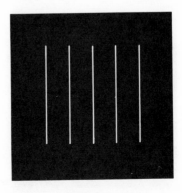

FIGURE 15.4

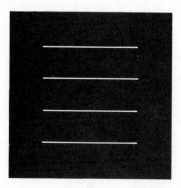

FIGURE 15.5

PARALLEL LINES *are lines running side by side in the same direction, and are always at the same distance from one another throughout their whole length. They may be straight or curved, vertical, oblique, or horizontal.*

Draw on the board parallel vertical (Figure 15.4), horizontal (Figure 15.5), and oblique lines (Figure 15.6), and require the pupils to repeat them on their slates, without turning their slates. This is an exercise to which you should frequently revert. When the pupils have drawn two lines parallel, require them to draw a third in the center between the two, and thus let them continue to halve the spaces between the lines, until the lines are very close together. The pencil should have a fine point for this work, and no two lines should be allowed to touch each other. This is excellent practice. As soon as the pupils have acquired some

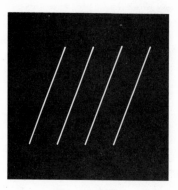

FIGURE 15.6

skill in judging distances, require them to draw parallel lines of definite length, as one inch, two inches, etc.

Pupils should have a clear understanding of parallel lines. There are two things requisite to make lines parallel: they must lie side by side, and they must have the same direction. When, therefore, we want two parallel vertical or two parallel horizontal lines, it is not enough to say, "Draw two vertical lines," or, "Draw two horizontal lines"; for in neither case need the lines be drawn side by side. Nor is it enough, when two parallel lines are wanted, simply to draw them side by side; for side by side does not necessarily mean that the lines must have exactly the same direction. Hence, we must say parallel vertical lines, parallel perpendicular lines, parallel oblique lines, or parallel horizontal lines, as the case may be, if we would say just what we mean. As further progress is made in this course of drawing, it will be more clearly seen why so much stress is laid upon the exact use of terms.

See that the pupils always have long and well-pointed pencils: they should never be allowed to draw with stubs or blunt pencils. To make sure that the pencils are always in good condition, keep them in a box under your own charge, to be distributed and taken up at every lesson. Appoint some one of the pupils from day to day, to sharpen the pencils, doing the work where it will not disturb the school. Without good material, it is impossible to draw rapidly and well.

The pencil should be held about an inch and a half from the point, and so held that the hand will not come between the eye and the space where the line is to be drawn, obstructing the vision.

When drawing straight lines in different directions, as horizontal, vertical, and oblique instead of turning the slate or paper, turn the hand. Observe these two things: always keep the hand and fingers in a position of freedom; never let the hand obstruct the sight.

Draw the shortest lines with the fingers alone; those somewhat longer draw with the hand, using the wrist joint, the next grade draw with the fore-arm, using the elbow joint; those longer yet, which will usually be on the blackboard, draw with the whole arm, using the shoulder joint. Occasionally, in drawing a very long horizontal line on the blackboard, it is necessary to carry the body forward as the line is drawn. It is best, when drawing a vertical line on the blackboard, to stand directly in front of where the line is to be drawn, with the side partially turned towards the board, and far enough away to let the hand, when the arm is extended, fall easily carrying the crayon down. Never draw a line with a jerky movement, but always with a uniform motion, and slow enough for the eye to follow.

Dividing Straight Lines and Judging Distances

Draw on the blackboard a vertical line(1), and divide it into two equal parts. Explain that the dividing mark is in the center of the line. Draw another line (2), and divide it into four equal parts; first, by dividing it into two equal parts, and then each of the halves into two other equal parts. Draw another line (3), and divide it into three equal parts. Dividing a line into three equal parts is more difficult than dividing it into

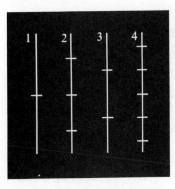

FIGURE 15.7

two equal parts. Draw another line (4), and divide it into six equal parts; first, by dividing it into two equal parts, and then each of the halves into three equal parts. While the teacher draws these lines on the blackboard, the pupils should draw lines of a given length on their slates, and divide them into halves, quarters, thirds, and sixths, following the teacher. Exactness in the division of lines should not be expected on the part of young pupils at first. It is sufficient, if they get the idea. Accuracy will come by practice. In these early stages, permit the pupils to correct their faults in free measurement by the aid of the scale which accompanies each series of cards. This practice will be found the surest way of educating them to correct observation. Before resorting, however, to the use of the scale, the pupils should do their best with their eyes alone. Drawing and dividing lines in this manner should be practiced in connection with other lessons, until pupils acquire a considerable degree of skill in determining definite distances and proportions.

Young children, unless they have received positive instruction, seldom have any clear idea of the length of an inch, a foot, a yard, or mile, though they may have heard the words used hundreds of items. If questioned, they frequently give answers that astonish the questioner.

Suppose, further, that it is required to draw a line, but of no particular length, and to divide it into five, seven, eleven, thirteen, or any other prime number of equal parts. In that case, having drawn a line, divide it into four equal parts, and then add one part, to make five; or divide it into eight equal parts, and then erase one, leaving seven, if that is the number required. That is, first draw a line, and divide it into a composite number of parts, then add or erase, as may be required. This is not, of course, a suitable exercise for the youngest pupils.

Frequently ask the pupils how they would proceed to divide a line into any designated number of equal parts. If, for example, the number is six, the answer should be: Divide the line into two equal parts; then divide each part into three equal parts, giving six.

Combining Straight Lines – Angles

As soon as the pupils have acquired a knowledge of straight lines, they should begin to combine them. Draw on the blackboard a vertical line of definite length, say twelve inches, and then require the pupils to draw a similar line, say four inches long, on their slates.

At this stage, the lines should all be drawn of definite lengths. Having first been drawn by the aid of the eye alone, they should afterwards all be corrected by the scale. Such practice is the beginning of the study of proportion.

Having drawn the vertical line, next draw a horizontal line of the same length; draw it from the lower end and to the right of the vertical line. The two lines, thus united, form what children will call a corner, but what we will call an angle. This particular angle (Figure 15.8) is called a right angle, not, however, because it opens to the right.

FIGURE 15.8

A RIGHT ANGLE *is formed by the meeting of two straight, or right, lines perpendicular to each other.*

The pupils should be taught to distinguish clearly between a vertical line and a perpendicular line. A vertical line is always perpendicular; but a perpendicular line is not always vertical. One line is said to be perpendicular to another line when the two meet so as to form a square corner, or right angle; yet both lines, when considered with reference to their position, may be oblique. But one line is never said to be vertical to another. When a right angle has been formed on a slate by the meeting of a vertical line and a horizontal line, it will remain a right angle, though the slate be partly turned around, and the lines become oblique. When a knife is half open, it forms a right angle: the blade is perpendicular to the handle, in whatever position the knife may be held, while the handle is perpendicular to the blade. Frequently illustrate this important distinction between the words vertical and perpendicular, and always insist upon the pupils using the words correctly.

Now extend the horizontal line in Figure 15.8 the same distance to the left of the vertical line already drawn, and explain that the corner thus formed on the left is also a right angle. By next extending the vertical line the same distance below the horizontal line, two more right angles will be formed; and you will have four right angles meeting in a point, or at the center, as Figure 15.9

The size of an angle does not depend at all on the length of the lines forming it: for

AN ANGLE *is the difference in the direction of two lines which meet, or would meet if extended far enough.*

FIGURE 15.9

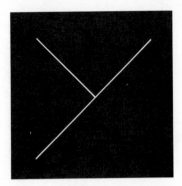

FIGURE 15.10

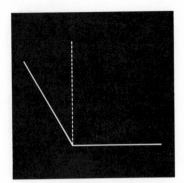

FIGURE 15.12

Therefore, the four angles meeting in Figure 15.9 would be no larger, though the lines were drawn longer.

Draw right angles on the board in various ways. Thus, draw a horizontal line; from its left end, draw a vertical line downwards. Again, draw a horizontal line; from its right end, draw a vertical line downwards; also, from above, draw a vertical line to join the right end of the horizontal line. Again, draw an oblique line; and, perpendicular to its center, draw another which will make two right angles on the first oblique line, as shown in Figure 15.10. Pupils repeat on their slates.

AN ACUTE ANGLE *is any angle less than a right angle.*

Draw a right angle, and, midway between the two lines, draw an oblique line meeting the first two in the corner, or vertex, of the angle, in Figure 15.11. This oblique line divides the right angle, and makes two sharper corners of it. These sharper corners are called acute angles, because they are sharper, or more pointed, than a right angle.

AN OBTUSE ANGLE *is an angle greater than a right angle.*

This figure in Figure 15.12 shows what is meant by "greater than a right angle." Draw a horizontal line as in Figure 15.13; then an oblique line, joining the horizontal line at its center; and then a third line, perpendicular to the second line. The union of the horizontal and oblique lines forms one acute angle and one obtuse angle; the former to the right of the oblique line, the latter to the left. The union of the two oblique lines forms two right an-

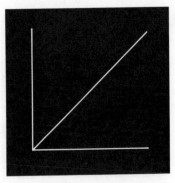

FIGURE 15.11

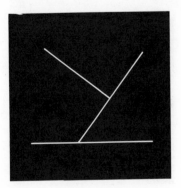

FIGURE 15.13

FIGURE 15.14

FIGURE 15.16

gles. Thus draw the different angles in various positions, and require the pupils to name the angles, until they can readily recognize them, however they may be drawn. Also require the pupils to make the different angles by placing two sticks in different positions. Explain clearly that an angle is the *difference in direction* of two lines, and not the lines themselves, nor the space between them. An angle is formed when two lines tend towards each other, though they do not always extend far enough to meet.

Good drawing models are the best objects with which to illustrate the principles of geometrical drawing.

The following letters drawn with single lines illustrate the different angles (Figure 15.14). Letters E, F, H, L, contain right angles. Letters M, N, V, W, Z, contain acute angles. Letters A, K, X, Y, contain acute and obtuse angles.

Combining Straight Lines — Triangles

A TRIANGLE *is a figure having three straight sides, enclosing three angles.*

A RIGHT-ANGLED TRIANGLE has one of *its angles a right angle* (Figure 15.15).

Draw a right angle, by joining the end of a vertical line to the end of a horizontal line. Draw an oblique line, joining the other ends of the lines. These three lines will give a three-sided figure, as at J, which is called a triangle, because it has three angles; and a right-angled triangle, because one of the angles is a right angle.

Here is a curious fact about triangles: The three angles are always equal to two right angles. If one is a right angle, as in the present instance, then the other two will be equal to a right angle. This may be easily illustrat-

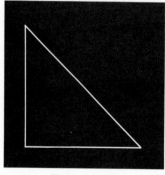

FIGURE 15.15

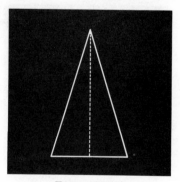

FIGURE 15.17

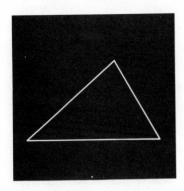

FIGURE 15.18

AN ISOSCELES TRIANGLE *has two only of its sides equal* (Figure 15.17).

Draw a horizontal line, and mark its center. From this center, draw a vertical line upwards. Join the end of the vertical line to the ends of the horizontal line by two oblique lines, as in Figure 15.17. Erase the vertical line, when an isosceles triangle will remain. The word isosceles means having equal legs, as this triangle has two equal sides. An equilateral triangle is an isosceles triangle; but all isosceles triangles are not equilateral.

A SCALENE TRIANGLE *has no two of its sides equal.*

Draw three straight lines of unequal length, uniting their ends, as in Figure 15.18. The word scalene means limping. This triangle can be placed on no one of its sides without leaning to the right or left.

ed with paper. Cut paper into triangles of various shapes; then cut off the corners of any one of the triangles, and lay them side by side, so that the points will be close together, when they will be found exactly to fill the space of two right angles. Mark the corners before they are cut off; otherwise, the right corners may not be laid together.

AN EQUILATERAL TRIANGLE *has three equal sides and three equal angles* (Figure 15.16).

It will require considerable practice to draw an equilateral triangle correctly. For the present, it will be sufficient if the pupils get the idea. They should name the lines forming the triangles, also the kinds of angles formed by the lines. A triangle is the strongest of all figures. The position of three sticks thus united cannot be changed without breaking one of the sticks.

Combining Straight Lines – Rectangular Figures

Any figure having four straight sides and four right angles is called A RECTANGLE.

A SQUARE *is a figure having four equal sides and four right angles.*

Draw a right angle opening to the right, with the horizontal and vertical lines of the same length. From the upper end of the vertical line draw towards the right a horizontal line of the same length as the one below. Next, draw a vertical line connecting the right ends of the two horizontal lines. Thus we have a square (Figure 15.19).

Let the pupils frequently name the lines, state if any are parallel, and also give the number and kind of angles the square contains.

The pupil having learned to draw a square, it will now be well for him to work within one of definite size.

FIGURE 15.19

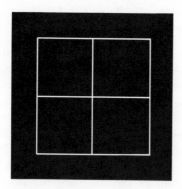

FIGURE 15.20

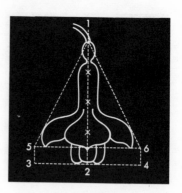

FIGURE 15.22

A DIAMETER OF A SQUARE *divides the square and its opposite sides into two equal parts.*

Draw a square as before. Divide each of its sides into two equal parts; connect the points of division by a vertical and a horizontal line, as in Figure 15.20. These lines give the diameters of the square, and, at the same time, divide it into four equal smaller squares.

Let the pupil name the kind and number of angles in these four squares.

DIAGONALS OF A SQUARE *are lines connecting the opposite angles of a square.*

Variation 1. Draw three squares united horizontally, and fill them in a similar manner. Continue the moulding below the rosettes.

Variation 2. Draw the square, its diagonals and diameters, and the circle at the cen-

ter. Then, instead of drawing the compound curves on the diagonals, draw them on the diameters, and the leaves on the diagonals. Finish.

CARD-EXERCISE: TOY CHURCH

Draw a square, and divide it into nine equal small squares. Erase the right two of the upper three. Divide the right and left sides of the remaining upper square into thirds, and the top into fourths. Through the lower points of division on the sides, and the outer points of division on the top, draw the inclining sides of the spire. The window occupies one-half the width of the square. Draw the vertical and horizontal lines belonging to the spire and body of the church; then add the lines for the roof, door, and windows. Draw the lower lines of the roof before the upper lines; observe that the ridge is level with the bottom of the spire (Figure 15.21).

CARD-EXERCISE: FUCHSIA CONVENTIONALIZED

Draw 1 2, and divide it into four equal parts (Figure 15.22). Make 3 4 equal to 1 2. Join ends of 3 4 to the upper end of 1 2 by oblique lines, and draw 5 6 through the center of the lower fourth of 1 2. Finish the form.

Variation. Draw a circle, and divide it into six equal parts by drawing three diameters. On every other semi-diameter, draw a form similar to this, with the stems of the three uniting at the center.

FIGURE 15.21

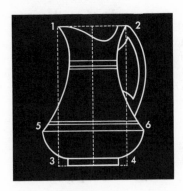

FIGURE 15.23

CARD-EXERCISE: PITCHER, ILLUSTRATING
COMPOUND CURVES

Divide the central vertical line into four equal
parts, and make 1 2, 3 4, equal to two of these
parts, and 5 6 equal to three (Figure 15.23).
Draw 1 3, 2 4. Finish, noting carefully where the
lines of the pitcher cross the dotted lines. The
width of the base of the pitcher is equal to one
part and a half of the vertical line.

Variation. Let the curve from 1 be unbroken at
5, rounding off to 3. Make the outline of the opposite side of the pitcher the same. Extend 1 2
half of its length beyond 2, and from its extremity
draw a straight line to a point just above 6. This
last line forms the outer line of the handle, to
which add the thickness; then put a spout,
curving above the left half of 1 2, and passing
through its center beneath the right half, but
turning up again to where the handle starts.

A design must vary somewhat according to the

material from which the object is to be made, as
silver, clay, wood, stone, cast or wrought iron.

CARD-EXERCISE: (A) A WATER-BOTTLE OF SIMPLE
CURVES AND STRAIGHT LINES

Draw the vertical line 1 2, and divide it into
fourths (Figure 15.24). Just above the lower
extremity, draw 3 4 equal to three-fourths of 1 2.
Draw the neck and stopper, which occupy the
upper half of 1 2, making the width of the neck
equal to two-thirds of 1 2. On the lower half of
the vertical line, draw simple curves, forming the
outline of the body of the bottle, as shown in
the copy. Draw the curves springing from 3 and
4. Finish.

In England the water-bottle is quite extensively
used in the sleeping-rooms of hotels and in private
houses. It will be seen that water put into it
must of necessity be kept pure.

(B) CANDLESTICK, CANDLE, AND EXTINGUISHER

Draw the central vertical line, and divide it
into four equal parts (Figure 15.25). Through
the lower point of division, draw 1 2 a little longer than three-fourths of the vertical line, and extending to the same distance on each side of it.
Make 3 4 equal to one-half of 1 2. The top of the
socket reaches to the center of the vertical line,
while the wick occupies the upper half of the upper fourth. Draw the curves carefully, most of
them being compound. Draw the outer curve of
the handle before drawing the inner. See that the
sides of the extinguisher have the same slope.
In this exercise but few exact measurements

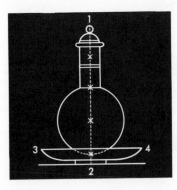

FIGURE 15.24

FIGURE 15.25

are given: it will, therefore, be a good one for the best pupils to draw on the blackboard from the book.

QUESTIONS

1. What is said of conventionalized forms?
2. When is it proper to imitate Nature exactly?
3. What is mentioned as the first step in original design?
4. How can the power of repetition in numbers on form be illustrated?
5. How far is it proper to use the blackboard?
6. Why should pupils in a class never draw from wall charts?

16. The Natural Way to Draw

KIMON NICOLAIDES

I assume that you are about to embark on a year of art study, and I plan to teach you as nearly as possible just what you would have learned if you had spent a year in one of my classes at the Art Students' League. I do not care who you are, what you can do, or where you have studied if you have studied at all. I am concerned only with showing you some things which I believe will help you to draw. My interest in this subject is a practical one, for my efforts consist in trying to develop artists.

The students who have come to my actual classes have been people of vastly differing experience, taste, background, and accomplishments. Some had studied a great deal, some not at all. Many were teachers themselves. I always ask them, as I am going to ask you, to approach these exercises from the beginning, exactly as if you were a beginner, whatever your preparation may have been. I believe that the reason for this will become apparent as you work. Each exercise develops from preceding ones, and it is conceivable that if you opened this book anywhere other

than at the beginning you would be misdirected rather than helped.

The arrangement of the text has been determined, not by subject matter, but by schedules for work, because the work is the important thing. Each section of reading matter is accompanied by a schedule representing fifteen hours of actual drawing. Begin your first day's work by reading the first section until you come to the direction that you are to draw for three hours according to Schedule 1A. *Then stop and draw.*

I ask that you follow the schedules explicitly because each one has been planned with care and for a definite purpose. You should not even read the succeeding paragraphs until you have spent the time drawing as directed. And that is true of the entire book, for the basic idea of its instruction is to have you arrive at the necessary relationship between thought and action. Each exercise has its place and carries a certain momentum. If you fail to do it at the time and for as long a time as you are instructed to, you disrupt that momentum. If you

*SOURCE: Reprinted from Kimon Nicolaides, *The Natural Way to Draw*, copyright 1941 by Anne Nicolaides. Boston: Houghton Mifflin Co., 1941, pp. 1–22, 221. In the original book this section was entitled "How to Use This Book."

feel that you fail with some exercise, that you do not understand it at all, simply practice it as best you can for the required time and then try the next. There are other exercises that will take up the slack provided the effort has been made.

In most courses of study of any sort the general idea prevails that it is to your credit to get through the work quickly. That is definitely not true in this study. If you are particularly apt, your advantage will lie, not in how much sooner you can "get the idea" and "finish," but in how much more you will be able to do at the end of a year's work than someone less gifted. What you are trying to learn is not the *exercise* — that should be easy, for I have tried to make each one as simple as possible. You are trying to learn to *draw*. The exercise is merely a constructive way for you to look at people and objects so that you may acquire the most knowledge from your efforts.

As you begin, try to develop the capacity of thinking of only one thing at one time. In these exercises I have attempted to isolate one by one what I consider the essential phases of, or the essential acts in, learning to draw. I turn the spotlight first on one, then another, so that by concentrating on a single idea you may be able most thoroughly to master it. The exercises eventually become welded and the habits thus formed will contribute to every drawing you make.

Don't worry if for the first three months your studies do not look like anything else called a drawing that you have ever seen. You should not care what your work looks like as long as you spend your time trying. The effort you make is not for one particular drawing, but for the experience you are having — and that will be true even when you are eighty years old.

I believe that entirely too much emphasis is placed upon the paintings and drawings that are made in art schools. If you go to a singing teacher, he will first give you breathing exercises, not a song. No one will expect

you to sing those exercises before an audience. Neither should you be expected to show off pictures as a result of your first exercises in drawing.

There is a vast difference between drawing and making drawings. The things you will do — over and over again — are but practice. They should represent to you only the result of an effort to study, the by-product of your mental and physical activity. Your progress is charted, not on paper, but in the increased knowledge with which you look at life around you.

Unfortunately most students, whether through their own fault or the fault of their instructors, seem to be dreadfully afraid of making technical mistakes. You should understand that these mistakes are unavoidable.

The Sooner You Make Your First Five Thousand Mistakes, the Sooner You Will Be Able to Correct Them

To keep the exercises clear, the book is written as if you were an enrolled student in an art school. However, I realize that there are many talented people who are not in a position to go to a school and yet who deserve some opportunity of guidance because of their ability and desire. In the hope that this book can serve as a teacher for such people, I have included the simplest and most practical details of instruction. Where no class is available, I suggest that you try to organize a small group to share the expense of a model. In such a group one student should be elected monitor so that there will not be any confusion.

As the exercises are described, it is assumed that a nude model is available. However, all the exercises may be done from the costumed model instead, except those in anatomy for which you can use casts. If you cannot afford or secure a model, call on your friends or family to pose for you whenever you can and work from landscapes and objects the rest of the time. You will find that, with a few exceptions, the exercises apply just as much to things as to people. I have made some suggestions as to the most suitable subjects from time to time, and you are expected to supplement your work by drawing such subjects, even if you work regularly from the model.

The model should be placed in the center of the room so that all the students can sit very close and can look at the pose from all angles. Sit in a straight chair and rest your drawing against the back of another chair in front of you. (For these exercises, this relaxed and familiar position is more suitable than sitting or standing at an easel.) If you work at night, use concealed lighting or overhead lights from more than one source, and if you work by day, do not allow sunlight to fall directly on the figure. Avoid anything that has the effect of a spotlight on the model

At the beginning of each exercise you will find a list of whatever *new* materials you will need. Most of these materials are readily procurable anywhere. All the materials suggested are cheap, and they are more suitable for these exercises than expensive ones, even if you can afford them.

You can make several studies from any pose by looking at the model from different positions. Use this method of adapting the pose to your needs if you work in some class where the schedule of this book is not being followed. When a pose is going on which does not fit your exercise, you can stop drawing the model and draw objects or the room or your classmates.

Whatever the circumstances in which you work — whether in a class or alone, with a model or without — your ultimate success depends on only one element, and that is yourself. It is fallacy to suppose that you can get the greatest results with a minimum of effort. There is no such thing as getting more than you put into anything. You expect a man who is guiding you through the mountains to save your energy and tell you

the best way, but you can't get any farther in that mountain than you *can* and *will* walk. My one idea is to direct you to make the right sort of effort, for if you do you are bound to win out.

If you have ever tried it, you will realize how difficult it is to speak clearly and concisely of art. One is always very close to contradictions. However, you will not simply read the things I have to say. You will act upon them, work at them, and therefore I believe that each of you will arrive at a proper index of these ideas through a natural and individual application of them. Each of you, in a way peculiar to yourself, will add something to them. The book has been planned to that end.

Contour and Gesture[1]

Correct Observation

The first function of an art student is to observe, to study nature. The artist's job in the beginning is not unlike the job of a writer. He must first reach out for raw material. He must spend much time making contact with actual objects.

Learning to draw is really a matter of learning to see — to see correctly — and that means a good deal more than merely looking with the eye. The sort of "seeing" I mean is an observation that utilizes as many of the five senses as can reach through the eye at one time. Although you use your eyes, you do not close up the other senses — rather, the reverse, because all the senses have a part in the sort of observation you are to make. For example, you know sandpaper by the way it feels when you touch it. You know a skunk more by odor than by appearance, an orange by the way it tastes. You recognize the difference between a piano and a violin when you hear them over the radio without seeing them at all.

[1] From Section 1 of *The Natural Way to Draw.*

SCHEDULE I

	A	B	C	D	E
Half Hour	Ex. 1: Contour (one drawing)	Ex. 2: Gesture (25 drawings)	Ex. 2: Gesture (25 drawings)	Ex. 2: Gesture (25 drawings)	Ex. 2: Gesture (25 drawings)
Half Hour	Ex. 1: Contour (one drawing)	Ex. 1: Contour (one drawing)	Ex. 1: Contour (one drawing)	Ex. 1: Contour (one drawing)	Ex. 3: Cross Contours (one sheet of drawings)
Quarter Hour	Ex. 1: Contour (one drawing)	Ex. 2: Gesture (15 drawings)	Ex. 2: Gesture (15 drawings)	Ex. 2: Gesture (15 drawings)	Ex. 2: Gesture (15 drawings)
Quarter Hour	Rest	Rest	Rest	Rest	Rest
Half Hour	Ex. 1: Contour (one drawing)	Ex. 2: Gesture (25 drawings)	Ex. 2: Gesture (25 drawings)	Ex. 2: Gesture (25 drawings)	Ex. 2: Gesture (25 drawings)
One Hour	Ex. 1: Contour (one or two drawings)	Ex. 1: Contour (one or two drawings)	Ex. 1: Contour (one or two drawings)	Ex. 1: Contour (one or two drawings)	Ex. 1: Contour (one or two drawings)

This schedule represents fifteen hours of actual drawing, which I have divided for convenience into five three-hour lessons — A, B, C, D, and E. You may, of course, divide the work into seven two-hour lessons or fourteen one-hour lessons, omitting the rest period if you shorten the time. The model is usually allowed to rest during five minutes of each half hour, so the half-hour pose is actually only twenty-five minutes. The longer poses should be fairly simple at first and should show various views of the figure — back and side as well as front.

Because pictures are made to be seen, too much emphasis (and too much dependence) is apt to be placed upon seeing. Actually, we see *through* the eyes rather than with them. It is necessary to test everything you see with what you can discover through the other senses — hearing, taste, smell, and touch — and their accumulated experience. If you attempt to rely on the eyes alone, they can sometimes actually mislead you.

I think you will realize that this is true if you imagine that a man from Mars or some planet totally different from ours is looking for the first time at a landscape on the earth. He *sees* what you see, but he does not *know* what you know. Where he sees only a square white spot in the distance, you recognize a house having four walls within which are rooms and people. A cock's crow informs you that there is a barnyard behind the house. Your mouth puckers at the sight of a green persimmon which may look to him like luscious fruit or a stone.

If you and the man from Mars sit down side by side to draw, the results will be vastly different. He will try to draw the strange things he sees, as far as he can, in terms of the things his senses have known during his life on Mars. You, whether consciously or not, will draw what you see in the light of your experience with those and similar things on earth. The results will be intelligible, the one to the other, only where the experiences happen to have been similar. But if you both start out and explore that landscape on foot, touching every object, inhaling every odor, both will approach closer to what it is.

A man can usually draw the thing he knows best whether he is an artist or not. A golfer can draw a golf club, a yachtsman can make an intelligible drawing of a sail. This is a thing with which he has had real experience, a thing he has touched and used. Many other things which he has seen as often, but not used, he would not even attempt to draw.

FIGURE 16.1 "A Woman Playing the Violin" by Clara Crampton. (The artist has been blind since birth.) You need not rely on the eyes alone. Courtesy of The Lighthouse, The New York Association for the Blind.

The Sense of Touch

Merely to see, therefore, is not enough. It is necessary to have a fresh, vivid, physical contact with the object you draw through as many of the senses as possible — and especially through the sense of touch.

Our understanding of what we see is based to a large extent on touch (see Figure 16.1). Advertising experts realize this and place sample objects in stores where people can touch them. If you close your eyes and someone puts into your hands an object that you haven't seen, you can doubtless tell what that object is without opening your eyes. You can probably draw it from the experience of touch without ever having seen it. If you go into a dark room to get a book, you will not bring back a vase by mistake even though the two are side by side.

I read recently of a girl whose sight was suddenly gained after a lifetime of blindness. As long as she was blind, she was able to move about the house with ease. When she began to see, she could not walk across the

FIGURE 16.2 "Still life with fruit and flowers" by Henri Matisse. Courtesy of Peter Matisse Gallery, Beverly Hills.

room without stumbling over furniture. Her difficulty lay in the fact that she could not yet coordinate her new sense of sight with what she had previously learned through the sense of touch.

The first exercise, which you are about to attempt, is planned consciously to bring into play your sense of touch and to coordinate it with your sense of sight for the purpose of drawing.

Look at the edge of your chair. Then rub your finger against it many times, sometimes slowly and sometimes quickly. Compare the idea of the edge which the touch of your finger gives with the idea you had from merely looking at it. In this exercise you will try to combine both those experiences — that of touching with simply looking.

EXERCISE I: CONTOUR DRAWING

Materials: Use a 3B (medium soft) drawing pencil with a very fine point (sharpened on sandpaper) and a piece of cream-colored manila wrapping paper about fifteen by twenty inches in size. Manila paper usually comes in large sheets which may be cut into four pieces of that size. You may use, also, the kind sold as "shelf paper" provided it is not glazed. Fasten the paper with large paper clips to a piece of prestwood or a stiff piece of cardboard. Wear an eyeshade. Do not use an eraser until you come to Exercise 28.

Sit close to the model or object which you intend to draw and lean forward in your chair. Focus your eyes on some point — any point will do — along the contour of the model. (The contour approximates what is usually spoken of as the outline or edge.) Place the point of your pencil on the paper. Imagine that your pencil point is touching the model instead of the paper. Without taking your eyes off the model, *wait* until you are *convinced* that the pencil is touching that point on the model upon which your eyes are fastened.

Then move your eye *slowly* along the contour of the model and move the pencil *slowly* along the paper. As you do this, keep the conviction that the pencil point is actually touching the contour. Be guided more by the sense of touch than by sight. *This means that you must draw without looking at the paper,* continuously looking at the model.

Exactly coordinate the pencil with the eye. Your eye may be tempted at first to move faster than your pencil, but do not let it get ahead. Consider only the point that you are working on at the moment with no regard for any other part of the figure.

Often you will find that the contour you are drawing will leave the edge of the figure and turn inside, coming eventually to an apparent end (see Figure 16.3). When this happens, glance down at the paper in order to locate a new starting point. This new starting point should pick up at that point on the edge where the contour turned inward. Thus, you will glance down at the paper several times during the course of one study, but do not draw while you are looking at the paper. As in the beginning, place the pencil point on the paper, fix your eyes on the model, and wait until you are convinced that the pencil is touching the model before you draw.

Not all of the contours lie along the outer edge of the figure. For example, if you have a front view of the face, you will see definite contours along the nose and the mouth which have no apparent connection with the contours at the edge. As far as the time for your study permits, draw these "inside

FIGURE 16.3   Student contour drawing. *Let the lines sprawl all over the paper.*

is no point in finishing any one contour study. In fact, a contour study is not a thing that can be "finished." It is having a particular type of experience, which can continue as long as you have the patience to look. If in the time allowed you get only halfway around the figure, it doesn't matter. So much the better! But if you finish long before the time is up, the chances are that you are not approaching the study in the right way. A contour drawing is like climbing a mountain as contrasted with flying over it in an airplane. It is not a quick glance at the mountain from far away, but a slow, painstaking climb over it, step by step.

Do not worry about the "proportions" of the figure. That problem will take care of itself in time. And do not be misled by shadows. When you touch the figure, it will feel the same to your hand whether the part you touch happens at the moment to be light or in shadow. Your pencil moves, not on the edge of a shadow, but on the edge of the actual form (see Figure 16.4).

At first, no matter how hard you try, you may find it difficult to break the habit of looking at the paper while you draw. You may even look down without knowing it. Ask a friend to check up on you for a few minutes by calling out to you every time you look at the paper. Then you will find out whether you looked too often and whether you made the mistake of drawing while you were looking.

This exercise should be used in drawing subjects of all sorts. At first, choose the contours of the landscape which seem most tangible, as the curve of a hill or the edge of a tree-trunk. Any objects may be used (see Figure 16.5), although those which have been formed by nature or affected by long use will offer the greatest amount of variation, as a flower, a stone, a piece of fruit, or an old shoe. Draw yourself by looking in the mirror, your own hand or foot, a piece of material. It is the experience, not the subject, that is important.

FIGURE 16.4 Student contour drawing. *Draw without looking at the paper, continuously looking at the model.*

contours" exactly as you draw the outside ones. Draw anything that your pencil can rest on and be guided along. *Develop the absolute conviction that you are touching the model.*

This exercise should be done slowly, searchingly, sensitively. Take your time. Do not be too impatient or too quick. There

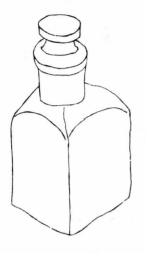

FIGURE 16.5   *Draw anything.*

Contour Versus Outline

"Contour" is commonly defined as "the outline of a figure or body," but for the purposes of this study we are making a definite, if perhaps arbitrary, distinction between "contour" and "outline."

We think of an outline as a diagram or silhouette, flat and two-dimensional. It is the sort of thing you make when you place your hand flat on a piece of paper and trace around the fingers with a pencil — you cannot even tell from the drawing whether the palm or the back of the hand faced downward. Contour has a three-dimensional quality; that is, it indicates the thickness as well as the length and width of the form it surrounds (see Figure 16.6).

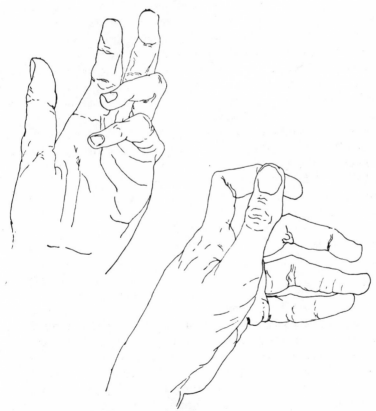

FIGURE 16.6   Student contour drawing.

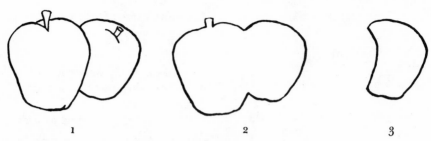

FIGURE 16.7   *Draw for three hours as directed in Schedule 1A. If you have not read the section, "How to Use This Book," read it now.*

We do not think of a line as a contour unless it follows the sense of touch, whereas an outline may follow the eye alone (Figure 16.7). Place two apples on a table, one slightly in front of the other but not touching it, as in Part 1. Part 2 shows the visual outline of both apples. Part 3 shows the visual outline of the second apple. Neither Part 2 nor Part 3 could possibly be a contour drawing because, in both, the line follows the eye and not the sense of touch. If you feel you are touching the edge, you will not jump from the edge of the first apple to the edge of the second without lifting your pencil, as in Part 2, just as you cannot actually touch the second apple with your finger at that place until you have lifted your finger from the first apple.   As an outline, Part 3 shows what you *see* of the second apple only, but if you think in terms of contour or touch, part of that line belongs to the first apple and not to the second. The outlines in both Part 2 and Part 3 are visual illusions. A contour can never be an illusion because it touches the actual thing.

Two Types of Study

The way to learn to draw is by drawing. People who make art must not merely know about it. For an artist, the important thing is not how much he knows, but how much he can do. A scientist may know all about aeronautics without being able to handle an airplane. It is only by flying that he can develop the senses for flying. If I were asked what one thing more than any other would teach a student how to draw, I should answer, "Drawing — incessantly, furiously, painstakingly drawing."

Probably you realize already that contour drawing is of the type which is to be done "painstakingly." On the other hand, gesture drawing, which you will begin today, is to be done "furiously." In order to concentrate, one can act furiously over a short space of time or one can work with calm determination, quietly, over a long extended period. In learning to draw, both kinds of effort are necessary and the one makes a precise balance for the other. In long studies you will develop an understanding of the structure of the model, how it is made — by which I mean something more fundamental than anatomy alone. In quick studies you will consider the function of action, life, or expression — I call it *gesture*.

The quick sketches made by most students are exactly what they are called — quick sketches — which to my way of thinking is very bad practice. In fact, anything that is sketchy is bad practice. The word "sketch" suggests something that is not completed. Quick studies, on the contrary, should indicate that there has been real study and a completion of the thing studied, representing a certain kind of concentration even though the study is quick. The way to concentrate in a short space of time is to concentrate on only one phase of the model. Naturally, I try to select an important phase and I have chosen the gesture.

Quick sketches are often used simply to "loosen up" the student and not as a means of penetrating study. Often students do them well and are quite surprised at the results, which are far beyond any knowledge they have. The reason is that by working quickly they accidentally find the gesture. The gesture is a feeler which reaches out and guides them to knowledge.

Materials: Use a 3B or 4B pencil (keeping the point blunt and thick) and sheets of cream manila paper about ten by fifteen inches in size. (This is half the size used for contour drawing.) Use both sides of the paper, but put only one drawing on each side. Since you will make a great many gesture drawings, you may substitute for manila an even cheaper paper known as newsprint. Keep an ample supply of paper on hand.

The model is asked to take a very active pose for a minute or less and to change without pause from one pose to the next. If you have no model — or, frequently, even if you do — you should go to some place where you are likely to see people actively moving about. A playground, a football game, a bargain basement, a busy street, a lumber mill, a swimming hole, a building under construction, will give you excellent opportunities to study gesture.

As the model takes the pose, or as the people you watch move, you are to draw, letting your pencil swing around the paper almost at will, being impelled by the sense of the action you feel. Draw rapidly and continuously in a ceaseless line, from top to bottom, around and around, *without taking you pencil off the paper.* Let the pencil roam, reporting the gesture.

You Should Draw, Not What the Thing Looks Like, Nor Even What It Is, but What It Is Doing

Feel how the figure lifts or droops — pushes forward here — pulls back there — pushes out here — drops down easily there (Figure 16.8). Suppose that the model takes the pose of a fighter with fists clenched and jaw thrust forward angrily. Try to draw the actual *thrust* of the jaw, the *clenching* of the hand. A drawing of prize fighters should show the *push*, from foot to fist, behind their blows that makes them hurt.

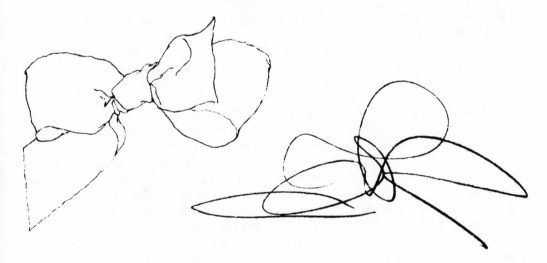

FIGURE 16.8   In contour drawing you touch the edge of the form. In gesture drawing you feel the movement of the whole.

FIGURE 16.9   Student gesture drawings. *Draw not what the thing looks like, not even what it is, but what it is doing.*

If the model leans over to pick up an object, you will draw the actual bend and twist of the torso, the reaching downward of the arm, the grasping of the hand. The drawing may be meaningless to a person who looks at it, or to you yourself after you have forgotten the pose. There may be nothing in it to suggest the shape of the figure, or the figure may be somewhat apparent. That does not matter.

As the pencil roams, it will sometimes strike the edge of the form, but more often it will travel through the center of forms and often it will run outside of the figure, even out of the paper altogether. Do not hinder it. Let it move at will. Above all, do not *try* to follow edges.

It is only the action, the gesture, that you are trying to respond to here, not the details of the structure. You must discover — and feel — that the gesture is dynamic, moving, not static. Gesture has no precise edges, no exact shape, no jelled form. The forms are in the act of changing. Gesture is movement in space (Figure 16.9).

To be able to see the gesture, you must be able to feel it in your own body. You should feel that you are doing whatever the model is doing. If the model stoops or reaches, pushes or relaxes, you should feel that your own muscles likewise stoop or reach, push or relax. *If you do not respond in like manner to what the model is doing, you cannot understand what you see.* If you do not feel as

FIGURE 16.10   Student gesture drawings.

the model feels, your drawing is only a map or a plan.

Like contour, gesture is closely related to the tactile experience. In contour drawing you feel that you are touching the edge of the form with your finger (or pencil). In gesture drawing you feel the movement of the whole form in your whole body.

The focus should be on the entire figure and you should *keep the whole thing going at once*. Try to feel the entire thing as a unit — a unit of energy, a unit of movement. Sometimes I let new students begin to draw on a five-minute pose and then, after one minute, ask the model to step down from the stand. The students stop drawing with surprise. I tell them to go ahead and draw, that they had started to draw and must have had something in mind; but usually they are unable to continue. The truth is that they had started with some little thing, such as the hair, and had not even looked at the pose as a whole. In the

first five seconds you should put something down that indicates every part of the body in the pose. Remind yourself of this once in a while by limiting a group of gesture studies to five or ten seconds each.

It doesn't matter where you begin to draw, with what part of the figure, because immediately you are drawing the whole thing, and during the minute that you draw you will be constantly passing from one end of the body to the other and from one part to another. In general, do not start with the head. Offhand, the only times I can think of when the head would be the natural starting place for an action would be when a man is standing on his head or hanging on the gallows.

Sometimes students ask whether they should think of gesture in this or that or the other way. My answer to that is that you should rely on sensation rather than thought. Simply respond with your muscles to what the model is doing as you watch, and let your pencil record that response automatically, without deliberation (Figure 16.10). Loosen up. Relax. Most of the time your instinct will guide you, sometimes guide you the better, if you can learn to let it act swiftly and directly without questioning it. Let yourself learn to reason with the pencil, with the impulses that are set up between you and the model. In short, listen to yourself think; do not always insist on forcing yourself to think. There are many things in life that you cannot get by a brutal approach. You must invite them.

If your model complains that he or she "can't think of any more poses," suggest the following: typical poses from all sports such as boxing, tennis, fencing; positions used in dancing; ordinary daily acts such as putting on one's clothes; typical movements in various kinds of work such as those of a farmer, a mechanic, a builder, a ditch-digger; poses expressive of different emotions such as fear, joy, weariness. The model should use all sorts of positions — standing, sitting, stooping, kneeling, lying down, leaning on something — and you should draw all sorts of views, front, back, and side. The poses should be natural and vigorous rather than artificial. Some of them should be quite twisted up and contorted.

Scribbling

My students eventually began to call these studies "scribble drawings." They are like scribbling rather than like printing or writing carefully, as if one were trying to write very fast and were thinking more of the meaning than of the way the thing looks, paying no attention to penmanship or spelling, punctuation or grammar.

One student said of his first gesture drawings that they looked like "nothing but a tangle of fishing line" (Figure 16.11). The drawing may look meaningless, but the benefits that you have at the moment of react-

FIGURE 16.11 *In the first five seconds put something down that indicates every part of the body in the pose.*

ing to the gesture will pay large dividends eventually. Before your studies from this book are over, you will have made hundreds of these scribble drawings. You will never exhibit one of them — they are considered purely as an exercise — yet they will give you an understanding and power which will eventually find its way into all your work. No matter what path you pursue, you keep going back to gesture.

Feel free to use a great deal of paper and do not ever worry about "spoiling" it — that is one of our reasons for using cheap paper. I notice that students working at their best, thinking only of the gesture and not making pictures, often throw their drawings into the trash-can without even looking at them. A few should be kept and dated as a record of your progress, but the rest may be tossed aside as carelessly as yesterday's newspaper. Results are best when they come from the right kind of unselfconscious effort.

More About Contour

Like many other students, you may have trouble drawing slowly enough in the contour exercise. Try making your next contour study with the left hand instead of the right (or the reverse if you are naturally left-handed). This should have the effect of slowing you up and, since your left hand is less trained, you will find it less easy to relapse into some way of drawing which you had already mastered.

This is a suggestion which may be applied to other exercises that we shall take up. Each exercise is meant to constitute in some way a new experience even if you have been drawing for twenty years. The use of your untrained hand may give you something of the advantage that a beginner always has — the advantage of a fresh approach.

When you looked at your first completed contour drawing, you probably laughed. No doubt the lines sprawled all over the paper, the ends did not meet in places, and one leg or arm may have been much bigger than the other. That should not worry you at all. In fact, you will really have cause for worry only if your drawing looks too "correct," for that will probably mean either that you have looked at the paper too often or have tried too hard to keep the proportions in your mind.

The time you spend counts only if you are having the correct experience, and in this exercise that experience is a physical one through the sense of touch. After you have drawn the contour of the model's arm, pass your fingers slowly along the contour of your own arm. If the sensation of touch is just as strong in the first act as in the second you have made a good start regardless of what the drawing looks like.

Contour drawing allows for concentrated effort in looking at the model rather than the usual divided effort of looking alternately at paper and model, which exercises

FIGURE 16.12   A gesture drawing is like scribbling rather than like printing carefully — *think more of the meaning than of the way the thing looks.*

mainly the muscles of the neck. In other words, the act of putting marks on the paper does not interrupt the experience of looking at the model. For that reason, you are able most effectively to follow forms to their logical conclusion, to learn where and how they relate to other forms. The parts of the figure are fairly simple in themselves — an arm, a finger, or a foot. But the way they fit together, the arm into the shoulder, the foot into the leg, is very difficult. They fit, not in a static way, but always in motion (Figure 16.12). Most students never settle down and follow out a form with all its nuances of movement, all the delicate transitions from one part to another. This exercise enables you to perceive those transitions because you follow closely the living form without taking your eyes off it.

Because the experience of looking at the model is not interrupted by looking at the paper, the drawing becomes a more truthful record of that one experience. If you made one leg longer than the other, it is probably because you spent more time looking at it. You may have done that simply because you had more patience than when you were drawing the other leg. Or you may have done it because the leg was closer to you, because more weight was on it, or because the position or turn of the leg attracted your interest. If you are drawing a model with very long arms, you may make the arms even longer than they are because your attention is attracted to their unusual length and you keep looking at them.

You need not think of these things. They happen subconsciously or, perhaps, accidentally. But, whether you know it or not, you are developing a sense of proportion, which may be a very different thing from a knowledge of proportion, but is equally important — for the creative artist, more important.

Draw for three hours as directed in Schedule 1 C.

The Contour in Space

The contour of any form in nature is never on one plane, but, as you follow it, is constantly turning in space. Assume that the model's arm hangs straight down at his side and that you are drawing the outer contour downward from the shoulder to the wrist. You will find, if you really are looking closely at the contour, that neither your eye nor the pencil can move straight down. Because the arm goes around as well as down, the contour seems sometimes to turn back away from you and then forward again toward you. Thus you will feel that you are sometimes drawing back into the paper and sometimes forward, as well as downward.

Draw for three hours as directed in Schedule 1 D.

EXERCISE 3: CROSS CONTOURS

This exercise calls for the same materials as the previous contour study, which it supplements. Like many of the exercises in this book,

it grew out of the effort to explain a particular point to a particular student. One night in my class I found a student who did not understand contour drawing, but was making outlines. In the attempt (a successful one) to show him what a contour really is, I explained that if he fixed his eye on the outside contour and moved straight across the body from one side to the other, he would be following a contour even though it was not at the edge of the figure. The value of this as an exercise then occurred to me.

Fix your eyes on a point on any one of the outside contours of the model, pencil on paper, as you did in the first exercise. Move both pencil and eyes across the figure at approximately a right angle to the contour you were touching when you started. For example, if your pencil was touching a point at the waist on a front view of the figure, you would not move it either up along the ribs or down along the thigh as previously, but straight across the abdomen. There is no visible line to guide you, but actually there is a contour from any point to any other point on the form.

If the position of the body changes, one of these cross contours, as we call them, may become an outside contour. For example, a line straight across the shoulders on the back of an erect figure may become the top contour if the figure bends over.

FIGURE 16.13

The line of a cross contour follows around the shape of the figure somewhat as a barrel hoop follows the rounded shape of a barrel. It dips down into the hollows and rises up over the muscles much as a piece of adhesive tape would if placed along the line you expect to draw. A contour on a leg, for example (Figure 16.13), can never be thought of as a line on a flat thing (Figure 16.14), because the leg is not flat.

FIGURE 16.14

Cross contours are different from the inside contours you have already drawn, such as that around the nose. An inside contour is at the edge of a clearly defined form even though that form does not happen to be at the edge of the whole figure. A cross contour may begin or end at any point on the body which your pencil happens to touch. It would be possible to make a cross contour simply by placing two dots at random on the figure and drawing between them a line which follows the shape of the form.

As a rule, draw horizontal contours — that is, those at a right angle to the outside edge. Sometimes, however, it is helpful to follow a vertical contour such as one from the collar bone down the chest, the ribs, the pelvic region, and the front of the leg. These contours may be drawn haphazardly on the paper — one across the forehead followed by another across the chest. They need not be connected or in place, and to an uninitiated observer they will be entirely meaningless.

The study of cross contours should continue what contour drawing has already begun — to help you make a real and seemingly physical contact with the model through the sense of touch.

Draw for three hours as directed in Schedule 1 E. It is important that you should not read on until you have finished Schedule 1.

Let's repeat what I said the very first time you sat down to draw. That is — drawing depends on seeing. Seeing depends on knowing. Knowing comes from a constant effort to encompass reality with all of your senses, all that is *you*. You are never to be concerned with appearances to an extent which prevents reality of content. It is necessary to rid yourself of the tyranny of the object as it appears. The quality of absoluteness, the note of authority, that the artist seeks depends upon a more complete understanding than the eyes alone can give. To what the eye can see the artist adds feeling and thought. He can, if he wishes, relate for us the adventures of his soul in the midst of life.

If your student efforts are based upon a sincere attempt to experience nature, you will know that you are on the right track and picture making will take care of itself. The job is to get at the truth — the truth as you will be able to understand it *first hand*, arrived at by the use of all your senses. When you are really enthralled, really stimulated, by a force other than the visual, strange-looking things are apt to occur, but you will not judge your work by formula or conventional standards. You may feel that there is no real necessity for remaining visually truthful or even structurally truthful in relation to the moment. There is always a bigger truth undiscovered — unsaid — uncharted until you meet it.

17. The Child as Painter

VICTOR D'AMICO

Painting is a natural expression of childhood, and one of the best media for stimulating creative response. Its fluid movement and ease of control make it pleasing to most children. It encourages spontaneity and originality in the most stubborn and inhibited nature. With the proper attention and direction, the tense, the academic, and the timid can be reborn through painting into a world of freedom and satisfaction. Both the spontaneity expected of the beginner, and the deliberate concentration required of the gifted artist, may be attained through this medium.

Painting is a general and persistent art with children, and one to which the majority of them return, even though they become interested in other activities. It ranges from a play expression on the lower levels, to a fine and specialized art on the upper levels. By its natural appeal to the creative sense, it evokes amazing results from the very young child, and by the same appeal to the conscious mind of the older student, it causes him to produce works of aesthetic merit and satisfaction.

Therefore, painting as an expression of art changes at different age levels because children of various ages employ and respond to it differently. For example, the young child uses it as a medium of release or play, while the older child, like the adult, regards it as a specialized activity. The young child employs the aesthetic values intuitively, and the older child uses them consciously.

Media and materials should be different for the demands and purposes of the various ages. For example, while oil paints are an excellent medium for the frequent changes and working-over necessary for advanced students, they are too complex for the spontaneous and free approach of young children. The subject matter of painting also goes through a peculiar cycle of change. At first there are the abstract dynamic patterns and splashes of color used by the child of the preschool or primary grades. From these develops a use of symbols, representing objects or things, in the early elementary grades, which changes into realistic and naturalistic expression at adolescence. However, there is often a re-

*SOURCE: Reprinted from Victor D'Amico, *Creative Teaching in Art*. Scranton, Pennsylvania: International Textbook Co. (1942), pp. 27–37.

turn in late adolescence to a conscious use of abstraction and of design for itself.

While we shall consider painting as a fine art, our greatest concern with it will be as a general creative expression. We shall, therefore, lay greater emphasis on the effect it has upon the child, than on the standard of work he attains. One may assume, however, that if the teaching is good the work will be good.

The Development of the Child as Painter

The young child from four to six years of age is a "born painter." The brush is more natural to him than the pencil. In his use of the brush the child is relaxed and free; his movements are poised and rhythmic, he is drawing with his arm and body. When a child uses a pencil he becomes tense, and obviously labors to squeeze a free idea out of the hard point. Therefore, the choice of the brush is important. It should be a resilient, flexible, responsive brush of camel's hair or Russian sable. It should be large and full, and should be used with such responsive pigment as water color, tempera, or poster paint. Water color is a good medium, not only because it is free-moving, but also because its running element allows for happy accidents in painting quality or color-mixing which, though unintentional, reveal new possibilities to the child and fill him with the curiosity to explore. Teachers often dislike transparent colors because they run. This fault may be avoided if each child works on an inclined or a flat table. In the case of vertical work, as in murals, the poster paints, thinned out with water for transparency, are recommended because they have body and can be controlled. Oils, however, should not be given to the young child, as they are too complex and difficult to manage. The paper should be large enough to accommodate the child's conception of space, allowing him the

opportunity of working out his idea on a large scale.

The child's development at this stage is indeed both rapid and eventful. He begins with mere daubing of paint, often without response to color. Then color consciousness dawns, demonstrated by the juxtaposition of colors or the mixing of color on the paper. It is a real experience to watch a child who has just discovered that two colors mixed together will produce a new color. A pattern period comes next, during which the child makes various designs of stripes, dots, or swirls. This pattern-making proceeds to a height of abstraction, demonstrated by grand dynamic masses of design and color well composed and balanced. Then comes a period of symbolism, indicating that the real world of people and things has broken into the child's consciousness. He represents them by self-devised symbols which appear flat and static. From this point the child gradually grows toward representation, when he is trying to communicate his ideas or imaginings through pictures. This young artist makes no previous drawing, but attacks the paper boldly with brush and paint, feeling his composition and design subconsciously as he goes along. There is very little teaching to be done in the dogmatic sense, but the teacher can encourage the child to work large, to use the space, to recognize the limits of the paper, and to use fresh, clean color when his brush is muddy. While the teacher has little control over the child's design, there is much he can do to enrich the child's experience and provide inspiration.

From the ages of six to ten, as the child grows into the representation and communication of ideas, the teacher can help to stimulate him by planning trips to the zoo and aquarium, or visits to places of interest in the neighborhood — the bakery or fruit market, the pet shop or the flower nursery.

While the effort should be made to keep the child working spontaneously, it may be necessary at times for him to use a pencil or a small tool to represent the detail in which he has become interested. When the quality of a painting depends on the fine pattern of line, a transparent medium, such as water color, should be used to preserve the fresh quality of the original lines. A child often faces bitter disappointment when he discovers that an opaque color has obliterated his careful and precious work.

In the upper years of elementary school, especially in the fifth and sixth grades, the child becomes a conscious designer, that is, he consciously seeks and considers the elements of design — line, mass, and color. It is very important that he experience them as a need or as a property in his own work; he should not be required to learn them theoretically in the hope of applying them later. The reason for this procedure is that the child will know more about the use of line, mass, and color if he learns it by working with these elements creatively, than if he learns it theoretically or through artificially devised problems. His effort to make the picture intelligible and effective will naturally arouse in him the desire to know how to employ these elements of design. The teacher can help him achieve this knowledge by revealing the special principle of design which will solve the problem. In this way the teaching meets a need felt by the child.

The most effective teaching, then, results when the principle taught coincides with a desire or interest on the part of the child, and when the child takes part in solving the problem. For example, a child will readily learn and remember the principle of balance when he realizes that the success of a definite piece of work depends on its use. A child may draw or paint a picture which is obviously unbalanced because all of the drawing is placed on one half

of the paper while the other half is left blank. He may feel that something is wrong, but he cannot detect what it is, or if he does, he may not know how to rectify it. The teacher can help him by calling his attention to the unused space, suggesting, although not telling him, that he may find his solution through it. By wise direction, he may get the child to realize that he can spread the drawing out over the blank area, or that he may add more drawing on the blank part to balance the part already drawn. In this way the child learns through self-discovery and actual experience and not through subservience to an empty principle.

While the child of four or six years of age possesses little or no sense of form other than a sense of line, flat mass, and color, the child of nine or ten attains a suggestion of form in the use of perspective. He suggests form by the contour lines of objects in perspective, by the receding of houses and buildings, by slight suggestion of foreshortenings in figures, and by the difference in size of the near and the far objects in his picture. He has, however, no sense of the change of form within a mass or surface, for this concept belongs to a later stage. Like the younger child, he fills in the areas with flat or blended color.

By the time the child is nine or ten years old, he has usually developed a good sense of dark and light value and some sense of pattern or texture. These elements are often apparent in the very young child's work, but they are more noticeable in that of older children. The child's experience should include as many painting media as possible, and the more advanced children may attempt some work in oils. Tempera and water color are the most successful media to use at this stage, and the bristle brush is especially suitable for large work. The child should work on both a large and a small scale, for while working in the large scale keeps his expression bold and free, working in the small scale satisfies his desire for details and small work. Large work is a valuable experience for most young children, but its value is apt to be overrated. There are times when most children wish to work small because their idea demands a small area and a tool which will express delicate pattern and detail. At such times the teacher should be sensitive to this need and try to meet it. Then there are those who by nature work small, in little patterns and fine line. A large scale medium might inhibit this type of child and thus destroy the purpose of the experience. The teacher should, therefore, be conscious of such exceptions as these and make the experience fit the need. It will be profitable to use the easel often to encourage spontaneous work, and to go about the neighborhood and city for new material and inspiration. Diverse subject matter is an important element at this stage, and the teacher will do well to keep the art activity alive through constant change of subjects. The other studies in the school, especially history, literature, and current events, should help to furnish a variety of materials for pictorial use.

Between the ages of ten and fourteen the child gains dexterity in drawing and painting and can deal with almost all subjects. His interest in the human figure is keen and he can easily avail himself of the opportunity to work directly from the model (especially from the seventh grade on) in free-brush work, putting in imaginary backgrounds. Self-portraits in poster paints or chalks, poses by classmates, especially group poses, are particularly popular. In these years the young artist is gaining a sense of composition through the arrangement of the various elements in his paintings, and acquiring a feeling of line and of dark and light values through the medium of his paint brush. His sense of form in painting and color is still elementary and

is revealed mainly through line contours and perspective.

From about fourteen to eighteen years of age, the developing artist perceives the true element of form. For example, he learns that by variations in the color and value of an object, form is achieved. He can be made to see that the color in a bowl moves and changes through light to dark, from the side where it receives the light to the opposite side away from the light. He also becomes conscious of edges, noticing that some edges of an object are sharp and clear, while others are soft and indistinct, and some entirely lost. He relates objects to the background and, to his amazement and satisfaction, discovers that colors affect each other, that a yellow vase against a green background appears different from the way it appears against a red background.

Fortunately, not all these problems confront the student simultaneously, or he would be completely baffled and perhaps inhibited. The teacher should be careful to have him consider one problem at a time in a progressive order, working from the simple to the complex. For example, the student must gain a thorough understanding of the use of line if he is to express pattern, form, and texture. He must have a similar experience with dark and light, and finally with color. It is important, however, to emphasize that these experiences should not be divided into definite periods so that the student works only with line for an indefinite period until it dulls his enthusiasm or inhibits his use of other elements. It is probably advisable to work in cycles in which the student continuously experiences the three elements of line, form, and color, but to give emphasis to one element in a given cycle. Also, it is not important to begin with line and proceed to color. For some it may be better to begin with color or value. This order of procedure will depend on the particular needs of each student. Let us say that during a certain period the student will explore the full potentialities of line in design, but will use value and color subordinately. When the student is studying color, it will be wise to give him at first a simple palette with a few colors and to increase his palette as he gains power. In addition to the problem of color value, there will arise the problem of painting texture and technique. The student will have to decide on the expression that is best for him, and learn by a technique all his own, how to portray the texture of an object in a given painting. He should keep in mind the elementary consideration that the painting should follow the form. A most helpful means of studying form will be found in the analysis of works of masters like van Gogh or Cézanne, whose technique reveals the concept of painting following form, and, at the same time, keeps the character of the artist's own personality distinct. The student must be careful, however, not to imitate the work of the masters, and the teacher should not give the class a set procedure which might develop into a set pattern, but should aim to develop meaning instead of mannerisms in his students.

The Teaching Process

The teaching of painting should be, as far as possible, related to the original work on an individual basis. That is, the study of form should be associated with the definite problem that a student encounters in his original painting. Also, the student should be confronted with only those problems that are within the range of his understanding. It is to be expected, with the varying capacities and intelligence of children at this age, that individuals will develop at different rates of speed and that their ability to grow will depend on their ability to understand and assimilate new concepts through their own experiences. However, the teacher learns to be a better critic of his students as he learns their aptitudes by watching them.

Group exercises and problems should be employed only to meet general group needs, such as painting from the life model to master the figure. Set-up or posed problems, such as still life, should be avoided or used with discrimination, as many problems of this kind tend to atrophy the originality and produce formalities and stereotyped results. They make the student dependent on models and tend to emphasize technique above original expression. The Mexican teacher's method — his use of two studios, one for imaginative work, the other for studying drawing and painting of objects and figures — may be helpful at this stage. When a student encounters a problem in his creative work he goes into the study studio and works until he has mastered it. Then he returns to his original composition. In this way the originative concept is emphasized. Of course, it is not essential to have two studios to work out this method. The student may merely stop his original project and make a special study of the problem which has puzzled him, and when he has solved it he may return to his original project. Formal results are also the outgrowth of the tendency on the part of teachers to give directions too specifically in dictated steps, instead of allowing the child to solve his problem in his own way.

As a general rule, we can assume that any process or approach is wrong if it develops a pattern within a group, regardless of its soundness of principle, or the startling results which it produces. Even modern and progressive teachers often set their pattern on students so that it is easy to recognize by the style of a student's painting with whom he has studied. A good teacher will demand the same individual quality and personal approach to a study problem or exercise that he does to the original work. The individual expression is always more to be considered than skill or draftsmanship.

The Problem of Composition

Composition, the structure upon which creative painting is built, is an ever-present problem with the artist. As has been stated, young children use the elements of composition more or less intuitively, but the older child, lacking this sensitiveness, must consider them consciously. That is, the older student must be aware of how to use these elements in his own work and must be able to recognize their presence in works of others as well as in the subject matter he chooses. At this point it must be definitely explained that by *the conscious use of the elements of composition*, we do not mean that the child must master the rules and go on a hunt for particular compositions that will fit his rules. Nor do we hope that he will go out with the scientist's eye, to analyze and dissect every painting or scene to discover whether or not it is done according to prescribed law. There is too much of the mind in such a process, and too little of the spirit. Good composition requires intellect and emotion. The artist not only recognizes the use of the elements of design, but also feels them. It is important, therefore, for the young artist to focus his attention on these elements for themselves, so that he may both feel and recognize their intrinsic qualities as aesthetic values. Subject matter for creative work involves so many complex problems that the beginner is easily misled or attracted by factors of secondary importance, such as correct drawing, realism, or detail. It is important therefore, that the child study his subject in order to decide or to discover its design elements. For example, let us suppose that on one of his excursions into the city a child chooses a group of apartment houses as a likely subject. In looking at it, he sees that the scene spreads out and he recognizes it as a horizontal composition. Studying it further he discovers that the main lines are horizontal and vertical. Therefore, he transfers his impressions imaginatively to his paper to see how it will best fit the shape. He may at once realize that he must use his paper horizontally and proceed to plan the picture to fit it. He feels that the picture must have a focus, or "a point of interest," as the artist calls it. This point of interest may be an action, a building, or a person or it may be a number of persons or things. Then comes the problem of dark and light which the artist meets consciously or subconsciously. For example, are the tenement houses in the picture to be dark against a light sky, or light against dark? Are the people in the street to be dark or light against the buildings? Thus the picture is built up toward color.

It is important to mention that this analysis of and emphasis on composition should be undertaken after the student has gained a freedom and power of expression, and when he indicates a desire or need for it. If the student has had a great deal of experience with spontaneous painting in imaginative work and in working from observation, he will have a feeling or an intuition for design which will prepare him for a more studied approach. By the time the student has reached high school he should be able to consider composition as a serious conscious study. However, it is necessary to realize that the structural elements of composition should be integrated with the idea or character of the painting, that they should not be obvious or labored, lest the observer be made too aware of their use. While all true artists are masters of composition, one is not immediately conscious of it. One is more concerned with the individual idea or style of the artist. At least the elements that go to make up the picture are blended into an integrated whole to which the observer responds.

18. To Do and Not to See: The Teacher of Art

JOSHUA TAYLOR

A favorite sport of college faculties is to lament the poor preparation of entering students, to wonder audibly just what the students have been doing through their formative years. Yet if the source of the trouble were analyzed, it might be discovered that a major factor was the kind of preparation the colleges have given their teachers. In no subject is this more true than in art or, for that matter, in the arts in general.

A study of the visual arts — which is what "art" usually refers to in the public schools — was late in making its appearance in university curriculums and almost as late in turning up in primary and secondary schools. The hireling drawing teacher, like the music and dancing masters, was very often a person apart. When, however, the self-conscious study of art did find acceptance in the formal school curriculum, it took hold rapidly and made the most of its opportunities.

Not very long ago the child in primary school was still invariably taught to copy line by line or square by square a drawing his teacher put on the board. Or a benign visiting supervisor would amaze the young by showing how, with a few deft snips of the scissors, one could cut a duck from folded paper. In high school, instruction was divided between lettering and poster-making and an earnest, but rather aimless, sort of sketching known as "freehand drawing." So far as direct copying is concerned, which was to instill discipline or develop manual dexterity in the child, the practice has long been obsolete in the more progressive schools. In fact, the very word "copy" is looked upon with scorn. The magic word for some years past has been "create."

One might be cheered at this transition from "copy" to "create" if only he could be sure of just what "create" has meant to the art teacher. At its introduction it bore the reassuring overtones of Dewey and the blessings of the newly established child psychologists. "Creative art" — it is difficult to imagine an art that is not creative

*SOURCE: Reprinted from *Journal of General Education*, XII (January 1959), pp. 60–68.

— was an inspirational catchword that gave impetus to an astonishing variety of activities. Yet, on closer inspection, it would seem that in practice "create" has more often than not meant simply to make or to do. Since what are called "creative projects" have, through the systematic training of our teachers, become quite standardized, they offer about the same degree of originality as painting by the numbers or expertly cutting a duck. Under the impact of much psychological study of children's art, the word "creative" in recent years has largely given way to the equally vague but inspirational term "expressive," but the results in all but the youngest students are much the same.

In the 1890's an uplifting missionary fervor concerning art was generated, and committees and organizations were formed to promote an increased appreciation of the fine arts. The enthusiasm was allied to the new Renaissance ideal, and eventually much serious effort was spent introducing into the schools courses in art appreciation and the history of art. But the formalities of instruction outlasted the initiating spirit, and such courses are most likely remembered by those who took them for their anecdotes of the Old Masters, the spot recognition of Great Paintings, and the homely recollections of schoolteacher tours of Greece. The image of art that emerged was one of venerable age: of antiqued furniture, gesso copies of Renaissance frames, and mementos from Florence. The new "art is doing" enthusiasm swept this quiet sentimental pleasure away, along with copying by squares and "disciplining the eye," and one cannot weep seriously for its passing. Yet it would be too bad if nothing comparable appeared to take its place.

There are areas in school art education in which the rigorous studies of psychologists and art educators which have produced these changes have been of enormous value. The recreative freedom now afforded

the youngest students is doubtless healthful and constructive. But "art" to a child of five fulfills a different function than it does to a youth of fourteen. The psychologists are certainly very much aware of this; yet the pattern of art education remains curiously the same for all ages. It is the education of the adolescent who is ready to prepare for adulthood that has suffered, and it is with this situation that the present article is concerned.

The young child, given the necessary implements, needs only encouragement, not instruction, to paint or to model contentedly. He takes delight in splashing about with materials and is quite unselfconscious about color mixing, composition, and other burdensome matters that bother adults. A seven-year-old, with hardly a perceptible suggestion from his teacher, can produce an abstraction or the picture of a train with admirable spontaneity. Talent is something noted and talked about by eager parents and teachers, not by children. They are concerned with doing and are not too critical of the final product.

But this happy state of innocence does not last long. At a surprisingly early age the child becomes aware that some of his friends are more able than he. Unless the tasks outlined in the art class are on a depressingly low and casual level, differences in ability become painfully obvious. An ability to draw, manual dexterity, a sharp eye for visual tricks, all begin to count. The happy, unified class in art with everyone contentedly doing things threatens to break apart, with those who have ability being outrageously admired or despised by those who have not. The resourceful teacher, however —and, to be resourceful, he spends many hours in summer schools and dutifully reads trade magazines—knows just what to do to save the situation. He comes up with a new technique or a fascinating new material to pique the interest of all and keep all hands occupied. Clay modeling gives way to simple, then more complex, ceramics, which can then be complicated with the problems of glazing. Enameled metal, mosaic, and other technical attractions lead on from there. Some activity is within the manual ability of everyone, and no one need feel inferior.

Depending on how progressive the school system is or how crowded the schools, this art-room activity will extend through elementary and even through high school. At the moment that easy "self-expression" lags, technical busywork takes over. Yet, if this is a graded progression of training, to what does it lead? What is the goal toward which the gradually more difficult problems are directed?

It would be encouraging to believe that, with all the equipment that goes into the well-established modern art room, even into the less well equipped, not only a new skill of hand but a taste for sound craftsmanship might result. The idea that everyone should perfect himself in some manual craft is not a poor one, especially in a culture depending so much on mechanization. A hasty look at the average exhibition of upper-grade and high-school art is enough to dispel any illusion that one might have about craftsmanship. Obviously, the students have played at the craft, not worked at it. Aside from the exceptional student, the work is technically poor and the design routine. Discouragingly enough, the students appear satisfied with their poor work. So far as achievement is concerned, it seems far below that of the old-fashioned carpenter shop and the sewing class. The clever techniques of ceramics and bent metal the student will soon forget; they are not, in spite of the teachers' hopes, going to enrich the idle hours of his later life. The work has served its purpose as a recreational activity and belongs to childhood.

The other achievement toward which we are told general training in art is directed is the development of artistic sensitivity or taste in matters of daily life. The success is not impressive. To judge from the reproductions that first-year college students select, the clothes they choose, the furniture they prefer, their taste is molded far more by popular magazines than by their schooling. Their training has been to do, not judge, works, and the fact that they have made jewelry does not seem to render their judgment more acute in buying it, any more than the fact that they have painted a picture makes Picasso more accessible. Since they were not aware of the nature of the choices they were making as they worked, or probably even aware that they were making choices, they are unaware that they have a capacity for personal judgment and follow sheeplike the lures of popular fads, quite as readily as if they had had no education at all.

Although almost every student entering college has spent many hours of his education in art classes of some description, he is likely to panic when faced with the assignment of trying out some previously discussed compositional ideas for himself—an assignment he encounters in a required first-year course at the University of Chicago —and acts often as if he had never seen two colors together before. Furthermore, when the works are turned in, there is rarely a correlation between quality and prior school classes in art. If anything, the students who were "good" in art have picked up so many mannerisms and gimmicks, which they use without meaning, that their work in particular lacks serious quality. Surely some modicum of confident judgment should emerge from their time spent with art.

One might even hope that a high-school student who schedules some hours in art might gain from them an inkling of the fact that art can be a serious part of his emotional and intellectual life. But this is the greatest disappointment of all. There seems to be little correlation between commendable activity in the art room and sensitivity to great works of art. For most high school students, anything beyond the technique of the arts remains a closed book.

The adolescent is highly aware of his own shortcomings and the capacities of others. He has early discovered that some things which he can do only adequately, others do well. Although he may still be forced to "take" art, if it is not his métier he will rarely follow the work seriously and often will belittle its importance in order to save face. A similar situation exists in music. The basis of most teaching of music in the schools is singing. If a child becomes conscious that he cannot sing as well as others, he is forced to decide that music is not for him. A high school principal once confessed to his staff that he had always yearned to learn more of music as a child but was denied its pleasure because he could not carry a tune. And the elementary ability to play an instrument through the standard repertory of a school band is not the answer.

Actually, by the time they finish high school, relatively few students consider themselves "good" in art. The majority have decided that they have no capacity in this direction and are often suspicious of those who do. In consequence they want little to do with the subject. Even worse are those with little ability who have become quite satisfied with their own mediocre productions and are placidly unaware that art has anything more to offer.

But, unfortunately, the chances that even the student who was good in art will develop a genuine judgment and appreciation are not heartening, for training based wholly on technical doing can destroy the judgment of the artistically inclined as well as repel those with little artistic interest. Value in art for the schooled becomes too often a relative technical matter or remains a superficial and unexamined preference. No matter how satisfied the teacher may be with some chance spontaneous effect that suggests to him a valid work of art, the adoles-

cent student is likely to judge the work on the basis of "how well done." And behind that "well" stands a rigid and narrow concept of art that his schooling has had no reason to touch. The possibility of art as a means for sharing a profound experience with others or of giving new human insight has not in the slightest way been glimpsed.

Yet, with all its shortcomings, art teaching in the schools, as far as it goes, is doubtless better than it once was. One can hardly argue for the reinstatement of mimicking exercises or rote lessons in authoritarian taste. The fault has been that the obsessive "doing" has crowded its way into areas in which it does not belong: it serves not only as an admirable therapeutic practice but as a substitute for art itself. Educators in their zeal have failed to distinguish between artistic activity for the child and art for the growing adult. It is not that the student cannot continue to profit from doing; but for the nascent adult simply doing is not sufficient. If the experience is to be worthwhile, it must engage his intellectual faculties. To placate his intellectual restlessness with technical complications is not to educate, not to mature, but to beguile and stultify.

It is the point of early adolescence at which the eager intellect begins to reach out for values, when the canny child secretly realizes that the artistic products of his own hands are not to be taken too seriously, that the existing system breaks down. At this moment, the child should be made aware that what he has striven for, others have achieved, and their successes remain for him to enjoy. In his way he has been learning the grammar of a language in which artists have created a profound and revealing literature. What he has learned of color, composition, even of technical procedures, can suddenly assume a new, adult meaning. The impact of art need no longer be bound for him by the limits of his own dexterity but can extend itself over an infinite range, inviting new inquiry and exploration. And exploration now is not experiment with techniques but the pursuit of an experience in which many human values play a part. If art invites back into its orbit a consideration of a wide range of human experience, there is no longer the temptation for a student to isolate the judgments of "art class" from his serious private world. Art can become a clarification and focus of many of the ideas and feelings of which he is now aware. It becomes not a "cultural" subject but a very real part of his new and complex adult life.

Two questions, however, arise. Just how does one go about developing this delicate transition from childish doing to adult apprehending, and what kind of teacher is necessary for the successful operation? The second of these is clearly the more important, since any system is only as good as the teacher and a sound teacher will find his own means. It is at the training of these teachers that the university should look with care, to determine whether it is fulfilling its responsibility in the matter.

The training of teachers of art for the public schools over the last twenty-five years has become a much discussed speciality. When it was first decided to divide teaching chores in the elementary schools among especially prepared teachers, there was a scramble on the part of the teachers to take, and of the universities to provide, more special "subject-matter" courses. At this point the whole matter of training teachers of art for the schools was reconsidered. In the case of history, nature study, or government the problem of what a teacher should know was elementary compared to that of art. What is, quite specifically, the subject matter of art? A variety of factors ranging from theories of child psychology to reflections of a new dogmatic artistic taste decreed the importance of artistic practice. Problems, things to do, became the chief concern of the harried teacher, and manufacturers of school supplies obliged by turning out an endless variety of novel materials, gaudy, foolproof, and nontoxic. From a modest supply of modeling clay, watercolors, and colored papers the stock of the art room swelled to contain kilns, presses, and patented foundries. Naturally, the teacher had to run to keep up with this progress, and more and more teacher-training courses were devoted to "how to do."

The elementary-school teacher must now be an amateur psychologist, on the one hand, and a purveyor of fascinating artistic tricks, on the other. The average high school teacher of art should—although probably not a practicing artist himself—know how to paint, draft, make a variety of prints, and produce ceramics and sculpture. Both must be capable of absorbing into practice each new material as it comes on the market. To make sure that teachers are so equipped, many states have legislated the number of practice courses a candidate must have and organized their examinations around such material. It is little wonder that the incipient art teacher, with a program further cluttered with required courses in educational theory, is likely to be the least well informed person in the area on the general matters of art. He is rarely a practicing artist and rarely a knowledgeable person in the history and criticism of art. Historical and theoretical studies in art are cut to a minimum in his program, as are other unnecessary studies, such as literature. He becomes a specialist in "how to do" and has little opportunity to think of artistic reasons why—although he is usually well armed with psychological explanations. This possibly explains why the teacher of art is not necessarily the member of the faculty most likely to be found at art exhibitions and is likely to be as baffled as the average layman by current tendencies in art. He is not, moreover, embarrassed to admit that he knows rather little of art outside the work of his students and their age group. On the rare occasion of classes visiting the local museum, a museum do-cent—who knows about pictures—takes charge, not the teacher.

Obviously, a teacher so trained and so limited is not likely to be the one to move the student to an awareness that art is more than the skill of devising a serigraph stencil. The subtle joys of appreciation are learned more from example than from curriculum. If the teacher is unaware of artistic values but, at the urging of principals and super-visors, bases judgment chiefly on the win-ning of poster contests, the students can hardly be expected to do otherwise.

What, then, should the training of a teacher of art be? In the first place, there should be a distinction made in the schools between vocational training in art and that available to the general student. While both might begin at the same place, the vocational training should move toward a technical discipline inconsistent with the abilities and aims of the student intending to specialize in other fields. The playing with materials that goes on in many a school art room should not be misconstrued as training in a craft. If a craft is to be taught, it should be taught thoroughly, with due respect to technical excellence. Actually, such vocational training in art has little place in the average high school but might be carried on more advantageously in a vocational institution. Students who have little manual capacity and have no inten-tion of pursuing a vocation of art (and this would include the majority of students) should not be cut off from art by these tech-nical restrictions, any more than they should be allowed to lower standards in professional classes. They should join with their more dextrous fellows in art classes not based primarily on practice.

The teacher of vocational courses in art should be thoroughly trained in his craft and, if possible, should be a practicing art-ist. One might hope, of course, that he might also be a person of well-rounded edu-cation. To hold this image of the art teacher as the sole ideal for all students, however, would be to miss important possibilities in the teaching of art and to misuse the talents of captive artists, forcing them to dissipate their energies on unreceptive subjects. For the majority of students, those who have no intention of going into the field profession-ally, the teacher of art might well be of a different sort and should be trained for his particular task, not as if he were to teach only future painters.

To be sure, the prospective general teach-er of art should have some training in the practice of art and should have some talent for it, although there is no need for his fancying himself an artist. He should, first of all, have a broad general education in the humanities, out of which his study of art should grow naturally and not be considered a thing apart. His initial studio training should be basic, directed toward the devel-opment of visual judgment, an under-standing of two- and three-dimensional composition, and a sensitivity to the relation-ship of artistic form to material structure. This basic study should be sufficiently broad in its foundation to comprehend a wide variety of forms of art. The training should strive consiouously to develop visual sensitivity and critical capacities rather than to perfect manual skills.

Closely linked to this studio training should be the analytical study of works of art so that matters of composition and form do not separate themselves from artistic content. The close association between the analysis of works by great artists, past and present, and studio practice should serve as a model of procedure for the future teacher, suggesting ways in which a bridge can be formed between what a student does him-self and what is to be found in the work of an artist. Toward this end, imitating styles and copying details is not an efficient way to study. The student should be taught to use his eyes, not simply caricature with his hand. The quality of great works should not be reduced to a beginner's level, but the student should learn to respect transcendent artistic quality. He should discover that there is such a thing as creative looking as well as creative painting.

To support this combined training in analysis and doing, the prospective teacher should have a survey of the history of art, studying all major periods, including his own. In such a survey it is more important that he learn to look with genuine sympathy and comprehension on a wide variety of expressions than to memorize the clichés standing for historical processes. In this study there should be two points of specialization: he should pursue one historical field further, to understand the meaning of historical research in art, and he should have further preparation in art and theory leading to the art of his own time. If the teacher is to make the art surrounding his students come alive for them, he must not be ignorant of its aims and its sources.

The third increment of the student's specialized training might be placed under the heading of education courses, for the courses would be devoted to both educational theory and practical problems for the classroom. It is under this latter category that training in the various popular technical projects might fall. If the basic studio training has been sound, the study of different technical procedures need not be difficult.

Contrary to most present practice, the training in judgment must be basic and the study of techniques secondary, not the other way around. To suppose that if a person works long enough at a particular craft he will automatically develop a widely applicable artistic judgment is a fallacy continuously and embarrassingly demonstrated by many art-school graduates. There must be a conscious intellectual effort to accompany the training of the hand. One can readily forgive an artist for not being able to judge works of art different from his own or for

being verbally inarticulate; one cannot so easily forgive a teacher.

The ideal teacher of art, then, for all but the most specialized professional training, should be a person broadly educated in the arts, with a developed taste and the capacity for making clear the nature and bases of his judgments. He should be alive to the full content of art, not just its technical execution, and recognize it as a serious and meaningful human endeavor. At the same time, he should be sufficiently trained in the techniques of art to lead the students through their own work to an understanding of the works of others. He should be capable, in other words, of taking students through the period in which they are satisfied simply to make things and, still utilizing this desire to do, lead them at the crucial moment to a realization that these very means in the hands of an artist may continue to provide them with many rewarding experiences.

Lurking behind the reasoning of this article is a dissatisfaction with an assumption, first broached in the handicraft movements of the last century, which has become dangerously widespread. It is the assumption that craft and art are in all important respects synonymous. Much good came out of this idea in its original application, and much fresh artistic material was revealed. But its crude application has led to regrettable results. While a sensitively designed pot may be a great and satisfying work of art, it is not interchangeable in the experience it affords with a painting by Rembrandt or Picasso. The appreciation of each has its value, but they are quite distinct. Although they may employ the same language, they speak in different dialects, and the study of one does not explain the other.

What has happened in the art classes of our schools is the result of the determined effort to restore the importance of craft, which was threatened with extinction by commerce. This is thoroughly commendable. No one now doubts that crafts are worthwhile. But in this righteous pursuit, the less readily teachable forms of art — painting and sculpture, for example—were dropped or, worse, made a by-product of the crafts. The humanistic insight, the exploration of new ranges of the mind that art affords, as a result remains closed to our students, even when the students become mature enough to value it.

Old classes in mechanical perspective and freehand drawing have been replaced with equally unrevealing courses in silk-screen Christmas cards or "free-form" jewelry. If under pressure from occupational therapists these craft shops must be retained as constituted beyond the primary grades in nonvocational schools, a clear distinction should be made between courses that set out to study art and hobby courses in what often turn out to be uncraftsmanly crafts. Such a separation would be regrettable, since, as has been suggested, much can be gained from an initial combination of the two. But a drastic move may be necessary for the study of art to regain a respectable and useful role in the upper grades and high school—a move so drastic as to redefine dramatically the difference between the joy of working with the hands and that of apprehending with the mind. But, to effect such redefinition, we must train teachers who are worthy exponents of their humanistic heritage.

19. The Effect of a "Depth" vs. a "Breadth" Method of Art Instruction at the Ninth Grade Level

KENNETH R. BEITTEL, EDWARD L. MATTIL, *Principal Investigators*
HERBERT J. BURGART, ROBERT C. BURKHART, CLARENCE KINCAID,
ROBERT STEWART, *Research Associates*

Introduction

This study compares the effectiveness of a "depth" method of art instruction, using closely related experiences in similar media, with a "breadth" approach, using a variety of different experiences in dissimilar media. The effectiveness of each method was determined by comparing groups instructed under the "breadth" and "depth" programs with each other and with a control group. The basis for the comparisons was on mean gains and losses on the spontaneity and the aesthetic quality of the pupils' art products. These product scores were also correlated with measures of an ideational self-determining personality orientation. The product judgments were compared to these measures of personality structure in order to determine the creative ideational values of the "depth" and "breadth" approaches for the individual student.

Background of "Depth" versus "Breadth" Programs

Many teachers and supervisors through general observation and practice have developed convictions regarding the superiority of the "depth" or "breadth" methods of instruction. The merits of the depth and breadth methods have been argued but not often studied. These methods are generally described as follows:

Depth

A teaching program which allows a sustained long-term concentration in one specific area of study. There may be variety within this area but the different activities are such that they permit an easy transition from one problem to another. This approach stimulates both sequential and cumulative learning.

*SOURCE: Reprinted from *Studies in Art Education*, III, 1 (Fall 1961), pp. 75–87.

Breadth

A teaching program in which a variety of well-chosen subjects and activities are dispersed in such a way as to accommodate differences in the interests and experiences of the pupils. A strong supporting argument is the maintenance of pupil interest while providing for a survey introduction to many media. The breadth program is the approach which has been most widely accepted in the junior high schools.

This study was designed for ninth grade because this was the terminal year of mandatory art instruction in this particular junior high school. This provided a representative population. The study was conducted in a nonuniversity middle-sized city in Pennsylvania. All instruction was handled by one highly skilled art teacher not trained at Penn State. Three sections of boys and girls were selected from nine available sections on the basis of the similarity and normality of these sections in the means and standard deviations of their IQ scores. This assured some normal population distribution within reason in each of these groups. One group was selected randomly as the control group. It was taught exactly according to the previous year's course of study for ninth grade. This program of study was essentially a breadth approach. A second section of pupils, the breadth group, was taught according to a prescribed course of study developed for this experiment, using a variety of topics and activities. Each activity had some enrichment through films, slides, books, etc. The third section of 27 pupils, the "depth" group, was also taught by a prescribed course outline prepared for this study. Painting was the "depth" activity. It included a variety of media, a study of the history of painting and acquaintance with contemporary paintings, etc.

The "depth group" program was enriched by films, slides, and books furnished as part of the research project. Based on prior experience, the "depth" group was thought by the art teacher at the outset to be the slowest group creatively. The program for each group was sufficiently flexible in operation to permit the teacher to work naturally within her individual classroom approach.

This study began with each student producing two paintings based on a common motivation. These were used to determine the individual and the group beginning levels of performance prior to the treatment. The depth group was a somewhat weaker group in art performance according to these judgments. During the pre-treatment period the test battery was given to all groups under the supervision of the research team. The testing was conducted by the Department of Art Education, Pennsylvania State University. From October to May the art teacher carried out the three programs as planned. At the end of this time, a post-treatment battery of tests was given. During the months following, the full set of each student's art products was evaluated to determine the representative level of his art achievements. Using this estimated level as a standard or constant, the judges then estimated progress, regression, or no change as a result of the treatment. Both the spontaneity and the aesthetic quality of the individual students' work were evaluated and were scored separately in all these estimates.

Development of the Test Batteries

The pre-post battery of personality tests were developed by Burkhart and Kincaid—refining and revising the Beittel Art Appreciation Test (1) and an Ideational Social Self-Determination Test (6) so as to determine the spontaneity and deliberateness of pupils' creative personality structure. In addition, the art works produced during the treatment were judged for spontaneity, aesthetic quality, and for direction of change or progress. Two supplementary test batteries, including spatial, general creativity, and personality scales were given to determine their usefulness at this level. However, the pre-post personality measures and art criteria developed specifically for this study were the most sensitive to progress in art and generally most useful of those employed, possibly because they were standardized concurrently using junior high school population samples. The criterion and personality measurement problem are thus seen as one in experimental studies. They must be considered together.

The Judgments of Spontaneity and Aesthetic Quality

Five highly trained judges with experience extending over several years evaluated the art products. All of these judges have their doctorates in art education from various institutions. In the first judging task, the judges evaluated each work in terms of spontaneous handling and deliberate handling. The judgments were made on an 8 point scale or continuum ranging from spontaneous, 8, to deliberate, 1. *Spontaneous Handling* is defined in terms of freedom or ease in movement in the use of materials and rendering of forms. *Deliberate Handling* is a judgment of the stiffness of the handling of the total work—of the placement and treatment of the material. (For further details see note (7).)

The second judging task was for aesthetic quality. The art works were judged on a 5 point scale or continuum. The judgments of the art products completed at the beginning of the experiment indicated that aesthetic quality and spontaneity-deliberateness are independent and separate in these works. In the preliminary works, factor analyses revealed that organization and design characteristics associated with Aesthetic

Quality appeared in the more deliberate beginning works while more varied and expressive uses of imagery and materials appeared in the more spontaneous beginning products, unassociated, however, with much Aesthetic Quality.

In the post-judgments of the students' total series of works, however, Aesthetic Quality and Spontaneity are significantly related. As the school year progressed those students who developed more spontaneous ways of working showed in their products an increase in Aesthetic Quality. Those who were or became more deliberate either failed to change or regressed aesthetically. This is indicated by the (.01 level) correlation .693 found between Progress in Spontaneity and Progress in Aesthetic Quality. This relationship will be discussed more fully in the analysis of the experimental findings.

The problems connected with judgments of Aesthetic Quality and Spontaneity provided findings of importance going beyond the consideration of judge reliability. The preliminary judgment of the beginning pictures was very stable. The works resulted from the same motivation and they were judged one at a time. The highest interjudge agreement was for Spontaneity (average $r = .786$) and then somewhat lower for Aesthetic Quality ($r = .756$). As the judgement tasks became more varied the judge agreement decreased because of the increased variety of topics and number of works (usually five) to be evaluated at one time. The judge agreement for Aesthetic Quality was .740 and for spontaneity .682. However, the judgment of progress brings in new difficulty since Spontaneity and Aesthetic Quality are intercorrelated. The average for judge agreement, therefore, dropped to .650 for Progress in Spontaneity and to .630 for Progress in Aesthetic Quality. In general, progress is the most difficult judgment to make. However, the average of these six judgments is .707. The general reliability was above expectation. The range of work appeared to the judges to be narrower and more limited at this grade level than on the college level in introductory classes or for the high school elective art classes. Within this limited range the judge agreement is reliable and statistically significant. (Tables I, II, and III summarize this additional information on judging.)

TABLE I

Intercorrelations of Separate Judges with Judge Totals for Four Post-Test Judgments

Judges	Aesthetic Quality	Progress in Aesthetic Quality	Spontaneity	Progress in Spontaneity	Judge Average
1	.750	.740	.790	.760	.760
2	.690	.750	.520	.520	.620
3	.670	.600	.730	.760	.690
4	.770	.590	.670	.470	.650
5	.810	.490	.700	.640	.651
Average by Types of Judgment	.740	.634	.682	.650	.675

NOTE: Judge two was lowest in the judgment of Spontaneity and judges two and four were low in the judgment of Progress in Spontaneity. Both according to the factor analysis failed to take into account ART QUALITY as a factor in Progress in Spontaneity. Judge five was low in the judgment of Progress in Aesthetic Quality.

TABLE II

Table of Average Interrelations for Six Judgments of Ninth Grade Art Products

1. Spontaneity (Preliminary)	.786
2. Aesthetic Quality (Preliminary)	.756
3. Aesthetic Quality (Concluding)	.740
4. Spontaneity (Concluding)	.682
5. Progress in Spontaneity (Concluding)	.650
6. Progress in Aesthetic Quality (Concluding)	.630
Average of all judgments for this study	.707

TABLE III

Varimax Rotation of Principal Components in Factor Analysis of Preliminary Test Battery

	Spatial—Verbal Intelligence Factor I	Ink Blot Form Perception Factor II	Aesthetic Orientation Factor III	Spontaneous Deliberate Continuum Factor IV	Ideational Openness Factor V	Process Involvement Factor VI	Art Experience Factor VII
1. IQ	665						867
2. AEI					-314		
3. HF	743				782		
4. DIT							
5. KSB		447	534				
6. SR	800						
7. BAT			708	-360			
8. RAT-ACT.		805					
9. RAT-NEG.		-696					-266
10. PIT						805	
11. RAT-SYM.		887					
12. BRIT-LETTERS	557				364	-443	
13. BRIT-IF	379				462	520	
14. WATER-G			547		403		
15. WATER-S-D				807			
16. STREETS-G			800				
17. STREETS-S-D				748			-364
% of variance accounted for	15.8	12.9	11.1	10.0	7.6	6.4	5.2

Total variance accounted for 69%

Statistical Analysis

Both the pretest and posttest batteries were intercorrelated and factor-analyzed. Tests of significance of differences in mean gains were used to determine the direction of progress or regression with respect to both the art products and the pre-post tests. The findings of a nonexperimental or descriptive nature tend to replicate Burkhart's earlier study (6). Those of an experimental nature tend to confirm the hypothesis of the present study.

Over a year's period of instruction with enriched programs at the ninth grade level, a group instructed by a "depth" approach will be superior to a "breadth" group or a control group, and a "breadth" approach will surpass a control or normal approach, as measured by progress in spontaneity, aesthetic quality and related creative personality dimensions.

That is:

Depth Group > Breadth Group > Control Group as determined by four criterion measures:

(1) Ideational   Self-Determination —
    Called the DIT (6)
(2) Beittel's Appreciation Test as revised by Burkhart-Kincaid — Called the BAT
(3) Progress in Aesthetic Quality
(4) Progress in Spontaneity
(NOTE: A combination of criterion measures three and four will be referred to as ART QUALITY in this study.)

Descriptive Findings of Importance

Spatial and Verbal Intelligence came up as an independent factor associated with fluency but unrelated to the art creativity factors. This occurred also in the concluding battery. The Rorschach Ink Blot Test also came up as an independent factor. The form used was developed for group administration by Stone (6). In general, it can be noted here that the Rorschach group test does not relate to either personality scales or criterion judgments of creativity in the art area.

Several independent and expected creativity factors also emerged on the preliminary test battery analysis. This included an Aesthetic Orientation Factor, a Spontaneous-Deliberate Continuum Factor, an Ideational Openness Factor, and a Process Involvement Factor, and lastly an Art Experience Factor. Of these the only significant loadings relating to the criteria or pictorial evaluations were for the Aesthetic Orientation, Spontaneity and Ideational Openness Factors.

Table III presents significant rotated factor loadings derived from factor analysis of the preliminary test battery. (Further description of the 17 measures will be found in the appendix to this chapter.)

Experimental Findings of Importance Regarding Progress in Art (Total Population)

Those findings which have a direct relationship for all students regardless of instructional methods relating to progress in art activities will now be discussed.

First, the Progress Factor of the Post-Test Battery will be considered as it relates to an analysis of growth and development in art under the varied conditions of this experiment, as determined through a factor analysis. This factor is identified as a Progress Factor because it has its highest loading on Progress in Aesthetic Quality (.790) and Progress in Spontaneity (.722). Most of this progress occurred in the depth group as was indicated by the high loading (.714) on this group rather than on the breadth or control group. However, some individuals did progress also in each of these groups. The other important high loadings found under this factor are on the Ideational Self-

Determination Test (.588) and the Beittel Art Appreciation Test (.551). The manner in which these tests relate to progress will be discussed more fully in an analysis of gain scores with respect to mean differences in these groups. However, the BAT (Beittel Art Appreciation) post-test correlated at the .01 level of significance (.382) with Progress in Spontaneity and with Progress in Aesthetic Quality (.287). The Ideational Self-Determination Test correlated at the .01 level (.357) with Progress in Aesthetic Quality at the same level (.311) with Progress in Spontaneity. The BAT also correlated with Spontaneity at the .01 level (.361) as did the Word-Question Test[1] Divergent Score (.298). The only other .01 correlate with Spontaneity was the Omnibus Paired-Word Test (.318), which is primarily a measure of personality flexibility or responsiveness. These personality measures are, therefore, useful in predicting Progress in Aesthetic Quality and in Spontaneity as early as the ninth grade level.

Four Analyses of Art Performance Judgments

According to a separate factor analysis of the judge scores, ART QUALITY is associated with Spontaneity and Aesthetic Quality and both must be present if any significant progress is to occur. The various interrelationships of ART QUALITY with (1) Aesthetic Quality, (2) Progress in Aesthetic Quality, (3) Spontaneity, and (4) Progress in Spontaneity are more specifically delineated in Table IV.

Some further conclusions can be made from this table with reference to the judgment of progress. First, ART QUALITY does encompass more than the usual aesthetic considerations (note the conclusion to Factor One) and it is clearly evident in

[1]This is a test asking the respondent to ask as many questions of an open nonfactual nature as possible about a common object—e.g., ice—in a short time. Developed by Burkhart. See *Studies in Art Education*, III, 1 (Fall 1961), pp. 18–39.

loadings related to Spontaneity. A judge or teacher who remains narrow in his orientation to ART QUALITY is unable to make reliable judgments of progress in art according to this analysis. Independently, Aesthetic Quality and Spontaneity are negatively related to the determination of Progress in Art. Only when both are taken into consideration together and are seen to move in a positive direction is there apparently any significant progress. Though it is important to be able to separate both these aspects of ART QUALITY to aid the student in his total growth, it is absolutely essential to grasp the relationship of one to the other in the determination of his Progress in Art. Thus both the traditional design approach, stressing aesthetic sensitivity, and an expressive materials approach, stressing spontaneity, may have negative values when isolated from each other (note conclusion to Factor II on Table IV).

Experimental Findings Relating to the Depth, Breadth, and Control Methods Of Instruction

In relation to the findings concerning the breadth-depth experiment, it is important to point out that a significant drop occurred for all groups in the measures of personality structure during the school year, as seen in the mean differences on the pre and post-test scores on both the Ideational Self-Determination Test and the Beittel Art Appreciation Test. At the elementary level it has been noted by Torrance (10) that an unexplained sharp dip in general creativity occurs at the fourth grade level. It may also be that a similar drop occurs around the ninth grade or at the time when there is a shift into a college preparation centered subject area curriculum. At least in this study of a year's duration there is a significant decline in interest in new or different theories, ideas and experiences, and a drift toward a more factual viewpoint for stu-

TABLE IV

Factors Relating to Art Quality as Determined From Art Product Judgments Factor Analysis

FACTOR I: ART QUALITY as a Factor in Aesthetic Quality and Spontaneity
1. The relationship of ART QUALITY to Aesthetic Quality 871
2. The relationship of ART QUALITY to Progress in Aesthetic Quality 444
3. The relationship of ART QUALITY to Spontaneity 666
4. The relationship of ART QUALITY to Progress in Spontaneity 521
                    (26.4% variance accounted for by this factor)
Conclusion: ART QUALITY is present significantly in all these various relationships
            as a central factor.

FACTOR II: Progress in Art as a QUALITY Factor.
1. The relationship of progress in ART QUALITY to Aesthetic Quality . . . .   −.334
2. The relationship of progress in ART QUALITY to Progress in Aesthetic Quality.   .800
3. The relationship of progress in ART QUALITY to Spontaneity . . . .   −.519
4. The relationship of progress in ART QUALITY to Progress in Spontaneity 746
                    (21.4% variance accounted for by this factor)
Conclusion: There is a negative relationship between progress in ART QUALITY and
            Aesthetic Quality (−.334) and progress in ART QUALITY and Spon-
            taneity (−.519). Progress in art appears as a product of both Progress in
            Aesthetic Quality (.800) and Progress in Spontaneity (.746). *Since alone
            these two attributes appear separate and negatively related to ART QUALITY
            they must therefore be acquired together to result in progress in quality in art.*

FACTOR III: Spontaneity in Art as a QUALITY Factor.
1. The relationship of Spontaneity to Aesthetic Quality . . . .   −.284
2. The relationship of Spontaneity to Progress in Aesthetic Quality 062
3. The relationship of Spontaneity to ART QUALITY 488
4. The relationship of Spontaneity to Progress in Spontaneity 167
                    (8.2% variance accounted for by this factor)
Conclusion: Spontaneity is not a factor in determining Aesthetic Quality (−.284).
            Neither Progress in Aesthetic Quality (.062) nor Progress in Spontaneity is
            related significantly to Spontaneity as such. There is, however, a significant
            relationship (.488) between Spontaneity and ART QUALITY which ap-
            pears as the significant variable for this factor.

FACTOR IV: Progress in Aesthetic Quality as an ART QUALITY Factor.
Conclusion: No significant loading appears under this last factor other than a .220
            loading on ART QUALITY. The whole complex of the various aspects of
            the work of art is what in the end must be sensed, and no one aspect or one
            part is apparently predictive of the quality of the whole.

dents as a whole. This suggests that study on a larger scale focusing on academic acceleration might be of real importance in arriving at a more complete understanding of the problems inherent in our present educational system where the develop-ment of creative personalities is a concern.

In this respect the Depth Group is important because its losses on these measures were not significant, while both other groups lost significantly (see Table V). Related to

TABLE V

Experimental Group Mean Gains or Losses on the Four
Criterion Measures and Their Levels of
Significance Within Groups

		Depth	Breadth	Control
DIT (Divergent Ideational Test)	M. Gain	−2.81	− 9.13	−13.38
	Sig.	———	Sig. Loss	Sig. Loss
BAT (Beittel Appreciation Test)	M. Gain	−4.11	−10.09	−21.97
	Sig.	———	Sig. Loss	Sig. Loss
Progress in Aesthetic Quality	M. Gain	4.09	1.22	1.38
	Sig.	Sig. Gain	———	———
Progress in Spontaneity	M. Gain	3.70	− 3.23	− 1.31
	Sig.	Sig. Gain	Sig. Loss	———

this is the fact that the Depth Group did register significant gains in Aesthetic Quality while the others did not. Most important, the Depth Group gained significantly in Spontaneity while the Breadth Group lost significantly. It may be that the opportunity to work creatively in depth is what enabled the students in the Depth Group to resist regression in their ideational creativity more successfully than the students in other groups. Art in depth can be seen here to play at least a sustaining role in the development of creativity in personality structure against more factually oriented educational forces. It should be noted, however, that the correlations for combined groups between Progress in Spontaneity and the Beittel Art Appreciation test (.382), and between the Ideational Self-Determination test and Progress in Aesthetic Quality (.357) and Progress in Spontaneity (.311), indicate that ideational creativity is clearly related to the achievement of progress in ART QUALITY regardless of instructional or methodological differences. It may be that the better pupils are good regardless of how they are taught because they are capable of being more self-deter-

mining in general, both ideationally and artistically.

Methods, however, make a difference when it comes to groups, as is shown by the fact that there were six .01 intercorrelations with the various art criteria in the Depth Group versus one significant one in the Breadth Group. It is informative to compare the two groups in this respect one criterion at a time.

Here it is interesting to note that in instances where a total group is developing there is more sensitivity on the part of these criterion measures than when instructional methods are mixed and progress is not uniform. In general the intercorrelates in the Depth Group suggest that this form of instruction will allow for a wider range of differences to be reflected by the art product than when instruction aims for Breadth. It appears that Depth allows for more of the whole person to be related to his art activities than does Breadth.

In the analysis of mean gains between the experimental groups according to the "t" test, the Depth Group differed significantly from the Breadth and Control Groups in six out of eight comparisons, and all changes

TABLE VI

Table of Significant Correlates of the Four Art Product Measures in Depth and Breadth Groups

Measure	Aesthetic Quality	Progress in Aesthetic Quality	Spontaneity	Progress In Spontaneity
1. Basic Social Concepts		.385-D		
3. Correctness of Expression	.554-D		.458-D	.400-D
5. Interpretation of Literature			.433-B .380-D	.387-D
6. Vocabulary			.459-D	.399-D
8. Omnibus Paired Word			.488-B	
12. Relationship Test Composition	.409-D		.414-D	
13. Beittel Art Appreciation Post Test			.365-D	
15. Ideational Self-Determination (DIT-Post)		.462-D		
22. VVRT-Action			.512-D	
23. VVRT-Abstraction		.381-D	.499-D	
30. World-Question Divergency	.411-D			
38. Art Experience Index	-.431-B			
40. Kieselbach (Pre)	.407-B			
41. Beittel Art Appreciation (Pre)	.433-D			
42. Rorschach Action	.408-B		.603-B	-.439-B
43. Rorschach Negative Space	.488-D			

Depth Group—19 .01 & .05 intercorrelations
Breadth Group—7 .01 & .05 intercorrelations

Depth group—6 .01 Correlations
Breadth group—1 .01 Correlation

TABLE VII

Tests of Significance of Difference of Mean Gains Between
the Three Experimental Groups

Depth	Breadth	Control
DIT (Ideational Self-Determination Test)	———	Sig. .01, D > C
BAT (Beittel's Art Appreciation Test)	———	Sig. .01, D > C
Progress in Aesthetic Quality	Sig. .05, D > B	Sig. .05, D > C
Progress in Spontaneity	Sig. .01, D > B	Sig. .01, D > C
Breadth		
DIT (Ideational Self-Determination Test)		———
BAT (Beittel's Art Appreciation Test)		Sig. .05, B > C
Progress in Aesthetic Quality		———
Progress in Spontaneity		———

Conclusion:
D > C 4 out of 4 comparisons
D > B 2 out of 4 comparisons
B > C 1 out of 4 comparisons

were in the predicted direction. In all four comparisons the Depth Group exceeded the Control Group. In one out of four instances the Breadth Group exceeded the Control Group. (See Table VII.)

These experimental findings indicate some of the conditions necessary for progress in art. Where a drive for depth and involvement is made possible through sustained work in a limited area of creativity it is possible to hold and perhaps develop a positive, aesthetic, self-determining orientation. Only over a series of works where progress can be discerned and evaluation can take place is it likely that an entire group of students will grow not only in their creativity in art but perhaps as individuals.

Summary

Two teaching methods were used in this experiment, the "breadth" and "depth." The breadth method is obviously the more popular, and certainly the more widely used of the two. The study showed that the

less popular method, the "depth" method, produced the greatest gain in individual student progress over a one-year period. Anecdotal data indicated that students say they prefer a variety of experiences, or the breadth method. This may have caused certain resistance against the "depth" approach which may in turn have lessened the gains under the method though these gains were strong. However, if these students had held an initially favorable attitude toward perseverance and long-term projects their gains might have been even greater. The study suggests that it may be well to begin earlier with boys and girls in engaging in sustained long-term projects of depth and with less yielding to their restless demands for variety. There is in fact some evidence in this and other studies by the authors that some kinds of activities that students appear to want and are insistent upon have little learning value for them, while some learning experiences that they show some real resistance to have some educational value for them. Initial student desires and resistance in this study were not a good positive predictor of the educational value of the types of instruction given. In another study (9) at the ninth grade level reported in this journal it is a major conclusion that student "dissatisfaction" is related to progress rather than their "satisfaction." Certainly a better method than student preferences for determining the kinds of learning activities that students need in art is the amount of learning value observable in their various products and processes and this is, of course, precisely the function of having continuous research going on in our classrooms. It is certainly evident also that one of the important advantages for both the students and the teacher of the "depth" approach is that it makes observable progress an unavoidable issue, challenge, and instructional requirement.

BIBLIOGRAPHY

1. BEITTEL, KENNETH R. "Experimental Studies of the Aesthetic Attitudes of College Students." *Research Yearbook*, National Art Education Association, 1957, pp. 47–61.
2. BEITTEL, KENNETH R., HERBERT J. BURGART, and ROBERT C. BURKHART. "Creative Personality and General Creativity Measures in Relation to Art Performance Criteria in a Large General Education College Class." The Penna. State Univ., 1961. Unpublished study.
3. BRITTAIN, W. LAMBERT. "An Experiment Toward Measuring Creativity." *Research Yearbook*, The National Art Education Association, 1957, pp. 36–46.
4. BURGART, HERBERT J. "Art in Higher Education: The Relationship of Art Experience to Personality, General Creativity, and Art Performance." *Studies in Art Education*, Vol. 11, No. 2, Spring 1961.
5. BURKHART, ROBERT C. "An Analysis of Individuality of Art Expression at the Senior High Level." *Research Yearbook*, The National Art Education Association, 1959.
6. ———. "Spontaneity and Deliberateness as a Creativity Personality Continuum, etc. *Studies in Art Education*, Vol. 2, No. 1, Fall 1960.
7. ———. *Spontaneous and Deliberate Ways of Learning*. International Textbook Company, in press.
8. ———. "The Relationship of Separate Criteria for Creativity in Art and Student Teaching to Four Personality Factors." *Studies in Art Education*, Vol. 3, No. 1, Fall 1961 (this issue).
9. LIENARD, M. "What is the Relationship of Children's Satisfaction With Their Art Products to Improvement In Art?" *Studies in Art Education*, Vol. 3, No. 1, Fall 1961.
10. TORRANCE, E. PAUL. "Factors Affecting Creative Thinking In Children." Bureau of Educational Research, University of Minnesota. (Mimeographed copy.)

APPENDIX

DEFINITION OF VARIABLES OF PRELIMINARY BATTERY

1. IQ — California test of mental maturity.
2. AEI — Art experience index, an object measure of previous formal art experience (4).
3. HF — Hidden figures, a test of spatial ability developed by Thurstone (6).
4. DIT — Divergent Ideational Test, a test developed from the Omnibus Personality Inventory (6), principally originated by Frank Barron.
5. KSB — Kieselbach Test of Aesthetic Discrimination (6).
6. SR — Spatial Relations Test of the Psychological Corporation (6).
7. BAT — Beittel Appreciation Test (1), as reoriented in terms of the Spontaneous-Deliberate Continuum (6).
8. RAT — Act., Group Rorschach Sub-Scale developed by Stone (6).
9. RAT-Neg. — Group Rorschach Sub-Scale developed by Burgart for this study to show perception of forms in negative space.
10. PIT — Process Involvement Test, a verbal check list operating through process recall and developed by Burkhart (5).
11. RAT-Sym. — Group Rorschach (see 9 above) scored for responses emphasizing symmetry.
12. BRIT-LETTERS — a test of predictive fluency requiring construction of letter forms from two given parts. Test developed by Brittain (3).

13. BRIT-IF — a test of ideational fluency requiring classification of concrete objects shown in drawings into various category groupings. Developed by Brittain (3).

14. WATER-G — Gestalt aesthetic judgment of art products on a stimulus topic: water.

15. WATER-S-D — Judgment of spontaneity —

deliberateness on the same topic and works as on 14 above.

16. STREETS-G — Gestalt aesthetic judgment of art products on a stimulus topic: city streets.

17. STREETS-S-D — Judgment of spontaneity-deliberateness on the same topic and works as on 16 above.

20. The Aesthetic Method of Education

HERBERT READ

So far, without deliberate intention, the impression created in this book (referring to *The Grass Roots of Art*) may have been gloomy. The indictment which has been drawn against modern civilization is a severe one, and the material conditions of salvation, when extracted from human history, seem to accord little with the many amenities to which we have become accustomed. My philosophy, however, is not a negative one, and in the remaining two lectures I hope to present you with positive proposals, which, though they entail a revolution in our way of life, are not impossible of achievement if we become urgently aware of the necessity for change.

I have repeatedly drawn attention to *sensibility* as the human quality underlying all processes involving skill, all achievements displaying taste, and I said that the first requirement in any civilization with pretensions to cultural values is a system of education or upbringing which not only preserves the innate sensibility of the child, but makes this the basis of mental development.

I now return to that fundamental question.

In all our attempts to define the place of art in society we are continually struggling against the general notion that art is unnatural — that the artist is a rare and eccentric individual, having little or nothing in common with the common man. But it is only greatness that is uncommon, only genius that is eccentric. The appreciation of good form, the perception of rhythm and harmony, the instinct to make things shapely and efficient — these are normal human characteristics, innate rather than acquired, and certainly present in the child from its earliest years. We teach art to children — or perhaps we don't — but what we do not sufficiently realize is that children are artists in any case, just as inevitably as they are walkers or singers, talkers or players of games. Art is merely one method of human expression — the method which makes use of the expressive line, of expressive color, of plastic form. There is an art of children, just as there is an art of savages or an art of adults. The mistake we make is to assume

✳SOURCE: Reprinted from *The Grass Roots of Art* (Ch. V). New York: Meridian (1961).

that this activity in children, the existence of which we can hardly deny, is merely a naive and clumsy attempt to imitate an adult activity. An imitative element is present in all childish activities, but the desire is never to imitate for the sake of imitation, but to communicate something in a common language. The drive behind all such childish efforts is an inner subjective need, not a monkey-like reflex, not an "aping," as we say, of adult behavior.

It is very important to admit the truth of this observation, for on such an admission depends the choice between teaching the child to imitate adult standards and recognizing that the child has standards of its own, appropriate to its age and expressive needs and gradually evolving to cope with widening circles of experience. This is a basic distinction in education generally, but for the moment I am only concerned with the effect it has on our attitude towards the aesthetic activity in children.

We are all prepared to admit that art is an affair of the emotions, perhaps also of intuitions and of the intelligence, and we ought therefore to realize that it is not merely a question of the simple growth of a separate faculty, the gradual maturation of a skill. Let us rather consider the analogy of love. The love of a child is one thing, and though the psychoanalysts have taken away our belief in its complete innocence, nevertheless we know that infancy, childhood, adolescence, and maturity represent so many stages in the development of the emotion of love which differ *in kind*. However much we may be deceived by the apparent thread of continuity represented by the uniqueness of each personality, we know that the transition from one stage of emotional development to another is often sudden and cataclysmic. The child of yesterday, attached to its parents by bonds of affection, is suddenly today the victim of a passion which makes of it a new being.

The art of the child is the art of a human being with perceptions and emotions, reactions and fantasies, which differ in nature from the perceptions and emotions, reactions and fantasies of the adult. Instead, therefore, of judging the art of children by adult standards, we should be acting more scientifically if we were to compare it with the art of savages and of primitive men generally. Many of the observations which have been made about primitive art can be applied to the art of children. In both cases we are dealing with what Lévy-Bruhl has called *a pre-logical* state of mentality, and the many characteristics which are common to both types of art spring from this fact. The art of children must be studied, not as the child's feeble effort to imitate the plastic modes of expression practised by the civilized adult, but as the child's direct and unsophisticated expression of its own world of feeling. Once we have adopted this correct attitude towards the art of children, once we have an understanding of the place which plastic modes of expression occupy in the child's emotional life, then our methods of teaching children must change radically, and the place which art should occupy in the scheme of education takes on an altogether new significance.

In the researches and experiments which have led to this new understanding of the art of children, no one country can claim preeminence. It was Rousseau who first taught us to respect the emotional integrity of the child's world of vision: but Rousseau, from our point of view, is still an intellectualist fully aware of the sensational basis of the child's mode of perception, but using it for rational ends. You will remember that he would have Emile cultivate the art of drawing, but "not so much for art's sake, as to give him exactness of eye and flexibility of hand." He would take good care, he said, not to provide Emile with a drawing master, who would only set him to copy copies and to draw from drawings: "Nature should be his only teacher, and things his only models." Rousseau specifically excludes drawing from memory, for fear lest his pupil should substitute "absurd and fantastic forms for the real truth of things, and lose his sense of proportion and his taste for the beauties of nature."

I think it was Ruskin who first realized that a distinction must be made between drawing from observation, whether of works of art or of nature, and drawing as a spontaneous activity, a form of expression dictated by inner needs, like speech. At any rate, in his *Elements of Drawing*, published in 1857, he suggested that it was "not advisable to engage a child (under the age of twelve or fourteen) in any but the most voluntary practice of art. If it has a talent for drawing, it will be continually scrawling on what paper it can get; and should be allowed to scrawl at its own free will, due praise being given for every appearance of care, of truth, in its efforts. It should be allowed to amuse itself with cheap colors almost as soon as it has sense enough to wish for them." These remarks of Ruskin's inspired one of his followers, a teacher called Ebenezer Cooke, to experiment in English schools. Ebenezer Cooke's experiments came to the notice of the leading English psychologist of the period, James Sully, and the result was a book, *Studies of Childhood*, published in 1896, which gave a firm psychological foundation to the study of this activity in children. Meanwhile the subject had been pursued in other countries — by Corrado Ricci in Italy and by Bernard Perez in France. During the past forty years quite an extensive literature has grown up round the subject, in America as well as in Europe, and certain teachers, such as Franz Cizek in Vienna and Marion Richardson in London, have carried out practical experiments in art teaching which have been significant enough to arouse considerable interest in the educational world. I have given a detailed account of this work elsewhere,[1] and here I will only summarize, very briefly and simply, the conclusions that have been derived from the observation of this creative activity in children and the claims that we now make for the practice of a free mode of plastic expression during the course of education.

Let me begin by making clear what we do *not* claim. We do not claim that we are teaching children to observe external objects with exactness. We are not attempting to sharpen the child's powers of observation, of classification, of memory. All that is a pedagogical activity which we are content to leave to the science master, and we would agree that a certain type of drawing or design should be taught, like writing and numeration, in conjunction with scientific observation: it is a necessary form of notation or record. It is a skill which becomes appropriate at the secondary stage of education.

In the second place — and it is most important to appreciate this point — we are *not* attempting to create professional artists. To become a competent painter or sculptor in the professional sense will require a long and arduous training in technique, and this vocational instruction should be given (as it is at present) in institutions specially devoted to the purpose. We teach children to speak, but we do not expect them all to be orators: we teach them to write, but we do not expect them all to be poets. In the same way, we teach them to draw and paint and model without any expectation that art will necessarily become their exclusive vocation in life.

What we do teach children by all these means is a particular medium of expression. Sounds, words, lines, colors — all these are the

---

[1] *Education Through Art*. rev. ed. New York: Pantheon, 1958.

raw materials out of which the child has to learn to communicate with the outer world. He has also at his command certain gestures, which he combines with sounds, words, lines and colors. In his difficulty — for it is enormously difficult at first for the child to make himself understood — he will use everything that comes to hand; he makes a total effort to express himself, to express his inner feelings and desires.

Normally the parent and teacher make every effort to understand the *verbal* signs which the child makes: we listen to the first babblings of the baby and try to construe them into words. How patiently we guide and encourage the child in his efforts, first to talk and then to write!

But the child has also at his command this other language of line and color, and he could often say by this means things for which he still lacks the words. He can express his emotions and desires, his perceptions and daydreams, by signs and symbols, by approximate representations. But more often than not his efforts in this direction receive no encouragement from the teacher, and even less from the parent. This activity, which should fluorish as naturally as speech, is discouraged and becomes atrophied. The child is then visually dumb, a word which originally meant stupid.

But if we do encourage the child to develop his visual communications, his language of images, a new direction for expansion and growth is opened up for him. We might say that one of our aims, and perhaps the chief one, should be to give the child the necessary confidence and skill to develop a new but quite natural medium of expression — to make the language of symbols as much a trained habit as the language of signs, to give the pictograph the same significance as the phonetic alphabet. But our secondary aim is to encourage the child to reveal its personality, its innate character-

istics. For the parent and the teacher a child's drawings become a new window into the child's mind.

But there is more to be discovered than the psychology of the individual child. As we gather and correlate this plastic imagery produced by children, we learn much about children in general, about their common characteristics and their mental development. And finally, but not in my opinion least important, we learn much about the nature of the aesthetic activity, about the place of art in life and in the evolution of mankind. For what these children produce is not merely line and color, but line and color (form, too, and cubic volume) which are significant and expressive, and which are significant and expressive quite naturally and instinctively. We learn, in short, that the primary elements of art — the factors which make it emotionally effective — are given to it by man's own nature and needs, and are not the creation of man's consciousness and intellect.

It would be wrong to give the impression that the aesthetic method in education is generally accepted in English schools. Such experiments are not part of an official policy, though they have the sympathy of many directors of education. It should be realized that the English educational system is still to a large extent decentralized. There is a central authority, the Ministry of Education, but there are also the numerous Local Education Authorities, and these preserve a large measure of autonomy. And then we have our so-called public schools, which are very private and exclusive, and numerous schools of a more or less independent character, run by religious communities or even by private individuals. This loose structure permits a degree of experiment which would not be possible under a rigidly totalitarian system. I do not want to suggest that experiments are confined to schools of a more or less private character; on the

FIGURE 20.1a "One of the Three Witches from Macbeth," by a girl of thirteen.

FIGURE 20.1b "The Family," by a boy of thirteen from an East End school in London.

contrary, some of the most interesting experimental work has taken place under authorities such as the London County Council, and anywhere one might find an enterprising director of education willing and able to try out new ideas in the schools under his control. The type of work illustrated in the accompanying Figures comes from no particular type of school, nor from the children of any particular class of society. It comes from elementary schools in the East End of London and from fashionable private schools, from secondary schools and schools for epileptic children. One thing that has been demonstrated beyond any doubt is that the aesthetic faculty is present in every child as a birthright, and that it can be made to blossom in the most unlikely surroundings — in gloomy industrial slums no less than in the

beautiful precincts of a school like Eton or Winchester. Of course, as the child grows and its perceptions feed more or less consciously on its environment, this environment begins to be reflected in the subject matter of the child's art. But only in the subject matter. The style can develop independently of the content. It is not the method of teaching.

If you now ask me: What is this method of teaching practiced in schools which produce the paintings I have shown, my answer can only be in the most general terms. I am not myself a teacher, and I do not like to dictate to those who carry on this most difficult vocation. But I observe teachers and I note the results: I see that certain methods lead to results which I consider good, other methods to results which I consider bad, or

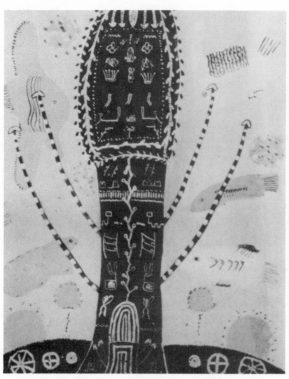

FIGURE 20.1c "Composition with Fish," by a secondary school girl of fourteen.

FIGURE 20.1d "Bedtime Story" by a girl of eleven (L.C.C. school).

to no results at all. It is easier to describe the methods which have bad results than those which have good results, for the former are definite and decisive, the latter infinitely subtle and uncertain. The bad results are always produced by a method which is too conscious and deliberate, by a discipline which is imposed from without, which is the command of a drill sergeant. The good results are produced apparently by no method at all, or by a system of hints and suggestions, and the discipline which undoubtedly exists, and *must* exist, arises out of the activity itself, is in fact a kind of concentration on tools and materials, an absorption in concrete things. The good teacher is not a dictator, but rather a pupil more advanced in technique than the others, more conscious of the aim to be achieved and the means that must be adopted, who works with the chil-

dren, sympathizes with them and encourages them, gives them that priceless possession which is self-confidence. It is only fear that prevents the child from being an artist — fear that its private world of fantasy will seem ridiculous to the adult, fear that its expressive signs and symbols will not be adequate. Cast out fear from the child and you have then released all its potentialities for emotional growth and maturation.

That, of course, is not the final stage of education. You have liberated the child from fear, but beyond liberation there must be the more positive world of cooperation. You have liberated the child by means of sympathy and understanding, and the same faculties must be used to create human bonds, social bonds, until the individual child finds his fulfillment in the adult world of the community. That is the general purpose of education, but I know of no methods so effective for this purpose as those which are in a concrete sense *creative*. As individuals we create to communicate: we create a language out of sounds, we create a pictorial language out of line and color. But every language, even the language of art, is a communal creation; it represents an agreed system of signs, to be used in common. Art is a bond. It is not a bond which should be the exclusive privilege of a class, of a tiny group of connoisseurs and artists. Art should be an integral part of our communal life, as it was in Ancient Greece, as it was in the Middle Ages; and it should enter our lives at their formative stage, as a natural function of human relationships, as the language of form and color, as universal and as innocent as the language of words.

It may be objected that when I speak of the language of form and color, I am confining myself to a much narrower conception of art than was prevalent in Ancient Greece or in the Middle Ages. In all our discussions of the place of art in education, there is admittedly a tendency to confine our observations to pictorial art. We think of art as predominantly visual, and we seem to ignore those other modes of expression, whether of speech or of sound, which are also forms of art of equal importance. By confining my observations in this lecture to children's drawings, I may seem to be guilty of the same neglect, not only of music and poetry, but even of sculpture and architecture. Let me therefore make it perfectly clear to you that anything I have to say about the art of children, and its importance in education, applies to all the arts. At the same time I think there is something more than mere convenience in the preference we give in this matter to pictorial art. Plato betrayed a similar partiality for the art of music, and nearly all his illustrations were drawn from that art. Again, I don't think it was merely

a question of convenience for Plato. We choose the illustrations which are most apt — that is to say, we resort to the art which the civilization we live in finds most utilitarian. Music, in Plato's time, was the normal adjunct to the religious festivals and public entertainments in which the Athenian public indulged: it was the accompaniment to their daily life. We cannot say the same of music nowadays: it is still there, in the background, especially if our neighbor leaves his radio on all day. But in modern life music is a subordinate art and does not compare, in the range and power of its appeal, to the stream of pictorial images which passes into the public consciousness through the channels of the press, the cinema, advertisements and illustrated books. The eye, perhaps, has a certain priority among our organs of sensation. I am not giving pictorial art more importance for this reason; I am merely defending the convenient use we make, and should make, of the pictorial image as a means of propaganda, even as a means of education. But the means is not the end; the end is the development of a balanced aesthetic awareness which is expressed in all media — not only in painting, but also in sculpture, weaving, embroidery, music, dancing, poetry and drama.

There is one further point to note: art is a natural discipline. In an obvious sense, art is a discipline imposed by the tool and the material — a child cannot use a pencil or a pen, a brush or a potter's wheel, without discovering that in order to be expressive, hand and eye must work in an instinctive unison. Art in this way produces an integration of the senses which we call *skill*, and which is one of the most fundamental purposes of any system of education. But art is also a discipline in another and a more profound sense. There is in the very process of perception, and in this complementary process of expression, an instinctive tendency to *form*. The formal perfection of most primitive works of art, achieved without any system of instruction, has often been a subject for wonder and astonishment. The unsophisticated art of children, before any instruction is given, has the same tendency towards formal organization — not only balance of composition and selective emphasis of significant detail, but also towards expressive line and harmonious color. Natural expression has its own instinctive form, and this would seem to suggest that the aim of education should be to seize on this innate sense of discipline, in order to develop and mature it, rather than to impose on the child a system of discipline which may be alien to its nature and harmful to its mental growth.

When the mental growth of the child has been impeded, and its psyche distorted (with results which are definitely neurotic and even delinquent), then there is much evidence which suggests that the practice of a creative art may have a therapeutic effect, gradually leading the child back to a balanced psychological disposition. The wider claims which are made for the place of art in education do not stop short at the achievement of a balanced personality for each individual child: that integration of the personality which is aimed at is an integration within the group or community to which the child belongs. We have never dared to trace the connections between the disordered state of our civilization and our traditional systems of education. If our schools were producing naturally and normally personalities which we could describe as balanced, integrated or harmonious, we should not be able to tolerate a condition of universal disunity and mutual distrust. We should therefore re-examine our whole tradition of education since the Renaissance and dare to ask ourselves whether it has been generally productive of individual serenity and social harmony. We might then have to confess that in our exclusive preoccupation with knowledge and science, we had omitted to educate those human faculties which are

connected with the emotional and integrative aspects of human life — that we had carefully nurtured inhuman monsters, with certain organs of the intelligence gigantically enlarged, others completely atrophied. I am not making scientific assertions; I am merely pointing out that in certain directions we have not dared to question the presuppositions of our academic traditions and that at the same time these presuppositions have a clear connection with the character of our civilization.

I hope I have now made it clear that what I have called the development of a balanced aesthetic awareness is not an end in itself. Our aim is the same as Plato's — the moral and intellectual wholeness or health of mankind — and art is for me, as it was for Plato, a means to this end. But that has not been the general purpose of education since the Renaissance. I think one might go so far as to say that since the rise of scholasticism in the Middle Ages, education has taken many forms, but essentially, during all these centuries, its aim has been to increase the powers of the intellect, to discipline the emotions and to build up a knowledge and understanding of the natural world. That aim has been pursued with such consistency and singleness of mind that, according to some anatomists, the very structure of the human brain has been altered and physiological tensions have been set up which are definitely perceptible as processes alien to the organisms as a whole.[2] I am not capable of handling the evidence, but I think it is worth noting in passing that there is some biological evidence for the belief (or rather, since it is contrary to the common belief, the heresy) that human nature can be changed.

Those people, the majority, who believe that human nature cannot be changed, usually make this dogma a basis for their

[2] Cf. Trigant Burrow, *Biology of Human Conflict* (New York: The Macmillan Co., 1937), p. 117.

further belief that we shall never abolish war. Man is a fighting animal, they say, and since there is no possibility of changing his nature, he will continue to fight until, presumably, the human race, like the Kilkenny cats, is no more. This is, of course, a very illogical and unscientific point of view. We know that some human beings are aggressive and others unaggressive; that some communities are martial in spirit, others pacific. We now have a hypothesis — the so-called frustration-aggression hypothesis — which offers a comprehensive explanation of this duplicity in human nature. Aggression, it asserts, is always a consequence of frustration. Avoid frustration and we shall thereby eliminate the psychological basis of war and all other forms of aggression.[3]

It seems to come to this: we could change human nature if we could avoid the frustration of certain instinctual drives which are part of the inherited characteristics of each human being. I do not wish on the present occasion to spend any time discussing the nature of these instincts; we are all aware of their existence, and we know that their perversion results in the formation of what we call "bad habits." Education, from this point of view, is the teaching of "good habits" — but how do innate instinctual drives which are presumably in their origin ethically neutral, or merely egotistical, become "good" habits rather than "bad" habits? That, as Plato and Aristotle recognized long ago, is the crux of the educational problem, and it is still a problem, which, in spite of Plato and Aristotle and all the educational philosophers who followed them, remains unsolved.

It remains unsolved in practice, but not, I think, in theory. The theory was formulated at the beginning, by Plato and Aristotle, but that theory has never yet been put into practice. We might go so far as to say that

the theory has never yet been taken seriously. Why?

To restate the theory is to risk the displeasure of all those who have had their grounding in these classical commonplaces. But in statements and restatements, everything depends on the emphasis given to particular aspects of a theory, and it is a wrong emphasis which in this particular case has been responsible for an age-long misunderstanding.

The theory begins with a clear distinction between *moral* and *intellectual* virtue. I need not elaborate the distinction, but please observe that once two things have been separated, it is possible henceforth to treat them separately — to hand over the teaching of moral virtue to one institution and the teaching of intellectual virtue to another. That is, in effect, what happened during the Renaissance: the teaching of moral virtue became the exclusive concern of the Church, the teaching of intellectual virtue the exclusive concern of the State. The Church has never pretended to teach moral virtue on Platonic lines, so the fact that the Church has failed to carry out its assignment is merely what a Platonist would expect. What is important to emphasize is that the State (in which term I include all secular institutions permitted or authorized to act in the name of the State), relieved of the necessity of inculcating moral virtue, was able to concentrate on that immense development of rational thought which has culminated in the atomic bomb. So overwhelming was the progress in this direction that intellectual values began, in the seventeenth century if not earlier, to invade the province of moral education, until we arrive at the paradoxical situation in which even ethics is held to be a *science*, subject to quantitative laws.[4]

Leaving on one side intellectual virtue, the development of which may or may not be justified by the immense structure of

[3]Cf. John Dollard and others, *Frustration and Aggression*, Institute of Human Relations, Yale University (New Haven, 1937).

[4]Cf. C. H. Waddington, *The Scientific Attitude* (Middlesex: Penguin Books, 1948).

modern philosophy and science, we should direct our attention to the fate of moral virtue, which Plato and Aristotle regarded not merely as of equal importance, but even as having a certain priority in education. These Greek philosophers said again and again that all the intellectual virtue man is capable of is not only useless, but indeed dangerous, unless it is grafted on to a stock of moral goodness. By ignoring the essential priority of moral virtue, our systems of education are merely putting dangerous instruments into the hands of people whose instinctual life may be, not merely unformed, but even evilly disposed.

The only method of moral education developed in the modern world is education by precept. These are the laws, these are the commandments, this is done and that is not done by the best people: obey, conform, go and do likewise. If we could assume that these laws and commandments were perfect, ordained by God, and not the mere accumulation of customs and superstitions, there might be some virtue in such a system. We know that human beings are very apt to learn by imitation, especially social imitation. But if they are imitating an imperfect pattern, no improvement takes place. We merely propagate one another's vices, along with a few convenient virtues. For this reason we must look outside human society for the pattern of moral virtue, and the only pattern outside ourselves is our environment, in so far as that is enduring. Look into the structure of the physical universe: there, said Plato and Aristotle, you will find the pattern of moral virtue. Repeat that pattern in your lives, impress it on your souls, do this habitually and especially in childhood, and then goodness will become second nature to you.

Plato did not put forward this theory as a likely hypothesis; he attempted to give it a logical demonstration. It was already evident to the Greeks that certain laws are exhibited in the structure of the physical universe: laws of harmony and proportion, of balance and rhythm. Modern physics has, of course, enormously reinforced the early perceptions of Greek science in this respect. The same laws, Plato was quick to perceive, are also exhibited in the most perfect and efficient forms of human activity: in music, in dancing, in gymnastics, in the rhythms of poetry and the harmonies of painting or sculpture. The inference was then simple enough — so simple that for twenty-four centuries it has seemed too bold and revolutionary. Make the rhythmic arts the basis of your methods of education, said Plato. Then, quite naturally, quite inevitably, you instill into children that sense of form or grace which is the foundation of moral goodness. That is the theory, simple and inflexible, which Plato taught in the *Laws* no less eloquently than in the *Republic*. It is simple, it is clear; the only mystery is why the world has for so long neglected it.[5]

There are many possible explanations of this mystery. To the Christian world of the Middle Ages, in so far as it was known to them, such a theory must have seemed pagan, humanistic, without divine sanction. More difficult to explain is the failure of the Renaissance to revive the theory with any sense of actuality. It is true that the theory was rediscovered and restated — by Alberti, for example. But by then moral education had become hopelessly confused with religious instruction, and this confusion was to be deepened by the Reformation. With the growth of puritanism an immense paradox was foisted on the world: the supposed antagonism of art and religion, of grace and goodness. In England, and in the United States, we still live within the limits of that moral blackout.

In general, two great mental changes are necessary before we can hope to give Plato's theory of education a trial: a return to the

[5]Recently it has been brilliantly restated by Hans Kayser, in *Akróasis, die Lehre von der Harmonie der Welt* (Basle, 1946).

Platonic ideal of moral virtue, which involves what we call "a change of heart"; and a true appreciation of the significance of the creative activity. The change of heart may be forced upon us by our desperate straits — it is the wider problem of the crisis of our civilization. But one change is implicated in the other, and I have failed if I have not persuaded you that a true appreciation of the creative activity is the best hope of a solution of our moral crisis. The means by which we can achieve the moral revolution are themselves the substance of an enduring culture.

21. The Logic of Teaching in the Arts

B. OTHANEL SMITH

It is the purpose of this essay to examine the logic of teaching in the domain of valuation and in the area of appreciation in the arts. In the course of exploring this aspect of teaching, we shall deal briefly with the meaning of "teaching." It is hoped that the use of the word "logic" in connection with "teaching" will not alarm anyone. True, logic has seldom been a fashionable subject and many teachers will doubt its usefulness. But any teacher who tries to lead a class through the lines of reasoning upon which a conclusion rests will sense instantly the logical aspects of his enterprise and the necessity of understanding them.

Meaning of "Teaching"

Almost everything we have come to know about teaching — or what we think we know about it — has been drawn by speculation from philosophy and psychology, salted with a bit of practical wisdom. We have not typically gone into the classroom to find out from actual observation what teaching is. Consequently, when we read in the books about problem-teaching,

lecture-teaching, question-answer teaching, project teaching, individualized teaching, or any other of the so-called methods of teaching, we are reading about what an author thinks the teacher ought to do according to the teachings of philosophy and psychology. The author does not tell us what a teacher actually does when he teaches. Yet how can we prescribe how the teacher should teach unless we can describe teaching as an observable and modifiable form of behavior?

To most of us, it seems obvious that matters of fact are determined by observation. But we have been slow to follow this maxim in our study of teaching, preferring to go along with the ancient Greeks, who believed in thinking rather than looking. Aristotle held that women have fewer teeth than men. He was married twice, but it never occurred to him to peer into his wives' mouths to test his belief. Of course, Aristotle was a genius in anybody's book, but his mistakes about nature and women only underline the fact that there is no substitute for observation when you want to know facts. If we want to know what teach-

*SOURCE: Reprinted from *Teachers College Record*, LXIII, 3 (December 1961), pp. 176–83.

ing is, the place to begin is in the classroom. Teaching is describable in terms of what teachers actually do rather than what we think they ought to do. At least, it seems reasonable to hold that teachers do teach and that what they do when they teach is what constitutes teaching.

In a recent study (1961)[1] we made intensive observations of the behavior of teachers in the classroom to find out what they do when they teach. These observations are made from a special point of view — that of the logic of teaching. It is an important angle from which to look at teaching, no less important for the teacher of art or music or literature than for other teachers.

To study teaching as it actually goes on in the classroom, one must have a record of the teacher's performance. Of course, the most complete record would consist of films and sound recordings. But to get such a full account of teaching is very expensive. Instead, we have made tape recordings of classroom discussion, supplemented by notes taken on the spot by an observer. We have tape-recorded about 125 class periods in various academic subjects in grades nine through twelve.

From an analysis of these recordings, we conclude that teachers generally do two sorts of things: (1) They show how to do something, and (2) they say or tell something. The saying or telling is much the greater part of what the teacher does. We might, of course, have surmised that teaching consists in these two things from what we know about our language. The words "teach" and "show" have a common Teutonic origin. If this were not so, we would still assume the close association between teaching and showing from what we know about early man. Although the origins of teaching are lost in man's obscure

[1]The analysis reported herein was made pursuant to a contract with the U. S. Office of Education, Department of Health, Education, and Welfare.

beginnings, it is easy to conjecture that it first took the form of showing the young how to do simple hand work and other physical tasks.

It may be further surmised that as language grew and the experience of the race became stored in the language, teaching took on the form of saying and telling. Certain things, such as the deeds of heroes long dead, ideas about the spirits and gods, and explanations of events, could not be shown. They could only be talked about; thus, teaching came to include a form of talking.

Thus showing and saying or telling make up what we call teaching. No one can teach anything to anybody without either showing him something or saying something to him. Of course, the words "showing," "telling," and "saying" are vague and ambiguous. But they are clear enough for present purposes if we remember that we are using "showing" in the sense of showing *how* rather than in the sense of merely displaying or exhibiting, and that we are using "saying" or "telling" to mean narrating and relating as well as stating that such and such is the case, as it is the case that this is a beautiful day or that cats prowl.

Language of Teaching

Whether or not showing or saying is predominant in a teacher's behavior depends to a large extent upon what he is teaching. The teaching of history and literature, for example, depends primarily upon words, that is, upon talking about something or upon verbal exchanges between teacher and students. We cannot teach history by showing students how to "do" history. One does not learn how to do history as he learns to do sums in arithmetic or to mix paints. He learns history in the sense of learning what is said about the past; he learns to talk about the past. And the same can be said of the teaching and learning of literature. On the other hand, the teaching of typing, for example, leans heavily upon acts of showing. Although a teacher may tell a student how to type, it is often more effective to show him how to do it. Obviously, teaching the history and appreciation of art is like the teaching of history and literature. It is largely a verbal activity; it cannot be carried on without the use of language. But the teaching of art in the sense of teaching how to make art objects requires showing how as well as telling how.

To understand teaching in terms of verbal behavior, it must be kept in mind that talking is itself a form of doing or acting. This point can hardly be overemphasized, since we are so much accustomed to associating verbal behavior with passivity. We have been told that if the teacher does all the talking, no learning is going on at all. This view has been pounded into our heads for almost fifty years in spite of the obvious fact that no one ever taught anybody anything without talking.

What are some of the actions that a teacher uses language to perform? There are at least three sorts: logical actions, directive actions, and admonitory actions. These actions are readily observed in the verbal behavior of teachers at work in the classroom. We shall not go into the details of how the analysis of these behaviors was made. Suffice it to say that classroom discourse, taped and transcribed, was analyzed into units which we call episodes. An episode consists of a verbal exchange between a teacher and one or more students. The episode typically opens with a question asked either by the student or by the teacher. The exchange usually ends in some form of reinforcing comment by the teacher, either in such expressions as "okay" or "all right" or in the simple repetition, with approval, of what the student said. Between the opening and the close is the body of the episode, which may involve a number of verbal exchanges.

Here is the simplest form of an episode. The teacher asks, "Who was Woodrow Wilson?" A student says, "He was the twenty-eighth president of the United States." The teacher says, "All right." But an episode may also be very complex, involving a large number of exchanges between teacher and students and among the students themselves. Our tape transcriptions were analyzed into some 3,300 episodes which we could classify into categories of logic.

Let us indicate a little more clearly what we mean by a logical category by giving an example of a simple episode and then showing the various standpoints from which it can be viewed for purposes of classification. Suppose a teacher asks, "What is a noun?" A student replies, "A noun is the name of a place or thing," and the teacher says, "Okay!" If we ask about the effect of this verbal exchange upon the student — Does it upset him emotionally? Does it motivate him to learn about nouns? — we are asking a psychological question. If we ask whether or not the definition of a noun given by the student is acceptable by authorities in the field of English, we are asking a content question. But if we ask whether or not the definition, as given by the student, meets the logical criteria for being a definition, then the question is a logical one. Any episode which can be evaluated by the rules of logic falls into what we call logical categories.

Verbal Actions

Our studies show that the logical actions which teachers perform, or which they require their students to perform, are varied and complex. By analyzing the verbal behavior of the classroom, we have found twelve types of logical actions: defining, describing, designating, stating, reporting, substituting, valuating, opining, classifying, comparing and contrasting, conditional inferring, and explaining. We have also identified a nonlogical category which we call "classroom management." We cannot say for sure that these logical actions are typical of all teaching, but we do think that subsequent investigations would bear out the claim that these actions are found in the classroom discourse of all subjects and grades.

It is reasonable to suppose, therefore, that teaching will be improved when teachers learn to perform these logical actions more effectively. About 75 per cent of classroom discourse is concerned with the manipulation of subject matter. Because the manipulation of content nearly always involves logical operations, to improve the way these operations are handled and performed in the classroom is to improve teaching. Thus, a direct way to improve teaching is to increase the teacher's ability to deal with and perform these logical actions, to improve his way of dealing with logical aspects of classroom discourse.

The other two forms of verbal action previously mentioned, directive and admonitory actions, are, naturally, very important aspects of teaching performance. And they are, of course, nonlogical actions. The teacher uses words to direct the student in certain activities. Instead of showing the student how something is done (for example, instead of actually performing such overt acts as placing the hands properly on the keyboard of a typewriter), the teacher may tell the student to do thus-and-so. Verbal actions of this sort frequently occur in the teaching of skills, especially those involving overt action, such as the skills entailed by painting or performance on a musical instrument.

It is important to note that directive verbal behavior is effective only when the acts which students are to perform are repetitive. Repetitive acts can be diagnosed,

and the individual performing them may thus be informed of his mistakes. Whatever can be repeated forms a pattern, and errors show up as deviations from the pattern. For example, there are patterns for typing, dancing, and for producing certain effects in color and sound. Directive actions help the student learn to perform within the patterns of such activities. But when the acts of the student are creative rather than repetitive, directive teaching behavior is irrelevant. No person can tell another how to be creative.

Admonitory action involves the teacher's approval or disapproval. He advises and enjoins. He tells students that their work is good or that they could have done better. All these are verbal actions, although the teacher may also use gestures and other natural expressions like frowns or smiles. But in admonishing the student with "John, you had better quiet down," he hardly expects the student to remember his words. He is concerned with the emotional impact of his words rather than with any knowledge they may convey.

Valuation and Appreciation

What has this analysis of teaching to do with the teaching of art? After all, it stresses the logical aspects of teaching and emphasizes the role of language. And one may naturally ask what bearing have logic and language on art. The answer is that they have much to do with the teaching of art because they bear directly upon the teaching of appreciation.

To appreciate is to recognize the worth of something, to value it highly, to appraise or estimate its worth. Appreciation is not the same thing as enjoyment. To enjoy is to like something, to feel the pleasure of it, to respond to it positively. If one enjoys a work of art, he likes it. Or he may appreciate it but not enjoy it. It would be self-contradictory to say, "I enjoy Matisse's 'White Plumes,' but I do not like it." At least, if someone were to say this, we would be entitled to ask him for some special explanation. On the other hand, it would not be self-contradictory to say, "I appreciate 'White Plumes,' but I do not like it." For the meaning of "appreciation" does not include the meaning of "liking." Neither would it be contradictory to say, "I enjoy 'White Plumes,' but I do not appreciate it," although we are not likely to hear anyone talk this way.

We can say, then, that appreciation has logical dimensions, whereas enjoyment is a psychological matter and has no logical aspects at all. Suppose I were to say, "I appreciate Matisse's 'White Plumes.'" It would be sensible for you to ask for evidence, for you to demand of me the facts and rules by which I decided upon the value of "White Plumes" as a work of art. If I fail to present such evidence, you may rightly doubt that I appreciate the painting. You may think with good reason that I was putting up a front. For appreciation involves judgments or conclusions; judgments and conclusions are logical matters, requiring evidence for their support. And I have produced no evidence to support my claim to appreciation.

But suppose you were to say, "I enjoy 'White Plumes.'" Then it would be odd for me to ask you for evidence that you enjoy it. Enjoyment is a psychological process or state, not something that rests upon proof. Your statement that you enjoy something is not a conclusion or judgment, but a report of how you feel about something. You may say, were I to question you, that you enjoy the painting even though I seem to doubt that you do. And you may go on to say that if I watch you when you are looking at the painting, I will see that you are enjoying it. But if such observations do not convince me, you can still maintain that you do like Matisse's "White Plumes."

It would be somewhat like my trying to convince you that you do not have a headache when in fact your head is aching terribly.

Logically speaking, appreciating a work of art is comparable to deciding upon the desirability of a course of action, upon the truth of a statement or upon the moral rightness of conduct. To appreciate a work of art is to make a decision about it — to decide, for example, whether or not it is beautiful or original, whether it belongs to this school or that, or whether it expresses some significant aspect of culture. In short, to appreciate a work of art is not to describe it in any way, but to render a judgment about it.

Appreciation is thus logically oriented. To teach one how to handle appreciation questions is necessarily to be involved in performing certain logical operations —defining, valuing, explaining. These operations make up about 25 per cent of teaching performance in general. And it is reasonable to suppose that they comprise a considerable part of teaching in the domain of appreciation.

The Appreciative Decision

The role of logic in dealing with questions of appreciation underscores the kinship between art teaching and teaching in other fields. It is often assumed that teaching students to appreciate art is unlike teaching in other subjects, and some people say it is not really teaching at all, that appreciation is caught, not taught. These are both mistaken notions. Teaching students how to handle questions of appreciation is not essentially different from teaching them how to deal with questions of valuation in any field of learning. When teaching in the domain of valuation is performed thoroughly, it involves three things: a set of criteria or rules or standards for judging, a set of facts, and a judgment of how well the facts satisfy the criteria or standards. These same requirements hold for teaching in the domain of art appreciation because appreciation is a form of valuation.

Let us give some examples of valuation questions to show more concretely that appreciation questions are the same sort of thing:

1. In a study of *Cry the Beloved Country*, the teacher asks, "Is the law just that says that a man should be hanged who accidentally kills another man because he's frightened while robbing the man's house?"

2. In a history class, the teacher asks, "Do you think it's a safe assumption that Jackson would decide today, as he did a hundred and thirty years ago, on the same issue?"

3. In another class, a boy asks: "These magazines about true stories — Are those things really true?"

4. In an art class, a student asks, "Is it fair for an artist to use his medium to promote a point of view?"

5. In a literature class, the teacher asks, "Do you think it's true that one can arrange for another's happiness?"

6. In a physics class, the teacher asks, "Is friction good or bad?"

Such questions ask the student to decide something — to decide whether or not an assumption is safe, a statement is true, a law is just, an artist is fair, friction is good.

To make such decisions wisely requires a consideration of both facts and criteria. But all too often, when the student makes a decision in these cases, the teacher either accepts or rejects it without regard for the facts and criteria involved. This practice of disregarding facts and criteria is probably the chief defect of teaching in the domain of valuation. For example, here is an episode that is typical of the way value questions are handled in class:

Student: These magazines about true stories — are those things really true?

Teacher: Well, I don't know whether that's a magazine or whether these articles are true.

Student: Well — it is — people send in their stories.

Teacher: Yes.

The point of this verbal exchange hinges on the uses of the word "true" and the ways of deciding the truth-value of a statement. But this fact is not recognized by the teacher, or else he chooses not to deal with it. As a result, the value question is passed over, and in consequence, the students fail to learn the difference between facts and criteria of judgment, and they also miss the experience of thinking through a value question to a justifiable judgment.

Questions of Criteria

A more appropriate way of dealing with the student's question of "Are these stories really true?" is to raise the further question of what is meant by "true." The student held that whatever a person writes from his own experience is true, and he concluded from this that what is printed in the true-story magazines is true because it is written from personal experience. Now, the teacher could have helped the class analyze logically the student's conclusion about the truth of the stories. He could have called attention to fact that the word "true" is a value term, that whether a statement is true or not is, in the final analysis, a matter of decision rather than a matter of fact, and that we use criteria to decide whether a statement is either true or false.

Specifically, the teacher could have helped the class see that the student's criterion of "true" was "Whatever a person writes from his own experience is true." This criterion could then have been put in the context of other criteria, and the basis of decision would have been profitably broadened. He could have suggested that some individuals hold the criterion that whatever is revealed is true, that others insist that whatever is intuited is true, that still others maintain that any statement which accords with observations is true, etc. Unless these various criteria are recognized by the students, the value question is dealt with at a very superficial level.

Once the diversity of possible criteria is recognized, differences of opinion will arise as to which criterion can best be used in the particular case. Until these differences are somewhat reconciled, there is no common ground for deciding the question of whether or not what is said in the stories is "true." Hence, the first thing to do when dealing with value questions in the classroom is to help the students to uncover the criteria which are being used and to select from among possible criteria those which are useful in answering relevant questions of value.

The next step is to examine the situation to see whether or not the facts of the case meet the criteria. Let us suppose, for purposes of illustration, that the student's criterion — that anything a person writes from his own experience is true — is an acceptable one. The factual question now to be faced is whether or not the stories in the true-story magazines are based upon personal experience. If they are, then by this criterion the stories are true. If it can be shown that these stories are not based upon personal experiences, then by the *same* criterion they are false. If one cannot find out what the stories are based upon, then their truth is indeterminate and one has to say that he does not know whether they are true or not.

These, then, are the phases involved in handling value questions in the classroom: first, identify and decide upon the criteria or standards of judgment; second, examine the situation to see whether or not the observed facts meet the criteria; and finally, in terms of the criteria and facts, decide

upon the value of the objects in question.

Valuation in the arts follows the same pattern. In dealing with value questions, the art teacher must be concerned with the facts and the criteria. If he deals with the facts alone, he may expand the student's enjoyment of art without necessarily increasing his appreciation of it. He may help the student analyze a painting by raising factual questions. For example, he may ask whether or not it is painted with brush strokes that follow the form; he may ask whether the painting consists mainly of floating squares of color, or he may ask whether nearby objects are diminished and the more remote ones increased in size. Then he may go on to ask about the effects accomplished by these various techniques. These are all factual questions, and a discussion of them may help the student understand a painting and thereby expand the range of things he may enjoy. But discussion of such questions does not lead to appreciation unless it is coupled with a discussion or analysis of some set of criteria by which value decisions are ultimately made.

Standards of Taste

At this point, however, the teacher may be (and usually understandably is) faced by a bewildering number of criteria. He will be faced by those which the students propose, and, in addition, by traditional value criteria inherited from previous periods in the history of art and aesthetic taste. For example, in times past, beauty in art was associated with beauty of the subject. Hence the skillful representation of a beautiful subject was — by this criterion — the essence of a beautiful painting. At another time, nobility of subject matter was held to be essential to beauty in art. Hence, if art was to imitate nature, it had to imitate nature in its ideal form. Then, as everyone knows, there came a revolt against content.

Form, pure form, and not subject matter became the criterion of artistic beauty; a work of art was beautiful to the extent that its subject matter was refined away and pure design remained. Then some individuals came to hold that art is beautiful to the extent that its form consists in soft and flowing lines and subtle curves, whereas others stressed sharp lines and angles. Still other persons tended to associate beauty with a work of art which aroused the emotions. Of course, as any art teacher knows, this is a pitifully short list of standards of taste. But it will serve our purpose here.

What is a teacher to do when faced with such a congeries of criteria? For one thing, it is well for him to help the student see that criteria for deciding the aesthetic value of art shift from time to time, from one school of art to another, from one cultural phase to another. In this respect, the art teacher's task is no different from that of a teacher in any other subject in which attempts are made to deal with value questions. It is characteristic of value questions that the criteria by which they are settled are constantly in flux and beset with controversy.

For another thing, the teacher can direct the students to an examination of the various criteria themselves and to choosing those to be used in making their judgments. It is important here for the students to understand that when they decide upon criteria, they are by this choice determining what facts about the work of art are relevant and worth considering. They are also deciding at the same time the justification they will give for their judgment of the work of art in question. If the students are asked why they think the particular work is beautiful or good, they can answer logically only by reference to the criteria they have chosen and the facts observed about the work of art itself. In other words, questions which ask for explanations in art are answered by the same logic as similar questions in mathematics, English, social studies, and science.

In suggesting the handling of art appreciation in terms of logic, what we are saying is open to the objection that we are calling for a return to the old academic tradition in art — substituting understanding for intuition, reason for imagination, facts and rules for happiness and pleasure, logic for feeling. This objection is ill founded. There is not the slightest evidence that the use of logic in teaching impedes the intuitive or imaginative processes. Nor are the feelings neutralized by the performance of logical operations. It is true, however, that the use of reason and logic increases neither the intuitive nor the imaginative abilities. Indeed, we do not know how to develop these abilities through instruction or, for that matter, in any other way. The significance of what we have been suggesting boils down to the question of what we wish to accomplish by instruction in art appreciation. If we want students to be disciplined in the processes of making value judgments, to be skilled in the handling of value questions, to be alert to the pitfalls of reasoning and prudent in making decisions and taking actions, and to be perceptive of the deeper aspects of art, then a renewed emphasis upon the logical aspects of teaching in the arts, as well as in other subjects, seems clearly called for.

SUGGESTED READINGS FOR PART IV

ALBERS, JOSEF. *Interaction of Color.* New Haven: Yale University Press, 1963.

HELLER, JULES. *Printmaking Today: an introduction to the graphic arts.* New York: Holt, Rinehart and Winston, Inc., 1958.

KEPES, GYORGY. *Language of Vision.* Chicago: Paul Theobald, 1944.

KLEE, PAUL. *Pedagogical Sketchbook* (Introduction and Translation by Sibyl Moholy-Nagy). New York: Frederick A. Praeger, 1953.

MATTIL, EDWARD L. *Meaning in Crafts.* Englewood Cliffs: Prentice-Hall, Inc., 1959.

MOHOLY-NAGY, LAZLO. *Vision in Motion.* Chicago: Paul Theobald, 1956.

PERRINE, VAN DEARING. *Let the Child Draw.* New York: Frederick A. Stokes Co., 1936.

SHERMAN, HOYT. *Drawing by Seeing.* New York: Hinds, Hayden and Eldredge, 1947.

STRUPPECK, JULES. *The Creation of Sculpture.* New York: Henry Holt and Company, 1952.

TAYLOR, JOSHUA C. *Learning to Look: a handbook for the visual arts.* Chicago: University of Chicago Press, 1957.

PART V

WHAT DOES RESEARCH SAY ABOUT CREATIVITY IN ART?

Although the concept of creativity was not always associated with art education, in recent years, perhaps more than any other concept, it has appeared in the literature of the field. When Walter Smith began his work in Boston, Massachusetts, in 1871, creativity was not a part of his conceptual view of art in education. For Smith art was a skill to be learned through prescribed instructional exercises. The youngster who mastered these graduated exercises was thus better able to use his skill in industry: art education was conceived of by Smith not as a means for developing the creative capacities of the student but as a kind of vocational training. Art contributed to breadwinning.

As education in the United States changed, so did art education, its means and its ends. The birth of the child study movement in the 1880's, the industrial expansion of the nation, the great influx of immigrants around the turn of the century placed new demands upon the school. Schooling broadened and the school became the melting-pot for Americanizing the new arrivals at our shores.

With the growth of the school there also developed a growing interest in the psychology of the human. The work of G. Stanley Hall influenced many who desired a more complete understanding of the maturing child, and American behaviorists, led by John Watson, tried to create rigorous scientific ways of studying human beings. Since the behaviorists wanted to use methods which would display some of the rigor of the physical sciences, they attempted to limit their observations to behavior, to avoid using methods which were difficult to replicate or which lacked the levels of objectivity that they valued. Thus, concepts such as "introspection" and the "mental event," to take only two examples, were considered unlikely to lead to the science of human behavior they desired to construct. Their emphasis on the observable, their concern with the physiological and with the carefully controlled animal experiment did not lend itself well to the support of or to interest in a concept as nebulous as creativity. The study of human creativity by behaviorists working in the early decades of this century was a rarity at best. After all, intuition, insight, and imagination were like "ghosts in the machine," and no respectable science could afford to concern itself with ghosts.

The concept of creativity while awkward for the behaviorists was much more acceptable to those working out of a Freudian frame of reference. Freud's first major work, *The Interpretation of Dreams*, was published in German in 1900 and had some influence on psychologists in this country shortly thereafter. But, perhaps the formal induction of Freudian psychology in the United States can be marked by Freud's visit to Clark University in 1909. It was at that time that G. Stanley Hall, then president of Clark and father of the Child Study Movement, invited Freud to Clark for a series of lectures. By the twenties, the avant-garde in psychological circles were using Freud's concepts in fields varying from psychiatry to education to child-rearing. To be sure, Freudianism did not permeate all or even most American schools, but it did have the support of many progressive educators who saw in its concern for the inner development of man, similarities to their own conception of the needs of the child. And it wasn't too long before the "unconscious" became a part of the language of progressive education. Margaret Naumberg, Ann Schumacher, and Hughes Mearns were only a few leaders in progressive circles who used a "dynamic" conception of the human in their views regarding education, the arts, and the growing child.

During the twenties and thirties progressive educators spoke of unlocking the creative powers of the child, of removing the barriers that hindered his creative development, of freeing the child so that he may create. If creativity had a tenuous relationship to art education before the twenties, surely this relationship was cemented firmly thereafter. Art was seen as one of the major vehicles for unfolding the child's creative capacities; and more often than not, when an article or an entire issue of a journal was to be devoted to "creativity," the cover displayed a group of children painting or working with clay. Creativity and work in the visual arts had become synonomous.

Art educators responded favorably to Freudian conceptions on a number of counts. First, they made provision for the imaginative life of man that was thought to be so important for the artist. Second, they tended to emphasize the affective and emotional life of man, which for most art educators is the lifeblood of art. But embracing the image of Freudian man and the use of metaphor and simile and methods of introspection was not without its costs. This view, and the view of creativity that was attached to it, did not lend itself to rigorous scientific study. But art educators were not scientists; indeed, some believed then as some believe today that science has no place in art education, that at best it can only contaminate the artistic processes. Art and creativity were more often thought of as mysteries and were discussed in poetic, even romantic terms. The scientific study of creativity during the thirties was not engaged in by art educators but by a small handful of psychologists who felt free enough to use psychological tools to study the never-never land of human behavior — creativity.

It was in the fifties, however, that the research in creativity came into full bloom. Perhaps the person who has done as much as anyone to contribute to this interest is J. P. Guilford, a psychologist working at the University of Southern California. In 1950, when Guilford was president of the American Psychological Association, he delivered, as his presidential address, a speech describing the approach he was going to use to study what he considered to be a neglected problem in psychology, the problem of understanding human creativity. His work, initiated in the fifties, and the work of others in different parts of the country — Stein at Chicago, Mooney at Ohio State, Parnes at Buffalo, Lowenfeld at Pennsylvania State, Taylor at Utah, and Torrance at Minnesota — began to provide an important body of data concerning man's creative development in both the sciences and the arts. The methods that were once rejected by art educators as being inappropriate for studying artistic creativity were now being employed by art educators at a number of institutions, and significant headway in the understanding of creativity was beginning to be made.

By no means have the findings concerning human creativity in the arts or elsewhere, for that matter, been conclusive. And there is relatively little in the way of hard knowledge to provide guidance to teachers attempting to develop the child's artistic creativity. The findings so far are suggestive; much more is available in the way of descriptive research findings than is available as experimental research findings.

In the work that has been undertaken in the study of artistic creativity a variety of research methods have been used and a number of objectives have been pursued. Some workers have concerned themselves with the problem of identifying those behaviors which constitute creative performance in art, while others have attempted to find personality correlates for persons judged highly creative in art. Still others have attempted to identify the working strategies that creative individuals use in going about their work in art. Some investigators have attempted to identify the types of instruction that seem conducive to creative productivity while others have attempted to identify types of creativity that children display in the visual arts.

Research in creativity has probably raised more questions than it has answered. How can creative work in art be distinguished from work that is merely bizarre? Is the same type of classroom environment conducive to creative performance for all students, or do different students need different types of environments in order to function creatively? How much experience in depth in art is needed before an individual is likely to function creatively? Does creative development in one area affect creative performance in another? Do art contests, art awards, and grading in art hamper or help the child's creative development? These and a host of other questions are now being raised. Old answers, often based on dogma and superstition, now seem inadequate, and art education is now reassessing some of its most cherished beliefs concerning the artistic development of man. The studies in this chapter are representative of the diversity of approaches that have been taken in the scientific study of creativity.

22. Creative Abilities in the Arts

J. P. GUILFORD

In 1950, the writer set forth some hypotheses concerning the component abilities that were believed to be needed to account for creativity (1). These hypotheses were developed by way of preparation for systematic studies of this phenomenon by a combination of experimental and factor-analytic approaches. In order to complete the setting of these studies, which is important in preparation for some of the things to follow, something must be said about the scope of the studies of creativity.

The aptitudes project[1] has not been confined to the study of creativity, but has investigated all types of thinking abilities, including also those traditionally known as reasoning abilities, and those we chose to include under the headings of planning and evaluation. This inclusiveness was fortunate, for we find that the whole area of thinking abilities or functions is rich with interelations and parallels. The under-

standing of some parts of this total area is very helpful in understanding others.

On the other hand, the studies of creativity proper, up to the present, have been more limited than they might have been. In setting up hypotheses concerning the component abilities in creativity, we were guided mostly by the kinds of creative activity recognized as such in scientists, engineers, inventors, and in supervisory and administrative personnel; in other words, types of personnel that are of concern in the military setting. We did tolerate the general hypothesis that the abilities that make these kinds of personnel creative might be the same as those that make the painter, the composer, the writer, and others creative, but we did not reject the contrary hypothesis, for we had no basis for doing so. To be sure, it would be a simpler outcome to find that the same qualities of fluency, flexibility, and originality, for example, account for performances of artists and scientists alike. But in our research we have never been very strongly influenced by the goal of simplicity.

[1]Under Contract N6onr-23810 with the Office of Naval Research, monitored by the Personnel and Training Branch.

*SOURCE: Reprinted from the *Psychological Review*, LXIV (1957), pp. 110–118, and based upon a paper presented in the symposium on "Aspects of Creativity" at the convention of the American Psychological Association, September 4, 1956, in Chicago, Illinois.

We have seen that all too often the compulsion of this goal has been unfortunately restrictive of the investigator's outlook.

We did favor the notion that creativity, whatever its range of application, is by no means a unity but is rather a collection of different component abilities or other traits. Our results have definitely supported this general point of view. They also suggest the hypothesis that in the areas of the performances of the graphic artist and the composer, at least, we shall find new factors; factors that are distinct from those that are important in creativity of scientists, technologists, and managers, yet that are parallel to them. It is from the information concerning abilities that we have already investigated that we can deduce something about creative abilities that we should find to be important in the arts. The artistic, creative abilities that I shall mention are thus mainly hypothetical, but I should say that there are better precedents for these hypotheses than for those presented in 1950. We have made a beginning toward relating some of the known factors to the art of writing. It is hoped that the presentation of the hypotheses in this article will stimulate other investigators to test them in connection with other arts as well.

In general, the support for the expected factors thought to be important in the arts lies in the systematic nature of the whole collection of thinking factors, also the memory factors. Enough of the thinking and memory factors are known for us to see the lines of a system. A conception of the entire collection of intellectual factors has been presented in a recent issue of the *Psychological Bulletin* (2). It will pay us to review briefly the features of that system that are relevant in support of factors that are predicted to be important in the arts.

The System of Intellectual Factors

One of the significant principles of the system is that the factors fall into three parallel groups, depending upon the kind of material involved in the activity. Let us think of them as being in three parallel columns. Psychologists have had a long-standing recognition that different abilities are involved in verbal tests on the one hand and nonverbal tests on the other. In nonverbal tests the psychological material dealt with by the examinee is in the form of figures, letters, numbers, or other symbols. Our project results show that we must make a further distinction within the nonverbal area. The consequence is that the intellectual factors tend to come in groups of three parallel abilities or traits. For example, there are three abilities for seeing relationships between things. One of them applies to relations between perceived figures. A second has to do with relations between meanings or concepts. There is a third relations-seeing factor that has to do with the ability to see relationships between such materials as letters, numbers, or other simple symbols. In the latter case, it is neither their figural nor their meaning properties that determine the relationships; it is some other property. We have called this category of factors the "structural" group. In everyday life, the structural type of thinking is perhaps most evident in mathematics. It does not appear that the structural factors have much significance for the arts, as such, and we shall have to look for the significant artistic abilities among the figural and conceptual factors.

One or two additional comments will help to show just where the artistic-creative factors fit into the general scheme of intellect. The thinking factors seem to fall into three general groups of another kind, in a cross classification. This grouping is based upon the kind of *action* performed. There is a group of *cognition* factors, a group of *production* factors, and a group of *evaluation* factors. We become aware of the things with which we are confronted; we produce something of our own in response to that awareness, or something that it calls for; and we

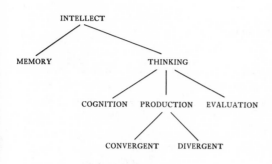

Figure 22.1

for example, qualities of fluency, flexibility, and originality. These come under the category of the divergent-thinking aspect. While they may contribute toward reaching one right answer where that is demanded, they are more obvious in activities where this is not the case. In the arts there is usually *no* one right answer. Some answers are regarded as merely better than others. There is a matter of evaluation.

evaluate our products of thought. A total creative act involves all three aspects — cognition, production, and evaluation. A schematic view of all the classes of intellectual factors is shown in Figure 22.1

In view of the active nature of creative performances, the production aspects or steps are most conspicuous and probably most crucial. Among the productive-thinking abilities another logical distinction appears. With some productive-thinking factors, and the tests that measure them, thinking must at some time converge toward one right answer; the significant type of thinking involved has been called "convergent" thinking. With other productive-thinking factors and their tests, thinking need not come out with a unique answer; in fact, going off in different directions contributes to a better score in such tests. This type of thinking and these factors come under the heading of "divergent" thinking. It is in divergent thinking that we find the most obvious indications of creativity.

This does not mean that convergent thinking and divergent thinking never occur together. They frequently do, in a total act of problem solving. Creative steps are necessary in solving new problems. Actually, we can hardly say there is a problem unless the situation presents the necessity for new production of some kind. Factors are abstractions of components from total activities. Some of the components are recognized as being more creative than others,

Fluency Factors

Let us consider first the potential factors in the more obvious creative areas of fluency, flexibility, and originality. Our project results thus far have clearly indicated four fluency factors, two flexibility factors, and one originality factor. For the most part, our tests of these factors fall into the conceptual column. Table I is given to show the whole matrix of productive-thinking factors and their interrelationships.

Let us consider the fluency factors first. Two of them, *word fluency* and *associational fluency*, have to do with the production of single words. Tests of *word fluency* are best characterized by the fact that the words produced must meet specified structural requirements, such as listing words beginning with a certain letter or words ending in a certain suffix. Meanings or concepts are of no importance. The *word fluency* factor thus falls in the structural column. Parallel to it, the *association fluency* factor is measured by tests that involve listing words having some meaningful requirement, such as listing synonyms or opposites for a stimulus word. To complete this triad of factors, there should be one involving the production of letter combinations that satisfy certain *figural* requirements, such as the activity of producing monograms or other artistic effects with words.

The factor of *ideational fluency* stands alone at present in another incomplete triad. It is the ability to produce rapidly a succession of ideas meeting certain meaningful

TABLE I

A Table of the Productive-Thinking
Factors of the Divergent-Thinking Type

Type of Result Produced	Type of Content		
	Figural	Structural	Conceptual
Words		Word fluency	Associational fluency
Ideas			Ideational fluency
Expressions			Expressional fluency
Shifts	Flexibility of closure	Adaptive flexibility	Spontaneous flexibility
Novel responses			Originality
Details	Elaboration*		Elaboration*

*At present regarded as the same factor, but future results may indicate two separate factors.

requirements. The number of words produced in each response may be one or several. For example, tests of this factor may call for the listing of things round, of ideas about a man going up a ladder, of titles for a story plot, or of predictions of consequences of events. Quantity is important but quality is not.

A parallel factor in the figural column would be an ability to produce a variety of artistic ideas in limited time. Rough ideas for themes, rough sketches, and the like would be sufficient output so far as this ability is concerned. At this point we must face a question that has general significance, beyond the *ideational fluency* areas. This is the question of whether ability to produce numerous ideas in the graphic arts is the same as the ability to do so in music.

There is a precedent at one place in the system of intellectual factors for a distinction between visual and auditory functions. This occurs among the memory factors. We have an apparent triad of memory factors in all of which the learning and retention of associative connections between contents is the important thing, and a second triad in which memory for the contents themselves is essential. In the latter triad, there is an ability to remember the substance of meaningful verbal material. Parallel to it are two factors, rather than one, having to do with remembering substance in figural form. There is a factor of *visual memory*, and this is separate from a factor of *auditory memory*. The latter involves memory for such things as melodies and rhythms. We may regard melodies and rhythms as auditory figures.

The separation of two figural memory factors, visual and auditory, suggests that a similar distinction may be found elsewhere in the system, and hence possibly in the area of the production of figural ideas. This would mean that the ability to produce ideas in the graphic arts is distinct from the ability to produce ideas in music. With this separation of factors, we should have four ideational fluency factors, not forgetting the one in the structural column, rather than the one factor already known. There could even be a fifth ideational fluency factor connected with the kinesthetic sense, also in the figural column. This ability would presumably be of importance to the successful choreographer or creative acrobat.

The fourth known fluency factor is called *expressional fluency*. Thus far confined to verbal tests, this factor is recognized as an ability to put ideas into words. Tests requiring the putting of words together in appropriate, connected discourse are best measures of the factor. The distinction of this factor from *ideational fluency* is support for the common observation that it is one thing to have an idea and it is something else to be able to put it into words.

Three of the known fluency factors should go a long way to account for talent for writing. *Ideational fluency* should give the writer something to write about; *expressional fluency* should enable him to put it into appropriate words; and *associational fluency* should help to find words with the right shadings of meanings without the help of word-finding aids.

Is it likely that there are factors to complete a triad of expressional factors? The concept of expression is surely not foreign to the arts. Having a graphic or a musical idea is short of the total creative production. Putting the idea into appropriate organizations of figural material would be necessary to complete the process. And possibly, again, we shall find that expression in graphic form depends upon a different ability than expression in musical form, just as both differ from expression in verbal form.

A general conception of creativity that calls for so many distinctions and separations of function may be somewhat surprising to readers. Why, after all, should there not be much in common between having ideas in the graphic arts, in music, and in writing? Why should there not be much in common in expressing ideas in the different media?

Notice that I have referred to such abilities as being distinct; not necessarily as being independent or uncorrelated. I suspect that there *is* something in common among parallel factors. This should not preclude their statistical and experimental separation, provided that performances of these different kinds or with different materials are not perfectly correlated when correction is made for unreliability. I suggest that we proceed to find out whether the factors are statistically separable and, if so, whether they separate along the lines hypothesized or along some other lines. Then we can more appropriately raise the question about their interrelationships.

There is some evidence from everyday observation to lend support to the separateness of the expressive abilities. For example, the production of a popular song often involves the collaboration of a composer and a lyricist. To be sure, some individuals do both successfully. Actually, the correlation could be zero between these two performances, and yet there would be by chance *some* individuals who showed high status in both respects. The production of a motion picture, in which musical, graphic, and conceptual ideas are commonly expressed in blended combination, is a synthetic task of specialists, just as, more and more, even single cinema characters represent synthetic blends of talents of different performers.

Flexibility Factors

The two flexibility factors that we have found differ in more than one respect. One difference is that one factor is found in verbal tests and the other mostly in nonverbal tests. One therefore belongs in the conceptual column and the other in the structural column, or possibly they cut across structural and figural columns; we are not sure. The other difference is in the role that each factor plays or the degree of compulsion vs. freedom involved.

The conceptual flexibility factor is called *spontaneous flexibility* because the examinee shows flexibility on his own initiative; the test items do not necessarily require it. It is possible that this quality is a temperamental trait or a motivational trait rather than an ability; a disposition to avoid repeating oneself, or an urge to vary one's behavior. If this is true, the trait might be accounted for under the Hullian concept of "reactive inhibition," or under the concept of a general psychological refractory phase, or under the concept of satiation. Being quite general in its determination of behavior, such a trait might serve as the basis for very fanciful, creative imagination wherever it is found, for example, in artist and scientist alike.

The other factor in this area we have called *adaptive flexibility*, because it is important in the solution of problems—particularly those that require the discarding of familiar or habitual methods and striking out in new and unusual directions. We have more recently expected to find three factors of this kind, but thus far have not found them, probably because our test variations have been inadequate to effect their separation. To the extent that there are problems involved in the arts, this kind of ability or trait would seem to play a significant role. It remains to be seen whether an adaptive-flexibility factor that is unique to figural material is required.

Originality

The one factor of *originality* seems to be rather general, in one sense at least. That is, it is indicated by varied tests—tests that require unusual or uncommon responses, remote associations or connections, or clever responses. The use of an unusual variety of tests has provided much opportunity for a separation into two or more originality factors along the lines of such differences. All the tests have been verbal, or have involved verbal meanings in some way. We have as yet provided no opportunity for

finding a triad of originality factors, distinguished along the lines of the materials involved.

There is a possibility that the factor of *originality* will prove to be fundamentally a temperamental or motivational variable. For example, it might be a general set to be unconventional or to avoid repeating what other individuals do. A single trait of this kind could be expected to cut across material categories. There would then be one originality factor, not a triad. Some of our future research will be directed along these lines with regard to originality as well as with regard to flexibility.

We have already made a beginning toward relating fluency, flexibility, and originality factors to temperamental and motivational variables. At present, it does not appear that any of them can be accounted for on the basis of such nonaptitude variables as we are exploring in this connection. This leaves the way clear for testing the hypothesis that there are complete triads of factors in these three areas.

Other Factors Related to Creativity

In 1950, in addition to factors of fluency, flexibility, and originality, it was hypothesized that there would be an ability to see problems, an ability to analyze, an ability to synthesize, and an ability to redefine or reorganize objects of thought. The hypotheses concerning analyzing ability and synthesizing ability were rather decisively discredited by the results. In spite of the opportunities for such unitary abilities to make themselves known, they failed to appear. This does not mean that, in thinking, no such activities as analyzing and synthesizing take place, for too many activities can be described as such. The unitary abilities that individuals have in common and that have a bearing upon success, however, are better described otherwise. This kind of conclusion is not unique. No one would deny that we indulge in activities that are properly called thinking, and yet there is no generalized unitary ability to think. There are many thinking abilities, as previous discussion has demonstrated. An all-too-common error in psychology has been to assume that because a range of phenomena can be subsumed under a single name there is therefore a unitary function. Every such assumption must be tested by empirical procedures.

A factor was found that could be defined as the ability to see problems. It is a cognition factor rather than a production factor. It proved to be much less general than was originally expected, being confined to seeing defects and deficiencies in such practical matters as everyday gadgets and implements and in social institutions and practices. The tests that measure the factor have been exclusively verbal. Will the use of comparable nonverbal tests give us completion of a triad of problem-seeing factors? This hypothesis should be tested. To the extent that the artist has problems, we may suppose that there are individual differences in ability to recognize them. The problem might be in the form of the need for a theme or a particular kind of theme, or in the form of expression or treatment, or in the use of techniques and implements. Among these would be problems involving figural properties of things. The triad hypothesis would lead us to expect little correlation between the ability to detect *such* problems and the ability to detect the kind represented in verbal tests.

The factor of redefinition involves the ability to desert one interpretation or conception of use of an object, or part of an object, and to adapt it to some new function or use. For example, the cover glass of a watch can be removed and used as a condensing lens to start a fire. How readily can the individual arrive at such a transformation? How good is he at improvising in similar situations in general? This variable is a divergent-thinking factor that involves the production of a shift of meaning of an object. Are there parallel factors involved anywhere in the arts?

Actually, there is a factor of *visualization*, which seems to be to the figural column what *redefinition* is to the conceptual column. The factor of *visualization* is the ability to think of changes or transformations of a figural kind in visually perceived objects, or in objects visually thought of. The relation of such an ability to work in the visual arts can be readily imagined. There might even be such a factor in the auditory field, enabling a composer or arranger to produce variations on a theme with changes in use of phrases so radical that they take on new values or functions.

A factor of evaluative ability was hypothesized, not as a contributor to the production of creative results but as a means of determining whether such results are good, suitable, correct, or adequate. In our investigation of this area of thinking, we gave ample opportunity for more than one evaluative-ability factor to emerge. There are different bases or criteria by which a product is judged. One is its logical consistency with known facts. Another is its less-than-logical consistency with other experiences. There are also different kinds of products to be judged, depending upon the kind of materials involved. We included tests with both figural and verbal material. At the time of the study of evaluative abilities, the third category of structural materials had not yet been recognized.

We found three general evaluation factors. *Logical evaluation* is an ability to judge products on the basis of their logical consistency with given facts. A factor called *experiential evaluation* seemed to fit the picture of an ability to judge products in terms of consistency with past experiences. In the interpretation of this factor, if the emphasis is placed upon ability to make use of past experiences in the act of judging, it could be a rather general ability. If, however, emphasis is placed upon the past experiences we face the real possibility of many common factors of this kind, depending upon the more or less coherent bodies of information that people acquire, for example, mechanical, mathematical, and so on. As for the rest, the use of experience would be a rather specific matter.

A third factor, which was called *perceptual evaluation*, is of uncertain generality. It can readily be hypothesized that there are as many perceptual-evaluation factors as there are coherent areas of perceptual functioning. The variety of psychophysical judgments is, of course, almost unlimited. The tests that defined our *perceptual evaluation* factor emphasized comparisons of lengths of lines and total sizes of figures. The factor we found may therefore have been the more limited *length-estimation* factor that was previously known.

The whole area of evaluative abilities is still largely unexplored. I have hinted that we may expect to find a very large number of rather narrow evaluative-ability factors. As for evaluation in the arts, presumably the *logical-evaluation* factor would not apply. Experiential-evaluation abilities might account for aesthetic tastes in terms of aesthetic values. Perceptual-evaluation abilities would have much bearing on the acceptability of art forms, visual, auditory, or kinesthetic. They would perhaps be numerous and also generally of narrow scope.

The factors mentioned thus far are those we originally regarded as belonging in the creative category. Recognizing that some aspects of planning are also creative, certain newly obtained factors in that area could also be regarded as creative. But as the system of the intellectual factors developed, cutting across our original categories of reasoning, creativity, and planning, these category concepts have shrunk in importance. Furthermore, it became more apparent that, in the creative activity of everyday life, abilities other than those regarded

as primarily creative also play roles to some degree. For example, is it not likely that a large vocabulary is desirable for the creative writer? Should not the developer of ideas in descriptive geometry be able to think readily in terms of visual-spatial arrangements? These two examples imply the usefulness of the factors known as *verbal comprehension* and *spatial orientation*, respectively. Norman C. Meier has also emphasized the finding that individuals with recognized artistic talents are unusually able to observe and to remember clearly things they perceive (3). This implies a high degree of the factor known as *visual memory*, an ability to remember visual content. The factor of *auditory memory* may play a similar role for the composer.

Thus, a great number of primary mental abilities that would not be regarded as creative abilities nevertheless play their roles at times in creative work. We might say that minimal levels of such abilities are desirable, if not necessary, for success in various artistic activities. We might say that to that extent these are necessary but not sufficient conditions for creative production. The factors of fluency, flexibility, and originality, and the like not only are necessary but, when possessed in adequate amounts, are sufficient. All of this, of course, assumes adequate motivating conditions, also. In the process of surveying the resources of creative artists of any kind, therefore, whether this is for the sake of better understanding of talent or for the practical purposes of prediction and guidance, it would be well to ask whether any of the intellectual factors may play a significant role, and where and how, if so.

Summary

1. It is hypothesized that creative artistic talent is not a unitary or uniform commodity but is to be accounted for in terms of a large number of factors or primary mental

abilities. From what is already known, we would expect that the creative abilities of artists will be found to involve some factors other than those among creative abilities in fields such as science and management.

2. Of the known factors, certain ones, of fluency, flexibility, and originality, are the most obviously creative abilities. All of them come under a general class of factors known as productive-thinking abilities and in a subclass of divergent-thinking abilities.

3. A developing system of all the intellectual factors indicates the relationships of the more creative factors to one another and to other factors. From certain relationships and parallels, unknown factors that are probably important in the arts can be hypothesized with some confidence.

4. A full account of complete creative-artistic performance involves evaluative abilities and abilities that are not primarily creative, many of which are already known.

REFERENCES

1. GUILFORD, J. P. "Creativity," *Amer. Psychologist*, **5**, 1950, 444–454.
2. GUILFORD, J. P. "The Structure of Intellect," *Psychol. Bull.*, **53**, 1956, 267–293.
3. MEIER, N. C. "Factors in artistic aptitude: Final Summary of a Ten-Year Study of a Special Ability," *Psychol. Monogr.*, **51**, 1939, 140–158.

23. Strategies of Spontaneous, Divergent, and Academic Art Students

KENNETH R. BEITTEL *and* ROBERT C. BURKHART

We have recently discovered a new way, previously overlooked, in which students work in art. In the course of furthering our knowledge about Spontaneous and Deliberate students (7), we became progressively aware of a working strategy in art, distinct from both of these approaches, which seems most accurately described as Divergent. The word "Divergent" is employed because the objective of this strategy is primarily *discovery*, whereas the objective of the Spontaneous student is primarily *problem solving*. Both are originative ways of working, in contrast to Deliberate approaches, now referred to as Academic or Technical. The word "Deliberate" has been dropped in favor of the word "Academic," because the Divergent approach, in which thinking is emphasized over action, is a creative strategy which proceeds through deliberation toward discovery. This article describes, according to our present research, the distinctions between these three types of students and the strategies they consistently employ, touching on their interdisciplinary implications for education.

The outline of differing strategies becomes evident as detailed distinctions are made concerning the processes by which art products evolve. A strategy is thought of as a total system of behavior which includes both an individual's working procedures and his goals. Goals are directly related to procedures, and, conversely, procedures relate directly to goals. This means that as goals differ, as they do in differing strategies, procedures will differ.

In a dynamic strategy there is an open and a closed circuit to the system. The procedure and the objective can be either open or closed, but not both, as one must always be held constant as a means of control. With a Spontaneous student, the problem is held constant and the procedure is varied until an appropriate procedure emerges which leads to the solution of the problem. Thus, the innovation in Spontaneous work is procedural. This is a process orientation. The Divergent student varies the goal rather than the procedure. He controls the process in order to intellectually search for ideas which will lead to new discoveries. The former is more

*SOURCE: Reprinted from *Studies in Art Education*, V, 1 (Fall 1963), pp. 20–41.

like a trouble-shooter, the latter, the inventor. For the one the problem is the challenge; for the other, the discovery. In contrast, the Academic student chooses a known technique by which to proceed to a known goal. He thus operates under a static strategy. In focusing only on control, both procedure and objective are held constant and there is no innovative quality to the system. The Academic student is thus more like a technician who concentrates on competency. Alas!

With this introduction, we will now turn to an analysis of how these strategies manifest themselves in art products; and also how they are based on clear differences in the students' personality structure and problem-solving, discovery, and evaluative powers, suggesting that these are operational systems cutting across disciplines. Thus, they constitute different life orientations whose etiology must be further probed.

It was possible to identify these orientations through art work by holding the subject matter (stimulus) and medium constant as a basis for control and comparison. All of the examples shown in this article were done by members of a group of 47 junior art education majors participating in an art-learning experiment.[1] The drawings were done in pen-and-ink and brush from a complex still-life construction, photographs of which appear on the page of Divergent illustrations. Students worked in small groups from this stimulus for a period of four weeks without an instructor being present. Process shots, taken at three-minute intervals, supplied examples of strikingly different ways of working.

In art works the most critical point of detection determinant of the strategy is the beginning stage. Illustrations (a), (b), and

[1] U. S. Department of Health, Education, and Welfare, Office of Education. "Effect of Self-Reflective Training in Art on the Capacity for Creative Action," *Cooperative Research Project No. 1874.* University Park, Pa.: The Pennsylvania State University.

(c) — Spontaneous (p. 295) — show that Spontaneous students begin with a centrally placed, vaguely defined whole, organically developing their products with expansive thrusts, obtaining space through voids encircled by big, dark forms. They work kinesthetically seeking freedom in the development of their idea as an organic whole. Off-right-angle movements predominate. Spontaneous illustrations (d), (e), and (f) indicate their concerns for freedom of movement and show the range of individuality of expression evident at the high level. On a lower level, as in illustrations (g), (h), (i), and (j), the work is simpler, more literal in content, and suggestive of random trial-and-error, involving less control over the medium. Typically, Spontaneous students work toward more directness of statement, eliminating unessential procedures and detail. They rely on suggestion for expression. Observing the page of Spontaneous illustrations as a whole, one notices that there is very little reliance on contour, presketching, and elaboration through detail.

In the first photograph, taken after just three minutes of work, the Divergent student's way of working is clearly distinguished from that of the Spontaneous student. The Divergent student begins with a controlled contour drawing of a single element, which is already chosen for its particular value as a theme for development through variation.

Like the Spontaneous student, he places great importance on directness of statement; but unlike him, he is concerned with precision and clarity at any point and with every element. Utilization of error is common in Spontaneous strategies, and even large accidents may be turned to good use. The Divergent student, however, completes one part at a time, and it has to work. His freedom lies in the opportunity he has left himself for organizational innovation, because he desires to change the whole up to the very end. For the Spontaneous student error symbolizes the possibility of the overlooked exception, which might require new procedures and bring resolution to the problem. In searching for clarity and directness of statement, the Divergent student must rely on opposition and contrast for unexpected vividness. The sequence of Divergent illustrations (a) through (d) is a perfect example of the Divergent strategy. Using the chair sawed in half as a theme, in (a) one chair appears in the first three minutes; in (b) three chairs appear at six minutes; in (c) four chairs appear at nine minutes; and in (d), which is the conclusion, six chairs appear. This is a synthetic approach in which unity is achieved at the conclusion of the picture. In Divergent work complexity is progressive, and discovery through elaboration and enrichment is the objective. Spontaneous students begin with wholeness; their objective is to give increasing vitality to the whole through suggestive progressive interaction. The Spontaneous approach is more Beethoven-like; the Divergent more Bach-like.

Illustrations (f) and (g) indicate how a Divergent student took the entire still-life — illustration (e) — as a theme. Illustration (f) also shows how off-center placement is utilized to arrive at original compositions (see also (a)). By comparing (g) with (f), one observes how the theme was carried over from one week to the next and elaborated in three variations of size, placement, and treatment to increase the originality of the product through formal organizational invention. Thus, the route to discovery for the Divergent person is through organizational origination. Illustration (h) shows again variation of a theme through juxtaposition and comparison, in positive and negative visualizations, of the same element. In all of these examples discussed, there is a very strong emphasis on static positioning through right-angle placement. No middle tones, with the possible exception of decorative and contained textures, intervene between black and white. All edges are sharp

and clean. Space is achieved through static placement of solids projected into voids. This strategy requires control.

This tendency endlessly to vary the elements formally through alterations in shape, texture, and placement also appears in the work of a student working on a lower level. In this respect the flowerpot on the chair is interesting to focus on in (j). It has a different shape, texture, and placement on the chair in (k). This orientation is thus not dependent on skill, but upon inventiveness. The last illustrations, (l) through (n), are indicative of the lack of preconception connected with the Divergent synthetic discovery strategy in art. Though he conceives of each step with clarity, the Divergent student apparently does not know the step which will follow. He stops and thinks, and then consciously tries to make the next most unexpected, right, feasible connection. He gets satisfaction from surprising himself with his ability for originative improvisation on a theme. The series (l) through (n) gives some feeling of the unpredictable chaining of connections which the Divergent student values.

The Academic student is clearly distinguished in his initial stages from the Spontaneous and Divergent students. The Academic student tries early to commit himself to the total product; frequently through full-page contour drawing, crowding out room for variation and arrangement or for organic development of his concepts from a vague beginning, since he starts with precision. He begins with a contour, like the Divergent student, but not with an element or the intention of varying elements from their given position. He begins with a concept of the whole like the Spontaneous student, but unlike the latter he wants a precise statement which leaves little room for organic interaction with the medium. In this connection, the second shot reveals his use of applied textures. Once having determined the technique to be employed, such

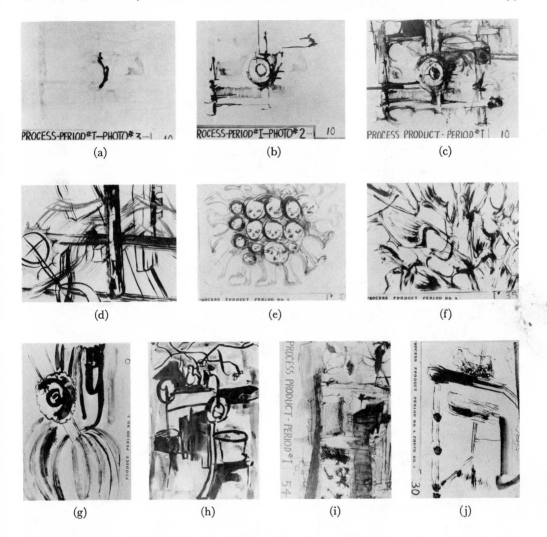

FIGURE 23.1   Illustration of art work of spontaneous students. a, b, and c — Process shots showing Spontaneous working strategy. d, e, and f — Examples of work of Spontaneous high students. g, h, i, and j — Examples of work of Spontaneous low students.

as the stippling seen in Academic illustrations (a) through (c), he mechanically applies it to the whole. Thus, neither vitality nor discovery are possible. These static techniques are frequently rendered in middle tones, avoiding extreme darks and lights except for an occasional accent. Thus, there is symbolized neither a direct action nor a direct statement of one's own. The higher Academic students have greater facility and mastery of a variety of techniques, as in examples (d) through (f), done by the same student who did the stippling. Here it is noteworthy that the realistic scale of the stimulus is retained, and there is no alteration of viewpoint toward the subject matter or exaggeration of elements. There is no continuity of individual style in the work of the better students. One of the reasons for retaining the stimulus in all its

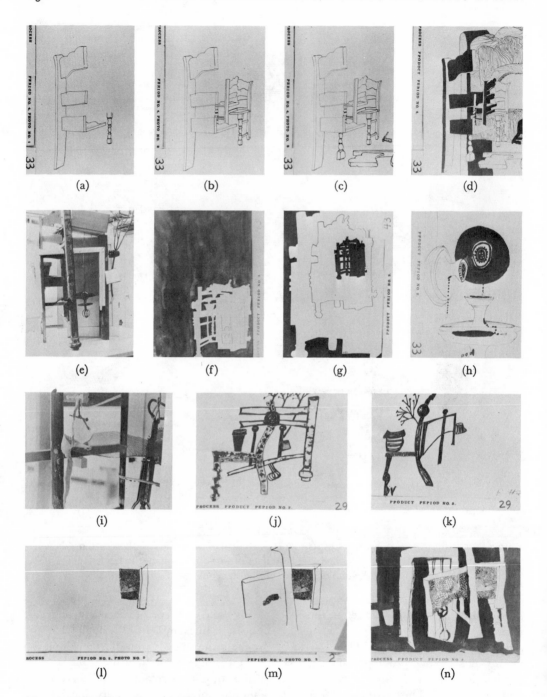

FIGURE 23.2   Illustrations of Still-life stimulus and art work of Divergent Students. a, b, c, and d — Process shots showing Divergent working strategy. e and i — Still-life stimulus from which art works were made. f, g, and h — Examples of "theme and variation" typical of Divergent students. j and k — Examples of works of Divergent low students. l, m, and n — Process shots showing unexpectedness in the emerging organization of a Divergent high student.

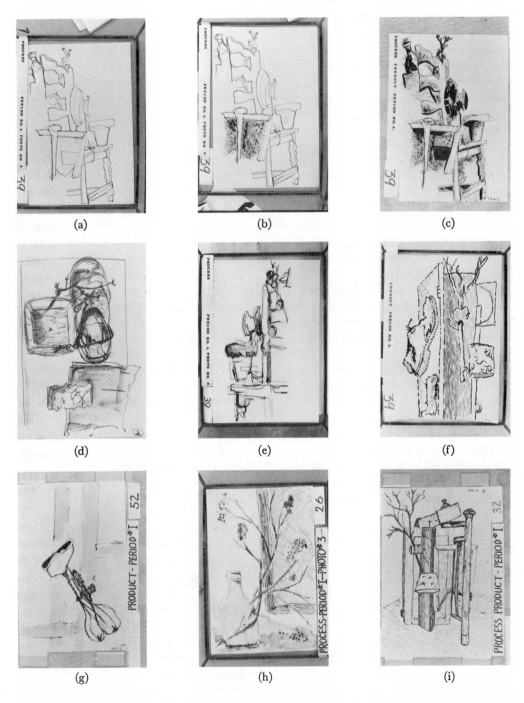

FIGURE 23.3   Illustrations of art work of Academic Students. a, b, and c — Process shots showing Academic working strategy. d, e, and f — Further examples of the work of the same student as in a, b, and c, showing diversity of styles and technical facility typical of an Academic high student. g, h, and i — Examples of works of Academic low students.

representational scale is the desire to demonstrate technical facility in drawing. Such students are often quite self-critical and concerned about ability to draw. They have an evident need for a known standard against which to judge their achievements in these respects. The lower student, as in (g) through (i), possesses less facility and sophistication, but has the same concreteness in objectives. The objective here is not open to the development of new processes unknown to the student, nor to the new organizational ideas.

One's strategy is an outgrowth of life-oriented purpose, and if that purpose is not innovative, the strategy becomes academic. The purpose is identifiable by the source to which the student looks for satisfaction. The Academic student looks to others for recognition for achievement through skill; the source of satisfaction is thus external. Both the Spontaneous and Divergent students achieve internal satisfaction from the reaffirmation of their creative resourcefulness through their strategies of work.

Students possessing these three strategies can be distinguished from each other almost on the same bases as in their art from paper-and-pencil tests of their visual and verbal process responses and preferences. Tests given four weeks before our studio learning experiment began are predictive of these strategies as discriminated on the basis of their later art works. This indicates that we are dealing with stable, operational life-systems. These distinctions are not only evident in process responses, but in measures of personality structure and in problem-solving and evaluative abilities.

The data upon which these comparisons are based are found in Tables I through VI, which represent 107 separate scales from 12 different tests. These tests are subjected to four-way comparisons, resulting in 105 significant distinctions, 44 at the .01 level and 61 at the .05 level of significance. Two-tailed tests of significance were performed for a more rigorous determination of differences, since this is the first time these three distinctions have been made between strategies. Approximately 25 per cent of all comparisons were significant. The group sizes used for comparison were as follows:

Spontaneous Strategy........N = 15
Divergent Strategy..........N = 15
Academic Strategy..........N = 17
High Performers.............N = 24
Low Performers.............N = 23

Visual and verbal process response patterns will be discussed first because they are predictors of strategy distinctions between groups. From the analysis of the art products comes an anticipated pattern of response which is borne out by Table I. It could be hypothesized that the Spontaneous group would be more active, freedom-seeking, and independent in the working process; would prefer pictorial sample revealing motion, directness, and diversity; and would as a result produce works showing more extensive application of the medium (blackness). In contrast, we would hypothesize that the Divergent student would be more concerned with control over the process, so as to be free to concentrate on organizational origination. Both groups, thus, seek freedom, but in different ways; one group through process involvement, the other through process control, in relation to their different innovative objectives. It is, therefore, to be expected that both groups would report more words connected with freedom, invention, involvement, and independence in the process than would the Academic group. These distinctions are found only in the verbal, not the pictorial, domain, because the same words have different strategy referents for Spontaneous and Divergent groups. For Spontaneous students freedom is related to the feeling of not being restricted in their process activity; for

Divergent students control over the process provides freedom for organizational innovation. One is thus a *freedom from restriction,* the other a *freedom for invention through control.*

In the visual measures (Table I) there are important distinctions between the groups, in that Spontaneous students prefer big, bold, active, dark, circular, organic process samples; whereas Divergent students prefer static, angular, linear, constructivistic, and organizationally distinctive process samples. Both types of students, however, prefer direct, definite, dark statements as compared with the Academic students. Academic students prefer tentative process samples over Divergent students, and control words over Spontaneous students, showing a more hesitant and less direct approach in their art activities.

These distinctions hold true for the various strategies, regardless of aesthetic quality, and are strikingly shown by the filled and empty cells of Table I. Note, for example, that there are no significant differences in the D > S and D > A cells under visual process preferences. Conversely, there are no control distinctions in the S > D and S > A cells. The only aesthetic distinctions on visual scales are between high and low art performers within these three strategy groups, indicating that the other distinctions are uncontaminated by aesthetic quality differences, and thus refer only to strategies. Differences in process involvement, however, as indicated by verbal scales, would be anticipated between high and low students across these groups. High students are much more involved in their creative work than low students in every group. This indicates that involvement and mastery go hand in hand.

It is important to point out that both visual and verbal tests have distinctive values, which as supplements to each other make each more understandable. They make simultaneous distinctions in different dimensions of creative activity and response, referring (1) to how the student feels and (2) to how he prefers to work.

Verbal responses unrelated to process recall from an art product stimulus are important in verifying that strategies deal with generalized life-related operational systems. In this connection the source of student responses established that these are preferred orientations. The SDT test instrument asks the student to choose two out of five words in each item on the basis of his preference without referring to any specific areas of activity. Five words were presented in order to elicit responses symbolic of a hierarchy of values between what were thought to be distinct personality orientations. The real meaning of the words, however, was not apparent until the three strategies were located. Instead of the ten possible distinctions contained in the original scoring, the three strategy distinctions now appear to account for most of the variance of choice patterns. The words presented, therefore, in Tables IV and V represent new scoring keys for distinguishing between these three personality styles according to those words which were found to make significant distinctions between groups.

It is obvious from reading the words in Table IV that the Spontaneous group is concerned with "pursuit," as contrasted with "control" and "preconception" in process which are the predominant orientations of the Divergent and Academic groups respectively. These orientations can be seen to extend from process distinctions to behavioral patterns related, respectively, to "exuberance," "self-restraint," and "propriety" in daily relationships as shown in Table V.

Further evidence that these are predominantly personality orientations will be discussed in relation to comparisons made on personality inventories, summarized in

Table II. Before proceeding to this discussion, it is important to point out the distinction between "control" and "self-restraint" as opposed to "preconception" and "propriety." These distinctions, which heretofore have been overlooked, are essential to the understanding of what constitutes a dynamic, as against a static, strategy in life. Orderly institutional change and stability in life-relationships are often associated with mastery of a discipline as seen in the thoughtful self-restraint of the Divergent personality. Both the Divergent and the Spontaneous personality are inevitably in conflict with the Academic, for the latter are fearful of change, and conceive of their function as the maintenance of the proper state of affairs. There has frequently been a positive supplementary relationship between Spontaneous and Divergent personalities; the one tends to focus on problems and the other tends to keep problems open. Since both are dynamic but different orientations, they are really not competitive; and where common purposes are recognized, their combined approach to problems is doubly dynamic. Whitehead's and Bertrand Russell's cooperation on *Principia Mathematica* is an example of scholarly cooperation between a Spontaneous and a Divergent mind.

Turning now to Table II, we see a similar basis for distinctions between the three strategies. Proceeding through the table, it is evident that the Spontaneous student possesses more social self-determination than either the Divergent or Academic student, and that both Spontaneous and Divergent are over the Academic in independence.

Both Divergent and Academic students come from supportive environments, but of differing kinds. Supplementary interview material indicates that Spontaneous students come from environments in which there is parental inconsistency and some turmoil, where as children they were unable to rely on parental authority for guidance, though there is no suppression of the in-

stinctual life of the child and limited indulgence. As a result, the Spontaneous student perceived his early life-relationships as problems to be solved by his own actions. The Divergent student, in contrast, has supportive parents who teach relative values, leaving defined areas for decision making to the child. Thus, the Divergent student early perceived life as allowing for discovery through his own decisions, but within the traditions of an open and a meaningful environment. Thus, they are rewarded for enriching their environment through their achievements. The Academic students, however, have effectively reinforcing authoritarian homes where clear distinctions between right and wrong are made on the basis of propriety, according to traditional and socially acceptable modes of behavior. The instinctual life of the child is suppressed in favor of right-wrong, compliant behavior. The preservation of the instinctual life of the child acts as a foundation for the dynamic action and thought of the Spontaneous and Divergent student, whereas the suppression of instinctual life seen in the Academic student leads to static behavior strategies. Moreover, both Spontaneous and Divergent students, in different ways, have to assume personal responsibilities for their decisions, whereas Academic students have this responsibility assumed by external authorities.

It is out of acting on his own behalf that the Spontaneous student develops the action orientation distinguishing him from Divergent and Academic students, as evidenced in several scales in Table II, where the Divergent student's self-restraining way of action is likewise evident. Both of these are in sharp contrast to the inaction orientation of the Academic student.

In the theory section of Table II, the Divergent student is clearly distinguished from both the Spontaneous and the Academic. We might speculate why this is so. Perhaps in being encouraged to make his own decisions and discoveries he is also being asked to demonstrate to himself his ability to do so. In a supportive environment in which relative values are stressed as a basis of decision-making, more ideas about actions have to be discussed. This delimits action as being guided by thoughtfulness.

In contrast, the Spontaneous student's self-regard is dependent upon achievements which come as a direct result of his actions. This distinction can be seen in the achievement section of Table II. This is the way he determines whether his decisions have been valid or useful ones. Achievement is the route to self-acceptance for the Spontaneous student. For the Academic student, however, achievement is a means for recognition

TABLE I*a*

Visual-Verbal Process Response Patterns

Process and Control Distinctions Between the Three Strategy Groups	Number of Scales and Direction of Differences							
	$S > D$	$S > A$	$D > S$	$D > A$	$S + D > A$	$A > S$	$A > D$	$H > L$
Visual								
Process diversity pictorial preference patterns (VM)	3				I			
Process directness pictorial preference patterns (VM)					I			
Process tentativeness pictorial preference patterns (VM)							I	
Process blackness application (IBM)	I	I						
Verbal								
Process involvement recall from product stimulus (Schwartz)	2	3		2	2			
Process orientation word selection patterns (SDT)	I	2						
Process independence and self-reliance (PIT)					I			
Visual								
Control over process pictorial preference patterns (VM)			3	2				
Verbal								
Control orientation word selection patterns (SDT)			I			I		
Total	7	6	4	4	5	I	I	

TABLE I*b*

Visual-Verbal Process Response Patterns (Continued)

High and Low Distinctions Across Strategy Groups	Number of Scales and Direction of Differences							
	$S > D$	$S > A$	$D > S$	$D > A$	$S + D > A$	$A > S$	$A > D$	$H > L$
Visual								
Aesthetic sophistication pictorial preference patterns (VM)								I
Aesthetic unique organization pictorial preference patterns (VM)								I
Verbal								
Process involvement recall from product stimulus (Schwartz)								4
Process orientation word selection patterns (SDT)								I
Total								7

or acceptance by authority. Thus, either Academic or Spontaneous students are in danger of focusing on achievement primarily for acceptance. On the other side, the Divergent student may not focus on achievement, because he has acceptance. Crutchfield (10) has indicated achievement is likely to be creative only when it is primarily "task-involved," and not "ego-involved."

Preceding information has indicated the concern of the Spontaneous student for problems. Part of a problem-solving orientation is sensing the presence of a problem before it is clearly defined. Words such as "unpredictable," "confound," "intangible," "unfocused," and "diffuse," preferred over all other groups by Spontaneous students, indicate an acceptance of uncertainty prior to the definition of the parameters of a real problem. Such students work in hope of making the problem progressively clearer, but they know that the problem can't be initially clear. The challenge to Spontaneous students lies in the tension between sensing the presence of a problem and accepting its intangibility, in that until the real question can be phrased, no answer can be forthcoming. Therefore, such students keep their processes open in order to gain information that will progressively delimit the problem. This is a deductive route which, by its very nature, must proceed in terms of abstractions relating particulars in pursuit of the problem. Procedural thinking must be abstract because it must encompass emerging particulars. There is little concern with preserving the uniqueness of the particular in pursuit, because the abstraction is what is important. The focus is on the formation of the system, not the detail which is to be processed as part of the whole problem.

The Divergent person focuses on the content in detail, not the system, because he perceives the system as being likely to be

TABLE II

Creative Capacity Inventory Response Patterns

Personality Inventory Distinctions Between and Across the Three Strategy Groups	Number of Scales and Direction of Differences							
	$S > D$	$S > A$	$D > S$	$D > A$	$S + D > A$	$A > S$	$A > D$	$H > L$
Social Relationships								
Social self-determination (ISSD)	1	1						2
Nonauthoritarionism (BBCI-X3)					1			
Nonconventionality orientation word section patterns (SDT)	1	1						
Social independence (BBCI-X3)					1			
Supportive environment in childhood (BBCI-X3)			1			1		
Social self-restraint orientation word selection patterns (SDT)			2			1		
Action Orientation								
Spontaneous flexibility (FAT)	1	1						
Flexibility (VVCI-X3)								1
Action orientation (BBCI-X3)		1						
Exuberance orientation word selection patterns (SDT)	1	1						
Self-restraint orientation word selection patterns (SDT)			1	1				
Theory Orientation								
Theoretical interests (ISSD)			1	2				2
Theory orientation word selection patterns (SDT)			1	1				
Achievement								
Achievement motivation (BBCI-X3)	2						1	

TABLE II

Creative Capacity Inventory Response Patterns (Continued)

Personality Inventory Distinctions Between and Across the Three Strategy Groups	Number of Scales and Direction of Differences							
	$S > D$	$S > A$	$D > S$	$D > A$	$S+D > A$	$A > S$	$A > D$	$H > L$
Aesthetic Concern								
Aesthetic interests (BBCI-X3)	I				I			
Sensitivity (to nature) (BBCI-X3)					I			
Problem Sensing								
Problem-sensitivity orientation word selection patterns (SDT)	I	I						
Pursuit word selection preferences (FAT)	I	I						
Acceptance of uncertainty (BBCI-X3)	I							
Ideational Concern								
Interest in exceptions (complexity) (ISSD)					2			I
Interest in exceptions (complexity) (BBCI-X3)					I			
Ideational word selection patterns (SDT)			I		I			
Creativity Self-Image								
Ideational and social self-determination total (ISSD)					I			I
Ideational self-determination total (ISSD)					I			
Creativity inventory total (BBCI-X3)					I			
Creativity self-rating (BBCI-X3)								I
Total	10	8	6	4	11	2	I	8

TABLE III

Problem Solving, Discovery and Evaluative Powers*

Interdisciplinary Creative Problem Solving and Discovery Power	Number of Scales and Direction of Differences			
	$S+D>A$	$S>A$	$D>A$	$H>L$
Discovery of common denominator (WET)	5	4	3	I
Divergent question power (personal and impersonal) (OQT)	2			
Remote associates test (RAT)				I
Art Evaluative Power				
Evaluative matching: art samples with own products	I			
Divergent recognition evaluative power				I
Total	8	4	3	3

*There were no problem-solving and evaluative distinctions between the Spontaneous and Divergent groups, suggesting that these strategies are equally successful creatively.

arbitrary, excluding, and possibly detrimental to the uniqueness of each particular. He therefore guards against prediction; his concern is for discovery, not for solutions. His is the belief that discovery can be approached in terms of its parts, and that the whole as an organization need not be grasped all of a piece or made as a whole. In focusing on discovery, he demonstrates new meanings attributable to varied organizations constructed from new perceptions of the same particulars. This is why theme and variation appeal to him, and why he must remain open to new alternatives. Both Spontaneous and Divergent groups, as indicated in Table II, are interested in exceptions; the Divergent person is stimulated to think of new alternatives and the Spontaneous person is challenged to expand his procedural systems.

In contrast, the Academic person lacks this ideational concern, because exceptions tend to break down the traditional structures upon which he relies for security through propriety. This is one of the reasons Academic students are weaker on problem-solving, discovery and evaluative powers, a weakness revealed in Table III. It is probably through the processing of exceptions of any type that evaluative power is developed. If exceptions are repeatedly brought to consciousness, in time this necessitates the development of some system for dealing with them. Spontaneous and Divergent students have, as a result, developed different styles of thought and value systems for sensing and utilizing exceptions in problem-solving, discovery, and evaluative situations. In a way, the Academic student has been protected from exceptions, or made to feel that they are unimportant. As a result, his problem-solving, discovery, and evaluative powers have never been adequately developed. Thus, the learning problem of the Academic student is distinctly different from either of the other groups. The reason, as we have indicated, is that his strategy is static rather than dynamic, be-

TABLE IV

Evident Process Distinctions Between the
Strategies on Work Checklist Inventory (SDT)

Pursuit in Process (Spontaneous Group)	Control in Process (Divergent Group)	Preconception in Process (Academic Group)
Searching	Disciplined	Cautious
Seeking	Structured	Careful
Ongoing	Decided	Comply
Emerging	Precise	Restrained
Evolving	Logical	Maintain
Persistent	Reason	Protect
Involvement	Design	Proven
Interaction	Accomplished	External
Evolution	Competent	Tangible
Risk	Capable	Dimension
Intuitive	Trained	Certain
Intrinsic	Polished	Still
Unpredictable	Routine	Documented
Confound	Regulated	Refined
Open	Deliberate	Redefined
Intangible	Completed	Credible
Unfocused	Practical	Principle
Indirect	Product	Regular
Fluid	Found	Reliable
Diffuse	Answer	Delineate
Diverse	Problematic	Controlled
New	Certainty	Condense
Originate	Ideas	Clarification
Divergent		Correlate
Extension		Formulation
Hypothesis		Uncomplicated
Relationship		Appropriate
Detached		
Aloof		
Question		
Problem		

cause of the repression of his instinctual life, because of his lack of opportunity to make his own decisions, and because both his goals and procedures are thereby defined in terms of compliance to established external standards of recognized authority figures. The focus on dynamic strategies indicates that the solution does not lie in the produc- tion of art products which are Spontaneous or Divergent in appearance. Self-reflective educational procedures need to be instituted which allow for the gradual correction and replacement of Academic behavioral pat- terns along nonthreat treatment lines of problem solving and discovery. Eventually, we feel, the evaluative objective of such a

TABLE V

Evident Behavioral Distinctions Between the
Strategies on Word Checklist Inventory (SDT)

Exuberance (Feeling) (Spontaneous Group)	Self Restraint (Thinking) (Divergent Group)	Propriety (Conditioned) (Academic Group)
Exuberant	Reserved	Proper
Feeling	Composed	Polite
Emotional	Stable	Serene
Excitable	Established	Civilized
Instinctive	Tolerant	Courtesy
Impressionable	Adaptive	Complimentary
Suggestible	Fashionable	Traditional
Passionate	Respectable	Conventional
Quick	Sociable	Minimize
Forthright	Broad	
Unpolished	Unemotional	
Erratic	Real	
Irregular		
Irrational		
Inconsistent		
Impetuous		
Subjective		
Self-absorbed		
Different		
Unconventional		

program must be the selection and development by the student, under guidance, of the more productive strategy.

The possession of a strategy, however, is no assurance of quality, though it insures individuality. The strategies are qualitative in character only in that they are dynamic systems for the achievement of quality. The achievement of quality within strategies is a distinct and different problem from the possession and acquisition of a strategy. A next step in the study of strategies is that of isolating educational conditions and student habits conducive to learning through their strategies. The discipline of learning within a strategy needs to be defined and distinguished from those conditions of learning that cut across strategies.

It is further possible that different content areas may require one strategy more than another. For example, a field geologist may, because of the nature of his subject area, need to operate Divergently. His field procedure is a rigorous one, but the objective has to be kept open for discovery through a systematic approach to organization of particulars into an unknown whole, originally perceived — if at all — through multiple hypotheses. In contrast, choosing an example from daily life, a diagnostician in medicine has to be able to determine through the choice of appropriate procedures the cause of a patient's illness. The psychology of career choice may well need to investigate the strategy requirements of various vocational fields and of differentiation within them.

Education to date has only been concerned with the problem-solving and not the discovery dimension of art, philosophy,

TABLE VI

Significant .01 Items from the Spontaneous
Flexibility Scale (F.A.T.) Indicating Academic Student
Orientation as Compared with Spontaneous
and Divergent Groups*

		Answer Is Scored	$A > S + D$	$A > S$	$A > D$
1.	I prefer courses in which the teacher tells me exactly what is expected of me.	True	X		
2.	When I do my homework, I try to plan my study time in advance and stick to it.	True	X		
3.	I believe in the old motto, "A place for every tool, and every tool in its place."	True	X		
4.	There is much truth to the saying, "The devil finds work for idle hands."	True	X		
5.	I often change my mind in following a specific course of action.	False	X		
6.	When introduced to people for the first time, I seldom remember their names.	False	X		
7.	One should not begin something he has no intention of finishing.	True		X	
8.	I prefer participating in group discussions rather than listening to a lecture.	True		X	
9.	I prefer to work with someone who is highly organized.	True			X
10.	Novelty for the sake of novelty is senseless.	True			X
11.	I'll try anything once.	False			X

*This table was added to give a further indication of how the Academic student thinks.

history, and science. Heretofore, discovery has always been considered as relating to problem solving. The entire body of evidence of this article indicates that discovery is singular and distinct from problem solving not only as a strategy but also as an end in itself. This points to a huge gap in our educational methodologies which are oriented toward education as problem solving. A new educational methodology must be constructed which deals with discovery as a way of learning. The educational implication of this idea far exceeds the content area of the visual arts in its importance.

APPENDIX

BRIEF DESCRIPTIONS OF MEASURES MENTIONED
IN TABLES I THROUGH V

1. *VM, or Visual Magila: An experimental exercise for visual preference patterns.* This test consists of 32 items, each of which contains five pictures from which two are to be chosen on the basis of preference. Pictures have the flavor of nonrepresentational process samples in black and white media. Each item has samples representing a process-control dimension; a masculine-feminine dimension (square, heavy, bold, dark, etc., as opposed to round, light, graceful, etc.); and a unique organizational dimension. These dimensions are so combined that there is in each item the following types of samples: (1) process-feminine, (2) process-masculine, (3) control-feminine, (4) control-masculine, and (5) unique organization. (See references 1, 2, 3.) (Developed by Beittel.)

2. *Process blackness application (IBM).* This is an actual IBM test score derived from inserting students' drawings made with IBM pencils on the Nitschke Drawing Behavior Samples Test (12) into an IBM test scoring machine for blackness count. Scores varied from 1 to 200. (Developed by Nitschke.)

3. *Process involvement recall from product stimulus (Schwartz).* There is an A and B form of this checklist on each of which 50 adjectives descriptive of process *feelings and thoughts* are presented for checking through recall on the student's part with his art object before him. (See reference 13.) (Developed by Bernard Schwartz.)

4. *Word selection preference patterns test (SDT).*

This is a 42-item test in which five words are presented to the subject on each item. As in the VM, the respondent is asked to choose only two. The five words represent choices originally labeled: (1) abstract orientation, (2) process orientation, (3) theory orientation, (4) impulsivity orientation, and (5) nonconventionality orientation. (See references 5 and 7.) (Developed by Beittel and Burkhart.)

5. *Process independence and self-reliance (PIT).* This is a test which presents to the student on each item five statements representing decisions or attitudes concerning independent work and the working process, and asks the student to rank these. (Developed by Penny Burkhart.)

6. *ISSD, or test of ideational and social self determination.* This is a test which has gone through three revisions and has proven useful in the description of creative action (See references 7, 8, and 9.) There are four scales: (1) complexity, (2) theoretical interest, (3) aesthetic interest, and (4) social self-determination. (Developed by Burkhart.)

7. *BBCI-X3, or experimental creativity inventory.* This is the third version of the BBCI series. There are 130 items, with 14 "content" scales. These are named: (1) originality, (2) general sensitivity, (3) flexibility, (4) interest, (5) independence, (6) action, (7) abstraction from perception, (7) inclusion of opposite, (8) confidence (risk), (9) humor, (10) fluency, (11) tension, (12) supportive environment, (13) skill, and (14) creative orientation (word pairs). (See references 2, 5, and 7.) (Developed by Beittel and H. J. Burgart.)

8. *FAT, or flexibility abstract orientation test.* This is a test of 80 items, 40 of which are of the self-descriptive statement type and 40 of which are word pairs. The statements reflect an action orientation typified by spontaneous flexibility, whereas the word pairs reflect a preference for abstract over concrete words. (Developed by Beittel, H. J. Burgart, and Burkhart.)

9. *WET, or word equation test.* This is a power test asking the student to find a common denominator or principle which will order three words (e.g., floor, chair, ceiling) and give an explanation for doing so. The student is asked to give as many common denominators within a given time period as possible. (Developed by Burkhart.)

10. *OQT, or object question or divergent question test.* This is a timed test in which the respondent is to ask "open" questions about common objects, such as "ice." The questions are to arouse interest and curiosity, and lead to a variety of responses which are neither factual nor capable of a "yes-no" answer. (See references 7 and 9.) (Developed by Burkhart.)

11. *RAT, or remote associates test.* In this test built by Sarnof Mednick (11), three words are presented in each item and the respondent is asked to discover a word which "mediates" a common association among them. An example is blue, cottage, rat; which words can be mediated by the remote associate "cheese."

12. *Art evaluative power.* This is a performance in evaluating in which the student is asked to do two things: (1) describe as many different criteria as possible that will rank eight pictorial samples and (2) find the sample of the eight most like a drawing of his own. The samples have known ranks according to spontaneous, divergent and formal criteria. Scores are derived for: (1) insight in evaluative matching, in which the student is scored when his evaluative ranking tendency corresponds with his own style of work, and (2) the student's ability to recognize the divergent dimension in the eight samples.

REFERENCES

1. BEITTEL, KENNETH R. "Construction and Reconstruction of Teaching Methods through Experimental Research." Research issue, *Eastern Arts Association Bulletin*, Vol. 19, No. 4, 1962.
2. BEITTEL, KENNETH R. "Creativity in the Visual Arts in Higher Education: Criteria, Predictors, Experimentation, and Their Interaction." Paper read at the University of Utah Research Conference on the Identification of Creative Scientific Talent, held in Brighton, Utah, 1962. To be published.
3. BEITTEL, KENNETH R. "Factor Analyses of Three Dimensions of the Art Judgment Complex: Criteria, Art Objects, and Judges." *Journal of Experimental Education.* In press, Fall 1963.
4. BEITTEL, KENNETH R. "On the Relationships between Art and General Creativity: A Biased History and Projection of a Partial Conquest." *School Review*, Vol. 12, No. 3, Autumn 1964, pp. 272-288.
5. BEITTEL, KENNETH R. "Predictors and Settings Relating to the Capacity for Creative Action in the Visual Arts." A Progress Report and data summary of studies analyzed or begun since January 1961, supported by National Science Foundation GL-17984. University Park, Pennsylvania: Department of Art Education, The Pennsylvania State University, January 1962. 88 pp.
6. BEITTEL, KENNETH R. and ROBERT C. BURKHART. "The Effect of Self-Reflective Training in Art on the Capacity for Creative Action." Project No. 1874, U. S. Office of Education Cooperative Research Program, October 1962-December 1964. University Park, Pennsylvania: The Pennsylvania State University.
7. BURKHART, ROBERT C. *Spontaneous and Deliberate Ways of Learning in Art.* Scranton: International Textbook Company, 1962.
8. BURKHART, ROBERT C. "The Creativity-Personality Continuum Based on Spontaneity and Deliberateness in Art." *Studies in Art Education*, Vol. II, Fall 1960, pp. 43-65.
9. BURKHART, ROBERT C. "The Interrelationship of Separate Criteria for Creativity in Art and Student Teaching to Four Personality Factors." *Studies in Art Education*, Vol. III, No. 1, Fall 1961.
10. CRUTCHFIELD, RICHARD S. "Conformity and Creative Thinking." *Contemporary Approaches to Creative Thinking.* (Edited by Howard E. Gruber, et al.) New York: Atherton Press, 1962. Chapter 4, pp. 120-140.
11. MEDNICK, SARNOF. "Associative Basis of the Creative Process." Paper read at the University of Utah Research Conference on the Identification of Creative Scientific Talent, held in Brighton, Utah, 1962. To be published.
12. NITSCHKE, EARL. *Some Advantages of Using Multiple Drawing Behavior Samples in Lieu of Regular Classwork.* Unpublished doctoral dissertation. University Park, Pennsylvania: The Pennsylvania State University, 1963.
13. SCHWARTZ, BERNARD. *The Effect of Duration of Working Time, Instruction, and Predicted Creative Level Upon the Over-all Aesthetic Quality and Process Characteristics of Art Projects.* Unpublished doctoral dissertation. University Park, Pennsylvania: The Pennsylvania State University, 1963.

24. Complexity—Simplicity As a Personality Dimension

FRANK BARRON

This is the fourth in a series of reports on the identification and measurement of a factor in perceptual preferences which seems to have considerable generality in human behavior. It may be described briefly as a bipolar factor which opposes a preference for perceiving and dealing with complexity to a preference for perceiving and dealing with simplicity, when both of these alternatives are phenomenally present and when a choice must be made between them. The kinds of phenomenal fields which have been the objects of the research to be reported here, and which seem to possess descriminable degrees of simplicity and complexity, are interpersonal relations and interpersonal psychodynamics, politics and economics, religion, relations to authority, attitude towards sensual experience, social conformity and adherence to tradition, and originality and intellectual independence.

As we shall point out more fully later, a somewhat similar factor had previously been identified in the field of esthetic preferences by Eysenck, who attempted also to construct a measure of it (4, 5). It was, however, rediscovered independently and more or less incidentally by Welsh, who published the first of the four reports referred to above (12). A new measure of it was developed by Welsh and the present writer (3). The latter explored some of its correlates in preferences for painting and in self-conception (2). In the present paper we shall deal with further correlations of this dimension with variables in several areas of behavior. Before this further work is reported, however, a brief review of the findings which led up to it seems in order.

[1]This study was carried on at the Institute of Personalities Assessment and Research, University of California, and was supported financially by the grant of the Rockefeller Foundation to that Institute. The writer ows a special debt of gratitude to the Director of the Institute, Dr. Donald W. MacKinnon, for his encouragement of the research and for his critical reading of the manuscript.

*SOURCE: Reprinted from the *Journal of Abnormal and Social Psychology*, XLVIII, No. 2 (1953), pp. 163–72.

The Welsh Figure Preference Test

This series of investigations began with the construction by Welsh of a test consisting of several hundred line drawings in black ink on 3 × 5-in. white cards. He intended it as a nonverbal psychiatric diagnostic instrument, and sought originally to develop scales to measure such variables as Hysteria, Depression, Schizophrenia, Paranoia, and so on. The subject (S) was asked to indicate for each figure whether he liked it or did not like it, and thus to sort the drawings into two groups according to his preferences.

The effort to develop a diagnostic instrument is still in progress, but did not immediately meet with success. In seeking to understand the nature of the preferences being expressed, however, Welsh carried out a factor analysis of various scales defined on the basis of his own judgment as to the stimulus-character of the drawings: e.g., bilaterally symmetrical figures, three-dimensional figures, figures with many projections, figures with few projections, ruled-line drawings, freehand drawings, angular figures, curved figures, and so on.

From this analysis, two factors emerged: an acceptance-rejection factor (expressing the general tendency of the subject either to like or to dislike the figures), and a second, bipolar factor, orthogonal to the first, whose poles, as determined by inspection of the figures, seemed to be simplicity (combined with a rather obvious, bilateral symmetry) and complexity (usually associated with a much less obvious kind of balance, which in previous reports has been referred to as "asymmetry").

This latter factor bears a close resemblance to that earlier identified by Eysenck, and named by him the K factor. Eysenck has demonstrated for a number of stimulus classes (colors, odors, paintings, polygons, poetry) the existence not only of a general factor of esthetic appreciation, but of a secondary, biopolar factor as well. The second factor presents the same polar opposition noted by Welsh, one pole being represented by preference for the simple polygon, the strong, obvious odor, the poem with the obvious rhyming scheme and the definite, unvarying, simple rhythm, and the simple, highly unified picture; at the other pole is preference for the more complex polygon, the more subtle odors, the poem with a less obvious rhythm and a more variable and loose rhyming scheme, and the complex, more diversified picture.

The Barron-Welsh Art Scale

A measure of this secondary, bipolar factor in the Figure Preference test was constructed in much the same incidental manner as that in which the factor had been discovered. It had happened that several artists were included in the control sample which Welsh had used for comparison with psychiatric patients, and these artists all clustered together at the complex-asymmetrical pole of the factor. The present writer, in search for measures of artistic discrimination for inclusion in a battery of assessment procedures, recalled this finding, and was led to wonder whether the factor was not significantly related to ability to discriminate the good from the poor in artistic productions. In any case, the Figure Preference test clearly consisted of stimulus material which might yield such a measure. The most straightforward way of checking on this seemed to be to give the entire 400-item test to a sample of artists and nonartists, and then to construct, by means of the item-analysis technique, a scale which would embody the differences between artists and nonartists in their preferences for the figures; and finally, of course, to cross validate the scale on new samples of artists and nonartists. This was accordingly done, and a highly reliable and valid scale resulted (3).

Inspection of the items in the scale quickly revealed that the secondary, bipolar factor which had emerged from the factor analysis was reproduced in the later empirically derived measure. The artists *liked* figures which were highly complex, asymmetrical, freehand rather than ruled, and rather restless and moving in their general effect. (Several artists, in reacting to them, had described them as "organic.") The figures which were *liked* by people in general, however, were relatively simple, often bilaterally symmetrical, and regularly predictable, following some cardinal principle which could be educed at a glance. These figures were described by artists as "static," "dull," "uninteresting."

This convergence of the results of factor-analytic and external-criterion methodologies seems especially worth noting. Factor analysis not only revealed the psychological unity in perceptual preferences with which we are here dealing, but in addition provided the clue to an extremely important external correlate which could be used for straightforward empirical scale derivation. The scale is now properly designated as an Art Scale, but can be equally properly construed as a measure of the factor found by Eysenck and by Welsh. It has both psychological unity and external predictive power. Most of the remainder of this paper will be devoted to what Cattell refers to as "peripheral validation," which consists essentially of an extension of the investigation to correlates of the factor in areas of behavior which are, prima facie, remote from that in which the factor was discovered. First, however, we shall review briefly some previously reported findings concerning the relationship of these figure preferences to preferences in paintings and to self-descriptions.

Art Preferences and Self-Description

The two test procedures which have already been analyzed and reported on (2) in relation to the Art Scale are the Gough Adjective Check-List (8) and a Painting Preference test assembled by the present writer. The former is a list of 279 common personally descriptive adjectives, from among which S is to select (by checking) those which he thinks describe himself; the latter consists of 105 postcard-size reproductions in color of paintings by a large number of European artists, which S is asked to sort into four groups according to the degree of his liking for the paintings.

The polarity noted in these three domains of figure preferences, art preferences, and adjective self-descriptions may best be summed up in this fashion:

I

In Figure Preferences
  Preferring what is simple, regularly predictable, following some cardinal principle which can be educed at a glance.
In Art Preferences
  Preferring themes involving religion, authority, aristocracy, and tradition.
In Adjective Self-Checks
  Contented, gentle, conservative, patient, peaceable, serious, individualistic, stable, worrying, timid, thrifty, dreamy, deliberate, moderate, modest, responsible, foresighted, conscientious.

II

In Figure Preferences
  Preferring what is complex, irregular, whimsical.
In Art Preferences
  Preferring what is radically experimental, sensational, sensual, esoteric, primitive, and naive.
In Adjective Self-Checks
  Gloomy, pessimistic, bitter, dissatisfied, emotional, pleasure-seeking, unstable, cool, irritable, aloof, sarcastic, spendthrift, distractible, demanding, indifferent, anxious, opinionated, temperamental, quick.

Further Results

The relationships cited in the preceding section were found in a sample of 40 male graduate students, from about a dozen departments of the University of California, who had taken part in weekend living-in assessments at the Institute of Personality Assessment and Research. These Ss had been carefully studied by means of a large number of objective tests and experimental procedures, and had also been interviewed concerning their personal history, their values and philosophical views, their professional aspirations, and so on. At the conclusion of the series of (four) assessments, they were all rated by the staff[2] on 40 variables which previous personality researches had indicated as being of general importance.

We are thus in a position to see how the simplicity-complexity dimension is manifested in many different areas of behavior, by correlating the Figure Preference measure with other variables. For the most part, we all restrict ourselves to relationships obtained in this one sample of 40 Ss. However, the scale was also given, together with some questionnaires, to a sample of over 100 male undergraduates in two Pennsylvania colleges, and the correlates of Complexity in that sample will be described. Data are also available from the assessment study of 80 other subjects (Ph.D. candidates and medical school seniors) who took a revised form of the test.

For ease of reporting, we shall adopt the technique of drawing a composite picture of two ideal, modal persons, the simple and the complex, on the basis of the correlational results. The statistical support for the portrait will be cited as we go along. Several cautions must be observed in interpreting such material, however. For one thing, since the picture is based entirely on group relationships, it will fail in some respects to do justice to unique patterning of the variables in individual cases. Like the average man, the composite simple or complex person would be hard to find.

In addition, one must be particularly cautious in evaluating the "goodness" and "badness" of the correlates of this dimension. As a previous report (2) pointed out, it is important to bear in mind that, in terms of the total constellation of factors making for personal effectiveness and professional prom-

[2]Staff members who participated in these assessments were D. W. MacKinnon, R. N. Sanford, Erik H. Erikson, R. S. Crutchfield, R. E. Harris, H. G. Gough, P. Dempsey, R. Taft, and the present writer. It need hardly be said that this entire research project is greatly indebted to the staff who contributed the ratings and carried out the assessment.

ise, simple persons and complex persons were equally represented among Ss who were rated as possessing that combination of attributes in high degree. This equal representation held also among the group of Ss with low ratings. One must conclude that both simplicity and complexity have their effective and ineffective aspects; they simply result in different sorts of merits and liabilities.

As we have indicated, in order to facilitate the reporting of the data, we shall adopt two conventions, one with regard to the scale and the other with regard to the designation of the Ss. The Barron-Welsh Art Scale will hereafter be referred to as a measure of the variable *Complexity*, since it is that feature of the scale which is of interest here, and since the scale is so scored that preferences like those of artists (hence, preference for the complex) earn S a high score, while preferences like those of people in general (i.e., preference for the simple) earn a low score. The designations *Complex person* and *Simple person* will be employed to indicate a modal high scorer and a modal low scorer, respectively, on this particular test.

The Correlational Composite

This description begins with personal tempo, which is usually a rather easily observed, surface attribute, complicated though its ramifications may be in the personal character. It is "surface" in the sense that it is what we are first presented with when we meet another person; we take in almost automatically such attributes as flow of speech, speed of response, rate and intensity of expressive movement, and expansiveness or constriction in interaction with the environment.

It will be recalled that on the Adjective Check-List our Complex Ss had described themselves as "quick" and "temperamental." The Simple Ss, on the other hand, had characterized themselves as "deliberate" and "dreamy." These self-descriptions would seem to be borne out by the staff's ratings of *S*s on such variables as Personal Tempo, Verbal Fluency, and Constriction. The correlations with Complexity are, respectively, .50, .29, and —.42.[3] Thus, the Complex person is more intensely expressive, expansive, and fluent in speech than the Simple person. The Simple person, on the other hand, is seen as being more natural and likeable, and also as more straightforward and lacking in duplicity. (Complexity correlates —.44 with Naturalness, —.27 with Likeability, and .56 with Deceitfulness, as rated by the staff.) This picture of easy and uncomplicated simplicity is further supported by staff ratings of such factors as Good Judgment, Adjustment, and Abundance Values, all of which go with preference for the simple figures. (The *r*'s with complexity are —.39, —.31 and —.34, respectively.)

"Adjustment" had here been defined as "getting along in the world as it is, adequate degree of social conformity, capacity to adapt to a wide range of conditions, ability to fit in." As we shall see later, this kind of adjustment is not an unmixed blessing; the "unadjusted" complex person, who does not fit in very well in the world as it is, sometimes perceives that world more accurately than does his better-adjusted fellow.

The negative correlation with Abundance Values, combined with the positive relationship of Complexity to Deceitfulness, merits some comment. Abundance Values was defined as "sense of security and optimism regarding the future, absence of fears of deprivation, of being exploited, and of being cheated." Deceitfulness was identified with "duplicity, lack of frankness, guile, subterfuge." Again, one recalls the adjective self-descriptions of the Complex people: gloomy, pessimistic, bitter, dissatisfied, demanding, pleasure-seeking, spendthrift. There is certainly some suggestion here of early oral deprivation, of pessimism concerning the source of supply, which is seen as untrustworthy and which must be coerced, or perhaps tricked, into yielding. It is as though the person had reason to believe that he would not "get what was coming" to him unless he made sure that he did, by whatever device might be available. It is this lack of infantile *trust* (as Erikson names it) that leads to adult duplicity and craftiness. Our aspect of complexity then (and perhaps a penalty sometimes attaching to it) is, to render it in the common phrase, a sort of "two-facedness," an inability to be wholly oneself at all times. The more simple, natural, and likeable person finds it easier to be always himself.

This suggested relationship of Complexity with the derivatives of orality (i.e., character traits determined in part by a relatively long and intense oral stage of development in the child) receives some slight support from several other correlations. If it is true, as clinical evidence generally indicates, that oral fixation leads to feminine character traits in men, one would expect to find Complexity related to masculinity-femininity measures. This proves to be the case, the *r* with the Minnesota Multiphasic Personality Inventory *Mf* being .18, that with the Strong Interest inventory *Mf* (which is so scored that the feminine man earns a low score) —.39. Rated Effeminacy, defined as "effeminate style and manner of behavior; softness," is also related to Complexity, the *r* being .29. Thus the Complex man has an attitude of acceptance toward his femininity showing itself in soft, gentle, and effeminate behavior. In the light of this, it is not surprising to find both Sentience ("seeking and enjoing sensuous impressions, sensitive, esthetic") and Sensuality ("acceptance of and capacity for sensual gratification") being related positively to Complexity (*r*'s of .25 and .26 respectively). This completes a picture of low but consistent cor-

[3]All correlations reported in this paper are based on *N*'s of 40, with the standard error therefore being .16.

relations of Complexity with some of the derivatives of orality.

The preference for Complexity is clearly associated with originality, artistic expression, and excellence of esthetic judgment. Originality was one of the three criterion variables around which the assessment research program was organized, and every subject was rated by the faculty members of his department on the degree of Originality he had displayed in his work. The Complex person is seen as more original, both by the assessment staff and by the faculty of his department. The correlation with the criterion ratings on Originality is .30.

Complexity is also related to Basic Good Taste as measured by a test which presents various alternative arrangements of formal design elements and asks S to choose the most aesthetically pleasing combination. This test, constructed by Sanford E. Gerard, is scored a priori in terms of known principles of composition. The correlation with Complexity is .44.

The Ss were also given a mosaic construction test devised by Turney, and known as the Turney Designs. In this test, the task is to construct a mosaic design in rectangular form from several hundred one-inch-square solid-colored pieces of pasteboard (20 different colors being represented). The designs were then rated by members of the Art Department of the University, in terms of the artistic merit of the productions. The ratings thus obtained correlate .40 with Complexity.

To be purely speculative for the moment, one might wonder whether there is not some relationship between the more enduring and intense oral stage of development in our complex Ss suggested by some of the data, and their evidently greater originality and sensitivity to the aesthetic character of objects. Fowler (7) has shown that oral character traits are significantly associated with textural responses to shading on the Rorschach, and psychoanalytic writers, particularly Rank, have emphasized the relationship between femininity and artistic productive-

ness in men. Sanford (personal communication) has noted tendency towards somewhat slower social development in the earlier years in original people, which would fit in nicely with the notion that a person must, as it were, have more commerce with himself and his feeling states and less with the environment during childhood if he is later to have sufficient communication with his own depths to produce the original thought. In this view, originality evidenced in maturity is to some extent dependent upon the degree to which the person in early childhood was faced with a complicated relationship to the maternal source of supply, combined with his capacity to persist in and eventually to achieve some mastery of this earliest problem situation. The argument would be that this primitive experience of phenomenal complexity sets a pattern of response which results in slower maturation, more tentativeness about the final form of organization, a resistance to early crystallization of the personality, and finally, greater complexity in one's view both of the outer and of the inner worlds.

Perhaps such speculation is unwarranted, however, and in any case it is clear that a great many other factors are involved in determining originality. What can be said is that originality and artistic creativeness and discrimination are related to the preference for complexity, and that the latter bears some relationship to sentience and femininity in men.

The Complex person's greater flexibility in thought processes is shown by a correlation of −.35 with rated Rigidity, defined as "inflexibility of thought and manner; stubborn, pedantic, unbending, firm." A 22-item scale for Rigidity, developed by Gough and Sanford, yielded an r of −.18 with Complexity. The two scales (Rigidity and Complexity) were later found to be related significantly and negatively to one another in a sample of medical students (r of −.36).

That repressive overcontrol may sometimes be associated with the preference for simplicity has already been indicated by the correlation of − .42 of Complexity with Constriction, and by another correlation of .50 with Impulsiveness. It is shown also in the relation of the Complexity measure to psychiatric variables which are scaled on the Minnesota Multiphasic Personality Inventory. With Hysteria, for example, Complexity correlates − .30, while with Schizophrenia it correlates .37, and with Psychopathic Deviate. 36. Thus Complexity goes along both with lack of control of impulse (the *Pd* scale) and with the failure of repression which characterizes the schizophrenic process. This is by no means to suggest that any of these graduate students showed schizophrenic tendencies of a pathological degree, but it is reasonable to suppose the *Sc* scale of the *MMPI* has built into it the correlates of the sort of free-floating symbolic activity and frank confrontation and expression of the unconscious which is often so startlingly present in schizophrenic patients. The *Hy* scale, on the other hand, picks up the tendency of *S* to repress aggressive and erotic impulses, or to render them innocuous by rationalization, reinterpretation, or gratification in a substitutive manner which will not cause conflict. At the risk of being oversimple, we might say that preference for the complex in the psychic life makes for a wider consciousness of impulse, while simplicity, when it is preferred, is maintained by a narrowing of that consciousness.

That the perceptual decision in favor of admitting complexity may make also for greater subjectively experienced anxiety is indicated by the correlation (.34) of Complexity with Overt Anxiety as measured by the Welsh Anxiety Index (11) on the MMPI. To tolerate complexity one must very often be able to tolerate anxiety as well, this finding would seem to say.

The negative correlation with *Hy* and the positive correlation, of about the same magnitude, with *Sc* would seem to fit well with a finding of Eysenck's that his own measure of

the Complexity-Simplicity dimension, the K test, correlates in this same direction with his Hysteria-Dysthymia factor.

Complexity is related negatively, although not significantly so, to Political-Economic Conservatism (− .22) and to Ethnocentrism (− .27), as measured by Form 60 of the Levinson-Sanford scale (10). These *r*'s are bound to be minimum estimates of the true relationship, since there was considerable restriction of range on both *PeC* and Ethnocentrism, the means being significantly lower than those of the general population. Some corroboration of this finding is furnished by attitudes expressed by *Ss* in the Pennsylvania sample, as we shall show later.

In addition to being less rather than more conservative, the person who prefers complexity is socially nonconformist. Staff ratings of Conformity correlate − .47 with Complexity, while the self-ratings of *Ss* on Conformity correlate − .53. Related to this is a correlation of − .29 between Complexity and Submissiveness, which was here defined as "deference, willingness to be led, compliance, over-ready acceptance of authority." In addition, Complexity correlates positively (.36) with the *F* scale of the MMPI. The *F* scale consists of items which are psychologically heterogeneous, the defining property of the scale being that all items in it have a low probability (about .1) of being answered on the scored direction. Thus, the higher the *F* score, the more likely it is that the subject holds a set of socially dissident and deviant opinions.

Complexity and Independence of Judgment

There is one further bit of information, of a rather intriguing nature, which bears on this question of conformity. Asch (1) has devised an experimental social situation in which *S* is put under pressure to conform to a group opinion which is false. In this experiment, there are from eight to sixteen ostensible *Ss*, only one of whom, however, is naïve; the rest are in the hire of the experimenter. The task is to judge which of three lines of variable length meets a standard line; or, put otherwise, to match the length of a given line with one of three lines which are themselves not equal to one another. The Ss, one by one, announce their judgment publicly. The naïve S is so placed as to be one of the last to announce his judgment. On the critical trials, the hired majority gives a prearranged false answer. The experimental variable is called Yielding, which is defined as agreeing with group opinion when it is in error. Yielding scores, in the prototypical experiment, range from 0 to 12, zero yielding being known as Independence.

In this experiment, approximately 25 per cent of all Ss are Independent, while the 25 per cent at the other extreme of the distribution Yield from 8 to 12 times. These two quartiles were selected for intensive personality study, in which the present writer participated as a test consultant and analyst. Among the tests employed in this part of the research was the measure of Complexity whose correlates we have been describing.

Since the experiment and the personality study of Ss will be fully reported elsewhere, we shall note here only that the mean difference in Complexity scores between the Independents and Yielders was in the predicted direction, i.e., Independents were more Complex. In a sample of 40 Haverford College students, the difference was significant at the .001 level, while in a sample of 60 Temple University students it was significant at the .05 level. For both groups combined, the difference was significant at the .01 level.

We have referred earlier to the negative relation of Complexity to Adjustment, part of the definition of which involved "an adequate degree of social conformity" and "ability to fit in." It is indeed a delicate question as to what, in social conformity, is an adequate degree thereof; different people seem to make different requirements of others in this matter. It is almost implicit in the design of the Asch experiment that to abandon the evidence of one's own senses in

favor of group opinion is carrying a good thing too far; while the popularity of many a modern nation within its own boundaries tends to become so categorical that even judicious dissent from this or that aspect of national policy may get labeled "disloyal," "deviationist" or, the shift in adaptation level in invective being what it is, something even worse.

In any event, it seems that these complex and independent Ss did not "fit in"; they faced up to the anxiety of being a minority of one, and continued to call the turn as they saw it. They accepted the fact that they held a different opinion from the rest of the group and they were able to persist in their belief in their own opinion. Some, indeed, were not surprised at all at this, and seemed to take pleasure in being among the Opposition; others were made extremely anxious, to the point of panic; while there were other independent and complex Ss who, while somewhat perturbed, went their own way with unassertive but firm confidence in their own judgment. In this latter group, independence seemed more genuinely critical and differentiated; and it is this sort of independence which, when it is allied with complexity, should prove constructively unadjusted and actually productive of original work rather than simply a deviant attitude.

RESPONSES TO AN
ATTITUDE QUESTIONNAIRE

In the same study, Asch and the present writer collaborated in the construction of a criterion-specific questionnaire, which consisted of 86 items which were especially selected, or written anew, to test particular hypotheses concerning personality differences between Independents and Yielders. Again, the results of this effort will be described in another publication; however, the results of an item analysis of the Independence questionnaire against the criterion of high or low score on Complexity may be given here. In this analysis, the Haverford and Temple groups were combined, and the questionnaire responses of the highest 27 per cent of scorers on the Complexity scale were compared with the lowest 27 per cent. Items which showed differences significant at the .05 level are given below.

Answered True by High Scorers on Complexity

1. The unfinished and the imperfect often have greater appeal for me than the completed and the polished.
2. I could cut my moorings . . . quit my home, my parents, and my friends . . . without suffering great regrets.
3. Politically I am probably something of a radical.
4. I think I take primarily an aesthetic view of experience.
5. I would enjoy the experience of living and working in a foreign country.
6. Many of my friends would probably be considered unconventional by other people.
7. Some of my friends think that my ideas are impractical, if not a bit wild.
8. I enjoy discarding the old and accepting the new.
9. When someone talks against certain groups or nationalities, I always speak up against such talk, even though it makes me unpopular.

Answered True by Low Scorers on Complexity

1. I don't like modern art.
2. Disobedience to the government is never justified.
3. Perfect balance is the essence of all good composition.
4. Straightforward reasoning appeals to me more than metaphors and the search for analogies.
5. It is a pretty callous person who does not feel love and gratitude towards his parents.
6. Things seem simpler as you learn more about them.
7. I much prefer symmetry to asymmetry.
8. Kindness and generosity are the most important qualities for a wife to have.
9. When a person has a problem or worry, it is best for him not to think about it, but to keep busy with more cheerful things.
10. It is the duty of a citizen to support his country, right or wrong.
11. Barring emergencies, I have a pretty good idea what I'll be doing for the next ten years.
12. I prefer team games to games in which one individual competes against another.

13. An invention which takes jobs away from people should be suppressed until new work can be found for them.

Since these *Ss* were all undergraduate students in Pennsylvania colleges, and their average age was 19, it is of some interest to compare their characteristics with the correlates of Complexity noted in the sample of California Ph.D. candidates. By grouping items, we may summarize the personality differences between the Complex and Simple persons in the Pennsylvania sample somewhat as follows:

The Complex person:

1. is artistic (4);
2. has unconventional friends, occasionally is visited by an impractical, not to say wild, idea, and would rather be creative and neurotic than normal and ordinary (6,7,10);
3. is politically somewhat radical, and can be militantly opposed to racial prejudice (3,9);
4. is aware of present imperfections, would welcome and has faith in future developments (1,2,5,8).

The Simple person:

1. doesn't like modern art (1);
2. particularly values kindness and generosity in a wife (as opposed to implied alternative values), and feels that the proper filial sentiments towards one's parents are love and gratitude (8,5);
3. feels that a citizen should support his country, right or wrong, and that disobedience to the government is never justified. Somewhat allied to this, he prefers a team effort to individual competition (2,10,12);
4. prefers symmetry to asymmetry, considers perfect balance the essence of good composition, and prefers straightforward reasoning to metaphors and the search for analogies (7,3,4);
5. has clear plans for the future, and considers that things seem simpler as you learn more about them (11,6);
6. believes that a person with a problem or worry should not think about it, and that inventions which take jobs away from people should be suppressed until new work can be found for them (9,13).

The general pattern is certainly similar to that shown by the correlations we have been reporting. In Pennsylvania as in California, preference for simplicity is associated with social conformity, respect for custom and ceremony, friendliness towards tradition, somewhat categorical moral judgment, an undeviating patriotism, and suppression of such troublesome new forces as inventions which would temporarily cause unemployment. This last item is almost prototypical of the simple person's orientation towards repression as a psychic mechanism. In the California sample, it was shown in the negative correlation of Complexity with Hysteria and the positive correlations with Psychopathic Deviate and Schizophrenia. Its derivatives appear in many other characteristic attitudes as well, such as acceptance or rejection of sensual experience, of conventional religion, of paintings of unclad ladies, and so on. For "invention," write "impulse," and it is not hard to see an analogy to the common clinical formulation of the function of repression in the hysterical character.

The correlates of preference for complexity in this undergraduate sample are, again, much like the correlates of the corresponding preference among the Ph.D. candidates. Complexity goes along with artistic interests, unconventionality, political radicalism, strong cathection of creativity as a value (even at the expense of "normality," as the item puts it), and a liking for change.

It seems evident that, at its best, preference for simplicity is associated with personal stability and balance, while at its worst it makes for categorical rejection of all that threatens disorder and disequilibrium. In its pathological aspect it produces stereotyped thinking, rigid and compulsive morality, and hatred of instinctual aggressive and erotic forces which might upset the precariously maintained balance.

There is a passage in Hugo's *Les Misérables* which is remarkably coincident with these observations. It occurs at that point in the narrative when Javert, the single-minded and merciless representative of the law, has turned his own world upside-down by allowing Jean Valjean, the outlaw whom he had so relentlessly pursued, and whom he finally had in his grasp, to escape. He says to himself, in this surprising moment, "There is something more then than duty." At this, "he was startled; his balances were disturbed; one of the scales fell into the abyss, the other flew into the sky. . . ."

. . . To be obliged to acknowledge this: infallibility is not infallible, there may be an error in the dogma, all is not said when a code has spoken, society is not perfect, authority is complicated with vacillation, a cracking is possible in the immutable, judges are men, the law may be deceived, the tribunals may be mistaken . . . to see a flaw in the immense blue crystal of the firmament!

. . . Certainly it was strange, that the fireman of order, the engineer of authority, mounted upon the blind iron-horse of the rigid path, could be thrown off by a ray of light! that the incommutable, the direct, the correct, the geometrical, the passive, the perfect, could bend!

. . . Until now all that he had above him had been in his sight *a smooth, simple, limpid surface; nothing there unknown, nothing obscure; nothing which was not definite, coordinated, concatenated, precise, exact, circumscribed, limited, shut in, all foreseen;* authority was a plane; no fall in it, no dizziness before it. Javert had never seen the unknown except below. *The irregular, the unexpected, the disorderly opening of chaos,* the possible slipping into an abyss; that belonged to inferior regions, to the rebellious, the wicked, the miserable.[4]

This passage brings together many observations made intuitively by Hugo and arrived at in a more pedestrian manner in this research. A precise simplicity is seen to be related to authority, dogma, tradition, morality, constriction, and repression; the opposite of all these things is typified by the flaw in the crystal, by the irregular, by disorderly chaos; such qualities as are to be found in the inferior regions, where reside the rebellious, the wicked, and the miserable. The emphasis here is pathological,

[4]Italics are Frank Barron's.

and the dichotomy absolute, but if we extend the range into normal behavior and admit the many shortcomings of the typology, there is considerable agreement between Hugo's intuition and this set of correlations.

Reservations and Discrepant Findings

So far as the correlational results in the California sample are concerned, it is evident that they must be accepted with some caution, since there is considerable possibility that chance error alone would account for some of the significant correlations. In addition, some variables would be correlated with one another in this sample but not in the general population, and a correlation of Complexity with just one of a set of atypically related variables would contribute to misleading correlations of the others of that set with the Complexity variable.

However, the findings from the Temple and Harverford nonassessment samples would tend to increase our confidence that many of the correlations found in the California assessment group would stand up when subjected to further investigation. There is also another source of evidence, although it is open to some question. The correlates of a revised and significantly different form of the Complexity measure in two other assessment samples (40 more Ph.D. candidates, and 40 medical school seniors) are known. In general, they are very much the same as those reported in this paper; in some cases, the r's are higher ($-.39$ with PeC, e.g., and .45 and .39 with Originality). However, there are some discrepant findings which should be noted, even though the Complexity measures are not strictly comparable.

In the first place, the negative relations of Complexity to Naturalness, Likeability, and Adjustment become zero-order in both the medical and graduate student samples. In addition, the positive relationship with Deceitfulness disappears, being slightly negative in the second sample of graduate students and exatly zero in the medical sample.

Several relationships which were zero in the first California sample become significantly positive in both of the succeeding samples. Complexity shows correlations with intellect of .42 and .41; with Breadth of Interest of .33 and .39; with Sense of Humor of .39 and .33; with Cathexis of Intellectual Activity of .42 and .29. (The correlations in the graduate school sample are given first, those in the medical sample second.)

Work is going forward on further investigation of these results. Within a year or so a sample of at least 200 Ss will have been assessed, which should yield fairly stable correlations. An effort is being made to develop other measures of the complexity-simplicity dimension, with some attention to capacity as well as preference for dealing with and resolving complex phenomenal fields. The scale is also being used in nonassessment settings, such as psychiatric clinics, and as stimulus material in memory experiments.

Summary

This paper has described the correlates of a bipolar factor in perceptual preferences which opposes a preference for perceiving and dealing with complexity to a preference for perceiving and dealing with simplicity, when both of these alternatives are phenomenally present and a choice is made between them. The correlates ramify through many areas of human behavior and attitudes, including interpersonal psychodynamics, interpersonal relations, and more broadly social spheres of behavior, such as politics, religion, group interaction, and the like.

It was emphasized that these types have both their effective and ineffective aspects, so far as human functioning is concerned. At times there is considerable merit in the simple view, while on other occasions some ease may profitably be sacrificed for greater phenomenal richness.

A measure of this factor was described, and its correlates were reported. Calling the factor variable *Complexity*, we note this pattern of relationships to it:

1. It is related positively to personal tempo, verbal fluency, impulsiveness, and expansiveness.

2. It is related negatively in one sample to naturalness, likeability, lack of deceitfulness, adjustment, and abundance values, but in other samples a revised form of the measure shows no significant relationship to these variables, so that the finding must await further checking before being credited.

3. It is related positively to originality, good taste, and artistic expression, and its revised form in two other samples shows significant positive correlations with intellect, sense of humor, breadth of interest, and cathexis of intellectual activity (none of which were significantly related to it in the first sample).

4. It is related positively to sensuality, sentience, aesthetic interest, effeminacy, and femininity in men.

5. It is related negatively to rigidity and constriction.

6. It is related negatively to control of impulse by repression, and positively to expression of impulse and to breakdown of repression.

7. It is related negatively to political-economic conservatism, to subservience to authority, to ethnocentrism, and to social conformity.

8. It is related positively to independence of judgment.

REFERENCES

1. Asch, S. E. Effect of group pressure upon the modifications and distortion of judgments. To appear.

2. Barron, F. Personality style and perceptual choice. *J. Pers.*, in press.

3. Barron, F., and G. S. Welsh. Artistic perception as a factor in personality style: Its measurement by a figure-preference test. *J. Psychol.*, 1952, 33, 199–203.

4. Eysenck, H. J. The general factor in aesthetic judgments. *Brit. J. Pscyhol.*, 1941, 31, 94–102.

5. Eysenck, H. J. "Type"-factors in aesthetic judgments. *Brit. J. Psychol.*, 1941, 31, 262–270.

6. Eysenck, H. J. *Dimensions of Personality.* London: Routledge, Kegan Paul, 1947.

7. Fowler, C. Personality correlates of the differential use of shading on the Rorschach test. Unpublished bachelor's thesis, Bennington College.

8. Gough, H. G. Predicting success in graduate training. A progress report. Berkeley: Univer. of California, Institute of Personality Assessment and Research, 1950. Hectographed.

9. Hugo, V. *Les Misérables.* New York: The Modern Library.

10. Levinson, D. J., and R. N. Sanford. A scale for the measurement of anti-Semitism. *J. Psychol.*, 1944, 17, 339–370.

11. Welsh, G. S. An anxiety index and an internalization ratio for the MMPI. *J. Consult. Psychol.* 1952, 16, 65–72.

12. Welsh, G. S. A projective figure-preference test for diagnosis of psychopathology: 1. A preliminary investigation. Unpublished doctor's thesis, Univer. of Minnesota, 1949.

25. A Typology of Creative Behavior in the Visual Arts

ELLIOT W. EISNER

Through research the conception of creativity has undergone an important change. Once considered an elusive, almost mystical gift belonging to a special few, creativity is now being seen as a capacity common to all men, one that should be effectively developed by the school. Once considered a rare type of behavior limited to the arts, creativity is now viewed as a mode of activity that penetrates, in some degree, almost all human action, and even educators who are usually chary of accepting new responsibilities for an already overloaded curriculum have become intrigued with the idea of educating for creativity.

Concern with the development of creativity has been a long standing one in art education. "Unlocking" the creative impulse has been one of the major functions of the teacher of art and while mere impulsivity has at times been confused with serious creative art, art education's concern with creativity has been real and sincere. Viktor Lowenfeld (8), and Herbert Read (9), and

Henry Shaffer-Simmern (11) are only a few who have made pioneering contributions to both the theory and practice of developing children's creativity in the arts. The recent flow of creativity research by psychologists is beginning to persuade those working in other academic fields that education for creativity is not the sole responsibility of those working in the arts. Thus, research undertaken on purely scientific grounds is providing some new and important directions in American education.

Of the major approaches that have been taken in the study of creativity, three have been prominent. Guilford (6), whose work has been especially influential, has postulated a set of factors and factorized tests that are theoretically relevant for understanding the structure of the human intellect. In his scheme, creativity is seen as a complex of a variety of unitary abilities which are displayed singly or in combination in the creative act. His factor-analytic methodologies have provided one major approach in study-

*SOURCE: An abbreviated version of this article appeared in the *American Educational Research Journal*, II, No. 3 (1965), pp. 125-136. It received the Palmer O. Johnson Award for the highest quality research published in that volume.

ing the problem and use of these tests has been widespread among workers in this area.

A second approach, taken by Blatt and Stein (3) and others, has been to study individuals who are known to be of high creative ability as evidenced through patents, discoveries, publications, inventions, and the like in the hope of finding common personality characteristics.

A third approach taken in the study of creativity has been the identification of process characteristics through examination of the completed product. This method, developed by Beittel and Burkhart (4), has been especially useful in the field of art education where the product's characteristics are indicative of the methods and modes of action employed by the artist. The constructs *spontaneous*, *divergent* and *academic* have proved useful for analyzing artistic process, and significant personality correlates have been found for individuals displaying these process-strategies.

The research reported here presents a fourth approach to the study of creativity. It represents an effort to formulate and test a typology of creative behavior in the visual arts.[1]

The treatment of *types* of creativity as distinct from the treatment of creativity in general may have several advantages. First, behaviors that are now excluded from the conception of creativity in general may be brought into a wider conception of creativity. Second, if an analysis of art works is undertaken with an eye to the different sort of "creativities" that they exhibit it might be possible to arrive at defensible views about the creative competencies that characterize different individuals. With such knowledge these competencies might be more efficiently encouraged.

The conception of types of creativity is based upon the various qualities and characteristics that have historically been considered creative in the visual arts. Analysis of children's art work, as well as that of adults, reveals that their qualities can be classified into a system of types. For example, some artists make their creative contribution through the treatment of form, others through selection of subject matter, some in the novel treatment of the conventional, others in the creation of the utterly new. Some children develop unique ways of combining media, others formulate new methods of expression; still others are able to confer aesthetic order to conventional visual elements. Creativity in art does not seem to be characterized by any simple unitary trait. Creativity, like art itself, has many faces. It was the purpose of this study to determine if it would be possible to identify systematically the types of creativity found in the art products of sixth-grade students, and to determine the relationship existing among these types.

Four types of creativity and two loci constitute the classes of the typology. The types are called (1) Boundary Pushing, (2) Inventing, (3) Boundary Breaking, and (4) Aesthetic Organizing. The loci are content and form.[2] The types are described *in general* as follows.

Boundary Pushing

In every culture objects are imbedded within various mental fields. These fields are bounded in such a way as to enable members of the culture to place the object in some meaningful context, usually the con-

[1]Specifically, the study attempted to determine if it would be possible to identify the type or types of creativity that preadolescent children display in their art products and to determine the relationships among the types. The study also investigated the relationship between each type of creativity and psychological health. These findings, however, are reported elsewhere.

[2]Content is defined as an attempt at representation and is evidenced by the presence of conventional signs. Form is defined by the presence of formal qualities. Thus, every visual art product contains formal qualities but may or may not contain conventional signs.

text in which it is normally found. These fields also act as a sort of psychic economy, a slicing up of the world so that objects within it can be meaningfully and efficiently classified. In addition, they provide the culture with a common set of object-field expectations that act to discourage bizarre actions on the part of individuals within that culture. The fields encourage and specify acceptable, stereotyped, and limited behavior on the part of individuals who behave within their limits.

Object-field expectations are learned early in life. Even before children learn to talk, they are taught that objects are to be used in specified ways. In their need to maintain decorum at home, parents set up "ground rules" through which socialization and acculturation are achieved. The child becomes socialized as he learns these rules and behaves within their limits. Yet if one studies the activities of the very young child, it is apparent that as soon as he is old enough to hold various sorts of objects he goes through various ordered stages with them. The child of two or three months smells objects, looks at them, feels them, hears them, and tastes them. He experiences the object through all of his senses. He seeks experience free from the social framework that later stereotypes and restricts his behavior and the objects' limits.

Ernest Schachtel (10) has made an important contribution towards understanding such behavior by emphasizing that infants as well as some adults have an openness to experience and *actively seek* commerce with the world, not merely to reduce tensions, as Freud has suggested, but to actualize themselves as humans. Schachtel's concepts of *activity-affect* and *embeddedness-affect* describe two distinct behavioral modes; the first is an active quest for experience, and the second a desire to return to a homeostatic intra-uterine state. While Schachtel believes that the balance between activity-affect and embeddedness-affect within any individual may be congenitally determined, he recognizes the possibility of changing the relationship between these levels through experience. "If the active coping behavior is encouraged, the infant will learn to rely more on its own activity. Conversely, an overprotective, or punitive mother may well prevent a congenitally active child from coping effectively with its environment. (10)"

Around four or five months of age, the child begins to experiment with objects in still other ways. He begins to explore their potential for stimulation by hitting one object against and with another. He "sees what happens" when he rolls one toy on top of another or moves a rattle against the slats of the crib. The child tests the reactions of people and objects by throwing spoons, toys, and cups from his high chair. Through exploration and experimentation he learns the probability pattern of his environment, he learns to predict what will occur if and when he decides to behave in certain ways.

At about nine or ten months of age the child begins to open up the objects of the world. He begins to take apart mechanically constructed objects; it is insufficient for him merely to explore the outside of things: now he must investigate the way in which reality is put together. A new toy commands interest only insofar as the child can explore its exterior without becoming bored with it. After this stage of exploration has passed, the child investigates its interior by pulling it apart and examining its parts. While this investigative phase is occurring, the child is concurrently being instructed by his parents as to proper modes of behavior. By the time he passes his first birthday, he has already begun to substitute the sounds of language for the objects that he previously knew in much different ways. The child learns to substitute the symbol and class of the object for the object itself. He learns to organize, abstract, and categorize and, indeed, he must if he is to get on adequately in the world. But in so learning, he pays a price that is exacted throughout his school experience. He relinquishes a portion of his imaginativeness and inquisitiveness focused in exploration, experimentation, and sensation, for a comfortable place within the social world. He may compensate for this by attuning his imagination to daydreaming and fantasy or by seeking stimulation from the imaginative works of others. In this way, his imagination is less mischievous. This aspect of socialization seems to be for the most part complete when educators state that somewhere along the line the creative powers of the young child have been lost.

The loss that both educators and parents speak of, however, is only a relative one and fortunately most children retain both the inclination and the ability to continue to explore and experiment with the limits of the conventional. This process of experimentation, of redefining the limits of common objects, may be called Boundary Pushing. Generally, Boundary Pushing is the ability to expand the limits that define the uses to which an object can be put, as well as the ability to place objects into classes from which they were previously excluded.

Some examples of such behavior may help in its clarification. In the area of technology, Boundary Pushing was demonstrated by the individual who first thought of installing electric shaver outlets in automobiles, thus extending the usual limits of both auto and shaver. It was also demonstrated by the person who first conceived of using rubber for the blades of electric fans and by the individual who first used nylon for the wheels of roller skates. In the classroom, Boundary Pushing is displayed by the child who uses numerals to create designs or pictures or who uses an inked eraser as a rubber stamp. Boundary Pushing is displayed in the recognition that plywood can be molded into a chair, that a cellophane strip can be used to open a package of cigarettes, and that a key can be used to open a can of coffee. Boundary Pushing is thus an ability to attain the possible by extending the given.

Inventing

Inventing, the second type of creativity in the typology, is an ability to employ the known in order to create an essentially new object or class of objects. The inventor does not merely extend the usual limits of the conventional; he creates a new object by restructuring the known. Edison, to use a classic case, best exemplifies the inventor, for his activities were not merely directed toward the novel implementation of known materials or objects but rather toward their combination and reconstruction. There is no need to list his inventive contributions here for they are well known. It is sufficient to point out that his contributions differ markedly from those produced by Boundary Pushing. The terminus of Inventing is the creation of a new product that may itself be creatively employed, thus being the subject of Boundary Pushing. Gutenberg, Bell, and Marconi are only a few of those who have displayed inventive behavior; and our recognition of their contributions combined with our general reluctance to call them scientists is indicative of the distinction we make at the commonsense level of the ways in which creativity is displayed.

In *Insight and Outlook* (5) Arthur Koestler discusses the creative process and his analysis of this process is similar to the description of Inventing. Koestler claims that creativity is primarily a bi-sociative process in which the creator finds that two fields usually considered separate could be made to dovetail to establish a new productive relationship. He believes that the ability to find this relationship emanates from motives resulting from aggression and that these motives are also exercised in the production of witticisms and humor.³ Specifically, in describing bi-sociation Koestler states:

. . . the creative originality of this matchmaking bi-sociation is not apparent in the smooth syllogistic scheme. The scheme gives the impression that the mental achievement consisted in drawing the conclusions. In fact the achievement was to bring two premises under one roof, as it were. The conclusion is merely the offspring of the marriage, arrived at by routine actions. In other words, syllogism and deductive reasoning are not the method of creative thought, they merely serve as its formal justification after the act (and as a scheme for repeating the process by analogy after the original bi-sociation of the two fields in which the premises are representatively located). The solutions of problems are not "invented" or "deducted" — they are "found"; they occur" (5).

He goes on further to give examples of such occurrences among which is Darwin's "find."

In Darwin's case the stick was Malthus's "An Essay on the Principle of Population," published in 1797 — more than forty years earlier. In it Darwin saw in a flash the "natural selector," the functional concept he was looking for:

This is the doctrine of Malthus, applied to the whole animal and vegetable kingdoms. As many more individuals of each species are born than can possibly survive; and as consequently there is a frequency recurring struggle for existence, it follows that any being, if it vary ever so slightly in manner profitable to itself, under the complex and sometimes varying condition of life will have a better chance of surviving and thus being *naturally selected* (5). (Underline is Darwin's)

The conception of Inventing used here holds that while the impetus for Inventing may lie in the discovery or the "find" of the congruence of two fields this find is not enough. From this find the individual must deduce ideas, structure and conclusions. It is from this process that the invention de-

³Research on creative adolescents carried out by Professors J. Getzels and P. Jackson indicates that a sense of humor is highly regarded by creative adolescents. This finding coincides with the position taken by Koestler on the relationship between creativity and humor.

velops — discovery must be succeeded by purposeful ordered activity for it is in this activity that the invention becomes manifest.

Boundary Breaking

Boundary Breaking is defined as the rejection or reversal of accepted assumptions and making the "given" problematic. This type of behavior is probably characterized by the highest level of cognition. In Boundary Breaking the individual sees gaps and limitations in present theories and proceeds to develop new premises which contain their own limits. Copernicus, for example, displayed Boundary Breaking behavior in his conceptual, if not theological, rejection of the theory that the earth was the center of the universe. His hypothesis that it was the earth that moved around the sun, and not vice versa, led him to develop a theory that, as far as we know, validly describes the astronomical system. His rejection of the then present knowledge — knowledge and theories that were limiting — allowed him to make a significant contribution toward helping man understand the universe. In the present era, Einstein's notion of simultaneity allowed him to develop new concepts useful for understanding nature through his theory of relativity. His questioning of previous theories of relationships in time and space allowed him to develop a theory from which better predictions of natural phenomena can be made.

Still another example of Boundary Breaking can be found in the work of Binet. "Binet's approach was the direct opposite of that of his predecessors. Instead of trying to find a single index of intelligence he went to the other extreme and deliberately searched for a multiplicity of indexes" (12). By making the given problematic and by reversing the approach taken by others, Binet set the pattern for over fifty years of intelligence testing.

Two behaviors characteristically displayed by Boundary Breakers — insight and imagination — might function in the following ways. Insight might help the Boundary Breaker grasp relationships between seemingly discrete events. It might also enable him to recognize incongruities or gaps in accepted explanations or descriptions. As he recognizes these gaps his imagination may come into play and enable him to generate images and/or ideas useful for closing these gaps. Through the production of these images and/or ideas he is able to reorganize or even reject the accepted in order to formulate a more comprehensive view of the relationships between the elements that gave impetus to the initial insight. Insight into gaps in contemporary theory or action and visions of the possible are probably insufficient to satisfy the Boundary Breaker unless he is able to establish an order and structure between the gaps he has "seen" and the ideas he has generated.

Aesthetic Organizing

Aesthetic Organizing, the fourth type of creativity constituting the typology, is characterized by the presence in objects of a high degree of coherence and harmony. The individual who is able to display this mode of creativity confers order and unity upon matter; his overriding concern is in the aesthetic organization of qualitative components.[4] Decisions concerning the placement of objects are made through the use of what may be called a qualitative creativity.

Individuals who are able to aesthetically organize components probably obtain a great deal of pleasure from doing so. This inclination towards aesthetic order also seems to be displayed in the way in which

[4]While aesthetic organization is present in the theoretical, what follows deals with the aesthetic organization of the qualitative.

forms are perceived. Barron (2) has shown that both creative artists and creative scientists show a greater preference for designs that are highly complex, asymmetrical and seemingly disorganized than do other less creative individuals. In this sense the aesthetic organizer may be an aesthetic seer as well, that is, he may obtain his aesthetic pleasures by seeing through disorder to identify orderly elements. Some artists and writers report that they are controlled by these urges and drives and admit to following their lead consciously rather than carefully preconceived plans of execution.

Expressionism as a painting style reflecting this type of cognitive activity capitalizes on the direct, spontaneous, emotionally charged use of form. The expressionist is very concerned about colors and shapes that portray, in vivid fashion, the feelings he is attempting to express. Form is his major expressive vehicle, and decisions regarding its treatment are made in response to the qualities emerging from his actions. Thus, the expressionist has to react to and see through the qualities he has created for their potential power to touch his aesthetic sensibilities.

It should be noted that a major difference exists between Aesthetic Organizing and the other three modes of creativity. In Boundary Breaking, Inventing, and Boundary Pushing, novelty is a defining characteristic. Either a new use for an object or a new object itself is created. In Aesthetic Organizing this may not necessarily be the case; no new object may have been created. The object upon which creativity was exercised, however, displays a high degree of coherence. Its parts hang together harmoniously. For most artists the aesthetic organization of form is a prime concern, but for children (and these are the subjects of this study), high aesthetic organizing ability is relatively rare. The pre-adolescent who is able to organize form to a high degree of coherence and harmony is often said to be gifted; and in this study this particular type of giftedness is considered one type of creativity.

Subjects and Instruments

Once having formulated the classes which constitute the typology the problem shifted to the empirical: Could the typology be used to identify types of creative characteristics displayed in childrens' art products? Such characteristics will be assumed to be evidence of particular types of behavior.

In order to answer this question specific criteria were deduced from each general description of the types. These criteria described the characteristics that would be present in each art product if the subject had displayed a particular type of creativity. For example, a subject who engaged in Aesthetic Organizing would produce a product with satisfying formal qualities. Its parts would hang together and it would be unified; balance between figure and ground would be achieved. A subject who engaged in Boundary Pushing would produce a product in which either form or content were used in a novel way, his treatment of these aspects of the art product would be original.

Eighty-five Ss attending the sixth grade of a midwestern private school constituted the sample. Of the eighty-five, thirty-nine Ss were girls. The median IQ of the sample was 128 with a range from 93 to 180. Where IQ measures other than the Stanford-Binet were used, scores were transposed to Stanford-Binet equivalents.

The subjects were asked to produce two types of art products. One product was a piece of sculpture made from one quarter pound of oil-base clay, a handful of colored toothpicks and a paper plate that was to be used as a base to make the sculpture movable. Instructions given to Ss were as follows:

"In the booth before you, you will find a paper plate, some colored toothpicks and some oil-base clay. You may build anything you wish out of the clay and toothpicks. The paper plate is to be used as a base so that whatever you make can be easily moved. You will have forty-five minutes to complete your work. You may begin."

To insure privacy all of the Ss worked in enclosed booths.

The second product consisted of a set of nine drawings made in a booklet $8''$ by $11\frac{1}{2}''$ in dimension. On each page of the booklet the Ss found an abstract line which was to be used as a starting point or stimulus for their drawing. A border line an inch and a half away from the edge of the page appeared on each page of the booklet. Ss had two minutes to work on each page and knew when the two minutes had elapsed by a signal given to them by the test administrator. Instructions were as follows:

"On each page of this booklet you will find some simple lines. You are to use your pencil to change each of the lines in any way you wish. You will have two minutes to work on each page so you will have to work rapidly. Wait for the signal before you begin. Once you complete one page don't turn to the next page until you are told to do so. You may begin."

Procedure and Treatment of Data

In order to identify the various types of creativity that each art product might display, three judges were selected. Each judge had had over five years of art teaching experience with children. In addition, each of the judges had considerable experience as a practicing visual artist. The judges met daily for two weeks to discuss the criteria and to practice using the criteria by judging the creative characteristics of work similar to those used in the study. When this period had expired, the judges believed that they had an adequate understanding of the criteria and their application and proceeded to the actual evaluation.

The products produced by the Ss were arranged in two large rooms and the judges, using a nine-point scale, independently evaluated each type of creativity at a time. After one evaluation was completed, the score sheet was handed in, another score sheet distributed, and the judge selected another point in the display at which to begin his next evaluation. This procedure, used to reduce halo effect, was duplicated throughout.

In order to determine interjudge agreement the data were treated in several ways: the raw scores assigned by each judge were transformed to standardized normal scores and summed. These summed scores for each judge were then intercorrelated to determine the level of interjudge agreement among the judges' *overall* assessment of creativity. Following this, interjudge agreement in *each medium* was ascertained, this time by correlating the summed standardized normal scores in each medium. Finally, the raw scores assigned to the products by each judge in each type and locus of creativity were intercorrelated. This procedure of determining interjudge agreement by gradually moving from a gross to successively more specific assessment of creativity made it possible to identify the points at which interjudge agreement diminished.

When each of the judge ratings was summed for an *overall* creativity score, interjudge agreement was rather high. The coefficients derived were .82, .78, and .72. When correlations of overall creativity scores in *each medium* were computed, the amount of interjudge agreement dropped slightly. The coefficients derived for drawings were .80, .79, and .71; for structures, .74, .65, and .61. Finally, when correlations for interjudge reliability were computed for *each type and locus in each medium*, the coefficients ranged from .90 to .10 with a median of .59 (see Table I).

Once having decided that the interjudge agreement was high enough to warrant use of the data it became possible to determine the relationships existing among the types

and other variables. The following questions guided the analysis.

1. What relationships exist among scores in each type of creativity within and between media?

2. Are relationships among the types for girls significantly different?

3. Do different relationships among types of creativity appear in subjects above and below the medium in intelligence?

4. What are the correlations between each of the types and the Stanford-Binet IQs?

To answer the first question the raw scores for each type of creativity were transformed to standardized normal scores and summed. Transformations were made to equalize the scales used by the judges and sums were computed to obtain a single creativity score for each type of creativity in each medium. These scores were then intercorrelated and are presented in Table II with coefficients for IQ. From the coefficients, three conclusions can be drawn. First, the relationship between creative performance in one medium and creative performance in another is low. (The median coefficient among r's between media is .11. This coefficient is not shown in Table II.) Second, the relationships among types of creativity in drawing are higher than among types of creativity in structures. Third, scores in Boundary Breaking in form and content were more highly correlated than were other types of creativity in form and content. In addition, scores on this type of creativity in structures were least highly correlated with scores in other types.

The virtual lack of relationship between creative performance in one medium and creative performance in another is consonant with the kinds of expectations critics have for the work of professional artists. Aside from a few outstanding exceptions such as Degas, Michelangelo, Picasso, and Moore, most artists display high-level

TABLE I

Interjudge Correlations Computed From Raw Data

Type and Locus of Creativity	Judges		
	A vs. B N = 85	A vs. C N = 85	B vs. C N = 85
Boundary Pushing–Content Structures	.80	.70	.90
Boundary Breaking–Form Structures	.88	.72	.75
Boundary Pushing–Form Drawings	.74	.58	.68
Aesthetic Organizing–Form Drawings	.55	.60	.76
Inventing-Content, Drawings	.52	.73	.60
Aesthetic Organizing–Form Structures	.58	.56	.68
Inventing–Form, Structures	.52	.62	.61
Inventing–Form, Drawings	.55	.57	.65
Boundary Pushing–Form Structures	.53	.53	.63
Inventing–Content Structures	.51	.47	.54
Boundary Pushing–Content Drawings	.39	.60	.49
Boundary Breaking–Form Drawings	.33	.38	.68
Boundary Breaking–Content Drawings	.10	.81	.42
Boundary Breaking–Content Structures	.27	.27	.76
Median	.53	.59	.66

Significance at the .01 level of confidence = .27

creativity in one or, at best, two media. When artists function creatively in more than one medium it is most often in media of the same kind, such as collage and drawing or sculpture and bas-relief. The apparent specificity of creative behavior in the visual arts is probably a function of the status of certain skills that are necessary in working in two rather than in three dimensions or in working in color rather than in black and white. The type of demands different media make upon an individual probably affect the extent to which he can employ those cognitive skills that exemplify or make possible creative thinking. A person unable to perceive depth might be able to function in a highly creative way in the production of mosaics but surely would be severely handicapped in the production of sculpture. Since the Ss in the study had about the same

TABLE II

Correlations Among Types and Loci of Creativity and IQ[1]

(N = 85)

Types and Loci of Creativity		IQ	Form, Structures				Content, Structures			Form, Drawings				Content, Drawings		
			B.P.	I.	B.B.	A.O.	B.P.	I.	B.B.	B.P.	I.	B.B.	A.O.	B.P.	I.	B.B.
	IQ		−.02	.05	−.04	−.01	.21	.18	−.09	.05	.16	.03	.07	.15	.01	−.15
Form, Structures	BP			.40	−.05	.76	.33	.32	−.03	.25	.19	.17	.25	.13	.27	.20
	I				−.30	.39	.02	.20	−.38	.13	.09	.04	.05	.13	.09	.04
	BB					.08	−.00	−.05	.64	.11	.16	.01	.18	−.04	−.04	.05
	AO						.34	.29	.10	.27	.14	−.03	.25	.07	.17	.04
Content, Structures	BP							.83	.22	.09	.06	.11	.18	.28	.18	−.05
	I								.05	.06	.07	.11	.16	.29	.21	−.06
	BB									−.04	−.03	−.02	.11	−.01	−.09	−.06
Form, Drawings	BP										.77	.26	.73	.52	.45	.39
	I											.39	.76	.60	.52	.45
	BB												.26	.33	.39	.50
	AO													.56	.55	.35
Content, Drawings	BP														.75	.36
	I															.57
	BB															

amount of experience with each medium they used, the character of the two media and the different types of abilities that these media elicit might account for the modest relationship between them.

Although the relationships between the several types of creative performance in one medium and the types of creative performance in another tend to be slight, seven significant relationships did emerge. Six of those seven relationships occur between types having the same locus. For example, Boundary Pushing in content in structures and in drawings is significantly correlated. Inventing in content in structures and Boundary Pushing in content in drawings are also significantly correlated. These relationships may be due to the type of mental set that the *S*s brought to their work. *S*s who obtained high creativity scores in the locus of *form* might have sought the stimulation of emerging formal qualities rather than the successful imposition of a preconceived idea or symbol upon the medium. They might have preferred to treat the medium as a partner rather than as a master, taking their cues from the unexpected emergence of forms that flowed from their actions.

Those who obtained high scores in the locus of *content* might have formulated a rather clear image of the idea they desired to represent. Once the idea was conceived, the medium became its material embodiment. Viktor Lowenfeld's concept of the visual and haptic continuum may be relevant here. Lowenfeld distinguishes between the visual and the haptic individual by characteristics found in the subject's art products.

"The visual type, the observer, usually approaches things from their appearance. He feels as a spectator . . . . Visually minded persons have a tendency to transform kinesthetic and tactile experiences into visual experience. . . .
The main intermediary for the haptic type of individual is the body-self. . . . In his art, the self is projected as the main actor of the picture whose formal characteristics are the resultant of a synthesis of bodily, emotional, and intellectual apprehensions of shape, and form. Size and shape are determined by the emotional value in size and importance" (7).

Creativity in the locus of content may take place in the context of an idea or concept, in the replication of a *symbolic* mental image. Creativity in the locus of form may take place in the context of the sensuous, in the aesthetic ordering of the qualitative. Concern with the formal necessitates reliance on the sensuous, since objective criteria for aesthetic quality are not available. Individuals who focus their creative efforts upon the treatment of form must, to a large extent, rely upon affective responses to the merging forms to determine subsequent action. Content oriented individuals may be less confident in their affective judgements and hence attempt to mirror what can be seen or to portray meanings through the use of symbols. It may prove valuable to conduct inquiries specifically designed to determine the extent to which form and content separate as loci of creativity outside, as they seem to do within, the field of the visual arts.

The third finding emerging from the correlation table isolates a particular mode of creative behavior. Of all types of creativity, Boundary Breaking, in both content and form, emerged as the most independent. Explanation for this may be found in the nature of Boundary Breaking itself. In order to engage in Boundary Breaking, the individual must reject and/or reverse, or both, the premises upon which the problem rests. For example, Alexander Calder's rejection of the assumption that sculpture had to be static was a precondition to his creation of moving sculpture, the mobile. Kandinsky's rejection of the assumption that painting must represent was a precondition for his creation of nonobjective painting. Individuals able to escape the limits of heavily embedded cultural expectations are always rare, and since Boundary Breaking is an instance of the most dramatic type of successful escape of such expectations, its rarity is not surprising.

One *S* who engaged in Boundary Breaking in structures used the paper plate, which was intended only as a base, as an integral part of his structure and, in addition, combined torn cardboard as a functional element. Another used the colored toothpicks not as a structural element in the clay but as a burden that was carried by the clay donkey that he built. In the drawings, one *S* carefully punched holes in the several pages so that his drawings had a relief quality. These *S*s rejected or reversed the premises on which the problem was built in order to develop novel solutions.

In order to determine whether different relationships existed among the types of creativity for each sex, the intercorrelations were computed for boys and girls separately. In 19 of 91 pairs of coefficients significance was attained by only one of the two coefficients in the pair. However, no pattern in the 19 could be identified.

A median split was made in the sample by IQ again to determine if differences existed in relationships among types of creativity for those differing in IQ. In this matrix an interesting pattern did emerge. Of 19 significant relationships between creative performance in one medium and creative performance in the other, *all* of 19 significant relationships occurred in the high IQ group. In other words, the high IQ subjects in this study appear more consistent in their level of creative performance between media than subjects in the lower half of the IQ distribution.

To determine if IQ as measured by Stanford-Binet is related to any of the types, Pearson coefficients of correlation were computed and are presented in Table II. As has been found in other studies, the relationships between creativity scores and the type of cognition assessed by IQ measures are overall. In no case in this study did a signifi-

cant relationship emerge between any of the types of creativity and IQ scores.

Summary

In this study creativity was differentiated according to its type and according to the location at which it was displayed within an art product. The typology then was used to evaluate two art products produced by eighty-five sixth grade students. One art product consisted of a nine-page drawing booklet and the other a three-dimensional structure made of clay and toothpicks. Each product was rated independently by three artistically experienced judges, using a nine-point scale. After degree of interjudge agreement had been determined, it was found that the relationship between creative performance in one medium and creative performance in another was low, the median coefficient being .27. It was found, however, that when significant coefficients among the types did occur, they occurred among types having the same locus; that is, creativity in form in one medium was most likely to be related to creativity in form in another medium, and creativity in content in one medium likely to be related to creativity in content in another medium.

One type of creativity, Boundary Breaking, was displayed much more rarely than the other types. While Boundary Pushing, Inventing, and Aesthetic Organizing were displayed in some degree by almost all subjects, Boundary Breaking was not. The difficulty in exercising this type of creativity may account for its rarity. No differences in the pattern of relationships among types of creativity for boys and for girls could be determined. However, when the sample was divided in half at the median IQ, those in the upper half of the sample appeared more consistent in their creative performance across media than those in the lower half. No significant relationships emerged between IQ scores and any of the types of creativity.

REFERENCES

1. BARKAN, M., and J. HAUSMAN. "Two pilot studies with the purpose of clarifying hypotheses for research into creative behavior." *Research in Art Education*, 1956, pp. 126–141.

2. BARRON, FRANK. "The psychology of imagination." *Scientific American*, 1958, **199,** September, 1958, pp. 150–166.

3. BLATT, S. J., and M. I. STEIN. "Some personality, value, and cognitive characteristics of the creative person." Paper presented at the 1957 meetings of the American Psychological Association.

4. BEITTEL, KENNETH R., and ROBERT C. BURKHART. "Strategies of Spontaneous, Divergent, and Academic Art Students." *Studies in Art Education*, 5: 20–41, Fall, 1963.

5. KOESTLER, A. *Insight and Outlook.* New York: The Macmillan Co., 1949.

6. GUILFORD, J. P., *et al.* A factor analytic study of creative thinking, II, administration of tests and analysis of results. *Psychological Laboratory*, University of Southern California, 1952.

7. LOWENFELD, V. *Creative and Mental Growth,* Third edition. New York: The Macmillan Co., 1957, p. 541.

8. LOWENFELD, V. *The Nature of Creative Activity.* New York: Harcourt Brace and Co., 1939, p. 272.

9. READ H. *Education Through Art.* New York: Pantheon Books, 1940.

10. SCHACHTEL, E. *Metamorphosis.* New York: Basic Books, Inc., 1959.

11. SCHAFFER-SIMMERN, H. *The Unfolding of Artistic Activity.* Berkeley: University of California Press, 1948.

12. STEPHENS, J. M. *Educational Psychology,* revised edition. New York: Holt and Co., 1951.

26. The Ability of College Art Majors to Recombine Ideas in Creative Thinking

V. R. FISICHELLI *and* L. WELCH

In a previous study[1] designed to observe the part played in creative thinking by the ability to recombine ideas according to plan, one of the present authors constructed a special test in which the subject was obliged to recombine familiar ideas according to four different plans. In that study the test performance of unselected college juniors and seniors was compared with that of a group of successful professional artists, and a statistically significant difference in mean performance score was found in favor of the professional group.

The test itself, which is described in greater detail in the study already mentioned, consists of four separately given parts: (1) constructing meaningful sentences, (2) constructing letters of the alphabet, (3) constructing a short story, and (4) constructing pieces of furniture from wooden blocks. The specific instructions for each part of the test are as follows:

[1] L. Welch, "Recombination of Ideas in Creative Thinking." *J. Appl. Psychol;* **30**, 1946, pp. 638–643.

Part I. Recombine the words of each group on the next page to make as many meaningful, grammatical sentences as possible. For example, here is a group of ten words: MEN SKY IS FIGHT THAT THE SLOW BRIGHT OF FOR which can be recombined into the following sentences:

> Men fight for the sky.
> The sky is bright.
> The fight is slow.
> Etc.

You will receive as much credit for a *short* sentence as for a long one. Your sentences do not have to be artistic, but they must be grammatical. There must be at least a subject and a predicate. You will receive credit for a sentence which is only slightly different from another. A word from the group can be used only once in the same sentence, but it may be used any number of times in other sentences. Only use words from the group that you are examining at the time. You may skip from one group to another if you like.

There are ten of these groups and you have only ten minutes in which to complete the test. Are there any questions? ... Do not turn the page until the examiner says "Start."

SOURCE: Journal of Applied Psychology, XXXI (1947), pp. 278–282. The authors are grateful to Miss Phyllis Arnoff for her gracious assistance in this investigation.

Part II. Make as many letters as possible using no more and no less than three straight lines. For example, the letter A is made with three straight lines, two slanting downward and one across. You will be given no credit for the letter A, since it is an example.

Make as many letters as possible using no more and no less than two straight lines.

Make as many letters as possible using no more and no less than one straight line and one semi-circle.

The time limit is three minutes.

(The three separate sets of instructions contained within this part were printed on the same page with considerable working space between them.)

Part III. On the next page you will be given a list of twenty words which you are to connect into a story. You must be certain to use the words in the order in which they appear on the list. If the first word on the list is "house" and the second word is "tree," you must first make use of the word "house" in your story and then make use of the word "tree." You must not skip any of the words.

Your story must be grammatical and logically related. It must have a beginning and an end. You will be rated on the number of words you can make use of in the time allotted. Write as fast as you can and underline each of the twenty words as you use it.

The time limit is three minutes.

Part IV. The object of this test is to construct, out of ten blocks on each trial, as many pieces of furniture or home furnishings as possible. The piece of furniture you construct must fit properly. It must be symmetrical and recognizable as a piece of furniture. Do not attempt to be futuristic. Use conventional forms. You must use a minimum of two blocks to construct a piece of furniture. You can use the same block over again to make another piece of furniture. You can make as many of the same type of furniture as you like. You will receive full credit for the same type that is only *slightly* different from another.

You have only ten minutes to complete this test. There are five trials; hence, you have only two minutes for each trial.

The subjects in this investigation were 25 female art majors in their junior and senior years at Hunter College. They were chosen from the upper class years to insure that they had all successfully passed the preliminary screening courses offered by the art department. These students were, thus, promising young artists with demonstrated talents and special abilities in their chosen field. The first three parts of the test were administered to them in group form. The fourth part was given individually at a uniform time and under uniform conditions.

TABLE I

The Mean Performance Scores and the Standard Deviations for Each Group
on Each Part of the Test

Parts	Professional Artists $N = 30$		Art Majors $N = 25$		Unselected Students $N = 48$	
	Mean	S.D.	Mean	S.D.	Mean	S.D.
I	17.7	7.2	21.9	7.6	18.0	4.2
II	12.5	1.9	13.2	1.0	6.7	1.8
III	11.4	4.1	7.3	2.5	9.1	3.2
IV	18.4	7.8	13.9	9.1	3.4	2.7
Total Score	60.5	12.3	56.4	15.1	37.6	7.0

Results

The test results of the 25 art majors in this study were compared with those of the two groups, professional artists and unselected upper class students, reported in the previous study. The mean scores and standard deviations for each group on each part of the test are shown in Table I. (See page 337.)

It will be seen that there is a striking difference in the overall score between the art majors and the unselected college students. The difference between the professional artists and the unselected students has already been mentioned in the previous study. The differences between the groups on the different parts of the test are not quite as striking. All of the differences, however, were put to test and some significant t values were obtained. The t values obtained for differences between the means of the three groups on each part of the test and between the overall scores are presented in Table II.

It appears that, for the overall test score, the difference between the unselected students and the art majors is statistically significant, while that between the art ma-

jors and the professional artists is not. Parts II and IV of the test seem to be especially important. The differences between the groups on these two parts seem to be consistently significant. On Part II, both the professional artists and the art majors receive significantly better scores than the unselected students. On Part IV, the professional artists are the best performers, the art majors second best, and the unselected students last. For Parts I and III of the test, which require constructions along literary lines, the differences between the groups are not consistently significant. On Part I, the order of best performance is art majors, unselected students, and professional artists. On Part III the order is professional artists, unselected students, and art majors.

In order to determine the reliability of the method of scoring the test three scorers worked independently on all papers. The degree of agreement between scorers ranged from .934 to .978. A list of acceptable constructions for Part IV of the test is now being prepared for future use. Although there was little disagreement between scorers, most of such disagreement was on this part of the test.

TABLE II

The *t* Values Obtained for Differences Between Means of Groups

Parts	Professional Artists and Art Majors	Professional Artists and Unselected Students	Art Majors and Unselected Students
I	2.1[1]	0.2	3.0[3]
II	1.5	13.2[3]	17.1[3]
III	4.4[3]	1.1	2.4[2]
IV	2.0[1]	10.2[3]	7.5[3]
Total Score	1.1	10.9[3]	7.2[3]

[1]$t_{05} = 2.0$.
[2]$t_{02} = 2.3$.
[3]$t_{01} = 2.6$.

In the previous study a correlation co-efficient of .27 was reported for the scores on this test and the Wonderlic Personnel Test. In this study the test scores were correlated with the general scholastic index of the subjects and a product-moment co-efficient of .45 was found, which, for 25 subjects, is significant at the five per cent level. Performance on the test for recombination of ideas appears, therefore, to be related to the general intelligence of the art major group in no minor degree. It is to be indicated, however, that the unselected students of the previous study were not, by comparison with the art majors, a less intelligent group. On the American Council of Education Psychological Test the mean score for art majors was 114.9 and for the unselected student, 122.7.

Summary and Conclusions

The purpose of this investigation was to determine the ability of a group of college art majors to recombine ideas in creative thinking. A special test, constructed by one of the present authors, was given in which the subject was obliged to recombine familiar ideas according to four different plans.

1. The performance of these art majors was compared with that of a group of professional artists and a group of unselected college students, both of which were examined in a previous study. The mean scores for the three groups are as follows: professional artists, 60.5; college art majors, 56.4; students unselected for major field of study, 37.6. The difference between the unselected students and the art majors is statistically significant while that between the art majors and the professional artists is not.

2. Parts II and IV of the test seem to have the most discriminative value where art is the field in question. For the three groups examined no consistent differences were obtained on the other parts of the test.

3. There is some tendency for the total test scores to be related to the general scholastic index of the art major group.

4. Finally, it should be mentioned that the function tested in this study was strictly a quantitative one, and apart from the fact that the recombined ideas of all subjects had to fit the simple criteria of conventional usage and symmetry of form, nothing was demonstrated concerning the qualities of their production.

27. Creativity and Culture

MORRIS I. STEIN

In this paper a series of hypotheses will be discussed regarding the personality of the creative individual, his work, the process through which he achieves it, and some of the relationships between these and the culture in which they appear. These hypotheses were developed in the course of studying the personalities of a small number of Chicago artists.[1] The tentative nature of the hypotheses should be emphasized — their validity is still in question. They are now being subjected to test in a study of chemists.

Let us start with a definition. The creative work is a novel work that is accepted as tenable or useful or satisfying by a group in some point in time. Each of the parts of this definition will be considered separately.

By "novel" I mean that the creative product did not exist previously in precisely the same form. It arises from a *reintegration* of already existing materials or knowledge;

when it is completed it contains elements that are new. The extent to which a work is novel depends on the extent to which it deviates from the traditional or the status quo. This may well depend on the nature of the problem that is attacked, the fund of knowledge or experience that exists in the field at the time, and the characteristics of the creative individual and those of the individuals with whom he is communicating.

Often, in studying creativity, we tend to restrict ourselves to a study of the genius because the "distance" between what he has done and what has existed is quite marked. Such an approach causes us to overlook a necessary distinction between the creative product and the creative experience. The child who fixes the bell on his tricycle for the first time may go through stages that are structurally similar to those which characterize the work of the genius. His finished product, however, is a return to a previously existing state of affairs. The product of an inventor's labor, on the other hand, may strike one as creative immediately because it did not exist previously. In

[1]The study of artists was supported by a grant in 1950 from the Social Science Research Committee of the University of Chicago. The study of chemists is now supported by the Research Division of Armour and Co., Chicago, Illinois.

*SOURCE: Reprinted from the *Journal of Psychology*, XXXVI (1953), pp. 311–322.

340

speaking of creativity, therefore, it is necessary to distinguish between internal and external frames of reference.

Turning to the characteristics of the creative experience or creative process and the personality of the creative individual, we adopt a bipolar point of view, in which there is an *interaction* between the creative individual and the problem on which he is working, or, in broader terms, and the environment in which he exists. To speak solely of the existence of the stresses and strains in the environment without due consideration of the individual, as some investigators do, or to deal primarily with the stresses and strains in the individual and to overlook the nature of the problem or the environment as other investigators do, is an arbitrary approach which is a consequence of the specialization in our profession today. Such separate emphases, however, can yield only partial insight and understanding.

The first question that arises in analyzing the creative process is the question of motivation: "Why does the individual create?" This does not differ from any other motivational problem. Therefore, in the early stages of the creative process, the individual experiences a state of disequilibrium — one might say that homeostasis is disturbed, or that there is a lack of closure, or, from a hedonistic point of view, that the individual experiences a lack of satisfaction with the existing state of affairs. On probing more deeply into the roots of the individual's personality, one may realize the historical factors and personal needs which determine the subject's *sensitivity* to such states. The creative person has a lower threshold, or greater sensitivity, for the gaps or the lack of closure that exist in the environment. The sensitivity to these gaps in any one case may stem largely from forces in the environment or from forces in the individual.

Associated with this sensitivity is the creative individual's capacity to *tolerate ambiguity* (1). By "capacity to tolerate ambiguity" I mean that the individual is capable of existing amidst a state of affairs in which he does not comprehend all that is going on, but he continues to effect resolution despite the present lack of homeostasis.

To summarize this early stage of the creative process; the creative individual may be characterized as a system in tension sensitive to the gaps in his experience and capable of maintaining this state of affairs. Some individuals go no further than this point in the creative process. Their creativity is manifested in the fact that they have played a critical role in calling the attention of others to the gaps that exist. But for others the creative process continues to the next stages — hypothesis formation and hypothesis testing. These individuals seek various solutions that would close the gap or that would effect closure.

To be capable of developing such hypotheses, it is suggested that just as there need be some communication between the individual and his environment (i.e., that which was termed sensitivity previously), so there need be communication between some or all of the inner personal regions. Stated somewhat differently, the creative individual is characterized by permeable boundaries that separate the self from the environment and that separate some or all of the regions within the self. At times when this permeability does not exist, it may be induced by the taking of drugs or alcohol as we find to be the case in many creative persons. Or it may exist when the person is distracted or devoting himself to other works.

The character of the inner personal region obviously varies with the nature of the work that is undertaken. For persons in one area (physics, for example) it may mean greater flexibility in the intellectual sphere, while for others, the artist, it appears as a greater flexibility in the emotional or affective sphere. To be sure, there is an interaction between the two spheres, and rigidity in one area may well impede developments in the other and sidetrack the creative process.

This interaction and some of its hazards are well illustrated in Schiller's response to a friend who complains of his lack of creative power. He says:

The reason for your complaint lies, it seems to me, in the constraint which your intellect imposes upon your imagination. Here I will make an observation, and illustrate it by an allegory. Apparently, it is not good — and indeed it hinders the creative work of the mind — if the intellect examines too closely the ideas already pouring in, as it were, at the gates. Regarded in isolation, an idea may be quite insignificant, and venturesome in the extreme, but it may acquire importance from an idea which follows it; perhaps, in a certain collocation with other ideas, which may seem equally absurd, it may be capable of furnishing a very serviceable link. The intellect cannot judge all those ideas unless it can retain them until it has considered them in connection with these other ideas. In the case of a creative mind, it seems to me, the intellect has withdrawn its watchers from the gates, and the ideas rush in pell-mell, and only then does it review and inspect the multitude. You worthy critics, or whatever you may call yourselves, are ashamed or afraid of the momentary and passing madness which is found in all real creators, the longer or shorter duration of which distinguishes the thinking artist from the dreamer. Hence your complaints of unfruitfulness, for you reject too soon and discriminate too severely (2, p. 193).

The "momentary and passing madness" is, I believe, a function of the permeability of the boundaries in the inner personal regions that are usually blocked from consciousness. The intensity of the "momentary and passing madness" is correlated with the depth to which the experience goes. For the artist it may go deeper into subjective experience than for the scientist. Instances of such experiences are described by many creative persons. Thus Zervos, in discussing Picasso's creative process, says:

His only wish has been desperately to be himself, in fact he acts according to suggestions which come to him from beyond his own limits. He sees

descending upon him a superior order of exigencies; he has a very clear impression that something compels him imperiously to empty his spirit of all that he has only just discovered, even before he has been able to control it, so that he can admit other suggestions. Hence his torturing doubts. But this anguish is not a misfortune for Picasso. It is just this which enables him to break down all his barriers, having the field of the possible free to him, and opening up to him the perspectives of the unknown (4, p. 109).

For some persons the creative process may stop during the stage of hypothesis formation. They develop too few hypotheses because of intellectual or emotional reasons, or in the process they become sidetracked by considering a specific intellectual matter that is not relevant to the demands of the moment, or they come upon a previously unresolved emotional difficulty that forces its attention upon them.

The process of hypothesis formation in the creative person is not a haphazard nor rigid process. It is a flexible one that is often characterized by either implicit or explicit direction. The creative individual's time perspective is oriented toward the future. He senses in the present how some aspects of the final form of the product are to appear. Thus Wertheimer, in discussing Einstein's thought processes while he was working on the theory of relativity, says:

Before the discovery that the crucial point, the solution, lay in the concept of time, more particularly in that of simultaneity, axiom played no rôle in the thought process — of this Einstein is sure. (The very moment he saw the gap, and realized the relevance of simultaneity, he knew this to be the crucial point for the solution.) But even afterward, the final five weeks, it was not the axioms that came first. "No really productive man thinks in such a paper fashion," said Einstein.

Later he added:

During all those years there was a feeling of direction, of going straight toward something concrete. It is, of course, very hard to express that feeling in words; but it was decidedly the case, and clearly to be distinguished from later considerations about the rational form of the solution. Of course, behind such a direction there is always something logical; but I have it in a kind of survey, in a way visually (6, p. 183).

It has been observed by some that in the course of the creative process the creative individual experiences depression. The hypothesis is suggested that this depression arises as a result of anxiety that is brought forward by the lack of direction just mentioned. The creative person no longer feels that he is going forward and still he cannot enjoy the present state. The lack of direction may be a consequence of an excessive number of hypotheses that occur to the subject and the feeling of inadequacy as to the possibilities of testing any of them. It may also arise as a result of his inability to communicate his ideas to others. Finally, as the result of the relaxation of the inner personal barriers, old unresolved tensions are brought to the surface which are the residues of earlier life experiences wherein the individual was realistically inadequate — thus there is a process of reinforcement. Indeed, for the creative individual this is only one point in a sequence of events, but for others it may be the end.

After the development of a series of hypotheses, or even simultaneously with them, there is testing of the hypotheses. The testing may vary with the area of the work. For one person it may involve the construction of practical models, while for others it may involve changing the features of a painting. In any case, it is suggested that when the final solution is attained, that is, when there is closure for the individual, he experiences a feeling of satisfaction with the final work, a feeling of exhilaration with the good gestalt. It is this feeling that is manifest in "Eureka" or "This is it!"

Some investigators in the area of creativity who have relied primarily on the Rorschach test have remarked, with some degree of dismay if not disturbance, that the records of their subjects contain responses that are to be found in the records of severely disturbed persons. These responses apparently occur in sufficiently large numbers so that the emotional stability of the subjects is questioned. I would like to suggest that this finding may result from any one or a combination of the following factors. It may indeed be an accurate reflection of the creative person's instability, and it is this instability which may result in the subject's being sensitive to the lack of closure in his environment. It was therefore suggested previously that in the inner personal regions there is communication between *some* or *all* of the regions. The creative person may not necessarily be completely integrated. Some of the factors that differentiate him from the neurotic or the more severely disturbed person, such as tolerance of ambiguity, direction, and a time perspective oriented to the future, have already been discussed. He is also different from the neurotic or psychotic in the next stage — that of communication, which will be discussed below. Furthermore, the Rorschach finding may be a manifestation of the extent to which the creative individual differs from others, and is congruent with his tendency to perceive accepted reality in a manner that differs from most people. By deviating from the traditional and status quo, the individual has achieved the first stage in arriving at the novel work. Furthermore, since many of the so-called "bad" signs in the Rorschach are inadequately formed *Gestalten*, his responses may reflect his ability or capacity to tolerate ambiguity in one area — the perceptual area. The Rorschach responses are then only a sample of an individual's behavior in one area, from which we may infer his behavior in other areas. Finally, to fixate completely on the disturbed aspects of a creative individual's personality is to emphasize a finding that may be an artifact of our present theory, which is oriented, possibly much too heavily, toward psychopathology, and an artifact of the experimental design, which does not take into account aspects of the personality for which the Rorschach is not necessarily the best. Mind you, it is not suggested that the Rorschach finding is invalid, but that it is only part of the story. The part that is not considered sufficiently is the creative person's ability to convey or to communicate his personal experiences to others so that they may react to it.

This brings us to the second part of the definition suggested above: that the creative work is tenable or useful or satisfying. These terms were selected to cover the areas of ideas, things, and aesthetic experiences respectively, although they may well be replaced by other terms. My essential purpose here is to develop the thesis that the results of the creative process must be communicated to others. Communication with the self alone is insufficient. The creative person must achieve, as Sullivan says in another context (5), "consensual validation." This may be clearer if we take the case of the psychotic person. Much of what the psychotic does has significance only within a narrow idiosyncratic framework. At times he may not even be able to communicate his experiences adequately, as one finds in the "word salads" and neologisms of the schizophrenic. And further, the ideas he has do not stand up under test. But the creative person is able to convey his experiences so that they can be tested, or, if he has tested them, so that they may be reacted to by others.

Suggesting that the creative work may be regarded as an element in communication implies at least two factors: (a) The creative person must have available to him means or media through which he can express himself. Just as each of us required training in language to convey our ideas, so it is obvious that to be creative in painting the artist needs some experience in the use of pigments, charcoal, etc., or to be creative in mathematics, and not in others. Such a study might well reveal the congruence that exists between the personalities of the subjects and the areas in which they have selected to work. (b) In the course of communicating his ideas, the creative person needs to abstract or eliminate certain aspects of his work which are completely of himself. In the final stages of communication, the individual must, as Mead would say, bear in mind the "others" with whom he is communicating. The extent to which this occurs varies with the area of work. Thus it is more prevalent in science than in art. But in either case there is a process of evaluation in which completely autistic factors, or the difficulties that were experienced in the course of arriving at a solution, are eliminated. Thus in Einstein's work:

The way the two triple sets of axioms are contrasted in the Einstein-Infeld book is not at all the way things happened in the process of actual thinking. This was merely a later formulation of the subject matter, just a question of how the thing could afterwards best be written. The axioms express essentials in a condensed form. Once one has found such things one enjoys formulating them in that way; but in this process they did not grow out of any manipulation of axioms (6, p. 183).

Similarly, we find that Zervos reports on Picasso's work:

I see for others, that is to say that I can put on canvas the sudden apparitions which force themselves on me. I don't know in advance what I am going to put on the canvas, any more than I decide in advance what colors to use. Whilst I work, I take no stock of what I am painting on the canvas. Every time I begin a picture, I feel as though I were throwing myself into the void. I never know if I shall fall on my feet again. It is only later that I begin to evaluate more exactly the result of my work (4, p. 109).

It should be indicated that at times the creative person may present his work so well after his evaluation that others regard it as "simple," and wonder why they never thought of it.

The next major portion in the definition of the creative work is acceptance by a group. It is suggested that the creative product is congruent with the needs or experiences of a group. It strikes a chord for the group as it does for the individual. The creative product "resonates" with the needs or experience of a group. The use of this word with regard to creativity reminds one of the resonance theory of hearing, in which it is postulated that different wavelengths of sound are heard because they strike different parts of the basilar membrane. To make an analogy between this and creativity, one might say that creative products resonate all along a responsive membrane. Thus certain art works resonate with feelings, while inventions resonate because they fulfill practical needs. In the case of art, it should be pointed out that there is not always a one-to-one relationship between what the artist attempted to express and what it resonated in the group. The conditions under which this does or does not occur are a matter for further investigation.

Acceptance by a group is significant. It provides the creative worker with his final test of reality, if you wish. The size of the group may vary. At times it may be only those on the "left bank," Greenwich Village, or the small number of persons who first gathered around Freud and Einstein. Individuals may seek out the creative person or he may have to proselytize them. The group provides the individual with necessary feedback so that he can clarify, alter, or make progress in his future work.

Finally, we arrive at the last point in our definition: that the creative work is accepted at some point in time. The historical point of view reflected by the phrase "some point in time" is inserted in the definition to account for the fact that some men, like Van Gogh, may not be considered creative in their own lifetime; as a matter of fact, some, like Socrates, pay dearly for their ideas. Yet when the works of art or the ideas are re-

discovered or are brought to attention at some future date, when the forces of society have changed, it is only then that these persons attain their rightful places in history Indeed in some areas of creativity there may be "universals," e.g., form and use of space in art with only content varying in time. But in determining the validity of such universals, one needs to be aware of the hazard that what we regard as the critical elements in the universals today is a function of ourselves, and it may not necessarily be congruent with the manner in which these works were regarded in their own times.

The discussion, up to this point, has been limited primarily to the creative individual and the creative process. Let us now turn to a consideration of the interaction between the processes described and culture.

If what was said previously regarding the sensitivity of the creative individual in relation to both his external and internal environments is valid, then it may be said that a culture fosters creativity to the extent that it provides an individual with the opportunity to experience its many facets. A culture that limits the freedom of a person to study in one or a variety of areas cuts down his opportunity to pick out the gaps that exist in the culture and also keeps him from learning the necessary media of communicating his feelings or ideas.

A culture also fosters creativity to the extent that its parent-child relationships and child-rearing techniques do or do not result in the setting up of rigid boundaries in the inner personal regions.[2] Techniques that result in excessive repression or guilt restrict internal freedom and interfere with the process of hypothesis formation. Attention must also be directed toward the broader aspects of education. For example, does the culture tolerate deviation from the traditional, the status quo, or does it insist upon

[2]Indeed, certain cultures set up rigid boundaries in certain regions and not others. This will no doubt affect the areas of creative work.

conformity, whether in politics science, or at school? Does the culture permit the individual to seek new experiences on his own, or do the bearers of culture (parents, teachers, and so on) "spoon-feed" the young so that they constantly find ready-made solutions available to them as they come upon a situation that is lacking in closure? Furthermore, to what extent do the adults accept or reward and thus reinforce the creative experience that the individual has had? For example, in the case I spoke of earlier — the child who fixed his tricycle bell — his experience could have been handled either by a depreciation of his experience and verbalized as, "Oh, anyone could have done that!" or the magnitude of his experience for himself could have been recognized and he could have been encouraged to seek similar experiences in the future. Experiences of this kind should be studied both in the home and in formal educational systems.

The stage of development of a culture obviously influences the means available to the individual for creative progress. Thus the modern physicist has new vistas open to him as a result of the recent developments in nuclear physics. From the experience in this area, it may be said that the variety of creative works that occur in a culture vary with the number of works that deviate markedly from the traditional and are accepted. Only with the acceptance of the theory of relativity and other findings was the present development of physics possible, and we may well expect many new discoveries and applications in this area.

The culture may be marked by strict adherence to a specific philosophy, and this too influences progress in the arts and sciences. Giedion (3) suggests how a mechanistic view of the universe has effected the work in many areas of inquiry. And in the course of modern history, we have seen how various political and religious movements have at times stimulated and then markedly limited progress. Points of view which are

developed in one area and studied by a worker in another way may aid the latter in sensitizing him to the gaps in his fund of knowledge. This is manifest in the recent developments in communication theory in the social sciences which were stimulated by the physicist. The extent to which progress is made in the new area of application may well depend on the rigidities of the philosophy that is adopted and/or on the manner in which it is interpreted and followed by those who accept it. For example, present-day mechanism and materialism have caused Giedion to suggest that we have been overlooking humanism, and he highlights the need for a man who can live in "equipoise."

Furthermore, philosophies of life undergo cyclic change as a result of a multitude of factors. When a "valley" appears, the extent to which a culture comes out of it depends on the extent to which it is capable of tolerating ambiguity and encourages and tolerates a diversity of viewpoints as a new philosophy is developed. Further research might therefore be centered around the comparison of creative works when there is a consistent *Weltanschauung* and when one is lacking or when there is a conflict of philosophies.

Finally we come to a specific aspect of the culture — the audience with whom the creative person communicates — the critic, the patron, the followers, and the population at large.

The critic plays a very significant sociological role in determining what the larger population has available to it as instances of creativity. When we started our study of creative artists, we had a difficult time in getting critics to agree on who was a creative painter. Reputable persons in the art world disagreed with each other. Now let us assume that one of the critics, as was the case, is the curator of a gallery. That person would hang the works of one artist and not the other. For some people, because of the prestige of a museum, this work now becomes a "creative" work. But what of the others? They have to wait to be "discovered" by other critics and this may even happen, if they are fortunate, in their own lifetime. It might be wise, therefore, to study the personalities of critics or the supporters of scientific research, since they play such important roles in determining what is creativity.

In some respects similar to both the critic and the supporter of scientific research is the patron of arts. He, by virtue of the fact that he contributes financially to the artist's support, must be communicated with. How much of the patron's needs enter into the artist's evaluation of his final work depends on the relationship that exists between the two. The patron, just as was said of the broader culture, may well direct and restrict the content of his artist's work, if not the manner in which he works, because of his financial position. This raises a more crucial question in our own time when there are few, if any, patrons of the arts who are comparable to the Medicis, let us say. Is there anything to the hypothesis that *one* of the factors resulting in the development of nonobjective art is the fact that the artist no longer is subservient to a patron and he can therefore express himself as he wishes?

In considering the final stages of the creative process, it was suggested that the creative work must strike a chord or resonate in some manner with the group that accepts it. If this hypothesis is valid, then it would follow that the personalities or the experiences of the group are in some manner similar to those of the creative individual. It may be further suggested that studies of creative products provide some data for making inferences regarding the needs of the group that are being statisfied. Thus it may be suggested that one of the factors involved in the acceptance of modern art today is that it represents a retreat or a rebellion, if you wish, against the materi-

alism and intellectualism that has marked much of our time. It is a voice speaking against a period in which there is a denial of certain feelings. To be sure, to make similar interpretations of previous cultures may be hazardous if this is accepted as the only evidence. We cannot completely put ourselves in the place of primitive man.

Finally, one must also consider the problem of communication between the creative individual and the population at large. In some areas of works, such as practical inventions, communication may exist with an extremely large portion of the population because they are aware of an invention's demonstrated usefulness. Indeed, communication may stop when it is necessary to understand the thinking that has gone into the development. Modern artists have been most vociferous in asking why their art is not appreciated more widely than it is, especially when they as individuals feel that they have captured the spirit and problems of the day. This raises the question whether in an "age of anxiety" some individuals do not find it safer for themselves not to be aware of the problems that exist around them. Just as society affects the creative process by developing individuals who cannot relax the boundaries in the internal and external regions, so the extent to which an audience does resonate with an art product is a reflection of the extent to which they as perceivers are capable of relaxing their defenses. Thus by studying the "nonappreciators" we can also learn a great deal of the culture.

In summary then: A definition of the creative work was presented. A creative work is a novel work that is accepted as tenable or useful or satisfying by a group in time. In line with this, it was hypothesized that studies of the personality of the creative individual may reveal a sensitivity to the gaps that exist in his own culture, and his creativity may be manifest in calling attention to these gaps or in finding a means of effecting closure, or his sensitivity to certain facets of this may result in his desire to communicate to others. In addition to sensitivity, attention was called to the creative individual's ability to tolerate ambiguity and to maintain direction as he develops and tests his hypotheses. The final product, considered as an element in communication, resonates with the needs or experiences of a group at some point in time. In considering cultural factors, it was hypothesized that the extent to which a variety of creative products are developed depends on the extent to which cultural influences permit the development of both freedom between the individual and his environment and freedom within the individual; or the extent to which the culture encourages diversity and tolerates the seeming ambiguity that such diversity suggests. We also considered certain aspects of the audience, specifically the critic, the patron, the appreciators, and the population at large, with whom the creative person communicates. The experimental problems involved in testing the hypotheses mentioned are numerous, but they are not insurmountable.

REFERENCES

1. FRENKEL-BRUNSWIK, E. "Intolerance of Ambiguity As an Emotional and Perceptual Personality Variable." In *Perception and Personality* (Bruner, J. S., & D. Krech, Eds.). Durham: Duke Univ. Press, 1949.

2. FREUD, S. *The Basic Writings of Sigmund Freud* (Brill, A. A., Ed.). New York: Random House, 1938.

3. GIEDION, S. *Mechanization Takes Command.* New York: Oxford Univ. Press, 1948.

4. READ, H. *Art Now.* New York: Pitman, 1948.

5. SULLIVAN, H. S. "Conceptions of Modern Psychiatry." Reprinted from *Psychiatry*, 3 (1940) and 8 (1945).

6. WERTHEIMER, M. *Productive Thinking.* New York: Harper, 1945.

SUGGESTED READINGS FOR PART V

1. BEITTEL, KENNETH R. "The Creativity Complex in the Visual Arts," *Studies in Art Education,* I (1959), 26–37.

2. BRITTAIN, W. LAMBERT, and KENNETH R. BEITTEL. "Analyses of Levels of Creative Performances in the Visual Arts," *The Journal of Aesthetics and Art Criticism,* XIX (1960), 83–90.

3. DREVDAHL, JOHN E. "Factors of Importance for Creativity," *Journal of Clinical Psychology,* XII (1956), 21–26.

4. LOWENFELD, VIKTOR. "Creative Intelligence," *Studies in Art Education,* I (1960), 22–25.

5. MACKINNON, DONALD W., Ed. *The Creative Person.* Berkeley: University of California, General Extension, 1962.

6. STEIN, MORRIS I., and SHIRLEY J. HEINZE. *Creativity and the Individual:* Summaries of Selected Literature in Psychology and Psychiatry. Glencoe, Illinois: The Free Press, 1960.

PART VI

HOW SHOULD ART
PERFORMANCE BE
EVALUATED?

Perhaps the question that should precede the title of this section is, Should art performance be evaluated? This is by no means a meaningless question. To a host of people working in the field of art education, evaluation is intimately related to grading, and grading, they say, should not occur in the field of art. For one, grading children's art products often creates anxieties and these anxieties hamper creative expression. The child needs to feel secure rather than anxious, supported by the teacher rather than threatened. Evaluating his work and grading it, which is the usual outcome of evaluation, tends to make the student feel both insecure and threatened.

Another argument put forth by those who look skeptically on evaluation is that art, by its nature, cannot be evaluated. They claim that criteria are applicable in the discursive and theoretical domains are not applicable in art. Art is a personal thing, it is a unique expression of a unique individual, it has no set rules and therefore it cannot be compared or evaluated.

The critics go on to state that when evaluation takes place the teacher tends to concern himself with the product and not with the process. And it is the process that the child undergoes in creating an art object and not the art object itself that is of the greatest importance. The process is important because it is this process which develops the creative powers of the child. It is this process which elicits the child's imaginative capacities and which engages his deepest and most personal feelings. One of the major purposes of art education, they hold, is to free the child from the restrictions of the outer world by developing those cognitive and affective abilities that art media elicit. If the product becomes the focus of the teacher's attention, it is likely to divert him from the central issue — the child's creative capacities — and is likely, therefore, to hamper the development of these capacities.

Another argument that is offered by those critical of evaluation of children's art is that one cannot justify one's likes and dislikes in art. Art preferences in the last analysis are a matter of taste and "In matters of taste there can be no dispute." Describing and even analyzing and comparing art products, these critics claim, is perfectly valid. Indeed, it is a necessary part of instruction in art, but evaluation, in the sense of making value judgments about the art produced in terms of its goodness or badness, is not appropriate because it cannot be defended. There is no empirical test for aesthetic quality in art, hence there is no justification for judgment about quality in art. The language of the critic may be persuasive, his style may be powerful and one might be swept into agreement with his judgment about a particular work, but this judgment is essentially personal and its validity cannot be tested.

Still another argument is that evaluation of a child's art product by an adult more often than not rests upon criteria that have little meaning or relevance to the child. The world of the child, the types of thought processes he uses, the way he considers his work in the field of art, are simply irrelevant to the type of criteria that an adult is likely to apply in evaluating his work. Psychologists have indicated that human beings go through a rather predictable sequence of stages in their cognitive development. The child in the elementary school is still undergoing this process of cognitive development. Perceptual powers too are in a state of evolution, hence the object produced in art is a product of these still immature levels of development. And to apply criteria through the eyes of an adult whose stages of perceptual and cognitive development have reached maturity is not only difficult and irrelevant to the child, it is unfair. It is unfair because it tends to make children feel responsible for meeting standards in art for which they lack readiness, hence the typical outcome is one of breeding a sense of failure and disappointment in the child.

As persuasive as these arguments may seem, those who endorse evaluation as a procedure in art instruction offer equally as persuasive counter arguments. Their grounds, like those who criticize evaluation of children's art, are numerous. Supporters of evaluation claim that the school has certain objectives that it wishes to attain. These objectives are developed not only for the school at large but for each of the subject areas constituting the curriculum. Instruction and content within these various subject areas are merely means for attaining educational ends, hence not to determine through evaluation that these ends have or have not been obtained is to remain ignorant of the effectiveness of the program. The field of art like other fields of study has objectives and if evaluation is not made, curricular changes can only occur by whim and fancy without the type of evidence that evaluation of student performance is likely to supply.

Another argument that is used to support evaluation practices in art is especially strong. This argument holds that if one claims that there are no applicable or justifiable criteria for determining quality in art, evaluation is not possible. But if this is so then there can be no instruction either, except of course for the teaching of mere technical skills and procedures. If a teacher cannot evaluate a student's art work, he cannot decide if the student is progressing or regressing in art, he cannot decide if the activities he has planned have been effective or if he should select one type of material or another for instructional purposes. If art is truly only a matter of taste, claim the supporters of evaluation, then why shouldn't the student's artistic taste be just as valid as the teacher's? But to accept this conclusion is to relinquish the teacher's claim to any artistic expertise and to render him virtually useless in the matter of instruction in art.

Those supporting evaluation of children's art claim that it is not necessary for the teacher to apply criteria that are irrelevant or meaningless to the child. They claim that children, even at the earliest ages in school, need and want criticism and that honest evaluative appraisal is necessary for the child. Such evaluation provides a sense of direction and a framework that is necessary for the child's security, the very thing which those who oppose evaluation claim to be so important. Without aesthetic criteria and a teacher who is skilled in their application, children soon become bewildered and disenchanted with their own work in art. The application of aesthetic criteria in evaluating children's art is a necessary condition for effective teaching.

It should be clear that the issues and arguments involved in the evaluation of children's art are far from settled. Few areas in the field of art education are as complex and vexing. Should children's art-work be evaluated? Can it be validly assessed? How should evaluations be made? Who should evaluate student work in art? What types of criteria should be applied? Is the process more important than the product. Are both equally as important? Should children's art-work be graded? Should children's work be compared? What about prizes and art contests? Are these an asset or detriment to the child and his development in art?

These are some of the questions that art educators have been concerned with. They are questions that classroom teachers face whenever they teach art. How do you answer these questions? The sections constituting this chapter represent some answers that have been developed by people who have given some thought to this complex area in the field of art education.

28. Criticism and Perception

JOHN DEWEY

Criticism is judgment, ideally as well as etymologically. Understanding of judgment is therefore the first condition for theory about the nature of criticism. Perceptions supply judgment with its material, whether the judgments pertain to physical nature, to politics or biography. The subject-matter of perception is the only thing that makes the difference in the judgments which ensue. Control of the subject-matter of perception for ensuring proper data for judgment is the key to the enormous distinction between the judgments the savage passes on natural events and that of a Newton or an Einstein. Since the matter of aesthetic criticism is the perception of aesthetic objects, natural and artistic criticism is always determined by the quality of first-hand perception; obtuseness in perception can never be made good by any amount of learning, however extensive, nor any command of abstract theory, however correct. Nor is it possible to exclude judgment from entering into aesthetic perception, or at least from supervening upon a first total unanalyzed qualitative impression.

Theoretically, it should therefore be possible to proceed at once from direct aesthetic experience to what is involved in judgment, the clues, being given on one side from the formed matter of works of art as they exist in perception, and, on the other side, from what is involved in judgment by the nature of its own structure. But, in fact, it is first necessary to clear the ground. For unreconciled differences as to the nature of judgment are reflected in theories of criticism, while diverse tendencies among the arts have given rise to opposed theories that are developed and asserted for the sake of justifying one movement and condemning another. Indeed, there is ground for holding that the most vital questions in aesthetic theory are generally to be found in controversies regarding special movements in some art, like "functionalism" in architecture, "pure" poetry or free verse in literature, "expressionism" in the drama, the "stream of consciousness" in the novel, "proletarian art" and the relation of the artist to economic conditions and revolutionary social activities. Such controversies may be at-

*SOURCE: Reprinted from John Dewey, *Art as Experience*, pp. 298–325.

tended with heat and prejudice. But they are more likely to be conducted with an eye directed upon concrete works of art than are lucubrations upon aesthetic theory in the abstract. Yet they complicate the theory of criticism with ideas and aims derived from external partisan movements.

It cannot be safely assumed at the outset that judgment is an act of intelligence performed upon the matter of direct perception in the interest of a more adequate perception. For judgment has also a legalistic meaning and import, as in Shakespeare's phrase, " a critic, nay, a night watchman." Following the signification supplied by the practice of the law, a judge, a critic, is one who pronounces an authoritative sentence. We hear constantly of the verdict of critics, and of the verdict of history pronounced upon works of art. Criticism is thought of as if its business were not explication of the content of an object as to substance and form, but a process of acquittal or condemnation on the basis of merits and demerits.

The judge — in the judicial sense — occupies a seat of social authority. His sentence determines the fate of an individual, perhaps of a cause, and upon occasion it settles the legitimacy of future courses of action. Desire for authority (and desire to be looked up to) animates the human breast. Much of our existence is keyed to the note of praise and blame, exculpation and disapproval. Hence there has emerged in theory, reflecting a widespread tendency in practice, a disposition to erect criticism into something "judicial." One cannot read widely in the outgivings of this school of criticism without seeing that much of it is of the compensatory type — the fact which has given rise to the gibe that critics are those who have failed in creation. Much criticism of the legalistic sort proceeds from subconscious self-distrust and a consequent appeal to authority for protection. Perception is obstructed and cut short by memory of an influence rule, and by the substitution of

precedent and prestige for direct experience. Desire for authoritative standing leads the critic to speak as if he were the attorney for established principles having unquestionable sovereignty.

Unfortunately such activities have infected the very conception of criticism. Judgment that is final, that settles a matter, is more congenial to unregenerate human nature than is the judgment that is a development in thought of a deeply realized perception. The original adequate experience is not easy to attain; its achievement is a test of native sensitiveness and of experience matured through wide contacts. A judgment as an act of controlled inquiry demands a rich background and a disciplined insight. It is much easier to "tell" people what they should believe than to discriminate and unify. And an audience that is itself habituated to being told, rather than schooled in thoughtful inquiry, likes to be told.

Judicial decision can be made only on the basis of general rules supposed to be applicable to all cases. The harm done by particular instances of judicial sentence, as particular, is much less serious than the net result in developing the notion and antecedent authoritative standards and precedents at hand by which to judge. The so-called classicism of the eighteenth century alleged that the ancients provided models from which rules could be derived. The influence of this belief extended from literature to other branches of art. Reynolds recommended to students of art the observance of the art-forms of Umbrian and Roman painters, and, warning them against others, said of Tintoretto that his inventions are "wild, capricious, extravagant and fantastic."

A temperate view of the importance of the models furnished by the past is given by Matthew Arnold. He says that the best way to discover "what poetry belongs to the class of the truly excellent, and *can therefore do us the most good*, is to have always in one's mind lines and expressions of the great masters, and to apply them as a touchstone to other poetry." He denies that he means that other poetry should be reduced to imitation, but says that such lines are an "infallible touchstone for detecting the presence or absence of high poetic quality." Aside from the moralistic element involved in the words I have taken the liberty of italicizing, the idea of an "infallible" test is bound, if acted upon, to limit direct response in perception, to introduce self-consciousness and reliance upon extraneous factors, all harmful to vital appreciation. Moreover, there is involved the question as to whether the masterpieces of the past are accepted as such because of personal response or on the authority of tradition and convention. Matthew Arnold is really assuming an ultimate dependence upon someone's personal power of just perception.

Representatives of the school of judicial criticism do not seem to be sure whether the masters are great because they observe certain rules or whether the rules now to be observed are derived from the practice of great men. In general, it is safe to assume, I think, that reliance upon rules is a weakened, a mitigated, version of a prior, more direct, admiration, finally become servile, of the work of outstanding personalities. But whether they are set up on their own account or are derived from masterpieces, standards, prescriptions, and rules are general while objects of art are individual. The former have no locus in time, a fact naïvely stated in calling them eternal. They belong neither here nor there. In applying to everything, they apply to nothing in particular. In order to get concreteness, they have to be referred for exemplification to the work of the "masters." Thus in fact they encourage imitation. The masters themselves usually serve an apprenticeship, but as they mature they absorb what they have learned into their own individual experience, vision, and style. They are masters precisely because they do not follow either models or rules but subdue both of these things to serve enlargement of personal experience. Tolstoi spoke as an artist when he said that "nothing so contributes to the perversion of art as these authorities set up by criticism." Once an artist is pronounced great "all his works are regarded as admirable and worthy of imitation. . . . Every false work extolled is a door through which hypocrites of art creep in."

If judicial critics do not learn modesty from the past they profess to esteem, it is not from lack of material. Their history is largely the record of egregious blunders. The commemorative exhibition of paintings by Renoir in Paris in the summer of 1933 was the occasion for exhuming some of the deliverances of official critics of fifty years before. The pronouncements vary from assertions that the paintings cause a nausea like that of sea-sickness, are products of diseased minds — a favorite statement — that they mix at random the most violent colors, to an assertion that they "are denials of all that is *permissible* [characteristic word] in painting, of everything called light, transparence and shade, clarity and design." As late as 1897, a group of academicians (always the favorites of judicial criticism) protested against the acceptance by the Luxembourg Museum of a collection of paintings by Renoir, Cézanne, and Monet, and one of them stated that it was impossible that the Institute should be silent in the presence of such a scandal as reception of a collection of insanities since it is the guardian of tradition — another idea characteristic of judicial criticism.[1]

There is, however, a certain lightness of touch usually associated with French criticism. For real majesty of pronunciamento we may turn to the outgivings of an

---

[1]The greater part of the collection is now in the Louvre—a sufficient comment on the competency of official criticism.

American critic on the occasion of the Armory exhibition in New York in 1913. Under the caption of the ineffectualness of Cézanne, it is said that the latter is "a second-rate impressionist who had now and then fair luck in painting a moderately good picture." The "crudities" of Van Gogh are disposed of as follows: "A moderately competent impressionist who was heavy-handed (!), and who had little idea of beauty and spoiled a lot of canvas with crude and unimportant pictures." Matisse is disposed of as one who has "relinquished all respect for technique, all feeling for his medium; content to daub his canvas with linear and tonal coarseness. Their negation of all that true art implies is significant of smug complacency . . . . They are not works of art but feeble impertinences." The reference to "true art" is characteristic of judicial criticism, never more injudicious than in this case with its reversal of what is significant in the artists mentioned: Van Gogh being explosive rather than heavy-handed; Matisse being a technician almost to a fault, and inherently decorative rather than coarse; while "second-rate" applied to Cézanne speaks for itself. Yet this critic had by this time accepted the impressionist painting of Manet and Monet — it was 1913 instead of twenty years earlier; and his spiritual offspring will doubtless hold up Cézanne and Matisse as standards by which to condemn some future movement in the art of painting.

The "criticism" just quoted was preceded by other remarks that indicate the nature of the fallacy that is always involved in legalistic criticism: confusion of a particular technique with aesthetic form. The critic in question quoted from a published comment of a visitor who was not a professional critic. The latter said, "I never heard a crowd of people talk so much about meaning and about life and so little about technique, values, tones, drawing, perspective, studies in blue and white, etc." Then the judicial critic adds: "We are grateful for this bit of concrete evidence of the fallacy which more than others threatens to mislead and completely obfuscate the too-confiding observers. To go to this exhibition with a solicitude about 'meaning' and about 'life' at the expense of matters of technique is not simply to beg the question; it is to give it away with both hands. In art, elements of 'meaning' and 'life' do not exist until the artist has mastered those technical processes by which he may or may not have genius to call them [sic] into being."

The unfairness of the implication that the author of the comment intended to rule out matters of technique is so characteristic of alleged judicial criticism that it is significant only because it indicates how completely the critic can think of technique only as it is identified with some one model of procedure. And this fact is deeply significant. It indicates the source of the failure of even the best of judicial criticism: its inability to cope with the emergence of new modes of life — of experiences that demand. new modes of expression. All of the post-impressionist painters (with the partial exception of Cézanne) had shown in their early works that they had command of the techniques of the masters that immediately preceded them. The influence of Courbet, Delacroix, even of Ingres, pervades them. But these techniques were suited to the rendering of old themes. As these painters matured, they had new visions; they saw the world in ways to which older painters were insensitive. Their new subject-matter demanded a new form. And because of the relativity of technique to form, they were compelled to experiment with the development of new technical procedures. An environment that is changed physically and spiritually demands new forms of expression.

I repeat that here we have exposed the inherent defect of even the best of judicial criticism. The very meaning of an important new movement in any art is that it expresses something new in human experience, some new mode of interaction of the live creature with his surroundings, and hence the release of powers previously cramped or inert. The manifestations of the movement therefore cannot be judged but only misjudged when form is identified with a familiar technique. Unless the critic is sensitive first of all to "meaning and life" as the matter which requires its own form, he is helpless in the presence of the emergence of experience that has a distinctively new character. Every professional person is subject to the influence of custom and inertia, and has to protect himself from its influences by a deliberate openness to life itself. The judicial critic erects the very things that are the dangers of his calling into a principle and norm.

The blundering ineptness of much that calls itself judicial criticism has called out a reaction to the opposite extreme. The protest takes the form of "impressionist" criticism. It is in effect, if not in words, a denial that criticism in the sense of judgment is possible, and an assertion that judgment should be replaced by statement of the responses of feeling and imagery the art object evokes. In theory, though not always in practice, such criticism reacts from the standardized "objectivity" of ready-made rules and precedents to the chaos of a subjectivity that lacks objective control, and would, if logically followed out, result in a medley of irrelevancies — and sometimes does. Jules Lemaître has given an almost canonical statement of the impressionistic point of view. He said: "Criticism, whatever be its pretensions, can never go beyond defining the impression which, at a given moment, is made on us by a work of art wherein the artist has himself recorded the impression which he received from the world at a certain hour."

The statement includes an implication which, when it is made explicit, goes far beyond the intention of the impressionist theory. To *define* an impression signifies a good deal more than just to utter it. Impressions, total qualitative unanalyzed effects that things and events make upon us, are the antecedents and beginnings of all judgments.[3] The beginning of a new idea, terminating perhaps in an elaborate judgment following upon extensive inquiry, is an impression, even in the case of a scientific man or philosopher. But to define an impression is to analyze it, and analysis can proceed only by going beyond the impression, by referring it to the grounds on which it rests and the consequences which it entails. And this procedure is judgment. Even if the one who communicates his impression confines his exposition of it, his demarcation and delimitation, to grounds that lie in his own temperament and personal history, taking the reader frankly into his confidence, he still goes beyond the bare impression to something objective in it. Thus he gives the reader ground for an "impression" on his own part that is more objectively grounded than any impression can be that is founded on a mere "it seems to me." For the experienced reader is then given the means of discriminating among different impressions of different persons on the basis of the bias and experience of the person who has them.

The reference to objective grounds having begun with statement of personal history cannot stop there. The biography of the one who defines his impression is not located inside his own body and mind. It is what it is because of interactions with the world outside, a world which in some of its aspects and phases is common with that of others. If the critic is wise, he judges the impression that occurs at a certain hour of his own history by considering the objective causes that have entered into that history. Unless he does so, at least implicitly, the discriminating reader has to perform

[3]See *ante*, p. 191.

the task for him — unless he surrenders himself blindly to the "authority" of the impression itself. In the latter case, there is no difference among impressions; the insight of a cultivated mind and the gush of the immature enthusiast stand on the same level.

The sentence quoted from Lemaître has another significant implication. It sets forth a proportion that is objective: as his subject-matter is to the artist, so is the work of art to the critic. If the artist is numb and if he does not impregnate some immediate impression with meanings derived from a prior rich funded experience, his product is meager and its form is mechanical. The case is not otherwise with a critic. There is an illicit suggestion contained in the reference to the impression of the artist as occurring at a "certain hour" and that of the critic as taking place "at a given moment." The suggestion is that because the impression exists at a particular moment, its import is limited to that brief space of time. The implication is the fundamental fallacy of impressionist criticism. Every experience, even that containing a conclusion due to long processes of inquiry and reflection, exists at a "given moment." To infer from this fact that its import and validity are affairs of that passing moment is to reduce all experience to a shifting kaleidoscope of meaningless incidents.

Moreover, the comparison of the attitude of a critic toward a work of art to that of the artist toward his subject-matter is so just as to be fatal to the impressionist theory. For the impression the artist has does not consist of impressions; it consists of objective material rendered by means of imaginative vision. The subject-matter is charged with meanings that issue from intercourse with a common world. The artist in the freest expression of his own responses is under weighty objective compulsions. The trouble with very much criticism, aside from the impressionist label, is that the critic does *not* take an attitude toward the work criti-cized that an artist takes toward the "impressions he has received from the world." The critic can go off into irrelevancies and arbitrary dicta much more readily than the artist, while failure to be controlled by subject-matter is much more evident to eye and ear than is a corresponding failure on the part of the critic. The tendency of the critic to dwell in a world apart is great enough in any case without being sanctioned by a special theory.

Were it not for the blunders made by the judicial critic, blunders that proceed from the theory he holds, the reaction of the impressionist theory would hardly have been called forth. Because the former set up false notions of objective values and objective standards, it was made easy for the impressionist critic to deny there are objective values at all. Because the former has virtually adopted a conception of standards that is of an external nature, derived from use of standards developed for practical ends, and legally defined, the latter has assumed there are no criteria of any sort. In its precise signification, a "standard" is unambiguous. It is a quantitative measure. The yard as a standard of length, the gallon as a standard of liquid capacity, are as precise as legal definitions can make them. The standard of liquid measure for Great Britain was defined, for example, by an act of Parliament in 1825. It is a container holding ten pounds avoirdupois of distilled water, weighed in air with the barometer at thirty inches and the Fahrenheit thermometer at sixty-two degrees.

There are three characteristics of a standard. It is a particular physical thing existing under specified physical conditions; it is *not* a value. The yard is a yard-stick, and the meter is a bar deposited in Paris. In the second place, standards are measures of definite things, of lengths, weights, capacities. The things measured are not values, although it is of great social value to be able to measure them, since the properties of things in the way of size, volume, weight, are important for commercial exchange. Finally, as standards of measure, standards define things with respect to *quantity*. To be able to measure quantities is a great aid to further judgments, but it is not itself a mode of judgment. The standard, being an external and public thing, is applied *physically*. The yard-stick is physically laid down upon the things measured to determine their length.

When, therefore, the word "standard" is used with respect to judgment of works of art, nothing but confusion results, unless the radical difference in the meaning now given standard from that of standards of measurement is noted. The critic is really judging, not measuring physical fact. He is concerned with something individual, not comparative — as is all measurement. His subject-matter is qualitative, not quantitative. There is no external and public thing, defined by law to be the same for all transactions, that can be physically applied. The child who can use a yard-stick can measure as well as the most experienced and mature person, if he can handle the stick, since measuring is not judgment but is a physical operation performed for the sake of determining value in exchange or in behalf of some further physical operation — as a carpenter measures the boards with which he builds. The same cannot be said of judgment of the value of an idea or the value of a work of art.

Because of failure of critics to realize the difference between the meaning of standard as applied in measurement and as used in judgment or criticism, Mr. Grudin can say of a critic who is a believer in a fixed standard with respect to works of art: "His procedure has been that of an excursion for words and notions to support his claims, wherever he could find them; and he has had to trust to the meanings he could read into already available odds and ends belonging to various fields and gathered into a

makeshift critical doctrine." And this, he adds with not too great severity, is the usual procedure followed by literary critics.

Yet it does not follow because of absence of a uniform and publicly determined external object, that objective criticism of art is impossible. What follows is that criticism is judgment; that like every judgment it involves a venture, a hypothetical element; that it is directed to qualities which are nevertheless qualities of an *object;* and that it is concerned with an individual object, not with making comparisons by means of an external preestablished rule between different things. The critic, because of the element of venture, reveals himself in his criticisms. He wanders into another field and confuses values when he departs from the object he is judging. Nowhere are comparisons so odious as in fine art.

Appreciation is said to occur with respect to values, and criticism is currently supposed to be a process of valuation. There is, of course, truth in the conception. But it is fraught, in current interpretation, with a host of equivocations. After all, one is concerned with the values of a poem, a stage-play, a painting. One is aware of them as qualities-in-qualitative-relations. One does not at the time categorize them *as* values. One may pronounce a play fine or "rotten." If one term such direct characterization valuing, then criticism is *not* valuing. It is a very different sort of thing than a direct ejaculation. Criticism is a search for the properties of the object that may justify the direct reaction. And yet, if the search is sincere and informed, it is not, when it is undertaken, concerned with values but with the objective properties of the object under consideration — if a painting, with its colors, lights, placings, volumes, in their relations to one another. It is a survey. The critic may or may not at the end pronounce definitely upon the total "value" of the object. If he does, his pronouncement will be more intelligent than it would otherwise have been, because his perceptive appreciation is now more instructed. But when he does sum up his judgment of the object, he will, if he is wary, do so in a way that is a summary of the outcome of his objective examination. He will realize that his assertion of "good" or "bad" in this and that degree is something the goodness or badness of which is itself to be tested by other persons in their direct perceptual commerce with the object. His criticism issues as a social document and can be checked by others to whom the same objective material is available. Hence the critic, if he is wise, even in making pronouncements of good and bad, of great and small in value, will lay more emphasis upon the objective traits that sustain his judgment than upon values in the sense of excellent and poor. Then his surveys may be of assistance in the direct experience of others, as a survey of a country is of help to the one who travels through it, while dicta about worth operate to limit personal experience.

If there are no standards for works of art and hence none for criticism (in the sense in which there are standards of measurement), there are nevertheless criteria in judgment, so that criticism does not fall in the field of mere impressionism. The discussion of form in relation to matter, of the meaning of medium in art, of the nature of the expressive object, has been an attempt on the part of the writer to discover some of these criteria. But such criteria are not rules or prescriptions. They are the result of an endeavor to find out what a work of art is as an experience: the kind of experience which constitutes it. As far as the conclusions are valid, they are of use as instrumentalities of personal experience, not as dictations of what the attitude of any one should be. Stating what a work of art is as an experience may render particular experiences of particular works of art more pertinent to the object experienced, more aware of its own content and intent. This is all

any criterion can do; and if and as far as the conclusions are invalid, better criteria are to be set forth by an improved examination of the nature of works of art in general as a mode of human experience.

Criticism is judgment. The material out of which judgment grows is the work, the object, but it is this object as it enters into the experience of the critic by interaction with his own sensitivity and his knowledge and funded store from past experiences. As to their content, therefore, judgments will vary with the concrete material that evokes them and that must sustain them if criticism is pertinent and valid. Nevertheless, judgments have a common form because they all have certain functions to perform. These functions are discrimination and unification. Judgment has to evoke a clearer consciousness of constituent parts and to discover how consistently these parts are related to form a whole. Theory gives the names of analysis and synthesis to the execution of these functions.

They cannot be separated from each other, because analysis is disclosure of parts as parts of a whole; of details and particulars as belonging to a total situation, a universe of discourse. This operation is the opposite of picking to pieces or dissection, even when something of the latter sort is required in order to make judgment possible. No rules can be laid for the performance of so delicate an act as determination of the significant parts of a whole, and of their respective places and weights in the whole. This is the reason, perhaps, why scholarly dissertations upon literature are so often merely scholastic enumerations of minutiae, and so-called criticisms of paintings are of the order of analyses of handwriting by experts.

Analytic judgment is a test of the mind of the critic, since mind, as organization into perceptions of meanings derived from past intercourse with objects, is the organ of discrimination. Hence the safeguard of the critic is a consuming informed interest. I say "consuming" because without natural sensitivity connected with an intense liking for certain subject-matters, a critic, having even a wide range of learning, will be so cold that there is no chance of his penetrating the heart of a work of art. He will remain on the outside. Yet, unless affection is informed with the insight that is the product of a rich and full experience, judgment will be one-sided or not rise above the level of gushy sentimentalism. Learning must be the fuel of warmth of interest. For the critic in the field of art, this informed interest signifies acquaintance with the tradition of his particular art; an acquaintance that is more than knowledge about it since it is derived from personal intimacy with the objects that have formed the tradition. In this sense acquaintance with masterpieces, and with less than masterpieces, is a "touchstone" of sensitiveness, though not a dictator of appraisals. For masterpieces themselves can be critically appreciated only as they are placed in the tradition to which they belong.

There is no art in which there is only a single tradition. The critic who is not intimately aware of a variety of traditions is of necessity limited and his criticisms will be one-sided to the point of distortion. The criticisms of post-impressionistic painting that were cited came from persons who thought they were expert because of exclusive initiation into a single tradition. In the plastic arts, there is the tradition of Negro, of Persian, of Egyptian, of Chinese and Japanese art, as well as the Florentine and Venetian traditions — to mention a few outstanding ones. It is because of lack of sense for the variety of traditions that unstable swings of fashion mark the attitude of different periods toward works of art — the overestimation of Raphael and the Roman school, for example, at the expense of Tintoretto and El Greco once current. Much of the unending and sterile contro-versy of critics adhering exclusively to "classicism" and "romanticism" has a like source. In the field of art, there are many mansions; artists have built them.

Through knowledge of a variety of conditions, the critic becomes aware of the vast variety of materials that are usable (since they have been used) in art. He is saved from the snap judgment that this or that work is aesthetically wrong because it has matter to which he is not accustomed, and when he comes across a work whose matter has no discoverable precedent he will be wary of uttering an offhand condemnation. Since form is always integral with matter, he will also, if his own experience is genuinely aesthetic, appreciate the multitude of special forms that exist and be safeguarded against identifying form with some technique that he has come to prefer. In short, not only will his general background be broadened, but he will become familiar, to the point of saturation, with a more fundamental matter, the conditions under which the subject-matter of varied modes of experience move to fulfillment. And this movement constitutes the objective and publicly accessible content of all works of art.

This knowledge of many traditions is no foe to discrimination. While I have spoken for the most part of the condemnations passed by judicial criticisms, it would be easily possible to quote as great egregious blunders in misplaced laudations. Absence of sympathetic acquaintance with a number of traditions leads the critic to a ready appreciation of academic works of art provided they are done with excellent technical facility. Seventeenth-century Italian painting was met with an acclaim that it was far from deserving simply because it pushed to an extreme, with technical skill, factors that earlier Italian art had held within bounds. Knowledge of a wide range of traditions is a condition of exact and severe discrimination. For only by means of such a knowledge can the critic detect the intent of an artist and the adequacy of his execution of intent. The history of criticism is filled with charges of carelessness and willfulness that would never have been brought if an adequate knowledge of traditions had been present, just as it is filled with praise for works that have no merit beyond a skillful use of materials.

In most cases, the discrimination of a critic has to be assisted by a knowledge of the development of an artist, as that is manifested in the succession of his works. Only rarely can an artist be criticized by a single specimen of his activity. The inability is not merely because Homer sometimes nods, but because understanding of the logic of the development of an artist is necessary to discrimination of his intent in any single work. Possession of this understanding broadens and refines the background without which judgment is blind and arbitrary. The words of Cézanne about the relation of exemplars of tradition to the artist are applicable to the critic. "Study of the Venetians, especially of Tintoretto, sets one upon a constant search for means of expression which will surely lead one to experience from nature one's own means of expression. . . . The Louvre is a good book to consult, but it is only an intermediary. The diversity of the scene of nature is the real prodigious study to be undertaken. . . . The Louvre is a book where we learn to read. But we should not be content to keep the formulae of our illustrious predecessors. Let us leave them so as to study beautiful nature and search to express it according to our personal temperament. Time and reflection gradually modify vision, and at last comprehension comes." Change the terms that need to be changed, and the procedure of the critic stands forth.

Critic and artist alike have their predilections. There are aspects of nature and life that are hard and others that are soft; that are austere, even bleak, and that have attractive charm; that are exciting and that

are pacifying and so on almost without end. Most "schools" of art exhibit a tendency in one direction or another. Then some original mode of vision seizes upon the tendency and carries it to its limit. There is, for example, the contrast between the "abstract" and the "concrete" — that is, the more familiar. Some artists work for extreme simplification, feeling that internal complexity leads to a superfluity that distracts attention; others take as their problem the multiplication of internal specifications to the utmost point consistent with organization.[2] There is again the difference between the frank and open approach and the indirect and allusive approach to vague matter that goes by the name of symbolism. There are artists who tend toward what Thomas Mann calls the dark and death and others who rejoice in light and air.

It goes without saying that every direction has difficulties and dangers that increase as it approaches its limit. The symbolic may lose itself in unintelligibility and the direct method in the banal. The "concrete" method ends in mere illustration and the "abstract" in scientific exercise, and so on. But yet each is justified when form and matter achieve equilibrium. The danger is that the critic, guided by personal predilection or more often by partisan conventionalism, will take some one procedure as his criterion of judgment and condemn all deviations from it as departures from art itself. He then misses the point of all art, the unity of form and matter, and misses it because he lacks adequate sympathy, in his natural and acquired one-sidedness, with the immense variety of interactions between the live creature and his world.

There is a unifying as well as a discriminating phase of judgment — technically known as synthesis in distinction from analysis. This unifying phase, even more

[2]While the two examples of animal art are given primarily to indicate the nature of "essence" in art, they also exemplify these two methods.

than the analytic, is a function of the creative response of the individual who judges. It is insight. There are no rules that can be laid down for its performance. It is at this point that criticism becomes itself an art — or else a mechanism worked by precept according to a ready-made blueprint. Analysis, discrimination, must result in unification. For to be a manifestation of judgment it must distinguish particulars and parts with respect to their weight and function in formation of an integral experience. Without a unifying point of view, based on the objective form of a work of art, criticism ends in enumeration of details. The critic operates after the manner of Robinson Crusoe when he sat down and made a credit and debit list of his blessings and troubles. The critic points out so many blemishes and so many merits, and strikes a balance. Since the object is an integral whole, if it is a work of art at all, such a method is as boring as it is irrelevant.

That the critic must discover some unifying strand or pattern running through all details does not signify that he must himself produce an integral whole. Sometimes critics of the better type substitute a work of art of their own for that they are professedly dealing with. The result may be art but it is not criticism. The unity the critic traces must be in the work of art as its characteristic. This statement does not signify that there is just one unifying idea or form in a work of art. There are many, in proportion to the richness of the object in question. What is meant is that the critic shall seize upon some strain or strand that is actually there, and bring it forth with such clearness that the reader has a new clue and guide in his own experience.

A painting may be brought to unity through relations of light, of planes, of color structurally employed, and a poem through predominant lyric or dramatic quality. And one and the same work of art presents different designs and different facets to different observers — as a sculptor may see different figures implicit in a block of stone. One mode of unification on the part of the critic is as legitimate as another — provided two conditions are fulfilled. One of them is that the theme and design which interest selects be really present in the work, and the other is the concrete exhibition of this supreme condition: the leading thesis must be shown to be consistently maintained throughout the parts of the work.

Goethe, for example, gave a notable manifestation of "synthetic" criticism in his account of the character of Hamlet. His conception of the essential character of Hamlet has enabled many a reader to see things in the play that otherwise would have escaped attention. It has served as a thread, or better as a centralizing force. Yet his conception is not the only way in which the elements of the play may be brought to a focus. Those who saw Edwin Booth's portrayal of the character may well have carried away the idea that the key to Hamlet as a human being is found in the lines spoken to Guildenstern after the latter had failed to play on a reed. "Why, look you now, how unworthy a thing you make of me! You would play upon me; would seem to know my stops; you would pluck out the heart of my mystery; you would sound me from my lowest note to the top of my compass; and there is much music, excellent voice, in this little organ; yet cannot you make it speak. 'S blood, do you think I am easier to be played upon than a pipe?"

It is customary to treat judgment and fallacies in intimate connection with each other. The two great fallacies of aesthetic criticism are reduction, and confusion of categories. The reductive fallacy results from oversimplification. It exists when some constituent of the work of art is isolated and then the whole is reduced to terms of this single isolated element. Generalized examples of this fallacy have been considered in previous chapters; for example, in the isolation of a sense-quality, like color or tone, from relations; isolation of the purely formal element; or again when a work of art is reduced to the exclusive representative values. The same principle applies when technique is taken apart from its connection with form. A more specific example is found in criticism made from a historical, political or economic point of view. There can be no doubt that the cultural milieu is inside as well as outside works of art. It enters as a genuine constituent, and acknowledgment of it is one element in a just discrimination. The sumptuousness of Venetian aristocracy and commercial wealth is a genuine constituent of the painting of Titian. But the fallacy of reducing his pictures to economic documents, as I once heard done by a "proletarian" guide in the Hermitage in Leningrad, is too evident to need mention were it not that it is a gross case of what often happens in modes so subtle as not to be readily perceptible. On the other hand, the religious simplicity and austerity of French twelfth-century statues and paintings, which come into them from their cultural milieu, is held up, apart from the strictly plastic qualities of the objects in question, as their essential aesthetic quality.

A more extreme form of the reductive fallacy exists when works of art are "explained" or "interpreted" on the basis of factors that are incidentally inside them. Much of so-called psychoanalytic "criticism" is of this nature. Factors that may — or may not — have played a part in the causative generation of a work of art are treated as if they "explained" the aesthetic content of the work of art itself. Yet the latter is just what it is whether a father or mother fixation, or a special regard for the susceptibilities of a wife, entered into its production. If the factors spoken of are real and not speculative, they are relevant to biography, but they are wholly impertinent as to the character of the work itself. If the latter has defects, they are blemishes to be

detected in the construction of the object itself. If an Oedipus complex is part of the work of art, it can be discovered on its own account. But psychoanalytic criticism is not the only kind that falls into this fallacy. It flourishes wherever some alleged occasion in the life of the artist, some biographical incident, is taken as if it were a kind of substitute for appreciation of the poem that resulted.[3]

The other chief mode in which this type of the reductive fallacy prevails is in so-called sociological criticism. Hawthorne's *Seven Gables*, Thoreau's *Walden*, Emerson's *Essays*, Mark Twain's *Huckleberry Finn* have an undoubted relation to the respective milieus in which they were produced. Historical and cultural information may throw light on the causes of their production. But when all is said and done, each one is just what it is artistically, and its aesthetic merits and demerits are within the work. Knowledge of social conditions of production is, when it is really knowledge, of genuine value. But it is no substitute for understanding of the object in its own qualities and relations. Migraine, eyestrain, indigestion may have played a part in the production of some works of literature; they may even account, from a causal point of view, for some of the qualities of the literature produced. But knowledge of them is an addition to medical lore of cause and effect, not to judgment of what was produced, even though the knowledge induce towards the author a moral charity we might not otherwise share.

We are thus brought to the other great fallacy of aesthetic judgment which indeed is mixed with the reductive fallacy: the confusion of categories. The historian, the physiologist, the biographer, the psychologist, all have their own problems and their

[3]Martin Schuetze, in his *Academic Illusions*, gives pertinent detailed examples of this kind of fallacy and shows them to be the stock-in-trade of entire schools of esthethic interpretation.

own leading conceptions that control the inquiries they undertake. Works of art provide them with relevant data in the pursuit of their special investigations. The historian of Greek life cannot construct his report of Greek life except by taking into account the monuments of Greek art; they are at least as relevant and as precious for his purpose as the political institutions of Athens and Sparta. The philosophic interpretations of the arts provided by Plato and Aristotle are indispensable documents for the historian of the intellectual life of Athens. But historic judgment is not aesthetic judgment. There are categories — that is, controlling conceptions of inquiry — appropriate to history, and only confusion results when they are used to control inquiry into art which also has its own ideas.

What is true of historical approach is true of the other modes of treatment. There are mathematical aspects of sculpture and painting as well as of architecture. Jay Hambidge has produced a treatise on the mathematics of Greek vases. An ingenious work has been produced on the mathematically formal elements of poetry. The biographer of Goethe or Melville would be derelict if he did not use their literary products when he is constructing a picture of their lives. The personal processes involved in construction of works of art are as precious data for the study of certain mental processes as records of procedures used by scientific inquirers are significant in the study of intellectual operations.

The phrase "confusion of categories" has an intellectualistic sound. Its practical counterpart is confusion of values.[4] Critics as well as theorists are given to the attempt to translate the distinctively aesthetic over into terms of some other kind of experience. The commonest form of this fallacy is to assume that the artist begins with material that has already a recognized status, moral,

[4]There is a significant chapter with this title in Buermeyer's *The Aesthetic Experience*.

philosophic, historical or whatever, and then renders it more palatable by emotional seasoning and imaginative dressing. The work of art is treated as if it were a reediting of values already current in other fields of experience.

There can be no doubt, for example, that religious values have exercised an almost incomparable influence upon art. For a long period in European history, Hebrew and Christian legends formed the staple material of all the arts. But this fact of itself tells us nothing about distinctively aesthetic values. Byzantine, Russian, Gothic and early Italian paintings are all equally "religious." But aesthetically each has its own qualities. Doubtless the different forms are connected with difference of religious thought and practice. But aesthetically the influence of the mosaic form is a more pertinent consideration. The question involved is the difference between material and matter so often referred to in previous discussions. The medium and effect are the important matters. For this reason, later works of art that have no religious content have a profoundly religious effect. I imagine the majestic art of "Paradise Lost" will be more, not less, admired, and the poem be more widely read, when rejection of its themes of Protestant theology has passed into indifference and forgetfulness. And this opinion does not imply that form is independent of matter. It implies that *artistic* substance is not identical with theme — any more than the form of the "Ancient Mariner" is identical with the story that is its theme. The *mis-en-scène* of Milton's portrayal of the dramatic action of great forces need not be aesthetically troublesome, any more than is that of the "Iliad," to the modern reader. There is a profound distinction between the vehicle of a work of art, the intellectual carrier through which an artist receives his subject-matter and transmits it to his immediate audience, and both the form and matter of this work.

The direct influence of scientific upon artistic values is much less than that of religion. It would be a brave critic who would assert that the artistic qualities of either Dante's or Milton's works are affected by acceptance of a cosmogony that no longer has scientific standing. As to the future, I think Wordsworth spoke truly when he said: "... if the labours of Men of science should ever create any material revolution, direct or indirect, in our condition and in the impressions which we habitually receive, the Poet will sleep then no more than at present ... he will be at his side, carrying sensation into the midst of the objects of science itself. The remotest discoveries of the Chemist, the Botanist, or Mineralogist, will be as proper objects of the Poet's art as any upon which it can be employed if the time should ever come when these things shall be familiar to us, and the relations under which they are contemplated by the followers of these respective sciences shall be manifestly and palpably material to us as enjoying and suffering beings." But poetry will not on that account be a popularization of science, nor will its characteristic values be those of science.

There are critics who confuse aesthetic values with philosophic values, especially with those laid down by philosophic moralists. T. S. Eliot, for example, says that "the truest philosophy is the best material for the greatest poet," and implies that what the poet does is to make philosophic content more viable by addition of sensuous and emotional qualities. Just what the "truest philosophy" is is a matter of some dispute. But critics of this school do not lack definite, not to say dogmatic, convictions on this point. Without any particular special competency in philosophic thought, they are ready to pronounce *ex cathedra* judgments, because they are committed to some conception of the relation of man to the universe that flourished in some past epoch. They regard its restoration as essential to the re-

demption of society from its present evil state. Fundamentally, their criticisms are moral receipes. Since great poets have had different philosophies, acceptance of their point of view entails that if we approve the philosophy of Dante we must condemn the poetry of Milton, and if we accept that of Lucretius we must find the poetry of both the others woefully defective. And where, upon the basis of any of these philosophies, does Goethe come in? And yet these are our great "philosophic" poets.

Ultimately all confusion of values proceeds from the same source — neglect of the intrinsic significance of the medium. The use of a particular medium, a special language having its own characteristics, is the source of every art, philosophic, scientific, technological and aesthetic. The arts of science, of politics, of history, and of painting and poetry all have finally the same *material;* that which is constituted by the interaction of the live creature with his surroundings. They differ in the media by which they convey and express this material, not in the material itself. Each one transforms some phase of the raw material of experience into new objects according to the purpose; each purpose demands a particular medium for its execution. Science used the medium that is adapted to the purpose of control and prediction, of increase of power; it is an art.[5] Under particular conditions, its matter may also be aesthetic. The purpose of aesthetic art being the enhancement of direct experience itself, it uses the medium fit for the accomplishment of that end. The necessary equipment of the critic is, first, to have the experience and then to elicit its constituent in terms of the medium used. Failure in either of these respects results inevitably in confusion of values. To treat poetry as having a philosophy, even a "true" philosophy, for its especial material is like supposing that literature has grammar for its material.

[5]This point I have emphasized in the "Quest for Certainty," Chapter IV.

An artist may, of course, *have* a philosophy and that philosophy may influence his artistic work. Because of the medium of words, which are already the product of social art and are already pregnant with moral meanings, the artist in literature is more often influenced by a philosophy than are artists who work with a plastic medium. Mr. Santayana is a poet who is also a philosopher and a critic. Moreover, he has stated the criterion which he employs in criticism, and the criterion is just the thing most critics do not state and apparently are not even aware of. Of Shakespeare he says, " . . . the cosmos eludes him; he does not seem to feel the need of framing that idea. He depicts human life in all its richness and variety, but leaves that life without a setting and consequently without a meaning." Since the various scenes and characters presented by Shakespeare have each its own setting, the passage evidently implies lack of a particular setting, namely of a total cosmic setting. That this absence is what is implied is not left a matter of conjecture; it is definitely stated. "There is no *fixed* conception of any forces, natural or moral, *dominating and transcending* our mortal energies." The complaint is of lack of "totality"; fullness is not wholeness. "What is required for *theoretic wholeness* is not this or that *system but some system.*"

In contrast with Shakespeare, Homer and Dante had a faith that "had enveloped the world of experience in a world of imagination in which *the ideals of the reason*, of the fancy and the heart had a natural expression." (None of the italics are in the original text.) His philosophic point of view, perhaps, is best summed up in a sentence occurring in a criticism of Browning: "The value of experience is not in experience but in the ideals which it reveals." And of Browning it is said that his "method is to penetrate by sympathy rather than to portray by intelligence" — a sentence one might suppose to be an admirable description of a dramatic poet rather than the adverse criticism it is intended to be.

There are philosophies and philosophies as well as criticisms and criticisms. There are points of view from which Shakespeare had a philosophy and had a philosophy that is more pertinent to the work of an artist than one which conceives the ideal of philosophy to be the enclosure of experience within and domination of its varied fullness by a transcendent ideal that only reason beyond experience can conceive. There is a philosophy which holds that nature and life offer in their plenitude many meanings and are capable through imagination of many renderings. In spite of the scope and dignity of the great historic philosophic systems, an artist may be instinctively repelled by the constraint imposed by acceptance of any system. If the important thing is "not this or that system but some system," why not accept, with Shakespeare, the free and varied system of nature itself as that works and moves in experience in many and diverse organizations of value? As compared with the movement and change of nature, the form that "reason" is said to prescribe may be that of a particular tradition which is a premature and one-sided synthesis in terms of a single and narrow aspect of experience. Art that is faithful to the many potentialities of organization, centering about a variety of interests and purposes, that nature offers — as was that of Shakespeare — may have not only a fullness but a wholeness and sanity absent from a philosophy of enclosure, transcendence, and fixity. The question for the critic is the adequacy of form to matter, and not that of the presence or absence of any particular form. The value of experience is not only in the ideals it reveals, but in its power to disclose many ideals, a power more germinal and more significant than any revealed ideal, since it includes them in its stride, shatters and remakes them. One may even reverse the statement and say the value of ideals lies in the experiences to which they lead.

There is one problem that artist, philosopher, and critic alike must face: the relation between permanence and change. The bias of philosophy in its more orthodox phase throughout the ages has been toward the unchanging, and that bias has affected the more serious critics — perhaps it is this bias which generates the judicial critic. It is overlooked that in art — and in nature as far as we can judge it through the medium of art — permanence is a function, a consequence, of changes in the relations they sustain to one another, not an antecedent principle. There is to be found in Browning's essay on Shelley what seems to me to come as near as criticism can come to a just statement of the relations between the unified and "total"; between the varied and moving, the "individual," and the "universal," so that I shall quote it at length. "If the subjective might seem to be the ultimate requirement of every age, the objective in its strictest sense must still retain its original value. For it is with this world, as starting point and basis alike, that we shall always have to concern ourselves; the world is not to be learned and thrown aside, but reverted to and relearned. The spiritual comprehension may be infinitely subtilized but its raw material must remain.

"There is a time when the general eye has, so to speak, absorbed its full of the phenomena around it, whether spiritual or material, and desires rather to learn the exacter significance of what it possesses than to receive any augmentation of what it possesses. Then is the opportunity for the poet of loftier vision to lift his fellows, with their half-apprehensions, up to his own sphere, by intensifying the import of details and rounding out the universal meaning. The influence of such an achievement will not soon die out. A tribe of successors (Homerides) working more or less in the same spirit dwell on his discoveries and reinforce his doctrine till, at unawares, the world is found to be

subsisting wholly on the shadow of a reality, on sentiments diluted from passions, on the traditon of a fact, the convention of a moral, the straw of last year's harvest. Then is the imperative call for the appearance of another sort of poet, who shall at once replace this intellectual rumination of food swallowed long ago by a supply of fresh and living swathe; getting at new substance by breaking up the assumed wholes into parts of independent and unclassed value, careless of the unknown laws for recombining them (it will be the business of yet another poet to suggest these hereafter), prodigal of objects for men's outer and not inner sight, shaping for their uses a new and different creation from the last, which it displaces by the right of life over death — to endure till, in the inevitable process, its very sufficiency to itself shall require, at length, an exposition of its affinity to something higher — when the positive yet conflicting facts shall again precipitate themselves under a harmonizing law. . . .

"All the bad poetry in the world (accounted poetry, that is, by its affinities) will be found to result from some one of the infinite degrees of discrepancies between the attributes of the poet's soul, occasioning a want of correspondency between his work and the varieties of nature — issuing in poetry, false under whatever form, which shows a thing not as it is to mankind generally, nor as it is to the particular describer, but as it is supposed to be for some unreal neutral mood, midway between both and of value to neither, and living its brief minute simply through the indolence of whoever accepts it in his inability to denounce a cheat."

Nature and life manifest not flux but continuity, and continuity involves forces and structures that endure through change; at least when they change, they do so more slowly than do surface incidents, and thus are, relatively, constant. But change is inevitable even though it be not for the better. It must be reckoned with. Moreover, changes are not all gradual; they culminate in sudden mutations, in transformations that at the time seem revolutionary, although in a later perspective they take their place in a logical development. All of these things hold of art. The critic, who is not as sensitive to signs of change as to the recurrent and enduring, uses the criterion of tradition without understanding its nature and appeals to the past for patterns and models without being aware that every past was once the imminent future of its past and is now the past, not absolutely, but of the change which constitutes the present.

Every critic, like every artist, has a bias, a predilection, that is bound up with the very existence of individuality. It is his task to convert it into an organ of sensitive perception and of intelligent insight, and to do so without surrendering the instinctive preference from which are derived direction and sincerity. But when his especial and selective mode of response is allowed to harden in a fixed mold, he becomes incapacitated for judging even the things to which his bias draws him. For they must be seen in the perspective of a world so multiform and so full that it contains an infinite variety of other qualities that attract and of other ways of response. Even the bewildering aspects of the world in which we live are material for art when they find the form through which they are actually expressed. A philosophy of experience that is keenly sensitive to the unnumbered interactions that are the material of experience is the philosophy from which a critic may most safely and surely draw his inspriation. How otherwise can a critic be animated by that sensitiveness to the varied movements toward completion in different total experiences that will enable him to direct the perceptions of others to a fuller and more ordered appreciation of the objective content of works of art?

For critical judgment not only grows out of the critic's experience of objective matter, and not only depends upon that for validity, but has for its office the deepening of just such experience in others. Scientific judgments not only end in increased control but for those who understand they add enlarged meanings to the things perceived and dealt with in daily contact with the world. The function of criticism is the reeducation of perception of works of art; it is an auxiliary in the process, a difficult process, of learning to see and hear. The conception that its business is to appraise, to judge in the legal and moral sense, arrests the perception of those who are influenced by the criticism that assumes this task. The moral office of criticism is performed indirectly. The individual who has an enlarged and quickened experience is one who should make himself his own appraisal. The way to help him is through the expansion of his own experience by the work of art to which criticism is subsidiary. The moral function of art itself is to remove prejudice, do away with the scales that keep the eye from seeing, tear away the veils due to wont and custom, perfect the power to perceive. The critic's office is to further this work, performed by the object of art. Obtrusion of his own approvals and condemnations, appraisals and ratings, is sign of failure to apprehend and perform the function of becoming a factor in the development of sincere personal experience. We lay hold of the full import of a work of art only as we go through in our own vital processes the processes the artist went through in producing the work. It is the critic's privilege to share in the promotion of this active process. His condemnation is that he so often arrests it.

29. After Betsy, What?

H. W. JANSON

"*L'art est fait pour troubler, la science rassure.*" — GEORGES BRAQUE, *Cahier, 1917–1947.*

Two years ago the Baltimore *News Post* ran three pictures side by side, challenging the reader to identify them correctly: one showed an abstract painting recently acquired by the Baltimore Museum, another was the work of a six-year-old child, and the third had been produced by Betsy, a chimpanzee of the same age in the Baltimore Zoo. Two months later Betsy's discoverer and sponsor, the director of the Zoo, put a group of her paintings on public display, and a number of them were sold for amounts adding up to a significant fraction of the cost of a mate for the talented young female. At this point the story was picked up by the wire services; it became, for a moment, national front-page news — both the *New York Times* and the *Herald-Tribune* carried it on March 12 — and even *Pravda* printed an account of it, suitably embroidered to illustrate the degeneracy of bourgeois art (it claimed that American museums had been eager to acquire these simian scrawlings).

Conservatives on our side of the Iron Curtain must have had similar thoughts.

Was not Betsy the ultimate weapon in a campaign they had been waging for the past hundred years against the "incompetence" of modern art? Their endlessly repeated contention that "any savage (or any child) can do better than that" could now be amended to include a reference to the infrahuman primates. For them the advent of Betsy was thus neither unexpected nor unwelcome. It is the rest of us, unable to share these certitudes and I-told-you-so's, that have found Betsy a real challenge. One critic, who spoke on "The Age of the Chimpanzee" at the 1957 convention of the American Federation of Art, confessed that he saw no clear-cut way to distinguish Betsy's work from Abstract Expressionism, the dominant trend in present-day painting. Both, he pointed out, could be described in the same terms: highly uncommunicative, uncritical, personal, spontaneous, exploiting chance effects, emphasizing the act of painting as an end in itself and thus rejecting all references to the outside world. Is this not, he asked, a deplorable narrowing and impoverishment? "Doesn't the world need

*SOURCE: Reprinted from the *Bulletin of Atomic Scientists*, XV, 2 (February 1959), pp. 68–71, 93.

the painter's praise any more?" Others, we may be sure, have been similarly troubled. And not without cause; for the resemblance of Betsy's work to Abstract Expressionism is too real to be disregarded, whatever the conclusions one may want to draw from it. Nor can we deny that at least some of Betsy's products have a measure of aesthetic appeal to the unprejudiced beholder. There is indeed no clear-cut way to tell the two apart in every instance. It might even be said that Betsy epitomizes the qualities that differentiate the Abstract Expressionists from the painters of the past (including such "old masters" as Picasso).

Betsy and Sputnik

Betsy has thus had a shock effect not unlike that of *Sputnik I*. These two shakers of confidence, appearing both within the same year, have become symbolic of our doubts and misgivings in their respective spheres. How lasting an impact Betsy will have is difficult to say, but she has in any event raised some fundamental questions about the aims of the avant-garde of modern painting. Surely the fact that her work — rightly or wrongly — has made serious people think of Abstract Expressionism (or *tachisme*, the French term for the same phenomenon) demands further exploration. Does it really mean that these painters are in danger of descending to an infrahuman level? Or could it be that apes are more human than we think? Neither possibility can be dismissed out of hand; men, after all, are not immune to behaving like brutes, while chimpanzees, thanks to the researches of Köhler, Yerkes, and others, are known to possess surprisingly near-human mental capacities. Our first problem, then, is how to classify Betsy's efforts. Can they be termed works of art properly speaking? If not, what are they, and what is their relation to Abstract Expressionism? The question is less simple than it may seem, for no

one fully knows what a work of art is, so that we have no uncontested generic definition to help us in a borderline case such as this. Perhaps it would be well to note in passing that our difficulty is not unique; biologists and biochemists find it equally troublesome to define a living organsim as against dead matter. Still, on the basis of our pre-Betsy experience we can venture a few generalizations: thus, while we habitually use the word "beauty" for both, a work of art must not be confused with a work of nature (except insofar as the latter term might be said to include all the works of man). We must, I believe, insist that the making of works of art is an exclusively human activity — indeed, a basic human activity, since we know of no human society totally unproductive in this respect.

But if works of art, properly so called, must be man-made, is it not obvious that Betsy's canvases can at best claim to be the poor relations of true works of art? The difficulty here lies in what we mean by "man-made." Do we (at least so far as the fine arts are concerned) necessarily mean "made by human hands" in the direct, physical sense? Is the actual shaping of materials an essential part of the creative act? Our ideas on this subject have undergone some startling changes in the course of time. The Greeks, who were the first to give any thought to the problem, regarded manual work of any kind as base and menial; understandably enough, therefore, they tended to view the artist's mental activity as something quite separate and of far higher rank than the work of his hands. The visible, material work of art was to them merely an imperfect echo of the invisible "original" in the artist's head. According to this view (which is not entirely extinct even today) the physical act of making the work of art is a sort of mechanical projection, a "carrying out," of a design fully shaped in the mind. Hence the fine arts were classed among the mechanical arts, or crafts, unfit for free men, rather than among the liberal

FIGURE 29.1   "Backyard on Tenth Street" by Wilhelm de Kooning. Courtesy of The Baltimore
Museum of Art.

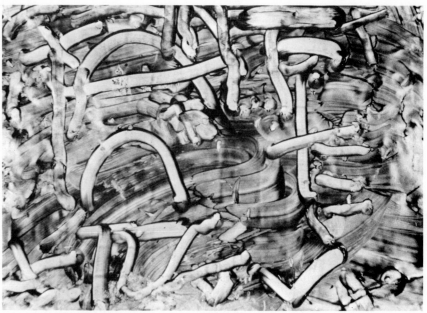

FIGURE 29.2   Interpretation of "Backyard on Tenth Street" by Alice Jones, age 6, First Grade.
Photo by *Baltimore News-Post* and *Sunday American.*

FIGURE 29.3   Painting by Betsy, age 6, Baltimore Zoo.
Photo by *Baltimore News-Post* and *Sunday American*.

arts; and mechanical arts they remained until the end of the Middle Ages. Hence also the Ancients had no reverence for the physical uniqueness of an artist's handiwork; a conscientious copy could easily replace the original, since the original itself was regarded as a "copy." Modern archaeologists are constantly struggling with the problem of originals versus copies in Greek and Roman sculpture for that reason, and the persistence of this attitude is attested by the continuing demand for copies of famous paintings or plaster casts of famous statues until far into the nineteenth century.

Today such copies and casts are out of vogue; we realize that an original loses its essential qualities in the process of being duplicated. But our awareness of the unique value of the original work of art is no sudden development. Its beginnings can be traced back some five hundred years, to the early Renaissance. There we encounter the earliest evidence that works of art were coming to be valued as embodiments of the artist's individual style; and since this style was as personal as a signature, it could be seen only in works that were autographic, i. e., originals. The new attitude gradually gave rise to a special appreciation of tentative, unfinished, and fragmentary works such as drawings and sketches, executed in a direct and spontaneous way that retained the full flavor of the author's "handwriting." Thus the physical making of the work of art achieved a new dignity and significance; the artist's hand was now viewed as a kind of seismographic needle recording every impulse of his mind. Liberated from the impersonal standards of craftsmanship, the fine arts at last joined the select company of the liberal arts. It was not until about a century ago, however, that the new attitude finally won out over the older one. Impressionism was the first movement in art whose very name proclaimed the victory of the sketch over the finished picture, of the How over the What, of Becoming over Being, of immediacy and spontaneity over deliberation. Yet the Impressionists and their successors — Fauves, Expressionists, Cubists — remained traditional in one respect; they still produced "likenesses," however tenuous their link with external reality. And to the extent that their aim was representational, their way of painting, "free" though it might be, retained an element of purposiveness, of method, of technical discipline.

Creative Process

Since then, we have had ample evidence that neither representation nor manual skill are essential to the creative process in the visual arts. In 1913 Braque and Picasso began to produce *papiers collés* and similar constructions of cut and pasted pieces of paper, bits of wood or other scraps of their material environment. The aesthetic importance of these objects is in no way diminished by the fact that the choice of ingredients was often accidental and that the act of assembling them demanded only the most elementary kind of manual dexterity. At their best such collages, although childishly simple in the technical sense, are masterpieces of controlled design. The Dadaists took over the invention itself but revolted against its formal severity; instead of cutting paper they preferred to tear it and to arrange the pieces "according to the laws of chance," so that not only the choice of materials but their shape and configuration as well were freed from premeditated control. The making of a work of art thus became "a lucky accident," and the artist's creative act was to make it possible for the accident to happen and to recognize it when it did. The ultimate expression of this attitude was the *objets trouvés* ("found objects") of Marcel Duchamp: mass-produced every-

day objects of our industrial civilization which he displayed, rechristened with intriguing titles, in Dadaist exhibitions. Clearly, these were his creations, even though he had not physically made them; he merely "found" them and communicated this discovery to the beholder by removing them from their customary setting and placing them on exhibit, with a label to point out their new identity. Here, then, we have the quintessential work of art — an act of the imagination made visible in a manner so simple and direct as to dispense with the trained hand entirely. After all, the one physical act involved in the "making" of an *objet trouvé*, the removal of the object from its nonaesthetic habitat, need not be performed by the artist himself.

If we acknowledge *objets trouvés* as authentic works of art — and I believe we must, however limited we may think their scope — then we shall have to extend the same recognition to Betsy's efforts; for they, too, are "man-made" even though painted by infrahuman hands. Köhler tells of a chimpanzee who had watched a man painting a wooden pole white and then, left alone with the brush and pot of paint, neatly painted a large stone. Betsy, we must assume, had no such specific model to imitate; she was merely supplied with paint and canvas and shown that these could be brought together. Doubtless she enjoyed making paint tracks with her fingers (and not only on the canvas, we may be sure). But was she watching for a "lucky accident" in the process? Did she suddenly stop and put aside a canvas because she liked what she saw and wanted it to stay that way? I rather suspect she stopped only when the game began to bore her; it was her keeper that watched for the "lucky accident" and snatched the canvas away from her at the strategic moment. And what determines the strategic moment? That depends on the keeper's expectation. If he responds only to realistic likenesses, he may well have to

FIGURE 29.4 "Satire on the
Romantic School of Painting,"
from "Un autre monde,"
1850. Grandville.

wait forever, since everything Betsy does will seem chaotic to him. If, on the other hand, he has some familiarity with Abstract Expressionism, he is likely to see "snatch-worthy" accidents at fairly frequent intervals. These may even have some genuine aesthetic appeal, but if they do the credit must go to the snatcher, since it was his imagination that recognized the "lucky accident" and caused him to remove it from Betty's clutches. Betsy herself is merely a source of random patterns, more manageable perhaps and capable of a greater variety of movements than the proverbial donkey's tail with a brush tied to it but essentially of the same order. Had her paintings been produced by a less anthropomorphic agent, they would in all likelihood have created much less of a stir. As it is, we have all been taken in to some extent by her performance, which through no fault of hers has become an object lesson in artistic gamesmanship ("how to give the appearance of painting a picture without actually doing so").

Ape as Painter

But Betsy was predestined to become a symbolic figure for another reason as well. Ever since the Middle Ages, it has been said that "art is the ape of nature," and the phrase has been cast in visual form countless times, so that the image of the ape as a painter is a thoroughly familiar one in Western art. Needless to say, these painting apes are for the most part either pedantic realists or superficial imitators of other (and greater) masters. Not until the mid-nineteenth century could the satire be reversed: the witty drawing on this page shows Delacroix and his fellow Romantics wielding the brush with an uncritical abandon that strikes us as

FIGURE 29.5 Detail from "St. Sebastian," by Andrea Mantegna, about 1460. Vienna, Kunsthistorisches Museum.

oddly prophetic of Betsy's behavior. The photographs of Betsy at the easel thus offer the startling spectacle of an allegory come alive. Even so, her paintings are not a valid argument against Abstract Expressionism; they are merely its by-products. We are, of course, free to reject the entire "accident-prone" aesthetic of which Betsy's work offers an extreme example, but we cannot legitimately do so on the ground that it is not art.

Abstract Expressionism itself, however revolutionary it may seem, is only the most recent stage of a development that has deep historic roots. The exploitation of the accidental is an essential aspect of all art, whether the artist takes advantage of chance formations in nature (as he did on the walls of caves in the Old Stone Age) or causes his own "accidents" on canvas. There is an element of the unexpected of chance discovery even in the most deliberate and controlled artistic effort, although it may be so thoroughly hidden by formal convention that its presence can only be surmised. What distinguishes the artist of today in this respect is, on the one hand, his comparative freedom from formal conventions (they are not wholly lacking even now, and probably never will be) and, on the other, a far greater awareness of the "creative accident." If we look for the beginnings of this characteristically modern attitude, we find them at the same point where we encounter the earliest concern with the physical uniqueness of the work of art: in the early Renaissance.

Thus Leone Battista Alberti explains the origin of sculpture on the basis of tree-trunks and clumps of earth having a chance resemblance to living forms, and Leonardo da Vinci describes our proneness to find images in clouds or cracking plaster. These passages were probably inspired by similar references among Ancient authors; but early Renaissance artists, unlike the Ancients, dared on occasion to make conscious use of chance images. Such at least is the conclusion forced upon us by the odd little horseman shown on the left, from the *Martyrdom of St. Sebastian* by Andrea Mantegna in the Vienna Museum. The figure occupies a tiny area (about $1\frac{3}{4}''$ square) in the upper left-hand corner of a panel two feet tall. That it is indeed an "accident" made explicit is indicated by the fact that its shape is only partly realized and that it has the color and texture of the cloud within which it is confined, so that the vast majority of beholders fail to notice its existence. Nor can it be explained on the basis of pictorial tradition, since there are no analogies to it in other paintings of the period. And no one has yet discovered a symbolic or narrative significance that might account for it as a rationally planned part of the composition. To all appearances, then, Mantegna discovered the figure in the process of painting the cloud, and became so fascinated with it that he not only let it stand but elaborated upon it a bit, thereby permitting us to share his pleasure in this irrational accident.

The path from Mantegna's diminutive burst of spontaneity to the complex chains of pictorial "accidents" in present-day art covers a span of five hundred years — the same five hundred years that encompass the growth of modern science. The two developments are, I believe, intimately linked to each other, even though they proceed along separate tracks. There are, to be sure, points of direct contact and cross-fertilization, but these generally lie along the periphery of either field, rather than at the center. Perhaps their relationship can be most aptly described in terms of the two faces of the same coin, the body of the coin, the substance common to both art and science, being the modern mind in its various stages of evolution since the fifteenth century. Did not the same impulse that brought about an awareness of the unique individuality of personal artistic style also encourage individual reasoning to claim primacy over time-honored belief? The battle against suprapersonal authority, whether of form or of intellectual tradition, could hardly be waged on one front alone; it had to be won or lost on both together. After all, original discovery in science is no less a feat of the individual imagination — even though a very different kind of feat — than original discovery in art. If, as Braque has observed, the purpose of science is to reassure us (by extending our grasp of the physical world) while that of art is to disturb us (probing the hidden recesses of our consciousness), it is hardly surprising that the capacity-to-disturb of the one should have grown during the past half-century at the same pace as the capacity-to-reassure of the other.

Postscript

When I wrote this essay six years ago, I was unaware that apes had been drawing and painting for the benefit of experimental psychologists ever since the time of the First World War. A recently published systematic study of the subject (Desmond Morris, *The Biology of Art*, London, 1962) has convinced me that my analysis of Betsy as a source of random patterns "creatively selected" by her keeper does not meet all the facts of the case. Morris' observations show that the picture-making behavior of apes follows a surprisingly strict evolutionary pattern, which follows step by step the development of drawing ability in human infants. Both run through the same sequence of stages — up to a point: and that point is reached when the child produces his first "image" (usually a face), an achievement linked to the development of articulate speech. The world of words, like the world of images, remains beyond the ape's capacity. When Morris tries to explain what he terms the "convergence" of modern art with that of the ape by suggesting that between 1900 and 1960 art has followed, in reverse, the evolution of picture-making by children from the age of two to the brink of adulthood, he compounds history and biology. But his analysis of the ape-infant relationship is most illuminating, though perhaps not quite in the way he intended. The very fact that the designs of both apes and infants do not have a random character but progress along a predictable path differentiates them from the "accident-prone" adult art of our day. To call them art at all seems as misleading as to call them abstract or nonobjective. Clearly, they deserve a term of their own: I propose "proto-art." The first, or "prefigurative" phase of proto-art we share with the infrahuman primates; the second, figurative, one is ours alone. And I like to think that what per-

mits the human infant to enter the second phase is the first stirring of that faculty described by Alberti and Leonardo in their discussions of chance images: the child suddenly discovers that one of the circle-and-dot designs he has been making happens to resemble a face. From that time on, he will know how to produce the same image at will. Yet I should hesitate to call him an artist, for the satisfaction he gets from his image-making is the pleasure of exploring his own faculties — the process rather than the result. The individual image has little importance for him, so that he is quite willing to discard it; after all, he can always do another one like it. Only much later, when he approaches adulthood, will the proto-artist discover that he needs the approval of outside beholders, and will preserve his work in the hope of finding an appreciative public. From that point on, his picture-making will no longer be determined by biological factors, but by the interaction between individual talent and the demands of society. Freed from the evolutionary pattern of proto-art, he is now free to produce works of art properly so called, if his gifts propel him in that direction.

May, 1964   H. W. JANSON

30. Evaluation of the Art Product

EDWARD C. WATERMAN

Aesthetically speaking, one of the most difficult tasks of the art educator is the evaluation of the art product.

Before the art product can be criticized or evaluated we must determine on what basis this is to be accomplished. Since most preliminary definitions of art included the art product as an end in itself, it becomes *terminably* valuable or has *intrinsic* value. If the art activity is controlled and leads to a product which has a specific utility it becomes *instrumentally* valuable or has *extrinsic* value. This might be stated less enigmatically by saying that intrinsically valued things are valued for their own sake and *extrinsically* valued things are appreciated and valued for their usefulness. It will prove interesting and fruitful if we examine the application of these values to art more closely, exemplified with analogies from daily life. We will find things can have both values, neither value, or either value.

Toward numerous and common human activities, many persons think only in terms of intrinsic value; those who love to sleep for the sake of sleep, the gourmets who "live to eat," and the sportsman who re-ceives an exhilarated feeling when playing tennis in the fresh air. But, all these activities have a common extrinsic value. They promote health which in turn helps to keep the human organism alive. A similar thing happens in art. The so-called fine arts in particular are usually referred to as ends in themselves, serving no purpose beyond being an object of art. It is true that the art product must justify its own existence, but an analysis of history proves that it usually also is a means to something more. It is also significant that the art product in the realm of the "fine arts" not only has the usual intrinsic value, but possesses the extrinsic value because it was explicitly intended as such by the artist. Tolstoy, through his writings, propagandized on behalf of the peasants; Grünewald's paintings conciliated the lives of Christ and the saints; the social status of Henry Moore has been augmented through his sculptures; all three added impetus to their power to earn money. On the other hand, from the spectators' viewpoint, the knowledge and enjoyment of reading "War and Peace" has obvious intrinsic values. The aesthetic ex-

*SOURCE: Reprinted from *Art Education* (April 1959), pp. 5-7, 10.

379

perience of examining Grünewald's *Alterpiece* or Moore's *Family* also has obvious intrinsic value. The use of the knowledge gained from reading "War and Peace" or just having seen works of art and being able to talk about them, gives the spectator a distinction in the eyes of his associates. This, then, for the spectator, is an extrinsic value.

Things thought of as singularly extrinsic can also be examined for their intrinsic value. Tools, machines, and other numerous gadgets which science gives us are usually thought of only in terms of what they can do. If we reflect a moment, however, it is obvious that any manufactured commodity can be made to possess that thing called *beauty* and in turn be valued for its own sake.

It is more difficult to discern things which have neither value, for man usually has a goal when he sets upon a task. One striking example, however, is the Victorian architecture of the 1890's. On the top of the more pretentious buildings was placed a small cupola complete with siding, a domed or peaked roof, and windows. It had, however, no access to its interior. This would lead us to believe that it was useless and had or has no apparent extrinsic value. To our way of thinking, it cannot be said that the cupola has intrinsic value because it is decorative, because as decoration it is superfluous. This brings up an important point. The "gingerbread" and garish decoration of this period had intrinsic value for the people of that period but do not have this value for us. For, while the elements of design or principles of art do not change, the subject matter and the way the elements are used will change. The reflection of the use of these elements and principles, and the subject, change with each culture and the social philosophy it promulgates. This being true, we can say that in the final analysis intrinsic values are central to the individual and are chronologically relative, or an intrinsically valued thing is valuable to an individual at a specific time.

Besides a change in either of one value, there also has occurred in history a change in stress from one value to the other. During the eighteenth century, for example, designers and architects were primarily interested in the intrinsic value of their work as manifested by *Louis Quanze* and *Louis Seize* furniture and buildings. Since then, about 1900, Louis Sullivan the iconoclast, broke away from the eclectic conventionalization of his predecessors and started a new movement that gained great impetus through the twentieth century. This movement, *"form follows function,"* pervades the lives of almost all of us.

Today, however, there seems to be a paradox to the "form follows function" rule. The many proselytes who advocate it contradict themselves by eclectically hanging an antique rug on the wall of one of their rooms, an Empire clock that does not work might be seen on the mantle shelf, and a useless seventeenth century American Betty lamp complete with tinder box will be prominently displayed on the foyer table. The aesthetic significance to this is that objects that at one time were primarily possessed for their extrinsic value are now kept only because they have a thing called "beauty." Additional significance lies in the fact that we can hazard a generalization and say from obsolescence of extrinsic values grows intrinsic values. Further credence can be added to this generalization by examining the artistic activity of primitive man. Although we have no way of knowing whether Cro-Magnon Man from the Upper Paleolithic Age valued his cave art intrinsically, there is strong evidence that we can be reasonably certain that he did value it extrinsically, not as an end in itself, but for worship in religious rituals and mystical adoration of nature. This is also true of other primitive societies, including the Minoan Thalassocracy and the Sumerians. The art products handed down to us from these societies are valued intrinsically.

We frequently think of them not in terms of their original use, but even go so far that in evaluating them we assume that their makers had the same attitude toward them which we have. The perspicuousness in discovering the difference between intrinsic and extrinsic value is obviously much more difficult than just seeing them.

Now that different examples of values have been manifested in art and daily human activity we can better understand the following intrinsic-extrinsic value standards.

The first is that the value of the end, whether intrinsic or extrinsic, is not relevant to the value of the mechanical or physical means. It would be foolish to argue that because automobiles are used for "getaway" cars, or the arrangement of criminal rendezvous, they are therefore not good machines for transportation. Again, the instrumental value of the perfect crime is not weakened by the foulness of the end. And so it is with art, the intrinsic or terminal value of a quintessential work of art is not mitigated by the fact that the subject matter is low in quality.

Secondly, the intrinsic value of the art product is irrelevant to the extrinsic value. Witness, for example, the aesthetic pleasure an artist receives from working on his canvas. His artistry does not necessarily result in an end product that has extrinsic value, yet no one can deny the intrinsic value of artistic creativity. "Thus, it is held that in the painting of a landscape the real or 'pure' beauty would consist of the satisfactions proffered by the relations of colors and lines and masses, while the pleasure we take in the ideas of tree, stream, meadow and hill would be irrelevant."[1]

Finally, the extrinsic value of a given product can be evaluated only by the actual empirical success of the product. A machine, for instance, has a high extrinsic value only if it does what it was intended to do. Standards of superiority can be annotated in relation to other machines which are intended to do the same thing. These standards are obvious; whether it can do it better than other machines, cheapness, speed, etc.

It is fairly easy to criticize a product made by man if we criticize only in terms of its extrinsic value. This is because extrinsic values are primarily *social* and can usually be judged *quantitatively*. For example, the empirical success of a chair can be judged in relation to other chairs and certain established quantitative criteria or standards which have been devised by man. Witness, for instance, the three most important things for which a chair is extrinsically and socially valued: the comfort it affords the user, the initial cost, and how long it will last as a chair before it must be discarded. The designer knows the quantitative standards he must use: the measurements of man (to insure comfort for the user) which determine the measurements of the chair, materials which are readily available to reduce the cost, and materials which are strong, in order that the life of the chair will be of a reasonable length of time. Other extrinsic standards used by furniture designers are obvious.

When we judge a chair for its beauty or how good an art product it is, we are judging the relative intrinsic value of the chair. We no longer think of the *quantitative social* standards but of the *qualitative individual* standards. This is, of course, more difficult and is of particular interest to us at this time.

Intrinsic values must likewise be judged by predicating the interest of the individual upon his variable satisfaction. Whatever it is an individual desires or needs has an intrinsic value for that individual. A rebuttalist might bring to bear the evidence that after the individual obtains what he wants he may no longer want it, which would extirpate the intrinsic value. This, however, does not prove that the value did not exist at one time. It proves, if anything, that human

[1]DeWitt H. Parker, *The Principles of Aesthetics*, 2nd edition (New York: Crofts, 1947), pp. 37–38.

beings are easily bored. Further, it does not prove but suggests the fanciful idea that man receives a greater intrinsic value (and satisfaction) from the quest for satisfaction than the possession of the satisfaction. If any given art product, therefore, elicits for one person a satisfaction of his aesthetic interests more than another given art product, the first art product has greater intrinsic value. Our rebuttalist will then state that it has greater value for *the* individual spectator, but does not have a greater value regardless of individuals. We say, however, that a value which no one values is not unlike an object or "sight" which no one can see. If no one values a thing, the thing has no value. Values must be values for man.

This is, of course, an individualistic and relativistic theory and individualism and relativism can be partially qualified in empirical practice by the fact the man possesses a high degree of homogeneity. For example, the *nurture* of man is dependent (sometimes accidentally) on the different social, religious, and economic groups to which he belongs. Different groups hold different values which include the value of art or the different areas of art. The *nature* of man is also of fundamental importance. It, too, separates man into different homogeneous groups. Man is born with certain intellectual capacities. These capacities are usually related to the chief area of interest of the individual and individuals with the same area of interest are homogeneous in nature.

This, however, accounts only for general areas of interest. A particular homogeneous group might have a general affinity toward modern art or more specifically the work of a particular modern artist. Yet, there might be a wide difference of opinion about the relative intrinsic or terminal value of a given work of art by the artist in question. This is because intrinsic values involve feeling, are individual, and are qualitative in nature.

The method of science has given us a philosophic way to judge the relative merit of extrinsically valued things through quantitative analysis. The things man holds more important or the things we hope they hold more important (the qualities of man and the qualities of the products of man's creative activity), however, fall outside the realm of scientific investigation because of their extreme variability. As we have said, we examine and judge the creative activities of man qualitatively or in a way in which Whitehead calls "aesthetic apprehension."[2]

When a person examines a work of art, he is judging and not measuring. Measuring involves a comparative standard, judgment does not. This is the fundamental difference between things quantitative and qualitative. The extrinsic value of an object may be *judged* through quantitative measurements with an explicit standard in mind. The intrinsic value of an object can be *judged* through qualitative criticism of the qualities of the object as it relates to *controlled* experience. In this sense, standards for measuring and standards for judgment are often confused. In the sense of qualitative measurement, there are no standards for criticism or judgment. But in order to keep us from falling into the bottomless chasm of impressionistic theoretical criticism, there are a few criteria for judgment, which apply to the arts, implicitly or explicitly recognized in analytical criticism and capable of formulation. They are complete exploitation of the media, the unique use of the media (when we read a sonnet we do not want to be made to think how much better the same thing could have been done in oils), subordination of ornamentation to form, relation of form to matter, etc. These criteria, however, are not "sure alls" or "cure alls" for the making of the perfect

[2]Alfred North Whitehead, *Science and the Modern World*, 2nd ed. (New York: Macmillan Co., 1925), p. 279.

art product. They can, which is just as important, help us to understand art as a manifestation of experience. In doing this, we become more aware of what we experience. And the art product as an experience elicits specific experiences from specific works of art relevant to the art product which is experienced.

Outside of intelligence, experience is a semichaotic confusion; movement without direction, matter without form, uncontrolled sounds, color without choice or discrimination, etc. The artist and spectator, however, in dealing with fragments of experience, intensify, clarify, and interpret the experience. The arts suggest the ultimate goal of all ordered experience, the concept of man living in an ordered and creative society.

Criteria for a more ordered experience in art naturally precedes disciplinary judgment. The criteria do not inhibit the creative process because they are not limitations; rather they open new vistas to the understanding, to the imagination, and to experience. It is not what we *cannot* do, it is, through understanding, what we *can* do.

31. Evaluating Children's Art

ELLIOT W. EISNER

The evaluation of children's art has been and continues to be one of the most vexing problems in the teaching of art. Making judgments about the adequacy of a child's art work is no easy task. Neither the criteria nor the standards to be applied are easily selected. Furthermore, the literature in art education shows no strong consensus concerning the "best" ways to evaluate. Research findings too are inconclusive. Questions about the desirability of art contests, grading art work, displaying all work regardless of quality, lack a definitive answer. The lack of definitive research findings provides no consolation to the classroom teacher facing thirty or more children. Decisions need to be made. Neither the teacher nor the children can wait; the teacher must act.

The problem of determining the best criteria to use in evaluation is not merely a methodological one. Such a problem rests upon a philosophical base. Deciding upon what is best as a means also implies that in the long run the means selected will contribute to the achievement of the larger ends sought. Thus, any method used to evaluate a child's work should be consonant with not only the particular purposes of art education, but also the larger scheme of education of which it is a part.

It is my purpose here to deal with some major ideas regarding evaluation in general, and to relate them specifically to the evaluation of children's art. Evaluating performance is difficult in any curriculum area. It is especially difficult in art because the nature of the field does not lend itself to the neat categories that are more easily applied to other fields.

Evaluation has a fairly specific meaning in education. It is a *judgment of the adequacy of behavior as compared to a set of educational objectives*. This conception of evaluation rests upon the assumption that educational activities are purposefully planned and that they are formulated to achieve specific ends. While this conception of evaluation is commonplace in education, it is not as common in art education. If it were employed in the teaching of art, it would require first a clear formulation of objectives for each activity included in the art curriculum. Second, it would require that the objectives be stated in terms of desired student behavior rather

*SOURCE: Reprinted from *School Arts*, Vol. 63, No. 1 (September, 1963), pp. 20–22.

than in terms of behaviors to be displayed by the teacher. Third, it would require that objectives be so clearly stated that they would be useful in determining if the objectives have or have not been achieved. When purposes and objectives are vague or ambiguous one is hard pressed to know exactly to what they refer.

Being clear about one's teaching purposes does not necessarily mean that activities be rigid or that standards be tight. Clarity of purpose is more likely to be useful in the selection of activities designed to reach certain ends than purposes which are diffuse. Clarity of purpose and efficiency in means are desired in the academic areas; it seems reasonable to aspire for no less in the teaching of art.

Objectives in teaching art are not always preplanned. What the student produces and what he learns are not always foreseen. The teacher is often faced with the task of trying to exploit the accidental and ephemeral qualities that are displayed in the work. Thus, if a student happens upon an imaginative use of color in a project designed to further knowledge of composition, the teacher may decide to shift his objectives for that student in order to capitalize upon the student's accidental discovery. This implies flexible purposing on the part of the teacher. It is in these unplanned flexible modifications that teaching becomes most artistic. The teacher recognizes that something valuable can be taught, takes advantage of the unique situation to try to teach it, and evaluates the student's performance with the particular objectives he formulated when he decided to make the shift.

The use of clearly formulated objectives in the evaluation process is an important aid to the teacher, but objectives alone will not provide evidence that the student has progressed. In order to determine progress and growth the student's work must be compared. The most common method of comparison in American schools is that of comparing individual performance to group performance. The classroom, the grade level, the national norm, all provide a comparative base for making judgments about the student's achievement. While such a method provides valuable data, it does not provide evidence of change. Knowing the relative rank of an individual child in a particular classroom tells a great deal about his relation to others but nothing about his progress. In order to determine progress, past and present performance must be compared.

The lack of standardized achievement tests in the field of art has enabled the field to avoid some of the evaluation practices that characterize many of the academic areas where standardized tests are available. However, with the growth of research in art education we may someday have and use standardized tests in art. While such tests might be useful for comparing large groups, they are of little use for evaluating individual achievement. And it is the individual child and not the statistical abstraction that the teacher faces. However, the practice of comparing children's performances has not totally escaped art education. Although art teachers, I believe, have been generally more sensitive to individual performance, the practice of comparing a student's products to those of his classmates is still used as an important method for judging achievement. The use of such a method is reflected in the concept of developmental levels in art. This concept is essentially a statistical one. It says simply that most children at a given age level produce art work having particular characteristics. While developmental levels in art are very useful for making general descriptions of groups, they cannot justifiably be used prescriptively. That is, it is illogical to conclude that a particular child *ought* to perform in a certain way simply because most children of his age do.

As simple and as reasonable as this might

sound in theory, it is seldom employed in practice. Assigning grades and evaluating progress on the basis of large-scale group comparisons is characteristic of American schools. Parents, teachers, and principals all desire their children, students, and teachers to be above average and somehow overlook the fact that if by some magic all such individuals were improved by 80 per cent, half would still be below average.

Our enchantment with group comparison is clearly reflected in the way grades are assigned. In general, average performance earns an average grade, above average performance, excellent or superior grades. The student is most often graded, in art as elsewhere, on his relative rank in class. His relationship to others determines how well he is doing. Such a system of grading is further confused by sandwiching an absolute description — excellent — between two comparative descriptions — average and superior! Thus, theoretically a student who is excellent has met certain standards; while one that is superior is better than most. Is it any wonder that confusion over grading exists?

Another shortcoming of using a class or grade level comparison as the dominant method for evaluating children's art work is the widely accepted myth that children in the fifth grade, for example, are fifth graders. Our knowledge of individual differences is often put aside in grading and placement practices in the school. The most common criterion for grade placement and achievement expectations is chronological age. Yet, if the same standardized tests are used in a classroom to determine the range of academic achievement, grade levels dissolve into a convenient fiction. For example, on the average, there is a four-year range in school readiness in first grade students. In the eighth grade, in the average classroom, there is an eight-year range in reading achievement. In the middle of the

academic year for any grade level only from 15 to 20 per cent of the students are achieving at grade level in each academic area. As yet we do not have such data for art performance, but it is reasonable to expect that similar findings will emerge.

What we will probably find is that as children become older, the range of art ability for each age increases. As the range of ability expands through the grades, the need for differentiating the art curriculum increases. Teachers should encourage these differences and plan so that those who are ready and able to move more quickly are provided with the kind of instruction that will make such progress possible. Conversely, those who achieve at a slower rate should be provided with instruction that makes provision for their natural learning pace without being concerned with falling behind. In short, I believe elementary schools should maximize individual differences despite their lock-step grade structure. And since art programs need not impose identical expectations and activities upon students merely because they are of the same age, it follows that criteria used for evaluating performance should also be differentiated. Comparing the child's work to that of his peers need not be the dominant method of evaluation.

There is an alternative to group comparison that might be well to explore. That alternative is one of comparing a student's work to his previous work and to use such a comparison as the *primary basis* for making judgments about growth. Indeed, if growth, in the Deweyan sense, should be the ultimate goal that schools should seek to attain, it is illogical to measure growth by comparing an individual to others. If we want to know if a child has gotten taller, it is fruitless to find out if he is above average in height. The analogy holds true for evaluating achievement in art.

Using an individual comparative base is

not only desirable on logical grounds, it also serves to improve instruction. It provides opportunities for diagnosing strengths and weaknesses in art performance. With such diagnosis it may be possible to plan activities specifically designed to help individual students.

If schools kept a portfolio of samples of each student's art work throughout the grades, it would be possible for teachers to consult these sources in planning art programs designed to meet the needs of particular students. Activities thus planned would rest upon a clear set of educational objectives in art, a longitudinal view of the student's past performance, and empirical evidence concerning the student's weaknesses and strengths in art. Such a portfolio could also be used by the student to help him recognize his own progress. It could present dramatic evidence of change that often goes unrecognized by those students who frequently underestimate their own progress.

The use of art products as the primary data for comparison can be supplemented by material written by the student at intervals during the school year. If the student can be encouraged to indicate his interest, understanding, and general attitude toward his own work, the teacher can obtain valuable information about factors that might otherwise go unnoticed. Students who are "doing well in art" in the eyes of the teacher may have serious misgivings about their own work. Such attitudes can build up and can lead to a rejection of art as a satisfying field of human experience. They can convince the student that he has no aptitude for art. How many adults, who are products of older art education programs, are convinced that they have neither talent nor interest in art?

By obtaining short descriptions from the student about his interest and satisfaction in art, the teacher is placed in a position of being able to provide encouragement and

support at those strategic moments when they are most in need. All the teacher has to observe is the student's overt behavior and art products. He can only surmise what the student's covert attitudes are. But the student has direct access to his own feelings and can, when student-teacher relations allow, describe how he feels about his own adequacy in art and his satisfaction in it. It would be sad indeed if we overlooked the attitudes that the student develops toward art in our eagerness to enable him to become responsive to and productive in the field.

In suggesting the use of educational objectives for evaluation and individual past performance as a means of determining progress I realize that many practical difficulties might ensue. Traditional expectations are not easy to dismiss. Both children and parents like to know where they stand in relation to others. Such a desire is further fostered by our culture. The use of material symbols works quite well as signs of success. It would be foolhardy to think that values and expectations as pervasive as these can easily be changed. Comparing achievement between groups and individuals is part of our national scene, yet when the schools use it as a primary method for evaluating and grading students it tends to encourage the slow-moving child to disregard his own achievements. Since the school rewards achievement based upon group status, there is little reason for him to think highly of his individual progress. The student needs to recognize his own progress in art as well as to recognize the achievements of others. This recognition is more likely to take place when he is encouraged to measure his own achievement in terms of his own growth rather than by limiting his comparison to the work of others.

In the last analysis differentiating the evaluative criteria for children of different abilities is based upon a conception of educational equality. Equality of educational opportunity means not only that all children have access to education but that all children have equal treatment. Equal treatment does not mean sameness of treatment. It means that all students are provided with the kinds of opportunities that are commensurate with their abilities and that expectations in performance are differentiated on the same basis. Providing an equal opportunity in art education, as in education in general, is after all a goal worthy of our aspirations.

32. Evaluation of Art Teaching

COMMITTEE ON THE FUNCTION OF ART IN GENERAL EDUCATION

In recent years a mounting interest in measurement has been exhibited in the educational world. In the various teaching areas much effort has been expended on the development of instruments to measure more exactly and objectively what students were learning. But in the face of this movement art teachers have, on the whole, remained aloof, unconvinced; they have not shared the general enthusiasm and at times have protested against the bases of it.

Various considerations have entered into this attitude: First, art teachers have undoubtedly been repelled by the more extreme statements of measurers — for example, that whatever exists can be measured. To art teachers, as to many others concerned with the wider aspects of educational experience, such a statement seems patently open to criticism. How, they ask, could one measure some of the values most significant in the art experience? How can sheer enjoyment of an experience be measured? Can any instrument register the personal release which comes through listening to a symphony or through expressing one's emo-tion in the painting of a picture? Can means be found to weigh the degree of personal integrity represented by a piece of sculpture? If, on the other hand, art work is to be judged only by its lesser but more objective manifestations, then the movement proceeds on delusive assumptions.

A second consideration which has caused art teachers to be dubious is the unsatisfactory nature of their experience thus far with testing. Use of the written test—the easiest and most obvious approach in measurement —has brought difficulties in its train. In the form in which these tests have attained prominence they have tended to measure chiefly information about art, and as art teachers consider this quite incidental to their real aims, they dislike having it stressed as of high importance. On the one hand such stress gives to administrators and other laymen a fallacious impression of the purpose of the arts. On the other hand the continued use of such tests in school testing programs may serve, by the pressure it exerts, to distract even art teachers themselves from the aims they most desire.

*SOURCE: Reprinted from *The Visual Arts in General Education: A Report of the Committee on the Function of Art in General Education for the Commission on Secondary School Curriculum.* Copyright, 1939, Progressive Education Association; Copyright, 1940, D. Appleton-Century Company, Inc. Reprinted by permission of Appleton-Century-Crofts.

The efforts thus far to extend the functions of the written test to the measurement of "appreciation" are likewise disappointing. In a commonly used instrument of this sort pupils are asked to look at a series of small reproductions of art objects and indicate the ones they prefer. Such a procedure, it is obvious, violates outrageously a proper conception of appreciation. It is for most purposes unimportant which object a child prefers, provided he has some personal reason for liking it which gives it value to him. If he sees in the object something which excites his imagination and gives it real meaning to him, then he appreciates that object. The fact that others do not respond as he does or that most people like another object better is irrelevant. And to say that "discrimination" rather than "appreciation" is being measured meets the objection only verbally. The procedure is therefore decidedly questionable in its assumptions as to the nature of appreciation. Moreover it is doubtful that any one could in a short test period "appreciate" a large number of pictures in any way that matters. It is doubtful also that he could have any genuine art experience with the small halftone reproductions necessarily used in such tests, though even the use of better pictures would not remove the chief objections inherent in the procedure.

Whether written tests must necessarily confine themselves to such gross and perversive functions is another story. The fact remains that since art teaching has been judged in this way by city-wide and state-wide testing programs many teachers tend to rebel at the very mention of a written test on the arts.

A third basis of apprehensiveness regarding tests is found in the tendency of measurers and other laymen to judge the student's development through the arts by his works alone, to fix attention on the quality of his product rather than on the subtler meanings

and values it represents for him. Attempts at measurement easily fall into this difficulty by the very nature of their search for objectivity and by their added desire to find bases of comparison. For the art teacher the product itself must be subordinate to personality values; in the realm of personality growth and expression, comparisons are especially odious. The student's work is, it is true, an important source of data as to what is happening to him, but not the only source. For example, the teacher who wishes to know whether a student's attitudes toward the arts have changed during his studio experience can form some idea from the way he goes about his work and from what he says about it, but this cannot be done with any certainty merely by looking at his products.

One real danger in relying exclusively upon the student's work to judge what he has learned is the increasing tendency, as time goes on, to judge his achievement by standards of what a work of art should be, despite determination not to do so. Teachers say that John needs to improve the quality of his line and Mary needs to handle color better, forgetting that John may need far more to learn to trust his own judgment and Mary may need far more to learn to accept criticism impersonally or to learn how to improve her own appearance. This is not to say, of course, that the teachers should ignore the product, but it is to say that concentration upon the product tends naturally to force more and more consideration of what the product needs rather than of what the student needs. The products help to disclose his need, but they do not tell the whole story and they may distract attention from the young person himself.

With but brief time available, with hundreds of works in progress, and with students wanting help on all of them, teachers may tend to think chiefly of what will enable the student to get better objective results. One boy's style is getting cramped — he needs to work large for a time; another's color is getting muddy — he needs to experiment with pure colors. Thus unless definite precautions are taken to compel attention to aims other than the quality of the art products, the energy of the teacher is expended chiefly in making better artists of students.

Another danger in stressing the art product as a means of evaluation is the danger of encouraging competitiveness. Too many factors in the student's environment already tend in this direction — the cultural climate of thinking, the marking system, and also the parents' own solicitude that the child do well in his work. Even without this pressure from the outside the adolescent tends to place undue importance on the quality of his product. Concerned as he is with achieving adult status, with demonstrating his effectiveness to a world which questions his readiness for full membership, the student tends in any event to be unduly self-conscious, unduly introspective, to feel himself unduly inadequate. To find his products the object of appraisal, of comparison, can only heighten tendencies which need to be reduced rather than increased.

The Committee is quite sympathetic to these considerations and shares the misgivings which grow out of them. To surrender the more significant values of the art experience on the altar of objectivity and comparison would be a needless tragedy. But because art teaching deals with the more intangible, the more elusive, it must take every precaution in its power not to be misled as to its effectiveness, not to be satisfied with verbal statements or with classroom demonstration only. The newer testing movement at its best is making a real contribution through its inquiry into the application, the employment of what is learned; it is contributing to a healthy skepticism regarding so-called learning which does reveal itself sooner or later in changed living — in growing sensitivities, in heightened appreciation, in more adequate outlook, in enriched enjoyment, as well as in the more objective respects. Here is an area of inquiry which art teachers must respect and find worthy of their own study.

The Committee believes, moreover, that the prevailing conception of evaluation, by its stress on "measuring" and "testing," has diverted attention unjustifiably to end results and so has given an emasculated conception of the possibilities inherent in appraisal; it believes that a better and more fruitful view would open up new potentialities within the teaching process itself. From these various considerations, certain aspects of the problem are to be discussed further.

A Broader Conception of Evaluation

Most teachers think of evaluation as the final step in the art experience, an appraisal by them of the student's work, a sort of "last judgment" of that particular experience closing then irrevocably for all time. For many teachers evaluation begins only when they are pressed to make a decision about the student in the form of a symbol, a mark. They then proceed to sum up in adding-machine fashion the student's merits or demerits — the number of times he has succeeded or failed in response to questions in the class and the number of successes and failures found in his portfolio. On this basis a rating is given. That such a conception of evaluation is held by most is not strange; it has prevailed in education for many years. Probably the teacher was himself appraised in this way as a student and is still being so appraised by his principal.

But without at this time discussing the merit and grading system — an evil unto itself and deserving of separate discussion

— consider the inadequacy of such a conception of appraisal. Actually evaluation begins with the inception of the art experience, at the moment teacher and student come together and regard each other. It starts with emotional response on the part of both. The student tries to discover whether he is going to like the teacher and the work together; the teacher attempts to learn what sort of individual the student is and to decide what will constitute fruitful ways of dealing with him. The instructor observes the young person's attitude toward the other students, and toward the situation, and makes mental notes as to what would be likely to appeal to him. But obviously the process does not end there. Constant watch must be kept for further data throwing light on the student's needs and potentialities. The teacher must stand ready continually to review his estimate and to alter his procedure accordingly.

The evaluation process in this sense goes on constantly as emerging factors are weighed to gain a total picture of the individual and his changing, progressive relationship to art experiences. Whenever the teacher assesses the needs of the individual in order to decide what to recommend as a next step, evaluation goes on, must go on. And whenever the teacher takes account of the situation in this fashion he must, as a correlative, make an estimate of his own teaching procedures in order to confirm or revise them as means to the values he wishes for the student. There is no reason whatever to restrict an evaluation program to written tests. Most of the teacher's appraising will be informal and subjective, as he observes what his pupils are doing and talks with them about their interests and problems.

The basic consideration, then, is to determine whether teaching procedures are adequate to help students learn the really important things it is desired to teach them. The major function of a conscious evaluation program may well be to suggest a wider range of elements to look for than the usual ones having to do with the quality of the students' expression of their ideas and feelings in art media.

It is highly desirable to know, for example, whether students have such an interest in the arts that it functions in their living; whether they are becoming increasingly sensitive to art values in their daily lives; whether they are developing sound attitudes toward the arts and expressing them in their behavior, or whether their ideas and understandings are fallacious; whether art experiences are contributing to their emotional adjustment, their independence, and so on; whether the student has a wholesome attitude toward his classmates and adults; whether he is social or antisocial or merely withdrawn. Perhaps instead the students are really learning to be insensitive to art values in their daily living, as so many artists are; perhaps they are becoming hostile or indifferent to the arts; perhaps they are growing to be conflicted and maladjusted beings, using art as an escape.

As was stated earlier in the chapter, the student's product is an important aid to evaluation. As each individual's handwriting or his English compositions have marks of his own individuality, so also do his art works. The product should not, however, be appraised alone, but in relation to all other known elements in the student's behavior. If the art expression is free and unhampered, it may reveal phases of the student's development not discoverable otherwise, for through the language of graphic symbols a student will often say things about himself that he will not say in other media of expression. For example, a weak line in drawing may reveal not only weakness in representing a visual perception but also a weakness in character. Likewise, organization or chaos in art work may indicate integrating or disintegrating attitudes in the student.

Suggested Lines of Appraisal

In an evaluation program of the sort here proposed it is obvious that the teacher's own behavior and method of working must receive central consideration. This is a continuing obligation for all teachers, no matter how efficient. Methods which succeed admirably at one time and with some students may fail at another time or with different students; the facet of the teacher's personality which helps him to gain the confidence of one individual may have the opposite effect on another. The art technique which succeeds with one student may not succeed with another. The good teacher, therefore, like the good artist or scientist, learns to adjust his procedures to the situation he is dealing with, to evaluate them continually as he evaluates the status and needs of the student, for it is unrealistic to think of shortages or needs in students without correlatively giving thought to better ways of meeting these needs. The suggestions following are accordingly designed to help the teacher make such an examination of his individual student's needs.

Regarding his own approach to the teaching situation, the teacher will wish to make inquiries such as these:

Do I take account of the fact that personality development is inherently involved in all art experiences?

The teacher of art should evaluate not only the art elements in the experience; his insight should be sufficiently broad to envisage the larger factors of personality growth.

He should ask: Am I sensitive to indications of the student's mental, physical, and emotional needs? Do I look for indications of his development in social adjustment? Do I look at his behavior as a whole for evidence of his growth, or do I look merely at the art work he produces? Am I aware of individual personalities in my group?

Each student in a class is entitled to consideration on his own account and in terms of his own potentialities, and the teacher should establish sufficient personal contact with the students to know their individual differences.

Inquiries such as these should be made: Do I see my class as a unit, or as a group of persons both like and unlike each other? Am I aware of the needs and potentialities of each? Are my aims and procedures sufficiently flexible to allow for all differences of temperament, intelligence, and artistic ability? Am I sensitive to the needs, interests and capacities of my students?

Often a teacher is so acutely aware of his own interests and needs that he inadvertently teaches with them in view rather than the students' problems. To avoid this pitfall, especially when one is in a role of authority, requires special effort. Even when the teacher conscientiously attempts to take his cues from the students, he may draw on his own adolescence as a means of understanding them without taking into account that his experience may have been very different from theirs. It is common also for the teacher to set up his own superiorities as standards and to expect the student to excel in the same techniques, habits, or skills. Or, conversely, he may come to admire and hold up for emulation those who exhibit attainments he himself lacks.

The teacher should ask: Is my effort directed toward securing the student's own expression? Or do I project my own needs and interests upon my class?

Am I a sufficiently creative person to recognize and respect creativeness in others?

Must the teacher be a creative person in order to recognize and appraise creativeness in others? Surely, he must because creative experience has values of its own which can be identified and appraised only by one who is himself creative; and the wider and more varied the teacher's experience, the greater will be his opportunity to recognize and to give expression to a variety of creative expression.

To cover this point the teacher should ask such questions as the following: Am I creative with art media, or have I abandoned such efforts? Do I display imagination, ingenuity, sensitivity in my teachings, or do I expect the same materials and same procedures to suit all students and all classes, year after year? Do I reach out for new ideas which will contribute to creativeness in dealing with my students and with problems of living? Do I reorganize my own life wherever feasible to secure greater effectiveness, or do I merely accept what exists or what comes? Do I deal with individuals in a way to elicit creative response?

Creativeness is so personal and so delicate that it is often difficult to recognize and it is even more difficult to germinate. Therefore the teacher must encourage its growth at the outset, even at the expense of many other values. Only a teacher who is highly sensitive to his students can estimate the creativeness of their expression, for evidence of creativeness must be sought not in the product which is turned out but in the student himself. With some students the product may be very crude or it may be weak and unformed, but it may nevertheless represent a definite reorganization of the individual's own insights and values. Often in the desire to achieve good art work the teacher has no patience to wait for the individual to develop his own creative power, but instead imposes another's more successful expression on him, thereby destroying the opportunity for individual growth.

Creativeness is unlikely to arise unless the student feels that he is valued as a person with his own feelings and aims and that any sincere effort at expression will be respected. The situation should be of the sort to encourage thoughtfulness, resource-

fulness, and desire to experiment. It should moreover be recognized that creation is not the making of something entirely new out of nothing, but rather it is the achieving of a new integration out of existing thoughts, values, materials, elements. Thus an atmosphere rich in stimulation serves to open lines of thought and feeling.

The teacher should therefore ask: Do I see each individual as a person with potentialities and need for expression? Do I enter sympathetically into his aims on his own terms to help him to clarify his desires and to find means to express them? Do I supply, through my own efforts, through class discussion, through provision of materials, the rich play of suggestion necessary to fructification of ideas? Do I refrain from procedures which bias or coerce him to my way of thinking or doing? Do the students feel that I regard their initiative as highly important? Do I strive in all my associations with them to build independence rather than dependence?

Do I evaluate student expression in terms of adolescent capacities or by adult standards?

A basic principle of art expression at any level is that the artist objectify what he himself sees and feels. But with young people this principle is one of the most frequently violated. Too often a teacher sensitive in other respects sets up adult standards as his criteria and tends to evaluate the student's work in these terms. This is largely due to ignorance of proper standards of adolescent achievement. And since the student is himself desirous of achieving adult recognition, he becomes an easy victim to this practice.

The teacher should ask, therefore: Are my criteria based on the student's own needs and abilities? Am I evaluating his work in terms of his own level? Am I evaluating it in terms of his own aims and abilities?

Am I sensitive to the relationship of studio experiences with other areas of living?

The art teacher must look with a discerning eye at the studio experience to insure that it makes for insight into and enrichment of other areas of living. He should accordingly be himself possessed of broad insight and understanding. Here, again, the wider, richer, and more meaningful his own experience, the greater the contribution he can make to his students' growth. Exchange of experiences with other teachers in other fields of study helps him to extend and to clarify his judgment in those fields and at the same time to use the combined resources for meeting students' needs. Interest and participation in community affairs will reveal many places where art is needed in the social life.

The teacher should ask: Am I sensitive to the wider significance of art, or do I confine my attention for the most part to my own field? Am I a student of life — of human beings and of the social life — so I can discover continually new ways for art to contribute? Through what specific means can I increase my sensibilities in these broader areas?

Regarding the learning experiences he promotes, the teacher will wish to ask questions such as these:

Will the experience contribute to the growth of the student's personality?

The importance of any experience in art lies in what it does to the individual, not in the kind of art work produced; thus evaluation must be made in terms of the student, not of the product. If the product is weak or poor, it may signify weakness or poor quality of development, and the teacher should seek to help the person, not change the product. When the student has changed, then the product will change also, and its change will be an evidence of growth in the personality of the creator.

The object in evaluating art experiences for their potentialities in growth is, of course, to nourish worthy characteristics and to discourage the unworthy, to confirm and enrich desirable habits and attitudes and strive to alter those which are undesirable. For example, if an egocentric tendency is discovered, the teacher may make it contribute to the student's development by giving him a position of responsibility in a stage crew or in a group working on a mural, where the trait may be altered by opportunity to direct and yet share with others in contributing to a large purpose outside of himself.

In studying personality needs of the student, the teacher will inquire regarding many points: What kind of individual is this student? Is he pleasant or unpleasant, aggressive or retiring, creative or unimaginative, unique or commonplace? Is he a well-balanced individual, the kind that one likes to have around? What are his social patterns of behavior? Is he sensitive to and considerate of other people? Is he outgoing and interested in others? Does he work well with a group? Can he subject his ego to group thinking and working when the situation demands it? What kind of interests does he have? Are his interests growing in variety and richness? Does he have opinions of his own? How did he come by them? Can he work out his ideas? Can he manage himself, or must he be supervised?

Does the experience arouse the student's interest?

Artists would agree that an experience which is not interesting lacks the essence, the *sine qua non*, of the art experience. But in addition an experience which is not interesting lacks dynamic, for interest in its psychological sense means exactly the pull on the individual of a situation or a factor in it, such a going-out to it that he wishes to do something about it. In a new situation the pull comes because a previous interest now sees a way of extending itself.

An art experience, for example, may be interesting because of its subject-matter, the medium, or the function, or because of all of those. Adolescent boys may be interested in drawing war scenes because of the subject-matter, or in modeling athletes because of the medium, clay, or in making modern jewelry because of its utility value, or they may enjoy making etchings of sailboats because the activity possesses several values. One student may identify himself with a problem in abstract design because of his ability to solve mathematical problems; another may be challenged by the technical requirements of a situation. In the case of any particular individual the elements of appeal will be those which grow out of his own peculiar make-up.

But it is a primary fact that a new activity which has no relationship to the present values and experiences of the student can have no "pulling power" for him, can arouse no real desire to exert effort. Perhaps a relationship to his interests exists and help from the teacher or further exploration by himself will disclose it. If not, there can be no psychological basis of appeal, of awakening dynamic.

The teacher should ask, then: What evidence do I see that interest does exist? Is the student taking hold of the experience himself? Does he display the eagerness to work at it which would indicate that he is identifying himself with it? Does the experience seem to establish an outlet, mental, emotional, or physical, for him? If not, what relationships to him and his living do I see in it which make me feel that it is appropriate and fruitful for him? Can I open these relationships in a way to arouse his interest? If not, am I merely pressing him to do something which has interest and value for me or for other students but not for him? Will the values likely to come from such a course outweigh the disadvantages in his case?

The teacher should ask further: How fruitful is his present basis of interest? Is it one I wish to see grow, or has it elements of

disintegration in it for him (for example, enjoyment of exciting war scenes)? Does it manifest a deeper disturbance which I should give attention to (for example, frustration)?

Does the experience allow the student to express something of his own self?

It is not a simple matter to judge whether another's experience comes from within himself, for it requires intimate knowledge of the person and of the situation. Many products made under the guise of self-expression are imitations of the ideas of someone else, perhaps the teacher, perhaps some favorite artist. The teacher must, therefore, know how to recognize the naïve statements that bespeak the self and nourish it into being and must foster experiences which allow and encourage the student to say something of his own.

He should ask, for example: Is the individual striving to say something of his own, to relate an experience significant to him? Or does the experience involve mere production as in the representation of a still life? Does the experience provoke thought and arouse eagerness to act? What evidence is there of his own individuality? A question should also be asked regarding the method used: Is the student being allowed to experiment with the medium in his own way or is each step dictated by the teacher, so that initiative and imagination are stifled?

Will the experience extend the student's present interests and capacities?

Experiences in art which do not include elements of growth for the student may be interesting at the outset but will soon cease to challenge. If, on the other hand, the present interest is extended to include new elements or to employ new abilities, the experience will have more satisfaction as well as greater value for the student. If enjoyment and interest are to continue, the expression should involve problems, it should stimulate endeavor, it should lead to learnings and activities that reach beyond the former range. For example, painting a picture may lead to an interest in color or composition. It may, by the demand to meet a new problem, require experimentation and acquisition of new abilities or suggest further fields of exploration; a student who finds it a problem to represent action in a football game may experiment, may try to work out the new and difficult poses from those he knows how to draw, and in doing so discover new facts about figure drawing.

The teacher should ask: Does the experience present new stimulation to the student? Does it arouse his curiosity? Does it call for new visual perceptions? Does it keep him striving toward further growth?

Is the student growing in ability to criticize himself and to make use of the criticism of others?

Ability to profit by criticism is extremely important to one who wishes to achieve improvement — whether in his techniques, in his art products, or in clarity and refinement of the point of view he expresses through these. A critical attitude implies an analytical state of mind in which one evaluates the elements in one's situation in order to achieve more satisfactory integration of them; when this is coupled with discernment as to values, it functions as good judgment. One who wishes to grow in this respect must be willing to study rigorously both his point of view and his products to see whether his own present best can be further extended. He must grow in power to analyze and to discriminate.

Facility in using the criticism of others is an essential to such growth. This is in itself something of an art. It requires open-mindedness, so that suggestions may be entertained and canvassed for their full value; it requires confidence in one's own point of view, such respect for one's own convictions

and ideas that one is free and secure in entertaining the views of others; it requires also discrimination, for one's position should not be merely laid aside, but rather examined for its worth and then remade in part or entirely as the new insight directs; it requires determination to act on the insight gained. Ability to employ criticism in this way requires control and self-discipline and is an evidence of power for which nothing else substitutes; it is one of the most important elements in differentiating persons.

The teacher should note the student's behavior in these respects: Does he study his work and his procedures to improve them? Does he learn increasingly to criticize his efforts? How does he respond to suggestions of others — does he build up a defense against them; does he incorporate them too readily and without evaluation; does he display receptiveness, comprehension, ingenuity? The evidence in answer to these questions will, of course, be relative — persons of the highest integrity exhibit such qualities in varying degree on different occasions. If, however, the evidence is negative, the teacher should ask himself the reason and attempt to get at the cause. Does it arise from fear of failure, from insecurity, from an unsocial attitude, from cocksureness, or from some other cause?

Will the experience help the student to grow in sensibility to art values?

The experience should extend the individual's awareness of art values and make him sensitive and receptive to their use. If he is painting a picture, he should grow in knowledge and understanding of the underlying values that make a good picture; he should also grow in sensitivity so that the presence of these values affects him pleasantly and their absence annoys or concerns him. Needless to say, the mere capacity to recite art principles is not necessarily an evidence of awareness. The student demonstrates his awareness by exhibiting the values in his own work and by the way he responds to them in works of others.

Will the experience increase the student's awareness of wider relationships?

Experience in art should develop in the student conceptions which increase his insight into other fields of study and living as well as into the arts, thereby adding enrichment to all. This seeing of wider and deeper meanings is an important element of the art experience. As he builds a conception or sensitivity in art he should come to sense its bearing in other areas of living.

For example, once he has gained the concept of himself as an individual it should have a reference much wider than his own experience; it should help him to understand and appreciate people. Though he may not like Salvador Dali, the Surrealist, he should be able to respect the uniqueness which makes Dali what he is in art; similarly he should be able to respect the uniqueness in all individuals. He should, in other words, be able to look sympathetically for another's idiom just as he expects others to search for and respect his own. As he grasps the meaning of creativeness in art media he should be helped to see how creativeness can enter into all areas of living. As he comes to understand the values in self-expression he should be helped to see the social bearing of the conception: how democracy is an attempt to carry these values into all areas of living for all people; how social institutions may further or thwart the realization of this aim.

The test in this aspect of the art experience will be found in the answers to questions such as the following: Is the teaching of a kind to break down compartmentalization of experience? What use does the student make in other experiences of the insights or techniques acquired in art, and vice versa? Are the conceptions he is acquiring in the arts carrying over into his

living to cause him to display there greater sensitiveness and understanding? Does the art experience tend to unify and illuminate the other aspects of living?

To determine the effects of experiences in art on the life of the student, the teacher should look to the student's day-by-day behavior; only by his findings there can he estimate the extent to which the work in art is influencing the student's life processes. Questions such as the following should be asked: Is the student a happier, more effective personality because of his work in art?

Queries of the sort suggested earlier for canvassing personality needs should be raised with reference to the student's daily living. The teacher should make observations along various lines: Are undesirable traits tending to disappear? Are his gifts being used to better advantage? Are his excellences being extended? Has his personal attractiveness increased? Can he deal more effectively with his environment? Does he get along better with his associates? Does he have more or deeper interests and enjoyments? What evidences do I find on points such as these?

Is there evidence in his personal appearance of sensitivity to art values?

It is not necessary or desirable that dress should conform to one set of standards; it is, on the other hand, essential that it express personality. Slickly combed hair and decorous clothing might, even if they could be enforced, be inapt in the adolescent boy whose desire is for free, untrammeled expression and release from petty conventions. But to the girl who is striving for femininity, bizarre or careless dressing would be equally unsuitable. Such questions as these should, therefore, be raised: Does the student employ the help art can give to enhance his good points? Does he dress with an awareness of the necessity that his clothing express his own character? Does he dress appropriately and tastefully?

Have the studio experiences affected his leisure time pursuits?

What are the student's hobbies? Does he continue any art expression on his own initiative? Does he go to museums and galleries through his own volition or only because of teacher persuasion? Who are his favorite artists? What moving pictures does he enjoy most? Does he go to plays? Which plays? What in particular does he enjoy about them? What magazines and books does he read?

What other evidence is there of the effectiveness of his art experiences?

Is the student sensitive to aesthetic values, or lack of them, in his own immediate environment? What pictures hang in his room at home, and who selected them? Is he concerned with the aesthetic improvement of his community or does he take the *status quo* for granted? What that is ugly or thwarting in the lives of people has he become aware of? What evidences do I see in his living of a conception of art broader than the traditional studio variety?

Written Work as an Aid to Appraisal

No other means of evaluation can take the place of constant informal scrutiny by the teacher of his own processes and of the student's developing needs. But, assuming this, there is no reason why teachers should not supplement such inquiries by written exercises or questionnaires wherever these fit in appropriately. For example, on many of the items mentioned in the preceding paragraphs it would be helpful to have more information than can be conveniently got from all members of the class through informal conversations. The teacher may wish, then, to experiment with aids of this sort for purposes of his own illumination. Some of the ends that might be served in this way are the following:

First, written work or questionnaires may be used to reveal the interests and preferences of the students and so to give indication of what to include in the program, of the particular media of expression to be offered.

Second, they may be used to determine to what extent the experience actually offered was counted important by the student. Obviously, the teacher should not make important conclusions on limited or superficial data. He should not conclude that etching is a poor medium for adolescents merely because the majority of a group declare that they did not like the experience they had in it; it may be that the experience was presented under unfortunate conditions.

Third, the written exercise may be used to ascertain how well a particular art concept has been mastered — for example, the organization of the graphic elements of a picture into a harmonious whole. Here the student may be shown an original work of art, in painting, sculpture, or some other field, and asked to criticize it or to react to specific questions. Through his answers the teacher will see what the student has learned to take into account. The results of the test should not, of course, be employed to brand the student as poor in taste or insensitive, but to indicate areas in which he needs help.

Fourth, questionnaires or written assignments may be of definite assistance in securing information of other sorts. They may supply data along the previously mentioned lines of inquiry as to the student's living, his leisure-time pursuits, the wider effectiveness of his art experiences, and the like. They can reveal what students think about the place of the arts in this civilization; whether they think the habitual practice and enjoyment of the arts are normal, adult, manly, and important; what they conceive to be the responsibilities of a citizen for the appearance of his own home, his place of business, and his community; what they think of building codes, zoning restrictions, and similar regulations; their opinion as to the provision made for art experiences in school and community; what the functions of a museum should be; what they consider the chief problems of the artist in contemporary society. Many other areas could be surveyed in similar fashion.

Records, Grades, Reports

In order to follow the student's progress effectively, the teacher will need considerable evidence as to his behavior and should continually make notes, mental and otherwise, of factors to be taken into account. One who is at all sensitive to personality growth will do this almost unconsciously, but for best results definite anecdotal records in written form should be kept in addition. Some teachers find it helpful to jot down notes while the students are at work. Some keep files on their students, including their own reactions to the students as well as statements and remarks made by the students themselves. Other teachers also make notes on the back of the student's art work after the class has been dismissed; if such a plan is followed it is important that the remarks do not fall into the hands of the students. The record might wherever feasible include also photographs of the students at work and of their productions.

When the time comes for the teacher to make a summarized evaluation, he should base it on a consideration of the student's total experience. The appraisal should not appear as a final judgment of something that is finished, but should be stated and regarded as data for future direction of both the student and teacher. Thus it may be like the doctor's periodic check-up and prescription for healthy living.

Obviously it is impossible to make reports with such constructive reference if the traditional plan of marking is used. The grading system which employs a symbol such as a letter or a numeral is repugnant to teachers of art but is still used in most schools. It is inconceivable that a letter such as A, B, C, or a numeral expressed in percentages can ever represent an adequate picture of the status of the child or of the growth he has made, and it is an equally inadequate measure of creative development. Indeed most teachers maintain a mark can represent nothing whatever of real significance regarding the art experience of the pupil. Yet the grade is regarded as an objective by most students and is at times used as a weapon by the teacher.

An emphasis on grades leads, in addition, to false standards. The student who accepts the usual system of grading, with marks as a symbol of success, will not be able to think in terms of the intrinsic rewards of emotional satisfaction and adequate use of his powers. Again to mark all students on the basis of what the most gifted in the class can do drives the less gifted student farther from his own conceptions and increasingly undermines his faith in himself. Even with grades removed, the sense of failure will persist if the better student's achievements are held up as a standard of performance. If a proper relationship is to be established between students of varying interests and capacities in the arts, the teacher must help each student to evaluate his art experiences in terms of his own aims and abilities. The development of power to make such evaluations intelligently may be prevented by a false idea of success or failure. Because the effects of such a rating system upon the student are so hurtful, its use should be either modified or abandoned. The Committee recommends the latter course wherever possible.

The most satisfactory type of report thus far devised is the written statement that indicates as specifically as possible the status of the student in behavior and accomplishment and makes recommendations for further direction. Though this method imposes a burden on the teacher, its results warrant the effort put into it; nothing is as satisfactory as the personal statement for each student. But in cases where a teacher meets several large classes, he may have to adopt a simplified version of this method. A fairly successful substitute for the personally written statement is provided by preparing several form letters carefully planned to cover a variety of types of students and a range of common difficulties. The teacher then selects from his mimeographed supply the form best suited to the particular student and makes necessary changes in longhand. The entire statement is then retyped by the stenographic office. For the student who does not fall into any of the form groups, the teacher writes a special report.

It is quite evident that these suggestions as to records are not wholly adequate and that the problem is of extreme importance, worthy of extensive research; but the Committee is at a loss to suggest better methods at the present time. We are convinced, however, that the anecdotal record is far superior to the system which accords grades or symbols.

SUGGESTED READINGS FOR PART VI

EISNER, ELLIOT W. "A Paradigm for the Analysis of Visual Problem Solving," *Studies in Art Education*, III, 1 (1961), 47–54.

GREENE, THEODORE MEYER. *The Arts and the Art of Criticism*, Part IV. Princeton: Princeton University Press, 1947.

PEPPER, STEPHEN C. *The Basis of Criticism in the Arts*. Cambridge: Harvard University Press, 1956.

STEINBERG, LEO. "The Eye is Part of the Mind," in *Reflections on Art*, 243–261. Edited by Susanne K. Langer. Baltimore: The Johns Hopkins Press, 1958.

THORNDIKE, EDWARD L. "The Measurement of Achievement in Drawings," *Teachers College Record*, XIV, 5 (1913), 1–38.

ZIFF, PAUL. "Reasons in Art Criticism," in *Philosophy and Education*, 219–236. Edited by Israel Scheffler. Boston: Allyn and Bacon, Inc., 1958.

PART VII

WHAT CAN ART EDUCATION CONTRIBUTE TO SOCIETY?

The typical art teacher who finds himself caught up in the daily affairs of the school — who is harassed by bells, schedules and hordes of students, and yet who is also striving to achieve specific, if limited, teaching objectives — is apt to take lightly so weighty a question as the role of art education in society. If he does, it is only because the subject seems so remote and abstract; the question of "ultimate goals," he may think, surely cannot be connected in any intimate and vivid way with his ongoing experience in the school. That there is, or should be, such a connection and that art teachers are in desperate need of a large view of the relations holding between their individual efforts and societal values remains, of course, to be demonstrated. The following articles attempt through various approaches to describe such relations and prescribe a social role for art and art education.

Before the reader moves on to the various answers contained in the articles, some introductory remarks seem appropriate, if only to strike a note of urgency regarding what is partly a scientific and partly a political or philosophic problem, or, rather, a series of interrelated problems involving social facts and values. The first point we may consider is this: Seldom do critics of American schools seriously question the social value of public instruction in reading, writing, arithmetic and now even science; the objectives of literacy for all citizens, skill with numbers, basic knowledge about the world, together with health education and the inculcation of certain basic moral and social precepts and practices are commonly shared objectives. No, most critical arguments tend to focus upon such issues as "why Johnny can't read" (here the debate is between the phonics and "word method" advocates) and how

403

we should organize the school (competing schemes are the self-contained classroom, team teaching and the nongraded school). Generally speaking, the response within the field of education to criticism consists of efforts to find the most effective means of achieving socially accepted or acceptable goals in public school instruction. While there is not complete accord as to what specific modes of inquiry are appropriate in attacking such problems, educators and critics of education widely hold these problems to be common-sensical, technological or scientific in nature; that is, ideally they will be resolved by discussion and debate, by practical testing or by empirical inquiry. One might characterize that kind of criticism and response which limits itself to the evaluation of pedagogical techniques or educational *means* as conservative in nature, for it tends not to question existing social values. The several Conant reports on American education fall into this category. Parenthetically, it may be mentioned that recommendations by conservative critics for improving art education in the schools are conspicuous by their absence.

On the other hand, criticism that does challenge the *status quo*, that does question social values in contemporary American life and education may be identified as either liberal or reactionary in spirit: the former is based on the view that education itself is a means — even *the* means — for reconstructing society in the image of projected democratic ideals; the latter seems bent upon having the schools revert to an image of "the good old days," McGuffey's Readers and all. While reactionary art critics who are both informed and influential are scarce, apparently a considerable number of citizens holds reactionary beliefs and attitudes toward art that are influential if not informed. And these beliefs and attitudes probably affect the success of art education (or lack of it) in the public schools more than all overt criticism combined. The following statements culled from a "letter to the editor" of a Midwestern newspaper reflect this undercurrent:

This type of "beatnikism" [exemplified by award-winning paintings at the State Fair] with its demoralizing influence upon society certainly should not be afforded the dignity of being called "art." It seems about time that the pendulum swing back to the side of sanity.

We are told to "learn to appreciate and understand" this type of thing, but what frame of mind does it require to do this when a mass of smears, blobs, and drips are involved? Or, perhaps a blank plainness that borders upon nothing.

If the "artist" is hereby expressing his feelings and attitudes toward life he is to be pitied and not praised. . . .

This "hodgepodge" and confusion in art is but one of the disintegrating and degenerating influences upon society, making it an easier prey to the alien ideologies that threaten our very existence.

The writer, evidently miffed that "exhibitors of beautiful 'still-life' and scenery" did not win the awards, seems to be suggesting that artists and art teachers do have a role as moral agent in society but that some of them (the prize-winners) either are not living up to it or have forgotten it.

On the liberal side of the ledger, we find, of course, numerous statements of avant-garde artists and critics and many art teachers. Among American educators and philosophers John Dewey possibly has done more than any other individual to promote the idea that art and art education are vital elements in democratic society. And among political leaders and statesmen John F. Kennedy was a champion of the arts. He gave a clear glimpse of his insight into the role of the arts in society in the last essay he wrote on the subject, which appeared in the March 28, 1964, issue of *Saturday Review:*

to understand that the arts incarnate the creativity of a free alitarian society can promote the arts in its own way — that it ductions of opera and ballet, as it can arrange for the restora- uildings. But art means more than the resuscitation of the past: nfined search for new ways of expressing the experience of the future. When the creative impulse cannot flourish freely, when thods and objects, when it is deprived of spontaneity, then socie-

ave expressed themselves with the eloquence of a President ong been saying much the same thing about the arts as a

lly illustrated by the contrasting views, above, is that in an cher must expect a vigorous and wide-ranging debate over education in the nation, community and the school. Our must encourage and join in this debate, for if he does not w of the value of an aesthetic education and creativity for all ositive influence of artists on society, he may lose by default. m will be filled — if not by those professionally informed in nen by those who are not. It is a truism in ethics that when a se to act, he *chooses* not to act: not choosing is actually a choice ve choices open to him) to let matters stand, in somewhat the way a gambler decides to let his bet ride on the same number while playing roulette. The art teacher's gamble, if he chooses not to debate, is that in the general debate over educational issues strong criticism and response from any quarter stand a good chance of reducing his teaching effectiveness with students, forcing a change in his instructional goals and curricular offerings in art, or even threatening his job. For example, the mere shifting of critical attention away from the arts toward the sciences sometimes results in a corresponding shift in student interest and motivation, and in the school's budgetary allocations for staff and physical facilities. So the stakes are high enough to warrant debate. Teaching, of course, is the central task of the art teacher. But also he must, with other citizens, accept the challenge to clarify and establish the role of education in society.

33. Democracy, Education, and Art

FRANCIS T. VILLEMAIN

We are living at a time when ideological schisms and their reinforcing circumstances are playing a major part in the growing threat to the continued existence of the human race in any form with which we are familiar. If philosophic reason is to contribute to the amelioration of our plight, it would appear that certain reformations of our great social quarrels may be in order. A basis for hoping that our intellectual climate might submit to modification rests on the contention that an investigation into a neglected area of study might provide findings capable of producing more fruitful disputes than those under which we presently labor.

Virtually untouched in the history of thought has been the exploration of the interrelations among democracy, art and mass education — indeed, the latter two are usually thought to cast no light whatsoever on the great civilizational problems of men. This assumption has yielded an intellectual tragedy, for it has directed philo-

sophic minds away from sustained analyses of aesthetic experience and its connection with educative processes and democratically ordered social life. The result has been truncated conceptions of both education and democracy as well as the most superficial grasp of the nature and potential functions of the several arts in schools and civilization. But this claim will not appear plausible until it can be shown that the three conceptions can be fruitfully interrelated.

I

The widespread assumption that analyses of artistic enterprises are not particularly relevant to an understanding of the nature of education and democracy is undoubtedly due to a singularly inadequate conception of art. The erroneous notion may well be interpreted as reflecting an historic account of the socially insulated status of certain art forms in various social orders. An examina-

∗SOURCE: Reprinted from *Educational Theory*, XIV, 1 (January 1964), pp. 1–15.

This is a copy of a paper presented at the Thirteenth International Congress of Philosophy, Mexico City, Mexico, September 12, 1963. The paper has had the benefit of criticisms and suggestions made by Professors Joe R. Burnett (University of Illinois), N. L. Champlin (Wayne State University), and George Eastman (University of Toledo).

407

tion of the history of the arts reveals times when certain of the arts were employed as symbols of political and economic power, of a way of life, and a set of values that held the welfare of the entire group in contempt, of a social order in which the conspicuous consumption of elegances by an elite required the perpetuation of a barren existence for the vast sweep of humanity.

Familiarity with this facet of the history of the arts seems to have led some to conclude that art is something necessarily disconnected, independent, and unrelated in any significant way to the social order in which it occurs or to other than artistic spheres of experience. The fallacy committed by this line of reasoning is not difficult to identify. Confusing a historic account of the arts, both inaccurate and incomplete at that, with a critically forged conception of the potential functions of the arts can certainly lead to the conclusion that art is a passive mode of indulgence, an esoteric affair, a dandification of the trivial, uncreative life, and a way of exhibiting the social status of an aristocratic, propertied, or governing elite. Unfortunately, a popular view of art perpetuates this confusion and thus perpetuates a theory of art that presupposes a social structure built upon a division between a laboring, productive, active, practicing group and a leisure, acquisitive, passive, nonproductive group.

Building new societies, whether on the North American continent in the eighteenth century or in Africa in the twentieth, depends upon creative, active, productive processes. Since art is taken to be part and parcel of a life of passive self-gratification, it is accordingly relegated, at best, to a minor role. This aim of active social participation and personal productivity has been joined with the general welfare tradition of Locke, Mill, and Rousseau. Both ideals are grounds for rejecting a social structure devised to make paramount the self-indulgence of a social minority at whatever expense to

the balance of the community. Thus the social base required for implementing the distorted view of art is antithetical to Enlightenment thought from the seventeenth century to the present.

The idea that the function of art is to gratify inconsequential, if not antisocial, impulses is often joined to the notion that art is generated and sustained only in a social setting that maintains the hierarchial division between those who consume and those who labor in their behalf. It is no wonder, therefore, that art would be suspect to Enlightenment thinkers. If art is social froth obtained in an aristocratically oriented society, then it surely holds no promise of contributing either to the meaning or to the realization of democracy. And, if it has nothing to do with what really matters in human affairs, then it certainly has no significant place in education.

Such an outlook makes of art something we superimpose on experience — like a dust jacket on a book. It is something nice to have but essentially superficial; it is disconnected from the sweep of experience. It is something for filling up idle moments. And to be engaged in the arts is, of course, a dilettantism, excusable only if proper provision has been made for things of genuine consequence. Art neither flows from, acts to modify, nor significantly contributes to the central concerns of democratic men. It is delightful trivia.

This view of art was the product of social arrangements that democratic thought rejects. Oddly enough, in one form or another, the identification of art with undemocratic social patterns persists. Its adherents are found in every profession and segment of society. The institution and profession of education is no exception. Here we find professors of education, school administrators, and even art educators still holding to the view that art is a civilizational and educational luxury, something provided only as important social and educational matters have been mastered. Herbert Spencer states the position well:

Accomplishments, the fine arts, *belles-lettres*, and all those things which, as we say, constitute the efflorescence of civilization, should be wholly subordinate to that knowledge and discipline in which civilization rests. *As they occupy the leisure part of life, so should they occupy the leisure part of education.*[1]

It is only fair to note that a measure of democratization appears with the qualification that art should be generously available to all. In keeping with the general welfare idea that a human good should not be arbitrarily curtailed but broadly distributed, art, the luxury item of a privileged few, properly becomes a commodity for all to consume. However, this is but an addendum to the view of art under consideration. The view itself remains unmodified and, it is to be argued, in error.

To recognize that this view of art is intimately associated with certain social arrangments is not to claim that no other factors were involved in its production. For some purposes it would be important to delineate a host of generating and sustaining influences which gave rise to the outlook. For the present limited purpose, however, it is sufficient to single out one factor. The focus upon predemocratic social arrangements will help to direct attention to the inadequacy of the conception presently at hand. Suggested is the idea that those who reject the undemocratic social base which has supported certain art forms upon occasion understandably overgeneralize their rejection. Limited data can lead one to an unsound characterization and evaluation of art. Art forms have functioned as extravagances and trivia in unacceptable social contexts and are, therefore, suspect if accorded importance in life and education. But it certainly does not follow that the only

view of art consistent with the democratic tradition must depreciate the artistic enterprise to the point that art is seen to have no vital connection with the ongoing life of a civilization.

Quite another view is suggested by John Dewey when he says: "As long as art is the beauty parlor of civilization, neither art nor civilization is secure."[2] One of America's prominent philosophers and a major contributor to the literature of democracy, Dewey claims that the ideal human community is dependent upon its aesthetic component. Rather than art as a Spencerian "efflorescence," it is a condition of the realization of democracy, conceived as an ideal that lends a distinctive character to all aspects of life. If such a view is tenable, then significant revisions in democratic educational and social theory are in order.

Dewey's is a radical departure from historic accounts of art and its role in human affairs. But it is remarkably continuous with a development in thought referred to by intellectual historians as the "modern mind." The difficulties in delineating crisply the "modern mind" are readily granted. But it probably can be safely said that the modern mind in part is marked by a distinctive conceptual structure. Such a structure assigns a central function to those explanatory conceptions making reference to procedure, operations, processes.

Modern thought continues to use terms appropriate to earlier conceptual structures. But here an important point must be noted. The meanings of many of these familiar words have been transformed. With the change of meaning comes a change in what is talked about. This shift in both language and subject matters for inquiry has occurred not only in the physical sciences but in philosophy and the social sciences as well. It has resulted in accounts of experience, of intelligence and mind that are stated in what

[1]Herbert Spencer, *Education: Intellectual, Moral and Physical* (New York: D. Appleton and Company, 1896), pp. 74–75.

[2]John Dewey, *Art as Experience* (New York: Minton, Balch and Company, 1934), p. 344.

have come to be known as "behavioral terms." Dewey was prone to point out that the most appropriate words for identifying and inquiring into human life, among them thought, mind, and intelligence, are adverbs or verbs.

Within the framework of process, activity, and behavior, art is differently defined. Art no longer denotes things. It denotes a kind of behaving which may involve painting, music, architecture and the like. Art is to be understood as an affair of experience, or better still, it is an experiencing. On the other hand, a caution needs to be noted. A behavioristic or process-oriented conception of experience parts company with the historic account of experience as an organism's absorption of environmental stimuli. The new formulation holds experience to be a purposive transaction between a Homo sapiens and its context. It is an affair of reciprocal acting and being acted upon, of functioning in a manner so as to achieve, as a consequence of the activity, some sought-after outcome. Art as experience, like any other achieved experience, is a deliberately controlled process. It is purposive. And if experiencing includes the active role of purpose, then art experience, upon examination, will exhibit means being so ordered that ends sought after are obtained.

Still, if art is a behavior in which means are ordered towards objectives, then how is art to be distinguished from experience which is not art? In order to gain a sound answer it will be useful to make focal in this analysis the matters of primary interest to professional artists. For example: the musician has in the foreground of his attention such matters as dissonance and atonality; the architect, texture and horizontality; the painter, cubism and linearity; the poet, lyricism and onomatopoeia. These elements are often called the feelings or emotions with which artists work. But such terms are usually defined with the language of physiology, and thereby taken to refer to chemi-

cal, electronic, or muscular states of affairs. Since such concepts do not direct attention to the central concerns of artists, they should be avoided and more appropriate terminology introduced. Accordingly the working materials, the means or "stuff" with which artists work, may collectively be called the *qualities* of experience. We speak of the loneliness of the moment, the Gothicness of a building, the formalness of clothing. In such cases we name distinguishable qualities — the various "nesses" of experience — discernible in a given experience. Artistic experience is primarily concerned with these sorts of matters. Art is the ordering, manipulating, refashioning of these qualities toward still further qualities.

Another term that has submitted to modification is intelligence. It was and still is restricted to the manipulation of the discursive symbols of knowledge. However, it is appropriate to indicate that if intelligence is taken to be a behavior in which all manner of means are methodologically ordered to ends-in-view, then the above analysis of artistic behavior turns out to be an affair of intelligence. When art is conceived as the constructing and organizing of the qualities of experience, it may be thought of as an instance of man's *qualitative intelligence* in action.

This is philosophic heresy for those scholars in psychology, philosophy, and education who tend to equate intelligence with cognitive processes. To compound the heresy we may add the idea that art is properly defined as intelligence achieved in the qualitative domain of experience, and the idea that cognitive operations themselves depend upon this qualitative intelligence. Art is something which filters throughout all occasions wherein man is purposive. We cannot have an experience devoid of a "suchness," a unique quality that sets it off from other experiences. Indeed, intelligence achieved in cognitive processes is utterly dependent upon the maintenance and ordering of qualities. The distinguishing of one item from another under a microscope, the mustering and maintenance of those qualities that permit concentration, the imaginative rejuxtaposition of qualities that are the potential subject matters for fresh scientific inquiry and a condition of the development of new hypotheses — all are facets of qualitative intelligence lending support to cognitive processes.

To say that art or qualitative intelligence pervades all experience is not to suggest that everyone is an amateur musician, novelist, painter, and dancer during every conscious moment. This is patently absurd. What we can empirically defend is the claim that qualitative orderings, the ever-present aesthetic component of experience, are in a spectrum of relationships with cognitive activity. Qualitative mediations are instrumental to focally cognitive operations at one end of the spectrum, while on the other they become focal with cognitive elements assuming the instrumental role. When qualities are of equal if not primary interest, when they become the ends to be obtained, we have the experience of music, painting, poetry, architecture, and the like.

Experience wherein qualities — the stuff of art — are focal is not reserved for the concert hall or museum. It may be gained in many contexts. When living is designed with an eye to the qualities that ought to permeate the living, and these qualities are prized as intrinsic goods, when we have the aesthetic in the foreground of our attention, the experience is as much an affair of art as that obtainable in the presence of a painting.

Rather than construe art as an intruder in life, we do well to look upon qualitative thought as that which makes the Homo sapiens become human. The act, in a sense both primitive and sophisticated, of distinguishing a something from a something else, a chair from a table, a me from a you, an X from a Y, requires the perception, or more accurately the construction, of a qualitative discrimination.[3] Without qualitative thinking, rational processes would not develop. Qualitative manipulations are thus indigenous to human life. They may at moments become refined and elaborated into what we call "fine" art. ("Fine" art is, however, an unfortunate term. Through the meanings attending the term we tend to perpetuate the notion that other art experiences are less than fine — or that "fine" art is somehow disconnected, preciously so, from the balance of life.) At other moments qualitative thought acts as a backdrop for cognitive thought.

This conception of art is an alternative to views which use art to name something that is honored, taken as the epitome of degeneration, or about which there is complete indifference. Art as qualitative intelligence simply locates a distinguishable phase of experience without offering a valuation that it is all worthwhile, all evil, or something in between. Art is thus stripped of any honorific meanings. And it is this which sets the stage for valuational enterprises. Qualitative processes are subject to assessment.

Frequently overlooked is the fact that some qualitative ventures curtail and misdirect behaviors. At times they may lead to confinement in a psychiatric hospital. Other focally aesthetic undertakings foster and expand the entire domain of intelligence. Some qualitative ventures, both personal and social, may well be encouraged and sustained. Some art should be avoided like the plague, and some art should be sought out and made the locus of the *summum bonum*. All encompassing generalizations, whether to the effect that art is a luxury, a frill, or the sublime achievement of the race, fail to make these important qualifications and hence are unsound. Upon occasion a given qualitative ordering may be

[3]For recent studies in sensory deprivation which appear to lend support to this claim see Philip Solomon *et al.*, *Sensory Deprivation* (Cambridge: Harvard University Press, 1961).

an "efflorescence." But upon another occasion a differing aesthetic process may be the source of standards for an entire civilization. In this capacity the achievements of our qualitative intelligence may act as a source of ethics. In so far as artistic activity sets standards for experience not otherwise available, one can grasp the significance of Dewey's point that art may be "more moral than moralities."[4]

II

The precarious and peripheral place now occupied by the "fine" arts and those who teach them in our schools is partially due to the faulty conception of art to which reference has been made. Yet, even if this notion is rejected, a tremendous block to the extension of art still looms before us. The minor place of the "fine" arts in the schools reflects the place they have in society. Also reflected is a widely affirmed historic pattern of values. This historic value pattern is diametrically opposed to a value system which holds some forms of art experience to be of central if not supreme worth. Widely embraced are the values which minimize or exclude artistic activity from schooling. Nurtured in the young is a view of the good life that dismisses art from any vital role in their own lives.

Perhaps the best way to lay bare these highly suspect values is to employ an illustration gained from a mind that represents and is a product of American democratic traditions. Professor George S. Counts on occasion will ask a class to identify the type of man they would seek as a speaker for a graduation exercise of a school. Invariably the president of the chamber of commerce, the director of the local industry, the president of the bank, or a political figure will be specified. Here are the leaders of the community, the outstanding men, or, if you will, those who tend to have approxi-

[4] *Ibid.*, p. 348.

mated the ideal. But what is being honored by these choices? It is the ability to manage property, humans and monies profitably. It is the amassment of either political or economic power, and the acquisition of wealth. Surely these are not the defining characteristics of the good life.

Such values have had an awesome influence upon the curricula, the objectives of education at every level, and upon programs of teacher education as well. Their implementation has produced educational systems that forward the value scheme of crass utilitarianism. When so oriented, education prepares students with the competence required to obtain these valued ends in their adult years. Although other and conflicting values are also operative, it seems undeniable that in large measure the schools of the western world are preoccupied with an educational experience that is directed toward the good life defined in utilitarian terms. Since fine art experience is of little use in gaining such ends, it has been granted the most limited role in curricula.

But consider the cost. As long as ideals are stated in terms of economic and physical well-being or managerial and political power, then the aesthetic dimensions of experience will necessarily be neglected and left impoverished. To the extent that crass utilitarian values remain operative in the schools of sovereign peoples, to that extent these schools embrace the same sort of values that direct and provide the philosophic bases for education in the Soviet Union. For, as we frame in the minds of our young the horizons of the good life as political and economic power and physical well-being, we move in an orientation that has much in common with that of the Soviet school system. Both forms of utilitarianism are incompatible with the vision of the good life which holds the ultimate goods for man to be located in the qualities of an ever-growing shared experience. And yet, this is a hallmark of a redefined democratic outlook. An essentially education-aesthetic conception of the good life holds the promise of providing learning situations calculated to build the foundations of a democratic civilization. Anything less may serve to jeopardize that which helps to distinguish a democratic from a nondemocratic way of life.

Plainly a democratic education must provide children with competencies which permit them to take part in the economic and political arenas of the society. However, there is a crucial difference between a thoroughgoing democratic conception of the role of these areas of experience in life and that of sheer utilitarianism. In the democratic value framework, political and economic institutions and practices are means to the good life rather than goods in themselves. The schools of free men fall short of democratic affirmations when they, like totalitarian schools, make political, economic, material, and physical states of affairs more than a prelude to the qualities of shared experience.

This weakness in education needs shoring up if we are to strengthen the arts in the schools. A major problem is thus set for education. It is to help children to see economic, political and material matters not as goods in themselves but as instruments of the good life. In this capacity they are appraisable as means to adequate art experience. They are conditions to be sought, modified and justified in the light of their contribution to the attainment of the goods of human community. Until they are so conceived, the place of art experience in schools and in society, when sanctioned at all, will be subordinated to the office of a means in the service of nonart ends. When this is their major role, art experience is truncated, its distinctive contribution to life is vitiated, its range of potentialities is subverted.

A prominent movement in education may appear as a source of support for those seeking a secure place for art. We are hear-ing voices of well-meaning men who in increasing numbers are vigorously disparaging the technological-scientific prowess of modern men. This is coupled with depreciations of the schooling which produces professional men and cultivates the method of science and its use upon the problems of contemporary life — both prerequisites to our maintaining and extending industrial and technological achievements. In these circles the term "specialist" is hardly a term of endearment. It is used as an epithet.

One segment of this group is troubled with the lack of concern with the aesthetic dimension of experience and sees science and professionalization, in both society and education, as the enemies of the artistic. This group includes people of worthy social purpose. Nevertheless they are misguided in their attempts to strengthen the role of reflection and the aesthetic experience. To attack the scientific movement and the specialization required in order to direct technological advances is to fight the wrong enemy. The problem is misconceived. There is no need of curtailing specialization or scientific thinking in order to forward the arts. If one sees art and science as interdependent and continuous spheres of experience rather than as enemies, then the problem has shifted. It becomes one of infusing all types of education and our society with adequate art experience, while at the same time making use of the assistance that only science and technology can give. The problem is not to curtail the obvious resource of science and technology but to enlarge and redirect their problems so that they may more effectively provide the conditions necessary for widespread art experience.

Apologies for our industrial might, our technological competencies and our scientific mentality are out of order for those committed to the welfare of all and not merely to a self-appointed elite. In medicine, food production, shelter, and hosts of other areas, science and technology have demonstrated their ability to make tremendous contributions. Those who make educational proposals out of a historic vacuum and hence look with jaundiced eye upon science and technology fail to see the significance of events of the recent past. The western democracies could not have survived the last world conflict without the help of science, technology, and industrial power. Such resources made it possible to defend and extend some of the finest ideals of western civilization, including the right to disparage the contribution. We have no need to make the past the authoritative source of direction and content for education. Nor need we deny the obvious contributions to the general welfare of our technological-scientific advances and rule these out of the schools. Neither group offers an outlook that will properly build art into modern civilization. Both fail to see how only science, technology, and an industrial civilization can provide not only the necessary conditions for widespread art experience but also aesthetic objects themselves.

Another group is asking us to hark back to previous eras for educational patterns. This segment of the educational revivalist movement would have us return to the three R's as the fundamental elements of schooling. It is crystal clear that such an education cannot provide a distinctively democratic education for any civilization. Since the three R's are also important to totalitarian schools, such as those of Nazi Germany and the Soviet Union, to ground our education on these elements is in no way to guarantee an education which will strengthen democratic values and foster the evolution of democratic civilizations. In our time an education based only upon the three R's is a disservice to the young. Only a three R's education does not fit the young for the moral responsibilities of democracy; it does not provide the critical competencies or understandings required for life in a community

of free men; it does not build the loyalties basic to a free civilization; nor does it provide for that prize of creative living, an art experience that generates communication and continuous expansion.

There may be several things at work to drive pedagogues into such a proposal for the schools. But one may well suspect that educators embracing such an outlook may have lost the fortitude required to confront the issues, crises, and disturbances of the contemporary scene. Teachers can avoid the poignant problems of the current international situation. In retreating to the sanctuary of the three R's, they turn their backs upon the difficulties found in the arena of controversy, out of which is built the decisions that direct a democratic community. Three R's education is a simple education. It provides a dangerously over simplified grasp of the problems and prospects of free men. Such education reflects an amateurish, simple-minded grasp of the problems, responsibilities and potentialities of an education in and for democracy in the latter part of the twentieth century. The three R's movement is a direct challenge to those educators who would conceive of art as central to life, who are committed to democratic values, and who hold socially productive qualitative processes to be not only a condition of the realization of a democratic society but also a supreme objective of this distinctive human achievement.

A societal orientation to education reveals another source of opposition to democratically oriented educators. We are suffering under a sustained and extensive assault upon the critical-creative processes of free minds. It has been influential in the schools, in other vital spots in our civilization and throughout the world. In some instances the attack upon free minds is being carried out by those who camouflage themselves with the verbal affirmations of free men but whose actions are calculated to breed conformity, and uncritical acceptance of ideas and practices. Intellectual inertia, at heart the suffocation of constructive criticism, is the result of the fear they sow and the coercion they effect through a variety of means. To advance themselves they use the difficult movements and problems of free men as occasions to advance their purposes rather than solve their problems. While such men proclaim themselves enemies of the worldwide totalitarian movement, communism, more accurately named Bolshevism, they employ the methods of all totalitarians. With these practices they strive to gain the twin bases of all totalitarian societies: the power to designate orthodoxies and the power to command uncritical conformity.

What then is the significance of this move toward intellectual anesthesia for those concerned with art experience which is conducive to the continuous refinement and extensive shoring? History provides ample testimony to the fact that leaders of economic, religious, and political groups have found it desirable to channel thought carefully in both the domains of the "fine" arts and knowledge. Perhaps the earliest recorded decisions on the part of both political and religious leaders concerning the proper place and character of the arts occured during the eighth and ninth centuries A.D. In what is known as the iconoclast controversy, claims and edicts were issued in which mosaics, sculpture, and other objects were either held to be improper parts of church rituals or exactly the contrary.[5] In this dispute, aesthetic adequacy and the proper functions of aesthetic objects was being determined by popes and emperors — not art-

ists. These political and ecclesiastical authorities evoked standards sanctioned by their religious beliefs, and, incidentally, came out with competing conclusions.

It should be noted that while the emperor, Leo III, argued against images, and he is reported to have appealed to Christian doctrine in support of his opposition to images in the church, historians have offered another explanation.

. . . Perhaps, however, the experience which he gained later on may have brought him to the reflection, that the conversion of the Jews, which he so greatly desired, would be made much easier by the removal of the images. Many suppose that, in this way, he endeavored to make his Saracen neighbours more favourable, and to pave their way into the Church.[6]

The practice of turning to political, economic, and religious doctrines and ideals for criteria with which to regulate the work of painters, poets, and musicians has been continued into the present. A good illustration of this sort of curtailment of artistic activity is found in the text of the draft program of the Soviet Communist party presented to its Twenty-second Congress held in October of 1961.

The party considers that the paramount task in the ideological field in the present period is to educate all working people in a spirit of ideological integrity and devotion to communism, and cultivate in them a Communist attitude to labor and the social economy, to eliminate completely the survivals of bourgeois views and morals, to insure the all-round, harmonious development of the individual, to create a truly rich spiritual culture.

. . . The party calls for the education of the population as a whole in the spirit of scientific communism and strives to insure that all working people master the ideas of Marxism-Leninism, that they fully understand the course and perspectives of world development, take a correct view of international and domestic events and consciously build their life on Communist lines.

[5]See: Henry Bettenson (ed.), *Documents of the Christian Church* (London: Oxford University Press, 1943), pp. 129–130; H. J. Schroeder, *Disciplinary Decrees of the General Councils* (St. Louis: B. Heder Book Company, 1937), pp. 141–156; Philip Hughes, *The Church in Crisis: A History of the General Councils* (Garden City: Hanover House, 1961), pp. 145–163; and several papers in volume Number Seven and Number Eight of the *Dunbarton Oaks Papers* (Cambridge: Harvard University Press, 1953).

[6]Charles Joseph Hefele, *A History of the Councils of the Church* (Edinburgh: T. and T. Clark, 1896), Vol. V, p. 270. Also see pp. 260–341.

Communist ideas and Communist deeds should blend organically in the behavior of every person and in the activities of all collectives and organizations.

Soviet literature and art, imbued with optimism and dynamic Communist ideas are great factors in ideological education and cultivate in Soviet people the qualities of builders of a new world. They must be a source of happiness and inspiration to millions of people, must express their will, their sentiments and ideas, must enrich them ideologically and educate them morally.

The high-road of literature and art lies through the strengthening of links with the life of the people, through faithful and highly artistic depiction of the richness and versatility of Socialist reality, inspired and vivid portrayal of all that is new and genuinely Communist, and exposure of all that hinders the progress of society.[7]

When artists are required to conform to doctrines from political, religious, or economic spheres, their range of experimental activity is seriously curtailed. The birth of aesthetic orthodoxy is evidenced by the suffocation of new departures and new criteria of adequacy.

Still another relation between adequately conducted art experience and this creeping paralysis of the mind is of import to those responsible for the nurture of the young. Educators do well to recognize that in the long run one of the most powerful resistance movements they can build to all forms of totalitarianism is the mentality which is fundamentally nurtured in creative-critical processes — the mentality built in adequately conducted art experience. A society habituated in this process will not tolerate efforts to impose intellectual conformity, for the creative-critical mentality is one that is perpetually appraising and remaking, evaluating and reconstructing. Since this is a revolutionary activity at heart, socially responsible creativity is a major protagonist to all sorts of conformity movements.

Wagner, Debussy, Stravinsky, Schonberg and others have in recent years developed

[7]"Text of Soviet Party's Draft Program," *The New York Times*, August 1, 1961, pp. 19–20.

modes of musical composition which have permitted an epoch-making expansion of musical possibilities. Cézanne helped to evolve painting qualities which opened the door to revolutionary developments in easel painting. Sullivan, Gropius, le Corbusier, van der Rohe and Wright introduced architectural qualities by means of which other people were enabled to produce a range of pace-setting architectural styles.

There is an empirical fact dramatically exhibited by these and other movements. The employment of certain qualities induces the reconstruction, the expansion, and refinement of man's aesthetic experience. It is precisely this sharing, rebuilding, and extension of men's qualitative intelligences that constitutes educative experience in art. This may appear to be a misuse of the word "education." However, in a generic sense of "education," in a sense that includes but passes well beyond schooling, aesthetic processes are an affair of education. Such is also the case in perhaps more important but less spectacular instances than those mentioned above. The qualities evoked in an industrial plant or a labor union office, or even in the intimacy of a home setting, may perform as genuinely educative functions as do those of the "fine arts."

Two major claims about aesthetic processes may now be made to converge upon each other. As suggested above, aesthetic practice may generate aesthetic developments; it may be educative. Also suggested was the idea that this qualitative thinking is a condition of the successful initiation and maintenance of cognitive processes. Art experience, as here defined, may be as thoroughly educative as anything we can designate in human experience. Indeed, the two claims about aesthetic processes enlarge the scope to be covered by the term education.

Although the conception of art as qualitative intelligence expands the meaning and importance of the idea of education — indeed leads to a redefinition of education — it does not specify which educative experiences are to be systematically pursued. The terms art and education are not to be reified. They do not refer to entities possessing inherent worth. They are simply tables for something to be assessed. They are not shorthand substitutes for statements identifying something deemed a human good. The proposed conception of art and the enriched conception of education do not solve the problem of selecting and rejecting among alternative educative experiences, of giving direction to educative practice. However, these conceptions do contribute to the problem of developing an educational ethic. They permit a more precise designation of the province for which educational valuations are appropriate. And it will be shown that they also help to reconstruct that moral outlook whose continued existence is now at stake — the democratic ethic.

To suggest that the meaning of democracy is malleable approaches the boundaries of blasphemy, in the eyes of some. They conclude that revisionists are undemocratic. The historical record casts doubt upon this conclusion. One of the early meanings of democracy referred to representative government resting upon the foundation of a sovereign people. This essentially political conception has not been abandoned but refined and augmented. A major shift in meaning occurred when the idea of consent of the governed was fused with the notion that human goods should be abundantly distributed among the governed. Here we find the democratic idea taking a new dimension of meaning — it is a name for a way of life in which human goods pervade the community. Thus we speak of the democratic way of life and subsume under it a set of political meanings. It is plain, therefore, that the democratic idea has undergone mutations during its celebrated history.

Several things need to be carefully noted about this latter day conception of democracy. When democracy is conceived as a way of life, it is an ethical frame of reference knowing no limitations with respect to its application to human life. This sweeping pertinence has helped create modern confusions about democracy. The right to universal well-being, often expressed in the phrase "dignity and worth of the individual," in turn requires a specification of the nature of the goods to be realized through corporate activity. The advent of what we generally call modern industrial society with its continuing crisis relationship between nation states and the attending array of new problems and possibilities makes the drafting of a bill of particulars exceedingly difficult. As it stands, democracy does not spell out for man's modern milieu what to seek and avoid at every point. This uncertainty about what is good and right for all men in a world of unfamiliar events, things, difficulties and potentialities seems to cause some disenchantment with democracy.

Perhaps a further unfolding of the meaning of democracy will help to resolve the moral malaise of contemporary men. To be avoided is the popular idea that democracy is a catalog of specific goods to be obtained. Democracy may best be construed as a structure of ideas which releases and gives form to the process of moral reasoning and judgment. This means that the delineation of social goals should be a continuing affair. It is the function of the democratic ethical affirmation to provide a format which will sustain the process of restating and enlarging goals and reconstructing the institutional and physical circumstances through which goals are brought to fruition. Take, for example, the ideal of equality of opportunity and treating persons as ends and not as mere means which is part of this format: nothing is said here about the character life ought to exhibit for any one man or for all men. Such statements help to structure deliberations that issue into substantive judgments about concrete situations.

This framework as well as the specifics is subject to refinement. Notable contributions are now being made by such students of democracy as Sidney Hook, Charles Frankel, and Edmond Cahn. In Cahn's dissection of the anatomy of democratic citizenship, he finds "prevention, reparation, and protest" as the "tools and techniques by which responsibility expresses itself and builds outlets for its own discharge."[8] This conception is an excellent example of a proposed refinement of the democratic ethical framework.

Another shift in the meaning of democracy helps to improve the effort to designate human goods. The sound historic idea which holds each person deserving of a life worth living, of realizing a measure of well being, may be expanded in the light of the preceding analysis of art. And if the conception of art as an affair of intelligence is added to the historic affirmation of personal worth and well-being, then the locus of human goods becomes one with the qualities of life available to men. The adequacy of these qualities is as one with their educational consequences. The qualities which extend and refine the qualities of life, those which foster shared qualitative enhancements, become the human good in a democratic society. This is to propose that the greatest good to be obtained in civilization is socially educative art experience. When human ideals are viewed as aesthetic-educational affairs the democratic ethical framework turns out to be a conceptual structure devised to release men's qualitative and discursive intelligence in the service of expanding art experience.

Now it may be said that the nuclear impasse, the deeply troubled underdeveloped areas of the world, set problems of such magnitude that we must delay the deliberate

[8]Edmond Cahn, *The Predicament of Democratic Man.* New York: Macmillan Company (1961), p. 49.

cultivation of the artistic experience of men throughout the world. If this is true, then we should set aside the meaning of democracy as here proposed. However, the democratic ethic as stated above is not nostalgic sentimentalism. If employed in thought, it clarifies our view of the problems we have in the world. It is a tool for making a fresh analysis of the crisis situation in which we find ourselves in the latter part of the twentieth century. The reformations and interrelations offered for democracy, education, and art modify the usual intellectual framework employed for making sweeping social diagnoses and prescriptions. With the proposed changes, the characterization of the international and national problems and prospects of men is significantly altered, and perhaps more amenable to fruitful resolution and of greater worth.

Granted, with no reluctance, that the survival of all political democracies is inexorably linked to the extension of political democracy in those societies where it is absent. And most assuredly the fostering of political democracy will involve revolutions. In the United States the growth of political democracy was in significant measure due to the fact that it served to implement the economic and religious interests of powerful groups. For a host of now familiar reasons, Americans and others embracing political democracy cannot expect to have their economic and religious patterns, or even their form of political democracy, followed in regions of the world where there are vastly different histories and traditions. This is particularly true in some culturally deprived areas of the world. It is self-defeating for us to make such attempts. However, we can help make the democratic ethic viable in non or even undemocratic societies. To those who will listen we can demonstrate and cite historic evidence to prove that it is the only instrumentality that serves to mold all manner of institutions, procedures, and events to the realization of an ever increasing availability of worthy qualities of experience for men. Such an outlook should prove to be contagious. In addition, we can, through economic aid, the Peace Corps, trade arrangements, cultural exchanges, and the like, help to sustain those groups and social arrangements forwarding the democratic ethic and similarly hinder those jeopardizing its development. In so doing, it is of utmost importance that we be responsive to the qualities of life that are indigenous to each nation. Some may well prove to be resources to other societies, and deserve to be imported. Some we will do well to sustain and others curtail. And the utmost care must be directed to the selection of the qualities one nation attempts to introduce into the life of another. America's rock-and-roll is hardly a substitute for almost any music of primitive peoples. The tourist souvenirs at vacation resorts in the United States are hardly a substitute for the native art of India, the Scandinavian peninsula, or most African tribes.

Overlooked and underestimated is the importance of the educational influence in the qualitative experience of other peoples that is exerted through the qualities we bring to each other in person, through our artifacts, and those we create in our international disputes. The appropriateness and adequacy of these qualities may act to nurture or to suppress the development of democracy and its human goals.

In overly brief terms, we have here the long run frontier, the international relations problem of democratic civilizations. And it is not, as we are accustomed to think, primarily an economic, political, or military problem, however much they are involved. It is an aesthetic-educational frontier.

The growing edge within all modern civilizations, no less than in our international relations, is aesthetic. From a historic perspective, it is fair to conclude that by and large the scientifically and technologically advanced democracies have succeeded in mastering their physical environment. They have successfully forged political instruments appropriate to their histories and prevailing conditions. Their economics, however imperfect, are at least far more amenable to control and modification than ever before. Their major industries are designed to produce for increasingly large markets. They have become what Professor Galbraith has so appropriately called "affluent" societies.

Hopefully, the *focal* problems of these civilizations no longer will need to be those dealing with their internal economic and physical matters, governmental structures, and the mastery of scientific instruments. Accomplishments in these areas have provided the conditions which will permit these societies to open up another, a new frontier.[9]

These societies continue to have great tasks to perform in such areas as health and government. They also continue to have major social and technological problems attending the development of extensive production. New economic and political relations with other nations continue to arise. But these matters do not constitute the new fundamental challenge. In the latter part of the twentieth century, mankind is on the threshold of a cultural renaissance. Now present are the social and physical foundations upon which we can build an artistic-educational expression of the highest order — an expression which could dip deeply into the lives of all and which could produce unprecedented resources for extending the democratic ethic to mankind.

[9]This may be overly optimistic; perhaps the day has not yet arrived. However it is interesting to note that no less an economist than J. M. Keynes looked forward to such a time. In 1931 he wrote in a "Preface" that "the author of these essays, for all his crookings, still hopes and believes that the day is not far off when the Economic Problem will take the back seat where it belongs, and that the arena of the heart and head will be occupied, or reoccupied, by our real problems — the problems of life and of human relations, of creation and behaviour and religion." J. M. Keynes, *Essays in Persuasion* (New York: W. W. Norton and Company, 1963), p. vii.

34. Transition in Art Education: Changing Conceptions of Curriculum Content and Teaching

MANUEL BARKAN

Our own field of art education — and indeed all of education — is now well beyond the threshold of a period of accelerated transition and significant change. Favored ideas and goals, which for some time have been assumed to be the proper bases for wise curriculum content and sound teaching practice, are now being held up to question. Accepted assumptions about the proper characteristics and dimensions of both art and education are now being viewed with increasing skepticism and doubt. Many of our established assumptions and goals are beginning to be challenged because of misgivings, debated because of changes in opinion, and opposed because of dissent.

If I were inclined to make prophetic judgments, and if I were a betting man, I would here and now predict that the next decade will bring some truly fundamental changes in the theory and practice of art education, changes which will be com-

parable only to those overwhelming transformations that took place within our profession during the late nineteen twenties and early thirties.

The clues which lead me to make such a claim lie in the content and character of the current debate about professional issues in art education. And, as I go on to point to these clues, let me urge you not to overlook for a moment the significance of the theme selected for this conference by the officers of the Western Arts Association: "Transition in Art Education." It is very different from the themes of many an earlier conference. Clearly it does not carry any of the meaning of a holding operation. Rather, it asserts that changes are in the offing, and ideas are on the move.

When basic ideas are in the process of transformation, there is and must be an inevitable grinding of opinions one upon the other. There must be inevitable controver-

*SOURCE: Reprinted from *Art Education*, Vol. 15, No. 7 (October, 1962), pp. 12–18, 27.

sy and debate, because old ideas, by their very nature, cannot and do not change unless and until they are challenged by new ones. Such a debate, I believe, is now in the making within the profession of art education.

To exemplify the nature of the current debate, I want to examine three clusters of assumptions which have been among the strongest guidelines in determining the nature of curriculum content and teaching procedures in art education. All of them are very popular in our field, but they are now beginning to be viewed with increasing misgivings and doubt: the *first* pertains to conceptions about how a person to be educated in art should be treated — whether as a "whole" person or as an artist; a *second* is concerned with the problem of criteria for understanding and judging works of art; and a *third* cluster of assumptions deals with a crucial aspect of any teaching program which seeks to encourage individual expressiveness, so much admired and aspired to by members of the art education profession. Here I am referring specifically to prevailing conceptions about experiences with art media in the teaching of art. I shall discuss in some detail the broad background and dimensions of the present-day controversies about these assumptions in order to show wherein the field of art education, as we know it, is now in transition.

In order to grasp the significance of the transformation of ideas now emerging, it is necessary to recapitulate some of the history of ideas in our field. A historical perspective is *always* necessary, because awareness of *when* and *why* many current and prevailing ideas came into being sharpens our sensitivity to the current signs and signals of changes which are now in process. I am here simply repeating the eternal verity that history is not only interesting and useful but it is absolutely essential. Only by backing away to take a somewhat longer look than is customary in our day-to-day ac-

tivities, can one hope to better distinguish some of the characteristics of the whole forest from the qualities of the many individual trees. Let me further emphasize the importance of a historical perspective if we are to control the current transformation of ideas toward positive directions. The philosopher George Santayana once wrote. "Those who ignore history are condemned to repeat it." With this admonition, I shall begin my analysis of changing conceptions of curriculum content and teaching in art education with a discussion of the first cluster of assumptions which I have just mentioned, the one pertaining to the way people ought to be treated so that they can become educated in art.

About twenty-five or thirty years ago there was a very powerful, and I think legitimate, reaction *against* the then prevailing academic strictures for the teaching of art. This reaction, along with other developments, led directly to our current conceptions about how a person ought to be treated if he is to become educated in art. Prevailing content and procedures which were then used in the teaching of art were rejected: Art was no longer to be taught through a series of tight exercises beginning with light and dark or rather shade and shadow drawings of cones and spheres on 8″ x 10″ manila paper using hard pencils. This was no longer to be followed, at a more advanced stage, with drawings from plaster casts of hands, feet, and heads. The accompaniment of careful study of the color wheel was also rejected, as was the required thorough acquaintance with a set of absolute and clearly formulated but static design principles.

The rejection of such teaching was a reaction against curriculum content and teaching procedures which were being recognized as leading to rigidity and the suppression of individuality. Furthermore, this reaction gave rise to the visionary, highly creative, and very serious formulation of a new and now familiar set of ideas and goals which are today peppered throughout almost all of the current literature on art education: art is free expression; everyone can learn to express; spontaneity is the key; art experiences are developmentally valuable; and finally, *the educational job is to teach the whole child rather than to try to make an artist out of him.*

Though these leading ideas first emerged in the late nineteen twenties and early and middle thirties, it took almost two decades until they became sufficiently widespread for the National Art Education Association to issue a policy statement in 1949 which read in part: "As an art teacher I believe that . . . Art experiences are essential to the fullest development of all people at all levels of growth . . . Art is especially well suited to such growth because it: encourages freedom of expression . . . Art classes should be taught with full recognition that . . . art is less a body of subject matter than a developmental activity."[1]

Now, it is precisely this same set of beliefs, or perhaps what has become of them, which is today being challenged. These beliefs are being reopened for a new level of examination, and they are hence being brought to a new level of questioning and doubt. Though these beliefs have placed an invaluable and indelible imprint on the development of art education during the past two decades, I would contend that they have also become the source of the popular and erroneous assumption among many if not most art teachers, and among educators in general too, that the job in our schools is to educate people not artists. I would also contend that in trying to bring art education to all people, well meaning but overzealous art teachers have themselves made learning in art appear to be all too simple, all too easy, and all too much fun. Is it really

any wonder that so very many art teachers complain about certain difficulties in their work, the fact that their sincere and energetic efforts are not being taken too seriously? Too many people perceive the study of art as child's play, hardly worthy of the time it takes. Far too many students, guidance officers, school administrators, and parents perceive art courses as places where easy credits are earned.

In pointing to such conditions which prevail this very day in most of our school systems, and indeed even in many of our universities, I am in no way overlooking the negative influences and the materialistic pressures of an American middle-class society which values the practical and the expedient. I am simply saying that the important and moving ideas in art education of the last generation have made their contribution, but they have now lost their cutting edge. In fact, these once creative ideas are now playing into the trap of those antihumanistic, anti-aesthetic forces within the general community, within our schools, and within the culture at large. This is precisely why these same ideas, assumptions, and their consequences are now beginning to be questioned both from within and from without the profession of art education.

The reaction against this cluster of favored assumptions about how a person to be educated in art ought to be treated has been gaining some momentum during the past two or three years. It is typified by many of the recent art education conference themes which have emphasized the return of art to art education; it is also evident both in the popular slogans and in the serious speculations among an increasing group of art teachers that the people who *teach* art should also *be* artists in their own right. The most eloquent statement I know about, however, regarding this general problem stems from the Woods Hole Conference of 1959, which curiously enough was primarily concerned with improvement in the teaching

[1] "As an Art Teacher I Believe That," *Art Education,* Journal of the National Art Education Association, II, No. 2 (March-April, 1949), p. 1.

of science, not art. Jerome S. Bruner, the Harvard psychologist, reported from that conference as follows: "The dominant view among men . . . engaged in preparing and teaching new curricula . . . lies in giving students an understanding of the *fundamental structure* of whatever subjects we choose to teach."[2] (Emphasis added.) In making this statement, Bruner does not deny any developmental values which can be derived from engagement in the study of a subject. All he is saying is that the key educational task is to give students an understanding of the fundamental structure of any subject we see fit to teach. When applied to the teaching of art, this would mean that there is a subject matter of the field of art, and it is important to teach it.

Having established his point about the significance of teaching the fundamental structure of any subject worth teaching, Professor Bruner turns his attention to the kind of behavior a person must learn, if he is to achieve understanding from the subject he is studying. ". . . Intellectual activity anywhere is the same, whether at the frontier of knowledge or in a third-grade classroom. What a scientist does at his desk or in his laboratory, what a literary critic does in reading a poem, are of the same order as what anybody else does when he is engaged in like activities — if he is to achieve understanding. The difference is in degree, not in kind."[3]

Taking into account the full meaning of Professor Bruner's statement, I don't think that I do him any injustice by saying that artistic activity anywhere is the same, whether at the frontier of art or in a third-grade classroom. What an artist does in his studio is of the same order as what anybody else does when he is engaged in like activities — if he is to achieve understanding. The difference is in degree, not in kind.

And now, if that statement were not yet strong enough to challenge some of our current and popular beliefs about how teachers should treat students, Professor Bruner, with attention to the teaching of science, provides, this powerful assertion: "The schoolboy learning physics *is* a physicist, and it is easier for him to learn physics behaving like a physicist than doing something else."[4] If Bruner would have been thinking about the teaching of art, I have no doubt that he would have written: The schoolboy learning art is an artist, and it is easier for him to learn art behaving like an artist than doing something else.

This, I suggest, is a fresh and challenging conception of what we ought to be doing in the teaching of art. It is by no means a matter of simple repetition of history. Far from it, because this new idea differs as much from our current beliefs about how we ought to educate children, as our current beliefs differ from the academic strictures which preceded them. And certainly, this new idea does not imply the slightest suggestion of academic rigidity. It simply asserts that to learn through art one must act like an artist.

Thus, our favored assumptions about how to treat people in the process of being educated in art are strongly contested. They are placed in serious doubt. Art education in transition must grapple with this issue in order to resolve it.

The second cluster of assumptions is about works of art and criteria for understanding and judging them. It too has a relevent sequence of historical antecedents, just as the first group of assumptions did. Some thirty years ago, the teaching of art appreciation was an accepted part of the content of any art program which was considered to be well developed. As taught in the public schools at that time, art appreciation consisted of the study of tiny prints, about the size of a

[2]Jerome S. Bruner, *The Process of Education* (Cambridge: Harvard University Press, 1961), p. 11.
[3]Ibid., p. 14.

[4]Ibid., p. 14.

playing card, of well-known paintings. These were carefully selected from the Renaissance and from the time up until the middle of the nineteenth century. On one side of these cards, there was a poor quality reproduction which could serve no other purpose than identification of the subject matter depicted in the painting; the other side carried some brief and superficial factual data about the artist, where and when he lived and worked. Students were taught to examine these cards in order to be able to identify the subjects in the paintings in relation to their titles and the names of the artists and their birth dates and dates of death — all of which they were expected to memorize for recitation and examination. The paintings selected for such study were of a specific character. They fit a particular criterion. In 1931, *The Course of Study in Art for Elementary Schools*, published by the Board of Education of the City of New York declared as its purpose: the "conversation . . . of acceptable ideals and canons of beauty against attempts to debase artistic taste and judgment."[5] This was the criterion used in the selection of works of art for study in art appreciation.

Now, I know that I need not remind you that by 1931 there was already a modest but substantial audience for paintings from Paris. The fifty-seventh street galleries in New York at that time had been showing paintings by Manet and Corot; the leading modern galleries were showing works by the Impressionists; and in November of 1929 the Museum of Modern Art had already presented its opening exhibition with a showing of works by Cézanne, Gauguin, Seurat and Van Gogh. In January of 1930, in fact, the Museum of Modern Art presented its second exhibition entitled "Painting in Paris." Included were the avant-garde of the day, at least as far as the United States

was concerned: Braque, Chagall, Chirico, Leger, Matisse, Miro, and Picasso.

The ferment and vitality from the art center of Paris had crossed the Atlantic through the Armory Show of 1913. By 1929, this ferment and vitality were clearly well established, at least in New York City. It is, therefore, no wonder that inquiring, perceptive, and progressive art teachers rejected the 1931 dictum of the New York City Board of Education, and refused to preserve: "the canons of beauty against attempts to debase artistic taste and judgment." Artistic taste, at that time, was in flux; and *adventurous* art teachers sensed the compelling nature of these new artistic forms which they were seeing. Though they knew that the old canons of beauty could no longer serve as criteria for judgment, more adequate criteria had not yet been formulated. Their reactions, therefore, came in the form of a rejection of *all* academic criteria.

There were other powerful developments worth recalling during these same years and just prior to them: William James and John Dewey had already made their impact on educational theory; the stories about Montessori and Cizek had already been imported to the United States; the famous Francis Parker School was conducting educational experimentation; Hughes Mearns had already published his signal work *Creative Power: The Education of Youth in the Creative Arts;*[6] and the progressive education and the child study movements were embracing the arts as the fertile and promising avenues for *creative development*. The child was perceived as the *center* of the educational enterprise with feelings, needs, and developmental capabilities which were *not to be violated*. The ideas developing in those years were perhaps most aptly embodied in the very title of Van Deering

---

[5]*Course of Study in Art for Elementary Schools* (Board of Education of the City of New York, December 1931), p. 5.

[6]Hughes Mearns, *Creative Power: The Education of Youth in the Creative Arts* (New York: Doubleday, Doran and Co., 1930).

Perrine's charming little book *Let The Child Draw*.[7] Don't teach him; don't show him; just *let* the child draw.

The educational *goals* thus incorporated into the teaching of art became the preservation of youthful spontaneity, the attention to developmental tendencies, and the absolute protection of children from adult standards. When these goals were coupled with the utter breakdown of academic criteria for the judgment of works of art, one of the outstanding results was the development of classroom practices which literally shielded children from looking at, enjoying, and studying the works of great artists. The study of art appreciation virtually disappeared from most schools, and many art teachers even argued strongly that looking at works of art was detrimental for children. It inhibited them from being creative, because they would surely copy what they saw rather than exploring, experimenting, and creating on their own. One key piece of evidence about this condition is the present poverty or even general absence in most schools of really good reproductions of art, let alone some originals of works by professional artists. In fact, most art teachers today might well ask themselves: what percentage of their annual budgets do they spend on fine reproductions? And indeed, they might also ask: what are their value judgments and decisions when the chips are down, when it is time for them to settle on those things they can afford to order or buy? Do they sacrifice some paint, or paper, or clay, or some other item of work material; or do they let the reproductions go by the board because they think that they cannot afford them?

There is a growing emphasis among some art teachers on the importance of sustained and continuous contact with great works of art. But this is a rather recent development in contemporary art education theory and practice. It stems from the discovery and the realization that the capacity for sensitive and knowledgeable judgment rests in large part on insights gained through acquaintance with and careful study of great works of art. Indeed, the capacity for sensitive judgment comes through having *lived* with great works. More art teachers are now becoming less afraid to confront children with paintings and sculpture by great artists of the past and the present. The controversy in art education today on this issue really hinges on the strong contention that learning in art requires careful attention to qualitative criteria that pertain to works of art.

There is the very strong probability that in the next several years we will witness renewed and energetic attention to the teaching of insightful observation of works of art. It will not come in the form of the art appreciation of the past, though there will probably be some of that. Rather, this renewed energy will be apparent in the creative development of teaching materials and courses in art history and criticism. These materials and courses will be based upon the rich research by such men as Etienne Gilson, Rene Huyghe and E. H. Gombrich. Such materials will be developed for use at all levels of instruction. Such courses will be developed in and for our secondary schools to challenge the mature needs and desires of young people, in order for them to better understand themselves through intimate study of great works of art. The efforts and accomplishments in the handful of school systems which have already instituted such experimental courses[8] will stimulate the transformation of ideas already in process. These developments will hasten the controversy and the debate on this issue.

If there is any art teacher who still doubts that our ideas, our goals, and our assumptions are in transition about confronting

[7]Van Deering Perrine, *Let the Child Draw* (New York: Frederick A. Stokes, 1936).

[8]Dearborn, Michigan, and Pittsburgh, Pennsylvania.

children with the works by professional artists in order for them to learn how to discover what is meaningful in the works, I would suggest a close examination of a popular magazine such as *School Arts*. Here is another place where one can find useful bits of evidence about current history which indicate changing emphases in the teaching of art.

School Arts is a good quality popular magazine, and though it exercises some leadership in *disseminating* ideas, it is not the kind of a journal which generates *new* ideas. It reflects sound educational ideas, but it does not carve out new directions. And, it is precisely because of this special nature and purpose of *School Arts* that it can serve as a useful barometer to gauge what is happening in our field. If you would examine your file of back issues, you will discover an important shift in editorial policy. Beginning for the first time with the April 1957 issue, *School Arts* has been publishing a regular feature entitled "Understanding Art."

Now, why would a magazine such as *School Arts* make such a change in editorial policy? In view of the strong assumptions and beliefs among many people in art education that "art is less a body of subject matter than a developmental activity," why would *School Arts* introduce a regular feature series on the works of artists who have influenced art history? In view of one of the most favored assumptions in art education about the detrimental nature and danger of imposing adult standards on children, why would *School Arts* begin to feature a series of articles to discuss and analyze the works by professional artists with emphasis on the criteria appropriate for judging them? When such materials are suddenly introduced and then regularly presented in a popular magazine, it is a certain sign that ideas about and attitudes toward the subject are already changing. Clearly, this is evidence of the history of art education in the making. Our assumptions about children, works of art, and criteria for judging works of art are all being challenged and changed before our very eyes. These changes are signs of the transition in and transformation of curriculum content and teaching in present-day art education.

My third cluster of assumptions pertains to prevailing conceptions within our profession about experience with art media in the teaching of art. In many respects, the effects of this group of assumptions are the ones which are most directly apparent in the day-to-day teaching of art now going on in the public schools. These are among the assumptions about curriculum content and teaching which are most obviously reflected in the daily events and occurrences in the art classrooms of the nation in terms of the types of things done and the kinds of materials worked with at all educational levels.

Any careful reading of the current literature in art education, both in books and in periodicals, would lead to the inescapable conclusion that virtually *all* art educators believe in using a variety of art media. Indeed, I don't think that I am overstating the case by saying that a great many art teachers judge the effectiveness of their teaching in terms of the number of different media they include. The *more* media they provide, the *better* they think they are teaching; the more varieties of media their children experience, the better they assume the learning to be. Talk to a great many art teachers, and by all means, talk to most undergraduate students who are preparing to become art teachers; and ask them to tell you something about a good art education program. Almost all will place experience with a wide variety of media uppermost on their list of values. Most of them are on a perpetual hunt not only for more media but also for new ones.

In preparing my material for this lecture, I thumbed through my file of 1961 issues of *School Arts* magazine. Let me read to you a group of titles I selected from among the special articles I found listed in the tables of contents: "Dip-Dribble Sculpture," "Paint and String Art," "Creating With Plaster," "Try Eggshell Mosaics," "Feather-rock, a New Carving Material," "Floor Tile Mosaics," "Try Erasable India Ink," and on and on.

So powerful is the art teacher's belief in more and new media that commercial suppliers of art materials to schools have adopted it, promoted it, and capitalized upon it. Here are two examples of the phraseology you can find in advertisements for art materials: "New, easy way to teach stained glass," claims one supplier; and "New medium for artistic expression and craft work," is announced by another. One manufacturer apparently decided that it had found a very good thing here; it simply appropriated the whole package by giving itself the "honorific" name of Nu-Media, spelled N-U-M-E-D-I-A.

Examine the current literature in art education with care to discover the very rare occasions one encounters any words of caution or doubt about this overriding emphasis among art teachers. What are the historical roots for these strong beliefs? Where did they stem from? What meaning did they have when they first developed? What is significant today in the overarching faith in varieties of new art media?

Make no mistake in thinking that in raising such questions I am arguing either for a reduced array of media in art instruction, or for any particular priority for certain media over others. I also hope that you won't interpret anything I have just said to mean that I have the slightest aversion to the several media I happened to mention. Quite the contrary! What I do intend to try to show, however, is not only that the historical events which led to the emphasis on varieties of media are long passed, but also that the historical reasons for expanding the scope of art media are no longer meaningful for today's prob-

lems in art education. Furthermore, I will try to explain why I believe that present problems in the teaching of art require new solutions in the form of new ideas about the utilization of media. In fact, I will try to show why our persistence in valuing variety and newness of art media, in its present form, is actually detrimental to what we in the profession of art education ought to be seeking to accomplish.

Thirty five years ago, the media used in public school art, as it was then called, consisted largely of medium hard pencils, small size oak tag and contour paper, crayons, pens and india ink, cakes of transparent water colors, and vine charcoal for more advanced students. Art was a two-dimensional activity, and even at that, the media used were restricted and limited. The reaction to these conditions stemmed simultaneously from two sources: one was the emerging movements of progressive education and child study; the second was the creative upheaval and turmoil in the world of the visual arts. The ideological power and energy of these two developments hammered out their imprint on this aspect of art education, as they did on virtually all of the others.

The progressive education movement of the late twenties and early thirties pounded away at those archaic school practices which in any way restricted the energetic exploration, experimentation, and creative formulation of purposive behaviors which children are capable of pursuing. The child study movement with its emphasis on the developmental needs and tendencies of children began to demonstrate how children can thrive and flourish when their physical, emotional, and sensual capacities are recognized, stimulated, and provided for. Rich, brilliant, and thick tempera colors with large brushes for smearing them onto soft absorbent newsprint paper; huge blocks of soft wood, light enough for children to pick up, move around, and use for arranging and modulating real environmental space;

sand for digging with all the muscular energy a youngster could muster to build something; and clay for rolling, smacking, and squeezing into worms, pancakes, pots, or just nothing at all — all of these media and more were brought into play for the sensual pleasure they provided and for the immense possibilities they opened for forming and shaping.

And from Paris there came the cubists to demonstrate that all of art is not of pencil, paint, and paper. Picasso, Braque and others invented the collage, and the first new medium of our era was born. If these artists could make pictures with bits of yesterday's newspaper, accented with the stub ends of a few burned matchsticks, then art could be made out of anything. The possibilities became *limitless*. Now, add to this the strong influence of the Bauhaus which was imported into the United States in the middle thirties. Different materials were recognized for their unique qualities of texture, tactile character, strength, and form potentialities. What is more, the Bauhaus taught us that the treatment of certain materials with different kinds of tools opened up a mathematically incalculable number of potential combinations for the invention and creation of all kinds of visual forms.

When all of these developments — the progressive education and child study movements, the influences of Parisian painting and the Bauhaus aesthetic ideology — are put together with the art teacher's perennial problem of managing on a skimpy budget, you have the makings of the quest for new and different media. This quest was completely sensible twenty-five years ago, because art teachers were throwing off the shackles of academic strictures and arbitrary rigid limitations. It continued to remain sensible even as late as 1949 when the National Art Education Association urged in its statement of policy that "Art instruction should encourage: exploration and experimentation in many media."[9]

[9] "As an Art Teacher I Believe That," *op. cit.*

In 1949, there was still some reason to argue the educational debate over the value of varieties of media. But, that battle has already long been won, and to continue on that course today is to follow a mirage. Just look at the media which have been admitted into the aesthetic experience by the New York School of Abstract Expressionist painters and sculptors — steel, stone, burlap, chicken wire, rags, found objects, and, for that matter, any kind of junk that happens to have a shape, color or texture that can be combined with something else. Is there really any art teacher now who is worth his salt and who is unable to develop and acquire just a reasonable array of media for his students to use?

The continuing quest for and emphasis on varieties of art media in planning curriculum and teaching are today detrimental to the purposes which art education ought to be trying to achieve. Now that the cupboard of media is literally burgeoning with possibilities, the demands upon art education are indeed in transition. There are more media available than we could possibly know what to do with. We are free to choose among any and all of them. Now the crucial questions are: How are we using this freedom we have? What are we doing in our teaching with our ever expanding catalogue of media? How are we using our wealth of media to serve educational purposes? In short, *what ought we to be educating for through the teaching of art?* As I see them, these are the questions at the heart of present-day problems in art education. If there is any transition now occurring in the ideology of art education, that transition must become apparent in our goals and in our teaching procedures.

In order to propose some possible answers to this final set of questions, I find it necessary to return to the point at which I concluded my discussion of the first cluster of assumptions, those which pertained to the way we treat people who are to become educated in art. I want to reiterate my paraphrase from Professor Jerome S. Bruner:

Artistic activity anywhere is the same, whether at the frontier of art or in a third-grade classroom. What an artist does in his studio is of the same order as what anybody else does when he is engaged in like activities — if he is to achieve understanding. The difference is in degree, not in kind. The schoolboy learning art is an artist, and it is easier for him to learn art behaving like an artist than doing something else.

If art education is to serve the American community as it should, our task is clear. If aesthetic significance is to make any appreciable imprint on how children grow up and conduct their lives, then we, the art teachers, must treat them as artists for whatever period of time they come to work with us. Our job, first and foremost, is to help them to behave like the artists they can become rather than doing something else. And our catalogue of media, new and old alike, serves no useful purpose whatsoever unless we use it to enable the schoolboy to engage in artistic activity. To do so means for us to teach toward aesthetic sensibility and not toward learning less and less about more and more media.

A wide variety of media is indeed essential for good teaching of art. But, it can also be a hindrance if children are expected to sample all of them. It is like the story about the famous school for ducks, where the young ducklings spent most of their time learning how to climb, and dig, and fly, instead of learning how to develop their capacities as elegant swimmers, because they already knew how to swim.

Different artists use different media, but no serious artist we know about flits from medium to medium. Among the most universal characteristics we can see in the artist are his dogged perseverance, his immersion in a medium, and his determination to make his chosen medium a part of himself in order to achieve the discipline and the skills which are involved. These are among the qualities of artistic dedication.

There *is* great value in a variety of media,

but the value is now being lost through the ways in which so very many art programs are organized, and the ways in which so many art teachers use the media at their command. Media are tools for teachers to use in teaching art, and for students to use in learning to behave like artists. Each, however — teachers while teaching and students while learning — need to use art media for distinctly different purposes.

The student, like the artist, needs some degree of exploration in order to find the medium he enjoys using, because through that medium he is able to formulate ideas of aesthetic significance at his level of development. Through his education in art, he needs to learn to come back again and again to work with the same medium. He needs to learn to finish many works and to begin even more of them. He needs to learn that to enjoy the thrill of creation requires him to shape his own purposes *now*, not later. In a certain sense, learning to create in art is no different from learning to create with verbal language. Just as it is not necessary, and in fact is a hindrance, for children to accumulate a huge vocabulary before they even try to write a story, so is it a hindrance if children collect knowledge through haphazard experiences with many different media before settling down to the serious business of behaving like artists. Children use the words at their disposal in order to say what they want to say. The important thing is that they write about ideas that interest them in story after story. In art, it is important for them to learn to like a medium and to use it to express their ideas in art work after art work.

For the teacher, all the media in the catalogue are teaching tools to be used for no other purpose than to teach children how to learn to behave like artists. This means creating the atmosphere of an artist's studio in the classroom. It means encouraging children to try different media for the primary purpose of discovering the one worth sticking with. It means using media selectively to help children achieve insights into important ideas and problems in their own work. It means having many media available for use by a whole class. But at the same time, it means teaching children how to make individual choices in order for each child to be able to exploit the medium of his choice for the fruits it can provide.

In conclusion, I want to read a brief and impressive passage by the renowned historian, Ralph N. Turner, who wrote that "The capacity of creativeness whether it operates as trial and error, reason, emotional sensitivity, sympathy, intuition, or spiritual aspiration, is the central part of history. Man, with the capacity of creativeness, can transform material factors and reshape goals, bring visions to reality. History is the formation and transformation of visions."[10]

Art education today is indeed in transition, but the way it will be transformed depends upon what we think it ought to become. If I may borrow a phrase from our youthful President: The educational frontier of the sixties in art is to make the aesthetic life a reality for ourselves and for our students. The least we must demand of ourselves is that, as art teachers, we should behave like artists. If we can achieve this, we will have transformed our visions.

[11]Ralph N. Turner, "Mankind from a New Summit," *The Saturday Review of Literature*, XXXV, No. 14 (April 5, 1952), p. 9.

35. Artist in the Schoolroom: A Modern Dilemma

FREDERICK M. LOGAN

The study of the arts in the humanistic tradition should be the aim of art teachers in the elementary schools and in the high schools, as it is in the college courses taught for the student seeking a liberal education — not a professional art education.

In the education of teachers of art there are current practices which interfere with this concept of the art teacher's most important service. Often these days, too intense a specialization is feared in the fields of science, of engineering, and of medicine; but a kind of intensive specialization is also present in the arts, and particularly in art courses for prospective teachers.

The artist on the lower East Side of New York City who lives and works in an old store loft has too much influence on the art teacher in a new high-school building on a forty-acre tract at the edge of a Midwestern city.

The artist, according to his own views and the conviction of magazine and museum personnel, is the sophisticate in art. The art teacher is the art provincial. The pro-vincial should, presumably, take his cue from the metropolitan sophisticate. This simplified view of the direction of art influences is probably, and unfortunately, subscribed to by the teacher as well.

If such a relationship has prevailed and is becoming stronger, it will hinder a healthy development in the arts by giving art teachers too limited a view of the potentialities of contemporary art and art education.

During the first fifty or more years of art teaching in grade and high schools most of the teachers were educated in normal schools. The Massachusetts Normal Art School was the first such instituion wholly devoted to the preparation of teachers of "industrial and fine arts," and early in the twentieth century the art department of the Teachers College, now affiliated with Columbia University, took over a national leadership. The kind of education these two schools encouraged among the many schools and art departments following their lead was one in which students were prepared, above all, to teach. Art graduates were to

*SOURCE: Reprinted from *Studies in Art Education*, II, 2 (Spring 1961), pp. 66–84.

teach art, of course, but with, it was hoped, the same dedication to the act of teaching that was expected of the prospective teachers of kindergarten, of the grades, and of the high schools.

Even in these days when baiting teachers colleges and schools of education is a popular intellectual pastime, an objective reading of the records to be found in journals of educational associations, in normal school catalogues and student annuals, and in publications of the work of leading scholars in the normal schools makes one aware of the enthusiasm for teaching which students and faculty alike possessed.

The great American dream of an educated democracy was to be achieved through the public schools, and the normal schools were providing the teachers to do the job. By the 1890's the normal schools were already converts to the need of a public-school education which should be more than a utilitarian grasp of reading, writing, and arithmetical skills. Art, music, home economics, and other humanizing disciplines were important. Obviously, normal schools would need to prepare these teachers. Relatively few graduates of the Pennsylvania Academy of Art, of the New York City Art Students' League, or of the Peter Cooper Union Art Department would expect to teach public schools in Van Wert, Ohio, or in Appleton, Wisconsin, any more than Harvard College graduates very often stayed in public-school teaching outside of New England. The normal schools were created because established colleges and special academies did not even consider the education of public-school teachers as a part of their function.

The art courses the normal schools developed were based on what was then known, or assumed to be true, of children's ability to learn about drawing and painting and a few crafts exercises. The courses taught to prospective art teachers were in some ways similar, and in other ways quite unlike, the work offered in the professional art schools. Normal school art departments were seeking a professionalism in teaching art.

A pronounced contrast to this art education approach of the period before 1941 is now in the ascendant. In the second decade after World War II, American colleges preparing men and women as teachers are emphasizing a greater depth of education in the subjects, in the content to be taught. History, geography, the sciences must be studied on a more thorough and mature level than was the case in the normal schools before 1941. In every aspect of teaching this emphasis is having its effect.

In the preparation of art teachers, college students in almost every art department in the country are being taught the studio disciplines of drawing, design, painting, sculpture, graphic arts, metal craft, ceramics, and other crafts, by artist-teachers who are professional in their accomplishments, even if few of them would, if they could, make a livelihood of the practice of art. The college art teachers are by the nature of their intensive work in art close in sympathy and often in acquaintance with some of the nationally known and exhibited artists in their field.

The emphasis, then, in the formal education of teachers of art is changing from that of inculcating a professional pride in teaching as a life work, to that of establishing in the student capabilities of development as an artist. Instead of assuming, as the normal school art faculty did, that a proper approach to teaching was more important than art training, we now operate on the basis that the process of teaching may have to be learned as a means of livelihood, but the college art student's initiation into professional art production is of the first importance. It is in the process of acquiring this artist professionalism that the student begins to see the independent metropolitan artist as his professional hero; he begins to assume that the artist's achievement, his sophistication in art, represents a goal, perhaps the only goal, to be sought after eagerly. This aim supplants the normal school graduate's ambition to become a fine teacher; and for many potentially excellent teachers of art it creates a dichotomy of ambitions which eventually becomes insupportable. At the time that some kind of resolution has to be made, the individual who elects to enter into or to continue in teaching is more than likely to do so with the acknowledged or suppressed conviction that to stay in the schools proves his incompetence to reach the goal which has been more exalted in his eyes from the time of his college career.

The end result of setting up the goals of the artist as applicable to both artist and teacher is to make less effectual the work of many teachers who have, through this process, come to lack pride in their teaching achievement.

The artist, often holding little or no part of the world's wealth, and almost always subsisting on a meager and irregular income, does have a pride in his professional occupation. It is a pride which is sustained by a complex combination of determination to succeed as an artist, in spite of the fact that the times seem so inimical to art; by a gregariously sustained feeling of martyrdom arising in response to this public neglect of the arts; and lastly, by the most incongruous fact of all, that an increasing number of magazines, museum publications, and books are being issued which discuss seriously the artist's work and intentions. The teachers have the regular income and the concomitant of a more stable life, but they are currently being deluged by disconcerting public doubts of the merit of their work. The artists live precariously but with the moral backing of a press which gives their work and their thought important stature, even while only a few of them make a livelihood from their art. Artists have had thrust upon them far more opportunities than they have wished for to make clear for the art press

what have been the motivations of their work. The responses are usually conscientious and honest, as it is difficult to resent seemingly sympathetic interest in one's work.

Any such effort on the part of an artist to phrase his most hopeful ambitions can be more unintentionally pathetic for him, and more damning of society's meager aesthetic expectations, than would be the most vindictive critical blast he could make. Often it is apparent that the artist exists in a world made too small by tight boundaries of general indifference and particularized hostility.

Willem de Kooning is an artist of integrity. He has achieved a critical and a financial success in the last decade. Important galleries and collectors own major pieces of his work for which they have paid prices high in comparison with those paid most living artists. Persons who do not like his work, which can be called "abstract-expressionist" in approach, and who like still less the vital (and ugly) images he painted in his series on "woman," are not justified in suggesting that he is simply riding a fad for the money he can make on it.

He was born in 1904. From 1919 on, he apprenticed to a painter, studied art, worked on the WPA Federal Art Project, and carried on his independent work. It was not until 1948 that he had his first one-man show, from which time he has done well in the sale of work. For any man to devote all his energy and skill to a problematical financial success from his young manhood to his forty-fourth year is not exactly the act of a money-hungry faker.

In a 1951 symposium de Kooning is quoted as saying: "Some painters, including myself, do not care what chair they are sitting on. It does not even have to be a comfortable one. They are too nervous to find out where they ought to sit. They do not want to 'sit in style.' Rather they have found that painting — any kind of painting — to be painting at all, in fact, is a way of living today, a style of living, so to speak. That is where the form of it lies. It is exactly in its uselessness that it is free. Those artists do not want to conform. They only want to be inspired."[1]

We know that a teacher does not have to be a "conformist" in the more confining sense of the word. A good teacher could not be. But a teacher is not able to insist on the approximation of freedom which men like de Kooning have purchased at the expense to themselves of many other valuable human experiences. All our society is at a stage where the "tyranny of the average" is powerful in its influence. The artist, whether he works, as did Michelangelo, for the rich and the powerful of his day, or whether he works in physical poverty in a direction of interest to only a few persons, has frequently been cut off from the life problems of the majority of his own contemporaries.

The teacher in America of the 1960's cannot be so cut off. The art teacher, more than the painter, is daily impelled by the very nature of teaching to provide interpretations of art. For the materials he needs as interpreter, he can turn to de Kooning, his paintings above all, and to what he has said, and what has been said of him. De Kooning can aid the teacher to understand the art of the recent past. De Kooning's "style of living" is one which he has found a necessary way of life to give himself the time and concentration for painting. The same "style" might not be necessary or desirable to another painter, but it cannot even be pined for by the teacher. It is a style of living for long-term contemplation, for expression of personal convictions through the painter's media. The teacher's contemplation has to be expended not only on objects of art but also upon the diverse individualities and possibilities of his students. "Freedom" in de Kooning's sense of the term is of

necessity a quite different freedom from that needed by the teacher.

Furthermore, de Kooning uses words which emotionally mean one thing but literally cannot mean what he seems to have said. To say that for painting — "it is exactly in its uselessness that it is free" — is not an adequate interpretation, for a student or teacher, of the artist's views.

If he believed painting to be useless de Kooning could not have painted his whole life.

He quotes the views of too many of our fellow citizens when he characterizes his life work with the term "useless." If painting is useless to the many millions of people whose obvious absence of sympathetic attitude de Kooning senses, then he is free of any demands or compulsions these millions may make on art. It is freedom from their unthinking demands which de Kooning seeks in using the term "useless" to describe what is of primary importance to him.

Again, speaking on the reverse of this view of the "mass" the teacher has to assume that a democratic society is educable, that individuals can grow, that children and adults are not as obtuse as they often act. The art teacher can no more be "free" of the average man and his progeny than de Kooning can be "free" of his paint and canvas.

American artists' expressions of faith are often stated in a kind of Hemingway brusqueness of manner and utter simplicity of vocabulary. At times this habit really makes impossible any attempt at more subtle interpretations of the artist's intent.

Theodor Werner, a West German artist, in the M O M A, The New Decade exhibition catalogue in 1955, is more helpful to our understanding than the "telegraphic" style permits, when he wrote:

Works of art are a kind of bulletin on the condition of man; his state of being, his participation in life, and his dangerous alienation from life.

[1] *Museum of Modern Art Bulletin, Volume* XXIII, Spring 1951.

Man seeks man.

The Creative is the compass with which he navigates around the cliffs of one-sided rationalization, mechanization, and around the dangers of becoming barren, empty, and a mass man. . . .

Homo sapiens struggles for his existence. He can only survive through existing. Only with the gentle force of the creative act will he master reality.[2]

In the world Mr. Werner knows, the artist is something of a lonely priest seeking a wholeness for himself and for his works in a world endangered by mechanization, a danger present not only to objects, but to people themselves. This view of the present-day painter as a hermit-like individual seeking some kind of truth, even if it is only a truth evident to himself and perhaps a few others, is not uncommon. For the teacher of art, Werner's views should provide a concept of the artist which has greater integrity than the image presented in picture magazines; and it might also encourage the teacher to achieve a similar integrity in the creative work of teaching.

Werner's insight into the creation of art and the spiritual journey of man is not one which would foster an adolescent search for "freedom" through superficial imitation of the "artist's life." It gives the teacher of art a deeper context for interpretative approaches to the painting of Werner and of other present-day artists. The cultural sophistication of Theodor Werner's thinking and the blunt words of de Kooning are in great contrast to artists' views which seek a kind of shorthand, implying hedonistic sneers at society.

The following statement comes from another exhibition catalogue. "I have tried to arrange things so that I can do what I want. No one ever likes the painting that I'm working on. I like this because this means that the things I'm thinking about in my

head are still mine (that is, no one has ever thought of them before) . . .

"One day you wake up and painting isn't mental gymnastics, it is not done to get a grade, it is not done to get in shows, nor is it done to stop thinking. *It's just done.*"[3]

Here, simplified, is the same isolation of the artist experienced by so many other men; the response to it is different. The chief value expressed by this artist is that of doing "what I want." The only reasons the artist gives for painting are discarded. The conclusion remaining is that painting is *"just done."*

The artist seems to wish that if man can do what he wants, he will then be able to paint somewhat as he breathes. In the rest of his statement he writes that stylistic continuity is not essential to him, that he supposes some people cannot get *ideas*, and that if you have enough time you can come up with something. He closes by saying somewhat ambiguously, "I hope that people will look at my things as individuals. I hope that my things will stand alone. I am right behind them."

Many artists preface brief essays by noting their inadequacy in words. They should do so. The art teacher, however, must work with the written and spoken word, as well as the media of art. For this reason the teacher should have or acquire a greater sophistication in the humanistic studies than many artists possess or make evident. Particularly, the art teacher must be capable of critical judgment in reading art publications of all sorts.

The artist quoted may wish that people will look at his things without reflecting the collective views of their relatives, clubs, churches, or neighbors. Or he may mean that he wishes people would look at his things separately, each one for itself, without regard to whether or not they are like his

[2]Museum of Modern Art. *The New Decade: 22 European Painters and Sculptors,* Statement by Theodor Werner. New York, 1955, p. 48.

[3]Museum of Modern Art. *Sixteen Americans,* Statement by Wally Hedrick. New York, 1959, p. 13.

other works. He may be telling us that he hopes his works will stand alone and not be compared to the work of his contemporaries or to the work of the past. Or he may be saying that he wants his works to stand alone because he is "behind them." Finally, he may be saying, like a bank, that he guarantees the value of his work by standing behind it.

Whatever impels the museum to seek artists' statements and whatever influences produce the artists' views, the art teacher should be among the most sympathetic of readers because of the light he may see thrown upon the artists' work. But he can absorb the valuable insights of this material in the same humanistically critical attitude with which he reads the work of critics and historians.

The sort of neoromantic natural man approach to the arts, which some artists believe to be essential, may not be, as they state it, an adequate framework for the teaching of the arts. Students in the art classes of America will be the future industrial workers, office people, salesmen, teachers, lawyers, doctors, scientists of all varieties, architects, designers, farmers, and so on through all the present and future vocations of society. In the adult art classes this vocational range of personnel is already very much with the art teacher. All of these children and adults bring with them an immensely diversified attitude toward aesthetic experience. As the teacher of art lives with their variety of responses, day after day, he cannot succeed as teacher if, more than anything else, he is aware of the negative qualities which the students express. He cannot permit himself to let his students become identified in his mind with the "mass," the "average," the "philistine" man, who prevents the "natural" artist from reaching his full development.

Furthermore, while the teacher must view each individual artist's writings critically, he should be interested in artists' writings

which can be considered great literature in the arts. Delacroix, Van Gogh, Louis Sullivan, Leonardo da Vinci, provide insights which interpret the work of hundreds of artists less able to express themselves in the written word.

Scattered more broadly through the country, forming very much less of a professionalized community, and much more closely attached to the heterogeneous communities where they live and work, are members of larger groups of people whose life work is concerned with art. These include all the artists designing objects and visual materials which serve so-called "practical" ends, and which yet call upon their producers for some kind and degree of aesthetic content. Architects, commercial artists, industrial designers, hand craftsmen, film and television artists, photographers, are at work on small and large assignments in every state in the nation.

In some degree, the architects' views of their work in relation to society, the architects' statements of intentions, are more easily grasped by the receptive students. Sometimes the teacher of art feels more closely identified in his own objectives to those expressed by men and women in design fields, especially architecture and regional urban planning, than he does to the ideas of the painters.

Doubtless the reason for this is that the members of the architect-designer group share with the art teacher a middle man or interpretive role in relation to clients and to the general public.

These artists, too, have been constantly urged to declare themselves as to the prospects they see for the practice of their work. Their responses are as various as is their work, and as are the localities in which they live. Yet in certain discouraging reflections they show an awarenesss of the cramped quarters, the confinement of vision, so keenly discerned by the painters and sculptors.

For ten years International Design Conferences have been held at Aspen, Colorado. The meetings have been widely attended and followed by artists and students for their clues to the state of design in Western industrial society.

From the 1960 Conference, comments by Olle Eksell, a Swedish artist-designer, were noted in the *Journal of Commercial Art* as follows:[4]

The biggest mistake a designer can make is to think he is a business man and forget he is an artist. Intuition is highly important to the artist. He must be free to play, to experiment."

At the same meeting, Craig Ellwood, architect, said in substance:

The corporation needs the designer even more than the designer needs the corporation. With competition and changing conditions the corporation will be forced to seek out the designer. The designer should remain apart, retain his separate identity; otherwise the corporation will swallow and frustrate him.

Designers and architects are now beginning to work together. New York's Seagram Building with its Four Seasons Restaurant is an example of the architect's maintaining control over everything, the building, the interiors, the graphics, down to the match covers. The effect is total and superior.

Taken together these quotations add another dimension to the teacher's rationale for the visual arts of today. The designers defend as stoutly as any painter the artist's need to exercise "intuition." They insist that the artist has the ability to create aesthetic values worth something to business, and which are not the achievement of business processes. Ellwood elaborates on the necessity for artists' collaboration on large scale projects if the projects are to be completed with aesthetic consistency as superior works of art.

These views assume that art in design and in architecture is attainable in community life. Every person living in some corner of the world, influenced by the worldwide industrial and economic organization of the twentieth century, will have to put up with the aesthetic failures of production, or they will enjoy the more satisfying successes of design in industry and in architecture.

Teachers find themselves pushed by the interest of their communities and their students to rely more frequently on the expressed objectives of artists in the design fields than upon those of the painters, when discussion gets started on the values of art to the layman.

Garrett Eckbo, a landscape architect speaking at an earlier Aspen Design Conference (1956), said in his paper:

The work of art without an audience has no meaning. . . . What does art do for its audience? It improves their understanding and experience of the world by communication, solution of specific problems, visual enrichment, creation of new relations between people and the world around them. It explores, especially, sensitive ways of communicating thoughts and feelings about the world: . . .[5]

This appeals to the teacher of art as a position to which he may subscribe. Something like it in the way of a philosophical conviction is an absolute essential to him if his work is to have any force and persuasiveness.

Since the children and adults to be taught are to be found everywhere, and buildings are designed and made wherever there are people, and industrially produced objects are sold wherever people can be tempted to want them, the designers are somewhat more geographically dispersed than are painters, and the teachers are still more scattered about the country than are the designers.

[4]All Aspen excerpts from: *Aspen*, The Journal of Commercial Art, Vol. 2, No. 7 (July 1960), pp. 9–22.

[5]Garrett Eckbo, *Profession of Design*. Print, Vol. X, No. 4 (Aug.-Sept. 1956), pp. 47–49.

Teachers by necessity are often provincials in the sense of isolation from art centers. Painters and sculptors tend to be metropolitan provincials isolated from the thought and feeling of people outside their small group of associates active in art or active in their concern with the arts.

Architects and designers occupy the middle position here. They are thickly localized in big cities and especially in New York, as are the painters. But there are thousands of them working over the country, and even the best publicized among them, most firmly established in New York, are forced to travel widely and frequently to meet and work with clients. Naturally their ideas on art seem more sanguine, less inclined to the pessimistic aspects of American potentialities. While the teacher of art has to be smart enough not to believe that office buildings, cheaply sheathed in glass and enameled metal, will revolutionize the art of architecture and make American cities the envy of Europe he can see the evidence that art in many of its design aspects is more pervasive in his own life and the life of his community than is the art of contemporary painting.

The architect-designer is less likely to be held up by the art teacher as a personal model whose life pattern the art teacher may hope to emulate.

The teacher will be grateful for the knowledge that aesthetic values are penetrating the national life broadly; nevertheless, his personal life story, which cannot be that of the single-minded professional artist in painting or sculpture, will have more similarities to that of the artist than it will to the life of the designer.

Whether the fact is justifiable or not, the teacher will earn less money annually than designers will. This lower economic rung he shares with the independent artist. In fact, there may be some interesting and rather curious economic relationships developing between the metropolitan artist and the provincial art teacher in the next decade.

It has become almost axiomatic that the artist does some part-time teaching at a salary level which is pitiful if his pay scale be projected to a full-time teaching job. And a large number of art teachers are selling their art work, produced on a part-time basis, at prices which are absurdly low if one were thinking of them as contributing to a wholly professional income.

Only the fact that the practice of the arts and of art education is comparatively thinly spread prevents the two groups from seriously undercutting each other economically in their respective professions. For the most part, the teaching done by the professional artists is of a sort not eagerly competed for by full-time teachers, and it is done in institutions in which pay scales are apt to be forced upward, if anything, by the example of the institutions employing full-time teachers. As to the sale of works of art made by teachers of art, this too is not keenly competitive. Most often purchasers of such work are venturing for the first time into the acquisition of an original piece. The sale of art teachers' work, at whatever price, is apt to create greater markets for art in the future rather than to be a present threat to the artist attempting a professional career.

Economically, the art teacher, like the independent artist, will in the foreseeable future live modestly. The teacher will benefit by the general upgrading of salaries which is slowly occurring. Some artists are benefiting by huge prices on highly publicized works, and many others are sharing in lesser degree in this price swing. Nevertheless, both groups seem destined to remain in lower economic positions than those enjoyed by the architect-designers.

It is in professional aspirations and attitudes that the teacher is necessarily at odds with the independent artist.

Adolph Gottlieb, in 1954, wrote something which at first reading may strike one as unwonted violence emerging from black despair. He said:

The artist is in a jungle and his fundamental problem is survival. Young artists find themselves in a brutally predatory society. . . . Contrary to popular opinion the artist is not utterly irresponsible, in fact he is the only member of society who accepts complete responsibility for the creation of art.[6]

These fragments culled from Gottlieb describe an atmosphere which few young people will admit exists, even if they are stranded dead center in it. If time brings one reluctantly to admit that Gottlieb's insight has validity, it seems more nearly an expression of stubborn devotion to art and to the importance of creating art than it does a product of despair.

The teacher of art is professionally educated in a curriculum which emphasizes his own development as a creator of art work. Lesser emphases are put upon his preparation for teaching art, on his knowledge of art history, and on his understanding of aesthetics.

The curriculum he presents for students from the ages of four to the indefinite upper ages of adult classes is devoted particularly to experiences in making art objects.

When he begins to put together a philosophical stand on which to base his professional life, he needs to find one appropriate to a teacher of art. A paraphrase from Gottlieb might do.

Possibly we are all in a jungle. Certainly the artist occasionally acts as if he were alone in the world, or at least abandoned by the world. But that is not true. If he is a denizen of a jungle, air-conditioned, macadamized, suburbanized, and noise ridden as it may be, then so are we all.

If the society is brutally predatory, then we are all in it. For the teacher, however, there is a significant difference. That same society has created schools, schools which are infinitely removed from perfection, but which from their inception to the present

day were in part created to seek a way out of, and an amelioration of, brutality and predatory ways of life. For the teacher not to recognize brutality when he is surrounded by it is virtually criminal. For him to assume that brutality cannot be curbed, or modified, or changed to constructive energies, is to abdicate one of his best functions as teacher.

Obviously, the teacher's seeming and inevitable reaction to his responsibilities admits of no ambiguity. The artist may appear to be loafing even while he is honestly "working" on his next effort. The teacher has no possibility of encouraging any doubts whatever. When students arrive in a classroom, the teacher is "responsible" on at least a caretaker's level, or he loses his job. But why could not the teacher of art make his own statement of absolutes in the following way?

"*The teacher of art is the only member of society who accepts as his 'complete responsibility' the teaching of art to his fellow citizens.* He teaches the practice of the arts, an understanding of aesthetic values of the culture, the history of art forms in Western and other cultures. He teaches small children some of the creative possibilities of expression in art materials. He teaches the prospective professional in art, and he teaches the adult who looks for the enlightenment and emotional satisfactions he suspects are to be found in art."

Certainly other persons and other agencies contribute to education in art; the museum personnel, gallery managers, retail sales people, artists of every persuasion, educate their contemporaries in art. Museums, books, magazines, television, retail shops, interior decorating firms, all take part in public education.

But just as the artist takes the primary responsibility for the creation of art, so the teacher takes primary responsibility for education in art.

To meet this responsibility he must de-

[6]Adolph Gottlieb, "The Artist and the Public," *Art in America*, Vol. 42, No. 4 (Dec. 1954), pp. 267–271.

velop diverse and, occasionally, opposing qualities. The creative quality of the productive artist should be part of the art teacher's makeup. As his teaching duties become more professional and his student days more distant, it is quite probable that his art work may become miscellaneous and less advanced over his youthful achievements than he might wish. As an active member of a school and a community he may move from occasional typographical designs for brochures to stage designing, to contributions to poster campaigns, or to building and grounds planning, as well as trying to retain his grasp of art in the area of his own interest, be it ceramics, painting, or graphic arts.

When new schools are built, he finds himself in the role of design consultant for his own art facilities and often for other parts of the plan. In his own home and in the community he may find himself absorbed in landscape planning. These are not far-fetched possibilities, nor are they tasks fit only for the uncreative or the unimaginative. They are not, in their varied nature and range, the kind of thing that the professional designer or artist is likely to be called in to do.

In hundreds of American communities they are things which the teacher of art is apt to find himself engaged upon. They keep his creative faculties alert and on the stretch. The jobs tackled and brought to completion become an example to students of the possibilities, the zest for a more conscious existence, which the art teacher's approach to life can stimulate. In such ways do art teachers continue their creative zeal.

The scholarly qualities of the teacher can, at times, be at war with his efforts as artist. He may be entirely aware that his own predisposition is toward a coloristically boisterous kind of romanticism; but he knows his history of modern art well enough and he interprets his psychology of learning objectively enough to know that a student's fascination with, let us say, mathematically precise forms and symmetrically handsome space organizations is an inclination which the teacher should respect and encourage.

As a scholar he knows that there have been societies which created works of art superior, in some respects, to those of our own day. He knows that the artists best rewarded in their lifetime may not be doing the work which will be greatly significant to future generations. Edwin Howland Blashfield was a popular and highly paid artist in 1910 when John Sloan, then thirty-nine years old, had sold only two or three paintings. Today, it is the Sloan paintings which are eagerly sought after.

For the art teacher, scholarship encourages a larger view of the present position of art, and of its past values, than he might wish to explore were he husbanding all his powers to expend as artist. The teacher cannot afford to view the art work of his own day and the possibilities of art in the immediate future only from the limited outlook of an upper Lexington Avenue sales gallery of contemporary painting. Not that the professional artist's vision is that limited either, but the sales gallery does occupy a frontal position in his landscape.

For the art teacher in America, it is the school system in all its ramifications which creates his working environment. He cannot wish so solid a structure out of his sight by attempting to play the part of the metropolitan artist. Instead of seeking some kind of refuge from the strain of coping with the complexities of any public school system, art teachers are being forced to learn their parts as members of the educational legislature. Their constituency is the field of the arts, but they have to deal with the whole faculty body and the executive branch of the school community to keep art education in a healthy growing condition and in favorable relationship to the over-all activities of the whole institution.

There are some current developments in the schools which are favorable to the arts, or which can be favorable if they are acted upon by alert art teachers. There are other tendencies being actively promoted which are downright frightening in their disregard of the arts. The art teacher's "complete responsibility" for the future of art education is more important than it has been in decades.

Not many years ago teachers of art began to realize that they themselves had created in the minds of parents, teachers, and principals very limiting objectives for art education, both in the elementary and in the high schools. For younger children we were insistent upon the great value of creative experience. The child's art activity was described as his best passport to a creative life.

And in the high school we added to creativity the value of preparing for "the creative use of leisure time." No more overworked cliché has appeared in all the writing on education.

Neither of these objectives goes far in developing an understanding of the humanistic values of the plastic and visual arts. Both objectives emphasize the development of expressive power on an individualistic basis. Neither objective specifically encourages teachers or students to be aware of the arts of mankind, of the aesthetic values which the historical and contemporary cultures of man have created.

We have been saying to the child of six or sixteen, "Find yourself. For the search, here is paint and a brush." But unless we are helping him to see what artists have already found and are still finding, he may "find himself" only in an isolated wilderness. For this is virtually the environment which many artists take for granted as the natural habitat of the painter and the sculptor. Certainly we can be hopeful that the child working in art forms is developing a creative outlook upon his world, is expressing in plastic means what he senses of its wonders. But if, as he grows older, the

emphasis is always on his direct form creation in art and seldom on the creative potentialities and accomplishments of art in the grownup world, is it not predictable that he will assume that art is for children, for isolated "artists," and not for the ordinary citizen busy at his normal responsibilities?

The art teacher can start educating young people to know the arts, to begin understanding art in historical perspective, to expect that works of art will be a part of their lives wherever they may be. Only by persistently teaching "art" as history is taught, as literature and science are taught, is the teacher going to help students see art as humanistic, that is, as "thought or action centering upon distinctively human interests." Too many high school graduates think of art class as time spent in painting or in "doing" other projects which are important only in the classroom, to be put aside along with other memories of childhood and youth.

To start them on the way to discriminating between Frank Lloyd Wright and Mies van der Rohe, art must be taught differently. Making such a discrimination is just as possible for a junior high-school student as grasping the difference between Louis XIV and King George V.

The most significant, and to art education the most alarming, development making strong headway in American junior and senior high-school education is the increased encouragement of superior students to eliminate from their programs most, or all, of the arts. Art, music, drama, dance, speech, all are categorized by implication as not for superior students.

The Conant study is somewhat responsible for emphasis on the prolonged study of English, mathematics, science, social studies, and foreign languages by all superior students. As Dr. Conant himself is a writer and scientist, his pressure has been very effective in these areas. We should not, however, overlook the fact that Conant, in the reports which are being used as practical handbooks for school improvement by thousands of administrators and school boards, makes an issue of urging the best students to include the study of art and music among their elective studies. Already the stimulus of this thinking has made changes in secondary education. The art teacher could be sharing with music, drama, literature, and creative writing and dance teachers some leadership in meeting current challenges to the validity of education in art.

In order to cope with the problem, the art teacher will have to get some knowledge of the curricular pattern in his school. He will have to be acquainted with the guidance program. He will need enough of this kind of background to serve on curriculum committees; and if he is not named to work with curriculum, he should insist on being represented at some expense to his own time.

What he is likely to find is that most of the other disciplines are slowly stepping up their demands upon the students. Art classes can profitably do likewise. The gifted and/or greatly interested student can easily accomplish far more in high-school art classes than he has been doing. What that more can be is important; for it should not be merely added assignments, but work requiring greater depth of perception, of skills, of individual growth in a variety of media. The least an accelerated art program will do is to eliminate the credit-sponging spectator. The more important accomplishment will be a gradual increase in the number of more able students enrolling in art.

Beyond this simple step, the art teacher who does the most for art education will devise approaches by which he can interest the most able of high-school students in the study of art. Since there are no standardized blueprints for these ventures, he must make his own.

We may be certain that Dr. Conant intends art and music courses to be as stimulating and substantial as a first-rate class in English literature or a senior class in physics when he urges the best of high-school students to include art and music electives in all or part of their senior high-school years. Too many art courses are conducted as havens from the more rigorous demands of the academic day. This condition of affairs in "the art room" is often remembered affectionately by students who have plenty of self-direction and art ability, for they find it possible to do a great many things exactly as they like. Or in less productive manner they can and do join the other group commonly enrolled in art classes, the students who are present in body only and are willing to settle for the lowest passing grades. The casual loafing about in a too permissive art room is indefensible.

More than being indefensible, it cannot be supposed that such an environment is adequate for the work of a group of superior students. A fresh, organized approach to the subject of the visual and plastic arts is called for if the high school art program is to provide a valid humanities course in the senior high school.

In many superior high schools the realization of this relationship of the arts to other humanistic studies is encouraging teachers to begin classes in art history, in art appreciation, in surveys of contemporary arts, in understanding visual and plastic arts. The courses are variously taught. Some are developed chronologically on a world-history-of-art approach. Some are planned as courses in appreciation with the various media — painting, sculpture, architecture — treated as units and emphasizing the contemporary world. In some schools, studio experiences planned to complement the insights gained from slides, discussions, readings, and lectures are important in the work, and in others, no studio approaches are used. The students enrolling in these classes include those who take as much art work as they can, as well as those who never enroll in the studio work.

Already, teachers who are conducting or planning such courses find that their teaching becomes more demanding of their time than it had been before, but that the necessity for extended reading and study on an organized basis has considerably enhanced their own art interests and the work of their studio classes as well.

If developments of this nature continue to spread in art education, we may find art teachers perforce removed even more from the orbit of the professional artist. Inevitably the growth of such teaching in the arts will push the art teacher closer to the scholarly concerns of the philosopher, the critic, and the historian.

In my view, the results would immeasurably improve general education in the arts and in the long run be much more successful in expanding the quality and quantity of public understanding of the visual and plastic arts.

Teachers cannot afford to stop creating in the arts. Neither are they in a position to stop studying both the educational process and their students. They cannot risk losing track of the more promising new work in all the arts. It is with all of these aspects of the social pattern they must create.

They have to find their own way to comprehend their multiple preparation and function. No other practice of profession in the arts is like theirs, and as a consequence they have to make their own standards, not being misled by the forlorn hope that they can safely create a dual personality on a kind of Jekyll and Hyde pattern.

Teaching art is enough of a challenge to absorb the talent and energy of many of the best young people who want to work in the arts. It is a responsibility which is in the old-fashioned Victorian sense a privilege. A teacher can dedicate a lifetime to opening the senses and the intelligence of young and older students to the arts of painting, sculpture, architecture, and the associated arts.

There are few human occupations as rewarding as that of teaching. While it is true that no teacher of art can be ignorant of the most compelling art forms of his own era and of the past, it should also be evident that all teachers of art should hold themselves equal to artists, designers, and architects in their pride of profession.

36. Frontiers for an Experimentalist Philosophy of Education

FRANCIS T. VILLEMAIN *and* NATHANIEL L. CHAMPLIN

I

Dewey's educational theory is primarily a philosophy of scientific learning more broadly conceived than heretofore since such learning, he feels, not only should comply with a scientific format but should also be addressed to the problems of free men. But this educational theory does not do justice to the richness of Dewey's thought, nor is it entirely compatible with a major element in his thinking. In certain writings not concerned directly with schooling there is a cluster of ideas which, if developed, would bring about a major change both in Dewey's educational theory and in the broad reaches of contemporary experimentalism. This set of ideas, we believe, locates an instrument of no less power than scientific method, an instrument capable of being employed in the construction, direction, and assessment of human life.

For some people it might seem inappropriate to turn to Dewey's general writings when the task is one of developing his educational theory. It could be argued that his general philosophy is really about other matters and not relevant directly to the work of the schools. Such a view would be unacceptable to Dewey. He subsumes schooling under the more generally defined concept of education. "Schooling is a part of the work of education, but education in its full meaning includes all the influences that go to form the attitudes and dispositions (of desire as well as of belief), which constitute dominant habits of mind and character."[1]

In his major educational document, *Democracy and Education*, Dewey defines philosophy in such a way that any separation between philosophy and educational theory is untenable. To maintain this separation is to block the creative exploitation of Dewey's thought and, at the same time, to ignore and violate his vision of the subject matter and purposes of philosophic reflec-

[1] John Dewey, *Liberalism and Social Action* (New York: Putnam, 1935), p. 58.

*SOURCE: Reprinted from *The Antioch Review*, XIX, 3 (Fall 1959).

tion. On the other hand, to move with Dewey's thought is to press into service the full sweep of his philosophic themes in order to have an educational theory as comprehensive as he envisioned it to be: "If we are willing to conceive education as the process of forming fundamental dispositions, intellectual and emotional, toward nature and fellow men, philosophy may even be defined as the general theory of education."[2]

Philosophical writings that do not deal explicitly with schooling are to be taken as part of a general educational theory and, as such, are properly used for contributing to the development of conceptions about and directives for education in the schools. Following this Deweyan directive, "philosophy of education" refers to a critically developed organization of ideas in which general conceptions uniquely relevant to schooling are at once featured and systematically unified with a general theory of education. This unification may act to modify both general theory and schooling directives.

II

While Dewey is a recognized spokesman on such matters as pragmatism and democracy, these matters do not encompass the heart of his philosophy. An examination of his theory of experience and his vision of the *summum bonum* shows him to be a philosopher of art above all else. As a major interpreter of Dewey says, art experience "is the central theme in all of Dewey's thinking . . . . His educational, social, scientific and logical contributions, technical as they can become, are all geared to this end."

In the Dewey view of the nature of experience, the aesthetic is so central that we cannot have an experience without it. Indeed, it is the defining characteristic of "an experience." Dewey writes: "An experience has a unity that gives it its name,

that meal, that storm, that rupture of friendship. The existence of this unity is constituted by a single quality that pervades the entire experience in spite of the variation of its constituent parts."[3] Since " . . . the aesthetic is no intruder in experience from without . . .," we cannot escape qualities nor need we apologize for them. The qualitative or aesthetic is generic to all experience.

We have here a preliminary set of notions. First, it is being argued that the qualitative is not to be set off as a type of experience that is independent of still other forms of experience. Rather, it is woven into the fabric of all "normally complete experience." Second, the qualitative or aesthetic is ever present whether the experience is primarily of a painting or of a mathematical formula. Third, qualities are not to be construed as a superfluous luxury nor as a contamination of "pure" experience. And fourth, since qualities *just are*, they are candidates for evaluation or assessment.

Dewey finds these qualities performing a function vital to the perpetuation of things that dearly matter: " . . . the immediate existence of quality, and of dominant and pervasive quality, is the background, the point of departure, and the regulative principle of all thinking."[4] This is an extremely sweeping claim. Even our language, Dewey tells us, becomes a "meaningless jumble" when it proceeds without reference to the "pervasively qualitative." The qualitative sets the necessary framework in which cognitive operations are released. But there is more to it than this. What Dewey calls "pervasive quality" functions in a regulative capacity. "Without its controlling presence, there is no way to determine the relevancy, weight or coherence of any designated distinction or relation. The universe of ex-

---

[2]John Dewey, *Democracy and Education* (New York: Macmillan, 1916), p. 383.

[3]John Dewey, *Art as Experience* (New York: Minton, Balch, 1934), pp. 37, 46.
[4]John Dewey, *Philosophy and Civilization* (New York: Minton, Balch, 1931), p. 116.

perience surrounds and regulates the universe of discourse . . . ."[5] And further: . . . such qualities permeate and color *all* the objects and events that are involved in an experience."

Dewey goes on to say that we think in terms of the relations of qualities. There is "qualitative thought." In his view this kind of thinking is as demanding as the kind we do "in terms of symbols, verbal and mathematical." The distinction to be noted is that we can think about qualities — as Dewey is doing in his writing — and we can think with qualities. That is, qualities are themselves thoughts. Particularly this second point prompts the conclusion that the process of creating, deploying, working, and reworking qualities is a form of intelligence. Where he was centrally concerned with this in *Art as Experience*, Dewey writes, "Any idea that ignores the necessary role of intelligence in production of works of art is based upon identification of thinking with use of one special kind of material, verbal signs and words. An incredible amount . . . of intelligence . . . is exercised in perception of qualitative relations . . . ."[6] This process of qualitative thinking is a "doing or making." When the outcome sought by the doing and making is itself a quality, and when this quality has acted in a regulative way over the doing and making, we have a case of that kind of intelligence which is art. As Dewey puts it: "The doing or making is artistic when the perceived result is of such a nature that its qualities as perceived have controlled the question of production."

There are experimentalists who would be reluctant to grant that such doing and making is intelligence. They would be quite willing to call it art. Even Dewey, elsewhere in his writings, equates intelligence with the processes of empirical inquiry. But any activity which is purposive and

focally preoccupied with a qualitative consequence fits not only Dewey's theory of art but also his general theory of intelligence. The Dewey of *Experience and Nature* writes:

"Thought," reason, intelligence, whatever the word we choose to use, is existentially an adjective (or better an adverb), not a noun. It is disposition of activity, a quality of that conduct which foresees consequences of existing events, and which uses what is foreseen as a plan and method of administering affairs.[7]

It is important to point out at this juncture that a conception describing art as an affair of intelligence does not for Dewey make art a special case of cognition. Consistent with his experimentalism, Dewey insisted upon art as an affair of qualitative relating. His theory of art is not subsumed under his general theory of knowledge. Of course his is a *theory* of art and, as such, is to be examined from the vantage point of standards which apply to any theory. But it is a theory about something which itself is not an affair of theory or of knowing. In a reply to Croce, he makes this crystal clear.

. . . Croce assumes that I have written about art with the intention of bringing it within the scope of pragmatic philosophy. . . . The actual fact is that I have consistently treated the pragmatic theory as a theory of *knowing*, and as confined within the limits of the field of specifically cognitive subject-matter. And in addition I have specifically rejected the idea that aesthetic subject-matter is a form of knowledge. . . .[8]

The fact that Dewey makes use of illustrative instances in such fields as painting, music, and architecture might reinforce the thought that his is simply a theory of "fine art." But while Dewey turns to such areas as these to obtain empirical data for the support of his conclusions, he does not take these areas to exhaust what is meant by artistic "doing and making." Again, the

[5]John Dewey, *Logic: The Theory of Inquiry* (New York: Henry Holt, 1938), pp. 68–69.
[6]John Dewey, *Art as Experience*, pp. 46, 50–51.
[7]John Dewey, *Experience and Nature* (Chicago: Open Court, 1925), pp. 158–159.
[8]John Dewey, "A Comment on the Foregoing Criticism," *The Journal of Aesthetics and Art Criticism*, Vol. VI, No. 3, March 1948, p. 207.

aesthetic or qualitative is generic to all experience. Any experience can become art
experience — not simply those labelled
"fine arts" experience.

Nor does Dewey rest his case with this
analysis. He makes a staggering claim
— the claim of claims — for the qualitative. The ultimate goals for human life, the
locus of the good, are seen to reside in art
experience. "Art — the mode of activity
that is charged with meanings capable of
immediately enjoyed possession — is the
complete culmination of nature, and . . .
'science' is properly a handmaiden that
conducts natural events to this happy issue."[9]

Such a statement as this should lay to
rest the notion that Dewey makes knowing
operations, or the scientific method, the
final good for human life. Science, law,
medicine, schooling, or any human activity
or social arrangement is, in the last analysis, to be assessed in terms of its adequacy
as a "handmaiden" (an *instrumental* office)
to the perpetuation and refinement of experience focally aesthetic. "Aesthetic experience is a manifestation, a record and
celebration of the life of a civilization, a
means of promoting its development, and
is also the ultimate judgment upon the quality of a civilization."[10] To which must be
added a warning: "As long as art is the
beauty parlor of civilization, neither art
nor civilization is secure."

III

The development of a complete and coherent philosophy of education which does
justice to the foregoing conceptions concerning art was not undertaken by Dewey, nor
has it appeared to be a task of compelling
importance to Dewey's students. The full-
blown Deweyan philosophy of education
awaits the perception of the qualitative-

aesthetic theme and of the strengthened
relations between this part of his thought
and the great themes which make up his
educational theory. Such a philosophy
would in no way depreciate the role and
procedure of empirical inquiry in the educational situation. The import might well be
even greater. But such an educational outlook, while encompassing the body of educational writings herein held as incomplete,
would, in the final analysis, be a philosophy
of art education writ large.

A promising approach to this frontier task
for a Deweyan-based philosophy of education is the same one Dewey used in studying
and building his theory of art experience.
This approach is distinguished from others
by the fact that it attempts to reach generalizations about, or to locate governing agencies for, relationships between acts and
consequences — between means and ends.
The inquiries conducted toward gaining
such conclusions are here called "methodological inquiries." Logicians have, of course,
been carrying on such inquiries for years.
The laws of logic delineated by logicians
are prescriptions to be followed in relating
theoretical materials. But this interest in
delineating regulative devices for governing
conduct has rarely been directed to qualitative materials.[11]

Dewey's thought is pioneering in this respect. He conceived the arts in such a way
as to tender them amenable to a study
which could reach methodological conclusions. It must be born in mind that he made
the arts an affair of intelligence which, in
turn, he defined as an activity of deliberately controlled means-ends relating. And to

[9]John Dewey, *Experience and Nature*, p. 358.
[10]John Dewey, *Art as Experience*, pp. 326, 344.

[11]It is interesting to note that Dewey, who shared a
great deal with Aristotle, should come to do to the
arts in general what Aristotle, for the first time in
the history of thought, did to tragic drama. This
places both men solidly in the tradition of uniquely
practiced methodological inquiry; uniquely so, for
both Dewey and Aristotle conducted this sort of inquiry into the arts as well as into cognitive operations.

say that the arts are controlled is to say that they are subject to a regulative device which patterns the relating of means to ends.

Methodological inquiry studies conduct which reveals and submits to deliberate and self-imposed pattern. Such inquiry must produce theory about these orderings. Hence, not any subject matter is a proper object for such investigations. Nor are concepts from just any field of knowledge appropriate.

Dewey seems to be struggling to maintain this methodological approach to the qualitative. By emphasizing and depending upon such concepts as "meaning," "thought," "means," "ends," "control," and "order," he deemphasizes and, at times, actually rejects concepts from such fields as psychology, physiology, and neurology. His disposition toward methodological language and away from concepts receiving their meaning in other fields is sound on at least two grounds. First, nonmethodological conceptions cannot contribute either to a definition of art experience or to a theory about it. Second, such conceptions are further unsuitable because as terms they do not represent (stand for) things which can be studied methodologically. They fail to represent the distinctive character of the matters examined.

This point on the appropriateness of concepts with respect to any given inquiry deserves an illustration and further analysis. One cannot describe onomatopoeia by describing the vibrations of the ear drums, the electronic impulses of the nervous system, the light waves reflected from typewritten pages, or the muscular contractions of the larynx when in the presence of an instance of this form of poetic construction. When in seeking to describe some discrimination made in experience (for example, the onomatopoeia) we use language which refers simply to elements which sustain or produce the discriminated, we have committed the reductive fallacy. We leave the distinc-

tive thing we are talking about undescribed. Or we may leave our readers and ourselves with a case of mistaken identity. Needless to say, Dewey criticizes this fallacy throughout his writings.

In no way is this to be taken as saying that other-than-methodological modes of constructing knowledge claims are menial and unworthy of vigorous pursuit. Different modes of inquiry, with different concepts, locate and study different things. Their subject matters, together with the language they use to locate and describe these subject matters, should not be confused with each other. The choice of one over another is dependent upon the problem to which one is addressed.

The problem of education requires methodological theory — conceptions which direct educators in their selection of the procedures, the means and the objectives of their undertaking. A philosophy of education which fails to provide educators with direction at these crucial points may still be a hymn to the profession, but it will not release professional performance in education. Since, however, methodological discourse provides knowledge expressly about procedures identifying subject matters to be manipulated and goals to be obtained — all matters of, for, and by experience — it *does* release the professional activity of the teacher.

Educational theorists within the Deweyan tradition have work to do on two broad fronts. First, there must be a major expansion and systemization of methodological knowledge about the qualitative which would include its bearing upon and relation to cognitive operations. Second, there must be a reexamination of Dewey's insightful educational themes with a view toward their integration with this new knowledge. Work on both of these broad fronts is work that will entail the reconstruction of theory all along the line.

IV

Traditionally the term "quality" has been used to refer to a standard of excellence or to an attribute of something. An alternative, and methodological, definition must be fashioned if we are to extend Dewey's analysis of the qualitative. Such terms as "method," "means," "end-in-view," "thought," "symbols," "mediation," and "control" are foundational to methodological inquiries — so much so that this sort of inquiry cannot proceed without them. Literally, they define the subject matters of these inquiries. If such terms cannot apply to what is designated by the term "qualitative," then plainly, methodological discourse is irrelevant.

Suppose, to illustrate, we do as Dewey did: we turn to the arts. A college authority commissions an architect to design a classroom building. Having been informed of the budget, the site, the space requirements, the activities to take place, the health and safety conditions, building codes, and such matters as these, the architect still lacks that which will permit him to design the building. He will have to ask the college authority whether it wants a Georgian, Classical, Cape Cod, Swiss Chalet, California Ranch, Jacobean, Norman Fortress, Gothic, or Modern International building. Once this has been determined, the architect has a format which will release his designing activity. He will know whether the building is to be tall and slender or long and horizontal; he will also know whether it will be light and airy or heavy and ponderous; or whether it will depend primarily upon wood, stone, glass, or concrete.

If the style selected is Gothic, the term "Gothic" does not provide the format. But it does *refer* to a host of structures that are differentiated from other structures by virtue of what they have in common. This commonality or pervasiveness is a regulative device. It sets the format or pattern, prescribes the elements employed in the designing, and acts as a point of reference for determining what is to be rejected as inappropriate. For example, the architect will not use a glass block wall studded with aluminum frame windows, or fluted columns to support a picture window. The building will not be a horizontal structure nestling into the grade of the terrain. While it is true that the architect must confront qualities as relevant *means*, and although he may eliminate certain Gothic elements, still the fact that these elements are possible *means* is determined by that to which we refer with the term "Gothicness." This regulative device whch controls or directs the designing procedure is the architect's *method*.

Method, as one distinction, may be joined by a second and third. Our architect will no doubt design a building which will be a distinct example. This distinctiveness — sharing in the commonality of Gothicness — is his specific *end-in-view*. Further, he has a range of *means* by which he attains the end-in-view, the distinctiveness — means in the sense that they are the elements which are incorporated into and produce the end. The end emerges from the components selected and organized and is thus other than any one or a mere collection of these means. He builds his building by orchestrating method-authorized components, i.e., fenestration, elongation, filigree, volume juxtaposition, spatial modulation — each of which receives a character prescribed by the method followed and the end sought.

If quality is a matter for methodological definition at the most general level, it is also a matter of meaning. Since meaning is an affair of *instituted* connections or relationships (sometimes and inadequately called "perceived," "given," "felt," or "intuited") then quality too must be such an affair. For what we refer to by the terms "Gothicness," "redness," or "joviality," at one and the same time emerges out of and exhibits instituted connections or relationships. The quality designated by the term "redness" is not obtained save as a relationship of contrast is instituted. When we have the quality of redness, we have a constructed contrast. This methodologically described circumstance must be present in order that a quality gain its status. Clearly, therefore, any quality is obtained only as these relationships are present, or better still, as the connection or relations are *presented*. In less methodological language, this same event has been called "direct," "immediate," or "had in the present." Indeed, art experience has been distinguished as *immediate* rather than *mediate* and thus held to be outside of the bounds of methodological inquiry. But in rigorous methodological language qualities are affairs of presented or exhibited relationships; and these relationships constitute their meaning. And if qualities are meanings, they are symbols. Qualities represent the instituted relations out of which they emerge and which they help to present. Discriminations of some "itness" and "thatness" are products of constructed interconnections, and they both stand for and display these relations.

Our departure from current usage, which locates symbol as an element of cognitive processes, is warranted to the extent that the concept "symbol" rests primarily upon the notion of representation (as demanded by Charles Peirce) leaving open the question as to what is to be represented, whether things, events, processes, or relationships between terms or people. But we now have a different species of symbol. This other, or what may be termed "qualitative symbol," differs from that employed in cognitive procedures, herein referred to as "theoretical symbol." The difference is primarily one of emphasis. No hard and fast boundaries can be erected. However, one can be

distinguished from another. A distinguishing feature of the qualitative symbol is that it presents what it represents. A distinguishing feature of the theoretical symbol is that it represents without displaying or placing before us what it represents. Each type of symbolic function has its own proper and improper mode of usage. The point to be made is that the qualitative *does* submit to methodological analysis. And the qualitative is continuous with and as thoroughgoing an affair of human intelligence as the deliberately ordered conduct of empirical knowing. The latter, tragically, is usually taken to exhaust what is "intellectual."

V

Students of Dewey who have made philosophy of education primarily a philosophy of democratized inquiry have in the main gained support from the Dewey of *How We Think*, *Logic: The Theory of Inquiry*, and *Democracy and Education*. In these works we find Dewey's most influential, refined and extended analysis of thought and intelligence. Still, however important such analysis has become, it is addressed primarily to the task of describing the manipulations of theoretical symbols. A *general theory* of intelligence must come to include a conception of qualitative intelligence and the indicated analyses.

In Dewey's most general account, intelligence is occasioned by and operative within what is called "problematic" or "indeterminate" situations. Room is thus left for an *other than* scientific intelligence. But the detailed descriptions of the problematic situation and its role in schooling fail to include an explicit account of how problems and procedures may be dominantly qualitative rather than dominantly theoretical. Dewey does little more than note the role of the qualitative in those problem situations which are dominantly theoretical. Accordingly, when it comes to organizing learning situations in the schools, teachers are expected to provide situations which are patterned after the broadly conceived procedures of empirical inquiry. Anything "more than this" is dismissed as "atmosphere," "frill," "nonmethod," "irrational," "nonintellectual," "emotional," and "subjective." Physiological, biological or psychotherapeutic language becomes the language of the more sophisticated. Such restricted conceptions of learning, together with the dismissal of the *more or other than theoretical* (dismissals never made by Dewey) fog the vision of the full range of resources and potentialities of deliberately nurtured learning.

In the absence of methodological theory, the children in our schools receive a corresponding neglect in not having potential qualities built into their lives to think, prize, enjoy, and share with others. Since, as Dewey would remind us, no experience can proceed without the qualitative, school life necessarily includes qualities. But these qualities are included indiscriminately and inadvertently. Accident, restrictive interpretation, and arbitrarily "packaged" and isolated units reign in the absence of a systematic account of the qualitative in life and education. The qualitative as methodologically identified and described becomes, therefore, a vast sweep of matters to be built critically into the means, ends, and methods of the schools — matters to be injected systematically into the nurture and experiences provided the young.

Learning is properly conceived as occurring only in a problematic situation, where some end-in-view is being sought. But the fact must be recognized that ends-in-view are to be found in a spectrum ranging from problems dominantly qualitative to, at the other extreme, problems which are predominantly theoretical. A given substantive instance of a problem may be such that the end-in-view is predominantly theoretical and, therefore, requires

methods and means which are largely theoretical. The former instance places the theoretical in an instrumental relation to qualitative resolution. And in the latter instance qualitative orderings are in the service of ends which are singularly theoretical.

This expanded account of the "seat of learning," the problematic situation, should be integrated from the standpoint of valuation with the most sweeping educational criterion Dewey would have us use, the criterion by which we judge all educational criteria. Criticized and defended widely, Dewey's formulation and justification of this criterion still stands as the most adequate for the philosophy of experimentalism. "The educational process has no end beyond itself; it is its own end. . . . Since in reality there is nothing to which growth is relative save more growth, there is nothing to which education is subordinate save more education."[12] He raises questions and forwards responses in the following:

. . . from the standpoint of growth as education and education as growth the question is whether growth in this direction promotes or retards growth in general. Does this form of growth create conditions for further growth, or does it set up conditions that shut off the person who has grown in this particular direction from the occasions, stimuli, and opportunities for continuing growth in new directions? What is the effect of growth in a special direction upon the attitudes and habits which alone open up avenues for development in other lines? I shall leave you to answer these questions, saying simply that when and *only* when development in a particular line conduces to continuing growth does it answer to the criterion of education as growing. For the conception is one that must find universal and not specialized limited application.[13]

This "growth for the sake of further growth" criterion does not specify substantive objectives for education. It need not do so. That is not its function. It functions to

[12]John Dewey, *Democracy and Education*, pp. 59–60.
[13]John Dewey, *Experience and Education* (New York: Macmillan, 1938), p. 29.

help in the appraisal of criteria on the one hand unique to theoretical "growings," and on the other hand unique to qualitative "growings." Qualitative methods are, in this view, properly appraised in terms of their contribution to the refinement and extension of qualitative ordering. So, too, would be the case in theoretical orderings.

But this criterion does not reflect as fully as it might the judgment concerning the locus of the *summum bonum* for men as required by an aesthetically oriented philosophy of education. Since the ultimate goal for men is seen as the attainment and continual reconstruction of art experience or qualitative intelligence, then the criterion, "growth for the sake of further growth," must yield to reformulation. All manner of experiencings and learnings are to be judged as growths if they contribute in the final analysis to growths which are focally qualitative. A philosophy of education which embraces this principle is then a philosophy of art education. As such, it places the theoretical in the service of the aesthetic or qualitative.

We can be clearer about the purposes of the schools, as they are formulated with the foregoing generalizations, only as we consider the impact of schools so guided upon civilization. The issue is not whether or not the schools *should* have an impact upon civilization. The fact of the case is that they inescapably do. Neutrality is a myth. Dewey points to the issue as being one of determining what the inpact *should be* "with the maximum possible of courageous intelligence and responsibility," rather than with blind chance. As the title *Democracy and Education* suggests, he sees the school as a social institution and as charged with the responsibility for contributing directly to the great social problem of preserving and extending our democratic heritage. Further, the democratic commitment is not only a conception about a kind of society the school should attempt to foster, but also a conception which defines attributes of

schooling itself. The latter is necessary if the former is to be obtained. As methodologist, Dewey says, "as are the means used so are the actual ends achieved."[14] Democracy, therefore, is not limited to political, governmental, or economic arrangements. It is a personal, school and civilization ideal.

A democratic society is seen to be in a constant state of flux. Its "keynote" is in the demand for the "participation of every mature human being in formation of the values that regulate the living of men together."[15] Its "foundation" rests upon a shared procedure in which the directives for social change are both developed and tested in the process of that change. It is a way of life which depends upon the critical intelligence of all its members, upon unhampered social inquiry. If it has a faith, such a faith centers in human intelligence and shared experience. Indeed, Dewey finds this to be the distinguishing trait of his vision of the ideal life.

And, finally, the Deweyan educational perspective is revealed as he affirms the individual as the seat of moral worth. If democracy has moral meaning, it gains this meaning as all political, economic, industrial, and other arrangements contribute to the "all-around growth" of every member of the society. Here is democracy as an educational conception: "Since the process of experience is capable of being educative, faith in democracy is all one with faith in experience and education."[16]

Dewey's democratic social outlook upon the schools and their place in civilization may now be joined with the theme of qualitative intelligence. Dewey heralds this fusion in *A Common Faith*, where he establishes the distinction between "religion"

[14]John Dewey, *Liberalism and Social Action*, p. 86.
[15]John Dewey, "Democracy and Educational Administration," *School and Society*, Vol. 45, No. 1162 (April 3, 1937), p. 457.
[16]John Dewey, "Creative Democracy—The Task Before Us," *The Philosopher of the Common Man* (New York: Putnam, 1940), p. 227.

and "the religious." The former makes reference to institutionalized beliefs and practices, while the latter is looked upon as a quality which may be said to pervade a wide variety of experiences, aesthetic, scientific, political, moral, and others. If democracy is a distinctive and overarching ideal proposed for mankind and conceived as pervading all facets of social life, then it is to be revealed in those instances Dewey finds to have religious quality. "Any activity pursued in behalf of an ideal end against obstacles and in spite of threats of personal loss because of conviction of its general and enduring value is religious in quality."[17] This thoroughgoing rejection of hedonism is joined by the acceptance of a creatively demanding conservatism. Dewey reminds us that what we prize most dearly is not of ourselves, but are the products of the past doings, makings, strivings, sufferings, and creatings of the "continuous human community" with which we are linked. Ours is the task of conserving, rectifying, and making more widely and generously shared these prizings.

[17]John Dewey, *A Common Faith* (New Haven: Yale, 1934), p. 9.

There is but a small step to take from this set of notions advanced by John Dewey. His conception of democracy describes what must be present in order to obtain what is envisioned by the indicated redefinition. Democracy, reconceived, is that quality of experience which pervades social life, and in so doing contributes to the attainment of the fullest possible growth of all toward qualitative ideals. So defined, democracy is a conception about an aesthetic-religious affair.

Democratic public education is that form of education which provides this sort of religious experience. Methodologically viewed, such an educational task is one with the deliberate nurture of those qualities in the lives of the young which should permeate the schools and life in the civilization. This aesthetic-social objective is one of developing competence in shared qualitative and theoretical intelligence that will enable men to move toward the religious ideal that is democracy. It is an ideal that holds the promise of qualitative extensions and refinements common to all people — the infinite reconstruction of our qualitative intelligence. It is in truth the democratization of art experience.

37. Role of the Arts in Education

LAWRENCE K. FRANK

Education in the arts and arts in education are two closely related, but distinguishable, aspects of a question which needs to be thoroughly discussed from various viewpoints. In this paper I would like to present some considerations on both aspects which I hope others will examine and elaborate if they find them fruitful.

Education in the arts apparently covers a wide range of endeavors, from the teaching of techniques and skills in various media to teaching of art history and art appreciation, and training for research in the arts and their diverse uses, as in psychotherapy[1].

With the development of nonrepresentative and abstract art, what Ortega y Gasset[2] has called "the dehumanization of the arts," there seems to be a radical break with traditional art patterns, of which there are similar developments in other fields. Thus, in poetry we see less of the traditional descriptions of nature as more of the poets offer their own personal feelings, imagery and fantasy; in music less of the traditional melody and harmonic patterns and more of a seemingly unpatterned, even random or erratic, composition such as that by Cage. Likewise in drama and in novels there are many new forms and patterns indicating a rejection of the familiar and traditional.[3]

If the arts are breaking away from traditional patterns, this may be considered a period of "productive disintegration," a time for rejecting the past, for renouncing and relinquishing the customary and familiar, in order to clear the way for new creative endeavor, an emancipation which Brewster Ghiselin has stated to be necessary for creative work.[4]

These developments imply that education in the arts may call for more concern for the emerging new climate of opinion, the new concepts and assumptions, the new ways of thinking, the new criteria of credibility which the scientific advances of the past

[1]Manuel Barkan, *A Foundation For Art Education* (New York: Ronald Press, 1955).
[2]Jose Ortega y Gasset, *The Dehumanization of the Arts*, Anchor paperback (Garden City: Doubleday, 1956).
[3]See writings of Thomas Munro, *Journal of Aesthetics and Art Criticism*.
[4]Brewster Ghiselin, *The Creative Process*, Mentor paperback (New York: New American Library, 1955).

*SOURCE: Reprinted from *Studies in Art Education* I, 2 (Spring 1960), pp. 26–34.

sixty years have developed, notably in modern physics. Thus it may be highly desirable that in the education of the artist, he become aware of these alterations in traditional conception, these new patterns of thinking and of perceiving the world, so that he can live and work "at the height of his times," as Ortega y Gasset has urged, and can interpret graphically the more recent transformations in our cultural world. Indeed, no more important task confronts the creative mind than that of creating new symbols and new patterns of perception.

While no one should venture to tell the artist what he should do and how he should work, we may remind him that he can still be true to tradition, can pay his debt to the past, by doing for today what his predecessors did for their day, namely, translating the then new concepts and assumptions, the then new world views, into graphic symbols and designs.[5] Already many artists have been doing this, since much of the painting beginning in the first decade of this century seems to be an expression of what the physicists were formulating as space-time and as relativity, namely, that one observes the world always from a given position in space-time. The painter could then see and paint the front, the back and sides, the inside and the outside, because he was painting from inside the picture, not outside, as in representative art.

What then, we may ask, can art education wisely and fruitfully offer that will orient the student and evoke his creative capacities? Will it help the student to become self-consciously aware of the current patterns as transitional, not necessarily to be copied or emulated, but to be viewed as points of departure for his own explorations? How much will it help or confuse the student to

hear about and discuss some of the major issues being debated in the philosophy of science today? How much should he be given some understanding of what recent studies of perception[6] and studies of artistic and scientific capacities and talents are showing, and especially how perception is patterned by concepts and often distorted by emotions and feelings?

Should art education, in other words, enlarge its ambience and try to orient the student to the major intellectual and scientific developments taking place today? Should art education guide him to see how, in all the arts, painting, sculpture, music, dance, architecture, drama, poetry, novels, there are many explorations, experiments, transformations going on, as there are similar innovations in science, philosophy and even religion? Thereby the art student may become aware of the emerging climate of opinion in which he lives and can work creatively.[7]

I raise these questions since they seem to me to be relevant, if not essential, to a critical examination of art education, especially since there is an increasing concern for creativity and an earnest desire to discover how we can evoke creative endeavors in more young people. I personally believe that this emphasis upon creativity is an expression of the realization that our traditional culture is disintegrating and that we must endeavor to renew or recreate our culture if we are not to suffer further demoralization and failure of nerve.[8]

What is called existentialism may be viewed as the consternation and anxiety aroused in those who have suddenly recog-

[5]Cf. Erwin Panofsky, *Meaning in the Visual Arts,* Anchor paperback (Garden City: Doubleday, 1955). Wylie Spyher, *Four Stages in Rennaissance Style,* Anchor paperback (Garden City: Doubleday, 1955).

[6]Robert R. Blake, and Glenn U. Ramsey, *Perception, — An Approach to Personality* (New York: Ronald Press 1951). Gibson, J. J. *Perception of the Visual World* (Boston: Houghton Mifflin, 1950). Gyorgy Kepes, *The Language of Vision* (Chicago: Paul Theobold, 1951).
[7]Cf. Gyorgy Kepes, *The New Landscape* (Chicago: Paul Theobold, 1957).
[8]Cf. the writer's paper, "Creativity: An Enquiry," *Western Arts Association Bulletin.*

nized that we have lived in a symbolic cultural world which is breaking down, leaving them more or less bewildered at the loss of the traditional assumptions, the familiar "as if" world they grew up in and took for granted. A culture, like an artistic creation, may be viewed as a virtual world, to use Susanne Langer's expression for the arts.[9] Today the traditional, virtual world of Western people has disintegrated and we face the necessity of making new patterns and new projections to give our lives order and meaning. An awareness of this may evoke more creative responses from art students and art educators.

This, then, brings me to the question of the role of art in education where, as I see it, the most urgent educational task is to displace the now obsolete, even archaic, concepts and assumptions derived from the past, and replace them with the new concepts that have been developed during the past sixty years, chiefly in theoretical physics and cosmology. Just as Newtonian concepts and assumptions provided the framework for the Enlightenment[10] and gave rise to the creative work of the eighteenth and nineteenth centuries in many fields of thought and artistic creative endeavor, so the new concepts recently formulated offer possibility of immense advances when and as they are communicated through education so that children and youth can begin to live in this new climate of opinion.[11]

Now such a task cannot be achieved by the usual technique of verbal instruction because it involves the difficult process of un-learning, that is, of giving up, relinquishing, rejecting accepted concepts, and replacing these with a new awareness and altered patterns of perception. This rarely takes place through verbalization because the words used by a teacher or writer are almost inevitably interpreted in terms of the old, accepted concepts, what we expect and believe, and so they become useless as instrumentalities for unlearning.

The most promising approach to unlearning is through presentation of new concepts, chiefly graphically, for visual perception, so that the picture, the image, the design thus presented will make the old, familiar words or new expressions meaningful. That is to say, a picture, a design, a visual presentation can be seen and grasped if it is clearly perceived and accompanied by new verbal symbols which become meaningful in terms of what is perceived visually.

Here, as I see it, the artist can contribute enormously to education, especially less formal, less didactic education, since he can provide the nonverbal presentations by which communication of new concepts can take place.[12] I am not thinking here of fabricating "visual aids" which, as the word aid implies, are considered as purely subsidiary to the seemingly all-important verbal communication, the traditional spoken or written presentations. Usually visual aids are just that — illustrations for the words are considered the primary mode of communication.

If we think of graphic communication, especially artistic presentations, as the major mode or instrumentality for creating awareness, for communicating concepts, and for patterning perceptions, we will see how important it is in education where the major task today is to communicate the new

[9]Susanne Langer, *Feeling and Form* (New York, Charles Scribner and Sons, 1953).

[10]Cf. Crane Brinton, *Ideas and Men* (Englewood Cliffs: Prentice Hall, 1950), reprinted in part in New American Library, Mentor paperback and *Making of the Modern Mind;* F. S. C Northrop, *Meeting of East and West* (New York: Macmillan, 1946) , see chapters III and IV; H. J. Muller, *The Uses of the Past* (New York: Oxford University Press, 1952), reprinted in the New American Library, Mentor paperback.

[11]Cf. the writer's Burton lecture, "The School as Agent for Cultural Renewal," *Harvard School of Education* (Cambridge, Mass.: Harvard Press, 1959), also "Cultural Implications of Man in Space," *Annals New York Academy of Sciences*, April 1958, **72**, pp. 195–211.

[12]Jurgen Ruesch, and Weldon Keyes, *Non-Verbal Communication*, (Berkeley: University of California Press, 1956).

concepts that are remaking our lives. Some of this communication can be made by models, physical models of the processes or operations or configurations we wish to convey, such as the three-dimensional models of molecules showing where each atom is located in the molecular configuration; two-dimensional diagrams or charts also will be useful. But to convey the full meaning and significance of new concepts, they need to be presented visually as in films, but also artistically.

For example, an architectural draftsman or engineer can draw a detailed plan of a building, a machine, a vehicle, but it will communicate only to those who are experienced in interpreting his drawings its often esoteric symbols and detailed figures. To communicate the essentials and meaning of a building, of a machine, of a vehicle, we need an artistic representation that is not cluttered up with unnecessary details but which gives the configuration or pattern that can be visually perceived and understood by viewing it as an organized whole.

The communication of new concepts, of new patterns of thinking and perceiving, not didactically as in lectures or textbooks, but as an experience that reorients the beholder, has been the ages-old role of the arts which has infused their communication with feeling tones that made them aesthetically significant and persistent. As Browning once said, "We learn to love that which we first see painted." And similarly, we may say we learn to understand and to perceive the world as it is artistically presented when the artist combines the *eidos* and the *ethos* of a culture in an aesthetic experience.[13]

Recognition of the communicative process and of the transactional process may offer fruitful leads for art education.[14]

Briefly, communication theory emphasizes that a message, presented or coded in some pattern, linguistic, graphic, tactual, has to be transmitted, subject to distortion and confusion by "noise" (any nonpatterned, extraneous events accompanying or interfering with the message); has to be received and decoded or interpreted by the recipient who understands it as he decodes and interprets it according to his life experience. Art, graphic and plastic, may be viewed as nonverbal communication employing all the resources of form, pattern, configuration, figure on ground and color, to enhance or clarify the message, relying upon signals, signs and symbols in varying combinations[15] to convey the artist's meaning and to provide an aesthetic experience, sometimes with little or no cognitive content. An understanding of communication processes may be of considerable help in art education as giving the art student a more sophisticated approach to his problems.

The transactional process involves a revision of our traditional assumptions about knowledge. For centuries knowledge has been regarded as a mysterious third substance, occurring out in space between the world and the individual. Knowledge has been considered as something that could be imparted to others or acquired, although no one could ever locate this substance in space or time, or give it any of the usual properties of substances.

Some years ago Dewey and Bentley in their book, *Knowing and the Known,*[16] proposed that we drop the idea of knowledge and speak of *knowing* as a dynamic cognitive relation which the knower establishes with the known or to be known. This focuses attention, then, on the activity of the knower who, in order to establish a new "knowing" relation to the world, needs to have a new

---

[13]Cf. the writer's paper, "Reconstruction Through the Arts," *Journal of Aesthetics,* 1946.

[14]Jurgen Ruesch, and Gregory Bateson, *Communication, The Matrix of Psychiatry* (New York: Newton, 1951).

[15]Cf. the writer's "Tactile Communication," *Genetic Psychology Monograph,* **56** (1957), pp. 209–255; see especially the discussion of signals, signs and symbols, pp. 211–212.

[16]John and Bentley Dewey, *Knowing and the Known* (Boston: Beacon Press, 1948).

awareness and a patterned perception so that he can relate cognitively to aspects of the world which he previously ignored or failed to perceive. This transactional process involves a circular, reciprocal relationship, of projecting or imputing meaning into situations and events or people, and then responding to that meaning which the individual has himself projected into situations or people.

Here we see how graphic and plastic art operates to give the viewer a transactional knowing approach to the world whereby he may discover and perceive new aspects of which he was previously unaware. Thus, arts can function as the primary agency for education since they provide communication to which the recipient responds in new ways, investing situations and people with the meaning and significance which the creative artist has revealed to him and has made aesthetically compelling.

The earlier reference to the need for presentation of our new concepts and assumptions which the arts can uniquely provide finds in communication theory and transactional process a strong reinforcement and specific procedure for achieving such results through the arts. The arts provide occasions for learning that gives rise to thinking.[17]

It will not be easy nor simple to provide in art education what may be needed for these purposes. If we are to give art students this reorientation in scientific thinking so that they will understand these new concepts and new assumptions, these new ways of perceiving and understanding the world, we must create the nonverbal anological communications that will convey the meaning of these concepts which words alone cannot do. We cannot expect art students to take endless courses in the sciences which for the most part are concerned with techniques and method and detailed factual findings and generalization, expressed in language. The

orientation of the art student will not be fostered by these conventional courses because usually they fail to communicate the concepts of a science and give little understanding of what science means or what the terms imply. Indeed, many scientific workers are unable to formulate their often unspoken concepts and assumptions, being preoccupied with generalizations from empirical studies which are guided by preconceptions they rarely recognize or can express. For grasping the new concepts and learning to perceive the world anew, we need to be helped in *unlearning*, in giving up our familiar assumptions which block new learning and new perceptions.

Accordingly, it may be necessary for art educators to develop the special kind of conceptual orientation and nonverbal communications to modern science which they need for their students, utilizing graphic and nonverbal materials so far as possible.[18] The use of physical models, diagrams, pictures, etc., is being recognized in the new teaching materials for physics, proposed by the Committee on Teaching of Physical Science, now issued by Educational Services, Inc. (Watertown, Mass.).

In so far as the artists of the future, who are today's students, may receive this reorientation, we may look forward to a period in which the contemporary artists, like their predecessors in the great transitional phases of European culture, will communicate the new perceptions, the new concepts of nature and new images of man,[19] whereby our culture may be renewed and revivified as it has been before. This is a prospect of immense significance which art educators may find sufficiently stimulating and provocative to evoke the efforts necessary to achieve such results.[20] But the best we

[17]Cf. Jerome, Bruner, "Learning and Thinking," *Harvard Educational Review*, **29** (Summer 1959), pp. 184–192.

[18]See Gyorgy Kepes, *The New Landscape* (Chicago: Paul Theobold, 1957).
[19]Cf. L. K. Frank, *Nature and Human Nature: Man's New Image of Himself* (New Brunswick, N. J.: Rutgers University Press, 1951).
[20]Horace M. Kallen, *A Study of Liberty* (Antioch Press, 1959).

can do today is to open the doors and to expose art students to this prospect and to these new materials, recognizing that how they will utilize such experience we cannot predict and must not try to control. Our task is to evoke and raise the level of their aspirations and to give them access to the new concepts and assumptions which they can use creatively as they contribute to the advancement of Western European culture, as artists have done throughout the centuries.

The emphasis above is on the cognitive, conceptual aspects of art education. But this should be corrected and enlarged by a recognition of our urgent need for more genuine aesthetic experiences, especially for art students who may be given chiefly ideas and techniques. As we face a world increasingly ordered and technologically managed, with ever increasing requirements for disciplined thinking and performance, we require more aesthetic experience in which, without thinking or reflection, without critical caution or cognitive patterning, we can resonate to the experience, especially those experiences which are provided by the creative imagination of the artist. Just as we need the physiological vitamins in order to utilize our foodstuffs, so we need the "psychological vitamins" of aesthetic experience to enable us to maintain some balance, sanity, mental health, in coping with our life experience and for functional efficiency and sensibilities. Lack of aesthetic experience may be as handicapping as is sensory deprivation recently studied.[21] As D. H. Lawrence remarked long ago, "It is the way our sympathies flow and recoil that really determines our lives."

Aesthetic experiences are essentially non-cognitive, dynamic relations with events in which for the moment we can live fully and wholly, forgetful of time and space, as we resonate to the situation. Apparently, Zen Buddhism seeks this kind of aesthetic relation to the world. Accordingly, let us guard against too much emphasis on the cognitive, conceptual education, as this paper may seem to suggest, and reiterate that art is for man's enjoyment and awakening for experiences he needs as a personality who lives in a symbolic cultural world, a product of creative artistic imagination that must be continually renewed to have any vitality and relevance to man's changing ways of living, and his rising level of aspiration. Creative work arises from aesthetic experiencing which evokes creative effort in utilizing concepts, images and designs.

If art education should be oriented in the direction here suggested, it is likely that art education will be more effective and will receive a larger and more generous recognition by administrators and curriculum planners. The arts still wait for full acceptance in educational programs in which they are indispensable and urgently needed. As Whitehead has remarked: "Those societies which cannot combine reverence for their symbols with freedom of revision, must ultimately decay, either from anarchy or from atrophy of a life stilled by useless shadows."[22]

[21]Cf. Jerome Bruner, "The Cognitive Consequences of Early Sensory Deprivation," *Psychosomatic Medicine* (April 1959) to appear in a volume *Sensory Deprivation and Social Isolation* (Cambridge, Mass.: Harvard Press).

[22]Alfred N. Whitehead, *Symbolism, Its Meaning and Effect* (New York: Macmillan, 1927). See Chapter, "Uses of Symbolism."

38. The Case for Art Education

HARRY S. BROUDY

It irks the art teacher to have art regarded as a luxury item on the school's bill of fare. For one thing no one likes to think of his life's work as easily dispensable, and experience has shown that when school money is scarce art is among the first activities to be dispensed with. Nevertheless, only fine and highly cherished objects are regarded as luxuries, and one may question whether the attempt to convince the public that art and music are as useful as arithmetic and science would be wise strategy even if the claim could be justified.

The claim has dubious validity. That artistic activity produces important results is true. Individual enjoyment is one such result and social control or discipline is another. But the sort of art that does this for most people most of the time is not the kind that has to be studied in school. The popular arts via the mass media furnish massive doses of enjoyment to the masses of people and likewise shape their feelings with respect to what in our culture is to be cherished, admired, loved, and hated.

We learn how to feel about love, death, success, war, and peace in the movies, popular fiction, the top 20 tunes in the jukebox, the advertising layouts in our magazines and newspapers. These arts present in perceptual form images or models that objectify and exhibit the current fashion in what is desirable and repulsive.

The popular arts of a people, whether they set out to do so or not, celebrate the values of that people. When these values are put into song and story they evoke feelings that become stylized and serve to educate the young and the old alike. Advertisers use art media to make the public yearn for their products; governments can, if they put their minds to it, shape the feelings of their people with respect to leaders and their policies.

But to reiterate, this use of art demands no formal training on the part of the young. Living in the group they will be controlled by the art forms of that group. The teaching of art in the schools makes sense only if there is an art to which ordinary daily experience does not give the pupil access, if access to it will give him something not to be found in ordinary transactions with popular art, and if this requires formal training.

*SOURCE: Reprinted from *Art Education* (January 1960), pp. 7–8, 19.

Is there an art to which ordinary routines of life do not give the pupil adequate access? In one sense the answer is no, because anyone, if he tries hard enough, can visit museums and libraries; listen to concerts and recordings. We are justly proud of the accessibility of all types of art objects, and the techniques of the mass media deserve much of the credit for it.

In another sense, however, certain realms of art are effectively closed off from many people. When considerable facility or acquaintance with the methods of making or viewing an art object is required for appreciation, ignorance is as effective a bar as a wall. Poor readers cannot do much with Proust's novels and a lack of familiarity with Greek mythology makes for a frustrating experience with Milton's *Paradise Lost.*

That is one reason for the irritation of the untutored viewer *vis a vis* abstract painting. He looks for what is not there and he does not know what to do with what is there. This irritation is sometimes relieved by suggesting that the painting be viewed as a piece of wall paper or floor covering. Hard as this is on the soul of the artist, it does, however, halt the viewer's frantic search for familiar themes and objects.

Serious art, by and large, does make demands that popular art does not: sensitive discrimination, awareness of form, some familiarity with technique, and, above all, an active and concentrated attention. Insofar as this is the case, serious art is not easily accessible to the untutored.

Because facility with serious art requires skill and knowledge not acquired incidentally, it makes sense for the school to offer a program of art education. But because such training entails effort that the child may be reluctant to exert, to require it of everyone calls for a promise to the child and to society. To the child must be promised enjoyment and satisfaction above and beyond that afforded by the popular arts; to society must be promised a strengthening of the people's

commitment to its ideals and aspirations, and, what may be even more important, a constant examination and evaluation of them.

There are two lines of argument that we can follow to justify these promises. One is that in the experience of the race, epoch after epoch has produced men who testify to the power and value of serious art. Why one cannot predict that some of our children and perhaps all of them will experience the same sort of reaction after similar training is hard to understand, yet so convinced are educators that aesthetic experience is no more than a capricious and individual matter of taste that they find this sort of evidence unconvincing.

The other line of argument consists in putting forward a theory that tries to show how art in general and serious art in particular functions in man's attempt to achieve the good life.

From the days of Plato to our own times many have tried to interpret what art does. For Plato himself, art by embodying harmony and order in delightfully sensuous forms induces harmony and order into the individual soul. So potent did he believe art to be that he insisted on having the stories and poems taught to the young censored. He was afraid lest certain types of music make boys effeminate. Nor did he believe that stories depicting gods and heroes in immoral escapades would do much for character education.

Susanne K. Langer speaks of art as shaping our inner life. Art introduces order into the chaotic realm of our emotions by holding up before us images of shaped feeling.[1]

Freud and Sir Herbert Read, among others, see art as stemming from man's struggle with his submerged animal impulses to love and destruction. Art on this view somehow plumbs the nether region of

[1]*Aesthetic Form and Education,* Michael F. Andrews, ed. (Syracuse: Syracuse University Press, 1958).

the unconscious and performs for us the rite of ennobling our unconscious transactions with our primordial lusts. The artist, so to speak, is our substitute for neurosis.

Gyorgy Kepes notes that we respond to the images of the artist because their forms and harmonies touch us at various levels of our being: sensational, rational, and emotional.[2]

As the industrial revolution swept into high gear William Morris warned that the rhythmic joy of work had been destroyed. Repeatedly we have been told that everyday life in our times no longer provides us with the models of wholeness and harmony that were once vouchsafed to the peasant in his natural setting. Art is more and more relied upon to restore the wholeness of human experience.

Summing it up, the theoretical justification for education in serious art lies in the claim that it trains the feeling side of life just as other studies train the intellectual side and still others perfect bodily skills, and that it does so in a way that goes beyond the educative effects of popular art.

Two problems seem to emerge if we take this line of persuasion with school boards and parents. First, whether even with respect to serious art the school need do more than provide an environment in which the child's natural expressive impulses are allowed to manifest themselves in paint, clay, etc., with a maximum of freedom and a minimum of technical requirements. If this is the case, then it need not require much more than time in the program, a wide variety of materials, and an encouraging teacher. The upsurge of Sunday painting indicates that perhaps not even this much is a prerequisite for adult artistic activity.

Casting doubt on this approach is the well-nigh universal testimony of artists and

connoisseurs in all fields that their achievements do not come naturally. On the contrary, they complain with almost tedious uniformity about the hard work their artistic endeavors entail. Serious art on the producing or the appreciating side is not for the lazy, nor presumably for the untrained. If, however, there is nothing systematic to teach, no special way of teaching it, and no effort required to learning it, the fuss about the art program is much ado about nothing.

The second point is that a program of art education which proposes to train pupils for the appreciation of serious art is not innocuous; it can be dangerous.

Serious art presents us with models of feeling that are neither so familiar nor so safe as those presented by the popular arts. Popular art gives aesthetic form to the values that most of the people are enjoying or would like to enjoy in a manner approved by the social order. Just as there are standard models of cars and refrigerators, so there are standard ways of feeling about love, war, marriage, death, home, etc. In the popular song, picture, photograph, movie, and story the average man recognizes his everyday problems and the standard solutions.

Serious art, on the other hand, tries to disclose modes of feelings that in our ordinary life we rarely experience, and would probably prefer not to experience at all. Most of us do not want to engage in heroic episodes of love, war, or politics, but in every epoch a few works of art depict mankind in such heroic and convincing roles that we see in them our species at its best. These works become certified as "great" works of art, but not always by their contemporary publics.

Contemporary art when serious criticizes the values of its culture. Sometimes this criticism is in the form of a protest; at others, it simply experiments freely with emotions and their expression in unusual forms.

Serious art, whether in its classical or contemporaneous form, whether freely ex-

[2]"Comments on Art" in *New Knowledge in Human Values*, Abraham H. Maslow, ed. (New York: Harper & Brothers, 1959), pp. 86 ff.

perimental or definitely idealistic, confronts the child with models of experience and feeling that are not typical of the life going on around him. The images it offers the child are not mirrors of life but projections of what life *might* feel like. All of these images are distortions. Some are interesting and important; some border on the insane, and a few disclose visions of feeling that haul mankind up another rung on the ladder of civilization.

All of which means that when the school takes serious art seriously it cannot expose the immature pupil to anything and everything, and this in turn presupposes a high order of aesthetic sophistication and competence on the part of all teachers who have a part in the program.

So conceived and defended a case can be made out for art education as an integral part of general education. That school boards and other appropriating agencies will be convinced is not so certain. They represent the tension between the conventional and the experimental that is never absent from a changing society. The artistic experience is intermittent and celebrative; it gives meaning and glow to life but it neither creates life nor sustains. The school must pay attention to all aspects of living — economic, intellectual, moral, and social — and if it must make a choice between preserving and sustaining life, on one hand, and making it glow, on the other, there is no question as to what it will have to choose. But we no longer face such a hard choice. If we did, we would not be discussing art education at all.

SUGGESTED READINGS FOR PART VII

BAYER, HERBERT, WALTER GROPIUS, and ILSE GROPIUS, editors. *Bauhaus, 1919–1928*. New York: The Museum of Modern Art, 1938.

FAULKNER, RAY, EDWIN ZIEGFELD, and GERALD HILL. *Art Today*. Fourth edition. New York: Holt, Rinehart and Winston, 1963.

GIEDION, SIGFRIED. *Space, Time and Architecture*. Third edition enlarged. Cambridge: Harvard University Press, 1956.

LOGAN, FREDERICK M. *Growth of Art in American Schools*. New York: Harper and Brothers, 1955.

MUNRO, THOMAS. *Art Education: Its Philosophy and Psychology*. New York: The Liberal Arts Press, 1956.

National Society for the Study of Education. *Art in American Life and Education* (40th yearbook). Bloomington, Illinois: Public School Publishing Company, 1941.

ORTEGA y GASSET, JOSE. *The Dehumanization of Art, and other writings on art and culture*. Garden City, New York: Doubleday & Company, Inc. (Anchor Books), 1956.

PLEKHANOV, G. V. *Art and Social Life*. London: Lawrence and Wishart, Ltd., 1953.

READ, HERBERT. *Education Through Art*. New York: Pantheon Books, Inc., 1958.

Index